MICROSOFT® .NET

DISTRIBUTED APPLICATIONS: INTEGRATING XML WEB SERVICES AND .NET REMOTING

Matthew MacDonald

PUBLISHED BY
Microsoft Press
A Division of Microsoft Corporation
One Microsoft Way
Redmond, Washington 98052-6399

Library of Congress Cataloging-in-Publication Data pending.

Printed and bound in the United States of America.

1 2 3 4 5 6 7 8 9 QWT 8 7 6 5 4 3

Distributed in Canada by H.B. Fenn and Company Ltd.

A CIP catalogue record for this book is available from the British Library.

Microsoft Press books are available through booksellers and distributors worldwide. For further information about international editions, contact your local Microsoft Corporation office or contact Microsoft Press International directly at fax (425) 936-7329. Visit our Web site at www.microsoft.com/mspress. Send comments to: *mspinput@microsoft.com.*

Acquisitions Editor: Anne Hamilton
Project Editor: Sally Stickney
Technical Editor: Marc Young

Body Part No. X09-35337

For Faria. You make it all worthwhile.

Contents at a Glance

Table of Contents

Part III Case Studies

Acknowledgments

Writing this book was a challenge. It's no easy feat to balance tutorials, real-world examples, and architectural guidance in a single work, and many times I wished I could focus exclusively on just one of these topics. I could never have finished this book without the help of many others, including the insightful developers on the DevelopMentor lists and the miscellaneous Microsoft architects who took time to answer my questions. I'm happy to report that the .NET community is alive and well—sharing tips and undocumented secrets in countless periodicals and books and on Web sites.

I owe a heartfelt thanks to many individuals at Microsoft Press, including Anne Hamilton, who "rescued" the book, and Sally Stickney, who guided it expertly through its Everett revision. This book also had the benefit of expert copyediting from Ina Chang, and no less than three excellent technical reviewers. Terrence Joubert and Ryan Payet provided feedback for the first revision, and Marc Young verified the book for Visual Studio .NET 2003. I'm indebted to all these individuals, as well as numerous others at Microsoft Press who have worked tirelessly behind the scenes to ensure that indexing, figures, and page settings were successful. In addition, I'd like to thank Lisa Thibault, Linda Bump, and Elise Walter at New Riders, who helped the book make the leap from proposal to its first revision.

Finally, I would like to thank my parents (all four of them) and my loving wife. Without the support of these individuals, nothing would ever get done.

Introduction

It's been roughly seven years since distributed application architecture first gained recognition in the business world. Back then, exciting new technologies such as COM/DCOM and CORBA/IIOP promised to revolutionize the way that large-scale, resource-intensive applications were built. Instead of trying to host a single monolithic application on a single computer, distributed architecture allowed software to be modeled as a group of objects communicating across different machines. Best of all, these machines no longer needed to be proprietary mainframes—instead, developers could use inexpensive servers running the Microsoft Windows operating system. Increasing the overall throughput of the system was often as easy as just adding an extra computer to the mix.

All this has made distributed programming one of the most exciting and hotly pursued areas of software programming, but it hasn't made up for some critical stumbling blocks. Quite simply, distributed applications are complicated. Programming a distributed application on the Windows platform requires a solid understanding of Microsoft's COM standard, its enterprise software and component services (such as SQL Server and COM+), and a healthy dose of painfully won experience. And no matter how skilled the programmer, a distributed programming project can quickly mushroom into a collection of versioning nightmares, interoperability headaches, and unexpected performance bottlenecks.

These problems are the key factors behind the creation of Microsoft's .NET platform. Microsoft .NET provides an entirely new model for creating components, communicating across computers, and accessing data—one that is optimized for distributed applications on every level. This framework still requires a healthy investment of developer time and a fairly steep learning curve for novice programmers. After the basics are mastered, however, .NET makes it dramatically easier to create truly scalable software systems.

This book explores distributed programming with .NET. It details the key .NET technologies you need to master and explains the best practices for distributed application architecture with .NET. Best of all, it shows you how the separate .NET technologies can all fit together.

Who Should Read This Book

This book is aimed at developers who have already learned the fundamentals of Microsoft .NET and want to graduate to the arena of distributed programming. This audience includes developers who have heard the hype about disconnected data, XML-based standards, and XML Web services but haven't yet seen the practical payoff. It also includes programmers who have a basic understanding of individual .NET technologies but want to learn the benefits and tradeoffs of using them in realistic applications.

.NET basics such as events, metadata, and the common language runtime (CLR) are not discussed in this book (and would make an incredibly boring rehash for most professional developers). If you want to design distributed .NET applications but you are new to .NET, your best bet is to begin with a comprehensive introduction to C# or Microsoft Visual Basic .NET. Many excellent books in print accomplish this goal (including my own, *The Book of VB .NET*, from No Starch Press).

The Focus of This Book

This book examines the architecture and best practices that lead to performance, security, and scalability in distributed applications. As part of this strategy, it's vital to explain not just how to use .NET technologies but also when each one is appropriate and how to integrate them together in a real-world solution.

You've probably already heard the marketing hype about .NET features such as disconnected data and XML Web services. Although these technologies are remarkable, they each have individual strengths and weaknesses. Using them wisely involves understanding when they are best suited—and when they will only lead to additional headaches.

This book also takes a critical look at application architecture issues. It considers the *real* gains and losses incurred when moving from two-tier to *n*-tier architecture and shows you how to tailor your designs for the problem or project at hand. Distributed application design sometimes involves compromises, such as balancing scalability against complexity and performance against standardization. This book covers the strategies for determining the best mix.

The Three-Part Structure of This Book

Microsoft .NET is a rich framework with hundreds of interesting nooks and crannies. For the computer author, this presents a unique danger: it's all too easy to become distracted with a subset of intriguing features and write a whole book without delving into the real core issues. This book is designed in three logical parts to avoid this danger.

Part I: Key Technologies

The first part of this book introduces each .NET technology from a distributed programming point of view. To keep the book relentlessly in focus, each chapter opens with a section that explains the role this feature plays in a distributed system. As a side effect, many interesting aspects of .NET don't appear in this book—everything from custom controls to file I/O. In return, the book makes room for a more comprehensive look at enterprise application issues. Here are some of the topics explored:

- Understanding components and component hosts
- Bridging the gap to other platforms with XML and XML Web services
- Communicating between distributed components with .NET Remoting
- Developing a data-transfer plan and handling concurrency issues with disconnected data
- Improving responsiveness with multithreaded clients and handling contention and synchronization issues
- Creating thread pools and Windows services
- Using Message Queuing for asynchronous, decoupled communication
- Using COM+ component services to enable transactions, JIT activation, object pooling, and more for your components

The chapters in the first part of the book include sparse code examples that focus on concepts rather than toy applications, which would only dilute the content. Instead, where appropriate, you are directed to a full example in the case study portion of the book (Part III).

Part II: Developing an Architecture

The second part of this book considers application architecture: how to build the parts of a distributed application so that they will perform reliably and can scale to support large numbers of clients. These are some of the topics covered:

- The performance limitations of object-oriented design
- The fundamentals of stateless programming
- The best way to transport data, communicate errors, and monitor the performance of your application
- How to design a database for optimum performance—and how to code against it without breaking encapsulation
- How to use encryption and secure your code from the transport level to the application code
- How to manage distributed application deployment by using self-updating applications and XML Web services

Part III: Case Studies

The final part of the book presents several complete case studies that show you how to integrate the .NET technologies discussed in the first two parts of the book into a distributed application. The following three examples are considered:

- **Invoicer.NET** Invoicer.NET coordinates the sales of employees in the field. The interesting part of this example is that it shows a phased migration path from a "traditional" approach—using Microsoft Excel and Microsoft Access—to a .NET solution, without requiring a full rewrite. This case study also tackles considerations for dealing with "disconnected" systems.
- **Transact.NET** Transact.NET is an order-fulfillment system that shows the key techniques to integrate XML Web services and Message Queuing in order to provide real-time notification. XML Web services provide the client order interface, and Message Queuing is the backbone that delivers notification messages.
- **SuperCompute.NET** SuperCompute.NET is a work-request application that performs requested tasks asynchronously and lets clients pick up the results later. It demonstrates how distributed application architecture allows clients to harness the CPU power of a server.

Of course, the case studies are not complete, read-to-release professional applications. Instead, each case study includes just enough code to show a well-designed solution framework for a common problem scenario. You can enhance these frameworks by adding additional security, performance optimizations, or additional features (particularly in the client applications, which lack the niceties that most users expect from a Windows GUI). Ideally, the case studies will show you how to choose and combine different .NET technologies and get you started with the best practices for .NET solution architecture.

The final chapter (Chapter 19) points you to a few interesting URLs where you can download additional distributed application case studies. These case studies, which are architected by various Microsoft teams, provide best practices for ASP.NET, ADO.NET, and XML Web services. Some of them even have associated white papers on MSDN describing the design process.

System Requirements

You'll need the following software to work through the samples in this book:

- Microsoft Visual Studio .NET or Visual Studio .NET 2003
- Microsoft Windows 2000, Windows XP, or Windows Server 2003

The minimum hardware specification for development is a 450-MHz Pentium II-class processor, with a minimum of 128 MB of RAM if you're running Windows 2000 and 256 MB of RAM if you're running Windows XP, Windows 2000 Server, or Windows Server 2003. You'll need about 5 GB of free hard-disk space to install Visual Studio .NET 2003. These values are bare minimums, and your development life will be much easier on a system with ample RAM and free disk space.

Code Samples

Most of the code shown in this book is presented and analyzed in individual snippets. In the interest of brevity (and to save you from having to wade through pages of basic boilerplate), some of the more pedestrian details are left out, such as the Windows designer code needed to create form controls. To download the complete case studies in their most recent, up-to-date format, browse to the companion site for this book, *http://microsoft.com/mspress/books/6723.asp*. Click the Companion Content link in the More Information box on the right side of the page to bring up the companion content Web page. You'll find additional content at my Web site, *http://www.prosetech.com*.

> **Note** The code in this book has been tested with versions 1.0 and 1.1 of the .NET Framework. In most cases, these two platforms work almost exactly the same, although .NET 1.1 (which is a part of Visual Studio .NET 2003) includes a slew of minor bug fixes and performance enhancements. In the rare cases where the Visual Studio .NET 2003 behavior differs from that of the original Visual Studio .NET, the text makes special mention of the differences. Code shortcuts that are not available in .NET 1.0 code are not used.

Variable Naming

In the past, Microsoft favored a variation of Hungarian notation when naming variables. That meant, for example, that a Visual Basic integer variable would start with the prefix *int* (as in *intCount*). But in the world of .NET, where memory management is handled automatically, data types can change without any serious consequences and the majority of variables are storing references to full-fledged objects. Hungarian notation is starting to show its age.

The new Microsoft standard is to avoid variable prefixes, especially for properties and methods visible to other classes. This style is similar to the standard used for COM components and controls, and it makes a great deal of sense for code transparency. Data types no longer pose the problems they once did, because Visual Studio .NET will spot invalid conversions and refuse to compile.

In this book, data type prefixes are not used for variables. The only significant exception is with control variables, for which it is still a useful trick to distinguish between different types of controls (such as *txtUserName* and *lstUserCountry*) and with some data objects. Of course, when you create your own programs, you are free to follow whatever variable naming convention you prefer, provided you make the effort to adopt a complete consistency across all your projects (and ideally across all the projects in your organization).

Feedback

This book is designed to be the best tutorial for learning .NET distributed application technologies and concepts. Toward that end, your comments and suggestions are extremely helpful. You can send complaints, adulation, and everything in between to me directly at *distribapps@prosetech.com*. I can't solve your .NET problems or critique your code, but I will benefit from information about what this book did right and wrong (and what it might have done in an utterly confusing way).

Microsoft Press Support

Every effort has been made to ensure the accuracy of the book and its companion content. Microsoft Press also provides corrections for books through the World Wide Web at the following address:

http://www.microsoft.com/mspress/support/

To query the Knowledge Base for book and companion content corrections, visit *http://www.microsoft.com/mspress/support/search.asp*.

In addition to sending feedback directly to the author, if you have comments, questions, or ideas regarding the presentation or use of this book or the companion content, you can send them to Microsoft using either of the following methods:

Postal Mail:

Microsoft Press
Attn: Microsoft .NET Distributed Applications: Integrating Web Services and Remoting Editor
One Microsoft Way
Redmond, WA 98052-6399

E-mail:

mspinput@microsoft.com

Please note that product support isn't offered through the above mail addresses. For support information regarding Microsoft Visual Studio .NET 2003, go to *http://msdn.microsoft.com/vstudio/*. You can also call Standard Support at (425) 635-7011 weekdays between 6 a.m. and 6 p.m. Pacific time, or you can search Microsoft's Support Online at *http://support.microsoft.com/support*.

Part I

Key Technologies

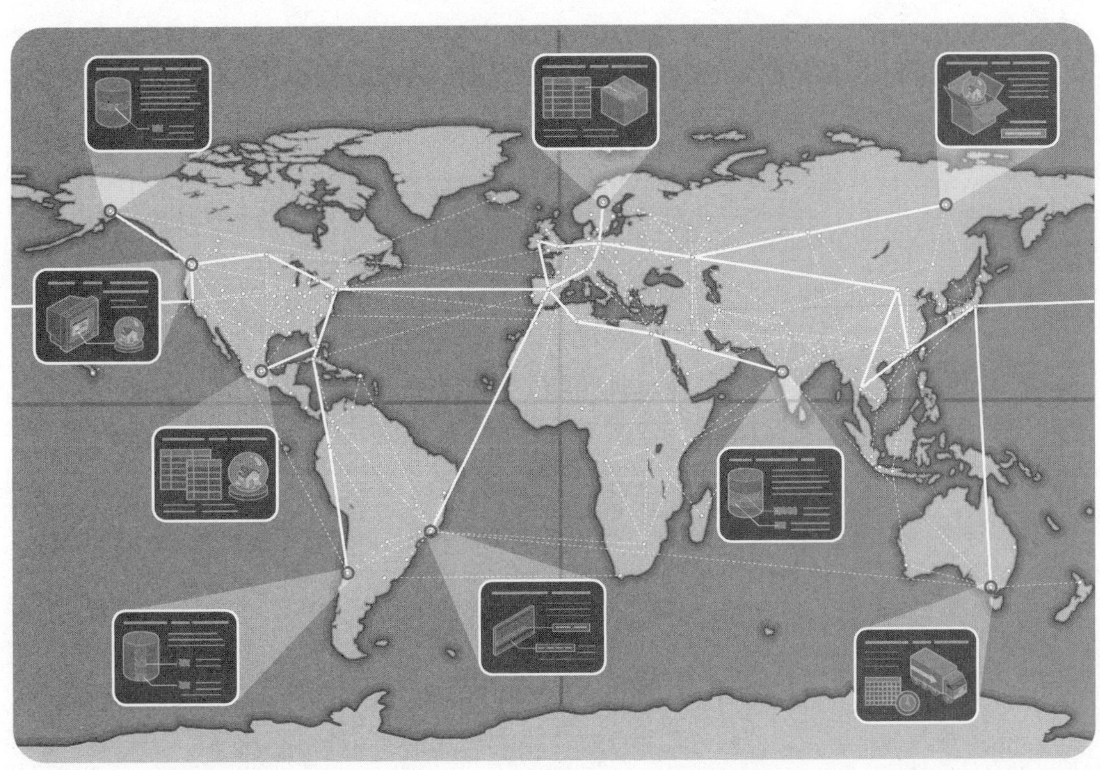

1

Understanding Distributed Architecture

In this chapter, we start on the ground floor and ask what distinguishes a distributed application from any other program. Although defining distributed applications might seem like an easy task, programmers (and programming authors) often misrepresent distributed architecture, equating it with component-based development or stateless design. To complicate matters, components in a distributed application can communicate in a variety of ways, particularly in Microsoft .NET, meaning that distributed application architecture isn't nearly as uniform as the client/server model.

This chapter introduces distributed architecture, and explains how a distributed application is partitioned into components and tiers and hosted on multiple computers. This chapter will also provide a practical look at some of the advantages—and complications—that this design introduces.

What Is a Distributed Application?

A distributed application is simply one that spreads its execution over more than one computer. Generally, the goal of distributed application architecture is to improve performance and scalability. The ideal distributed application can scale up to serve thousands of simultaneous clients just by adding additional computers.

You might adopt a distributed architecture for other reasons, however, including the following:

- To integrate code running in different environments, operating systems, and platforms. This is one of the primary goals of .NET XML Web services and one of the primary reasons for the adoption of XML standards in ADO.NET.
- To provide synchronization and live communication between multiple clients (for example, with a chat server). Implementation of this design in a traditional server would rely on heavy use of a database and frequent polling, and the server would be extremely pressed to support a large number of users.
- To support thin clients (for example, software on embedded devices) that have insufficient processing power to handle their data needs. As an extension of this principle, you might use a distributed application to allow a powerful server to handle a CPU-intensive calculation or even implement a peer-to-peer application in which each client shares in the processing work.

Many programming books obscure the idea of distributed applications by confusing distributed architecture with multitier design (or good design practices in general). For example, here are several hallmarks of a well-designed application that can apply just as easily (and sometimes more easily) to a client/server application as to a distributed application:

- Component-based code reuse
- Division of logic into business objects and data services objects
- Multithreading
- Disconnected, stateless use of data
- Transactional programming

These characteristics are often considered a part of distributed programming because they came to prominence at the same time developers were abandoning the outmoded code in poorly designed client/server software. They also play a heightened role in most distributed applications. This book covers all these topics, but it's important to understand that they apply to all enterprise applications, even those that use the client/server model.

To really understand the role of distributed programming, we need to back up and examine a little history.

Client/Server Architecture

Enterprise computing has evolved through several stages. It started with proprietary mainframes and monolithic applications. Later, it spread wildly to desktops and local area networks (LANs) with the client/server model, which suddenly allowed the lowly desktop computer to play a role in sophisticated business applications. The client/server model, for all its flaws, is probably the most successful single model of application design. It has persisted, unchanged, as the dominant application architecture until the past few years.

A typical client/server application is hosted by a server on an internal network. It's usually an all-in-one package that relies on a back-end database. Multiple clients run the application from different computers, as shown in Figure 1-1. In this case, we'll also assume that the server plays two roles: hosting the database software and hosting the application files. This is a common choice for a small-scale setup, but it's certainly not the only possibility (and rarely the best design in distributed architecture).

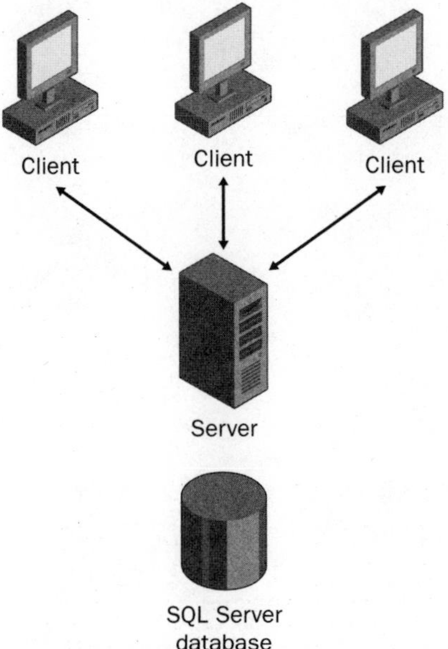

Figure 1-1 Basic client/server interaction

This deployment model provides two basic benefits. First of all, it ensures that every client can access the same version of the application. (Ideally, no client deployment is needed at all, but a few thorny problems often thwart that vision—all of which I cover a little later in this chapter.) Second, it centralizes all the back-end business information in one place: a server-side resource such as a database.

The defining characteristic of this design is that although the application is shared with multiple clients, it's really the clients rather than the server that perform all the work. That's because the central computer is little more than a file server. The client reads the appropriate executable and DLL files from the server's hard drive and loads them into its process space. It then uses its CPU and memory to run the program.

Inevitably, the server does perform some work. In this example, the server runs the relational database software, Microsoft SQL Server. When rows are retrieved or changes are applied to a table, SQL Server performs the low-level grunt work. To a certain extent, you can offload some additional responsibility to the server by adding stored procedures that encapsulate some of the business logic in the database.

Even in a client-server application, you are free to use a multi-layered design. For example, you can create middle-tier components that handle data access tasks such as retrieving data or committing changes, saving your application from needing to connect directly to the database. This approach improves organization, simplifies your code, and makes it easier to change data access details without modifying the application logic (and vice versa). The application is still a client/server application, however, because all the code is still executed on the client side, as illustrated in Figure 1-2.

Later chapters consider in more detail how you can divide an application into objects and tiers. For now, the important insight you should gain from all this is that adding more logical tiers to your application or placing your application files on different computers doesn't make your application distributed. As long as the client has the responsibility of executing all the code, the application is a client/server one.

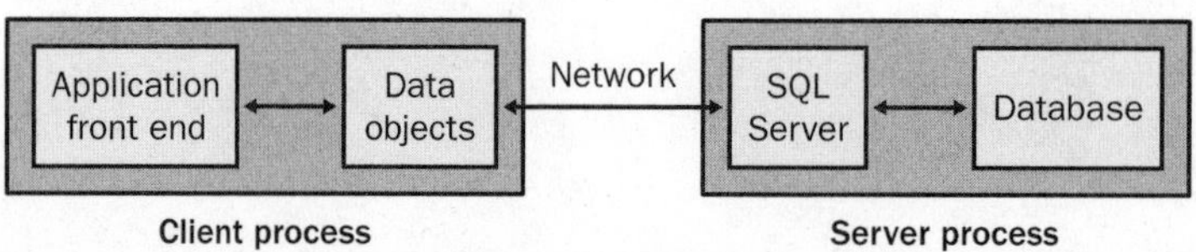

Figure 1-2 Client/server process usage

> **Note** Developers who are familiar with the concept of two-tier, three-tier, and multitier architecture might have noticed the absence of these terms in this chapter. These concepts help define the difference between client/server and distributed application *modeling*, but they don't designate where code is *executed*. (This difference between modeling and execution is also referred to as the difference between logical and physical partitioning.) In other words, using multitier design doesn't make a client/server application into a distributed application. Furthermore, solid multitier design practices are a good idea regardless of the type of application you're creating. Chapter 10 explores application architecture concepts in detail.

Problems with Client/Server Architecture

The inevitable question is, What's wrong with client/server design? Clearly, it can't accommodate easy client interaction because each client runs a separate instance of the application. Similarly, it doesn't allow for thin clients (sometimes derisively known as "feeble clients") because each client runs the application inside its own process space.

However, another more troubling problem exists. If this application needs to expand to serve not dozens but hundreds or thousands of simultaneous users, the server-side database quickly becomes a bottleneck. The overhead required to continuously release and create database connections for each client limits the performance and reduces the maximum number of clients that can be served simultaneously. This bottleneck has no easy solution in the client/server world.

The Real Database Bottleneck

It's often said that the problem with client/server development is that clients hold open connections to the database for their entire lifetime. This poor design restricts the maximum number of concurrent application users to the maximum number of connections that the database server (for example, SQL Server) can create at a time, introducing a significant bottleneck. However, this problem on its own doesn't tell the whole story about the limitations of client/server architecture. In fact, although this poor design is common in client/server code, it's just as easy to create in a distributed application. It all boils down to good coding practices. Whenever an application accesses a limited, shared resource such as a database connection, it should acquire it for the shortest amount of time possible. Ideally, an application should acquire the connection, perform a single update or query, and disconnect immediately.

Sometimes it seems that the world is filled with poorly written client/server applications. However, a well-written client/server application that behaves nicely—acquiring a database connection just long enough to perform a single database transaction—will still suffer from a fundamental bottleneck that distributed applications can avoid. The real problem is that just creating a connection involves a certain amount of work. This task requires a number of low-level operations, including validating the authentication information supplied by the client. This basic overhead is unavoidable, and it means that a client/server application has difficulty supporting a massive number of clients (thousands of simultaneous connections, rather than hundreds) even if they have relatively modest needs. The server tends to become tied up with the overhead of creating and releasing connections long before it has reached its maximum throughput or taxed the processing power of its CPU.

The database bottleneck problem exists with any server-side resource that's frequently used and expensive to create. It's this type of problem that effectively prevents almost all client/server programs from being able to expose their features to the wider audience of the Internet. Quite simply, they can't handle the load. Distributed applications, on the other hand, tackle this problem with the help of pooling, as discussed a little later in this chapter.

Is Deployment a Client/Server Problem?

In the client/server example discussed so far, the application is deployed on the server and the clients are more or less untouched. This approach is ideal because the application can be updated just by replacing the server-side files (although all the current clients must disconnect before you can take this step). Real life, however, is rarely as easy.

First of all, clients might require various system components. For example, an application that incorporates advanced user interface controls (particularly if written in Microsoft Visual Basic) can require various system DLLs and ActiveX controls, which are often distributed as part of Microsoft Internet Explorer, Office, or the Windows operating system. Alternatively, the application might make use of custom COM components that have been developed in-house. Before the application can use these components, they must be installed and registered on each client computer. In this situation, a dedicated setup program is the only practical approach. Unfortunately, every time the component is modified, a new setup program is usually required—and each client must run this setup before it can use the updated application. Clearly, the deployment picture has become much less pleasant.

These complications have led many developers to add "deployment hell" to the list of client/server drawbacks. The only problem is that this situation isn't unique to client/server applications. It's actually a fundamental stumbling block with COM, and distributed applications are rarely better off. If distributed applications use COM components directly, these components must be installed and registered. In theory, life should be simplified in a distributed application because components can be registered on the computers where they're executed (not on every client), but traditional DCOM often requires additional, more painful setup and configuration steps.

You've probably already heard about the .NET zero-touch deployment and support for side-by-side installation of different component versions. These features (dissected in the next chapter), along with the advanced support for version policies, remove the requirement for manual client-side setup. Don't be misled, however: this is a benefit for all .NET programmers, even those who create pure client/server programs. It has little to do with your choice of architecture.

Distributed Architecture

Distributed architecture rose to prominence as a way to respond to the scalability challenges inherent in the client/server model. The basic concept behind distributed applications is that at least some of the functionality runs remotely, in the process of another computer. The client-side application communicates with this remote component, sending instructions or retrieving information. Figure 1-3 shows a common design pattern, which uses a remote data access component. Notice that it incorporates three computers—the client and two other computers called *servers*, although the distinction between client and server here is really only skin-deep. In some distributed systems, these other computers might be ordinary workstations, in which case they're usually called *peers*.

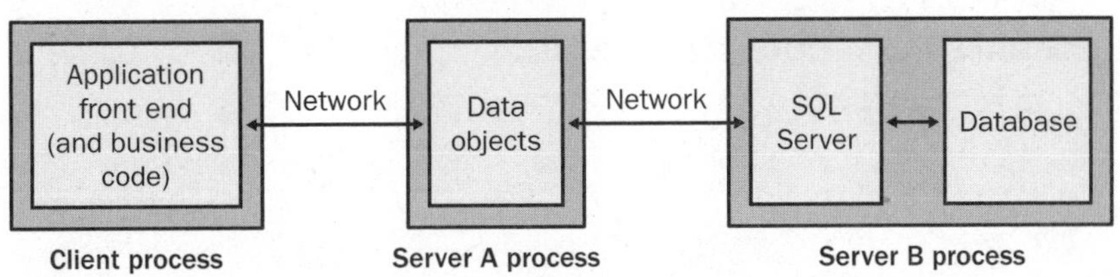

Figure 1-3 One example of a distributed application

Depending on the type of application, you can add multiple layers in this fashion. For example, you can add separate components for various tasks and spread them over different machines. Alternatively, you can just create several layers of components, which enables you to separate them to dedicated computers later. Similarly, you can decide how much of the work you want to offload to a given component. If you need to support a resource-starved client such as a mobile device, you can move all the logic to one or more servers, as illustrated in Figure 1-4. Generally, components are clearly divided into logical tiers that separate user services from business logic, which is in turn separated from data processing services (although this is not always the case in more freely structured peer-to-peer applications). Determining the best design for your needs is a difficult task and one we return to in the second part of this book.

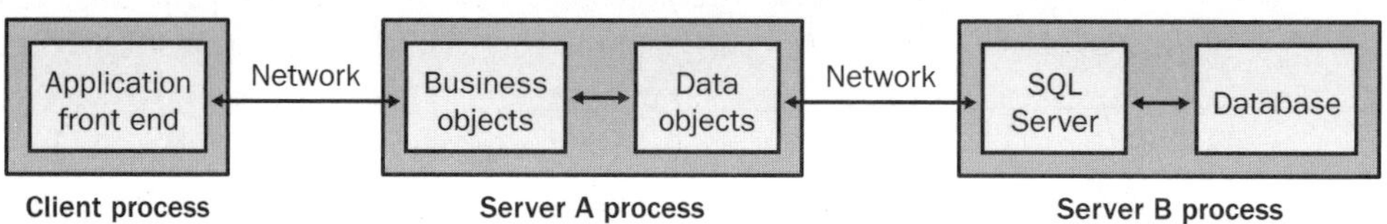

Figure 1-4 One way to implement three-tier design

Don't make the mistake of thinking you need to subdivide your program into dozens of layers to use multiple computers. Microsoft provides a clustering service with its Application Center 2000 product. This service allows a component to be hosted on a cluster of computers, which appear like one virtual computer to the client. When the client uses a component, the request is automatically routed to an available computer in the cluster. This design requires some additional configuration (mainly the installation and configuration of Application Center 2000), but it enables you to provide ironclad scalability for extremely high-volume applications. You can also use partitioned views and federated database servers to split database tables over a group of servers, which can then work together (simulating a single larger machine with the combined resources of all the constituent servers).

Advantages of Distributed Architecture

Allowing components to run on other computers provides some new capabilities, such as support for thin clients, cross-platform code integration, and distributed transactions. However, the key benefit is scalability. New computers can be incorporated into the system when additional computing power is needed. Stability is generally better (particularly if you're using clustering) because one computer can fail without derailing the entire application. The most obvious benefit appears when you need to access limited resources, such as database connections. With the help of some prebuilt Microsoft plumbing, you can enable features such as just-in-time activation and object pooling for your components. These features are part of the COM+ component services built into the Windows operating system. With pooling, an expensive resource such as a database connection isn't destroyed when the client finishes using it. Instead, it's maintained and provided to the next client, saving you the work of having to rebuild it from scratch.

Object Pools and Taxicabs

By far the best analogy I've heard to describe object pooling comes from Roger Sessions in his classic book on COM and DCOM. You can think of limited components as taxicabs with the sole goal of transporting you to the airport. If you dedicate a single taxicab to every passenger who needs to get to the airport, you'll quickly hit a traffic jam as the parking lot fills and streets become crowded with traffic. This situation is the equivalent of a poorly written client/server program that maintains a database connection over the life of the application. Other users need a taxi, but the application refuses to release them.

Another approach might be to create single-use taxis. You use the taxi to get to the airport and immediately destroy it when you arrive there. The parking lot remains empty, and new cars can continue to arrive. However, cars can be built only so quickly, and eventually the demand outstrips the ability to create and send new cars. This scenario is the equivalent of the well-written client/server application that releases database connections properly as soon as it doesn't need them.

The best approach, and the one closest to real life, is to create a pool of taxis. When a taxi finishes driving a passenger, it travels back to serve a new client. A dispatcher takes care of tracking new requests and matching them to available taxis. This dispatcher plays the same role as COM+ component services.

Traditionally, distributed programming also introduces programmers to the benefits of writing and reusing components in different languages, using tiers to make certain separate data services from business logic and creating components that can serve a variety of different platforms (such as Web applications and desktop applications). As the client/server example shows, however, all these features are available in client/server programs. They become more critical in distributed applications, but good application design is always worthwhile.

DCOM and the History of Distributed Applications

In most cases, the programming model for a distributed application is similar to the programming model for a client/server application because the remote communication process is abstracted away from the programmer. Microsoft has gone to extraordinary lengths to ensure that a programmer can call a method in a remote component just as easily as a method in a local component. The low-level network communication is completely transparent. The disadvantage is that the programmer can easily forget about the low-level reality and code components in a way that isn't well suited to distributed use.

The most important decision you make when creating a distributed application is determining how these components talk together. Traditionally, remote components are exposed through COM, and the network communication is handled by the DCOM standard—a protocol that carries its own baggage. DCOM has at least two fundamental problems: its distributed garbage collection system and its binary communication protocol.

Distributed Garbage Collection

DCOM uses keep-alive pinging, which is also known as distributed garbage collection. Under this system, the client automatically sends a periodic message to the distributed component. If this message isn't received after a certain interval of time, the object is automatically deallocated.

This system is required because DCOM uses ordinary COM components, which use reference counting to determine their lifetime. Without distributed garbage collection, a client could disconnect, fail to destroy the object, and leave it orphaned in server memory. After a while, these abandoned objects can drain precious memory from the server, gradually bringing it to a standstill.

In short, DCOM needs keep-alive pinging because it's based on ordinary COM objects, and COM doesn't provide any other way to manage object lifetime. However, distributed garbage collection increases network traffic needlessly and results in difficulty scaling to large numbers, particularly over slower wide area networks (WANs).

Complexity

DCOM is based on an intimidating multilayered protocol that incorporates services such as transport-level security. Microsoft programming languages and tools do a remarkable job of shielding developers (and their applications) from these complexities, but they still exist. Distributed DCOM components often require careful configuration on multiple computers and firewalls, over which they can't usually communicate. For these reasons, DCOM is poorly suited to distributed networks or heterogeneous networks that introduce computers from other platforms.

.NET Distributed Technologies

.NET addresses the problems that distributed application programmers have been grappling with for several years. However, .NET also recognizes that, depending on the application, there are several possible best approaches. For that reason, .NET includes a variety of distinct ways to use remote components. Developers who are adopting the .NET Framework for the first time face a good deal of confusion because they won't know where each technology fits into the overall picture of application design.

.NET Remoting

One of the most important distributed technologies in .NET is called *.NET Remoting*. .NET Remoting is really the .NET replacement for DCOM. It allows client applications to instantiate components on remote computers and use them like local components. However, .NET Remoting introduces a slew of much-needed refinements, including the capability to configure a component in code or through simple XML files, communicate using compact binary messages or platform-independent SOAP, and control object lifetime using flexible lease-based policies. .NET Remoting is also completely customizable and expandable—if you choose, you can write your own pluggable channels and sinks that can allow .NET Remoting to communicate according to entirely different standards.

.NET Remoting is the ideal choice for intranet scenarios. It typically provides the greatest performance and flexibility, especially if you want remote objects to maintain state or you need to create a peer-to-peer application. With .NET Remoting, you face a number of design decisions, including the protocol you want to use to communicate and the way your objects are created and destroyed. Figure 1-5 and Figure 1-6 show two sides of .NET Remoting: one in which components are created on a per-client basis and the other where a single component handles all client requests, which would be an impossible feat for a client/server application to duplicate.

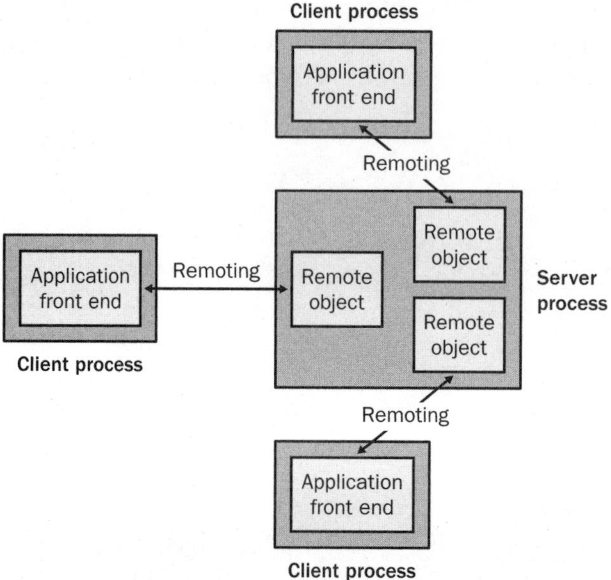

Figure 1-5 .NET Remoting with per-client objects

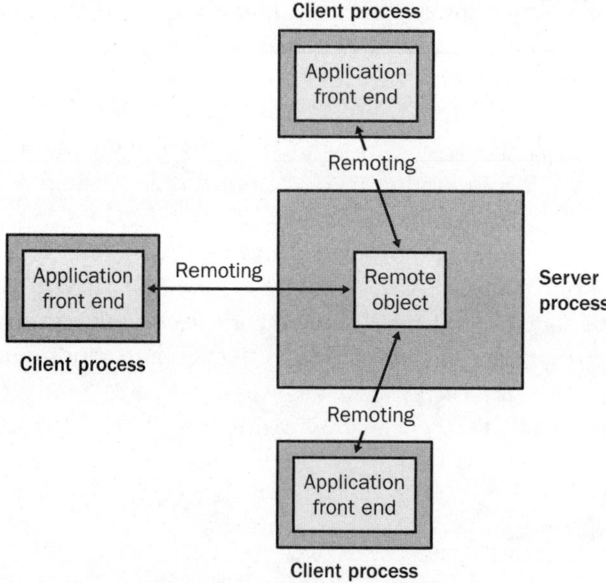

Figure 1-6 .NET Remoting with a singleton object

.NET Remoting can also be used across the Internet and even with third-party clients. It's at this point, however, that .NET Remoting starts to become blurred with another .NET technology: XML Web services. The following sections describe some of the differences.

XML Web Services

XML Web services are among the most wildly hyped features of Microsoft .NET. They allow a type of object communication that differs significantly from .NET Remoting (although it shares some of the low-level infrastructure):

- **XML Web services are designed with the Internet and integration across multiple platforms, languages, and operating systems in mind.** For that reason, it's extremely easy to call an XML Web service from a non-.NET platform.
- **XML Web services are designed with interapplication and interorganization use in mind.** In other words, you'll often expose a component through .NET Remoting to support your own applications. An XML Web service is more likely to provide basic functionality for other businesses to "plug in" to their own software. Toward that end, XML Web services support basic discovery and documentation. You can also use the Universal Description, Discovery, and Integration (UDDI) registry to publish information about XML Web services to the Internet and make them available to other interested businesses.
- **XML Web services are designed with simplicity in mind.** XML Web services are easy to write and don't require as much developer investment in planning and configuring how they work. This simplicity also means that XML Web services are more limited—for example, they're best suited to stateless solutions and don't support client notification or singleton use.
- **XML Web services always use SOAP messages to exchange information.** This means they can never communicate as efficiently as an object using .NET Remoting and a binary channel. It also means they can be consumed by clients on other platforms.

Figure 1-7 shows a remote XML Web service in use. Notice that the outline indicates that XML Web service objects are single-use only. They're created with each client call and destroyed at the end of a call. .NET Remoting objects can also work in this fashion; unlike XML Web services, however, they don't have to.

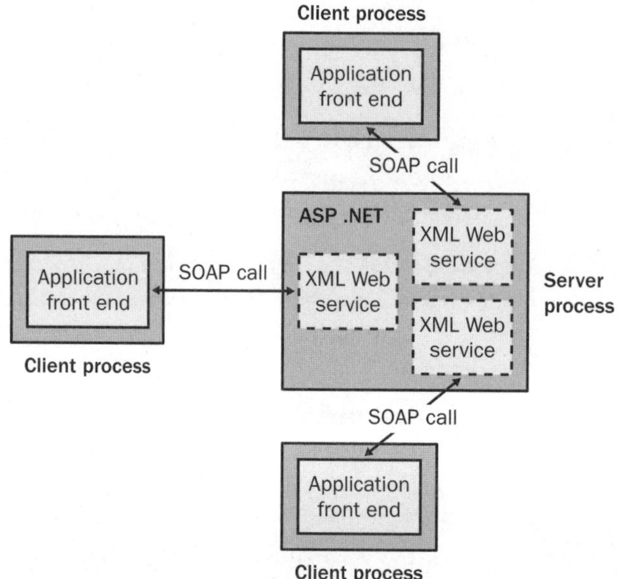

Figure 1-7 XML Web service calls

ASP.NET Applications

Finally, there are also ASP.NET Web applications, which are inherently distributed. ASP.NET applications rely on the ASP.NET worker process, which creates the appropriate Web page object with each client request and destroys it after it has finished processing. In that way, ASP.NET pages follow the exact same pattern as XML Web services. The only difference is that XML Web services are designed for middle-tier use and require another application to consume them. You can design this application, or a third-party developer can create it. With ASP.NET applications, however, the client is a simple Web browser that receives an ordinary HTML page.

The basic process for an ASP.NET application is as follows:

1. Microsoft Internet Information Services (IIS) receives a Web request for an ASP.NET (.aspx) file and passes the request on to the ASP.NET worker process. It compiles the file (if needed), caches a copy, and executes it.

2. The compiled file acts like a miniature program. It starts and runs all appropriate event handlers. At this stage, everything works together as a set of in-memory .NET objects.

3. When the code is finished, ASP.NET asks every control in the Web page to render itself.
4. The final HTML output is sent to the client.

ASP.NET programming does the best job of hiding the underlying reality of distributed programming from the user. Compilation takes place automatically, and the platform provides built-in services for handling state and improving performance through caching. In essence, an ASP.NET application is just a set of compiled ASP.NET pages that are continually started, executed, and completed on the Web server. The client has the illusion of interacting with a Web server but in reality sees only the final HTML output returned by the code after it has completed.

This book doesn't cover ASP.NET coding directly because many excellent books are dedicated to ASP.NET (including my own *ASP.NET: The Complete Reference*). Instead, this book concentrates on how to create components for a distributed system—whether it's a Web or desktop application. If you're creating a high-volume ASP.NET Web site that requires a transactional component to commit an order to a sales database, for example, you'll need to consider issues such as connection pooling and COM+ services, which this book examines. However, this book does not examine how to write the upper layer of ASP.NET user interface code.

Combining Distributed Technologies

Of course, you're also free to combine .NET Remoting, XML Web services, and ASP.NET pages according to your needs. For example, you might create an XML Web service that communicates through .NET Remoting with another component or create an application that uses XML Web services for some of its features and remote components for others. You'll see several examples of these blended solutions in the case study portion of this book (Part III).

> **Note** Unfortunately, the DCOM discussion in this chapter isn't just a history lesson. Depending on your .NET needs, you might need to rely on DCOM again. The most common reason is that you're using COM+ services, which require a COM/DCOM wrapper around your component. This situation is far from ideal and will likely change in the future as Microsoft creates a .NET version of COM+. Until then, you need to pay careful attention to these issues. Chapter 9 discusses when you can avoid these problems and how you can manage them.

Summary

This chapter tackled some essential theory. Like any developer, you'd probably like nothing more than to plunge into distributed application coding and start mastering .NET Remoting, XML Web services, and threading right away. However, it's keenly important that you understand the basic premise behind distributed applications before you start programming. That basic premise is this: Distributed architecture relies on executing portions of code on different computers, not just on the client. This code is wrapped up into a neat object, or component, as described in Chapter 2.

Of course, now that you've followed the evolution of application architecture, it should be obvious why we need distributed applications. Without them, it's extremely difficult to expose processing logic to a massive audience (eager e-commerce shoppers, for instance). For large-scale systems, distributed architecture ensures scalability, reliability, and flexibility for future design changes. It can also help software bridge the gap between modern-day applications and legacy systems.

There's one secret that programming authors don't want you to know: Although .NET makes distributed programming a good deal easier, distributed design still adds complexity, and it's not always the best solution, particularly for small-scale systems. If you're creating an internal system that doesn't need to use distributed architecture, you can still benefit a great deal from this book. Incorporating tricks such as multithreading, disconnected data, and stateless design can still improve your code and make it easier to remodel as a distributed application if the need arises in the future.

2

.NET Components

These days everyone knows what an object is and why these reusable units of logic are so critical for modern software programming. However, understanding the role components play in a distributed application isn't always as clear. In this chapter, we'll dissect these basic building blocks and start to plan a standard database component.

Along the way, we'll examine the difference between a simple class and a component and consider two essential class types for distributed applications. We'll also explore configuration files, the disposable pattern, and encapsulation. The chapter wraps up with an overview of assembly versioning and deployment. Here we'll consider how the common language runtime (CLR) resolves assembly references, and we'll examine the real advantages and sacrifices associated with shared assemblies. These basics form the groundwork for the advanced deployment techniques explored in Chapter 15.

What Is a Component?

Often, developers distinguish classes from components based on their use. Classes enable you to break up the functionality of your program into logical units. Components are classes that have a greater destiny: they are intended for use in more than one program.

Technically, components encapsulate one or more classes in compiled binary form. Components represent code that you might want to provide to another developer or just reuse in more than one of your own applications. Therefore, components need to have a higher standard of self-protection and they need a rigorously standardized interface. For example, components must restrict invalid data using property procedures, refrain from using parameters with cryptic names, and never include a combination of obscure methods that must be invoked in a specific order. All these considerations also apply to classes, but they are more critical for components. It's usually acceptable for a class to be tested according to the set way in which it will be used. The component programmer, however, has less control over how the code will be used and must consider every possibility.

Components are also versioned, maintained, and deployed individually. A developer uses a component in an application by adding a reference to a compiled assembly, not by copying a source code file into the project. Therefore, components are more self-sufficient than the average class. They represent reusable functionality at its best.

> **Note** One subtle difference between components and assemblies is that components define a logical grouping of classes around a specific feature set while assemblies are the physical DLL or EXE files that contain the compiled code. An assembly is a unit for the purposes of versioning, deployment, and the code-access security mechanism discussed in Chapter 13. It can contain any number of related components. It's also possible, but less likely, to find a single component spread out over more than one assembly. As a seasoned .NET developer, you already know that classes are built from properties, methods, and events, and you'd rightly be insulted if I reminded you of that. What's more important is determining how classes interact in a distributed system and how they divide their functionality into methods and properties.

The Component's Role in a Distributed System

In a distributed application, components contain classes that typically play one of two roles:

- A provider of services
- A container for information

Why the sharp distinction? In a distributed application, state is a critical issue (as discussed in Chapter 10). By using this distinction, you can separate classes that require state but don't provide much functionality (the information packages) from classes that provide a collection of utility functions and are entirely stateless (the service providers).

> **Note** Programming veterans might notice that I've studiously avoided bringing business objects into this discussion. In Chapter 10, we'll revisit the issue in more detail as we examine tiers and object modeling.

Service Providers

The most important role a class can play is that of a "provider of services" for your application. This type of class might provide services directly to the client front end, to another component, or to a third-party program that you have no interest in (as is often the case when you create a Web service). In this sense, a component has one goal: to facilitate the reuse and maintenance of a logically distinct piece of code. For example, you could design the perfect tracing or database class in a component, and then compile in a separate assembly. This is a pattern you'll see throughout this book.

Deciding to put functionality into a component doesn't mean much when you're dealing with distributed architecture. Any type of program can benefit from component-based programming. When you start thinking about partitioning your application into components, however, you open yourself to the possibility of hosting components out of process. Out-of-process components can still run on the same computer, or they can run on other computers. This is the essence of distributed application programming.

So how do you make a component that can be activated on another computer? It's a topic we'll return to in the next few chapters, but here's an overview of some possibilities:

- Classes that inherit from *System.MarshalByRefObject* directly or indirectly can be activated across computers using .NET Remoting.
- Classes that use the <*WebMethod*> attribute (and optionally inherit from *System.Web.Services.WebService*) can be accessed through ASP.NET as Web services.
- Classes that inherit from *System.EnterpriseServices.ServicedComponent* are serviced components and gain everything that COM+ has to offer, including object pooling and just-in-time activation.

Information Packages

You might also want to create a class that should never be executed out of process but is intended to be part of a component assembly. The most common example is creating an "information package"—basically, an object such as an *Account* class or a *UserInfo* class that contains a set of related properties that detail information about a single entity.

In this case, you might also want to add the <*Serializable*> attribute, which ensures that the component can be serialized and transmitted to other out-of-process components through .NET Remoting (no such step is necessary for XML Web services). We'll get into these considerations in more detail over the next few chapters.

Dissecting a Sample Component

One of the most common services that components are called on to provide is data access. Databases make ideal work for components for several reasons, including the following:

- **Databases require extraneous details.** This information (connection strings, field names, and so on) can complicate application logic. A well-written component encapsulates these details.
- **Databases are always in demand.** A typical application might call a database several times for different pieces of information. Placing this code in a database component ensures that the connection and querying details are handled in a consistent manner rather than copied to every corner of your code.
- **Relational databases aren't object-oriented.** However, components are. By placing a component between the database and the application, you gain the best of both worlds. The application programmer can work with the database using an object interface (and not worry about whether the retrieved information is being joined from multiple tables). The database, on the other hand, gets the SQL (or stored procedure calls) it requires.
- **Databases often change.** If new fields are added or stored procedure names are changed after the application is deployed, it's easier to change a single component rather than the entire application.
- **Database access code often changes.** This is a natural progression as you develop the fine-tuned code that ensures optimum per-

formance. After profiling your database or modifying the set of indexes, you might need to modify a query. Or, you might develop a database component during development that uses straightforward queries and then modify it to use better-performing stored procedures later on.

When you create an assembly with data access code, you'll often create two classes for each table. One class is the data package that represents the information your code needs to retrieve. The other class is the service provider that performs tasks such as updates and information retrieval. Depending on your needs, this service provider might provide methods that allow a single matching record to be retrieved and returned as an object and methods that return an entire collection or array of data objects.

Listing 2-1 shows a sample component that wraps a single Customers table. I've left out the actual data access details and shown just the skeletal structure for the information package and service provider. This example provides a good template for any data-based service provider. We'll revisit this class over the next few chapters.

```
'*******************************************************
'
' CustomerDetails Class
'
' A data component that encapsulates details about
' a particular customer.
'
'*******************************************************

Public Class CustomerDetails

    Private _ID As Integer
    Private _Name As String
    Private _Email As String
    Private _Password As String

    Public Sub New(customerID As Integer, password As String, _
      name As String, email As String)
        ' Note that the constructor assigns to the properties, not the
        ' private variables. This ensures that any required validation
        ' is performed in the property procedures, and invalid values
        ' can't get in through a back door.
        _ID = customerID
        _Password = password
        _Name = name
        _Email = email
    End Sub
```

Listing 2-1 The structure of a sample database component

```
    Public Sub New(name As String, email As String, _
      password As String)
        _Name = name
        _Email = email
        _Password = password
    End Sub

    Public Property ID() As Integer
        Get
            Return _ID
        End Get
        Set(ByVal Value As Integer)
            _ID = Value
        End Set
    End Property

    Public Property Name() As String
        Get
            Return _Name
        End Get
        Set(ByVal Value As String)
            _Name = Value
        End Set
    End Property

    Public Property Email() As String
        Get
            Return _Email
        End Get
        Set(ByVal Value As String)
            _Email = Value
        End Set
    End Property

    Public Property Password() As String
        Get
            Return _Password
        End Get
        Set(ByVal Value As String)
            _Password = Value
        End Set
    End Property

End Class
```

```
'*****************************************************
'
' CustomerDB Class
'
' A service provider component that encapsulates all data
' logic necessary to retrieve, update, or add a customer.
'
'*****************************************************

Public Class CustomerDB

    Private _ConnectionString As String = _
     "Data Source=MyServer;Initial Catalog=MyDb;" & _
     ""Integrated Security=SSPI"

    Public Function GetCustomer(ByVal customerID As Integer) _
      As CustomerDetails
        ' (Code omitted.)
    End Function

    Public Sub AddCustomer(ByVal customer As CustomerDetails)
        ' (Code omitted.)
    End Function

    Public Sub UpdateCustomer(ByVal customer As CustomerDetails)
        ' (Code omitted.)
    End Sub

End Class
```

Notice that the service provider class *CustomerDB* is entirely stateless. It uses a single static member variable to store the database connection string, which is hidden from the application programmer. The *CustomerDetails* class, on the other hand, is entirely stateful. It provides two constructors that ensure it is preloaded with valid data when it is created. The first constructor, which accepts all three pieces of information, is designed for use with the *GetCustomerDetails* method and *UpdateCustomer* method. The other constructor is designed for the client to use with the *AddCustomer* method. At this point, the client won't know the unique ID value because this is assigned automatically by the database.

You also might have noticed that the *CustomerDetails* class uses full property procedures even though a simpler class with public members would do just as well (as shown here):

```
Public Class CustomerDetails

    Public ID As Integer
    Public Name As String
    Public Email As String
    Public Password As String

End Class
```

Using full property procedures offers a few advantages, however, including the following:

- It enables you to perform some basic data checking and refuse invalid information. Don't take this approach too far, however, because rules are often better placed in a different location (such as at the user interface level or in a service provider method).
- It enables you to use data binding with arrays or collections of this class in Windows Forms and ASP.NET Web pages, which comes in handy.
- It provides a better level of design-time support. Property procedure settings can be configured through the Properties window in Visual Studio .NET; public variables cannot.

Essentially, it all boils down to one thing: Adding property procedures ensures that your class follows the rules of proper encapsulation.

Classes vs. Structures

Instead of using classes for your information packages, you can use structures. Structures are similar to classes, with some limitations. (For example, they don't support inheritance, although they do support interfaces, property procedures, and methods.) The key difference between a structure and a class is in how they are allocated in memory. Structures are value types, which means they behave differently for assignment and comparison operations than classes, which are reference types.

To get a better grasp of the difference, consider the following code, which manipulates two structure variables:

```
StructureA = StructureB
' StructureA now has a copy of the contents of StructureB.
' There are two duplicate structures in memory.

If StructureA.Equals(StructureB) Then
    ' This is True as long as the structures have the same content.
    ' This performs a full binary comparison that will be slow for
    ' large structures.
End If
```

Compare this with the behavior for two class instances:

```
ObjectA = ObjectB
' ObjectA and ObjectB now both point to the same thing.
' There is one object in memory, and two ways to access it.

If ObjectA Is ObjectB Then
    ' This is True if both ObjectA and ObjectB point to the same thing.
    ' This is False if they are separate, yet identical objects.
End If
```

Generally, structures provide the best performance for small objects (ones that store fewer than 16 bytes), whereas classes are more efficient for larger objects. Classes are also more common in Microsoft Visual Basic code because pre-.NET versions didn't include structures (although user-defined types provided similar but reduced functionality). To define a structure, you use the *Structure* keyword instead of the *Class* keyword:

```
Public Structure CustomerDetails

    Private _ID As Integer
    Private _Name As String
    Private _Email As String
    Private _Password As String

    ' (Property procedure and constructor code omitted.)

End Structure
```

Note that if you require value-type semantics and the ability to copy or compare the contents of class instances, you don't necessarily need to create a structure. Instead, you can implement interfaces such as *ICloneable* and *IComparable* when you create your class to support these features.

The *IComponent* Interface

To make matters a little confusing, the .NET Framework also defines a component as a class that implements the *System.ComponentModel.IComponent* interface or that derives from another class that implements *IComponent* (such as *System.ComponentModel.Component*). These *IComponent* classes have a few characteristics that distinguish them from ordinary classes:

- They provide a way to release resources deterministically. Because the *IComponent* interface extends the *System.IDisposable* interface, every component provides a *Dispose* method. When this method is invoked, the component immediately frees the resources it uses—assuming you've added the necessary code.
- They provide basic design-time support—that is, the ability to be hosted in the Microsoft Visual Studio .NET Toolbox, dragged and dropped on a form, and configured through the Properties window. This basic support is a free frill built into Visual Studio and the .NET Framework.

In this book, I use a slightly broader definition of components that includes any class or group of classes intended for reuse in different applications or for execution on different computers. This means, for example, that Web service classes are components. In strict .NET terms, Web services usually implement *IComponent* indirectly—but they don't need to.

If you'd like, you can change the *CustomerDB* and *CustomerDetails* classes into *IComponent*-supporting types. First of all, you can derive *CustomerDB* from the *System.ComponentModel.Component* class. Because this class derives from *System.MarshalByRefObject*, you won't only gain design-time support—you'll also gain the ability to execute the *CustomerDB* component on another computer and communicate with it through .NET Remoting. The following code shows the new *CustomerDB* class declaration:

```
Public Class CustomerDB
  Inherits System.ComponentModel.Component
```

CustomerDetails, on the other hand, can derive from *System.ComponentModel.MarshalByValueComponent*, which is a component type that can't be manipulated remotely. However, you can add the *<Serializable>* attribute and gain the ability to send objects based on this class from computer to computer using .NET Remoting:

```
<Serializable()> _
Public Class CustomerDetails
  Inherits System.ComponentModel.MarshalByValueComponent
```

We'll examine the <*Serializable*> attribute and the *MarshalByRefObject* class in more detail in Chapter 4 when we dive into .NET Remoting. For now, it's just important to understand that you can build on the basic *CustomerDB* and *CustomerDetails* classes by making them remotable (or turning them into Web services), and by adding design-time support through the *IComponent* interface.

Using Components at Design Time

You can access a component from another application in several ways after you compile it. The first way is to add a reference. (In Visual Studio .NET, you right-click on the project in Solution Explorer, choose Add Reference, and find the DLL assembly that contains your component.) You can then use the component classes as if they are a part of your own project:

```
Dim CustDB As New DataComponent.CustomerDB
CustDB.AddUser(New DataComponent.CustomerDetails( _
    "Matthew", "MacDonald", "opensesame"))
```

If these classes implement the *IComponent* interface, however, you have the choice of a second, similar approach that makes use of the design-time capabilities of components. In Visual Studio .NET, right-click on the Toolbox and choose Customize Toolbox. Then add the .NET assembly. Two new icons will appear in the Toolbox, one for each component (as shown in Figure 2-1). At the same time, a reference is added to your project.

Figure 2-1 Components in the Visual Studio .NET Toolbox

You can now create the component at design time by dragging it onto a Windows Form, a Web page, or a Web service. The first time you add the component to any part of a project, Visual Studio .NET adds the necessary assembly reference. The component then appears in a special component tray (as shown in Figure 2-2) and is added to the hidden designer code for the class you're creating. You can modify properties for this instance of the component through the Properties window. Typically, this ability to use the Properties window at design time isn't much more than a programming convenience.

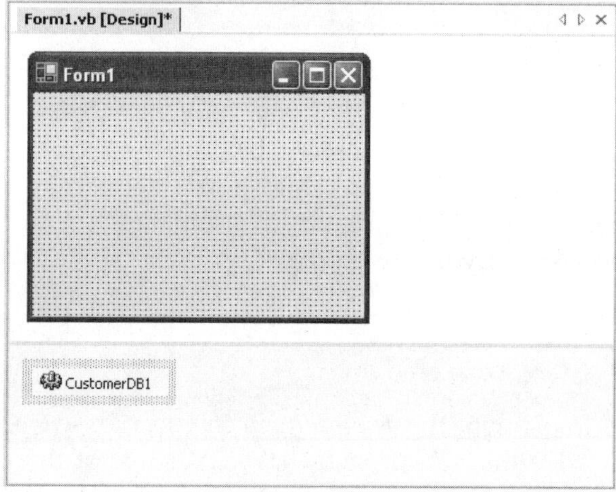

Figure 2-2 A component at design time

The final way to load a component from an assembly is through reflection (which is similar to late binding). This approach is slower, much more susceptible to runtime errors (for example, if you specify incorrect type information), and more difficult to program with. It's required in some situations where you might be examining a type that you don't know much about, but it's never used as part of a distributed system that you create. Reflection does serve a purpose when creating highly configurable applications, and we'll consider it in more detail in Chapter 15.

> **Note** Adding an assembly reference to a Visual Basic .NET project is quite different from referencing a COM component in a Visual Basic 6 project. In the .NET world, adding the reference actually copies the assembly DLL to your local application directory. This is because, by default, all components are private and can be located and used only if they are in the same directory as the application.

Resources and Disposable Classes

The CLR uses garbage collection to free up memory by deallocating objects that are no longer referenced in your application. This automatic memory management solves the problems traditionally faced by C++ developers, who needed to ruthlessly track and release every morsel of memory that came under their control. However, it also introduces the problem of nondeterministic finalization. Essentially, nondeterministic finalization means that when you release an object, it might remain in memory until system memory becomes scarce and the garbage collection service springs into action. This works well for ordinary classes but not so well for classes that hold unmanaged resources (such as file handles). In this case, these scarce resources are held onto long after they are needed, potentially reducing application performance or causing a contention error as more than one object competes for the same resource.

Components deal with the problem of nondeterministic finalization through the *IDisposable* interface, from which *IComponent* derives. To satisfy *IDisposable*, every class must provide a *Dispose* method that automatically releases resources. The drawback is that you need to rely on the client to call this method to clean up when a task is complete. Otherwise, the same performance and contention problems will remain. Many .NET classes, such as *FileStream* (which wraps a file handle), provide a *Dispose* method, which you should call when a task is complete, just before setting the object reference to *Nothing* or letting it go out of scope. In addition, these classes often add custom methods such as *Close*, which will implicitly call *Dispose*.

Using the Disposable Pattern in a Component-Derived Class

When you're creating classes that hold limited resources, you need to ensure that they follow the disposable pattern and release their resources explicitly. Ideally you won't need to maintain any resources in a class because this can seriously affect scalability. For example, the *CustomerDB* class creates, opens, and closes a database connection in each method to conserve that limited resource. This is the best design for a distributed application. Still, you might need to create a lower-level class that wraps a limited resource, which would then be used by a higher-level service provider class. (We'll consider one example of this design in Chapter 9.) If your resource class derives from a .NET *Component* class, you use the design pattern shown in Listing 2-2.

```
Public Class MyComponent
    Inherits System.ComponentModel.Component

    Protected Overloads Overrides Sub Dispose(disposing As Boolean)
        If disposing Then
            ' Disposal was triggered manually by the client.
            ' Call Dispose() on any contained objects.
        End If

        ' Release unmanaged resources.

        ' Call Dispose on the base class.
        MyBase.Dispose(disposing)
   End Sub

End Class
```

Listing 2-2 The disposable pattern in a component class

The client releasing your component won't call your *Dispose* method directly. Instead, the client calls a basic parameterless *Component.Dispose* method, which your class inherits. This method automatically calls your custom *Dispose* method. This allows a component to dispose of itself in two ways: in response to a *Dispose* method invocation (the preferred way) and when the object is garbage collected (if the client forgot to call *Dispose*). In the first case, the disposing parameter is *True*. In the latter case, it is *False*.

The reason for this extra layer of indirection is that it isn't safe to dispose an object that no longer exists. If the *Dispose* method has been called by the runtime, there is a good possibility that any contained objects have already been garbage collected, so your object shouldn't attempt to dispose of them again. If *Dispose* is called by the client, these objects will still exist and should be disposed of properly.

Using the Disposable Pattern in Non-*Component* Classes

In some cases, you won't be able to derive from *System.ComponentModel.Component*. For example, you might need to inherit functionality from another non-*Component* class. Because .NET doesn't support multiple inheritance, you must implement the *IComponent* or *IDisposable* interface on your own. The code you use to release resources is similar, but you must add a little more of the lower-level logic yourself. Namely, you need to add a *Dispose* method with no arguments, which the client calls directly. This method calls the custom *Dispose* method to release resources and then instructs .NET that garbage collection isn't needed because the object has already cleaned up after itself.

You also need to account for the possibility that the client will forget to use the *Dispose* method by adding a *Finalize* method. This method also triggers the custom *Dispose* method. Listing 2-3 shows a full example.

```
Public Class MyComponent
    Inherits MyBaseClass
    Implements System.ComponentModel.IComponent

    ' Implement IDisposable.
    ' This is the method the client calls to dispose the object.
    Public Overloads Sub Dispose()
       Dispose(True)

       ' Take the object out of the finalization queue so it won't be
       ' accidentally garbage collected twice.
       GC.SuppressFinalize(Me)
    End Sub

    ' This method is only called if the object is garbage
    ' collected without being properly disposed.
    Protected Overrides Sub Finalize()
        Dispose(False)
    End Sub

    ' The custom code for releasing resources goes here.
    Protected Overloads Overridable Sub Dispose(disposing As Boolean)
        If disposing Then
            ' Disposal was triggered manually by the client.
            ' Call Dispose() on any contained objects.
        End If

        ' Release unmanaged resources.
    End Sub

End Class
```

Listing 2-3 Implementing *IDispose* directly

Remember, if you don't need to use the *Disposable* pattern and add design-time support to your component, you don't need to worry about inheriting from the *Component* class or implementing the *IComponent* interface. However, it's important to understand how .NET defines components.

> **Note** If you're a seasoned enterprise programmer, you already know that you can't rely on clients to behave properly and follow details such as calling a *Dispose* method. That's one of the reasons that service provider classes are always stateless, thereby ensuring that these problems can't occur. However, you might need to develop a low-level disposable object to support your service provider class. (This is analogous to the way the stateless *CustomerDB* class uses the disposable *SqlConnection* class.) In this case, the client never directly interacts with the object and you can enforce proper disposal in your server-side code.

Connection Strings and Configuration Files

Sometimes you might see a variation of the service provider design that provides its connection string as a property or requires the connection string in its constructor. This design might seem like a good idea because it allows flexibility for the data access class to be used with different data sources or login information. However, this approach also creates its share of problems:

- It introduces one more area in which the component will be susceptible to client mistakes.
- It introduces one more area where security can be compromised because each client will need to know the database user ID and password.
- It can threaten connection pooling because minor changes in the connection string result in the creation of new pools, even if the string is still functionally equivalent.

Essentially, this approach infringes on the responsibilities of the data access class, which is designed to encapsulate all database-specific details. It also breaks the component's contract. In other words, the data access component can't guarantee that it will provide reliable database access if it can't be sure that the connection string is correct.

For all these reasons, it's usually best to place the connection string in the component itself or in a configuration file that it reads from the same directory. The configuration file approach is often the preferred one because it enables you to modify the connection string without recompiling the component. However, you might also need to take extra steps to secure the configuration file, which could otherwise be read by a client on the network (although you won't need to worry about Internet access because ASP.NET automatically handles HTTP requests for .config files and rejects them).

Every .NET application can have an associated configuration file in one of two locations:

- If you're creating a Web page, a Web service, or a component hosted in an ASP.NET application, the configuration file is always named web.config and is located in the virtual directory of your application.
- If you're creating any other type of application, the configuration file must be in the same directory as the executable and will have the same name as your application, plus the extension .config. Therefore, if your application has the executable file name myapp.exe, you can create a configuration file named myapp.exe.config that .NET will process automatically when the application is launched.

The configuration file can contain a great deal of additional information. Later in this chapter, for example, we'll consider the settings it contains for resolving assembly references. Custom settings, such as a connection string, are always added to a configuration section called *<appSettings>*. Every custom setting has a string value and a unique string key that identifies it. You define both in the configuration file.

In the following configuration file, for example, a setting named *ConnectionString* is added to the application. The connection string itself is split over two lines due to space constraints.

```
<?xml version="1.0"?>
<configuration>

  <appSettings>
    <add key="ConnectionString"
         value="Data Source=MyServer;Initial Catalog=MyDb;Integrated
                Security=SSPI" />
  </appSettings>

  <!-- Other configuration sections can go here,
       but aren't necessary. -->

</configuration>
```

> **Note** The configuration file is written in XML. In XML documents, white space is collapsed (although this doesn't include the text in between quotation marks, which is why the connection string value must be placed on one line.) You can't use Visual Basic syntax (for example, using the ampersand [&] to join strings or the underscore [_] to indicate a line break) because it has no meaning in XML. XML also defines a format for comments. In the preceding example, the text note *Other configuration sections can go here...* will be ignored because it is enclosed in XML comment markers.

You can retrieve custom settings in the constructor method for the component using the *System.Configuration.ConfigurationSettings* class. This class provides a shared property called *AppSettings*, which is a key/value dictionary exposing all the custom configuration settings. Here is the new constructor code for the *CustomerDB* class, which retrieves the connection string setting from the configuration file:

```
Public Sub New()
    ' Retrieve the connection string and store it in the
    ' private member variable.
    _ConnectionString = ConfigurationSettings.AppSettings( _
                         "ConnectionString")
End Sub
```

Note that this example assumes you've imported the *System.Configuration* namespace and therefore don't need to type the fully qualified name for the *ConfigurationSettings* class. Remember, you don't need to access the file directly by specifying a filename or a directory path. Configuration files, if they have the correct name and are located in the correct directory, are recognized and made available by .NET automatically.

Configuration files are favored over other methods of storing settings because they are never locked and can therefore be edited at any time. Configuration files are also convenient because they are tied to a particular directory, not a particular computer (as a registry setting would be). Therefore, if several clients load the same application from the same directory, they will share the same single connection string setting.

In some cases, depending on the deployment you use, a configuration file might give the client too much opportunity to modify the connection string and you might need to compile it directly in the class (as shown earlier) or retrieve it from a Web service.

> **Note** One potential caveat with configuration file settings is that they are associated with the host application, not the component assembly. In a simple scenario where a Windows application uses a local component, you must add any configuration settings to the configuration file for the Windows application. If you're creating a component that uses .NET Remoting, you need to add settings to the configuration file used by the server-side hosting program. Finally, in the case of a Web service, configuration settings must be entered in a web.config file in the corresponding virtual directory.

Configuration Files in Visual Studio .NET

When you create a Windows project with Visual Studio .NET, a configuration file won't be created automatically. However, you can easily add one. Just right-click on the project in Solution Explorer and choose Add, New Item. Then choose Application Configuration File under the Utility node (as shown in Figure 2-3).

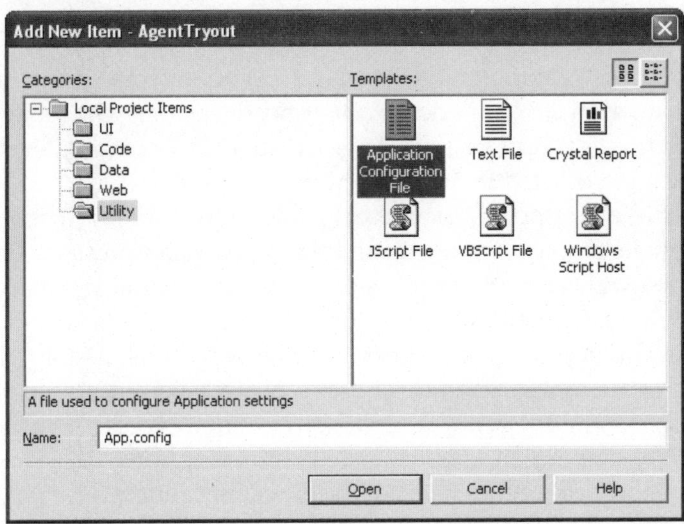

Figure 2-3 Adding a configuration file to a project

The application configuration file is automatically assigned the name app.config. You shouldn't change this name. When Visual Studio .NET compiles your project, it creates the configuration file in the appropriate directory, with the correct name. This enables you to rename your executable without needing to alter the configuration file. If you want to see the configuration file for yourself, choose Project, Show All Files from the menu. When you compile your project, you'll see the appropriate file appear in the Bin directory (as shown in Figure 2-4).

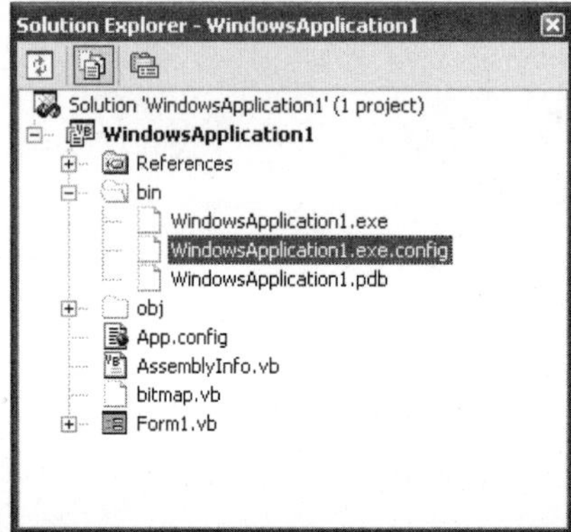

Figure 2-4 The automatically generated configuration file

Deploying an Assembly

In the past, the use of component-based development with distributed applications was plagued by constant deployment headaches. If you wanted to access Microsoft's rich set of COM+ services and create objects that were easy to reuse in any language, you had to write COM components, which had to be registered on multiple computers. If you tried another approach (such as creating your own low-level DLLs), you escaped the registration problem but were left out in the cold without easy reuse, versioning, or the ability to use distributed application essentials such as connection pooling.

In .NET, the deployment picture has improved considerably. After you've created a component and referenced it in a project, you just need to distribute the project and component assembly together. For a typical Windows application, that means copying the project executable along with the DLL assembly to the same directory on the server. When the client launches the application, it will find and use the required assembly painlessly. The Windows Registry doesn't play any role at all. In an ASP.NET application, the process is similar, except you deploy ASP.NET pages to a virtual directory on a Web server and any required assemblies to a Bin subdirectory of the virtual directory. Once again, the .NET Framework finds the required assembly automatically; reads all the metadata it needs about available classes, methods, events, and properties; and allows the client code to interact with it just as easily as if the class were a part of the Web page code. This process flows equally smoothly if the component is written in another language supported by .NET.

The only requirement is that the client computer have the .NET Framework installed. To install the .NET Framework, you can use the standard .NET redistributable (available for download from Microsoft and included with Visual Studio .NET). This redistributable supports the following operating systems:

- Windows 98
- Windows 98 Second Edition
- Windows Millennium Edition (Windows Me)
- Windows NT 4.0 (Workstation or Server) with Service Pack 6a
- Windows 2000 (Professional, Server, or Advanced Server)
- Windows XP (Home or Professional)
- Windows .NET Server
- Windows Server 2003

Internet Explorer 5.0 and Windows Installer 2.0 are also required. Keep in mind that these requirements apply to any clients that want to execute .NET code. If you're creating a Java client that talks to a .NET Web service or using an ASP.NET Web site that users can access through an ordinary browser, these requirements obviously don't apply.

Sharing Assemblies

Every experienced developer who learns about .NET's painless new deployment system has two questions:

- How do I update an assembly without breaking an application?
- How do I share an assembly between applications?

The answers to these questions depend on whether you're using private or shared assemblies. Shared assemblies are made globally available to every .NET application on the computer. Private assemblies are constrained to applications that know how to find them.

At this point, you're probably quietly concluding that you need to create shared assemblies to reuse important core pieces of functionality. Not so fast. There are some serious potential headaches that you probably haven't considered:

- Shared assemblies need a *strong name*, which guarantees that they won't conflict with any other component in the global assembly cache (GAC). To create this strong name, you have to sign the assembly with a public/private key pair.
- Like COM components, the GAC is computer-specific. This means you must install the component in the cache of the same computer that will run the client application. If you want to use a component with different instances of a Windows application, for example, you need to install the assembly on each and every client machine. Otherwise, when the client runs the application, the required component assembly won't be found.

The second problem is by far the most significant. Even if you're creating a component that you want to execute in the process space of another computer, the client still needs to be able to reference it. Otherwise, it won't have the information it needs about properties, methods, and events. For these reasons, it might make little sense to place a component in the computer-specific registry such as the GAC, especially if it needs to be used by applications running on several different machines. In this case, .NET's capability to load an assembly directly from an unregistered file is far superior.

So how can you share a private component among multiple applications in different directories? Well, one option would be to place a separate copy of the component into every application directory. This actually isn't such a bad idea. That way, you could theoretically update some applications with a new version of the component while ensuring that other applications use the original version. It's also incredibly easy. Unfortunately, you can't overwrite the assembly while it's in use, which presents one possible problem. (ASP.NET is one pleasant exception because it enables you to update private assemblies even when they are in use.) This system is also likely to lead to some level of disorder if you need to reuse a basic component with a large number of different applications. To implement a more consistent approach, you need to use a custom configuration file.

Searching for Private Assemblies

By default, .NET automatically searches the root directory of the application for any referenced assemblies. However, you can also instruct .NET to consider other locations. To do so, you need to create an application configuration file. As described earlier in this chapter, every configuration file has the same name as the .NET assembly, plus the extension .config (as in myapp.exe.config). If this file exists in the same directory, .NET reads and applies its settings automatically. The exception is with ASP.NET configuration files, which always use the fixed name web.config.

The *CodeBase* Element

The configuration file uses a simple XML-based format. Listing 2-4 is a sample configuration that specifically indicates that the private assembly DBComponent.dll is located in the subdirectory Components.

```
<?xml version="1.0"?>
<configuration>
  <runtime>
    <assemblyBinding xmlns="urn:schemas-microsoft-com:asm.v1">
      <dependentAssembly>
        <assemblyIdentity name="DBComponent" />
        <codeBase href="Components\DBComponent.dll" />
      </dependentAssembly>
    </assemblyBinding>
  </runtime>
</configuration>
```

Listing 2-4 A sample configuration file

You can provide explicit directory information for multiple assemblies in this fashion by adding additional *<dependent>* assembly elements:

```
<?xml version="1.0"?>
<configuration>
  <runtime>
    <assemblyBinding xmlns="urn:schemas-microsoft-com:asm.v1">
      <dependentAssembly>
        <assemblyIdentity name="DBComponent" />
        <codeBase href="Components\DBComponent.dll" />
      </dependentAssembly>
      <dependentAssembly>
        <assemblyIdentity name="LogComponent" />
        <codeBase href="Log\LogComponent.dll" />
      </dependentAssembly>
    </assemblyBinding>
  </runtime>
</configuration>
```

In this case, if the *LogComponent* or *DBComponent* assemblies reference other private assemblies, .NET will automatically search in the corresponding Components or Log directory. This makes it easy to distribute a group of related components without having to write too much information in the configuration file.

The *Probing* Element

Alternatively, you can use the *<probing>* element, which is far less invasive than it sounds. Probing is the process by which .NET searches for private assemblies that aren't specifically configured. By default, it tries these two locations:

```
AppPath\[Assembly Name].dll
AppPath\[Assembly Name]\[Assembly Name].dll
```

If you have specified culture information for the referenced assembly, it performs a similar lookup attempt but automatically searches in the culture-specific subdirectory rather than the application path.

You can configure this probing process to use other directories by adding the probing element to the configuration file. This element specifies valid subdirectories to search for any private assembly that can't be located, separated by semicolons. The following example searches both the Components and Log subdirectories:

```
<configuration>
   <runtime>
      <assemblyBinding xmlns="urn:schemas-microsoft-com:asm.v1">
         <probing privatePath="Components;Log"/>
      </assemblyBinding>
   </runtime>
</configuration>
```

The only limitation with code bases and probing is that they must point to a subdirectory of the application directory. Unfortunately, they can't point to a directory higher up the tree or to a directory on another drive.

Versioning Assemblies

Assemblies also need to be versioned. You specify the version number for your application by adding an *AssemblyInfo* attribute to a code file in your application. If you create your applications using Visual Studio .NET, you automatically have a file named AssemblyInfo.vb that contains several of these attributes, which enable you to set all the information you see in the Properties window when examining a compiled executable or DLL, including a brief description, the relevant company and copyrights, and so on. A typical AssemblyInfo.vb file might look like this:

```
<Assembly: AssemblyTitle("Sample Database Component")>
<Assembly: AssemblyDescription("Example of a service provider " & _
    "and information package")>
<Assembly: AssemblyCompany("ProseTech")>
<Assembly: AssemblyProduct("Sample Database Component")>
<Assembly: AssemblyCopyright("Copyright(C) 2001 ProseTech")>
<Assembly: AssemblyVersion("1.0.*")>
```

The version is the most important piece of information. All .NET version numbers are made up of four components. The first two represent the major and minor version numbers and are always set manually. The last two represent revision and build numbers. If you use the asterisk, as shown above, Visual Studio .NET automatically increments a sequential number for these values, ensuring that each compile generates a unique version number. However, you need to modify the code file when you want to specify a change to the major or minor version number.

If you're using a private assembly that doesn't have a strong name, version numbers have no effect. In other words, .NET will try to use the assembly in the current directory (or the indicated subdirectory) regardless of whether it is the same version that the original client was compiled with. This attempt will fail if the required types have changed (for example, if they have new methods or methods with different signatures). This is a major departure from COM programming and a significant convenience. However, programmers will have to keep this behavior in mind when introducing significant changes. As with COM programming, you can introduce new versions of a method by adding a new interface to your component so as not to disturb existing clients.

Shared Assemblies and the GAC

Now that I've criticized global assemblies, you might wonder who would use them. However, shared assemblies and the GAC also include some features that distributed programmers might require, including the following:

- **Enhanced versioning** Strong-named assemblies enable you to apply strict versioning policies, and the GAC enables you to install separate component versions side by side. The GAC also enables you to enforce proper versioning of server-side objects with .NET Remoting, as discussed in Chapter 11.

- **Identity protection** With a strong-named assembly, it's impossible for another organization to create a component that appears to be your own.
- **Shadow-copy updates** The GAC enables you to update components even when they're locked open by their clients. Under this system, the existing client continues to work with the old version while future requests from new clients can be redirected to the new component.
- **COM+ services** To use COM+ enterprise services (described in Chapter 9), your components must have a strong name and should be placed in the GAC. This is because the COM+ runtime needs to be able to locate them.

Generally, if you're certain that a component will be required on only one computer or if you need to enforce strict versioning, shared assemblies might make sense. For example, you can share a component with all the ASP.NET applications and Web services on a single Web server by placing it in that Web server's GAC.

> **Note** The distinction between strong-named assemblies and shared assemblies is important. Shared assemblies are assemblies that are placed in a central component registry called the GAC. Strong-named assemblies are digitally signed, cannot be tampered with or impersonated, and strictly enforce versioning policies. To be placed in the GAC, an assembly must have a strong name. However, you can create a strong-named private assembly that goes in the application directory. In this case, you still benefit from the increased security and version enforcement. This distinction is a source of much confusion for many new .NET programmers, and it's often misstated.

Installing a component into the GAC takes three steps, which the following sections summarize. The first two steps involve creating a strong name, which prevents naming conflicts in the GAC and ensures that your assemblies are uniquely identified. The final step is copying the assembly to the GAC. Note that these steps require a little command-line work. Currently, you cannot create a new key file or install a global assembly using Visual Studio .NET's graphical interface.

Step 1: Creating the Key

The first step is to use the sn.exe command-line utility included with the .NET Framework (typically in a directory such as C:\Program Files\Microsoft Visual Studio .NET\FrameworkSDK\Bin). The sn.exe utility, also called the strong-name tool, enables you to create a .snk file. Each .snk file contains a private and a public key. To create a key, you use the *-k* parameter and specify the filename:

```
sn -k MyKey.snk
```

Private and public keys provide a time-honored form of encryption. Anything encrypted with a private key can be read only with the corresponding public key. Anything encrypted with a public key can be read only with the corresponding private key.

In .NET, the private key is used to compile the assembly and should be carefully guarded. The public key is embedded inside the assembly. When an application uses the component, the CLR uses the public key to decode information from the assembly manifest. No one else can create an update to your assembly because others would need to have your original private key to encrypt it.

Step 2: Adding the Key to a Project

To add the key to a control project, you need to add an *Assembly* attribute to the AssemblyInfo.vb file that identifies the file:

```
<Assembly: AssemblyKeyFile("MyKey.snk")>
```

The next time you compile the project, the key information will be added to the assembly.

Step 3: Installing the Assembly in the GAC

You can install a signed assembly to the GAC using a dedicated setup program or the GACUtil.exe utility. You can even drag and drop the assembly to the C:\WINNT\Assembly directory in Windows Explorer, which installs it automatically (although you can't use the cut-and-paste approach). The Windows Explorer shell extension provides all the GACUtil.exe functionality, enabling you to view the list of assemblies in the GAC, the supported versions, and their public key tokens (which are required for specifying new binding policies in the configuration file). Figure 2-5 shows the GAC shell extension with multiple versions of the DBComponent assembly.

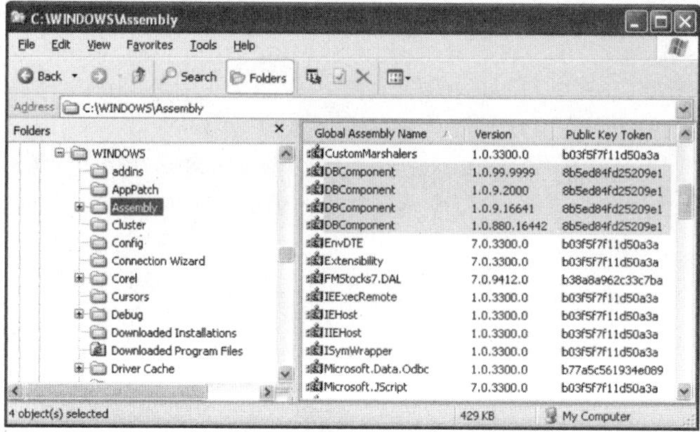

Figure 2-5 Multiple component versions in the GAC

Delayed Signing

If you decide to use strong-named assemblies, your key is your identity. In other words, any individual who has the private key can create "official" assemblies under your name. For that reason, many organizations guard their key pair carefully and won't distribute it even to developers.

Of course, this can create countless development headaches. If a component isn't usable until it's signed and the key pair isn't readily available, testing and debugging will grind to a halt. The solution is to use delayed signing.

With delayed signing, only the public key is provided to developers. The public key can be retrieved from a key pair file using the following syntax:

```
sn -p MyKey.snk MyPublicKey.snk
```

The developers must now add a special attribute to the source code to indicate that delayed signing will be used, and they must reference the public key file:

```
<Assembly: AssemblyDelaySign(True)>
<Assembly: AssemblyKeyFile("MyPublicKey.snk")>
```

When this assembly is built, the compiler adds the public key and reserves space for the private key. A trusted party can sign the assembly before it is released using the sn.exe utility with the *-R* parameter:

```
sn -R MyComponent.dll MyKey.snk
```

Of course, this doesn't solve the development problem because .NET still won't enable you to execute an assembly that lacks a proper signature. Fortunately, the sn.exe utility provides a *-Vr* option that enables you to disable signature verification for an assembly. Here's how you might disable verification for the MyComponent.dll file:

```
sn -Vr MyComponent.dll
```

Now when you use this assembly in a project, the verification process will be skipped. Because the public name is still present in the file, however, you can develop a client that will support the final, signed version. (As you'll see later in this chapter, clients store a hash of the public key of dependent assemblies in their manifest.)

This command doesn't actually modify the assembly. Instead, it just registers the assembly for verification skipping on the current computer. To reenable verification, use the *-Vu* option:

```
sn -Vu MyComponent.dll
```

> **Note** You can add one more step to the assembly deployment process, and add an Authenticode signature using a certificate. This step is typically taken by software publishers who want to give third-party clients the ability to verify the publishers identity. Unlike a strong name, an Authenticode signature requires that an organization provide some sort of credentials to a third-party Certificate Authority (like VeriSign). Authenticode signatures are beyond the scope of this book, but for more information refer to the MSDN documentation and the signcode.exe utility. Authenticode signatures are always applied after an assembly has been given a strong name.

Using Configuration Files with Shared Assemblies

You can still use the configuration files with shared assemblies. In fact, because the GAC can hold multiple versions of an assembly, configuration files become extremely useful for indicating the version that should be used with a particular client.

By default, a client will use only a strongly named assembly if it has the exact same version number as the assembly it was compiled with. If the client cannot find a suitable assembly, a *TypeLoadException* or *FileNotFoundException* will occur.

Every .NET application defines the components it requires in its manifest, which is a special portion of assembly metadata at the beginning of the compiled file. You can view this information using a handy utility included with the .NET Framework called ILDasm.exe (short for IL Disassembler). You can typically find this utility in a directory such as C:\Program Files\Microsoft Visual Studio .NET\FrameworkSDK\Bin.

Figure 2-6 shows ILDasm.exe viewing an ordinary Windows application that contains a single form. Using the assembly metadata, ILDasm.exe can determine all the classes it contains and provide information about their methods, properties, and events.

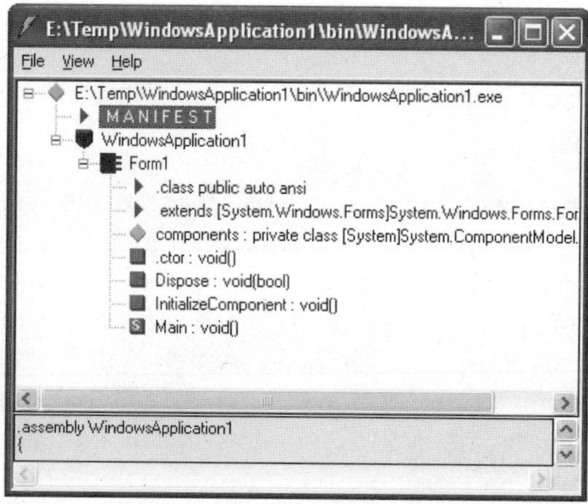

Figure 2-6 Viewing an assembly with ILDasm.exe

If you double-click the MANIFEST entry in the tree, you'll see a text listing like the one shown in Figure 2-7. The *.assembly extern* statements at the beginning of the manifest indicate the dependent assemblies and the required version numbers. In this case, the only dependencies are for some of the core assemblies included with the .NET Framework and the custom *DBComponent*. Because these are strong-named assemblies, the *.assembly extern* statements include a public key token, which is a hash of the assembly's public key.

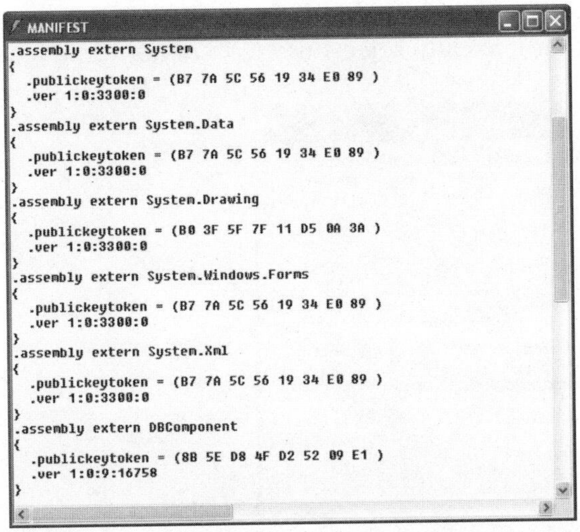

```
MANIFEST
.assembly extern System
{
  .publickeytoken = (B7 7A 5C 56 19 34 E0 89 )
  .ver 1:0:3300:0
}
.assembly extern System.Data
{
  .publickeytoken = (B7 7A 5C 56 19 34 E0 89 )
  .ver 1:0:3300:0
}
.assembly extern System.Drawing
{
  .publickeytoken = (B0 3F 5F 7F 11 D5 0A 3A )
  .ver 1:0:3300:0
}
.assembly extern System.Windows.Forms
{
  .publickeytoken = (B7 7A 5C 56 19 34 E0 89 )
  .ver 1:0:3300:0
}
.assembly extern System.Xml
{
  .publickeytoken = (B7 7A 5C 56 19 34 E0 89 )
  .ver 1:0:3300:0
}
.assembly extern DBComponent
{
  .publickeytoken = (8B 5E D8 4F D2 52 09 E1 )
  .ver 1:0:9:16758
}
```

Figure 2-7 Viewing assembly dependencies in the manifest

Verifying References at Run Time

Public keys are quite large. The CLR uses a hashing algorithm to create a smaller hash value, which it stores in the manifest. When you run the application, .NET locates the appropriate assembly, extracts its public key, runs the hashing algorithm, and compares the result with the value in the manifest. If these values don't match, the code isn't allowed to execute.

Conceptually, the hash value is a little like a checksum—it represents a larger value but doesn't contain all the original information. Unlike a checksum, the algorithm used to create a hash is complex enough that it can't be reverse-engineered. In other words, you can't create another document that will satisfy a given hash value without significant computing effort (on the scale of breaking an encrypted cipher).

.NET uses a similar technique to verify that a strong-named assembly hasn't been tampered with before loading it. In this case, the CLR hashes the contents of the assembly and compares them with a hash value embedded in the manifest. This hash value is even more difficult to tamper with because it is encrypted at compile time using your private key.

If the application can't find the required version of a dependent assembly in the GAC, it throws a *TypeLoadException* or *FileNotFoundException* (as shown in Figure 2-8). If there are multiple versions of the dependent assembly in the GAC, the application automatically selects the one it was compiled with.

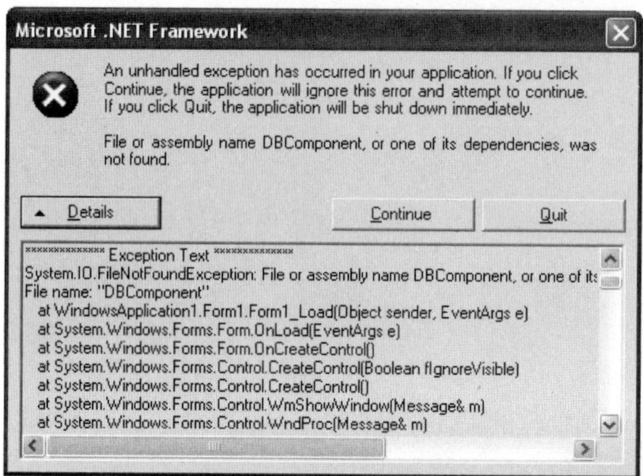

Figure 2-8 Failing to find the correct version of a strong-named assembly

> **Note** In an early beta version, .NET supported a feature called Quick Fix Engineering (QFE). Under this system, the assembly loader would require a match only for the major and minor revision numbers and would use the assembly with the highest build and revision numbers. Unfortunately, this system wasn't strict enough. Therefore, the release versions of .NET 1.0 and 1.1 require component versions to match exactly, guaranteeing that DLL Hell can never return.

If you want the application to use a different version of a dependent assembly, you have two options. First, you can recompile the client with a new version. This way, the new version number will be embedded in the client's manifest. Alternatively, you can apply a new version policy.

Versioning Policies with Strong-Named Assemblies

If you need to override the default binding behavior after an application has been deployed (either to direct a client or to use an older or newer version than it would use by default), you must create a configuration file. In the configuration file, you identify the assembly by name and by its public key token (which is displayed in the GAC). You can then add one or more *<bindingRedirect>* tags. Each redirect maps a single requested version, or a range of requested versions, to a specific new version. This version must be present in the GAC; otherwise, the application will throw an exception on startup.

The configuration file in Listing 2-5 maps versions 1.0.0.0 through 2.9.9.9 of a shared assembly named *DBComponent* to version 3.0.0.0.

```
<?xml version="1.0"?>
<configuration>
  <runtime>
    <assemblyBinding xmlns="urn:schemas-microsoft-com:asm.v1">
      <dependentAssembly>
        <assemblyIdentity name="DBComponent"
                          publicKeyToken="b03f5f7f11d50a3a"/>
        <bindingRedirect oldVersion="1.0.0.0-2.9.9.9"
                         newVersion="3.0.0.0" />
      </dependentAssembly>
    </assemblyBinding>
  </runtime>
</configuration>
```

Listing 2-5 Redirecting an assembly reference to a new version

Remember, you can use this technique only with assemblies that have strong names. Otherwise, .NET ignores the version information and assumes that any local assemblies are compatible.

Code Bases with Shared Assemblies

Shared assemblies also give you additional power with the *<codeBase>* element. Namely, you can specify any file or URL location from which the assembly should be downloaded. This little-considered feature enables you to partially solve deployment problems by allowing the client computer to automatically download the version of an assembly that it needs, according to the configuration file of the client application it is running.

Listing 2-6 automatically downloads version 2.0.0.0 of a component from a Web site (provided the client attempts to use this component).

```
<configuration>
   <runtime>
      <assemblyBinding xmlns="urn:schemas-microsoft-com:asm.v1">
         <dependentAssembly>
            <assemblyIdentity name="DBComponent"
                              publicKeyToken="b03f5f7f11d50a3a"/>
            <codeBase version="2.0.0.0"
                      href="http://www.prosetech.com/DBComponent.dll"/>
         </dependentAssembly>
      </assemblyBinding>
   </runtime>
</configuration>
```

Listing 2-6 Automated deployment through downloading

Note that when you use the *<codeBase>* tag with a shared assembly, you need to include the URI at the beginning of the address. Therefore, if you want to use a file path, you do it in the form *file:///g:\Components\DBComponent.dll* or *http://MyServer/Components/DBComponent.dll*. If the assembly is private, the *<codeBase>* tag must use a path relative to the application directory.

Downloading code in this manner can result in your assembly being placed into a lower security context and not being able to perform the work it needs to do. Before you can successfully use this technique to download assemblies from another computer, you need to modify code-access security settings, as described in Chapter 15. Chapter 15 also provides more information about automated deployment and downloading and presents some flexible techniques that don't require strong names.

> **Note** You can create and tweak configuration files using the .NET Framework Configuration tool that is included with the SDK. Just choose Settings, Control Panel, Administrative Tools, Microsoft .NET Framework Configuration from the Start menu. Among other things, this tool enables you to configure versioning policies and code bases for an application.

A Final Word About Assembly Binding

The assembly binding process can be complex, particularly for shared components. Figure 2-9 shows a high-level overview of the process.

You can use other .NET Framework features to configure how assembly binding takes place in even greater detail. For example, you can develop publisher policy or machine policy files that specify more generic assembly binding rules. However, these options (which are described on MSDN) continuously raise new versioning headaches. In a distributed application, the best deployment approaches don't require per-client configuration, which can complicate the setup immensely and introduce new problems when components are updated in the future.

Ideally, you will sidestep these issues by using private assemblies whenever possible. In a perfect world, the only consumer of a shared assembly will be a server-side component. This ensures that you can apply new version policies, if necessary, in a controlled environment. In a world with distributed clients, enforcing these policies might not be as easy.

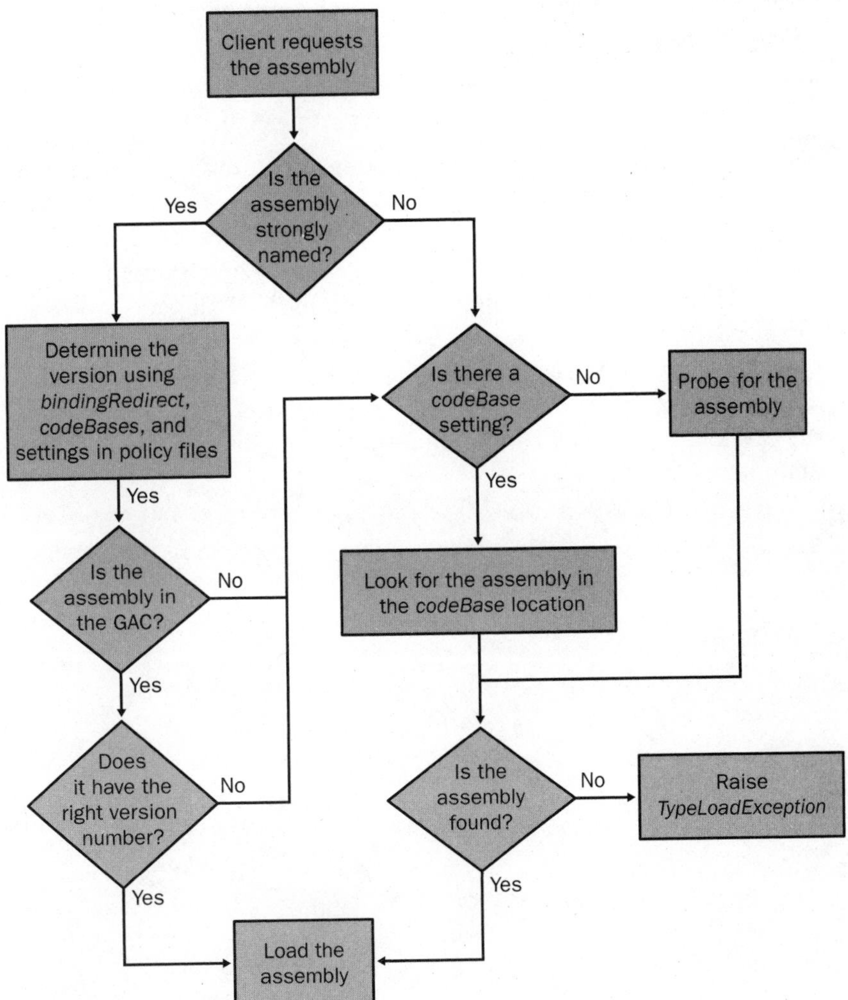

Figure 2-9 The assembly binding process

If you encounter an assembly binding problem that you can't resolve, you can use the Assembly Binding Log Viewer utility included with Visual Studio .NET (look for the file fuslogvw.exe, which you can run from the command line). This utility can be configured to track failed assembly binding attempts for applications in a specific directory, or across the entire computer.

Summary

This chapter covered .NET components, the fundamental ingredients for any distributed application. Along the way, I've intentionally glossed over several architecture issues. They'll return with a vengeance in Chapter 10, but first you need to have all the key .NET technologies at your fingertips.

We also took a lightning tour through .NET deployment basics, including how .NET resolves references to private or public assemblies. We'll return to this topic in Chapter 15 with advanced deployment techniques that can support a distributed application, including strategies you can use to create a self-upgrading program or a modular application that downloads required functionality transparently.

3

Disconnected Data: The Universal Language

I've often described the Microsoft .NET Framework as a collection of several not-so-minor revolutions bundled into a single platform, and data access is no exception. ActiveX Data Objects (ADO), Microsoft's previous COM-based data access technology, has been redesigned and rebuilt in the form of ADO.NET. And although ADO.NET bears some superficial similarities to ADO, it shifts the focus to distributed applications and the scalability considerations they entail. That isn't to say that you can't create a distributed application that connects to a database using ADO technology—in fact, with proper design practices, ADO still works like a charm. The problem is that many developers either ignored or forgot those best practices and created clumsy resource-intensive applications. ADO.NET is quite a bit more restrictive than ADO—it's designed to make these bad habits almost impossible.

ADO.NET isn't just a more restrictive version of ADO (although a skeptical programmer might make that claim). ADO.NET adds features that make it easier to send data to remote components, serialize it to XML, and make it available to software written in other languages. These features are all wrapped up in a special object called *DataSet*, which is an enriched data container that tracks changes and is optimized for translating data into XML. The features of the *DataSet* are far beyond ADO's primitive *Recordset* and include support for multiple tables, table relations, and column constraints. But the truth of the matter is that the *DataSet* is rarely used for updating data in an enterprise application. There are several reasons for this design pattern (all of which we'll explore in this chapter), but the dominant reason is that *DataSet* programming is complicated in an enterprise environment, where you must write additional code to handle the inevitable concurrency and stale data errors. Unfortunately, many beginning ADO.NET programmers fail to protect against these potential problems and don't realize the vulnerability of their code until it is deployed in a production environment. In most business applications, the additional details required to use disconnected batch updates are rarely worth the coding headaches. On the other hand, the *DataSet* is often an ideal one-way data transport, allowing data to be downloaded to a client in a single convenient package.

In this chapter, we'll focus on questions about how you should use ADO.NET and the *DataSet* in an enterprise application. I won't explain the entire ADO.NET model (because there are entire books on that subject). Instead, I'll identify the best ways to use the features of ADO.NET in a distributed system.

The Role of ADO.NET in a Distributed System

ADO.NET is a critical piece of almost any enterprise application simply because most applications need to access a database at some point. In this case, using the legacy ADO libraries makes little sense. They reduce performance (because execution must travel between your managed .NET code and the unmanaged ADO objects through a COM interop bridge) and add few useful features.

ADO.NET supports more than one model of data access. First of all, it uses a simple connection-based paradigm that enables you to execute individual commands. You'll find that this is the most useful aspect of ADO.NET for designing database components using the "service provider" design pattern introduced in Chapter 2. ADO.NET also provides disconnected data access, which is a quick-and-easy way to send information between tiers. In this case, the *DataSet* essentially takes the role of the "information package" component. It's an enticing option, but it strips away a layer of indirection (the custom information package class), potentially making your solution less generic and making it more difficult to update the client in response to data source changes.

Finally, ADO.NET can play a special role in a system that incorporates non-.NET clients. Internally, the *DataSet* stores information in a binary form optimized for XML output. That means you can look at the *DataSet* as an XML document without the danger of losing information. Clients in other programming languages won't know how to manipulate a *DataSet* object, but they can usually parse an XML document and schema, which makes it easy to transfer information around without needing to write your own error-prone conversion code. You'll read about this possibility at the end of this chapter.

The ADO.NET Object Family

The ADO.NET types are a part of the .NET Framework class library and are found in the namespaces that begin with *System.Data*.

Here's the 60-second overview:

- *System.Data* contains generic classes that are independent of the type of data source or the mechanism used to connect to it. The most important of these is the *DataSet*, which contains collections of other generic classes such as *DataTable*, *DataRow*, and *DataColumn*. There are also a number of generic interfaces (such as *IDbCommand* and *IDbConnection*) that are implemented by all provider-specific objects.
- *System.Data.SqlClient* contains the classes required to connect to a Microsoft SQL Server (7.0 or later) database using the highly efficient *Tabular Data Stream* (TDS) interface. In other words, these namespaces bypass several other potential layers, including OLE DB and ODBC. You'll use these classes to execute a direct command on a SQL Server database or to fill a *DataSet* with the results of a query.
- *System.Data.OleDb* contains the classes required to connect to most OLE DB providers. (OLE DB providers are included for all kinds of data sources, including Microsoft Access, SQL Server, and Oracle.) You can use these classes to execute a direct command on a data source through an OLE DB provider or to fill a *DataSet* with the results of a query.

Version 1.0 of the .NET Framework includes only these two providers: one that's generic for all OLE DB providers and one that's optimized for SQL Server. However, version 1.1 of the .NET Framework and Visual Studio .NET 2003 add the following new providers:

- *System.Data.OracleClient* contains the classes required to connect to an Oracle database (version 8.1.7 or later) using the optimized *Oracle Call Interface* (OCI).
- *System.Data.Odbc* contains the classes required to connect to most ODBC drivers' providers. ODBC drivers are included for all kinds of data sources and are configured through the *Data Sources* icon in Control Panel.

In addition, other vendors are sure to develop their own managed providers. The best strategy for the application programmer is to use the managed provider that's customized for the data source, if it's available, and thereby bypass as many intermediate layers as possible. Keep in mind that if you install a third-party provider, it is installed (generally in the GAC) as a separate DLL assembly, and you must reference this assembly before you can use the contained types. Third-party providers also won't be placed in a *System.Data* namespace (because *System* is reserved for the .NET Framework class library).

The Data Objects

At first, it might seem that Microsoft has broken with its long-standing tradition of cross-data-source compatibility. How else can you explain a separate namespace (and potentially a separate assembly) for every type of provider?

On closer examination, ADO.NET is generic in two ways:

- Although separate providers are required to connect to the data source, the *DataSet* object is generic. Therefore, a client can navigate and update a *DataSet* regardless of how it was created or where the information originated. All the details that are specific to the data provider can be encapsulated by a custom database component that you create.
- The provider-specific classes all inherit from a common class (in the *System.Data.Common* namespace) or implement a common interface (from the *System.Data* namespace). Therefore, the *SqlConnection* object exposes virtually the same properties and methods as the *OleDbConnection* and *OdbcConnection* objects. If you need to work with these objects generically in code, you can cast them to the appropriate interface (such as *IDbConnection*).

In some cases, classes or members are not directly inherited or implemented from a common base class or interface. (One example is the *SqlCommandBuilder* and *OleDbCommandBuilder* classes.) In this case, you'll still find that the classes included with different providers work essentially the same and almost always include properties and methods with exactly the same names. That means that examples written with one provider are easily translatable to another. Connection strings are one of the minor discrepancies.

So what are the basic ADO.NET objects? I won't describe them one by one here, but for ADO.NET novices, a quick overview is provided in Table 3-1.

Table 3-1 ADO.NET Core Provider Classes

Function	SQL Server Provider	OLE DB Provider	Oracle Provider	ODBC Provider
Connect to a data source	*SqlConnection*	*OleDbConnection*	*OracleConnection*	*OdbcConnection*
Execute a SQL statement	*SqlCommand*	*OleDbCommand*	*OracleCommand*	*OdbcCommand*
Execute an SQL stored procedure	*SqlCommand* (with any number of referenced *SqlParameter* objects)	*OleDbCommand* (with any number of referenced *OleDbParameter* objects)	*OracleCommand* (with any number of referenced *OracleParameter* objects)	*OdbcCommand* (with any number of referenced *OdbcParameter* objects)
Retrieve data with a fast-forward read-only	*SqlDataReader*	*OleDbDataReader*	*OracleDataReader*	*OdbcDataReader*
Transfer data to a *DataSet*	*SqlDataAdapter*	*OleDbDataAdapter*	*OracleDataAdapter*	*OdbcDataAdapter*
Apply *DataSet* changes to a data source	*SqlDataAdapter* (and, optionally, the *SqlCommandBuilder* helper class)	*OleDbDataAdapter* (and, optionally, the *OleDbCommandBuilder* helper class)	*OracleDataAdapter* (and, optionally, the *OracleCommandBuilder* helper class)	*OdbcDataAdapter* (and, optionally, the *OdbcCommandBuilder* helper class)
Manually initiate and manage a transaction	*SqlTransaction*	*OleDbTransaction*	*OracleTransaction*	*OdbcTransaction*
Catch an error from the data source (anything from invalid SQL to an error connecting)	*SqlException*	*OleDbException*	*OracleException*	*OdbcException*

Direct Data Source Interaction

The easiest form of access with ADO.NET is simple, connection-based access. With connection-based access, you have one of the following goals:

- **Execute a direct SQL *Update*, *Delete*, or *Insert* command.** You'll need to use the appropriate *IDbConnection* and *IDbCommand* objects.

- **Execute a query and retrieve the results as a read-only forward-only stream.** You'll need to use the appropriate *IDbConnection*, *IDbCommand*, and *IDataReader* objects.

The drawback of this strategy is that substantial data manipulation can result in substantial connection requests, potentially creating a bottleneck. For modest database usage, however, the simplicity and straightforwardness of this model outweighs most other considerations. Also, most ADO.NET providers support some form of connection pooling, which allows them to efficiently handle a large volume of short-lived requests.

The example in Listing 3-1 shows how the *CustomerDB* service provider class can use the ADO.NET objects to support record deletions, insertions, and updates.

```
Imports System.Data.SqlClient
Imports System.Data

Public Class CustomerDB

    Private ConnectionString As String = _
     "Data Source=localhost;Initial Catalog=Store;" & _
     "Integrated Security=SSPI"

    ' (GetCustomer and GetCustomers methods left out.)

    ' Inserts a customer record into the database.
    Public Sub AddCustomer(ByVal customer As CustomerDetails)
        Dim Sql As String = "INSERT INTO Customers "
        Sql &= "(FullName, EmailAddress, Password) VALUES ('"
        Sql &= customer.Name & "', '"
        Sql &= customer.Email & "', '"
        Sql &= customer.Password & "')"
        ExecuteNonQuery(Sql)
    End Sub

    ' Updates an existing customer record in the database.
    Public Sub UpdateCustomer(ByVal customer As CustomerDetails)
        Dim Sql As String = "UPDATE Customers SET "
        Sql &= "FullName='" & customer.Name
        Sql &= "', EmailAddress='" & customer.Email
        Sql &= "', Password='" & customer.Password
        Sql &= "' WHERE CustomerID=" & customer.ID.ToString()
        ExecuteNonQuery(Sql)
    End Sub
```

Listing 3-1 Adding ADO.NET code to the *CustomerDB* class

```
    ' Deletes a customer record in the database.
    Public Sub DeleteCustomer(ByVal customerID As Integer)
        Dim Sql As String = "DELETE FROM Customers WHERE CustomerID="
        Sql &= customerID.ToString()
        ExecuteNonQuery(Sql)
    End Sub

    ' Constructs and executes the appropriate database command.
    Private Sub ExecuteNonQuery(ByVal sql As String)
        Dim con As New SqlConnection(ConnectionString)
        Dim cmd As New SqlCommand(sql, con)

        Try
            con.Open()
            cmd.ExecuteNonQuery()
        Catch Err As Exception
            ' Use "caller inform" exception handling pattern.
            Throw New ApplicationException( _
             "Exception encountered when executing command.", Err)
        Finally
            con.Close()
        End Try
    End Sub

End Class
```

The *CustomerDB* class is organized so that a private *ExecuteNonQuery* method performs the database operation for all three tasks. The only difference is the supplied SQL text—in this design, the methods of the *CustomerDB* class just generate a dynamic SQL statement that identifies the field names and values. Using the ADO.NET objects, a new connection is opened, a direct command is executed, and the connection is closed immediately.

If an exception is encountered, the class doesn't try to remedy it because it probably indicates that the database is unavailable or the SQL text is invalid. Instead, an *ApplicationException* is thrown to the client, with the original *SqlException* packaged inside. This pattern is called *caller inform* because it ensures that the caller is notified that an unrecoverable error took place, but it uses a higher-level exception class that the client expects. This higher-level exception class could also be a custom exception class that you've defined.

With the caller inform pattern, the *ApplicationException* always includes the original *Exception* object nested inside. This approach can help the client diagnose the problem, but it might not be suitable in a secured environment, in which specific error information could inform a malicious user about potential vulnerabilities. In this case, create the *ApplicationException* object without nesting the original exception inside:

```
Throw New ApplicationException( _
  "Exception encountered when executing command.")
```

Connection Strings

Connection strings generally detail three types of information: what server to use, what database to use, and how to authenticate the connection. There also might be any number of additional vendor-specific settings.

In Listing 3-1, we use the *localhost* alias (which always refers to the current computer), the database named *Store*, and integrated security (which uses the currently logged-in Windows user to access the database).

```
Private ConnectionString As String = _
 "Data Source=localhost;Initial Catalog=Store;" & _
 "Integrated Security=SSPI"
```

If integrated security isn't supported, the connection must indicate a valid user and password combination. For a newly installed SQL Server database, the sa (system administrator) account is usually present, and often without a password.

```
Private ConnectionString As String = _
 "Data Source=localhost;Initial Catalog=Store;" & _
 "user id=sa;password="
```

If you're using the OLE DB provider, your connection string probably resembles the preceding example, with the addition of a Provider setting that identifies the OLE DB driver (or if you're using the ODBC .NET driver, you add a Driver attribute that identifies the DSN). The following connection string can be used to connect to an Oracle database through the MSDAORA OLE DB provider:

```
Private ConnectionString As String = _
 "Data Source=localhost;Initial Catalog=Store;" & _
 "user id=sa;password=;Provider=MSDAORA"
```

If you're using a third-party data provider, you might need to consult its documentation (or the MSDN class library reference) to determine the supported connection string values. For example, most databases support the Connect Timeout setting, which sets the number of seconds to wait for a connection before throwing an exception. (The SQL Server default is 15 seconds.)

Direct Queries and Data Readers

Queries are performed in a slightly different way. The SQL *Select* statement is executed through the command's *ExecuteReader* method, which returns a data reader. You can then step through the rows returned by the data reader one at a time from start to finish, using the *Read* method. The *GetCustomer* and *GetCustomers* methods shown in Listing 3-2 demonstrate this technique and create *CustomerDetails* objects to encapsulate the retrieved details. Lookup is based on customer ID, but you could make overloaded versions of this method that enable you to search by other criteria (such as the *FullName* field).

```
Public Class CustomerDB

    ' (Update, insert, and delete methods omitted.)

    ' Retrieves a single customer record from the database.
    Public Function GetCustomer(ByVal customerID As Integer) _
     As CustomerDetails
        Dim Sql As String = "SELECT * FROM Customers Where CustomerID="
        Sql &= customerID.ToString()

        Dim con As New SqlConnection(ConnectionString)
        Dim cmd As New SqlCommand(Sql, con)
        Dim Reader As SqlDataReader
        Dim Customer As New CustomerDetails()

        Try
            con.Open()
            Reader = cmd.ExecuteReader(CommandBehavior.SingleRow)
            Reader.Read()
            Customer.ID = Reader("CustomerID")
            Customer.Name = Reader("FullName")
            Customer.Email = Reader("EmailAddress")
            Customer.Password = Reader("Password")
        Catch Err As Exception
            ' Use caller inform pattern.
            Throw New ApplicationException( _
             "Exception encountered when executing command.", Err)
        Finally
            con.Close()
        End Try
```

Listing 3-2 Adding query methods to *CustomerDB*

```
        Return Customer
    End Function

    ' Retrieves all customer records into an ArrayList collection.
    ' Note that exposing this method allows client to invoke a
    ' potentially time-consuming query.
    Public Function GetCustomers() As ArrayList
        Dim Sql As String = "SELECT * FROM Customers"

        Dim con As New SqlConnection(ConnectionString)
        Dim cmd As New SqlCommand(Sql, con)
        Dim Reader As SqlDataReader
        Dim Customers As New ArrayList()
        Try
            con.Open()
            Reader = cmd.ExecuteReader()
            Do While Reader.Read()
                Dim Customer As New CustomerDetails()
                Customer.ID = Reader("CustomerID")
                Customer.Name = Reader("FullName")
                Customer.Email = Reader("EmailAddress")
                Customer.Password = Reader("Password")
                Customers.Add(Customer)
            Loop
        Catch Err As Exception
            ' Use caller inform pattern.
            Throw New ApplicationException( _
             "Exception encountered when executing command.", Err)
        Finally
            con.Close()
        End Try

        Return Customers
    End Function

End Class
```

Note that the *GetCustomer* method passes a special *CommandBehavior.SingleRow* parameter to the *ExecuteReader* method. This isn't required, but it does represent a little-known technique that can improve performance if you know you're retrieving only a single row. In this case, the code selects a record using its unique key number, which ensures that only a single item is returned.

Notice also that the *GetCustomers* method returns an *ArrayList* full of *CustomerDetails* objects. Alternatively, you can create a strongly typed custom collection class, such as the one shown in Listing 3-3.

```
Public Class CustomerDetailsCollection
    Inherits System.Collections.CollectionBase

    Public Sub Add(ByVal customer As CustomerDetails)
        Me.List.Add(customer)
    End Sub

    Public Sub Remove(ByVal Index As Integer)
        ' Check to see if there is an item at the supplied index.
        If Index > Count - 1 Or Index < 0 Then
            Throw New System.IndexOutOfRangeException()
        Else
            List.RemoveAt(Index)
        End If
    End Sub

    Public ReadOnly Property Item(ByVal Index As Integer) _
     As CustomerDetails
        Get
            ' The appropriate item is retrieved and
            ' explicitly cast to the CustomerDetails type.
            Return CType(List.Item(Index), CustomerDetails)
        End Get
    End Property

End Class
```

Listing 3-3 A custom collection for *CustomerDetails*

This technique ensures that the collection can only contain *CustomerDetails* objects, not any other type of object. The remarkable fact is that both the custom collection class and the *ArrayList* intrinsically support ASP.NET and Windows data binding. That means it takes just a few lines of code to display the results you retrieve without needing to iterate through each item. (As a disadvantage, it's usually harder to configure specific formatting details such as column order and size.)

Therefore, you can create a scalable database component that executes direct commands, returns custom objects, and even allows data binding, without resorting to the *DataSet*. Listing 3-4 shows the code for a simple form that uses the *CustomerDB* service provider class in this fashion.

```
Public Class BoundForm
    Inherits System.Windows.Forms.Form

    Friend WithEvents DataGrid1 As System.Windows.Forms.DataGrid
    ' (Designer code omitted.)

    Private Sub BoundForm_Load(ByVal sender As System.Object, _
      ByVal e As System.EventArgs) Handles MyBase.Load
        Dim DB As New CustomerDB()
        DataGrid1.DataSource = DB.GetCustomers()
    End Sub

End Class
```

Listing 3-4 A data bound form that uses *CustomerDB*

Figure 3-1 shows the sample output that displays when this form is used with the *CustomerDB* component.

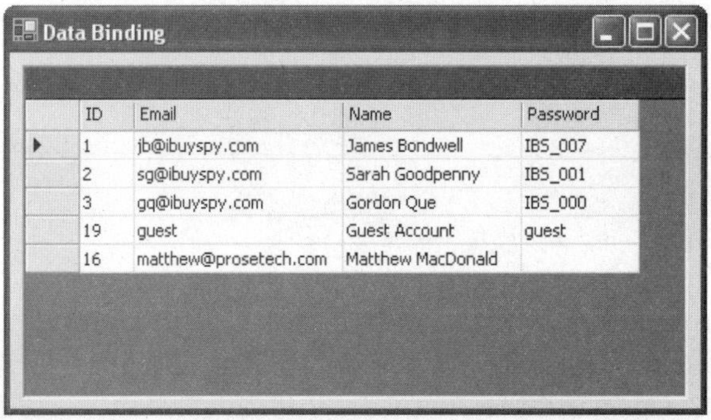

ID	Email	Name	Password
1	jb@ibuyspy.com	James Bondwell	IBS_007
2	sg@ibuyspy.com	Sarah Goodpenny	IBS_001
3	gq@ibuyspy.com	Gordon Que	IBS_000
19	guest	Guest Account	guest
16	matthew@prosetech.com	Matthew MacDonald	

Figure 3-1 Data binding without a *DataSet* object

Note In this discussion, you saw two command methods, *ExecuteReader* (for running queries and returning a set of rows) and *ExecuteNonQuery* (which returns only the number of affected rows). You can also use a third method, *ExecuteScalar*, which returns a single value. *ExecuteScalar* is ideal for using aggregate SQL functions (such as *Sum*, *Avg*, *Min*, *Max*, and *Count*) or for calling a stored procedure that returns a single data value.

Stored Procedures

Stored procedures—miniature SQL "programs" that are stored in the database—are a key part of any enterprise programming project. If you study Microsoft's platform samples (such as the IBuySpy case studies for ASP.NET), you'll see that they advocate a disciplined multilayered approach. The client Web page code interacts exclusively with a dedicated custom data component, which is similar to the *CustomerDB* class shown previously. The data component interacts with the data source through a layer of stored procedures, which in turn manipulate the underlying tables and records. This structured approach is shown in Figure 3-2.

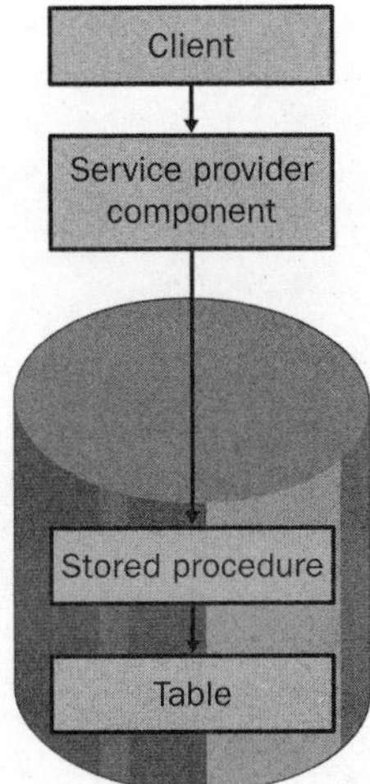

Figure 3-2 The ideal structured approach to data access

Some key advantages to stored procedures include the following:

- **They reduce the amount of data access code.** With stored procedures, work is offloaded to the server, simplifying your .NET code.
- **They improve encapsulation.** By using stored procedures, you can tighten security (by allowing access to certain specific procedures instead of granting full access to the whole underlying table) and combine a batch of commands into a single logical task. You can also modify and tweak this logic to fine-tuned perfection after the application has been deployed, without needing to recompile the client or data access components.
- **They often improve performance.** Performance improves because the database can create an optimized execution path when stored procedures are created, instead of performing the same work each time they are executed.

The last point depends on the database itself. For example, in SQL Server 2000, dynamic queries are compiled and cached much as stored procedures are. However, in many cases, stored procedures can still improve performance. One reason is that a single stored procedure can often replace dozens of differently structured (but similar) dynamic SQL queries. It's much easier to optimize a small set of stored procedures and create the optimal set of indexes than to sort through dozens of dynamic queries that are embedded into various applications. For more information about database optimization, refer to Chapter 12.

Generally, stored procedures take a little more effort because you need to work with the script-based SQL language. Listing 3-5 shows an example of a stored procedure that inserts a new customer record and then returns the automatically generated *CustomerID*.

```
CREATE Procedure CustomerAdd
(
    @FullName   nvarchar(50),
    @Email      nvarchar(50),
    @Password   nvarchar(50),
    @CustomerID int OUTPUT
)
AS

INSERT INTO Customers
(
    FullName,
    EMailAddress,
    Password
)

VALUES
(
    @FullName,
    @Email,
    @Password
)

SELECT
    @CustomerID = @@Identity
```

Listing 3-5 A stored procedure for adding a customer record

You can easily rewrite the *AddCustomer* method to use this stored procedure. As an added frill, this method now returns the unique *CustomerID*. (See Listing 3-6.)

```
Public Class CustomerDB

    ' (Other methods left out.)

    Public Function AddCustomer(ByVal customer As CustomerDetails) _
     As Integer

        ' Create the ADO.NET Connection and Command.
        Dim con As New SqlConnection(ConnectionString)
        Dim com As New SqlCommand("CustomerAdd", con)
        com.CommandType = CommandType.StoredProcedure
        Dim Param As SqlParameter

        ' Add the three input parameters.
        Param = com.Parameters.Add( _
         "@FullName", SqlDbType.NVarChar, 50)
        Param.Value = CustomerDetails.Name

        Param = com.Parameters.Add("@Email", SqlDbType.NVarChar, 50)
        Param.Value = CustomerDetails.Email

        Param = com.Parameters.Add("@Password", SqlDbType.NVarChar, 50)
        Param.Value = CustomerDetails.Password

        ' Add the output parameter.
        Param = com.Parameters.Add("@CustomerID", SqlDbType.Int)
        Param.Direction = ParameterDirection.Output

        Try
            con.Open()
            cmd.ExecuteNonQuery()
        Catch Err As Exception
            ' Use "caller inform" exception handling pattern.
            Throw New ApplicationException( _
             "Exception encountered when executing command.", Err)
        Finally
            con.Close()
        End Try

        ' Return the unique ID generated by the database.
        Return Param.Value

    End Function

End Class
```

Listing 3-6 Using the stored procedure in *CustomerDB*

As you can see, the use of stored procedures forces your code to specify more database details (such as the data types of various parameters). By using a disciplined database component, however, you can still maintain order.

Provider-Agnostic ADO.NET Code

It is possible to create a custom data component that can transparently work with any type of ADO.NET provider, by performing all your database operations through the generic interfaces in the *System.Data* namespace. This approach isn't always best—occasionally it might surrender some provider-specific functionality you need—but it can be indispensable in projects where more than one data source stores similar tables with different information or where you plan to migrate from one database product to another.

The basic approach is to start by creating the provider-specific command object that you need to use, with a small piece of conditional logic. From that point, you can create commands, data readers, and parameters, all by relying on methods and using the generic interfaces.

Listing 3-7 shows how you can apply this technique to the *GetCustomers* method. Note that the class constructor accepts an enumerated value that indicates the provider type. This allows the client to decide, at run time, which provider to use. The conditional portion of logic that creates the first provider-specific object is placed in a private *CreateConnection* function.

```
Imports System.Data.SqlClient
Imports System.Data.OleDb
Imports System.Data

Public Class CustomerDB

    ' (Other methods omitted.)

    ' Defines the supported providers types.
    Public Enum ProviderType
        SqlServer
        OleDb
    End Enum

    ' The provider this class will use.
    Public Provider As ProviderType

    Private SqlConnectionString As String = _
     "Data Source=localhost;Initial Catalog=Store;" & _
     "Integrated Security=SSPI"
```

Listing 3-7 *CustomerDB* with generic ADO.NET code

```
Private OleDbConnectionString As String = _
 "Data Source=localhost;Initial Catalog=Store;" & _
 "Integrated Security=SSPI;Provider=SQLOLEDB"

Public Sub New(provider As ProviderType)
    Me.Provider = provider
End Sub

Public Function GetCustomers() As ArrayList

    Dim Sql As String = "SELECT * FROM Customers"

    ' The connection object is generated through a private
    ' function.
    Dim con = CreateConnection()

    ' Interact with the command and data reader
    ' using the IDbCommand and IDataReader interfaces.
    Dim cmd As IDbCommand = con.CreateCommand()
    Dim Reader As IDataReader
    Dim Customers As New ArrayList()

    Try
        con.Open()
        Reader = cmd.ExecuteReader()
        Do While Reader.Read()
            Dim Customer As New CustomerDetails()
            Customer.ID = Reader("CustomerID")
            Customer.Name = Reader("FullName")
            Customer.Email = Reader("EmailAddress")
            Customer.Password = Reader("Password")
            Customers.Add(Customer)
        Loop

    Catch Err As Exception
        ' Use caller inform pattern.
        Throw New ApplicationException( _
         "Exception encountered when executing command.", Err)

    Finally
        con.Close()

    End Try

    Return Customers

End Function
```

```
    Private Function CreateConnection As IDbConnection

        ' Here we determine which object and connection string to use.
        ' This is the only provider-specific part of the code.
        Select Case Provider
            Case ProviderType.SqlServer
                Return New SqlConnection(SqlConnectionString)
            Case ProviderType.OleDb
                Return New OleDbConnection(SqlConnectionString)
        End Select

    End Function

End Class
```

A separate connection string is required for each data source. If you're using SQL Server, you can test this sample by connecting to the database through the SQL managed provider or the OLE DB provider for SQL Server (SQLOLEDB).

This approach does have some limitations—many of which Microsoft architects are working to remedy in future versions of .NET. Some of the problems include objects that don't use a common interface (like the command builders) and the use of provider-specific exceptions (such as *SqlException* and *OleDbException*).

Transactions

When many developers hear the word *transaction*, they automatically think of COM+ services or its predecessor, the curiously named Microsoft Transaction Service (MTS). That's because one of the early successes of MTS and COM+ was a new model for transaction enlistment that made it possible to create distributed transactions that could bind different data sources into one logical operation. This service is priceless when you need to integrate legacy systems and multiple database products in an evolving system. (In Chapter 9, we'll explore this service in more detail.)

However, you won't use COM+ distributed transactions when designing a new system. Instead, you'll rely on ordinary SQL transactions that are initiated and governed at the database level. This approach offers better performance and easier programming.

The best way to create a transaction is to encapsulate it entirely within a stored procedure. In that case, you won't see it in your client code. Listing 3-8 shows the basic structure used to initiate a transaction in SQL Server.

```
BEGIN TRANSACTION
   < SQL code here >

IF (@@ERROR > 0)
   ROLLBACK TRANSACTION
ELSE
  COMMIT TRANSACTION
```

Listing 3-8 A transaction in stored procedure code

You can also initiate the same type of transaction programmatically through .NET code. The disadvantage with this approach is that it requires the good behavior of the client. In other words, if a client forgets to initiate a transaction, it has the ability to perform an inconsistent update.

ADO.NET has provider-specific *IDbTransaction* objects that manage client-initiated transactions. You don't create this object directly; instead, you call the *BeginTransaction* method of the connection object. You can then enlist multiple commands and commit or roll back the transaction using the *IDbTransaction* methods when complete. Listing 3-9 shows a client-initiated transaction.

```
Dim Transaction As SqlTransaction = con.BeginTransaction()

' Enlist two commands (cmdA and cmdB) in the transaction.
' They will now succeed or fail as a unit.
cmdA.Transaction = Transaction
cmdB.Transaction = Transaction

' Execute the commands.
cmdA.ExecuteNonQuery()
cmdB.ExecuteNonQuery()

' Commit the transaction.
Transaction.Commit()
```

Listing 3-9 A client-initiated transaction

The *DataSet*

The *DataSet* is often described as an in-memory "cache" of relational data. Typically, the information in the *DataSet* closely resembles the raw data in the underlying data source. As the data source changes, it becomes more work to insulate the client against these changes and to ensure that the *DataSet* is still using the expected field names, data types, and data representations. The *DataSet* provides tools that make all of this possible, but they won't help if you don't realize all the assumptions that the client may make about the data in a *DataSet*. Worst of all, if the client uses the wrong table or column names, the mistake won't appear at compile time, because ADO.NET can't verify the string-based lookup on a *DataSet*. Instead, it will lead to a potentially frustrating run-time error.

The *DataSet* also has some remarkable advantages. Most important, the *DataSet* is a near-universal language for exchanging data with .NET and third-party clients:

- The *DataSet* is a core part of the .NET Framework. That means that any .NET client can interpret a *DataSet*. You don't need to distribute and add a reference to a proprietary assembly.
- The *DataSet* comes equipped with the capability to serialize itself to XML, which makes it easy to store a *DataSet* in a file, transmit it to a remote object, and even exchange the information with a client written in another language.

The *DataSet* also provides some advanced functionality that would be difficult to implement in your own custom class:

- The *DataSet* enables you to easily navigate through collections of data. You can even add *DataRelation* objects to allow the client to browse through master-detail relationships.
- The *DataSet* tracks changes. This allows the client to receive a *DataSet*, make a batch of changes, and submit them back to a service provider object, which then performs the updates. Without a *DataSet*, the client must call the remote object repeatedly, once for each update.

The *DataSet* uses the collection-based structure shown in Figure 3-3.

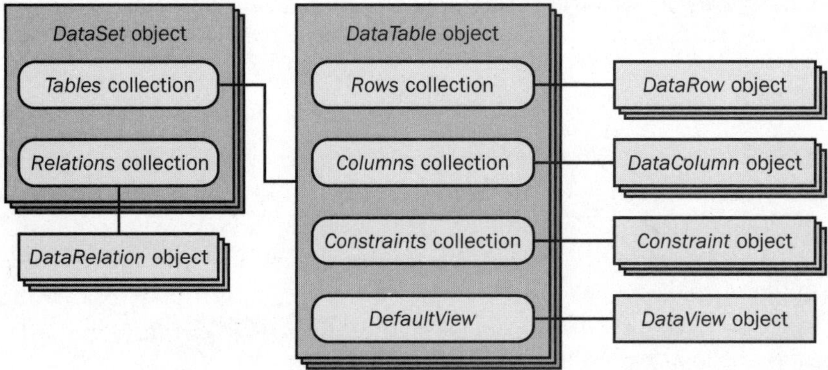

Figure 3-3 The *DataSet*

Creating a *DataSet*

To fill the *DataSet*, you need to use a special bridge called a *data adapter*. The data adapter is a provider-specific object that has two roles in life. First of all, you use it to retrieve the results from a query and insert them into a *DataTable* object. If you want to update the data source, you use the data adapter again. This time it examines the contents of a *DataTable* and executes the required SQL commands to insert, delete, and modify the original records.

When creating a data adapter, you can use a constructor that accepts a command object, as shown in the following code:

```
Dim Sql As String = "SELECT * FROM Customers"

Dim con As New SqlConnection(ConnectionString)
Dim cmd As New SqlCommand(Sql, con)
Dim Adapter As New SqlDataAdapter(cmd)
```

This command is placed in the *SelectCommand* property of the data adapter. Every data adapter can store references to four types of commands. It uses the *Delete*, *Insert*, and *Update* commands when changing the data source to correspond with *DataTable* changes, and the *Select* command when retrieving results from the data source and filling a *DataTable*. Figure 3-4 shows the data adapter's structure.

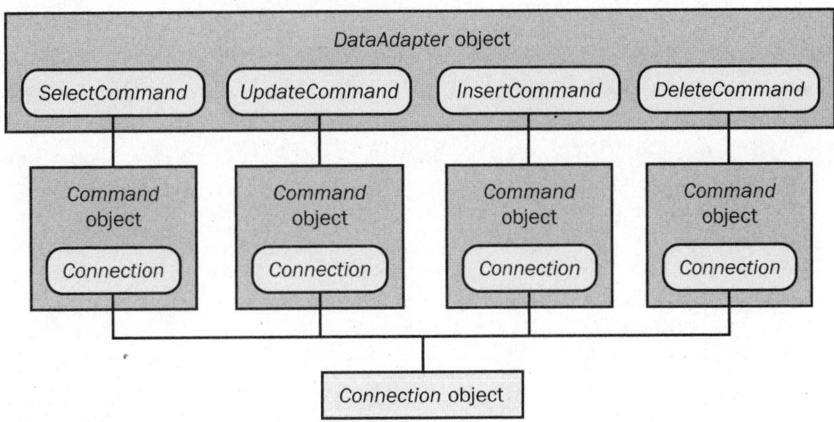

Figure 3-4 The data adapter

Using the data adapter is very straightforward. To fill a *DataTable*, you use the *Fill* method of the data adapter (for example, *SqlDataAdapter.Fill*). This method takes two parameters: a reference to the *DataSet* and the name of the table. If the named *DataTable* doesn't already exist in the *DataSet*, it will be created automatically.

```
' Create a new DataTable object named "Customers" in the DataSet ds.
Adapter.Fill(ds, "Customers")
```

If you want to fill multiple tables in a *DataSet*, you need to use the *Fill* method multiple times, once for each table. You'll also need to modify the *SelectCommand* property to enter the new query before each operation.

```
' Create a Customers table with the assigned command object.
Adapter.Fill(ds, "Customers")

' Modify the command.
Adapter.SelectCommand.CommandText = "SELECT * From ORDERS"

' Create a second Orders table in the same DataSet.
Adapter.Fill(ds, "Orders")
```

In a preceding example, we used an *ArrayList* of *CustomerDetails* objects with the *GetCustomers* method of a simple database component. This method can be tweaked to use a *DataSet* instead of the custom objects, as shown in Listing 3-10.

```
Public Function GetCustomers() As DataSet

    Dim Sql As String = "SELECT * FROM Customers"

    Dim con As New SqlConnection(ConnectionString)
    Dim cmd As New SqlCommand(Sql, con)
    Dim Adapter As New SqlDataAdapter(cmd)
    Dim ds As New DataSet()

    Try
        con.Open()
        Adapter.Fill(ds, "Customers")
    Catch Err As Exception
        ' Use caller inform pattern.
        Throw New ApplicationException( _
         "Exception encountered when executing command.", Err)
    Finally
        con.Close()
    End Try

    Return ds

End Function
```

Listing 3-10 Returning a *DataSet*

One interesting fact about this code is that only two statements need to be monitored for errors: opening the connection and filling the *DataSet* with the data adapter. The *Fill* method encapsulates all the logic needed to loop through the result set in a single line of code.

The client code requires no change. The *DataSet* can be bound to a Windows or an ASP.NET control just as easily as the *ArrayList* was in our earlier example. Listing 3-11 shows a data bound form with a *DataSet*.

```
Public Class BoundForm
    Inherits System.Windows.Forms.Form

    ' (Windows designer code omitted.)

    Private Sub BoundForm_Load(ByVal sender As System.Object, _
      ByVal e As System.EventArgs) Handles MyBase.Load
        Dim DB As New CustomerDB()
        DataGrid1.DataSource = DB.GetCustomers().Tables(0)
    End Sub

End Class
```

Listing 3-11 A data bound form with a *DataSet*

> **Note** In the *GetCustomers* example, a whole *DataSet* is returned even though it contains only one *DataTable*. This is the standard pattern. If you create a function that returns just a *DataTable*, it won't be able to work in a .NET XML Web service. The XML Web service serialization mechanism only supports the full *DataSet* object.

DataSet Indirection Through Column Mappings

One of the drawbacks to using a *DataSet* is that it strips away a layer of indirection between the data source and the client code. If you use a custom object such as *CustomerDetails*, for example, the data access code automatically assumes the responsibility of mapping the data source field names to the expected property names. Therefore, *EmailAddress* becomes *Email*, *FullName* becomes *Name*, and *CustomerID* becomes *ID*. The data class might also contain computed fields, adjust formatting, or replace a constant value in a field with a more descriptive enumerated value.

You can perform the same tasks by manually processing the *DataSet* after you fill it, but this makes it extremely difficult to update the data source based on *DataSet* changes. You would probably be forced to write additional code to examine the *DataSet* and perform the updates manually. This task is complicated, tedious, and prone to error.

Fortunately, ADO.NET provides one feature that can help you: column mappings. Column mappings are set at the data adapter level. They link a field in the data source with a differently named field in the *DataSet*. Listing 3-12 shows code that configures the data adapter to create a *DataSet* using the column names Email, Name, and ID.

```
' Create the new mapping, and attach it to the data adapter.
Dim CustomerMap As DataTableMapping
CustomerMap = Adapter.TableMappings.Add("Customers", "Customers")

' Define column mappings.
CustomerMap.ColumnMappings.Add("CustomerID", "ID")
CustomerMap.ColumnMappings.Add("FullName", "Name")
CustomerMap.ColumnMappings.Add("EmailAddress", "Email")

' Fill the DataSet.
Adapter.Fill(ds, "Customers")
```

Listing 3-12 Indirection with column mappings

The great advantage of column mappings is that they are bidirectional. In other words, the data adapter knows not only how to translate the data source information into the appropriate columns when performing a query but also how to modify the corresponding columns when performing an update.

You could explore other possible techniques to make the *DataSet* more generic and less error-prone. One idea is to create a separate class that stores a list of mappings between column names and field indexes. Alternatively, you can use a custom *DataSet*-derived class that adds an enumeration for table names and columns.

```
Public Class CustomerDS
    Inherits System.Data.DataSet

    Public Enum Fields
        ID = 0
        Name = 1
        Email = 2
        Password = 3
    End Enum

End Class
```

Because this class derives from *DataSet*, you can use it in exactly the same way with the *Fill* method of the data adapter. Just modify the *GetCustomers* code to create the correct type of object:

```
Dim ds As New CustomerDS()
```

The client can then use the enumerated values by name, ensuring that any mistakes are caught at compile time:

```
' Display the name of the first record.
MessageBox.Show(ds.Tables(0).Rows(0)(CustomerDS.Fields.Name))
```

As another benefit, index-based lookup is faster than name-based lookup. However, the obvious disadvantage is that you have now created a new custom class, and the client requires a reference to the appropriate assembly to use this type in its code. In other words, by extending the base .NET Framework classes, you might complicate deployment.

> **Note** ADO.NET also enables you to create strongly typed *DataSets* using the Visual Studio .NET IDE or the xsd.exe utility included with the .NET Framework. Typed *DataSets* are *DataSet*-derived classes that allow the client to access fields using property names (as in *CustomerRow.CustomerID*) rather than a string-based lookup (*CustomerRow("CustomerID")*. However, typed *DataSets* introduce all the problems of custom objects—namely, you need to distribute the appropriate assembly to every client. That means that typed *DataSets* are most useful on the server side. If you try to use typed *DataSets* with clients in a distributed system, you will only add a new distribution headache.

Navigating the *DataSet*

The *DataSet* uses an elegant collection-based syntax whereby the programmer steps through *DataTable* and *DataRow* objects. For example, here's the code to step through the customer *DataSet* and add each customer's name to a list control:

```
Dim Row As DataRow
For Each Row In ds.Tables(0).Rows
    lstNames.Items.Add(Row("Name"))
Next
```

The code in Listing 3-13 shows every field in every row of every table in a *DataSet*. It's written as a simple console application, but you could adapt it to display information in a Windows Forms page.

```
Dim Table As DataTable
For Each Table In ds.Tables
    Console.WriteLine(Table.TableName)

    Dim Row As DataRow
    For Each Row In Table.Rows
        Console.WriteLine()

        Dim Field As Object
        For Each Field In Row.ItemArray
            Console.Write(Field.ToString() & " ")
        Next
    Next
Next
```

Listing 3-13 Navigating all tables and fields in a *DataSet*

Checking for Deleted Rows

In Listing 3-13, the code iterates through all the rows. If you've deleted some of the rows by using the *DataRow.Delete* method, however, this code can cause a problem. The catch is that deleted rows don't actually disappear from the *DataTable.Rows* collection—if they did, ADO.NET wouldn't be able to delete them from the data source when you reconnected later and applied changes. Instead, the row remains but the *DataRow.RowState* property is set to *Deleted*. If you attempt to read a field value from a *DataRow* that is in this state, an exception is thrown.

To get around this idiosyncrasy, you can explicitly check the state of a row before you display it, as follows:

```
Dim Row As DataRow
For Each Row In ds.Tables(0).Rows
    If Row.RowState <> DataRowState.Deleted
        lstNames.Items.Add(Row("Name"))
    End If
Next
```

When you successfully apply these changes to the data source (by reconnecting and using the data adapter's *Update* method), the rows are removed from the *DataTable.Rows* collection because they are no longer needed.

Relations

You can also navigate through a *DataSet* by using table relations. One possible use of this technique is to allow a client to show a master-detail view of the information, without needing to query the data source more than once.

To use a relation in a *DataSet*, you need to add a *DataRelation* object that represents the relationship to the *DataSet.Relations* collection. There is currently no way to retrieve this information directly from the data source. That means that even if a foreign key relationship is defined in your database, you need to define it manually in your *DataSet* to use it. Listing 3-14 illustrates the concept with a *GetCustomersAndOrders* method.

```
Public Function GetCustomersAndOrders() As DataSet
    Dim SqlCustomers As String = "SELECT * FROM Customers"
    Dim SqlOrders As String = "SELECT * FROM Orders"

    Dim con As New SqlConnection(ConnectionString)
    Dim cmd As New SqlCommand(SqlCustomers, con)
    Dim Adapter As New SqlDataAdapter(cmd)
    Dim ds As New DataSet()

    Try
        con.Open()
        Adapter.Fill(ds, "Customers")
        Adapter.SelectCommand.CommandText = SqlOrders
        Adapter.Fill(ds, "Orders")
    Catch Err As Exception
        ' Use caller inform pattern.
        Throw New ApplicationException( _
         "Exception encountered when executing command.", Err)
    Finally
        con.Close()
    End Try

    ' Define the relationship is closed. Note that this step is performed
    '  after the connection is closed, because it doesn't
    '  use any information from the data source.
    Dim ParentCol, ChildCol As DataColumn
    ParentCol = ds.Tables(0).Columns("CustomerID")
    ChildCol = ds.Tables(1).Columns("CustomerID")
    Dim Relation As New DataRelation("CustomersOrders", _
                                     ParentCol, ChildCol)

    ' Add the relationship to the DataSet.
    ' This is the point where it takes effect, and an exception will
    '  be thrown if the existing data violates the relationship.
    ds.Relations.Add(Relation)

    Return ds
End Function
```

Listing 3-14 Returning a *DataSet* with a relation

The client can then move from a parent row to the child rows or from a child row to the parent row by using the *DataRow.GetChildRows* and *DataRow.GetParentRow* methods.

```
Dim ParentRow, ChildRow As DataRow

For Each ParentRow In ds.Tables("Customers").Rows
    ' Process parent row.
    For Each ChildRow In ParentRow.GetChildRows("CustomersOrders")
        ' Process child row.
    Next
Next
```

Listing 3-15 shows an implementation of this idea that fills a TreeView, which appears in Figure 3-5. The first level of nodes represents customers, and every customer node contains child nodes that represent orders.

```
Public Class RelationForm
    Inherits System.Windows.Forms.Form

    ' (Designer code omitted.)

    Private Sub RelationForm_Load(ByVal sender As System.Object, _
     ByVal e As System.EventArgs) Handles MyBase.Load

        Dim DB As New CustomerDB()
        Dim ds As DataSet = DB.GetCustomersAndOrders()

        Dim ParentRow, ChildRow As DataRow
        Dim ParentNode, ChildNode As TreeNode
        For Each ParentRow In ds.Tables("Customers").Rows

            ParentNode = TreeView1.Nodes.Add(ParentRow("FullName"))

            For Each ChildRow In _
             ParentRow.GetChildRows("CustomersOrders")

                ParentNode.Nodes.Add(ChildRow("OrderID"))

            Next

        Next

    End Sub

End Class
```

Listing 3-15 Displaying related rows in a TreeView

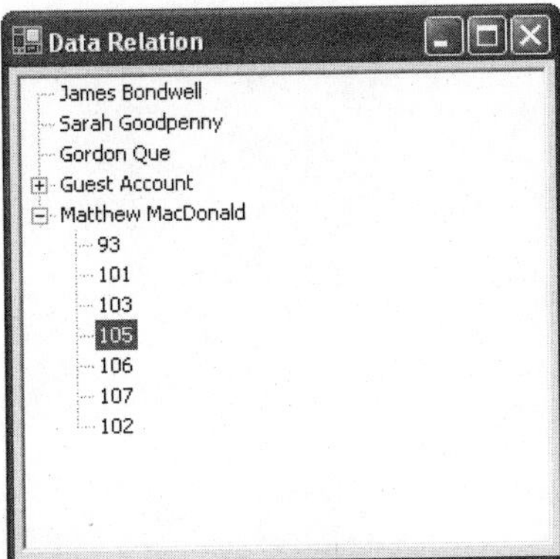

Figure 3-5 Using relations to fill a TreeView

After you define the relationship in the *DataSet*, you're bound by the same rules that govern any relationship: you can't delete a parent record if there are one or more linked child rows, and you can't create a child that references a nonexistent parent. Therefore, you might be prevented from adding a valid relationship to your *DataSet* if it contains only part of the data in the data source. One way to get around this problem is to create a *DataRelation* without creating the corresponding constraints. Simply use one of the *DataRelation* constructors that accepts the Boolean *createConstraints* parameter, as shown here:

```
' Don't create any DataSet constraints.
' The DataRelation will be used for navigation only,
' not to enforce relational integrity.
Dim Relation As New DataRelation("CustomersOrders", _
                                 ParentCol, ChildCol, false)
```

Embedding Data in a Control

Even though the TreeView doesn't support data binding, it's easy to populate it using *DataRelation* objects. You can extend this principle by embedding data in the control, using the *Tag* property supported by most .NET controls. The *Tag* property isn't used by .NET; instead, it's a container in which you can store any information you need in order to identify a control. For example, you can use the *Tag* property in a *TreeNode* object to track the unique ID that identifies the record in the data source. If the user asks to delete or modify this record, you can invoke the *DeleteCustomer* or *UpdateCustomer* method using the ID.

The *Tag* property isn't limited to simple numeric or text information. You can use it to store an entire object, including the *DataRow* that represents a given item. Consider Listing 3-16, for example, which stores the *DataRow* object for every order item.

```
Private Sub RelationForm_Load(ByVal sender As System.Object, _
 ByVal e As System.EventArgs) Handles MyBase.Load

    Dim DB As New CustomerDB()
    Dim ds As DataSet = DB.GetCustomersAndOrders()

    Dim ParentRow, ChildRow As DataRow
    Dim ParentNode, ChildNode As TreeNode
    For Each ParentRow In ds.Tables("Customers").Rows
        ParentNode = TreeView1.Nodes.Add(ParentRow("FullName"))
        For Each ChildRow In _
         ParentRow.GetChildRows("CustomersOrders")
            Dim NewNode As New TreeNode()
            NewNode.Text = ChildRow("OrderID")
            NewNode.Tag = ChildRow
            ParentNode.Nodes.Add(NewNode)
        Next
    Next

End Sub
```

Listing 3-16 Storing a *DataRow* in a *TreeNode*

When the user clicks a node, the *TreeView.AfterSelect* event handler (shown in Listing 3-17) retrieves this *DataRow* object and uses the field information to display the order date in a nearby text box, as shown in Figure 3-6.

```
Private Sub TreeView1_AfterSelect(ByVal sender As System.Object, _
 ByVal e As System.Windows.Forms.TreeViewEventArgs) _
 Handles TreeView1.AfterSelect

    Dim SelectedRow As DataRow = CType(e.Node.Tag, DataRow)
    If Not (SelectedRow Is Nothing) Then
        ' We must convert the date to a DateTime object in order to
        ' filter out just the date.
        lblDisplay.Text = "This item was ordered on " & _
         DateTime.Parse(SelectedRow("OrderDate")).ToShortDateString()
        lblDisplay.Text &= Environment.NewLine
        lblDisplay.Text &= "This item was shipped on " & _
         DateTime.Parse(SelectedRow("ShipDate")).ToShortDateString()
    End If

End Sub
```

Listing 3-17 Retrieving a *DataRow* from a *TreeNode* on selection

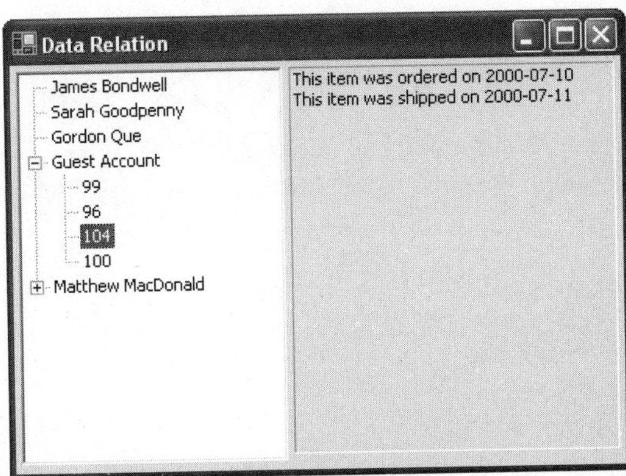

Figure 3-6 Using embedded data objects in a control

Will this approach waste extra memory? It depends on how your application is designed. If you're already storing a long-term reference to the *DataSet* (for example, in a form-level variable), the *Node.Tag* property just contains a reference to the appropriate *DataRow* object in the *DataSet*, and no extra memory is used. Keep in mind that retaining information on the client is always better than retrieving it multiple times. Generally, Windows clients have plentiful memory for storing the data you need. The real costs are incurred when transferring information over the network or when using server resources to execute a time-consuming query.

Updating from a *DataSet*

The *DataSet* allows clients to record an entire batch of changes and commit them in a single operation by using the *Update* method of the data adapter. You can use this batch update ability to extend the *CustomerDB* class, adding a *SubmitBatchChanges* method, as demonstrated in Listing 3-18.

```
Public Function SubmitBatchChanges(ds As DataSet) As DataSet
    ' We need to re-create the adapter with the original command object
    ' and Select query. With that information, the SqlCommandBuilder
    ' can generate the other data adapter commands.
    Dim Sql As String = "SELECT * FROM Customers"

    Dim con As New SqlConnection(ConnectionString)
    Dim cmd As New SqlCommand(Sql, con)
    Dim Adapter As New SqlDataAdapter(cmd)
```

Listing 3-18 Submitting batch changes

```
    ' Generate insert, delete, and update commands.
    Dim Builder As New SqlCommandBuilder(adapter)
    Adapter.InsertCommand = Builder.GetInsertCommand()
    Adapter.UpdateCommand = Builder.GetUpdateCommand()
    Adapter.DeleteCommand = Builder.GetDeleteCommand()

    Try
        con.Open()
        Adapter.Update(ds, "Customers")
    Catch Err As Exception
        ' Use caller inform pattern.
        Throw New ApplicationException( _
         "Exception encountered when executing command.", Err)
    Finally
        con.Close()
    End Try

    ' Return the updated DataSet.
    Return ds

End Function
```

When you call the *Update* method, the data adapter steps though the rows. For every changed row, it issues an update command. For every new row, it issues an insert command, and for every deleted row, it issues a delete command. This magic is possible because every *DataRow* actually stores information about its current value and the original value. The original value is the value that was retrieved from the data source (or the value that was committed the last time changes were applied with the *Update* method). The data adapter uses this information to locate the original row. It also uses the *DataRow.RowState* property to determine what action needs to be performed. For example, rows that must be inserted have the state *DataRowState.Added*.

After the change is applied, all the original values in the *DataSet* are updated to match the current values and the state of each row is set to *DataRowState.Unchanged*. This updated version of the *DataSet* is then sent back to the client. The client must use this updated version! Otherwise, the next time the client submits the *DataSet* for an update, the data adapter will try to reexecute the same changes.

The *SubmitBatchChanges* method shown earlier is not ideal for most distributed applications because it returns the entire *DataSet*. I'll introduce some more advanced optimizations in Chapter 12.

> **Note** The code in Listing 3-18 uses the helpful command builder. It examines the query that was used to fill the data adapter and generates the other commands required for inserting, deleting, and updating records. These commands closely resemble the direct *Update*, *Delete*, and *Insert* examples we used before except that they use the *Where* clause stringently, attempting to match every field. That means that if another user has changed any part of the record, the update will fail.

Update Issues

On paper, this approach looks phenomenal—it consolidates changes into a single step and reduces network traffic and database hits because changes are performed en masse. In fact, many .NET books focus exclusively on the *DataSet* and this batch change technique when describing ADO.NET, assuming that this is the best and only approach.

However, ADO.NET conceals an unpleasant secret: this remarkable new technique is not suitable for all distributed applications. In fact, if you study Microsoft's platform samples, you'll have trouble finding an example in which the *DataSet* is used to retrieve information, let alone to update a data source. Why is that? Quite simply, the *DataSet* increases complexity and the potential for error if you don't code carefully. It also reduces performance, unless you replace the autogenerated command builder logic with your own custom command objects for inserting, deleting, and updating records.

The following sections discuss some of these problems. Taken together, these problems are far from trivial. However, if you have a client that connects only intermittently and needs to perform a significant amount of work with multiple tables, using the disconnected *DataSet* may be the best option.

The *DataSet* Is Large

With the current implementation of the *SubmitBatchChanges* method shown in Listing 3-18, the client is encouraged to submit the entire *DataSet*, which could contain dozens of untouched rows. Therefore, even though database operations are performed less frequently, the network could face an overall slowdown as more information than is required is being sent over the wire to a remote database component. The client can code around this problem by submitting only the changed row using the *DataSet.GetChanges* method. However, the server can't ensure that the client will take this approach.

Automatically Generated Commands Perform Poorly

By default, the Command Builder creates commands that attempt to select a row by matching every field. Consider the following example:

```
"DELETE FROM Customers WHERE CustomerID=5 AND FullName='Matthew MacDonald' AND
EmailAddress='matthew@prosetech.com' AND ..."
```

This defensive approach won't perform as well as just selecting the record by its unique ID or using a stored procedure. And although you can customize the data adapter's update logic, it takes more work.

Concurrency Errors Are Common

Every enterprise application needs to consider concurrency problems, which can occur when two clients read and try to update the same information. Concurrency problems can affect any database code, but the problem is particularly common with the *DataSet* because the interval of time between retrieving the data and applying the changes is usually longer. Unfortunately, a single error can derail an entire batch of changes, and the problem won't be discovered until long after the user has made the change, when it might no longer be possible to correct it.

Update Problems Occur with Relationships

Changes aren't necessarily applied in the order you made them. That means that the data adapter might try to add a child row before adding the parent it refers to, which would generate an error from the data source if it has foreign key constraints defined. You can mitigate these problems to some extent by using the *DataSet.GetChanges* and *DataTable.GetChanges* methods to perform operations in the friendliest order.

Listing 3-19 illustrates how you might handle a *DataSet* with a parent Customers table and a child Orders table. Note that two different data adapters are used because different commands are needed to update each table.

```
' Split the DataSet ds.
Dim dsInserted, dsModified, dsDeleted As DataSet
dsInserted = dtParent.GetChanges(DataRowState.Added)
dsModified = dtParent.GetChanges(DataRowState.Modified)
dsDeleted = dtParent.GetChanges(DataRowState.Deleted)

' Add records to the parent table.
adapterCustomer.Update(dsInserted, "Customers")
adapterCustomer.Update(dsModified, "Customers")

' Now that insertions have been applied, this is a good place to
' commit all the changes in the child table.
adapterOrder.Update(ds.Tables("Orders"))

' Now that all child records are removed, it's safe to try to
' remove parent records.
adapterCustomer.Update(dsDeleted, "Customers")
```

Listing 3-19 Committing updates in phases

Order of updates isn't the only problem with relationships. Another problem occurs with autogenerated IDs. Suppose, for example, that you want to add a new parent and a new child. The child needs to refer to the parent using its unique ID. But because this ID is generated by the data source when the record is inserted, it won't be available until the update has been performed, even though the parent has been created in your disconnected *DataSet*. Unfortunately, there are only two ways around this headache: update the data source with new parent records before you add any child records, or carefully customize your data logic.

Validation Is Compromised

Generally, *DataSet* validation is performed by handling *DataTable* events such as *ColumnChanging*, *RowChanging*, and *RowDeleting*. These events fire as values are being modified. Unfortunately, it's up to the client to handle these events and disallow invalid values. By the time the entire batch of changes is submitted to the data component, it's hard to track inappropriate changes. With custom components, on the other hand, you can add code directly in your data objects to disallow certain values. It's also much easier to validate a single *CustomerDetails* object than a full *DataSet*.

Handling Errors

If you must use the batch update technique with a *DataSet*, the bare minimum is to catch any errors and report them to the user. Unfortunately, the standard *Try/Catch* block suffers from one serious problem: as soon as a single error occurs, the entire batch update is cancelled, potentially preventing other valid updates. To deal with this problem more flexibly, you need to handle the *RowUpdate* event or set the *ContinueUpdateOnError* property.

One common approach is to handle the *RowUpdate* event of the data adapter. This event provides a *RowUpdatedEventArgs* class that informs you if an error was encountered, indicates the relevant *DataRow*, and explains whether the attempted command was an *Insert*, *Delete*, or *Update*. If an error has occurred, you can then decide whether to allow this error to derail the entire update process (the default), or allow the data adapter to continue moving through the *DataTable* attempting updates. You signal that the update should continue by setting the *RowUpdatedEventArgs.Status* property to *SkipCurrentRow* when the *RowUpdate* event fires and an error is detected.

However, this technique is less suitable to a middle-tier component, which can't notify the user directly about any problems. Instead, a more useful approach is to set the data adapter's *ContinueUpdateOnError* property to *True*. If an error is encountered, the data adapter sets a text error message in the corresponding *DataRow.RowError* property. You can then use the *DataTable.GetErrors* method to retrieve all the *DataRow* objects that caused update errors and return this collection to the client, who will then notify the user or take alternative action. You'll put this technique to use in Chapter 12.

XML and Cross-Platform Data Exchange

As I mentioned earlier, the *DataSet* is invaluable when you need to share data with a non-.NET client. Almost every modern programming language can parse an XML document, making XML an ideal way to exchange shared data. Best of all, the *DataSet* exports data seamlessly to XML. That means you don't need to write any conversion code.

To create a simple test, we'll save the *DataSet* to a file using its built-in *WriteXml* method. (You also can save the XSD schema using the *WriteXmlSchema* method.)

```
Dim DB As New CustomerDB()
Dim ds As DataSet = DB.GetCustomers()
ds.WriteXml("c:\customers.xml")
```

The default representation uses a *DataSet* document tag, which contains *<Customer>* tags for every row in the Customers table. The *<Customer>* tags contain subtags for each field in an individual row. A portion of this file is shown in Listing 3-20.

```
<?xml version="1.0" standalone="yes"?>
<NewDataSet>
  <Customers>
    <CustomerID>1</CustomerID>
    <FullName>James Bondwell</FullName>
    <EmailAddress>jb@ibuyspy.com</EmailAddress>
    <Password>IBS_007</Password>
  </Customers>
  <Customers>
    <CustomerID>2</CustomerID>
    <FullName>Sarah Goodpenny</FullName>
    <EmailAddress>sg@ibuyspy.com</EmailAddress>
    <Password>IBS_001</Password>
  </Customers>
  <Customers>
    <CustomerID>3</CustomerID>
    <FullName>Gordon Que</FullName>
    <EmailAddress>gq@ibuyspy.com</EmailAddress>
    <Password>IBS_000</Password>
  </Customers>
</NewDataSet>
```

Listing 3-20 *DataSet* XML

To process this file, we'll use Visual Basic 6, with the help of the Microsoft COM-based MSXML parser (available for download from *http://msdn.microsoft.com/xml*). The client code simply opens the file and displays an entry in a list control for each customer, using the name and e-mail address, as illustrated in Listing 3-21 and Figure 3-7.

```
Private Sub Form_Load()

    Dim Doc As MSXML2.DOMDocument40
    Set Doc = New MSXML2.DOMDocument40

    Doc.async = False
    Doc.Load ("c:\customers.xml")

    Dim Child As MSXML2.IXMLDOMNode

    For Each Child In Doc.documentElement.childNodes
      ' The first node (offset 0) is the ID.
      ' The second node (offset 1) is the name.
      ' The third node (offset 2) is the email.
      lstNames.AddItem (Child.childNodes(1).Text & _
        " (" & Child.childNodes(2).Text & ")")
    Next

End Sub
```

Listing 3-21 Displaying the *DataSet* in Visual Basic 6

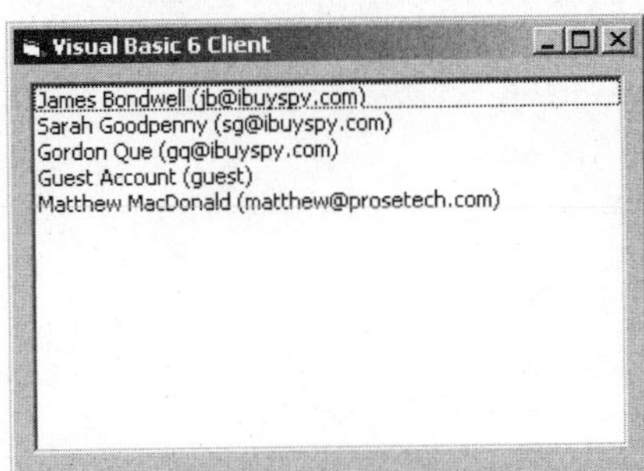

Figure 3-7 Reading the *DataSet* in a Visual Basic 6 client

This code demonstrates how easily *DataSet*-based information can be interpreted by a non-.NET client, but it doesn't provide a practical way to exchange the data. Typically, you'll want to create a .NET client that communicates directly with an XML Web service rather than one that relies on another component that saves the information to a file. In Chapter 5, I'll explain how to take this extra step.

> **Note** Unfortunately, the *DataSet* doesn't provide many options for tailoring the XML. If you need to support a client that expects different element names or a specific schema, you will have to manually process and modify the *DataSet* XML with the types in the *Systeml.Xml* namespace.

Summary

In this chapter, we examined the universal language of data exchange in .NET: ADO.NET providers and the *DataSet*. We also covered the basic architecture of and best practices for stored procedures and transactions. You also learned about a key design decision: whether to use custom objects or the *DataSet*. Finally, we took a realistic look at the drawbacks to and benefits of the *DataSet*.

It's important to remember that Microsoft's own designs tend to favor simple classes and structures over the *DataSet*, and that *DataSet*-based updates introduce additional headaches that might require far more effort than they are worth. Ultimately, the ideal niche for *DataSet* use may be in cross-platform programming, where its seamless XML conversion allows any client to retrieve and process the results of a query.

For more examples of information package and service provider classes that use ADO.NET code, refer to the case studies at the end of this book. All three case studies use data components as part of the solution.

4

.NET Remoting: A More Durable DCOM

Microsoft .NET Remoting is, at its simplest, a new way for components to communicate, even as they run in different processes or on different computers. To a degree, .NET Remoting can be considered a replacement for DCOM, the technology that allows COM components to talk across a network. Like DCOM, .NET Remoting is an ideal solution for use over internal networks and enables the application programmer to follow essentially the same programming model used to interact with local objects. Unlike DCOM, .NET Remoting is simple to configure and easy to scale. It also uses a "pluggable" architecture that makes it far more flexible than any previous standard. For that reason, you can use .NET Remoting in situations where DCOM rarely works, such as across a firewall or between computers on different platforms. In such cases, your remote components don't require any coding changes—you just adjust your .NET Remoting configuration files to specify a different message format or protocol for communication.

For developers who have toiled with DCOM, .NET Remoting will come as a welcome relief. However, some of the same problems that affect DCOM come into play with .NET Remoting. Namely, communicating with a component that is hosted in another process or on another computer is inherently slower than communicating with a locally instantiated component. .NET Remoting is therefore not always the best solution. Used wisely, it can be a fundamental building block for a scalable distributed system. Used recklessly—and Microsoft architects comment frequently that they see .NET Remoting being used in places where it isn't required—it can introduce new performance bottlenecks.

Even for experienced .NET developers, .NET Remoting is often a foreign subject. Because of its complexity, it hasn't received the same degree of attention as other innovations, such as .NET XML Web services. This chapter introduces .NET Remoting from the ground up, considers where it should and shouldn't be used, and highlights some of the common headaches that developers experience when starting out with it. It paves the way for later chapters and case studies in which we'll explore how remote components can interact with XML Web services in advanced distributed systems.

The Role of .NET Remoting in a Distributed System

Modern operating systems such as Microsoft Windows isolate applications and the memory they use from one another. This protection ensures that a flawed or maliciously designed program can't affect another running application. The cost of this protection is that interprocess communication is possible only through controlled channels, such as sockets or named pipes, and is slower and more complex.

.NET Remoting is a mechanism through which a .NET client application can interact with a .NET component that's part of another application domain (and often hosted on a different computer). Think of .NET Remoting as the key to full-blown distributed architecture. It enables you to split up entire portions of an application into separate physical locations. Other .NET technologies just aren't as ambitious. In Chapter 5, for example, you'll learn about XML Web services, which enable you to execute snippets of code on the Web server. By no stretch of the imagination can you consider an XML Web service a full-blown object. It can't raise events, provide a server-side user interface, or live longer than a single method call.

.NET Remoting imposes very few rules on application architecture. Unlike with XML Web services, you can even use .NET Remoting to design peer-to-peer applications in which individual clients communicate back and forth and there is no central server. In a typical enterprise application, however, you'll host utility components (the service providers) on separate computers and make these components available to clients through .NET Remoting. This approach allows database connections and other resources to be pooled among large numbers of clients and offloads some of the work from the client.

The actual remote component can be hosted in one of several different types of applications. It can be hosted in a Windows Forms or console application (which can be useful if you want to display running status information or an interface for configuring the component), in a dedicated Windows service (which allows automatic startup and provides good transparency), or even through Microsoft Internet Information Services (IIS) and the ASP.NET runtime (somewhat like an XML Web service). We'll consider all these possibilities throughout the book; we'll focus on the first, simplest approach in this chapter.

> **Note** We'll return to the difference between .NET Remoting and XML Web services in the next chapter. However, it's not too early to start considering one of the most important distinctions: .NET Remoting can use stateful objects, but XML Web services are always stateless helper classes. In other words, an XML Web service is created at the start of each client request and is destroyed after the response has been returned. XML Web services can serialize information to some type of storage between method calls, creating the illusion that they retain state, but they are never alive and active between client requests. Objects exposed through .NET Remoting have a much higher degree of independence. Even after the client has received a response, the remote object can continue executing.

.NET Remoting Fundamentals

In the world of .NET Remoting, there are essentially three types of classes:

- **Serializable classes** These classes, which are marked with the *<Serializable>* attribute, can be sent between processes, applications, and computers.
- **Remotable classes** These classes derive from *System.MarshalByRefObject* (or indirectly through another class that derives from *MarshalByRefObject*, such as *Component*). This provides them with the innate capability to be invoked remotely (outside of their application domain).
- **Ordinary classes** On their own, these classes can't be used in a .NET Remoting scenario for communication or for distributed execution. They might be used as a local part of an application, but that topic doesn't interest us in this chapter.

Figure 4-1 shows the role the remotable and serializable types play.

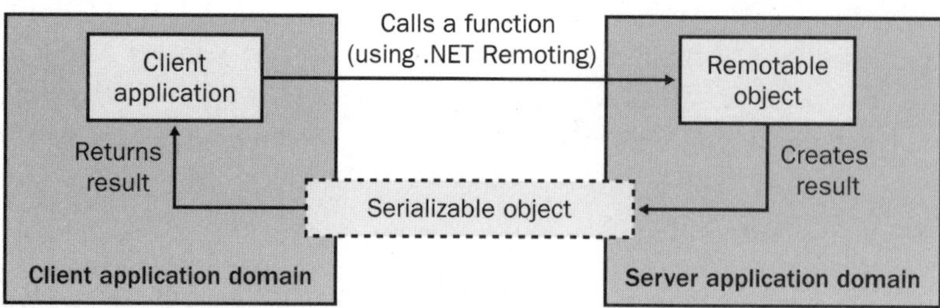

Figure 4-1 Remotable and serializable types

Serializable Classes

A serializable class generally plays the role of the "information package" (introduced in Chapter 2). .NET knows enough about a serializable class to convert all its information to a stream of bytes and reconstruct it in another process. In essence, a serializable object can be copied into any other application domain.

What Is an Application Domain?

Every .NET program consists of one or more threads inside an *application domain* (also called an *app domain*). The concept of an application domain is similar to the idea of Windows processes: application domains are isolated containers that can't communicate directly. In addition, if an application crashes in one application domain, it won't affect an application in another domain. Essentially, application domains have all the benefits of separate processes but have reduced overhead. Creating a separate application domain is handled by the .NET common language runtime (CLR) and doesn't require as much work as spawning a new process. For that reason, application domains are often described as "lightweight" processes.

Whenever you want to communicate with an object in another application domain, you need .NET Remoting. This is true regardless of whether the application domains are in separate computers or are hosted inside the same Windows process. You can retrieve a reference to an *AppDomain* object that represents the current application domain by using the static *AppDomain.CurrentDomain* property.

Many key .NET types are automatically serializable. These include everything from basic structures (including integers, floating-point numbers, and dates and times) to more sophisticated classes (such as strings, exceptions, and the *DataSet*). Table 4-1 provides a quick overview of some key serializable types in the .NET Framework. This is only a small fraction of the total number of serializable types available in the class library. To determine whether any other .NET type is serializable, look it up in the class library reference and check whether the type definition is preceded with the *<Serializable>* attribute, as shown here:

```
<Serializable()> _
Public Class Random
```

Table 4-1 Key Serializable Types

Category	Types
Simple value types	*Boolean, Byte, Char, DateTime, Decimal, Double, Enum, Guid, Int16, Int32, Int64, Sbyte, Single, TimeSpan, UInt16, UInt32,* and *UInt64*
Core classes	*Array, EventArgs, Exception, Random, String,* and almost all collection classes
Data classes	*DataSet, DataRow, DataRelation, DataTable,* and the native SQL Server–specific types

Keep in mind that when you serialize arrays or collections, the contained content must also be serializable. For example, you can serialize an array of *DataSet* objects but not a collection of *Buffer* objects (because the *System.Buffer* class is intended to represent direct access to unmanaged memory and therefore isn't serializable).

You can also create your own serializable types by simply applying the *<Serializable>* attribute. To re-create the serializable object in the new application domain, however, you must be sure that both the sender and recipient have a reference to the assembly that defines your custom type. Otherwise, the recipient will have a stream of bytes and no way to interpret it, which will lead to a run-time exception.

You should be aware of a few other serialization rules:

- **For the *<Serializable>* attribute to work, every member and property must also be serializable.** If you create a class that contains another custom class, this custom class must be serializable. If you derive from a parent class, this class must also be serializable.
- **When a class is serialized, every other object it references is also serialized.** This means, for example, that if you serialize the first item in a linked list, you actually end up transmitting the entire

list across application domains (because the first item points to the second, which points to the third, and so on). This can have unintended consequences for network bandwidth.

- **If there is any member variable you don't want copied, add the *<NonSerialized>* attribute just before it.** That way, the variable is reinitialized to an empty value when the object is copied. This proves useful if an object contains references that might not be valid in another application domain, such as a file handle.

Listing 4-1 shows the *CustomerDetails* information package from Chapter 1 recast as a serializable type.

```
<Serializable()> _
Public Class CustomerDetails

    Private _ID As Integer
    Private _Name As String
    Private _Email As String
    Private _Password As String

    ' (Remainder of code omitted.)

End Class
```

Listing 4-1 A serializable class

Listing 4-2 shows how to write the *CustomerDetails* class if we decide we shouldn't serialize the password for security reasons. It defaults to a blank string when transmitted across an application domain.

```
<Serializable()> _
Public Class CustomerDetails

    Private _ID As Integer
    Private _Name As String
    Private _Email As String
    <NonSerialized()> Private _Password As String

    ' (Remainder of code omitted.)

End Class
```

Listing 4-2 A partially serializable class

Note Serializable classes aren't used only in .NET Remoting. You can also use them programmatically to send a class to stream or a file. In these cases, you use the methods of the Binary Formatter (in the *System.Runtime.Serialization.Formatters.Binary* namespace) or the SOAP Formatter (in the *System.Runtime.Serialization.Formatters.Soap* namespace). Note that the Binary Formatter is part of the core mscorlib.dll assembly and is always available, whereas the SOAP Formatter requires a reference to the System.Runtime.Serialization.Formatters.Soap.dll assembly.

Remotable Classes

Every public property, method, and member variable in a class that derives from *System.MarshalByRefObject* can be used remotely. For example, Listing 4-3 shows how you might recast the *CustomerDB* service provider class so that it can be accessed from another computer using .NET Remoting.

```
Public Class CustomerDB
    Inherits System.MarshalByRefObject

    ' (The class code is unchanged.)

End Class
```

Listing 4-3 A remotable *CustomerDB*

With .NET Remoting, the communication process is governed through a proxy object. This approach is conceptually similar to the way that other distributed technologies work, including XML Web services and traditional COM/DCOM programming.

With proxy communication, your local code talks directly to a proxy object that "mimics" the remote object. When you call a method on the proxy object, it calls the remote object behind the scenes, waits for the response, and then returns the appropriate information to your code. This interception mechanism is a marvelous innovation for the application programmer, who doesn't need to worry about messy infrastructure details such as cross-domain or cross-process calls, network transport, or message formatting. Instead, the application communicates with a proxy object contained in its application domain. Even better, this proxy object behaves just like the original object would if it were instantiated locally.

In reality, the .NET Remoting architecture is a little more sophisticated. To start with, .NET Remoting proxies are slightly more complicated because there are actually two proxy layers (the transparent proxy that you communicate with directly and the real proxy that .NET uses to dispatch the message when it decides remote communication is necessary). However, this bit of plumbing isn't terribly significant. It's more important to understand how .NET Remoting divides the work among different types of services.

When communicating with a remote object, the proxy class doesn't actually perform all the required work. Instead, it communicates with a *formatter* that packages the client request or server response in the appropriate format. The formatter then communicates with a *transport channel* that transmits the information using the appropriate protocol. This multilayered approach enables developers to create their own formatters and channels and still use the same .NET Remoting model. In fact, you can change the channel and formatter used by an application without even recompiling the code. All you need to do is tweak a few configuration settings in an XML file.

Figure 4-2 shows how a method invocation is packaged on the client side and then unpacked on the server side. In this case, the information flows from the client to the server, but the return value also flows back to server to the client along the same path. Note that this diagram shows more detail than Figure 4-1, which ignores the proxy layer for the sake of simplicity.

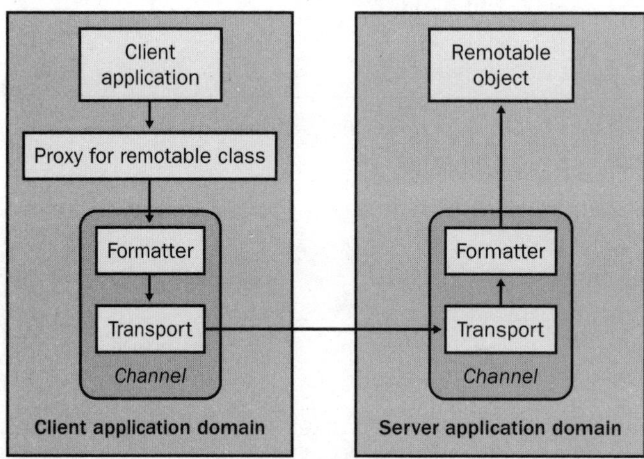

Figure 4-2 The multilayered .NET Remoting architecture

The formatter serializes the message to a binary or SOAP representation before it is sent. Incidentally, the formatter is only one possible channel sink that a message can pass through on its way to another process. If you like, you can create your own custom sinks and place them in the channel sink chain. These classes can intercept the communication (which you can manipulate using the *IMessage* interface) and provide additional services such as encryption, logging, or compression. The key concept is that channel sinks take effect on both the client and server. As you can see in Figure 4-2 and Figure 4-3, the server-side sinks are a mirror image of the client-side sinks.

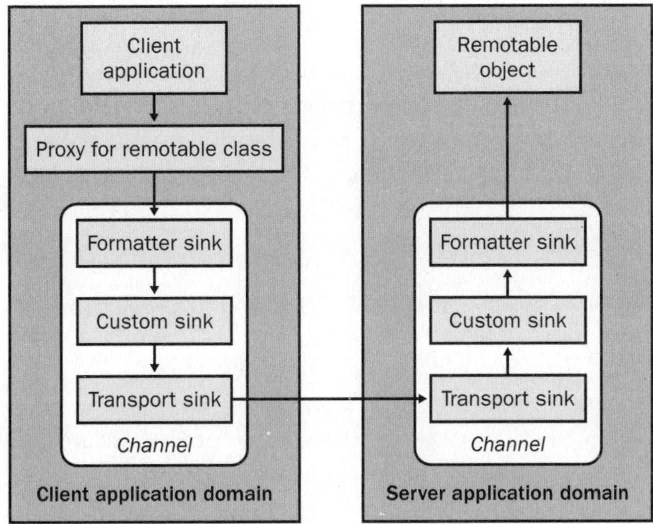

Figure 4-3 Interception with a custom sink

The last sink in the client side of the chain is always the transport sink, which is responsible for transmitting the message to the remote application domain. Figure 4-3 shows one example of how you might insert a custom sink into the chain. We won't discuss the creation of custom sink objects in this book because it's a low-level task best left to experienced infrastructure programmers (such as those at Microsoft).

The Remote Component Host

There's one other simplification that I've used so far. As described earlier, all *MarshalByRefObject* instances can be invoked remotely. However, just defining a *MarshalByRefObject* doesn't make it available to the client. What's needed is a dedicated server application—a program that listens for client requests and creates the appropriate objects.

Technically, it is possible to create a *MarshalByRefObject* that is also a component host, but this is likely to lead to a good deal of confusion. A better approach is to create a dedicated server-side application. This application can take one of several forms:

- A dedicated Windows service, which starts automatically when the server is switched on and requires no user intervention.
- A console application, which allows simple diagnostic or log information to be displayed on the screen.
- A full-fledged Windows application, which can provide a more sophisticated interface. Remember, however, that your remoted components probably won't interact with their component host. If you want to display information such as the currently connected clients, you might want to add a user interface class to the component itself or devise a more sophisticated logging strategy.

A component host needs to perform only two tasks. First, it creates the server-side channels that listen for client requests. When a client request is received, the .NET Remoting infrastructure automatically creates the required remote object in the same application domain as the component host.

After the component has been created, the component host also facilitates the communication between the object in its application domain and the remote client. However, the client never interacts directly with the component host. Figure 4-4 shows a simplified diagram of this relationship.

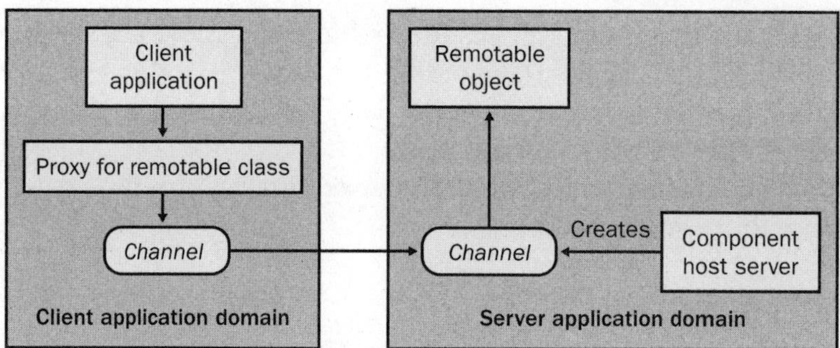

Figure 4-4 The role of the component host

In this chapter, we use a straightforward Windows application for a component host.

> **Note** The .NET Remoting infrastructure uses a thread pool to listen for client requests. That means that more than one client can create or use an object at the same time. If you design components that are shared between multiple clients, you must use the threading techniques discussed in Chapter 6 and Chapter 7.

Key .NET Remoting Design Decisions

As much as I'd like to jump straight into the typical "Hello World" example of .NET Remoting, you need to make a few fundamental choices before you even start to implement an architecture that incorporates .NET Remoting. These choices concern the type of activation, the object lifetime, and the message format and network transport used for communication.

Activation Modes

.NET Remoting supports three types of objects:

- ***SingleCall*** These stateless objects are automatically created with every method invocation and live for only the duration of that method. The client can keep and use the same reference, but every call results in the creation of a new object.
- **Client-activated** These objects are most similar to ordinary objects. They retain state, and each client receives a separate instance.
- **Singleton** This type of object retains state but shares it between every client. No matter how many clients connect, there is only ever one remote object instance.

The inevitable question is which activation type represents best design practices? *SingleCall* objects are usually ideal because they have a very low overhead. They don't consume any server resources when they aren't working, and they can easily be hosted on multiple servers with clustering because of their stateless design. They also match the "service provider" design pattern introduced in Chapter 2.

Client-activated objects, on the other hand, are often easier to program with because they resemble ordinary objects. The problem is that this false sense of familiarity can lead developers to use them in disastrous ways. Because client-activated objects retain state, for example, you might be tempted to use property procedures, member variables, and other object-oriented practices to simplify coding. Because of the nontrivial overhead required to make a network call, however, setting and retrieving properties individually can greatly slow down your application.

Singleton objects are probably the most difficult to manage properly. Because multiple clients can call methods at the same time, there is the potential for concurrency errors—subtle but serious problems that occur when data is modified simultaneously. Unfortunately, concurrency errors often don't appear in development testing and are difficult to repeat and diagnose. In addition, because of their state, singleton objects can't be used in load-balancing scenarios with multiple servers. Generally, you shouldn't use a singleton object unless you need to. In some peer-to-peer scenarios in which components need to share synchronized information, for instance, singleton objects are extremely attractive. Make sure, however, that you polish your threading skills by reading Chapter 6 and Chapter 7.

Object Lifetime

Singleton and client-activated objects have state, but they can't be allowed to live forever. Consider what would happen if a client were to forget to release the object or just disappear from view due to network problems. In these cases, the server-side objects they created would linger on in a useless zombie state, wasting valuable server resources. Multiplied by hundreds of clients over the period of several days, the server might be choked to a standstill by memory that was never properly released.

Clearly, a distributed component technology needs to take this danger into consideration. In .NET, this problem is dealt with using a lifetime leasing scheme. Essentially it works like this: An object is allowed to exist only for a fixed amount of time. If it needs to last longer, someone needs to renew its lease. This "someone" can be a dedicated lease sponsor, the client component, or the remote component itself. To ensure long-time stability and scalability of your system, however, you must implement a realistic, conservative leasing policy (as discussed a little later in this chapter).

> **Note** Lifetime leasing is a dramatic departure from DCOM, which uses keep-alive pinging (euphemistically known as *distributed garbage collection*) to manage object lifetime. Essentially, as soon as the pinging stops, the server assumes that the client had been disconnected and releases the object. The serious drawback to this technique is that the pinging is inherently unscalable in a large distributed system. Having hundreds of clients pinging remote components at the same time can significantly reduce network bandwidth and performance.

Server and Client Activation

To further complicate matters, singleton and *SingleCall* objects are both categorized as server-activated objects. The terms *server-activated object* (SAO) and *client-activated object* (CAO) turn up in the MSDN documentation and various publications. They cause a great deal of confusion.

For example, it's sometimes mistakenly said that lifetime leases apply only to client-activated objects, not server-activated objects. This just isn't true. Lifetime leases apply to both client-activated and singleton objects.

The real distinction between client-activated and server-activated objects is that a server-activated object isn't really created when a client instantiates it. Instead, it is created as needed. If the object is a *SingleCall* object or a singleton that doesn't exist yet, it's created with the first method call. Client-activated objects, on the other hand, are created when the client instantiates them.

Why is this distinction important? The difference is minor, except for one detail: client-activated objects can use parameterized constructors. Server-activated objects can be created only with the default (no parameter) constructor because they're not created directly by the client—they're created indirectly by the server.

Communication

The final decision you need to make when implementing a remote component is the communication format and transport to use. Although .NET uses a pluggable format that allows any type of formatter or channel, by default the .NET Framework ships with two formatters and two channels. These prebuilt choices serve most needs.

You can choose from two formatters:

- **Binary Formatter** The Binary Formatter serializes data to a compact, proprietary .NET format (although it doesn't compress the data). This formatter offers the best performance but can be used only by .NET applications.
- **SOAP Formatter** The SOAP Formatter serializes data to a SOAP message, which is a cross-platform XML-based plain-text format. Because clients on other platforms can create and send SOAP messages, this formatter can allow cross-platform communication with a remote .NET component. The SOAP format requires larger message sizes, however, and can therefore reduce overall performance. To get around this limitation, you can use the Binary Formatter or create objects that implement custom serialization. For example, the *DataSet* is an example of a class that uses custom serialization to optimize performance—it encodes its content into binary data, which is then inserted into the SOAP message.

There are also two channels:

- ***TcpChannel*** This channel uses the connection-based TCP protocol. It's ideal for internal networks.
- ***HttpChannel*** This channel uses the HTTP protocol, which is ideal for scenarios in which you need to communicate across the Internet. HTTP is based on the TCP/IP protocol, but it doesn't require a continuous connection. Instead, it communicates using request and response messages.

When defining a channel, you also need to choose a port number for the communication. Essentially, to communicate with a remote object you need the machine name (or IP address) and a port number (from 0 through 65,535) that maps to a network service and specific application. Choosing the correct port in a production environment might require some consultation with a network or firewall administrator in your organization. However, there are several rules of thumb:

- Ports 0 to 1023 are well-known ports and are often used by system services. All Web browsers connect to port 80 by default for HTTP. In general, you shouldn't use these ports for your applications.
- Ports 1024 to 41,9151 are registered ports that are available for use on most systems.

- Ports 49152 to 65,535 are dynamic or private ports.

I've actually simplified the issue slightly. When creating a connection, you have the choice of creating dedicated client and server channels, or bidirectional channels. With a dedicated client-server channel, the client invokes methods and the server returns information. However, the server can't invoke a method of the client object or raise an event to the client.

You can see all the prebuilt channels in the machine.config file (which is stored in the directory C:\[WinDir]\Microsoft.NET\Framework\[Version]\CONFIG). Each channel is given a friendly *id* attribute (which is the name you use in your configuration files) and more specific information about the underlying class, assembly, and version, as shown in Listing 4-4.

```
<channels>
    <channel id="http"
        type="System.Runtime.Remoting.Channels.Http.HttpChannel,
              System.Runtime.Remoting, Version=1.0.3300.0,
              Culture=neutral, PublicKeyToken=b77a5c561934e089"/>
    <channel id="http client"
        type="System.Runtime.Remoting.Channels.Http.HttpClientChannel,
              System.Runtime.Remoting, Version=1.0.3300.0,
              Culture=neutral, PublicKeyToken=b77a5c561934e089"/>
    <channel id="http server"
        type="System.Runtime.Remoting.Channels.Http.HttpServerChannel,
              System.Runtime.Remoting, Version=1.0.3300.0,
              Culture=neutral, PublicKeyToken=b77a5c561934e089"/>
    <channel id="tcp"
        type="System.Runtime.Remoting.Channels.Tcp.TcpChannel,
              System.Runtime.Remoting, Version=1.0.3300.0,
              Culture=neutral, PublicKeyToken=b77a5c561934e089"/>
    <channel id="tcp client"
        type="System.Runtime.Remoting.Channels.Tcp.TcpClientChannel,
              System.Runtime.Remoting, Version=1.0.3300.0,
              Culture=neutral, PublicKeyToken=b77a5c561934e089"/>
    <channel id="tcp server"
        type="System.Runtime.Remoting.Channels.Tcp.TcpServerChannel,
              System.Runtime.Remoting, Version=1.0.3300.0,
              Culture=neutral, PublicKeyToken=b77a5c561934e089"/>
</channels>
```

Listing 4-4 Channel templates in the machine.config file

If you want to, you can add your own defaults to the machine.config file. Doing so enables you, for example, to register a channel that always uses a certain port. However, these changes must then be applied to the machine.config file in every user's computer, which can be a tedious (and even risky) process.

> **Note** The .NET Framework also provides lower-level classes that enable you to create socket-based connections or send information over HTTP, FTP, or UDP manually. (See, for example, the *System.Net* and *System.Net.Sockets* namespaces.) These classes allow a great deal of flexibility and are probably required if you need optimum performance in a complicated peer-to-peer application (such as a multiplayer networked computer game). However, it's much less common to develop enterprise applications with these classes, both because it requires a good deal more code and because it can easily introduce unexpected vulnerabilities or unnoticed errors. It's also much less likely if you need to interoperate with components hosted on other platforms, languages, or operating systems. When designing distributed applications, you'll generally want to use the higher-level .NET Remoting Framework (or XML Web services) and concentrate on optimizing the database and network architecture instead of reinventing the wheel with custom networking code.

A Simple Remoting Server

So far we've explored a fair bit of information about the .NET Remoting architecture and its capabilities. It's time to dive into a complete example to see how it works in practice. This example requires three ingredients: the client application, the remote object, and the component host. You can develop and test the design on a single computer and modify the configuration later when you deploy it.

The easiest way to develop these three ingredients is to use separate Microsoft Visual Studio .NET projects. You can group them together into a single solution if you would like, but it's not required. In fact, you might want to try creating them in separate Visual Studio .NET instances first, which will help you understand each project's role and dependencies.

The Remote Object

First of all, we create a simple remotable class that provides a single method, named *GetActiveDomain*, which returns a string with the information about the current application domain where execution is taking place. (See Listing 4-5.) This class must be compiled into a DLL assembly, so if you're using Visual Studio .NET, you'll create this component as a class library project.

```
Public Class RemoteObject
    Inherits MarshalByRefObject

    ' Return the name of the current application domain.
    Public Function GetActiveDomain() As String
        Return AppDomain.CurrentDomain.FriendlyName
    End Function

End Class
```

Listing 4-5 A remotable object

That's it! You should now compile the remotable component before continuing.

The Component Host

The component host just creates the channel that listens for client requests. In .NET Remoting, there are two ways to configure and create a channel: directly in code or by loading a configuration file. In this example, we use a configuration file, which allows the settings to be modified without requiring a recompile. The settings are loaded using the shared helper method *RemotingConfiguration.Configure*. In this example, the component host itself is a Windows application named SimpleServer.exe, and the listening channel is configured when the *HostForm* Windows Form first loads (as shown in Listing 4-6).

```
Imports System.Runtime.Remoting

Public Class HostForm
    Inherits System.Windows.Forms.Form

    ' (Designer code omitted.)

    Private Sub HostForm_Load(ByVal sender As System.Object, _
     ByVal e As System.EventArgs) Handles MyBase.Load

        ' Start listening for client requests, according to the
        ' information specified in the configuration file.
        RemotingConfiguration.Configure("SimpleServer.exe.config")

    End Sub

End Class
```

Listing 4-6 A Windows Forms component host

The .NET Remoting configuration file is the same configuration file used for assembly dependencies and probing, as detailed in Chapter 2. This isn't required (you can actually use any filename), but it is recommended for simplicity. In a more sophisticated scenario, you might use several configuration files with different settings. The application then decides which one to use at run time or queries it directly from a database or an XML Web service.

The configuration file must be placed in the same directory as the executable. (So if you're testing in Visual Studio .NET, you use the Bin directory.) This configuration file defines the type of channel and identifies the type of object and the location where it can be found. Listing 4-7 shows the configuration file for the SimpleServer host application.

```
<configuration>
   <system.runtime.remoting>
      <application name="SimpleServer">
         <service>
            <activated
             type="RemoteObjects.RemoteObject, RemoteObjects"/>
         </service>
         <channels>
            <channel ref="tcp server" port="8080" />
         </channels>
      </application>
   </system.runtime.remoting>
</configuration>
```

Listing 4-7 The component host configuration file

In this example, the channel is identified as "*tcp server*", which is one of the channel aliases defined in the machine.config file. The assigned port number is 8080. If you want to use the HTTP channel instead, you just specify "*http server*".

The service (or remote object) is a client-activated type. Its fully qualified class name is *RemoteObjects.RemoteObject*, and it exists in the assembly *RemoteObjects*. (The .dll extension is assumed.) In this case, the assembly name matches the class name, but it doesn't need to. If the *RemoteObject* class were contained in an assembly called ServerObjects.dll, for example, you would rewrite the activation tag like this:

```
<activated type="RemoteObjects.RemoteObject, ServerObjects"/>
```

The configuration file also names the component host application; the client needs to use this name to connect to the listening channel:

```
<application name="SimpleServer">
```

The host application has a relatively simple life. Although it's currently created as a Windows Forms application (for the sake of convenience), it doesn't display any user interface. It also isn't notified when a client makes a request or when a remote object is created—all these steps take place automatically. However, the client application needs to be active in order to continue listening. As soon as the component host application ends, any current clients are disconnected (and all future clients are refused).

Alternatively, you can create the same component host as a console application, as shown in Listing 4-8.

```
Module ConsoleHost

    Sub Main()
        Console.WriteLine("About to configure channel.")
        RemotingConfiguration.Configure("SimpleServer.exe.config")

        Console.WriteLine("Listening has started.")
        Console.WriteLine("Press any key to stop listening and exit.")

        ' This next line is required to stop the program from ending
        ' prematurely. After the user presses a key, execution will
        ' resume, and the program will end when it reaches the end
        ' of this method.
        Console.ReadLine()
    End Sub

End Module
```

Listing 4-8 A console component host

One easily overlooked consideration is that .NET Remoting must be able to create the requested type inside the component host's application domain. In other words, if the component host is running on a remote server, the assembly that describes the remote object must be available in the server's global assembly cache (GAC) or in the same directory as the host application. This error is particularly tricky because it results in a run-time error, not a compile-time error. Visual Studio .NET (or the Visual Basic compiler) has no way of identifying that a component host requires the assembly for the remote object because its details are contained in a separate configuration file.

If you're developing in Visual Studio .NET, the easiest way to ensure that the component assembly is available is to add a reference to it. This way, whenever you compile the component host, the latest version of the remote object assembly is placed in the component host directory. If you're compiling your application at the command line, just make sure you manually copy the component assembly to the same directory.

The Client Application

In our example, the client application is also created as a Windows Forms project. Like the component host, the client requires a configuration file that tells it where to find the object. (Technically, because this is a client-activated object, the configuration file doesn't tell the client where to find the object so much as it tells the client on what machine it should instantiate the object. The remote machine must have a copy of the assembly and a listening component host.

The client configuration file is shown in Listing 4-9.

```
<configuration>
   <system.runtime.remoting>
      <application name="SimpleClient">
         <client url="tcp://localhost:8080/SimpleServer">
            <activated
             type="RemoteObjects.RemoteObject, RemoteObjects"/>
         </client>
         <channels>
            <channel ref="tcp client"/>
         </channels>
      </application>
   </system.runtime.remoting>
</configuration>
```

Listing 4-9 The client configuration file

This time, a client TCP/IP channel is defined:

```
<channel ref="tcp client"/>
```

The port number (8080) and the name of the component host are incorporated into a URL:

```
<client url="tcp://localhost:8080/SimpleServer">
```

The URL actually specifies five pieces of information—the protocol, the machine name, the port number, the application name, and the object identifier.

```
<client url="[Protocol]://[MachineName]:[Port]/[Application]/[Object]">
```

In the case of a client-activated object, the final object identifier portion is not required, because the client creates the object on its own.

In this example, the machine name is identified only as *localhost*, which is a loopback alias that always points to the current computer. Alternatively, you can use a machine name:

```
<client url="tcp://production:8080/SimpleServer">
```

Or an IP address:

```
<client url="tcp://226.116.109.100:8080/SimpleServer">
```

Finally, the configuration file identifies the type and assembly of the remote component:

```
<activated type="RemoteObjects.RemoteObject, RemoteObjects"/>
```

This configuration file is read and applied with a similar call to the *Remoting-Configuration.Configure* method:

```
RemotingConfiguration.Configure("SimpleClient.exe.config")
```

The client application also needs a reference to the component assembly of the remote object. Otherwise, you have no way to call its methods or set its properties in code because .NET won't be able to check the type metadata and validate your statements. Clearly, this requirement makes for a few distribution headaches. In Chapter 11, I'll explain how you can sidestep this problem with interfaces. If you're having trouble keeping this arrangement straight, refer to Figure 4-5, which shows all three projects and the required references. In this example, all projects are part of one Visual Studio .NET solution.

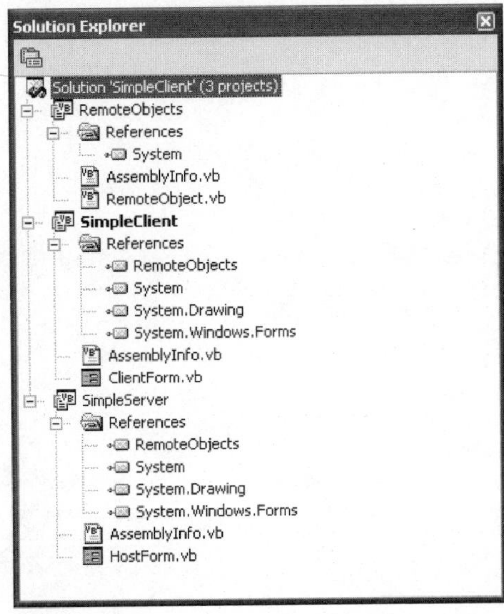

Figure 4-5 Three projects in a .NET Remoting solution

> **Note** Always remember that the client can't create an instance of a remote object unless it knows a bare minimum of information about that object! This point is critical but easily overlooked when you're starting out with .NET Remoting. In this example (which doesn't use interfaces), that means the client needs a reference to the remote object's assembly.

Finally, now that the client's channel is registered, the client can create the remote object as if it were a local object by using the *New* keyword. The sample program in Listing 4-10 does exactly that and tests the current location of the component.

```
Imports System.Runtime.Remoting

Public Class ClientForm

    ' (Designer code omitted.)

    Private Sub ClientForm_Load(ByVal sender As System.Object, _
      ByVal e As System.EventArgs) Handles MyBase.Load

        ' Configure the client.
        RemotingConfiguration.Configure("SimpleClient.exe.config")

        ' Display the current domain.
        MessageBox.Show("The client application is executing in: " & _
                        AppDomain.CurrentDomain.FriendlyName)

        ' Create the remote object, and determine what domain it is
        ' executing in.
        Dim RemoteObj As New RemoteObjects.RemoteObject()
        MessageBox.Show("The remote object is executing in: " & _
                        RemoteObj.GetActiveDomain)

    End Sub

End Class
```

Listing 4-10 The client test form

Remember that before you can start this program, you need to run the component host. Otherwise, the connection will be refused.

When you run this simple test program, two message boxes display in succession, as shown in Figure 4-6. Together they demonstrate that the remote component is running in a separate application domain.

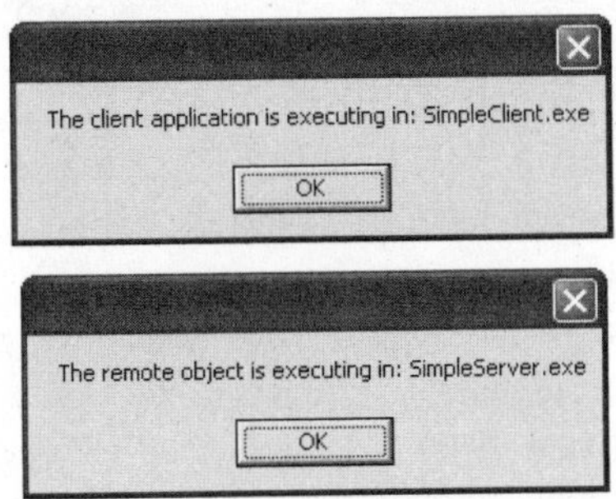

Figure 4-6 Interacting with a remote component

A Remotable Component with User Interface

To bring the point home, you might want to try a different test. This one is particularly interesting if you're testing on separate computers. Replace the *GetActiveDomain* function with the *ShowActiveDomain* subroutine shown here:

```
Public Class RemoteObject
    Inherits MarshalByRefObject

    Public Sub ShowActiveDomain()
        MessageBox.Show(AppDomain.CurrentDomain.FriendlyName)
    End Sub

End Class
```

Now, when you invoke this method you'll notice two interesting details. First, if you're running the client and component host on separate computers, the second message box appears on the remote computer because it is being displayed in the application domain of the component host. Second, the client application is stalled until you click OK to confirm the message. This example offers further proof that the component is really running remotely, and it hints at some of the reasons that middle-tier components shouldn't get involved in the user interface. If you want to provide tracking or diagnostic information, you'll generally want to design a separate component, as described in Chapter 14.

Testing with Visual Studio .NET

If you change any part of the component's code, you'll need to rebuild each of the three projects. First, change the component and rebuild it. Next, make sure you rebuild the server project (not just rerun it) by right-clicking on the project item and choosing Rebuild. This ensures that the modified component assembly is copied to the component host directory. (Otherwise, the component host will create the old version of the remote object when it receives a client request.) Finally, you can restart the client application.

When you understand .NET Remoting basics, the best choice is to combine projects in one solution. This makes it easy to set breakpoints and variable watches in the server code, client code, or remote object code and have them work transparently. Figure 4-7 shows the solution settings you need. When you start the project, both the component host project and the client project are compiled and executed. If you change the remote object, however, you need to manually recompile it as described earlier.

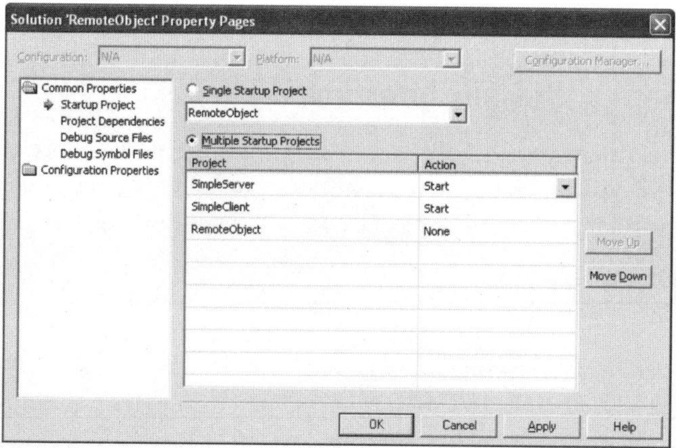

Figure 4-7 Solution settings for a .NET Remoting project

Using a Different Formatter

You might have noticed that the configuration file specifies the channel (the transport protocol for the communication) but not the formatter. That's because the TCP/IP channel defaults to binary format and the HTTP channel defaults to SOAP (XML-based text) communication. Although this is the default, other combinations can make sense. For example, you could use binary communication over an HTTP channel to allow .NET programs to communicate efficiently over the Internet and through a firewall.

In this case, you need to manually specify the formatter in the configuration file by adding a *<formatter>* tag inside the *<channel>* tag and set the *ref* attribute to *soap* or *binary*. Listing 4-11 shows how the server configuration file would look for this simple example if it were to use the HTTP channel with the Binary Formatter.

```
<configuration>
   <system.runtime.remoting>
      <application name="SimpleServer">
         <service>
            <activated type="RemoteObjects.RemoteObject,
                                 RemoteObjects"/>
         </service>
         <channels>
            <channel ref="http server" port="8080">
               <serverProviders>
                  <formatter ref="binary">
               </serverProviders>
             </channel>
         </channels>
      </application>
   </system.runtime.remoting>
</configuration>
```

Listing 4-11 A component host that uses the HTTP channel with the Binary Formatter

And the client's configuration file would look as shown in Listing 4-12.

```
<configuration>
   <system.runtime.remoting>
      <application name="SimpleClient">
         <client url="tcp://localhost:8080/SimpleServer">
            <activated
             type="RemoteObjects.RemoteObject, RemoteObjects"/>
         </client>
         <channels>
            <channel ref="http client" port="8080">
              <clientProviders>
                 <formatter ref="binary">
              </clientProviders>
            </channel>
         </channels>
      </application>
   </system.runtime.remoting>
</configuration>
```

Listing 4-12 A client that uses the HTTP channel with the Binary Formatter

Using Multiple Channels

You can create a component host that listens for connections on more than one channel. This scenario is most common if you need to support different types of clients. For example, local clients can use the faster binary TCP/IP connection, whereas remote clients connecting over the Internet can use SOAP over HTTP, as in the example shown in Listing 4-13.

```
<configuration>
   <system.runtime.remoting>
      <application name="SimpleServer">
         <service>
            <activated
             type="RemoteObjects.RemoteObject, RemoteObjects"/>
         </service>
         <channels>
            <channel ref="http server" port="8080">
            <channel ref="tcp server" port="8081">
         </channels>
      </application>
   </system.runtime.remoting>
</configuration>
```

Listing 4-13 A component host that supports multiple channels

The client can then choose the channel to use when it specifies the URI for the remote object.

Consider these points when using multiple channels:

- The only disadvantage to using multiple channels is that the listening process effectively ties them up, preventing any other application from using them. Therefore, if you run more than one component host on the same workstation, take care not to use the same ports. Alternatively, you can configure the servers to register channels programmatically, allowing dynamic port selection (a technique shown in Chapter 11).
- You can't register more than one channel of the same type using a configuration file (for example, two "*tcp server*" channels using different ports) because they have the same name. Chapter 11 shows how you can overcome this limitation with dynamic registration.
- A single component host can allow the creation of several different types of objects if you simply add additional *<activated>* or *<wellknown>* elements. However, you can't configure it so that some components are available through certain channels while others are

not. To implement this design, you need to create a separate component host or create a component host that creates separate application domains using the *CreateDomain* and *CreateInstance* methods of the *System.AppDomain* class.

- The number of objects a component host can create isn't in any way linked to the number of channels it uses. .NET handles all the infrastructure, automatically dispatching messages to the appropriate component instance, and a single channel can serve multiple clients.

SingleCall Objects

The preceding example uses a client-activated type because its behavior closely resembles that of an ordinary, in-process object. Remoting also provides two types of server-activated (or "well-known") objects, which the client must connect to using the specified URL. The first type is *SingleCall*.

SingleCall objects are the most efficient and common type of remotable object in an enterprise application because they are extremely lightweight and efficient. With a *SingleCall* object, the object is created at the beginning of every method invocation and released at the end. This ensures that valuable server memory is never retained for long. The client retains a reference to the proxy for the object as long as it wants, and the proxy creates the remote object with each call. If any defaults need to be set, they can be initialized in the class constructor, which will be executed with every call as the object is re-created.

In the simple example used so far, the remote object doesn't retain any state, so it's a perfect choice for a *SingleCall* object. You would need to modify the server configuration file as shown in Listing 4-14.

```
<configuration>
   <system.runtime.remoting>
      <application name="SimpleServer">
         <service>
            <wellknown mode="SingleCall"
                       type="RemoteObjects.RemoteObject, RemoteObjects"
                       objectUri="RemoteObject" />
         </service>
         <channels>
            <channel ref="tcp server" port="8080" />
         </channels>
      </application>
   </system.runtime.remoting>
</configuration>
```

Listing 4-14 A component host that provides a *SingleCall* object

Notice that the *<activated>* tag has been replaced with a *<wellknown>* tag and an *objectURI* has been added to uniquely identify the server-side object. The channel information doesn't need to change. Next you can update the client configuration file to use the *<wellknown>* tag and *objectURI*, as shown in Listing 4-15.

```
<configuration>
   <system.runtime.remoting>
      <application name="SimpleClient">
         <client url>
            <wellknown
                    type="RemoteObjects.RemoteObject, RemoteObjects"
                    url="tcp://localhost:8080/SimpleServer/RemoteObject"/>
         </client>
         <channels>
            <channel ref="tcp client"/>
         </channels>
      </application>
   </system.runtime.remoting>
</configuration>
```

Listing 4-15 A client that uses a *SingleCall* object

Service provider components are ideal for *SingleCall* objects over .NET Remoting. On the other hand, an object that requires a resource that is expensive to retrieve should not be *SingleCall*. Suppose, for example, that you create a server-side object that reads a large quantity of data from a database and provides aggregate information to the client. (You might use a design like this if clients are connecting over a slow Internet connection and the amount of raw data is extremely large.) In this case, you need to use a client-activated or singleton object so that the data can be retained; otherwise, the remote object would need to requery the database with each method call.

Singleton Objects

Singleton objects resemble client-activated objects in that they retain state; but the server, not the client, creates them. Only one instance of a singleton object is ever created, and it can serve any number of concurrent clients. Because the .NET Remoting services are multithreaded, clients can call methods on this object simultaneously. However, you must ensure that the object itself is thread-safe. If you modify a member variable in a singleton method, for example, you must ensure that you obtain an exclusive lock first. Otherwise, updates might be lost or inconsistent data might be applied.

We can alter the preceding example to use a singleton object without worrying. The single *GetActiveDomain* method just returns a static piece of information to the calling client, and this method can therefore be called concurrently without causing any problems.

The server configuration file looks the same as the *SingleCall* example, except for the different mode attribute, as shown in Listing 4-16.

```
<configuration>
   <system.runtime.remoting>
      <application name="SimpleServer">
         <service>
            <wellknown mode="Singleton"
                       type="RemoteObjects.RemoteObject, RemoteObjects"
                       objectUri="RemoteObject" />
         </service>
         <channels>
            <channel ref="tcp server" port="8080" />
         </channels>
      </application>
   </system.runtime.remoting>
</configuration>
```

Listing 4-16 A component host that uses a singleton object

The client configuration file looks exactly the same for the singleton object as for a *SingleCall* object.

Singleton objects are somewhat difficult to work with and can't be load-balanced over multiple computers. In some scenarios, however, such as those that involve synchronizing and communicating among multiple clients, a singleton object provides the most elegant solution. Chapter 7 takes a closer look at singleton objects and the threading techniques you need to use them safely.

Bidirectional Communication

The simple .NET Remoting examples developed so far support only one-way communication. That means the client can call methods, retrieve results, and use properties but can't respond to events or callbacks. In short, the server has no way of interacting with the client application except in response to the client.

In many enterprise applications, this simplified approach is ideal. In other cases, however, the server might need some mechanism to notify the client (for example, to signal that a time-consuming asynchronous task is complete or to send a message from another user in a chat application). In this case, a few changes are required.

First, you need to move from the client-server channels used so far to the bidirectional channels identified as *"tcp"* or *"http"* in the configuration file. Second, the client application needs to define a port used to listen for server communication. (In the simple client-server scenario, the underlying socket is closed when the communication is complete, so server-initiated interaction isn't possible.) To do this, you just specify a port number in the client configuration file. This can be the same port number (if you're testing on separate machines) or a different port number.

For example, you could define a TCP/IP port in the server configuration file like this:

```
<channel ref="tcp" port="8080" />
```

And one in the client configuration file as well:

```
<channel ref="tcp" port="8081" />
```

You have one alternative option. You can specify the port number *"0"* for the client, which instructs it to listen on a port that the CLR selects dynamically at run time. This is the most convenient and most common choice.

```
<channel ref="tcp" port="0" />
```

The next hurdle is that the client application needs at least one remotable *MarshalByRefObject* to receive the notification (which we'll call the *event listener*). Furthermore, the server application needs a reference to the assembly for this class so that it has enough information to use it—just as your client application requires a reference to the remote component assembly.

Assuming you meet these criteria, you have two options. You can define an event in the remote component class and handle the event with your client-side event listener class. Or you can pass a delegate that points to the listener class and allow the remote object to invoke that delegate. (Both of these approaches complicate life; if you need bidirectional communication, I encourage you to pay special attention to the section about interface-based programming in Chapter 11, which provides one way that you can simplify life with a shared component.)

Using Events

This section walks you through the steps needed to add an event to a remote object. Figure 4-8 shows the basic design pattern we'll use.

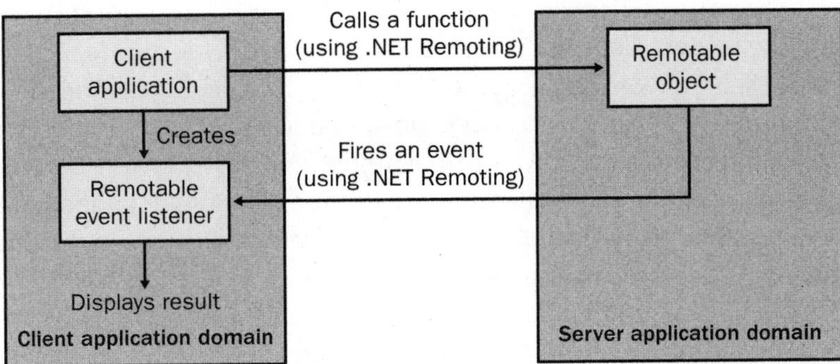

Figure 4-8 Handling an event with a remotable event listener

The first step is to define the event in the remote object and the custom *EventArgs* object, as shown in Listing 4-17.

```
Public Class RemoteObject
    Inherits MarshalByRefObject

    Public Event TaskComplete(ByVal sender As Object, _
     ByVal e As TaskCompleteEventArgs)

    ' (Other class code omitted.)

End Class

<Serializable()> _
Public Class TaskCompleteEventArgs
    Inherits EventArgs

    Public Result As Object

    Public Sub New(ByVal result As Object)
        Me.Result = result
    End Sub

End Class
```

Listing 4-17 Creating a remotable custom event

This event follows the .NET standard, passing a reference of the sending object and an *EventArgs* object with additional information. In this case, the *TaskCompleteEventArgs* object contains a *Result* property, which represents the result of a long-running server-side operation. Note that the *TaskCompleteEventArgs* object must be marked as serializable so it can be copied across application boundaries.

Next you need to create a remotable client-side component that can receive the event. This component *must* be implemented as a separate DLL assembly. Why? Both the server and client will need a reference to this object. The server needs the reference in order to be able to fire its event, while the client needs its reference in order to create the listener and receive the event. The .NET Framework does not allow applications to reference an executable assembly, so you need to use an assembly. Incidentally, you can overcome this limitation using the interface-based programming model explored in Chapter 11.

The event listener class simply defines two methods: one designed to receive the event and one that specifies an infinite lifetime, ensuring that the .NET Framework won't prematurely destroy this object (a consideration we'll explore in detail a little later in this chapter). When the event listener receives the event, it can raise another, local event to notify the client form class. In Listing 4-18, however, the event listener just displays a message box with the result.

```
Public Class EventListener
    Inherits MarshalByRefObject

    ' Handles the event.
    Public Sub TaskCompleted(ByVal sender As Object, _
      ByVal e As RemoteObjects.TaskCompleteEventArgs)

        System.Windows.Forms.MessageBox.Show( _
         "Event handler received result: " & e.Result.ToString())

    End Sub

    ' Ensures that this object will not be prematurely released.
    Public Overrides Function InitializeLifetimeService() As Object
        Return Nothing
    End Function

End Class
```

Listing 4-18 A listener class for a remote event

Here's where things become somewhat tangled. The *EventListener* component requires a reference to the *RemoteObject* assembly in order to know how to use the *TaskCompleteEventArgs* class. In turn, the component host needs to have access to the *EventListener* assembly so it knows how to communicate with that assembly. To sort out these tangled relationships, refer to Figure 4-9, which shows all four projects in the Visual Studio .NET Solution Explorer, along with their required references.

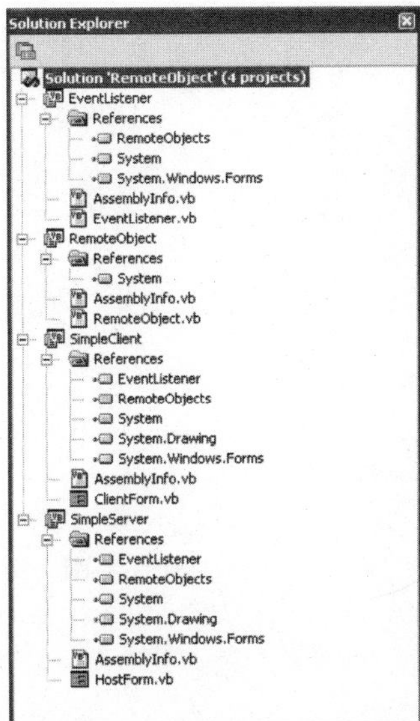

Figure 4-9 The remote event-handling solution

Next you need to add the method in the remote object that fires the event. The idea behind this event pattern is that the client submits a work request and returns to normal life while that work completes asynchronously. So far, we haven't looked at any threading concepts, so we'll implement this asynchronous processing by simply using a simple timer. The timer is enabled when the client calls *StartTask*. When the timer fires, it disables itself and calls back to the client, as shown in Listing 4-19.

```
Public Class RemoteObject
    Inherits MarshalByRefObject

    ' (Other class code omitted.)

    Private WithEvents tmrCallback As New System.Timers.Timer()

    ' Enable the timer.
    Public Sub StartTask()
        tmrCallback.Interval = 5000
        tmrCallback.Start()
    End Sub

    ' The timer fires. Disable the timer, and fire the event
    ' to the client.
```

Listing 4-19 Firing the remote event

```
    Private Sub tmrCallback_Elapsed(ByVal sender As System.Object, _
     ByVal e As System.Timers.ElapsedEventArgs) _
     Handles tmrCallback.Elapsed

        tmrCallback.Stop()

        ' For this simple test, we hardcode a result of 42.
        RaiseEvent TaskComplete(Me, New TaskCompleteEventArgs(42))

    End Sub

End Class
```

The client code is simple enough. It simply creates the *EventListener* object, hooks it up to the appropriate remote event, and calls the *StartTask* method. In our forms-based client, this happens in response to a button click, as shown in Listing 4-20.

```
Public Class ClientForm
    Inherits System.Windows.Forms.Form

    ' (Designer code omitted.)

    ' This is the class that will receive the event.
    ' The ClientForm can't handle the event directly, because it isn't
    ' a MarshalByRefObject.
    Private Listener As New EventListener.EventListener()

    Private Sub cmdSubmitRequest_Click(ByVal sender As System.Object, _
     ByVal e As System.EventArgs) Handles Button1.Click

        ' Hook up the event handler so it triggers the
        ' Listener.TaskCompleted() method.
        AddHandler RemoteObj.TaskComplete, _
                   AddressOf Listener.TaskCompleted

        ' Start the remote task.
        RemoteObj.StartTask()

    End Sub

End Class
```

Listing 4-20 Receiving the remote event

After a short delay, the callback fires and the client displays a message indicating that it received the result, as shown in Figure 4-10.

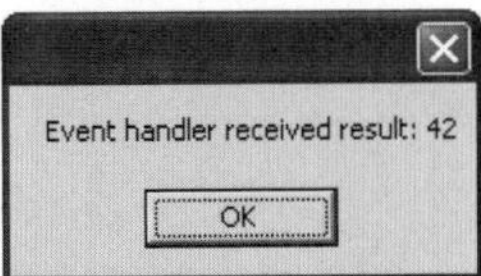

Figure 4-10 Handling an event from a remote component

Using Delegates

The event-based approach is a particularly good choice if you're using a singleton object that has several clients because they can all receive the same event. Alternatively, you can register a callback by passing a delegate to the remote object. The remote object can then call the delegate, in much the same way that it fired the event in the preceding example.

To understand delegates, you need to realize that the underlying *System.Delegate* class is serializable, so it can be copied across application boundaries. However, the delegate contains a *MarshalByRefObject* reference that points to a remote object using a proxy. Therefore, you can send a copy of a delegate to other components to tell them how to locate a given remote component.

To modify the preceding example for delegate-based event handling, you need to first define a delegate with a suitable signature in the remote class:

```
Public Delegate Sub TaskFinishedDelegate(result As Decimal)
```

You can use the same event listener class, but you need to modify it to accommodate the new signature, as shown in Listing 4-21.

```
Public Class EventListener
    Inherits MarshalByRefObject

    ' Handles the event.
    Public Sub TaskCompleted(result As Decimal)

        System.Windows.Forms.MessageBox.Show( _
         "Callback received result: " & result.ToString())

    End Sub

    ' Ensures that this object will not be prematurely released.
    Public Overrides Function InitializeLifetimeService() As Object
        Return Nothing
    End Function

End Class
```

Listing 4-21 A listener class for a remote callback

The remote object also needs only minor tweaking so that it accepts the delegate and stores it in a suitable member variable, as shown in Listing 4-22.

```
Public Class RemoteObject
    Inherits MarshalByRefObject

    ' (Other class code omitted.)

    Private WithEvents tmrCallback As New System.Timers.Timer()
    Private Callback As TaskCompletedDelegate

    Public Sub StartTask(callback as TaskCompletedDelegate)

        Me.Callback = callback
        tmrCallback.Interval = 5000
        tmrCallback.Start()

    End Sub

    Private Sub tmrCallback_Elapsed(ByVal sender As System.Object, _
     ByVal e As System.Timers.ElapsedEventArgs) _
     Handles tmrCallback.Elapsed

        tmrCallback.Stop()

        ' For this simple test, we hardcode a result of 42.
        Callback.Invoke(42)

    End Sub

End Class
```

Listing 4-22 Calling a client method remotely through a delegate

Finally, the client code calls the method and submits a delegate with a reference to the appropriate method, as shown in Listing 4-23.

```
Public Class ClientForm
    Inherits System.Windows.Forms.Form

    ' (Designer code omitted.)

    Private Listener As New EventListener.EventListener()

    Private Sub cmdSubmitRequest_Click(ByVal sender As System.Object, _
     ByVal e As System.EventArgs) Handles Button1.Click

        RemoteObj.StartTask( _
         New TaskCompleteDelegate(AddressOf Listener.TaskCompleted)

    End Sub

End Class
```

Listing 4-23 Receiving a remote call through a delegate

Configuring Object Lifetime

In the example used so far, no special code is used to configure the lifetime of the remote object. For a *SingleCall* object, no such code is required because the object is automatically destroyed at the end of each method call. For client-activated or singleton objects, however, the remote object is automatically destroyed if it is inactive for 2 minutes, provided it has been in existence for at least 5 minutes. These magic numbers are just the default properties of the lifetime lease automatically assigned to every remote object. They are encapsulated by the *ILease* interface in the *System.Runtime.Remoting.Lifetime* namespace. Table 4-2 lists the properties of the *ILease* interface.

Table 4-2 Lease Properties

Property	Description
CurrentLeaseTime	The amount of time remaining in the current lease, at the end of which the remote object is destroyed.
CurrentState	A value from the *LeaseState* enumeration. This can be *Active* (the lease hasn't yet expired), *Expired* (the lease has expired and can't be renewed), *Initial* (the lease has been created but isn't yet active), *Null* (the lease isn't initialized), or *Renewing* (the lease has expired and is seeking sponsorship).
InitialLeaseTime	The initial time that the object is kept in memory. This is the minimum amount of time that a remote object will live. The default is 5 minutes.
RenewOnCallTime	The minimum amount of time that the lease should be set to when the object is used. In other words, if *RenewOnCallTime* is 2 minutes (the default) and the *CurrentLeaseTime* is less than that, *RenewOnCallTime* is automatically increased 2 minutes every time the client invokes a remote method (or sets a remote property). This technique is known as *sliding expiration* and ensures that an object remains while it is being used.
SponsorshipTimeout	The amount of time that .NET waits for a lease sponsor to renew an expired lease. If no sponsor replies within this time (by default, 2 minutes), the object is destroyed.
LeaseManagerPollTime	This setting isn't provided through the *ILease* interface, but it is available as a configuration file setting. It determines the frequency with which the lease manager checks for expired leases. The default (10 seconds) means that the lease manager sleeps for 10 seconds after every check.

All remotable objects gain a special *MarshalByRefObject.GetLifeTimeService* method that returns the *ILease* instance currently assigned to the remote object. You can make use of this property to retrieve and examine the lease.

The next example modifies the Windows client to display information about the lease in a label control. (See Listing 4-24.) The client uses a timer and displays the current lease time in response to each timer tick. When you run the form, you'll see the lease time count down, as shown in Figure 4-11.

```
Imports System.Runtime.Remoting
Imports System.Runtime.Remoting.Lifetime

Public Class ClientForm
    Inherits System.Windows.Forms.Form

    ' (Designer code omitted.)

    Private RemoteObj As RemoteObjects.RemoteObject

    Private Sub ClientForm_Load(ByVal sender As System.Object, _
      ByVal e As System.EventArgs) Handles MyBase.Load

        ' Create the remote object.
        RemotingConfiguration.Configure("SimpleClient.exe.config")
        RemoteObj = New RemoteObjects.RemoteObject()

        ' Start the timer.
        tmrCheckLease.Interval = 1000
        tmrCheckLease.Start()

    End Sub

    ' When the timer fires, retrieve all the lease information and
    ' update the display.
    Private Sub tmrCheckLease_Tick(ByVal sender As System.Object, _
      ByVal e As System.EventArgs) Handles tmrCheckLease.Tick

        Try
            Dim Lease As ILease = RemoteObj.GetLifetimeService()
            If Not (Lease Is Nothing) Then

                ' Display current lease information.
                lblLease.Text = "Current State: "
                lblLease.Text &= Lease.CurrentState.ToString()
                lblLease.Text &= Environment.NewLine
                lblLease.Text &= "Initial Time Allocation: "
```

Listing 4-24 Tracking a lease

```
                lblLease.Text &= Lease.InitialLeaseTime.ToString()
                lblLease.Text &= Environment.NewLine
                lblLease.Text &= "Time Remaining: "
                lblLease.Text &= Lease.CurrentLeaseTime.ToString()

            End If

        Catch err As RemotingException
            lblLease.Text = err.ToString()
            tmrCheckLease.Stop()
        End Try

    End Sub

End Class
```

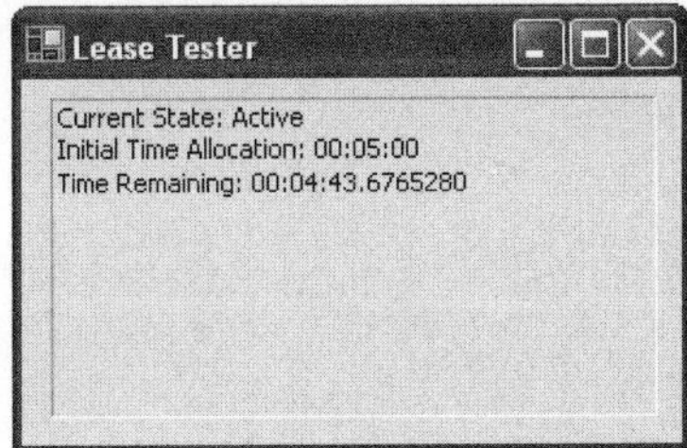

Figure 4-11 Tracking a remote object lease

When the lease dips below 2 minutes, something interesting happens. Because just retrieving the lease counts as interaction with the remote object, it automatically renews the lease lifetime to 2 minutes (according to the default *RenewOnCallTime*). This process happens perpetually, ensuring that the object is never destroyed. You can circumvent this behavior by retrieving and storing a reference to the *ILease* object when your program starts. First, create the *ILease* reference as a form-level variable:

```
Private Lease As ILease
```

Then retrieve the lease in the *Form.Load* event:

```
Private Sub ClientForm_Load(ByVal sender As System.Object, _
  ByVal e As System.EventArgs) Handles MyBase.Load

    ' (Other initialization code omitted.)
    Lease = RemoteObj.GetLifetimeService()

End Sub
```

Now, even though the lease is retrieved from the remote application domain, by using a direct reference you bypass the remote object to which it applies. When you run the program, you will see the lease count down until it reaches zero, the object is deallocated, and a *RemotingException* is thrown.

Modifying Lifetime

You can modify an object's lifetime in several ways. From the client's point of view, you can just call a method or set a property on the remote object, which automatically returns the lifetime to the *RenewOnCallTime* if it has dipped below this number. However, the client can't directly modify any of the *ILease* properties because they are all read-only. Instead, you can use the *ILease.Renew* method, which accepts a *TimeSpan* object and updates the *CurrentLeaseTime* accordingly.

To test the renewal method, you can add a *Renew* method to the lease test client, with the event handler shown in Listing 4-25.

```
Private Sub cmdRenew_Click(ByVal sender As System.Object, _
  ByVal e As System.EventArgs) Handles cmdRenew.Click

    ' Use the TimeSpan constructor for (Hours, Minutes, Seconds).
    Lease.Renew(New TimeSpan(0, 1, 0))

End Sub
```

Listing 4-25 Renewing a lease

If you click this button while the current lease time is greater than 1 minute, nothing happens. If you click this button after the lease time has dipped below 1 minute, it automatically resets the current lease time to 1 minute.

The component host can also play a hand in controlling the lifetime of the remote object. Generally, this is accomplished by setting lease defaults in the server configuration file, as shown in Listing 4-26. (These settings are case-sensitive and mirror the *ILease* properties, but with an initial lowercase letter.)

```
<configuration>
   <system.runtime.remoting>
      <application name="SimpleServer">
         <service>
            <activated
             type="RemoteObjects.RemoteObject, RemoteObjects"/>
```

Listing 4-26 Configuring lifetime in the host configuration file

```
        </service>
        <channels>
           <channel ref="tcp server" port="8080" />
        </channels>
        <lifetime leaseTime = "10M"
                  renewOnCallTime = "1M"
                  sponsorshipTimeout = "0"
                  leaseManagerPollTime = "30S" />
      </application>
   </system.runtime.remoting>
</configuration>
```

The lease settings apply to all the remote objects created by this component host in this application domain. Use a trailing *M* for minutes or an *S* to indicate seconds. In the preceding example, a remote object starts with an initial lifetime of 10 minutes and is renewed to 1 minute as required when the client interacts with it. By setting *sponsorshipTimeOut* to 0, we specify that the lease won't use any sponsors.

You can test these settings by running the lease client test. You also can try setting the *leaseTime* attribute to 0 minutes, which configures the remote object to have an infinite lifetime. In this case, the *GetLifetimeService* method returns a null reference (*Nothing*).

Alternatively, the remotable object can override the *InitializeLiftetimeService* method and take control of its own destiny. In this method, the remote object can modify the *ILease* properties, provided the lease hasn't yet been initialized. (See Listing 4-27.)

```
Public Overrides Function InitializeLifetimeService() As Object
    Dim Lease As ILease = MyBase.InitializeLifetimeService()

    ' Lease can only be configured if it is in an initial state.
    If Lease.CurrentState = LeaseState.Initial Then
        Lease.InitialLeaseTime = TimeSpan.FromMinutes(10)
        Lease.RenewOnCallTime = TimeSpan.FromMinutes(1)
    End If

    Return Lease

End Function
```

Listing 4-27. Overriding lease settings

If you want to set the object to have an infinite lifetime, you can bypass the leasing mechanism by returning a null reference, as shown in Listing 4-28.

```
Public Overrides Function InitializeLifetimeService() As Object
    Return Nothing
End Function
```

Listing 4-28 An object with an infinite lifetime

This is a common approach for a singleton object, which you often want to exist even when a client isn't using it.

Using a Leasing Sponsor

The last option is to use a leasing sponsor, which is a dedicated class that handles object renewal. When a lease manager discovers an expired lease, it first attempts to contact any registered sponsors. It then gives them the opportunity to renew the lease. This is generally better than manually renewing the lease in the client because you don't have to continuously check the current lease time. Instead, the sponsor is contacted only when necessary.

To create a sponsor, all you need is a class that implements *System.Runtime.Remoting.Lifetime.ISponsor* and derives from *MarshalByRefObject* (so that it can be called across a network). *ISponsor* defines a single method, called *Renewal*, which is called by the .NET runtime to extend the lifetime of registered objects. The class library also provides a *ClientSponsor* class that provides a default *ISponsor* implementation, complete with methods for registering and unregistering the sponsor and a *RenewalTime* property that sets the lease time that will be given to the remote object on renewal.

Listing 4-29 shows an example in which the lease sponsor is created in the same domain as the client application, ensuring that if the client is disconnected, the sponsor will also be unreachable (and the remote object will be destroyed). Figure 4-12 shows the arrangement.

```
Private Sponsor As New ClientSponsor()

Private Sub HostForm_Load(ByVal sender As System.Object, _
  ByVal e As System.EventArgs) Handles MyBase.Load

    ' Create the remote object.
    RemotingConfiguration.Configure("SimpleClient.exe.config")
    RemoteObj = New RemoteObjects.RemoteObject()
    ' Configure and register the sponsor.
    Sponsor.RenewalTime = TimeSpan.FromMinutes(5)
    Sponsor.Register(RemoteObj)
```

Listing 4-29 A custom lease sponsor

```
    ' Start the timer.
    tmrCheckLease.Interval = 1000
    tmrCheckLease.Start()

End Sub
```

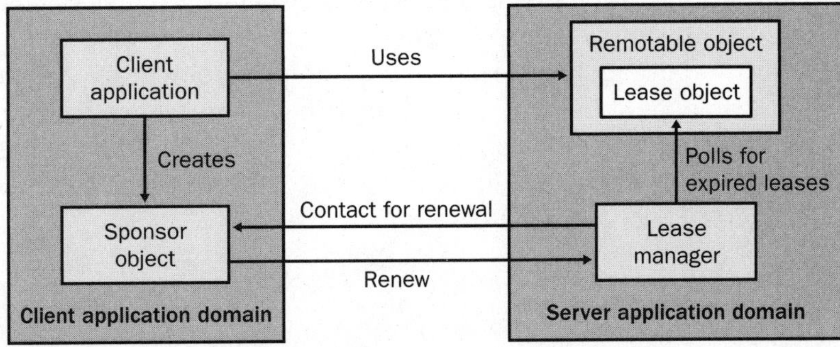

Figure 4-12 Using a lease sponsor

Figure 4-12 illuminates one other detail: The lease manager needs to contact the sponsor in the client's application domain. In other words, the lease manager will act like a client, and the sponsor will act like a server. For this reason, you need to modify the configuration file to use bidirectional channels:

```
<channel ref="tcp" port="0" />
```

When running the application, notice that the lease time actually dips below 0, into negative numbers. This is because the lease has expired but the lease sponsor hasn't yet been contacted. After the lease sponsor has been contacted, it responds with a renewal request and the time is reset to 5 minutes.

If necessary, the client can also retain a reference to the sponsor, which allows it to tweak the *RenewalTime* (for example, making it longer if the remote object is holding onto expensive server resources that could be time consuming to re-create). To switch off the sponsor, just unregister it:

```
Sponsor.Unregister(RemoteObj)
```

In version 1.1 of the .NET Framework, you need to explicitly allow full serialization in order to use a leasing sponsor. To do so, modify the channel portion of the client and server configuration file as shown here:

```
<channels>
  <channel ref="tcp" port="8080" >
  <serverProviders>
    <formatter ref="binary" typeFilterLevel="Full" />
  </serverProviders>
</channel>
```

> **Note** Leases are efficient because they require very little network traffic. Objects that are relatively lightweight can have long lease times for convenience. Objects that require resources that are expensive to re-create might also use a longer lease time or make use of a larger *RenewOnCallTime* to ensure that they are always retained if they are in use. (This provides a primitive type of caching.) On the other hand, objects that encapsulate important server resources or consume a large amount of memory will generally have short lease times, ensuring that they can be released as soon as the client has finished with them. In this case, you trade increased network traffic for more efficient use of server resources.

Common Remoting Exceptions

The .NET Remoting framework is quite friendly. If you make a mistake, you'll end up with a perplexing exception rather than a system problem or application crash. The .NET Remoting framework *is* complicated, however, and you're likely to encounter many trivial but frustrating problems when you're starting out with it. Most exceptions come in the form of the generic *System.Runtime.Remoting.RemotingException* class, with a description that provides a little more insight into the possible cause. Table 4-3 lists some common exceptions and messages and the problems that cause them.

Table 4-3 Common Remoting Exceptions

Exception	Message	Possible Cause
SocketException	No connection could be made because the target machine actively refused it.	You haven't started the component host, or the component host is listening on the wrong channel.
SocketException	No such host is known.	The host (machine) name can't be located on the network or over the Internet.
WebException	The underlying connection was closed: An unexpected error occurred on a receive.	You tried to connect to a TCP/IP server channel with an HTTP client channel.

Table 4-3 Common Remoting Exceptions *(continued)*

Exception	Message	Possible Cause
RemotingException	TCP channel protocol violation: expecting preamble.	You tried to connect to an HTTP server channel with a TCP/IP client channel.
RemotingException	Can't load type [type name].	The component host could not find the assembly required for the remote object.
SerializationException	The type [type name] isn't marked as serializable.	You can't return an object unless it is remotable (derives from *MarshalByRef_Object*) or serializable (marked with the <*Serializable*> attribute).
RemotingException	Object [URI] has been disconnected or doesn't exist at the server	The remote object might have been destroyed because its lease time expired.
RemotingException	The channel [channel name] is already registered.	You tried to define the same channel twice on the same machine. This could be caused by separate programs that are attempting to use the same channel (which isn't allowed), use of the wrong channel type (for example, using TCP when you really want to use TCP server and TCP client), or an attempt to use bidirectional communication over the same channel on the same machine.
RemotingException (root cause *ApplicationException*)	CONFIG file [filename] can't be read successfully: Invalid XML in file [filename].	You have mistyped an element in the .config file. (For example, you might have forgotten a required character or inserted an extra character.)

Summary

This chapter delved deep into one of the most flexible and sophisticated parts of distributed application development: .NET Remoting. .NET Remoting is a core part of .NET and an extremely flexible technology. Throughout the rest of this book, you'll encounter examples that employ .NET Remoting. Chapter 11 considers some advanced .NET Remoting techniques, such as dynamic registration and interface-based programming.

Remember that just because you *can* do something doesn't mean you *should*. Noted Microsoft architects have recently remarked that they've seen .NET Remoting being used in all the wrong places. If components are going to run on the same computer, for example, there's usually no reason to use .NET Remoting to communicate between them because it adds unnecessary overhead. Similarly, scattering components to different computers can help if you need sheer processing power; but if your needs are modest, the additional overhead required for network communication can contribute to an overall slowdown. The best advice is to design in several tiers and then look at the possibility of locating objects on other computers, where it makes practical sense.

We aren't quite ready to shift the discussion to architecture, however. First we need to fit a few more .NET technologies into the picture—starting with the next chapter, which discusses the revolution of XML Web services.

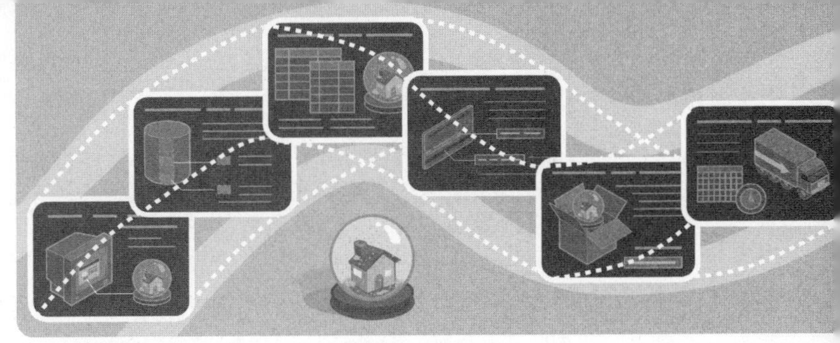

5

XML Web Services (RPC the Easy Way)

XML Web services are, depending on your point of view, a breath of fresh air after the complexities of Microsoft .NET Remoting or a simplified approach to distributed code execution that lacks a few key features. Both arguments contain at least a grain of truth. More accurately, XML Web services represent a new approach to distributed architecture, one that favors simplicity, best design practices, and cross-platform use over raw communication speed. XML Web services provide a simple, robust, and flexible way to make a remote procedure call (RPC).

Most introductory .NET books provide a brief introduction to XML Web services and describe some of the underlying standards such as WSDL and SOAP. This chapter takes a more practical approach. We start with a quick introduction to XML Web services, examine how the technology differs from .NET Remoting, and consider where XML Web services fit into the design of an enterprise application. We also examine how you can make use of ASP.NET platform services in an XML Web service, publish the availability of an XML Web service, and consume XML Web services from other platforms.

The Role of XML Web Services in a Distributed System

XML Web services play much the same role in an application as a component exposed through .NET Remoting. If you're new to XML Web services, you might first think of something like a Web site that enables you to look up the shipping date for a package or an investment site that enables you to get real-time price quotes. However, both of these examples are really entire Web applications. They might rely on a back-end XML Web service to actually retrieve the information, but they also include a user interface in the form of a Web page.

XML Web services, like any other type of middle-tier component, do not provide any type of user interface. They are used exclusively by other applications and are never invoked directly by end users. For example, you might create a package or a stock quote lookup XML Web service and then call this XML Web service from an ASP.NET Web application or a desktop Windows client.

.NET XML Web services are often identified as ASP.NET Web services because they represent an extension of the ASP.NET platform. In ASP.NET, every Web page acts like an individual application that runs briefly on the Web server when requested and returns an XML result over HTTP. ASP.NET is optimized for this task and uses multiple worker threads, automatic process recycling, output caching, and other enterprise-level features to ensure it can handle a large volume of clients. XML Web services work in much the same way as Web pages: They run briefly on the Web server and return a result in an XML markup (generally as a SOAP message). Much as ASP.NET Web pages create the illusion of a continuously running Web application, XML Web services can create the illusion of a stateful object. In reality, however, XML Web services are stateless components that are created and executed just-in-time when a client invokes an XML Web service method. This is one of the most dramatic departures from .NET Remoting, which provides the flexibility to allow singleton and client-activated objects that remain in memory under a set lease lifetime policy.

.NET Remoting vs. XML Web Services

XML Web services offer a simpler model for distributed applications than that provided by .NET Remoting. XML Web services are fine-tuned for Internet scenarios and cross-platform use. Although you can apply .NET Remoting in these scenarios, thanks to its SOAP formatter and HTTP channel, .NET Remoting is more suitable as a high-speed solution for binary communication between proprietary .NET components, usually over an internal network. And although XML Web services can't match the communication speed of .NET Remoting over a binary channel, they still lend themselves to high-performance designs thanks to their stateless nature and ASP.NET's multithreaded hosting service.

Here's a quick overview of the major differences between the XML Web service and .NET Remoting technologies:

- XML Web services are more restricted than objects exposed over .NET Remoting. An XML Web service works in a similar way to a *SingleCall* .NET Remoting object. It isn't possible to create a singleton or a client-activated object.
- Because of the restricted nature of XML Web services, the design issues are simplified. XML Web services are generally easier to create than remotable components (and easier to design well).
- Communication with .NET Remoting can be faster than XML Web service communication if you use a binary formatter. XML Web services support only SOAP message formatting, which uses larger XML text messages.
- XML Web services support open standards that target cross-platform use. For example, each .NET XML Web service has an associated WSDL document that describes how a client can interact with the service. Therefore, any client that can parse an XML message and connect over an HTTP channel can use an XML Web service, even if the client is written in Java and hosted on a UNIX computer.
- XML Web services are designed for use between companies and organizations. They can use a dynamic discovery mechanism or a UDDI registry that "advertises" services to interested parties over the Internet.
- XML Web services don't require a dedicated hosting program because they are always hosted by ASP.NET. That also means that they gain access to some impressive platform services, including data caching, Web farm–ready session state management, authentication, and an application collection for global, shareable objects. These features, if required, can be extremely difficult to re-create by hand in a component exposed through .NET Remoting.
- Because XML Web services work through Microsoft Internet Information Services (IIS) and ASP.NET, they can communicate with clients using the default HTTP channel (usually port 80). This means that consumers can use XML Web services just as easily as they can download HTML pages from the Internet. There's no need for an administrator to open additional ports on a firewall.

> **Note** The underlying technology that supports XML Web services overlaps with portions of the .NET Remoting framework. Part of the reason for this is that these technologies were developed simultaneously, before the .NET team realized the full potential of XML Web services. Chapter 11 examines the similarities a little more closely. For now, it helps to remember a broad distinction: If you are planning to provide functionality to clients over the Internet, XML Web services should be your first choice. If you need different capabilities or faster communication over a closed network, however, .NET Remoting is often a better option.
>
> According to Microsoft architects, .NET Remoting isn't designed to work in interop situations (for example, with Java clients) or when crossing trust boundaries (for example, exposing functionality to third-party clients or another business). These two basic rules of thumb can help you decide when to use .NET Remoting and when to use XML Web services. Incidentally, speculation abounds that XML Web services and .NET Remoting technology will be integrated in some future release of the .NET Framework, although this development isn't on the imminent horizon—and it won't help you plan today's generation of distributed applications.

XML Web Service Plumbing

XML Web services are based on a cluster of open standards. Table 5-1 lists the key players.

Table 5-1 XML Web Service Technologies

Standard	Description
WSDL (Web Services Description Language)	An XML-based format that describes everything a client needs to interact with an XML Web service. This includes the XML Web service's methods, the data types used for all parameters and return value, and the supported methods of communication.
HTTP (Hypertext Transfer Protocol)	The communication protocol used to send XML Web service requests and responses over the Internet.

Table 5-1 XML Web Service Technologies *(continued)*

Standard	Description
SOAP (Simple Object Access Protocol)	An XML-based format used to encode the information in XML Web service messages. SOAP includes a rich, cross-platform way of representing common data types (such as integers, strings, and arrays).
DISCO (Discovery)	DISCO is Microsoft's first crack at a lightweight way to create a simple list of XML Web service links. This can allow clients to discover the XML Web services offered by a particular organization. DISCO is slated for replacement by another similar standard called WS-Inspection, which was developed jointly with IBM.
UDDI (Universal Description, Discovery, and Integration)	The youngest and least evolved of the standards. UDDI is a business repository of XML Web service links designed to allow one business to find another based on the type of service, the business name, and so on. This specification is sure to go through many iterations before it becomes widely accepted.

So how do all these standards fit together? We'll begin with the process of creating the XML Web service, which can be summarized in three steps:

1. Create a dedicated virtual directory to host the XML Web service on your Web server, using IIS.
2. Code the custom XML Web service class, using the <*WebMethod*> attribute to mark each method that should be remotely callable. At its simplest, the XML Web service class is a collection of stateless methods. .NET takes care of the communication infrastructure that allows the client to discover and call these methods.
3. Deploy the XML Web service files to the virtual directory.

The second step is for the client to find and use your XML Web service:

1. The client finds the XML Web service, either through a predetermined URL or by using a discovery document or the UDDI registry.
2. The client requests the WSDL document that describes the XML Web service. .NET creates this document quickly and automatically by examining your XML Web service.

3. The client generates a proxy class based on the WSDL document. If the client is written using .NET, this step is performed automatically.

4. The client uses the proxy class much as it would use an XML Web service class if it were instantiated in the local process. Behind the scenes, the proxy sends a SOAP message to the XML Web service and receives a SOAP message result. The proxy class handles the Internet communication and SOAP formatting automatically (as shown in Figure 5-1).

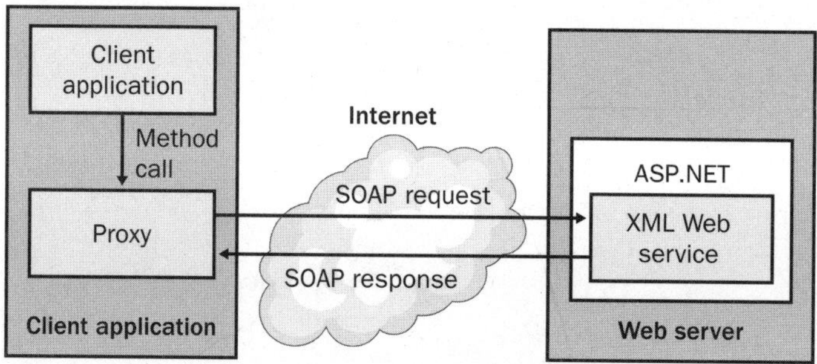

Figure 5-1 XML Web service interaction

This process is similar to .NET Remoting in several respects. First of all, the client communicates using a proxy class. The proxy class mimics the XML Web service and handles all the low-level details. Many programming platforms, including .NET, provide tools that create this proxy automatically.

The key difference is in how the proxy class is created. With .NET Remoting, the proxy object is generated dynamically. As soon as a .NET client instantiates a remote object, the runtime springs into action, creating the proxy based on the information in the assembly that describes the remote class. With XML Web services, the proxy class is created using the information found in the WSDL document. This is similar to the type of information contained in the assembly metadata, but it's stored in a cross-platform, human-readable XML format.

Another difference is the fact that the XML Web service proxy class is created during the development cycle. If the XML Web service changes, the proxy class must be manually regenerated. This process sidesteps the headaches required with .NET Remoting, where the client always needs a reference to the assembly that describes the remote component (or a supported interface). The WSDL document also contains enough information for non-.NET clients to communicate with the XML Web service on their own, without requiring a proprietary tool. We'll look at this issue at the end of the chapter.

The Role of IIS

With XML Web services, you don't worry about creating a server program that listens for requests and creates the required object. Instead, ASP.NET and IIS work together to perform this service for you.

IIS is the software that allows your computer to become a Web server and allows remote clients to download HTML pages (or run ASP.NET pages). IIS is included with Microsoft Windows 2000, Windows XP, and Windows .NET Server, but it isn't necessarily installed by default. To ensure that your computer has IIS installed, try typing the following into your Web browser: *http://localhost/localstart.asp*.

Here, *localhost* is the special "loopback" alias that always refers to the current computer. (Alternatively, you can use the specific server name or IP address.) *localstart.asp* is a traditional ASP file that is stored in the root directory of your computer's Web site home directory. If you receive an error when you attempt this request, you should check to make sure you have IIS installed.

To install IIS, follow these steps:

1. From the Start menu, choose Settings, Control Panel.
2. Select Add Or Remove Programs, and then click Add/Remove Windows Components.
3. Select Internet Information Services in the list, and click Next to install the appropriate files.

You must install IIS on your development computer even if the XML Web service will ultimately be hosted on a different Web server.

For those who aren't familiar with IIS, here are the key fundamentals you need to understand before you can create XML Web services:

- **IIS provides access to the Web server through virtual directories.** If you want to provide access to the C:\MyWeb directory, for example, you might create a virtual directory *http://[ComputerName]/MyWeb*. In this example, the virtual directory name (MyWeb) is the same as the physical directory name, but this isn't required. If your computer is accessible over the Internet (or an intranet), clients can browse to a Web page in the virtual directory. For example, you can view the HTML page C:\MyWeb\index.html by requesting *http://[ComputerName]/MyWeb/index.html*.
- **Virtual directories don't have the same permissions as normal directories.** By default, remote clients aren't allowed to browse the virtual directory, run executables, create files, or download

restricted file types (such as Microsoft Visual Basic source code files). You can configure some of these settings using IIS Manager and add further restrictions such as authentication requirements.

- **IIS handles your computer's Internet exposure.** However, it doesn't run ASP or ASP.NET pages or XML Web services. Instead, IIS maintains a list of registered file extensions. For example, ASP.NET pages (ASPX files) and XML Web services (.asmx files) are registered to the ASP.NET worker process. If IIS receives a request for one of these file types, it hands the work off to the ASP.NET worker process, which handles the rest of the work.

Creating a Virtual Directory

Before you create an XML Web service project in Visual Studio .NET, you should create a dedicated virtual directory. Otherwise, all your code files will be automatically located in a subdirectory of C:\Inetpub\wwwroot, which is the default home directory for IIS. This can cause a great deal of confusion, particularly when it comes time to move your XML Web service project to another computer.

Luckily, creating your own virtual directory is easy. Follow these steps:

1. Create the physical directory on your hard drive.
2. Start IIS Manager by choosing Settings, Control Panel, Administrative Tools, Internet Services Manager from the taskbar.
3. Start the Virtual Directory Wizard in IIS Manager by right-clicking on the Default Web Site item (under your computer in the tree) and choosing New, Virtual Directory from the shortcut menu.
4. Click Next to get started. Specify the alias, which is the name that your virtual directory will have for Web requests. Click Next to continue.
5. Specify the physical directory that will be exposed as the virtual directory. Click Next to continue.
6. The final wizard window gives you the chance to adjust the virtual directory permissions. The default settings allow clients to run ASP.NET pages and XML Web services but not make any modifications or upload files. This is the recommended configuration.
7. Click Next, and then click Finish to end the wizard. You will see the virtual directory in the IIS Manager tree display (as shown in Figure 5-2). After you have created a virtual directory, you can create a Web project in it using Visual Studio .NET.

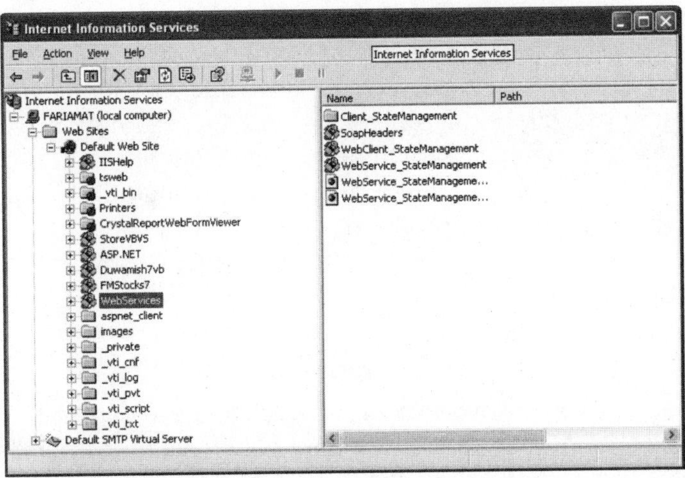

Figure 5-2 IIS Manager

The XML Web Service File Format

As mentioned earlier, XML Web services are special files with the extension .asmx. The ASP.NET worker process is registered to handle Web requests for this type of file. When it receives a request, it loads the .asmx file, compiles the appropriate class, executes the relevant Web method, and returns the result. This process is similar to the process used for ASP.NET pages (.aspx files). However, .aspx files contain significant information about the controls used on a Web page. The .asmx file is really just a text document that tells ASP.NET where it can find the relevant XML Web service class. Technically, you can create an .asmx file that contains the code itself, but it's almost always easier (and better in terms of organization) to place the XML Web service class in a separate file or dedicated assembly. This is also the model that Visual Studio .NET enforces.

The following sample .asmx file indicates that the XML Web service class called *MyWebService* can be found in a separate MyWebService.vb code file. ASP.NET is gracious enough to compile this file automatically when needed (a service that ordinary .NET components don't provide).

```
<%@ WebService Language="VB" Codebehind="MyWebService.vb"
    Class="MyWebService" %>
```

And here's a more typical example that indicates that the XML Web service class is named *MyWebService* and is already compiled into a DLL assembly called *MyAssembly*:

```
<%@ WebService Language="VB" Class="MyWebService,MyAssembly" %>
```

Most developers will program XML Web services with Visual Studio .NET. In this case, the .asmx file is created automatically. (In fact, Visual Studio .NET doesn't even display the contents of .asmx files in the integrated development environment [IDE], but if you use Notepad to examine these files, you'll see content similar to what's shown here.) Visual Studio .NET also compiles all the XML Web service classes in the project into a single DLL assembly. Therefore, when it comes time to deploy the completed project to a production Web server, all you need to do is copy the individual .asmx files and a single DLL assembly. You can safely leave the Visual Basic source code files behind.

> **Note** Every .asmx file contains a reference to one XML Web service. However, a given virtual directory can contain any number of .asmx files, and a Web server can contain any number of virtual directories. The important fact to remember is that each virtual directory acts like a separate ASP.NET application that runs in a dedicated process space and does not share any memory. This becomes important if you use the ASP.NET platform services. XML Web services in the same virtual directory use a common data cache and state collection, which XML Web services in different directories can't access.

Creating an XML Web Service

Actually creating an XML Web service class is easy, which is one of the reasons XML Web services have gained far more exposure than .NET Remoting. All you need to do is import the *System.Web.Services* namespace and add a <*WebMethod*> attribute to each method that you want to expose in the XML Web service.

```
<WebMethod()> _
Public Sub AddCustomer(ByVal customer As CustomerDetails)
    ' (Code omitted.)
End Sub
```

Optionally, you can set additional <*WebMethod*> properties to configure a text description for each Web method, which can help the client understand how your service works. You can also add a <*WebService*> attribute to your class declaration (although this isn't strictly required) to set a description for the entire service and associate an XML namespace with your service.

> **Note** XML Web service methods can't be overloaded. That means you can't create two versions of a single method that accept different parameters. Instead, you need to use distinct names (such as *GetCustomerByID* and *GetCustomerByName*). This is just one of the ways that XML Web service methods are not as fully featured as a local .NET class.

Listing 5-1 shows an example of the *CustomerDB* service provider component redesigned as an XML Web service. The differences are highlighted.

```
Imports System.Web.Services
Imports System.Data.SqlClient
Imports System.Data

' The XML namespace is not related to a .NET namespace.
' It simply associates a unique identifier that can be used
' to describe your service in the WSDL document.
' Typically, you will use a URL that you control.
<WebService(Namespace:="http://www.prosetech.com/", _
 Description:="Methods to interact with the Customers table.")> _
Public Class CustomerDB

    Private ConnectionString As String = _
     "Data Source=localhost;Initial Catalog=Store;" & _
     "Integrated Security=SSPI"

    <WebMethod(Description:="Add a new customer record.")> _
    Public Sub AddCustomer(ByVal customer As CustomerDetails)

        Dim Sql As String = "INSERT INTO Customers "
        Sql &= "(FullName, EmailAddress, Password) VALUES ('"
        Sql &= customer.Name & "', '"
        Sql &= customer.Email & "', '"
        Sql &= customer.Password & "')"
        ExecuteNonQuery(Sql)

    End Sub

    <WebMethod(Description:="Modify an existing customer record.")> _
    Public Sub UpdateCustomer(ByVal customer As CustomerDetails)
```

Listing 5-1 The *CustomerDB* service provider as an XML Web service

```
        Dim Sql As String = "INSERT INTO Customers "
        Sql &= "(FullName, EmailAddress, Password) VALUES ('"
        Sql &= customer.Name & "', '"
        Sql &= customer.Email & "', '"
        Sql &= customer.Password & "')"
        ExecuteNonQuery(Sql)

    End Sub

    <WebMethod(Description:="Modify an existing customer record.")> _
    Public Sub UpdateCustomer(ByVal customer As CustomerDetails)

        Dim Sql As String = "UPDATE Customers SET "
        Sql &= "FullName='" & customer.Name
        Sql &= "', EmailAddress='" & customer.Email
        Sql &= "', Password='" & customer.Password
        Sql &= "' WHERE CustomerID=" & customer.ID.ToString()
        ExecuteNonQuery(Sql)

    End Sub

    <WebMethod(Description:="Delete an existing customer record.")> _
    Public Sub DeleteCustomer(ByVal customerID As Integer)

        Dim Sql As String = "DELETE FROM Customers WHERE CustomerID="
        Sql &= customerID.ToString()
        ExecuteNonQuery(Sql)

    End Sub

    ' This private method is not remotely callable.
    Private Sub ExecuteNonQuery(ByVal sql As String)

        Dim con As New SqlConnection(ConnectionString)
        Dim cmd As New SqlCommand(sql, con)

        Try
            con.Open()
            cmd.ExecuteNonQuery()
        Catch Err As Exception
            Throw New ApplicationException( _
             "Exception encountered when executing command.", Err)
        Finally
            con.Close()
        End Try
```

```
End Sub

<WebMethod(Description:="Retrieve a single customer record.")> _
Public Function GetCustomer(ByVal customerID As Integer) _
 As CustomerDetails

    Dim Sql As String = "SELECT * FROM Customers Where CustomerID="
    Sql &= customerID.ToString()

    Dim con As New SqlConnection(ConnectionString)
    Dim cmd As New SqlCommand(Sql, con)
    Dim reader As SqlDataReader
    Dim Customer As New CustomerDetails()

    Try
        con.Open()
        reader = cmd.ExecuteReader(CommandBehavior.SingleRow)
        reader.Read()
        Customer.ID = reader("CustomerID")
        Customer.Name = reader("FullName")
        Customer.Email = reader("EmailAddress")
        Customer.Password = reader("Password")
    Catch Err As Exception
        Throw New ApplicationException( _
         "Exception encountered when executing command.", Err)
    Finally
        con.Close()
    End Try

    Return Customer

End Function

<WebMethod(Description:="Retrieve all customers in an array.")> _
Public Function GetCustomers() As CustomerDetails()

    Dim Sql As String = "SELECT * FROM Customers"

    Dim con As New SqlConnection(ConnectionString)
    Dim cmd As New SqlCommand(Sql, con)
    Dim reader As SqlDataReader
    Dim Customers As New ArrayList()

    Try
        con.Open()
        reader = cmd.ExecuteReader()
```

```
            Do While reader.Read()
                Dim Customer As New CustomerDetails()
                Customer.ID = reader("CustomerID")
                Customer.Name = reader("FullName")
                Customer.Email = reader("EmailAddress")
                Customer.Password = reader("Password")
                Customers.Add(Customer)
            Loop
        Catch Err As Exception
            Throw New ApplicationException( _
             "Exception encountered when executing command.", Err)
        Finally
            con.Close()
        End Try

        ' Now we convert the ArrayList to a strongly-typed array,
        ' which is easier fo the client to deal with.
        ' The ArrayList makes this possible through a handy
        ' ToArray() method.
        Return CType(Customers.ToArray(GetType(CustomerDetails)), _
          CustomerDetails())

    End Function

    <WebMethod(Description:="Retrieve all customers in a DataSet.")> _
    Public Function GetCustomersDS() As DataSet

        Dim Sql As String = "SELECT * FROM Customers"

        Dim con As New SqlConnection(ConnectionString)
        Dim cmd As New SqlCommand(Sql, con)
        Dim Adapter As New SqlDataAdapter(cmd)
        Dim ds As New DataSet

        Try
            con.Open()
            Adapter.Fill(ds, "Customers")
        Catch Err As Exception
            ' Use caller inform pattern.
            Throw New ApplicationException( _
             "Exception encountered when executing command.", Err)
        Finally
            con.Close()
        End Try

        Return ds
```

```
    End Function

End Class


Public Class CustomerDetails

    Public ID As Integer
    Public Name As String
    Public Email As String
    Public Password As String

End Class
```

> **Note** Although the code in Listing 5-1 throws an *ApplicationException* if a problem occurs, the client will actually receive a *SoapException* object, which contains a text message that describes the original application class. This is an inherent limitation with how .NET handles SOAP, and it reduces the efficiency of a client to check for specific error conditions. One way around this problem is for the XML Web service to throw a *SoapException* directly and store extra XML information in the *SoapException.Detail* property.

Remember, if you aren't designing your class with Visual Studio .NET, you also need to create the .asmx file that "advertises" the XML Web service to ASP.NET and move both files to a virtual directory. Visual Studio .NET performs these minor steps automatically.

Data Serialization

One difference you might have noticed in the XML Web service example is the downgraded *CustomerDetails* class. In the .NET Remoting example, the *CustomerDetails* class included full property procedures, several constructors, and a *<Serializable>* attribute. In an XML Web service, none of these is necessary. In fact, you could create property procedures and constructors, but the client wouldn't be able to use them. Instead, the client would receive a stripped-down version of the class that only uses public member variables (like the version shown in the preceding example).

Why the discrepancy? Even though XML Web services and .NET Remoting components can both send SOAP messages, they use different formatters.

Components exposed through .NET Remoting or saved to disk require the <*Serializable*> attribute and use the *SoapFormatter* class from the *System.Runtime.Serialization.Formatters.Soap* namespace. Web services, on the other hand, make use of the *XmlSerializer* class in the *System.Xml.Serialization* namespace. Both of these classes transform .NET objects into XML messages. The difference is that the *SoapFormatter* can exactly reproduce any serializable .NET object, provided it has the assembly metadata for the class. This involves some proprietary logic. The *XmlSerializer*, in contrast, is designed to support third-party clients who might understand little about .NET classes and assemblies. It uses predetermined rules to convert common data types. These rules, which are based on XSD and the SOAP standard, allow for the encoding of common data types, arrays, and custom structures but don't provide any standard way to represent code (such as constructors and property procedures). Therefore, these details are ignored.

Table 5-2 lists the data types supported in XML Web services and the SOAP standard.

Table 5-2 Data Types Supported in XML Web Services

Data Type	Description
Basic data types	Standard types such as integers and floating-point numbers, Boolean variables, dates and times, and strings are fully supported.
Enumerations	Enumerations types (defined by using the *Enum* keyword) are also fully supported.
Custom objects	You can pass any object you create based on a custom class or structure. The only limitation is that only data members can be transmitted. If you use a class with defined methods, the copy of the object that is transmitted will have only its properties and variables.
DataSet objects	*DataSet* objects are natively supported. They are returned as simple structures, which .NET clients can automatically convert to full *DataSet* objects. *DataTable* objects and *DataRow* objects, however, are not supported.
XmlNode objects	Objects based on *System.Xml.XmlNode* are representations of a portion of an XML document. Under the hood, all Web service data is passed as XML. This class enables you to directly support a portion of XML information whose structure might change.
Arrays and collections	You can use arrays and simple collections of any supported type, including *DataSet* objects, *XmlNode* objects, and custom objects.

What Is SOAP?

So far, we've been using the terms SOAP and XML almost interchangeably. Technically, SOAP is a set of tags based on XML. (You can think of XML as supplying the grammar, or ground rules, whereas SOAP defines the allowed vocabulary.) SOAP is used with Web method calls because it defines a very flexible way to encode common data types. It's thanks to SOAP that you can create an XML Web service that returns a *DataSet* or a custom structure such as *CustomerDetails*. You could encode the same information in ordinary XML, but there are so many possible variations that a client would never know what to expect.

SOAP is a key XML Web service format, but it isn't required. In fact, if clients don't support SOAP messages over HTTP, you can communicate using simple name-value pairs with HTTP *GET* (which passes parameter information in the query string) or HTTP *POST* (which passes parameter information in the body of the message). However, SOAP toolkits exist for most programming languages, including Java and COM-based Microsoft programming languages such as Visual C++ and Visual Basic. You'll almost always use SOAP encoding with your XML Web services, for the following reasons:

- Only SOAP allows the client to pass objects as parameters. In other words, the current version of the *UpdateCustomers* method wouldn't work over HTTP *GET* or HTTP *POST* because it requires a *CustomerDetails* object as a parameter. SOAP also provides support for *ByRef* parameters.
- SOAP is more standardized. .NET defines its own rules for encoding information in an HTTP *GET* or HTTP *POST* message.
- SOAP provides better exception support with .NET clients. If a method called over HTTP *GET* or if HTTP *POST* fails, it just returns an unhelpful HTTP error.

In this book, we won't discuss the low-level details of SOAP formatting any more than we'll discuss binary encoding in .NET Remoting or discuss HTTP headers. Although it never hurts to have a solid understanding of the protocols that support a given technology, these topics are peripheral to some of the real issues of application design. In fact, SOAP messages have been available to programmers, one way or another, for quite

(continued)

a while. However, it's only with .NET that they've gained much popularity with Microsoft programmers because the .NET Framework provides a simple, extensible abstraction on top of the low-level tedium. Learning how to master that abstraction (in this case, the XML Web services model) is more important than learning how various data types are encoded unless you need to mount a major cross-platform project.

Testing the XML Web Service

ASP.NET provides a simple way to test an XML Web service after you have deployed it to a virtual directory. If you request the .asmx file in a Web browser, you'll see an automatically generated test page that lists the available methods and the text descriptions you've added (as shown in Figure 5-3).

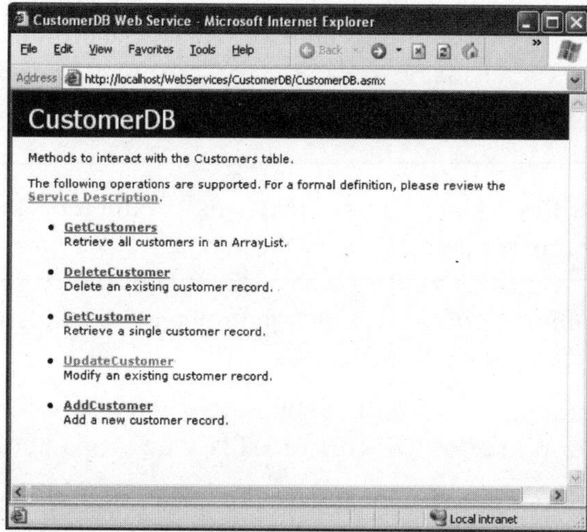

Figure 5-3 The *CustomerDB* test page

To test a Web method, you click one of the methods. A separate window will appear, with text boxes provided for parameters and with an Invoke button. When you click Invoke, the request message is sent, the XML Web service class is created, the Web method executes, the XML Web service class is destroyed, and the result is returned as an XML document that appears in the browser. Figure 5-4 shows the result of invoking the *GetCustomers* method from the test page. It returns an XML structure representing an array with five customers (two of which are collapsed in the screen shot).

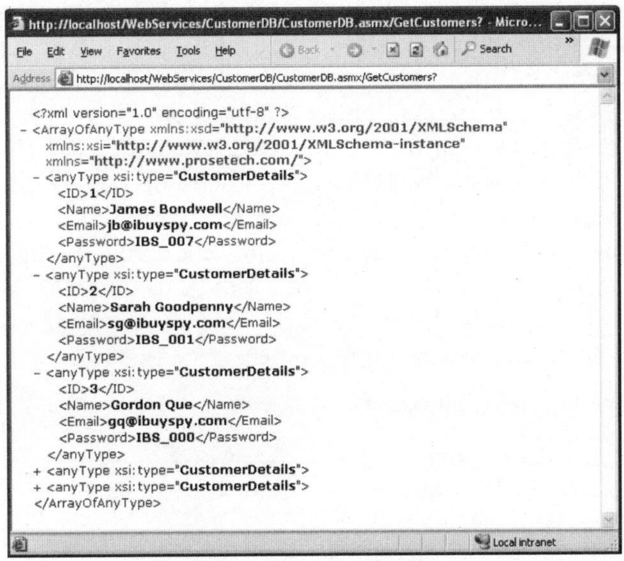

Figure 5-4 The result of invoking *GetCustomers*

It's important to understand that this technique does not require any special functionality from your Internet browser—it's simply a convenience provided by ASP.NET. If you were to type the exact same request string into a Netscape or Opera browser, you would receive the same test page and the same XML document. The request string is actually a request to the XML Web service using HTTP *GET*. It identifies the XML Web service, Web method, and any required parameters:

```
http://[Server]/[VirtualDirectory]/[AsmxFile]/[WebMethod]?[Arguments]
```

Here's the HTTP *GET* request required to get the list of all customers:

```
http://localhost/CustomerDB/CustomerDB.asmx/GetCustomers?
```

And here's another HTTP *GET* request string; this one retrieves information for the single customer record with the *CustomerID* of 1:

```
http://localhost/CustomerDB/CustomerDB.asmx/GetCustomer?customerID=1
```

Note that when you use the test page, the method of communication is HTTP *GET* (not SOAP). This means that you won't be able to test some methods in your browser, such as *UpdateCustomer*.

The WSDL Document

You also can request the WSDL document for your XML Web service by requesting the .asmx file with *?WSDL* appended to the end of the request string. (The test page links directly to this document; just click Service Description.) The WSDL document has the same role the IDL file does in COM programming, except it uses an XML-based syntax rather than a C-based syntax.

The WSDL document is far from compact. It's designed to be independent of communication protocols (like HTTP) and encoding methods (like SOAP), which gives it the ability to be used with future technologies. Unfortunately, this also means that the WSDL document requires a lengthy, multipart structure. If you browse through the WSDL document for the *CustomerDB* XML Web service, you'll find information about the supported methods and the custom-defined *CustomerDetails* class (excerpted here):

```
<s:complexType name="CustomerDetails">
  <s:sequence>
    <s:element minOccurs="1" maxOccurs="1" name="ID" type="s:int" />
    <s:element minOccurs="0" maxOccurs="1" name="Name"
               type="s:string" />
    <s:element minOccurs="0" maxOccurs="1" name="Email"
               type="s:string" />
    <s:element minOccurs="0" maxOccurs="1" name="Password"
               type="s:string" />
  </s:sequence>
</s:complexType>
```

Fortunately, there is little need to read the WSDL document directly. If you're creating a .NET client, you can create a proxy class based on the WSDL document automatically. The same feat is possible with many third-party tools in non-.NET languages.

Consuming the XML Web Service

.NET enables you to create an XML Web service proxy class in two ways. If you are using Visual Studio .NET, you can generate the proxy class using the Web reference feature (as shown in Figure 5-5). Just start a normal ASP.NET, Console, or Windows client project. Then right-click on the project in Solution Explorer and choose Add Web Reference. You can then enter the WSDL document location, or you can enter a Web URL that identifies a page or discovery document that links to the XML Web service and then browse to it using the appropriate link.

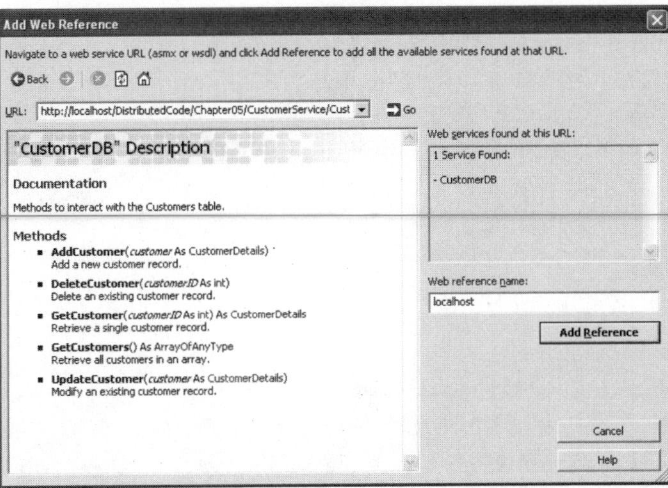

Figure 5-5 Adding a Visual Studio .NET Web reference

Figure 5-5 shows the version of the Add Web Reference dialog box that you'll see in Visual Studio .NET 2003. In earlier versions, the window is functionally equivalent but looks a little different. Visual Studio .NET 2003 also adds a few links that allow you to easily search for UDDI Web servers and browse the information they provide.

When you click Add Reference, the proxy class is generated in the language of the current project and is added to the project. By default, however, the proxy class is hidden because it shouldn't be modified directly. If you want to examine the proxy class, choose Project, Show All Files from the Visual Studio .NET menu. By default, the proxy class file has the name Reference.vb and is grouped under the server name in the Web References section of Solution Explorer (as shown in Figure 5-6).

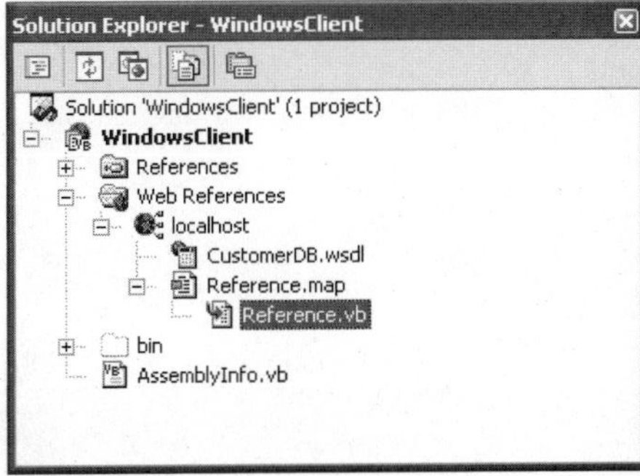

Figure 5-6 The Reference.vb proxy class file

Even if you aren't using Visual Studio .NET, you can still create the proxy class using the WSDL.exe command-line utility that is included with the .NET Framework. This utility is found in the .NET Framework directory, such as C:\Program Files\Microsoft.NET\FrameworkSDK\Bin.

The syntax for WSDL.exe is shown here. Table 5-3 describes each field.

```
wsdl /language:language  /protocol:protocol /namespace:myNameSpace
     /out:filename /username:username /password:password
     /domain:domain <url or path>
```

A typical WSDL.exe command looks something like this (split over two lines):

```
wsdl /language:VB /namespace:localhost
     http://localhost/CustomerDB/CustomerDB.asmx?WSDL
```

This creates a CustomerDB.vb proxy class file. You can then add this file to a client project or compile to a DLL using the vbc.exe command-line compiler, as shown here:

```
vbc /t:library CustomerDB.vb
```

Table 5-3 WSDL.exe Command-Line Parameters

Parameter	Description
Language	This is the language that the proxy class will use. The language really doesn't matter because you won't directly modify the proxy class code (because any changes are lost every time you regenerate it). The default is C#.
Protocol	Usually, you will omit this option and use the default (SOAP). However, you can also specify HTTP *GET* and HTTP *POST* for more limiting protocols.
Namespace	This is the .NET namespace that your proxy class will use. If you omit this parameter, no namespace is used and the classes in this file are available globally. For better organization, you should choose a logical namespace. Visual Studio .NET automatically uses the server name (for example, localhost).
Out	This enables you to specify the name for the generated file. By default, this is the name of the service followed by an extension indicating the language (for example, CustomerDB.vb).
Username, password, and domain	You should specify these values if the Web server requires authentication to access the virtual directory.
URL or path	This piece of information is always added at the end of the WSDL.exe command line. It specifies the location of the WSDL document for the Web service.

Examining the Proxy Class

It's not necessary to examine the proxy class, but doing so provides some interesting insights into how the .NET XML Web service framework works. Essentially, the proxy class mimics the XML Web service, reproducing every Web service method. The client then creates an instance of the proxy class and calls one of its methods. Behind the scenes, the proxy class packages the information into a SOAP request message, waits for the SOAP response message, and then converts the return value into a standard .NET data type, which it then passes back to the client.

Listing 5-2 shows a shortened version of the autogenerated *CustomerDB* proxy class. Notice that it includes a copy of the *CustomerDetails* class, which allows the client to use this type natively. The proxy class also includes specialized *Begin* and *End* versions of each Web method (as in *BeginGetCustomer* and *EndGetCustomer*), which allow the Web method to be called asynchronously. These methods, which aren't shown here, are examined in more detail in the next chapter.

```
Imports System.Web.Services
Imports System.Web.Services.Protocols
Imports System.Xml.Serialization

Namespace localhost

    <WebServiceBinding(Name:="CustomerDBSoap",
     [Namespace]:="http://www.prosetech.com/"), _
     XmlIncludeAttribute(GetType(System.Object()))> _
    Public Class CustomerDB
        Inherits SoapHttpClientProtocol

        Public Sub New()
            MyBase.New
            Me.Url = _

             "http://localhost/WebServices/CustomerDB/CustomerDB.asmx"
        End Sub

        <SoapDocumentMethod("AddCustomer"> _
        Public Sub AddCustomer(ByVal customer As CustomerDetails)
            Me.Invoke("AddCustomer", New Object() {customer})
        End Sub


        <SoapDocumentMethod("UpdateCustomer"> _
        Public Sub UpdateCustomer(ByVal customer As CustomerDetails)
```

Listing 5-2 The proxy class for the *CustomerDB* service

```
            Me.Invoke("UpdateCustomer", New Object() {customer})
        End Sub

        <SoapDocumentMethod("DeleteCustomer"> _
        Public Sub DeleteCustomer(ByVal customerID As Integer)
            Me.Invoke("DeleteCustomer", New Object() {customerID})
        End Sub

        <SoapDocumentMethod("GetCustomer"> _
        Public Function GetCustomer(ByVal customerID As Integer) _
         As CustomerDetails
            Dim results() As Object = Me.Invoke("GetCustomer", _
              New Object() {customerID})
            Return CType(results(0),CustomerDetails)
        End Function

        <SoapDocumentMethod("http://www.prosetech.com/GetCustomers"> _
        Public Function GetCustomers() As CustomerDetails()
            Dim results() As Object = Me.Invoke("GetCustomers", _
              New Object(-1) {})
            Return CType(results(0),CustomerDetails())
        End Function

        <SoapDocumentMethod("http://www.prosetech.com/GetCustomersDS"> _
        Public Function GetCustomersDS() As System.Data.DataSet
            Dim results() As Object = Me.Invoke("GetCustomersDS", _
              New Object(-1) {})
            Return CType(results(0),System.Data.DataSet)
        End Function

    End Class

    <System.Xml.Serialization.XmlTypeAttribute()>  _
    Public Class CustomerDetails
        Public ID As Integer
        Public Name As String
        Public Email As String
        Public Password As String
    End Class

End Namespace
```

The proxy class gains the ability to send SOAP messages over the Internet because it inherits from the *SoapHttpClientProtocol* class, which provides an *Invoke* method. Notice that each method receives a result as a generic object, which it then converts to the expected strongly typed class or structure.

By contrast, .NET Remoting uses its own dynamic proxy mechanism. .NET Remoting proxies are created at run time, whereas XML Web service proxies are created at design time. As a side effect, if the XML Web service changes, you must first recompile the XML Web service and then regenerate the proxy class. In Visual Studio .NET, you can accomplish this quickly by right-clicking on the Web reference in Solution Explorer and choosing Update Web Reference.

Using the Proxy Class

Using the proxy class is easy—in fact, it works just like any other object. Listing 5-3 and Figure 5-7 show a sample Windows client that gets the list of all customers and displays in a *DataGrid* control. This example is nearly identical to the local data component example in Chapter 3, even though the method call is invoked over the Internet. If you use Visual Studio .NET, you can even enter Break mode and single-step from the client code into the XML Web service code.

```
Public Class WindowsClient
    Inherits System.Windows.Forms.Form

    ' (Designer code omitted.)

    Private Sub WindowsClient_Load(ByVal sender As System.Object, _
      ByVal e As System.EventArgs) Handles MyBase.Load

        Dim DBProxy As New localhost.CustomerDB()
        DataGrid1.DataSource = DBProxy.GetCustomerDS().Tables(0)

    End Sub

End Class
```

Listing 5-3 A basic Windows client

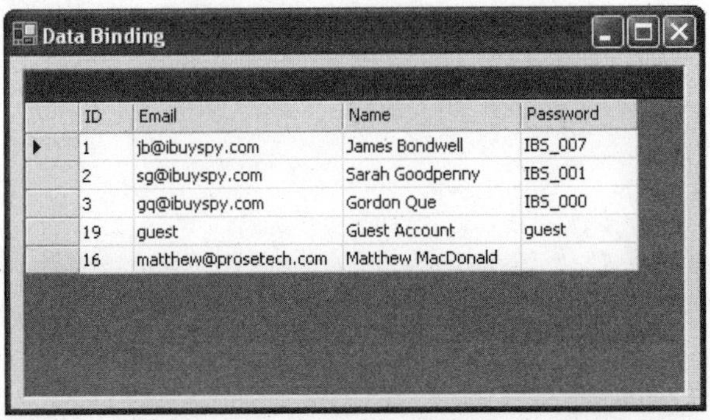

Data Binding

ID	Email	Name	Password
1	jb@ibuyspy.com	James Bondwell	IBS_007
2	sg@ibuyspy.com	Sarah Goodpenny	IBS_001
3	gq@ibuyspy.com	Gordon Que	IBS_000
19	guest	Guest Account	guest
16	matthew@prosetech.com	Matthew MacDonald	

Figure 5-7 Retrieving query results through an XML Web service

And here's an example that shows how you can interact with the *CustomerDetails* object defined by the XML Web service:

```
Public Class WindowsClient
    Inherits System.Windows.Forms.Form

    ' (Designer code omitted.)

    Private Sub WindowsClient_Load(ByVal sender As System.Object, _
      ByVal e As System.EventArgs) Handles MyBase.Load

        Dim DBProxy As New localhost.CustomerDB()
        Dim Customer As localhost.CustomerDetails
        Customer = DBProxy.GetCustomer(1)
        MessageBox.Show("CustomerID 1 is: " & Customer.Name)

    End Sub

End Class
```

Keep in mind that this is really just a remote procedure call. The XML Web service doesn't retain any state. Therefore, even though you retain a reference to the proxy class, the actual XML Web service instance is created at the beginning of every method invocation and is destroyed at the end. This means that you can't set instance variables or properties and expect the values to persist between method calls.

By default, the proxy sends its SOAP message over the default HTTP port used for Web traffic: 80. You can also tweak some proxy class settings to adjust this communication if needed. If you need to connect through a computer called MyProxyServer using port 80, for example, you can use the following code before you call any proxy methods:

```
Dim ConnectionProxy As New WebProxy("MyProxyServer", 80)
Dim DBProxy As New localhost.CustomerDB()
DBProxy.Proxy = WebProxy
```

Similarly, you can adjust the amount of time the proxy waits for a SOAP response before timing out and throwing an exception, as follows:

```
DBProxy.Timeout = 10000  ' 10000 milliseconds is 10 seconds.
```

Debugging Web Services

It's possible to debug an XML Web service in a separate instance of Visual Studio .NET or as part of a multiproject solution. However, you'll need to tweak the debugging settings so that your XML Web service code is compiled and loaded into the debugger. Otherwise, you won't be able to set breakpoints, use variable watches, or rely on any of the other indispensable Visual Studio .NET debugging features.

To enable XML Web service debugging, right-click on the project in Solution Explorer and choose properties. Then under the Configuration Properties | Debugging node, choose Wait For External Process To Connect, as shown in Figure 5-8. This instructs Visual Studio .NET to load the debugging symbols when you run the XML Web service, instead of simply showing the XML Web service test page.

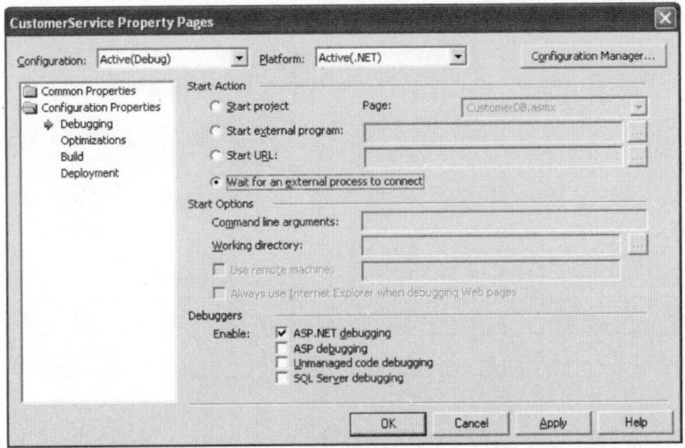

Figure 5-8 Configuring an XML Web service for debugging

If you're testing a compiled client or a client in another instance of Visual Studio .NET, just be sure to start the XML Web service project first in order to debug it. If you're creating a solution that includes both a client and an XML Web service, you can configure it to have multiple startup projects, exactly as you would with .NET Remoting. Simply right-click on the solution item in the Solution Explorer, and choose Properties. Figure 5-9 shows an example in which both an XML Web service and a client application are launched when the solution is started.

While testing an XML Web service, you might encounter the infamous "unable to start debugging on the server" error. This signals that Visual Studio .NET was able to compile the XML Web service but can't execute it in debug mode. Unfortunately, this problem can result because of countless different reasons. One common problem occurs if you install IIS after you install the .NET Framework. In this case, you can "repair" the .NET Framework using the original setup CD or DVD. Microsoft describes this process—and a number of other possible causes for this error—in a white paper at *http://msdn.microsoft.com/library/default.asp?url=/library/en-us/vsdebug/html/vxtbshttpservererrors.asp*. One common cause not mentioned is failing to create the virtual directory or trying to run a program after you've removed or modified the virtual directory. To correct these problems, modify the virtual directory settings in IIS Manager.

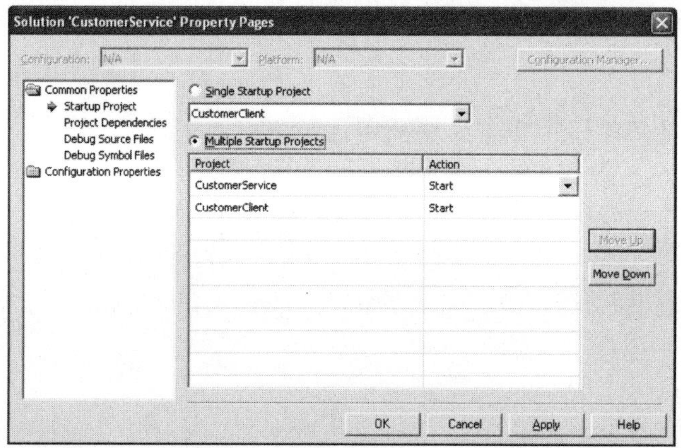

Figure 5-9 Starting an XML Web service and client

Another problem that can occur in Visual Studio .NET 2003 is a failure to authenticate. Visual Studio .NET 2003 attempts to access the local Web server using integrated Windows authentication, even if you have anonymous authentication enabled for the virtual directory. Thus, your virtual directory must allow both anonymous and Windows Integrated authentication. To allow for this, follow these steps:

1. Start IIS Manager.
2. Right-click the virtual directory for your application, and choose Properties. (Alternatively, you can configure authentication for all directories if you right-click the Web Sites folder and choose Properties.)
3. Select the Directory Security tab.
4. In the Anonymous access and authentication section, click the Edit button.
5. In the Authentication Methods dialog box, under Authenticated access, select Integrated Windows Authentication, as shown in Figure 5-10.

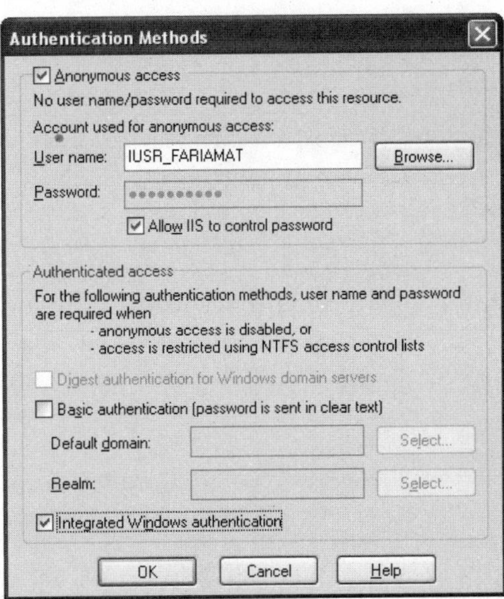

Figure 5-10 Enabling Windows authentication for debugging

6. Click OK to apply your changes.

ASP.NET Platform Services

The ASP.NET platform provides a rich set of services for all types of Web applications. You can harness many of these features in your XML Web services just by deriving your XML Web service class from *System.Web.Service.WebService*.

```
<WebService(Namespace:="http://www.prosetech.com/", _
 Description:="Methods to interact with the Customers table.")> _
Public Class CustomerDB
    Inherits WebService
```

By inheriting from *WebService*, your class gains four additional properties, as shown in Table 5-4. These features include a few heavyweights, such as authentication and caching, that we'll return to in later chapters. These prebuilt features are so useful that in many situations you'll find it easier to build a large-scale performance-optimal solution with XML Web services rather than .NET Remoting, even though .NET Remoting supports leaner binary communication.

Table 5-4 *WebService* Properties

Property	Description
Application	Provides a global collection where you can store any .NET object.
Context	Provides access to some ASP.NET intrinsic objects, such as *Request* and *Response*. Most of these aren't useful in XML Web services because you are interacting with a proxy class, not directly with the client. However, one object (*Cache*) is extremely useful for storing frequently used information. You'll learn how to master this object in Chapter 12.
Server	Provides server utility methods for tasks such as encoding HTML content and URL query strings. These features generally aren't useful in an XML Web service.
Session	Provides a collection where you can store information that's bound to the current request. However, this capability can easily waste server memory and is disabled by default.
User	Enables you to retrieve information about the client if it has logged on through the proxy class using some form of integrated IIS authentication. You'll learn about this option—and some more flexible alternatives—in Chapter 13.

You could also access these properties without deriving from *WebService*, by using the *System.Web.HttpContext* class.

SOAP Headers and SOAP Extensions

SOAP headers and extensions are great ways to extend the SOAP standard, and they add support for custom encryption, logging, compression, and authentication schemes. SOAP headers and extensions are also potential nightmares because they represent proprietary add-ons that you can apply to your XML Web services, potentially making them less generic and more difficult to support on other platforms. SOAP headers and extensions are also wedded to the SOAP standard, meaning you can't easily adapt a SOAP header authentication technique or SOAP extension logging approach to a .NET Remoting component that works over a TCP/IP channel with binary messages.

This chapter won't discuss SOAP headers and extensions. However, Chapter 13 and Chapter 18 show how you can use SOAP headers to implement security in conjunction with a custom ticket-based authentication system.

> **Note** Microsoft is also developing a number of XML Web service extensions based on emerging SOAP standards, particularly those related to security and authentication. These are known collectively as the Web Service Enhancements (WSE) and are available at *http://msdn.microsoft.com/webservices/building/wse*. As these standards continue to evolve, the WSE will likely change or be incorporated into a future release of the .NET platform.

Publishing an XML Web Service

Because XML Web services aim to share functionality between organizations, there needs to be some mechanism that enables an interested party to discover which XML Web services another entity offers. The most ambitious part of this strategy is the UDDI registry, which is still in its infancy. Essentially, UDDI is a specification that defines how an XML Web service registry should be organized and how XML Web services can be registered programmatically. There are currently several test UDDI implementations, including the Microsoft Registry at *http://uddi.microsoft.com/developer*. You can find general information about the UDDI standard at *http://www.uddi.org*. A link in a UDDI registry can point to a WSDL document or to a discovery document listing XML Web services. This book does not cover UDDI in any detail.

Microsoft also supports a simpler discovery standard. In the current version of Visual Studio .NET, this is DISCO (which is slated for replacement by a similar standard called WS-Inspection, as mentioned earlier). A DISCO document is essentially an XML file with a list of links to one or more WSDL documents. A client using Visual Studio .NET can enter the URL for a discovery document when adding a Web reference and can easily find the required XML Web service. Essentially, a discovery document offers a simple approach to sharing XML Web service URLs in a standardized format.

A typical discovery document has the extension .disco or .vsdisco and contains one or more *<contractRef>* elements, each of which points to a WSDL document. It can also contain *<discoveryRef>* links that point to other discovery files or *<schemaRef>* links that point to XSD documents. Here's an example that can allow a client to locate the *CustomerDB* XML Web service:

```
<?xml version="1.0" encoding="utf-8" ?>
<disco:discovery  xmlns:disco="http://schemas.xmlsoap.org/disco"
 xmlns:wsdl="http://schemas.xmlsoap.org/disco/wsdl">
```

```
  <wsdl:contractRef
   ref="http://MyServer/WebServices/CustomerDB.asmx?WSDL"/>
</disco:discovery>
```

Note that the example doesn't use the *localhost* reference because the client requires the real name of the server.

Microsoft also supports a dynamic discovery format. When a client requests this file, the Web server automatically creates a list of all the XML Web services in the given virtual directory and any subdirectories. You can specifically exclude search paths (typically to save time) by using the *<exclude>* attribute, although this doesn't stop the client from adding a reference to an XML Web service in one of these directories if it is not secured through IIS.

```
<?xml version="1.0" encoding="utf-8" ?>
<dynamicDiscovery
 xmlns="urn:schemas-dynamicdiscovery:disco.2000-03-17">
  <exclude path="_vti_cnf" />
  <exclude path="_vti_pvt" />
  <exclude path="_vti_log" />
  <exclude path="_vti_script" />
  <exclude path="_vti_txt" />
</dynamicDiscovery>
```

Cross-Platform XML Web Services

You've already seen how you can invoke an XML Web service in any browser using HTTP *GET* and the properly formatted query string. This gives you an idea of how easy it is for a non-.NET client to access an XML Web service. It just has to send the appropriate HTTP request and parse the retrieved XML document.

To test this technique, you can use the Microsoft XML COM library, which includes an *XMLHTTP* object that can send XML documents over the HTTP channel. This example (shown in Listing 5-4 and illustrated in Figure 5-11) uses Visual Basic 6 and Microsoft XML version 4 (msxml4.dll), but earlier versions will also work.

```
Private Sub Form_Load()

    Dim Transfer As XMLHTTP
    Set Transfer = New XMLHTTP

    ' Call the XML Web Service using HTTP GET.
    Transfer.open "GET", _
```

Listing 5-4 Consuming a .NET XML Web service in Visual Basic 6

```
     "http://localhost/WebServices/CustomerDB/CustomerDB.asmx/" & _
     GetCustomers", False
    Transfer.send

    ' Retrieve the XML response.
    Dim Doc As DOMDocument
    Set Doc = Transfer.responseXML

    ' Configure the MSFlexGrid control.
    MSFlexGrid1.TextMatrix(0, 0) = "ID"
    MSFlexGrid1.TextMatrix(0, 1) = "Name"
    MSFlexGrid1.TextMatrix(0, 2) = "Email"
    MSFlexGrid1.TextMatrix(0, 3) = "Password"

    ' Parse the response.
    Dim Child As MSXML2.IXMLDOMNode
    For Each Child In Doc.documentElement.childNodes

      ' The first node (offset 0) is the ID.
      ' The second node (offset 1) is the name.
      ' The third node (offset 2) is the email.
      ' The fourth node (offset 3) is the password.
      MSFlexGrid1.AddItem (Child.childNodes(0).Text & vbTab & _
       Child.childNodes(1).Text & vbTab & Child.childNodes(2).Text & _
       vbTab & Child.childNodes(3).Text)

    Next

End Sub
```

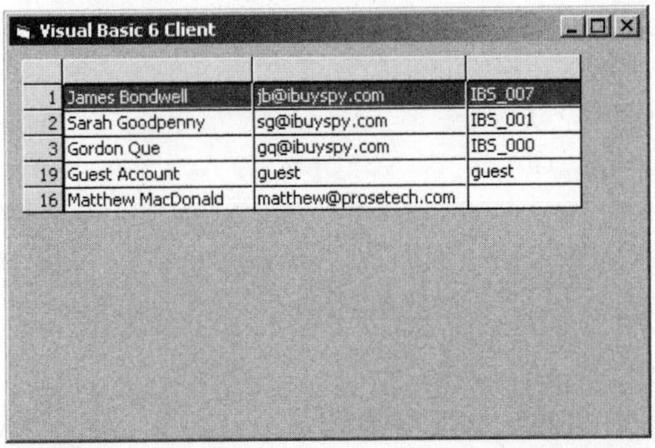

Figure 5-11 A Visual Basic 6 XML Web service client

Ideally, the client will use a slightly more advanced technique and will use SOAP messages. You can send and receive SOAP messages using the *XMLHTTP* object, but the client will need to shoulder the burden of manually creating the request message and processing the response. If the XML Web service changes, the client must also adapt. However, most platforms include more sophisticated tools that enable you to send SOAP messages using a higher-level abstraction and even create proxy classes by analyzing WSDL documents. Some examples include the following:

- Microsoft's SOAP Toolkit, which works with the previous generation of Visual Studio products (such as Visual Basic and C++)
- IBM's Web Service Development Kit
- Oracle's Web Integration Development Language
- Sun Microsystems's Sun ONE (Open Net Environment) offering, which now supports Web services written in the Java language
- Perl's SOAP::Lite kit, which provides basic SOAP functionality

Summary

This chapter has provided a lightning-quick introduction to XML Web services. I've steered away from many conventional topics (such as an examination of the SOAP standard), which are discussed to excess in most introductory .NET texts. Instead, this chapter has honed in on some more useful XML Web service topics, including cross-platform development, serialization, and ASP.NET platform services. The coming chapters show how you can work with XML Web services in even more flexible ways, including using asynchronous requests and authentication. I haven't introduced these topics yet because they represent techniques that can be applied with benefit to both XML Web services and .NET components exposed through .NET Remoting.

This chapter also touched on some topics that we won't return to in any detail, including ASP.NET pages and IIS configuration. If you would like to learn more about the ASP.NET platform and how to configure a Web server, you might be interested in a dedicated ASP.NET book, such as my *ASP.NET: The Complete Reference* (Osborne McGraw-Hill, 2002). Of course, you'll need to return to this book to learn many of the best practices to follow when you implement these features in an enterprise application.

Finally, if you would like to try interacting with a prebuilt XML Web service, the Internet provides many choices. You can try creating client applications for the following:

- Microsoft's TerraService (*http://terraservice.net*), which provides a free gateway to TerraServer, the multiterabyte database of satellite photography. You can use TerraService to download satellite images and display them in your .NET applications.
- Microsoft's MapPoint, which enables you to access high-quality maps and geographical information. MapPoint isn't free, but you can use a free trial of the XML Web service. See *http://msdn.microsoft.com/library/en-us/dnmapnet/html/mapintronet.asp* for information.

The basic services are on GotDotNet *(http://www.gotdotnet.com/playground/services*); they include tried-and-true favorites such as the thumbnail generator, the mail sender, and the quote of the day. Best of all, you can also see the .NET implementation code for the XML Web services.

6

Threaded Clients (Responsive Interfaces)

Microsoft .NET brings multithreading to the masses with the new set of classes in the *System.Threading* namespace. These classes wrap the intricacies of the Microsoft Windows API and make creating new threads as easy as declaring an object and invoking a method. But even though it's easy to create threads with the .NET class library, it's not as easy to manage them properly (and safely). To use threading successfully, developers need to adopt a different frame of mind and a few new habits. Without these best practices, a multithreaded application can appear to work correctly in the development environment but develop subtle and difficult-to-diagnose errors when deployed in the real world. These errors can compromise performance or, at worst, cause the program to fail or record invalid data.

This chapter examines the threading essentials every .NET developer requires. These include considerations such as callbacks, locking, and synchronization. We'll start with the basic support for asynchronous calls that's built in to the .NET Framework and consider how it can be used with XML Web services and remote components. The second half of the chapter tackles custom threaded objects and synchronization.

What Is Multithreading?

Multithreading allows your application to perform several tasks at the same time. In fact, "at the same time" isn't truly accurate. Unless your computer is equipped with multiple CPUs, it can execute only one instruction at a time.

(And even if you have multiple CPUs, your computer will almost always have far more threads in existence than it has processors.)

The truth of the matter is that when you use threads, you program as though these tasks were running independently. That means if you have two threads performing distinct tasks, you can't make any assumption about which thread will finish first.

Behind the scenes, the Windows operating system controls the life of all threads, acting a little like an administrator controlling access to a network supercomputer. Windows gives each thread a brief unit of time (called a *time slice*) to perform some work with the CPU, and then it freezes the thread in a state of suspended animation. A little bit later (perhaps only a few microseconds), the system unfreezes the application thread and allows it to perform a little more work. This invasive form of constant interruption is known as *preemptive multitasking*.

The most important thing to understand about threading is that it's all a matter of perception. For the most part, each thread behaves as though it is running exclusively and has complete control of the CPU. The controlling program acts as though the threads are running simultaneously. The user carries on as though the program can perform several tasks at once, perhaps even initiating multiple concurrent tasks, even though these tasks might complete more slowly when performed at the same time. Note that if you have more than one CPU, Windows might choose to execute different threads by using different CPUs, but this isn't necessary.

In a multithreaded program, each independent unit of execution is a thread. A complex application (or process) can have dozens of threads executing simultaneously. By using Task Manager in Windows, you can see all the executing processes, but you can't tell how many threads are in progress.

The Role of Threaded Clients in a Distributed System

This chapter is the first of two that deal with threading. This chapter looks at the role of threading in the client application. The next chapter discusses how threading can improve the server side. The central focus in this chapter is using threading to improve the performance and responsiveness of a client.

But does multithreading improve performance? It actually depends on the task. If you are writing an intensive number-crunching algorithm that performs several calculations, using threads won't reduce the total time required to complete the operation. In fact, because the separate threads are competing for the CPU and slight overhead is required to switch from thread to thread, a multithreaded approach will probably complete more slowly than a single-threaded solution. (This isn't necessarily true if your computer has more than one CPU, in which case multiple threads might allow Windows to optimize execution by using more than one CPU at the same time. However, relatively few client computers have more than one processor.)

On the other hand, if you have an operation that has some latency, multithreading can increase performance. If you have to make several XML Web service calls, for example, performing all of these calls at once from separate threads can save some significant time. If you invoke the methods consecutively, you'll spend time waiting for the first method to return and then spend time waiting for the second method to return, and so on. If you call the methods simultaneously, you can collapse your waiting time into one interval (as shown in Figure 6-1).

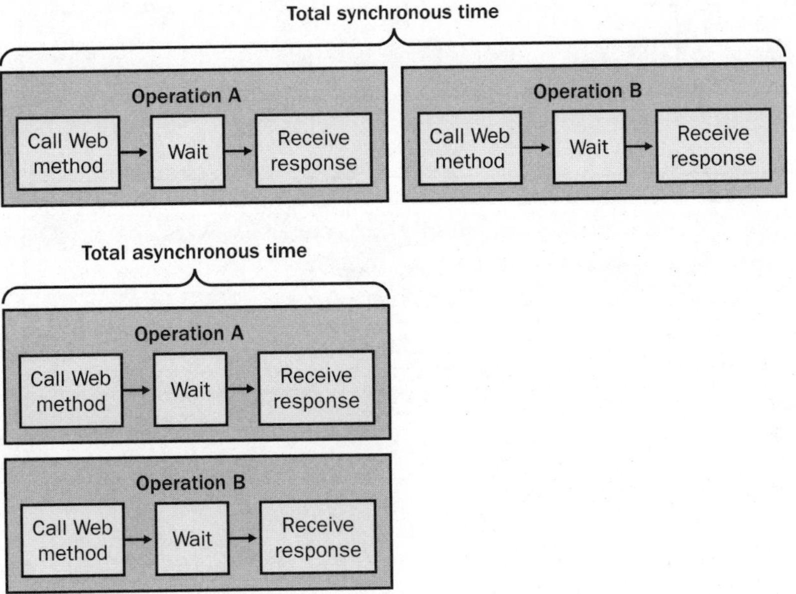

Figure 6-1 When operations involve waiting, asynchronous calls can dramatically improve performance.

The possible benefits of threading depend on the bottleneck. In the example shown in Figure 6-1, the client is being held back by the speed of its Internet connection. It needs to wait for the request message to be forwarded to its destination (the Web server) and for the response message to be routed back. A similar technique can be used to optimize a network or database call, which also incurs some overhead and entails some waiting. As a rule of thumb, the longer the wait, the more of advantage you can reap by using a multithreaded design.

If your threads are competing for finite resources on the client computer (such as the CPU), however, multithreading won't increase performance. Instead, it will cause all the operations to complete more slowly. In Figure 6-2, for example, the total time taken to complete the operations asynchronously is about the same as the time taken to complete them synchronously. In the asynchronous case, however, both operation A and operation B appear to take the full length of time before completing. In the synchronous case, operation A will complete more quickly. (Operation B will still take the full length of time because it won't be started until operation A ends.)

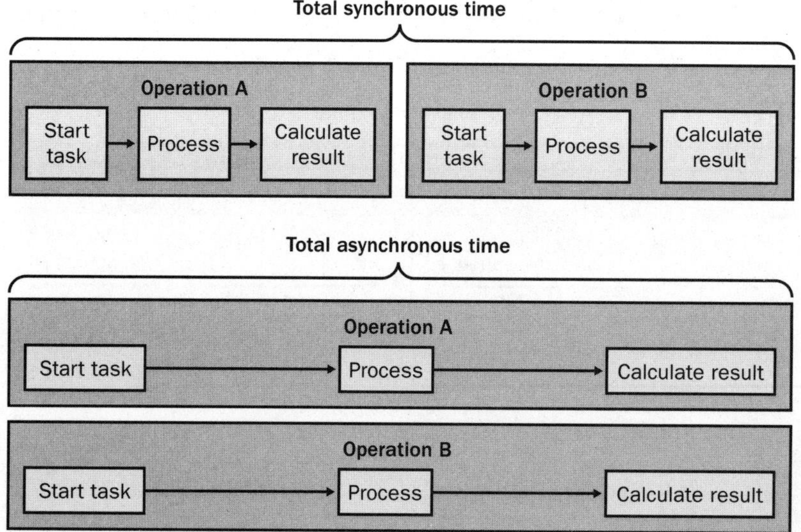

Figure 6-2 When operations involve a limited resource, asynchronous calls won't improve performance.

Of course, there's another reason to use multithreading. In many cases, particularly in the Internet world, a client uses threading to ensure that the user interface remains responsive. Imagine, for instance, that your application has a Get Info button that triggers a call to an XML Web service. If you don't use threading, the client will have to sit idly by while you download all the information. If you perform the call on a separate thread, however, the client can continue to interact with your user interface, performing different tasks. This might just be a user interface nicety, or it might have a genuinely useful purpose, such as enabling the user to cancel a long-running asynchronous process instead of forcing him to shut down the application. We'll look at an example at the end of this chapter that shows how threading can ensure a responsive client.

The value of threading also depends on the type of application. With a Windows application, multithreading is often used so that your code can perform several tasks while interacting with the user. With an ASP.NET application, however, this isn't the case. In an ASP.NET Web page, all the processing happens at once, and the final rendered HTML isn't sent to the client until all your code has finished executing. Therefore, using threading won't make the interface more responsive; it will just divide your tasks into more units of execution. (Of course, you might still use threading to collapse waiting times in certain scenarios. For example, if your ASP.NET Web page code needs to make multiple XML Web service calls, however, you can use threading to make all the calls at once, collapse your waiting time, and possibly return the page to the client a few seconds faster.)

Note Multithreaded programming isn't always in your best interest. It adds a new level of complexity to client programs and can introduce unusual errors, difficult-to-detect bugs, and other coding nightmares. Quite simply, threading properly is no easy feat. Threads also require additional overhead because the operating system must track and schedule them. If you won't see an obvious benefit from adding threading, don't be afraid to leave it (and the additional locking and synchronization concerns) behind.

Threading in .NET

There are essentially two ways to take advantage of multithreading with .NET:

- Create a new thread manually by using the *System.Threading.Thread* class.
- Use a .NET type that has built-in support for asynchronous use. This includes the types used for file I/O, the XML Web service proxy class, and the *Delegate* type.

This section focuses on the second approach, which provides most of the benefits of custom threading and shields you from many of the risks. Later in the chapter, we'll examine the first approach and custom threading.

Of course, it's also worth noting that many parts of a .NET application gain the benefits of threading completely for free. When you use the .NET printing classes, for example, the *PrintDocument.PrintPage* event is fired on a separate thread, allowing your application to remain responsive. Similarly, when you are hosting Web pages or XML Web services through ASP.NET, or components through .NET Remoting, the common language runtime (CLR) automatically uses a pool of worker threads to handle the requests of multiple clients simultaneously. These threads run separate instances of the component, which means that your code rarely needs to take this concurrent use into account. Similarly, if you are offloading the work from your applications to a relational database such as Microsoft SQL Server, you'll benefit from a tested, optimized product that uses a pool of worker threads to efficiently handle high request volumes and intensive file access.

Asynchronous Delegates

One of the basic building blocks in .NET is the *delegate*. Delegates are often described as type-safe function pointers. They are function pointers because they enable you to store a reference that "points" to a class method. They are type-safe because every delegate is defined with a fixed method signature. For example, you might create a delegate variable that can point to any method that takes two string parameters and returns an integer value. This is the delegate signature. You can't use this delegate to store a reference to a method with a different signature (for example, one that takes two string parameters and has no return value).

The two core delegate classes are as follows:

- ***System.Delegate*** The base delegate type, which can point to a single method. This is usually the type of delegate you'll use when you create a delegate on your own. This is also the type of delegate that this chapter explores.
- ***System.MulticastDelegate*** Represents a delegate that can point to more than one method at a time. This delegate is the basis for .NET event handling.

Suppose, for example, that you have a project that contains the following object:

```
Public Class ProductList

    Public Function GetTotal() As Decimal
        ' (Code omitted.)
    End Function

End Class
```

To create a delegate that points to *GetTotal*, you need to define the function signature. We'll call this *GetTotalDelegate*. Typically, you define this delegate inside the class consumer.

```
Public Delegate Function GetTotalDelegate() As Decimal
```

Now you can create a delegate variable based on *GetTotalDelegate* that can point to any function that accepts no parameters and returns a decimal result. Listing 6-1 is a code example that creates a *ProductList* object and a *GetTotalDelegate* that points to the appropriate *GetTotal* method.

```
' Declare the object.
Dim List As New ProductList()

' Declare the delegate variable.
Dim GetTotalPointer As New GetTotalDelegate(AddressOf List.GetTotal)

' Call List.GetTotal() through the delegate.
' This is the line that invokes the delegate.
Dim Total As Decimal
Total = GetTotalPointer()
```

Listing 6-1 Invoking a method through a delegate

So far, this is only an example of .NET basics. However, delegates are more interesting under the hood because they include built-in support for asynchronous execution.

Essentially, it works like this: Every time you define a delegate, .NET generates a custom delegate class. When you create a delegate and "point" it to a method, the custom delegate object stores a reference to the appropriate method. When you invoke the delegate, you are actually using the *Invoke* method in the custom delegate class.

The *Invoke* method provides synchronous execution, but the delegate class also includes two other methods—*BeginInvoke* and *EndInvoke*—that enable you to call the referenced method asynchronously on another thread. These asynchronous methods don't work the same as the basic *Invoke* method. *BeginInvoke* returns immediately, allowing your code to continue its work. *BeginInvoke* also returns a special *IAsyncResult* object that you can examine to determine when the asynchronous operation is complete. To pick up the results at a later time, you submit this *IAsyncResult* object to the *EndInvoke* method, which waits for the operation to complete if it hasn't already finished and returns the information in which you're interested.

Listing 6-2 shows the same code rewritten to use asynchronous delegates.

```
' Declare the object.
Dim List As New ProductList()

' Declare the delegate variable.
Dim GetTotalPointer As New GetTotalDelegate(AddressOf List.GetTotal)

' Call List.GetTotal() through BeginInvoke().
' Note that BeginInvoke always takes two extra parameters, and
' returns immediately.
Dim AsyncResult As IAsyncResult
AsyncResult = GetTotalPointer.BeginInvoke(Nothing, Nothing)

' (Perform some other work while the GetTotal() method is executing.)

' Retrieve the final result using the IAsyncResult.
Dim Total As Decimal = GetTotalPointer.EndInvoke(AsyncResult)
```

Listing 6-2 Invoking a method asynchronously through a delegate

Figure 6-3 diagrams how this code works.

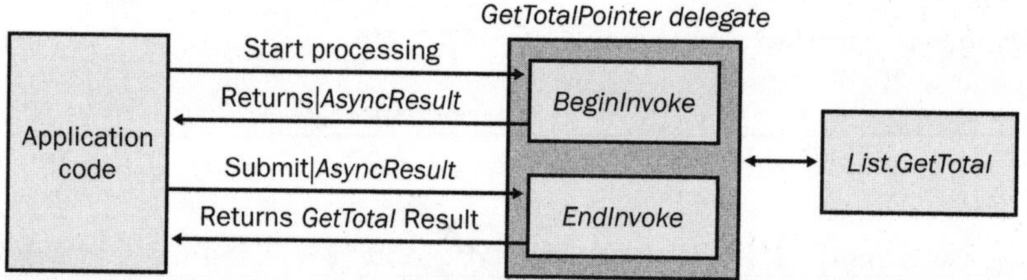

Figure 6-3 Calling a method asynchronously with a delegate

If the *GetTotal* method hasn't finished by the time you call *EndInvoke*, your code just waits for it to finish. In some cases, you might want to know whether the method is actually complete (and ready for pickup) before you call *EndInvoke* so that you won't risk a long wait. You can make this determination by examining the *IsCompleted* property of the *IAsyncResult* object, as shown in Listing 6-3. Checking this information repeatedly (for example, in a loop) is known as *polling*.

Part of the reason this delegate approach is so straightforward is because the asynchronous method doesn't have any other dependencies. It doesn't need to communicate its result or read information from another object. Thanks to this independence, you won't need to worry about synchronization or concurrency problems.

```
Dim List As New ProductList()
Dim GetTotalPointer As New GetTotalDelegate(AddressOf List.GetTotal)

' Call List.GetTotal() through BeginInvoke().
Dim AsyncResult As IAsyncResult
AsyncResult = GetTotalPointer.BeginInvoke(Nothing, Nothing)

' Loop until the method is complete.
Do Until AsyncResult.IsCompleted
    ' (Perform some additional work here.)
Loop

' Retrieve the final result.
Dim Total As Decimal = GetTotalPointer.EndInvoke(AsyncResult)
```

Listing 6-3 Polling to determine when an asynchronous method is complete

Table 6-1 shows the full set of *IAsyncResult* properties. Note that polling is rarely the most efficient approach. Generally, it's a better idea to use a callback or a wait handle. We'll look at these options parameters later in this chapter.

Table 6-1 ***IAsyncResult* Properties**

Property	Description
AsyncState	Returns the object that was supplied as the last parameter of the *BeginInvoke* call. This is useful when you're making multiple asynchronous calls at once because it enables you to associate an object with each call.
AsyncWaitHandle	Returns a *System.Threading.WaitHandle* object, which is primarily useful if you want to wait for a batch of asynchronous calls to complete.
CompletedSynchronously	Returns *True* if the method actually completed on the caller's thread. Typically, this will always be *False*. One possible exception is with asynchronous file I/O calls, where the work might be performed in the caller's thread if it is small (less than 64 KB).
IsCompleted	Returns *True* when the underlying method has completed. Otherwise, it returns *False*.

> **Note** You won't find *Invoke*, *BeginInvoke*, and *EndInvoke* in the class library reference for the *System.Delegate* type because these methods aren't a part of the basic delegate types. They are methods that .NET creates automatically when you define a delegate. (Technically, they are part of the custom delegate class that .NET builds behind the scenes.) If you think about it, you'll realize that this is a necessary fact of life because the *BeginInvoke* and *EndInvoke* have different signatures depending on the underlying method they are calling. For example, *BeginInvoke* always takes the parameters of the original method, along with two extra parameters, and *EndInvoke* always uses the return value of the original method. Thus, there's no way that they can be defined generically.

Asynchronous Remoting Calls

With .NET Remoting, the process is exactly the same. You can create a delegate variable that points to the method of a remote object and call it by using *BeginInvoke*. Technically, you aren't calling the remote object asynchronously—you're calling the transparent proxy asynchronously. (Remember, the transparent proxy is created automatically by the .NET Remoting infrastructure to manage communication between components in different application domains.) The proxy waits for the response from the remote object on a separate thread, as shown in Figure 6-4.

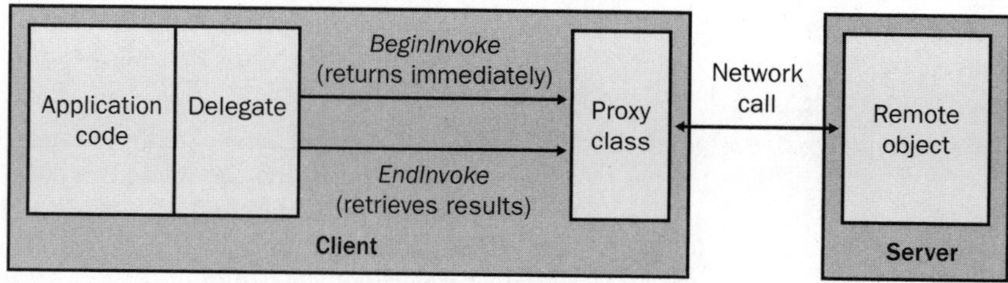

Figure 6-4 An asynchronous call to a remote component

Asynchronous Web Service Calls

It is possible to use delegates in much the same way with XML Web services, by creating a delegate variable that points to a proxy class method and calling this delegate asynchronously. However, you don't need to go to this extra work. When .NET generates a proxy class, it automatically adds additional methods that allow the XML Web service to be called asynchronously.

Suppose, for example, that you have the following Web method:

```
<WebMethod> _
Public Function GetStockQuote(ByVal Ticker As String) As Decimal
    ' (Code omitted.)
End Function
```

The proxy class will include a corresponding *GetStockQuote* method that calls this method synchronously. However, the proxy class will also include *BeginGetStockQuote* and *EndGetStockQuote* methods that call the Web service asynchronously. Listing 6-4 shows these three methods in the proxy class.

```
Public Function GetStockQuote(ByVal Ticker As String) As Decimal

    Dim results() As Object = Me.Invoke("GetStockQuote", _
                              New Object() {Ticker})
    Return CType(results(0), Decimal)

End Function

Public Function BeginGetStockQuote(ByVal Ticker As String, _
 ByVal callback As AsyncCallback, ByVal asyncState As Object) _
 As IAsyncResult

    Return Me.BeginInvoke("GetStockQuote", _
           New Object() {Ticker}, callback, asyncState)

End Function

Public Function EndGetStockQuote(ByVal asyncResult As IAsyncResult) _
 As Decimal

    Dim results() As Object = Me.EndInvoke(asyncResult)
    Return CType(results(0), Decimal)

End Function
```

Listing 6-4 Asynchronous support in the Web service proxy class

These methods mirror the *BeginInvoke* and *EndInvoke* methods. *BeginStockQuote* accepts the original string parameter, plus two optional ones, and returns an *IAsyncResult* instance. *EndGetStockQuote* accepts the *IAsyncResult* object and returns the *GetStockQuote* decimal return value.

To provide this magic, you'll notice that the proxy class code calls its own *BeginInvoke* method. This is actually one of the methods inherited from the base class *SoapHttpClientProtocol* (found in the *System.Web.Services.Protocols* namespace). All proxy classes that use SOAP communication derive from this class, and so they all have the ability to call Web methods asynchronously.

Wait Handles

With a wait handle, you can cause your program to wait until any one request in a batch of requests is complete or until all the requests have finished. All you need to do is use one of the shared methods of the *System.Threading.WaitHandle* class and provide it with an array of *WaitHandle* objects. You can retrieve a *WaitHandle* from the *IAsyncResult.AsyncWaitHandle* property.

Listing 6-5 shows an example that starts several XML Web service methods asynchronously and waits for them all to complete. Note that for this code to work as written, you need to import the *System.Threading* namespace.

```
' Call three methods asynchronously.
Dim Async1, Async2, Async3 As IAsyncResult
Async1 = Proxy.BeginGetStockQuote("MSFT", Nothing, Nothing)
Async2 = Proxy.BeginGetStockQuote("AMZN", Nothing, Nothing)
Async3 = Proxy.BeginGetStockQuote("EGRP", Nothing, Nothing)

' Create an array of WaitHandle objects.
Dim WaitHandles() As WaitHandle = {Async1.AsyncWaitHandle, _
                Async2.AsyncWaitHandle, Async3.AsyncWaitHandle}

' Wait for all the calls to finish.
WaitHandle.WaitAll(WaitHandles)

' You can now retrieve the results with Proxy.EndGetStockQuote().
```

Listing 6-5 Waiting for multiple asynchronous methods to complete

You also can instruct a wait handle to block the thread until any one of the method calls has finished. This can be a useful technique if you need to process a batch of data from different sources and the order in which you process it is not important, as shown in Listing 6-6.

```
' Call three methods asynchronously.
Dim Async1, Async2, Async3 As IAsyncResult
Async1 = Proxy.BeginGetStockQuote("MSFT", Nothing, Nothing)
Async2 = Proxy.BeginGetStockQuote("AMZN", Nothing, Nothing)
Async3 = Proxy.BeginGetStockQuote("EGRP", Nothing, Nothing)

' Create an array of WaitHandle objects.
Dim WaitHandles() As WaitHandle = {Async1.AsyncWaitHandle, _
                Async2.AsyncWaitHandle, Async3.AsyncWaitHandle}

' Wait for at least one call to finish.
WaitHandle.WaitAny(WaitHandles)

' You will need to check the IAsyncResult.IsCompleted property
' to determine which calls are finished.
```

Listing 6-6 Waiting for at least one asynchronous method to complete

The *WaitHandle* class also provides a single instance method, *WaitOne*, which just blocks the thread until the call is completed. It's analogous to using *EndInvoke*, except it doesn't return the information. (A separate *EndInvoke* call is still required.)

```
' Call three methods asynchronously.
Dim Async1, Async2, Async3 As IAsyncResult
Async1 = Proxy.BeginGetStockQuote("MSFT", Nothing, Nothing)
Async2 = Proxy.BeginGetStockQuote("AMZN", Nothing, Nothing)
Async3 = Proxy.BeginGetStockQuote("EGRP", Nothing, Nothing)

' Wait for them all to finish.
Async1.AsyncWaitHandle.WaitOne()
Async2.AsyncWaitHandle.WaitOne()
Async3.AsyncWaitHandle.WaitOne()
```

Finally, the *WaitHandle* class also provides overloaded versions of all these methods that enable you to specify a maximum wait time. If this time is reached and the method hasn't completed, your code continues. You specify the wait time with an integer representing a number of milliseconds or a *TimeSpan* object.

```
' Call one method asynchronously.
Dim Async1 As IAsyncResult
Async1 = Proxy.BeginGetStockQuote("MSFT", Nothing, Nothing)

' Wait for it to finish (or time out after 10 seconds).
Async1.AsyncWaitHandle.WaitOne(TimeSpan.FromSeconds(10), False)
```

Callbacks

Callbacks are one of the preferred ways to handle asynchronous calls because they simplify your code and eliminate the overhead of having to continuously poll a request that is in progress to see whether it has completed. The second-to-last parameter of the *BeginInvoke* method (or *BeginMethodName* in an XML Web service proxy class) accepts a reference to the method that you want triggered when the method call is complete.

To use a callback successfully, your callback method must have the same signature as the *System.AsyncCallback* delegate. That means it needs to accept a single *IAsyncResult* parameter. Here's an example:

```
Public Sub AsyncCallback(ByVal ar As IAsyncResult)
    ' (This code will be triggered when the method call is complete.)
End Sub
```

The callback code will then use the *IAsyncResult* object to call the appropriate *EndInvoke* method (or *EndMethodName* in a Web service proxy class) and retrieve the result.

Consider, for example, the *CustomerDB.GetCustomers* method introduced in Chapter 3, which returns a *DataSet* of customer information. You can call this method asynchronously with a callback by creating a delegate and using *BeginInvoke*. We'll walk through this process step by step.

First, you define the delegate. Notice that this delegate can be used generically with any method that requires no parameters and returns a *DataSet*.

```
Delegate Function GetDataSet() As DataSet
```

In addition, you need to create several form-level variables because the delegate variable must be accessible in more than one method (both the calling method and the callback).

```
Private DB As New CustomerDB()
Private GetData As New GetDataSet(AddressOf DB.GetCustomers)
```

Next, use the delegate to call the method:

```
GetData.BeginInvoke(AddressOf AsyncCallback, Nothing)
```

When the *DataSet* is returned from the remote component, the callback will be triggered:

```
Public Sub AsyncCallback(ByVal ar As IAsyncResult)

    Dim ds As DataSet = GetData.EndInvoke(ar)

    ' (Process the DataSet here.)

End Sub
```

> **Note** Although it's not strictly necessary, it's always good design practice to call *EndInvoke* even if you don't need to retrieve a return value. One reason is that your method call might have met with an error. Your code won't be notified of this exception until it attempts to call the *EndInvoke* method, at which point the exception will be rethrown.

Using callbacks seems fairly straightforward, but it actually involves several of the finer points of thread management. Here are some considerations:

- Callbacks don't indicate the method or delegate that triggered them. Therefore, if you are executing several asynchronous calls at the same time, you will either need to direct these to separate callback methods or use the *IAsyncResult.AsyncState* object.

- Callbacks are typically not executed on the same thread as the calling code. That means that they can execute at the same time as other code in your application, which opens your code up to a whole host of synchronization problems.
- When calling a remote component or XML Web service asynchronously, you are actually calling the proxy class asynchronously. Therefore, in a .NET Remoting scenario, you won't have to worry about using a bidirectional channel and listening for messages from the server because the server isn't triggering your callback. If this is at all hazy, refer back to Figure 6-4.

The first problem is the easiest to resolve. You just create an object that tracks the necessary information and submit it with the request. This object is automatically assigned to the *IAsyncResult.AsyncState* property and provided to the callback. Typically, this is a custom object that includes a reference to the delegate or proxy class that started the method invocation. For example, you can define the following state object for the stock quote XML Web service (as shown in Listing 6-7).

```
Public Class StockState

    Public Proxy As StockQuoteService
    Public Ticker As String

    Public Sub New(proxy As StockQuoteService, ticker As String)
        Me.Proxy = proxy
        Me.Ticker = ticker
    End Sub

End Class
```

Listing 6-7 A state object for the stock quote service

Before calling the method, you create an instance of the state object. You then submit the state object with the asynchronous call:

```
Dim Proxy As New StockQuoteService()

Dim State As New StockState(Proxy, "MSFT")
Proxy.BeginGetStockQuote("MSFT", AddressOf StockCallback, State)
```

The callback method can then retrieve all the information it needs from the state object. Remember, the *StockCallback* is providing the "answer" to your original asynchronous call. However, the answer isn't of much use if you don't remember what the original question was. The *StockState* object stores that information, including the proxy class you should use and the ticker value that was submitted, as shown in Listing 6-8. In this example, the stock information is written to a console window.

```
Public Sub StockCallback(ByVal ar As IAsyncResult)

    ' You must cast the AsyncState object to the correct type.
    Dim State As StockState = CType(ar.AsyncState, StockState)

    ' Retrieve the result.
    Dim Result As Decimal = StockState.Proxy.EndGetStockQuote(ar)

    ' Display the combined information.
    Dim Message As String
    Message = "Ticker: " & State.Ticker & " is at " & Result.ToString()
    Console.WriteLine(Message)

End Sub
```

Listing 6-8 A callback that uses a state object

The second problem—the fact that the callback executes on a separate thread—is more difficult to resolve and can lead to subtle, infuriating errors if it is not handled correctly. There is no easy way to pass information to another thread. You might think that you could solve the problem by raising a custom event. Unfortunately, this won't help at all because the event handler will execute on the same thread as the callback. Similarly, you might believe that you can avoid the problem by writing the retrieved information directly to the user interface. However, modifying the user interface from a thread other than the one that owns it is similarly problematic and is likely to lead to subtle, maddening problems.

Ultimately, if more than one thread needs to interact, you need to add some level of synchronization. We'll consider your options a little later in this chapter.

Asynchronous I/O

As you've seen, you can add threading to any type of code by placing it into a separate method and creating a delegate. In addition, the .NET Framework also includes asynchronous support in many classes, particularly those that deal with streams (and hence the code you use for direct socket connections over a network, downloading Web pages, and writing or reading files). You can recognize these methods by their name. When asynchronous methods exist, they always take the same name as the synchronous method versions, with *Begin* or *End* added to the beginning.

For example, you can use the *FileStream.BeginWrite* method to start an asynchronous write operation. This can enable you to save a large amount of data to disk without waiting for it to be completely written.

Here's how you initiate the operation:

```
Dim fs As New FileStream("c:\myfile.bmp", FileMode.Create, _
                         FileAccess.Write, FileShare.None)

fs.BeginWrite(ByteBuffer, 0, ByteBuffer.Length, _
              AddressOf FileWriteCallback, fs)
```

The following code is the callback that enables you to verify that it completed successfully. Note that because this code stores the *FileStream* as the state object, you can start any number of asynchronous file writing operations without any danger of getting them confused with each other.

```
Public Sub FileWriteCallback(ByVal ar As IAsyncResult)

    Dim fs As FileStream = CType(ar.AsyncState, FileStream)
    fs.EndWrite(ar)
    fs.Close()

End Sub
```

Custom Threading

So far, you've seen a number of ways to get asynchronous support for free from .NET. These techniques are ideal for making simple asynchronous calls to improve performance or to start a potentially time-consuming task without stalling the application. However, they are of much less help if you need to create intelligent, thread-aware code that communicates with other threads, runs for a long time to perform a variety of tasks, and allows variable levels of prioritization. To handle these cases, you need to take complete control of threading by using the *System.Threading.Thread* class and creating your own threaded objects.

To create a separate thread of execution in .NET, you create a new *Thread* object, identify the code it should execute, and start processing. In one respect, using the *Thread* object is like the delegate examples we considered before because the *Thread* class can point to only a single method. As with the delegate examples, this can be an instance method or a shared method. Unlike with the delegate examples, however, the *Thread* class has one basic limitation. The method it executes asynchronously must accept no parameters and have no return value. (In other words, it must match the signature of the *System.Threading.ThreadStart* delegate.)

The canonical threading example uses two threads that increment separate counters. To design this example, we'll use a command-line console application because the *Console* class is guaranteed to be thread-safe; multiple threads can call the *Console.WriteLine* method without causing any concurrency errors. The same is not necessarily true of the Windows user interface, where controls should be modified only from the thread that owns them. Listing 6-9 shows the full code.

```
Imports System.Threading

Module ThreadTest
    Public Sub Main()

        ' Define threads and point to code.
        Dim ThreadA As New Thread(AddressOf TaskA)
        Dim ThreadB As New Thread(AddressOf TaskB)

        ' Start threads.
        ThreadA.Start()
        ThreadB.Start()

        ' Pause to keep window open.
        Console.ReadLine()

    End Sub

    Private Sub TaskA()

        Dim i As Integer
        For i = 1 To 10
            Console.WriteLine("Task A at: " & i.ToString)

            ' Waste 1 second.
            WasteTime(1)
        Next

    End Sub

    Private Sub TaskB()

        Dim i As Integer
        For i = 1 To 10
            Console.WriteLine("Task B at: " & i.ToString)

            ' Waste 1 second.
            WasteTime(1)
        Next
```

Listing 6-9 A console application with two worker threads

```
    End Sub

    Private Sub WasteTime(ByVal seconds As Integer)

        Dim StartTime As DateTime = DateTime.Now
        Do
        Loop Until DateTime.Now > (StartTime.AddSeconds(seconds))

    End Sub

End Module
```

In this example, each thread runs a separate subroutine. This subroutine just counts from 1 to 10, delaying a second each time. The delay is implemented through another private method, *WasteTime*. Instead of using *WasteTime*, you could use the static *Thread.Sleep* method, which temporarily suspends your application for a number of milliseconds. However, I chose the *WasteTime* approach for several reasons:

- It illustrates that the *Thread* class initially targets one method but that this method can call any other code in your project.
- It demonstrates that more than one thread can call the same method at the same time without incurring any problems, unless they are trying to read from or write to the same variable at once. Each thread executes *WasteTime* separately, and there is no shared data, so no potential problems can occur.
- The *WasteTime* method doesn't actually pause the thread. From the thread's point of view, it is still at work, iterating several thousand times through a tight loop and comparing values. Even though each thread is inefficiently hogging the CPU, and neither thread is yielding for the other, the Windows operating system still ensures that they each get a chance to execute.

The output for this program demonstrates that each thread is given equal opportunity:

```
Task A at: 1
Task B at: 1
Task A at: 2
Task B at: 2
Task A at: 3
Task B at: 3
Task A at: 4
Task B at: 4
Task A at: 5
Task B at: 5
```

```
Task A at: 6
Task B at: 6
Task A at: 7
Task B at: 7
Task A at: 8
Task B at: 8
Task A at: 9
Task B at: 9
Task A at: 10
Task B at: 10
```

Table 6-2 indicates some of the properties of the *Thread* class. Note that you can retrieve a reference to the current thread by using the shared *Thread.CurrentThread* property. You can use this property in the *TaskA* or *TaskB* method to retrieve a reference to *ThreadA* or *ThreadB*, or you can use this in the *Main* method to retrieve a reference to the main thread of the console application, which you can configure just as you would any other thread.

Table 6-2 *Thread* Properties

Property	Description
IsAlive	Returns *True* unless the thread is stopped, aborted, or unstarted.
IsBackground	A thread is either a background thread or a foreground thread. Background threads are identical to foreground threads except they can't prevent a process from ending. After all the foreground threads in your application have terminated, the CLR automatically aborts all background threads that are still alive.
Name	Enables you to set a string name that identifies the thread. This is primarily useful during debugging.
Priority	One of the *ThreadPriority* values that indicate the scheduling priority of the thread as compared to other threads.
ThreadState	A combination of *ThreadState* values, which indicate whether the thread is started, running, waiting, a background thread, and so on. You can poll this property to find out when a thread has completed its work.

Thread Priorities

Threads might be created equal, but they don't need to stay that way. You can set the *Priority* property of any *Thread* object to one of the values from the *ThreadPriority* enumeration. Your choices, from highest to lowest priority, are as follows:

- *Highest*
- *AboveNormal*

- *Normal*
- *BelowNormal*
- *Lowest*

Thread priorities are mostly important in a relative sense. (For example, two threads at *Highest* priority compete for the CPU just as much as two threads at *Lowest* priority do.) However, when you use the higher priorities, you might steal time away from other applications and from your user interface thread, making the client computer generally less responsive.

You can test out thread priorities by modifying the *WasteTime* method in the Console example so that the wait is determined by the number of loop iterations rather than a fixed amount of time:

```
Private Sub WasteTime(ByVal loops As Integer)

    Dim i, j As Integer
    For i = 1 To loops
        For j = 1 To loops
        Next
    Next

End Sub
```

Now, if both *TaskA* and *TaskB* call *WasteTime* with the same sufficiently large parameter for loops (say, 10000), the one that has the highest priority will be able to wrest control and finish first.

Suppose, for example, that you start the threads like this:

```
Dim ThreadA As New Thread(AddressOf TaskA)
Dim ThreadB As New Thread(AddressOf TaskB)

ThreadA.Priority = ThreadPriority.AboveNormal
ThreadB.Priority = ThreadPriority.Normal

ThreadA.Start()
ThreadB.Start()
```

You are likely to see the following output:

```
Task A at: 1
Task A at: 2
Task A at: 3
Task A at: 4
Task A at: 5
Task A at: 6
Task A at: 7
Task B at: 1
Task A at: 8
```

```
Task A at: 9
Task A at: 10
Task B at: 2
Task B at: 3
Task B at: 4
Task B at: 5
Task B at: 6
Task B at: 7
Task B at: 8
Task B at: 9
Task B at: 10
```

> **Caution** *Thread starvation* describes the situation in which several threads are competing for CPU time and at least one of them is receiving insufficient resources to perform its work. This can lead to a thread that hangs around perpetually, never able to finish its task properly. To avoid thread starvation, don't use the higher thread priorities (or create a ridiculously large number of threads).

Thread Management

The *Thread* class also provides some useful methods that enable you to manage threads. For example, you can suspend a thread by using the *Suspend* method:

```
ThreadA.Suspend()
```

You can also call the *Join* method, which works similarly to a wait handle. It blocks the calling thread and waits for the referenced thread to end, either indefinitely or according to a set timeout:

```
' Wait up to 10 seconds.
ThreadA.Join(TimeSpan.FromSeconds(10))

' Perform a bitwise comparison to see if the ThreadState
' includes Stopped.
If (ThreadA.ThreadState And ThreadState.Stopped) = _
  ThreadState.Stopped Then
    ' The thread has completed.
Else
    ' After 10 seconds, the thread is still running.
End If
```

You can also kill a thread by using the *Abort* method. This throws a *ThreadAbortException*, which the thread can catch and use to clean up its resources before ending. However, the *ThreadAbortException* cannot be suppressed—even if your thread catches it, it will be thrown again as necessary until the thread finally gives in and terminates. You can test this by adding exception-handling code to the *TaskA* and *TaskB* methods in the console example, as shown in Listing 6-10.

```
Private Sub TaskA()

    Try
        Dim i As Integer
        For i = 1 To 10
            Console.WriteLine("Task A at :" & i.ToString)

            ' Waste 1 second.
            WasteTime(10000)
        Next

    Catch err As ThreadAbortException
        Console.WriteLine("Aborting Task A.")

    End Try

End Sub
```

Listing 6-10 Handling the *ThreadAbortException*

To see this error in action, abort the thread shortly after starting it:

```
ThreadA.Start()
ThreadB.Start()
ThreadA.Abort()
```

The output for this example is shown here:

```
Task B at: 1
Task A at: 1
Task B at: 2
Aborting Task A.
Task B at: 3
Task B at: 4
Task B at: 5
Task B at: 6
Task B at: 7
Task B at: 8
Task B at: 9
Task B at: 10
```

When you call the *Abort* method, the thread is not guaranteed to abort immediately (or at all). If the thread handles the *ThreadAbortException* but continues to perform work (for example, an infinite loop) in the *Catch* or *Finally* error-handling block, for instance, the thread might be stalled indefinitely. The *ThreadAbortException* is thrown again only when the error-handling code ends.

Even if a thread is well behaved, calling *Abort* only fires the exception—the thread might still take some time to handle the error. To ensure that a thread is terminated before continuing, it's recommended that you call *Join* on the thread after calling *Abort*.

```
ThreadA.Abort()
ThreadA.Join()
```

Also note that if *Abort* is called on a thread that has not yet started, the thread aborts immediately when it is started. If *Abort* is called on a thread that has been suspended, is sleeping, or is blocked, the thread is resumed or interrupted as needed automatically, and then it's aborted. When we look at custom threaded objects in the next section, we'll consider less invasive ways to tell a thread to stop executing.

Table 6-3 lists some of the most import methods of the *Thread* class. Note that these methods are written as though they act instantaneously, although this is not technically the case. For example, the *Thread.Start* method schedules a thread to be started. It won't actually begin until several time slices later, when the Windows operating system brings it to life.

Table 6-3 Thread Methods

Method	Description
Abort	Aggressively kills a thread using the *ThreadAbortException*.
Interrupt	If the thread is currently waiting (using synchronization code), blocked, or sleeping, this method puts it back on track.
Join	Waits until the thread terminates (or a specified timeout elapses).
ResetAbort	If the thread calls this method when handling the *ThreadAbortException*, the exception will not be thrown again and the thread will be allowed to continue living.
Resume	Returns a thread to life after it has been paused with the *Suspend* method.
Sleep	Pauses a thread for a specified number of milliseconds.
Start	Starts a thread executing for the first time. You cannot use *Start* to restart a thread after it ends.
Suspend	Pauses a thread for an indefinite amount of time.

Thread Debugging

When you debug with threads, it's imperative that you know which thread is executing a given segment of code. You can make this determination programmatically by using *Thread.CurrentThread* to retrieve a reference to the currently executing thread.

You should assign every thread in your program a unique string name by using the *Thread.Name* property, as shown in Listing 6-11. The *Thread.Name* property is "write once," so you can set it, but you can't modify it later.

```
Dim ThreadA As New Thread(AddressOf TaskA)
Dim ThreadB As New Thread(AddressOf TaskB)

Thread.CurrentThread.Name = "Console Main"
ThreadA.Name = "Task A"
ThreadB.Name = "Task B"

ThreadA.Start()
ThreadB.Start()
```

Listing 6-11 Identifying threads

You can then quickly test the current thread while debugging by using a command such as this:

```
' You can also use the less invasive Debug.WriteLine() method.
MessageBox.Show(Thread.CurrentThread.Name)
```

This code can prove extremely useful. In a complex multithreaded application, it's quite common to misidentify which thread is actually executing at a given point in time. This can lead to synchronization problems.

If you are using Visual Studio .NET, you have the benefit of the IDE's integrated support for debugging threads. This is a dramatic departure from earlier versions of Visual Basic, which can debug multithreaded applications only in an artificial single-threaded mode. The Visual Studio .NET debugging tools include a Threads window (Choose Debug, Windows, Threads to display it). This window shows all the currently executing threads in your program, identifies what code the thread is running (in the Location column), and indicates the thread that currently has the processor's attention with a yellow arrow (as shown in Figure 6-5).

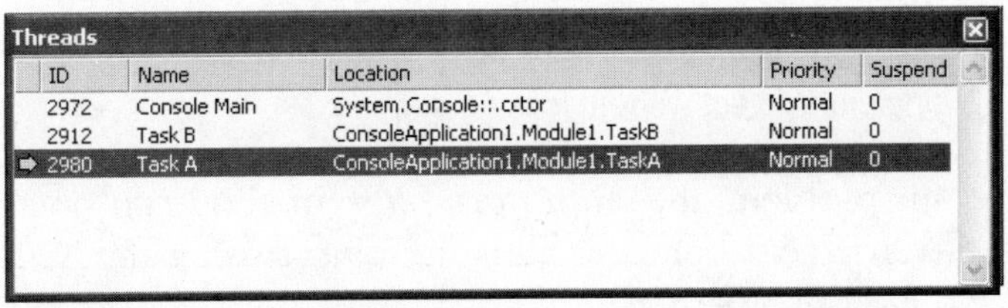

Threads

ID	Name	Location	Priority	Suspend
2972	Console Main	System.Console::.cctor	Normal	0
2912	Task B	ConsoleApplication1.Module1.TaskB	Normal	0
➡ 2980	Task A	ConsoleApplication1.Module1.TaskA	Normal	0

Figure 6-5 Debugging threads in Visual Studio .NET

If you pause your program's execution, you can even use the Threads window to set the active thread, freeze a thread so that it won't be available, or thaw a previously frozen thread.

Locking

The simple threading example we've created so far works well because the two tasks work independently. If you need to communicate between threads, life is not as simple. Trying to access an object on more than one thread at once is inherently dangerous. Threading problems are also infamously hard to diagnose because a single command in a high-level language such as Visual Basic .NET might actually compile to dozens of low-level machine-language instructions.

Locking enables you to obtain exclusive access to an object that's used by another thread. You can then safely modify the value without worrying that another thread might try to read or change it while your operation is in progress. Locking is built into Visual Basic .NET through the *SyncLock* statement. To demonstrate locking, we'll consider a simple example of a server-side object. The same technique applies when you design multithreaded clients; before we look at a full client example, however, we need to consider a couple of additional details.

Consider an object exposed through .NET Remoting as a *singleton*. This object maintains a collection of information supplied by clients in an *ArrayList*. Clients add a piece of information through the *AddInformation* method. If several clients call this method simultaneously, however, an error can occur, which will likely lead to losing at least one client's information (as shown in Listing 6-12).

```
Public Class InformationStorage
    Inherits MarshalByRefObject

    Private Information As New ArrayList()

    Public Sub AddInformation(info As String)

        Information.Add(info)

    End Sub

End Class
```

Listing 6-12 A singleton object without locking support

To solve this problem, the *AddInformation* method can obtain an exclusive lock on the *ArrayList* before it adds the object using the *SyncLock* statement, as shown in Listing 6-13.

```
Public Class InformationStorage
    Inherits MarshalByRefObject

    Private Information As New ArrayList()

    Public Sub AddInformation(info As String)

        SyncLock Information
            Information.Add(info)
        End SyncLock

    End Sub

End Class
```

Listing 6-13 A singleton object with locking

This approach efficiently solves the problem. The first client will obtain a lock on the *Information* collection. When another client attempts to access the *Information* collection, the CLR forces it to pause and wait until the lock is released. The CLR then allows the next waiting client to create its lock and gain exclusive access to the collection. You don't need to worry about keeping track of who made the first call; the CLR takes care of this queuing automatically and notifies clients as an object becomes available.

Locking is a common solution that guarantees data integrity with stateful components that are shared by multiple clients. A common question that developers have with locking is whether it reduces performance. Technically, locking always entails some slowdown because it forces clients to wait, effectively making a multithreaded program act like a single-threaded program for a short interval of time. However, the amount of performance slowdown varies dramatically depending on how coarse the lock is, how long it's held for, how many methods use the locked object, and how many clients are using the class that contains the locked object. In the preceding example, the slowdown would be noticeable if hundreds of clients were continuously adding information. However, the situation is dramatically different with the next example (shown in Listing 6-14), which uses *SyncLock* to safeguard a global counter that records how many times a method is called.

In this case, we can't use the *SyncLock* statement with the *GlobalCounter* variable because *SyncLock* works only with reference types, not value types. The only alternative is to lock the entire current instance of the *CountInvocations* class. This means that clients will not be able to call *any* methods of the *CountInvocations* object. Clearly, this lock is much coarser and has a less desirable effect on user concurrency.

```
Public Class CountInvocations
    Inherits MarshalByRefObject

    Private GlobalCounter As Integer

    Public Sub IncrementCounter()

        SyncLock Me
            GlobalCounter += 1
        End SyncLock

    End Sub

End Class
```

Listing 6-14 A coarser lock

Incidentally, you can solve this problem in two ways. One easy solution is to replace the *GlobalCounter* variable with an object that exposes an integer property. For example, an instance of the following *Counter* class can be locked:

```
Public Class Counter

    Public Count As Integer

End Class
```

Another possible solution is to use the specialized *System.Threading.Interlocked* class, which is designed to solve just this sort of problem with incrementing or decrementing an ordinary integer variable. The *Interlocked* class provides shared methods that increment or decrement a variable in a thread-safe manner as a single atomic operation, as shown in Listing 6-15.

```
Public Class CountInvocations
    Inherits MarshalByRefObject

    Private GlobalCounter As Integer

    Public Sub IncrementCounter()

        Interlocked.Increment(GlobalCounter)

    End Sub

End Class
```

Listing 6-15 Using the interlocked class

> **Tip** You might wonder why you need to lock the global counter in the first place. The problem is that the ordinary increment operation is actually shorthand for referring to two separate operations: reading a value and writing a value. Without synchronization, two clients might overlap. For example, they might both read the current counter value (say, 4) and both try to increment it to the next value (5). The end result is that the counter will be set to 5 twice rather than its rightful value of 6.

Race Conditions

With locking, you risk a couple of new problems. The first problem, race conditions, is really just a matter of not using the correct locking.

The example in Listing 6-16 shows the essence of a common race condition problem. A *ProcessValue* method obtains a lock when reading and writing a value, but it doesn't hold on to the lock for the time-consuming processing stage. This improves performance but raises the chance that another user will modify the value while the process is taking place.

```
Public Class CountInvocations
    Inherits MarshalByRefObject

    Private Value As Single

    Public Sub ProcessValue()

        SyncLock Me
            Dim ValueToProcess As Single = Value
        End SyncLock

        ' (Process ValueToProcess here).

        SyncLock Me
            Value = ValueToProcess
        End SyncLock

    End Sub

End Class
```

Listing 6-16 Potential grounds for a race condition

Race conditions can also be caused by unnoticed dependencies (for example, setting value A based on value B and C while another client is changing value C) or by the interference of more than one method.

There's no generic way to avoid a race condition. In the preceding situation, it might make sense to check that the current value equals the initially read value before making the update. Another choice is to use a Boolean member variable to keep track of whether the value is currently being processed and refuse to continue if it is.

Deadlocks

Whereas race conditions can lead to failed updates, deadlocks can stop a component from doing anything at all. Deadlocks are caused when two or more threads wait for each other to release a resource. For example, consider the two methods in Listing 6-17.

```
Public Sub MethodA()

    SyncLock ObjectA

        SyncLock ObjectB
            ' (Do something with A and B).
        End SyncLock

    End SyncLock

End Sub

Public Sub MethodB()

    SyncLock ObjectB

        SyncLock ObjectA
            ' (Do something with A and B).
        End SyncLock

    End SyncLock

End Sub
```

Listing 6-17 A likely candidate for a deadlock

Assume *MethodA* gets a hold of *ObjectA* and then tries to obtain a lock on *ObjectB*. In the meantime, *MethodB* obtains exclusive access to *ObjectB* and tries for *ObjectA*. Both methods will wait for each other to release an object, with neither method giving in. In this example, the culprits are nested *SyncLock* blocks. However, this situation is just as likely with separate objects that are trying to obtain locks on each other.

One of the problems with detecting and solving deadlocks is that they might not happen very often. (In fact, they might rely on a client calling just the right combination of methods.) The only way to avoid deadlock situations is through careful programming. Keep the following few guidelines in mind:

- Hold locks for as short a time as possible. Don't enclose code statements in a *SyncLock* block that don't need exclusive access to the object.
- Always obtain locks in the same order. If both *MethodA* and *MethodB* need *ObjectA* and *ObjectB*, for example, make sure they obtain locks in the same order. If that approach were used in the preceding example, one method would complete successfully while the other would wait politely.
- If you can't complete all your locks, release all your locks. In other words, if you achieve a lock on *ObjectA* but can't obtain one for *ObjectB*, release the lock on *ObjectA* and wait for a moment. This is the most difficult guideline to implement, and it can't be performed with the *SyncLock* statement alone. Instead, you need to have more fine-grained control of locks through the *Monitor* class.

Advanced Locking with the *Monitor* Class

The *SyncLock* statement is essentially a wrapper for another .NET class: *System.Threading.Monitor*. *Monitor* provides shared methods that enable you to test for locks, obtain locks, release locks, and notify other clients waiting for a locked object. Table 6-4 lists the methods of the *Monitor* class.

Table 6-4 *Monitor* Methods

Method	Description
Enter	Acquires a lock on an object. This action also marks the beginning of a critical section. Any other thread that attempts to access this object will block until the object is free.
TryEnter	Attempts to gain a lock on an object or times out after a specified number of seconds. Returns *True* if the lock was acquired or *False* if it wasn't.
Exit	Releases the lock on the object. This action marks the end of the critical section.
Wait	Releases the lock on the specified object and waits to acquire a new lock. An overloaded version of this method enables you to specify a timeout.
Pulse and *PulseAll*	Sends a signal to one or more waiting threads. The signal notifies a waiting thread that the state of the object has changed and the owner of the lock is ready to release the lock. The waiting thread is placed in the object's ready queue so that it might receive the lock for the object.

You can rewrite a block of *SyncLock* code using the *Monitor* class. For example, Listing 16-18 shows how to convert a *SyncLock* block into code that uses the *Monitor* class:

```
' SyncLock code.
SyncLock Obj
    ' (Use object here.)
End SyncLock

' Monitor equivalent of SyncLock code.
Try
    Monitor.Enter(Obj)
    ' (Use object here.)
Finally
    Monitor.Exit(Obj)
End Try
```

Listing 6-18 *SyncLock*-equivalent code with the *Monitor* class

In other words, the *SyncLock* statement uses exception-handling code that ensures that even if an error is generated, the lock is released on the object. This is a basic level of failsafe code required in any distributed application to prevent deadlocks.

In addition, you can make an intelligent attempt to acquire a lock using *TryEnter*, as shown in Listing 6-19.

```
If Monitor.TryEnter(Obj, TimeSpan.FromSeconds(60)) Then
    ' We have exclusive access to Obj.
    Try
        ' (Use object here.)
    Finally
        Monitor.Exit(Obj)
    End Try

Else
    ' After 60 seconds, the lock could still not be created.
    ' Log the error and thrown an exception to alert the client.

End If
```

Listing 6-19 Testing for a lock

This enables you to implement another safeguard against deadlocks. Namely, if you need to acquire a lock on more than one object, you should use *TryEnter* on the second object. If you can't acquire your second lock, you should release the first lock and try again later. This pattern is demonstrated in Listing 6-20.

```
' The TaskCompleted flag tracks is set once the operation is
' performed.
Dim TaskCompleted As Boolean = False

Do Until TaskCompleted
    ' Attempt to get the first lock for 10 seconds.
    If Monitor.TryEnter(ObjectA, TimeSpan.FromSeconds(10)) Then

        ' We have exclusive access on ObjectA.

        ' Attempt to get the second lock for 10 seconds.
        If Monitor.TryEnter(ObjectB, TimeSpan.FromSeconds(10)) Then
            ' We have exclusive access on ObjectA and ObjectB.
            ' (Perform task with ObjectA and ObjectB.)

            Monitor.Exit(ObjectB)
            TaskCompleted = True
        End If

        ' This releases the first lock, regardless of whether the
        ' task was completed.
        ' This ensures that other classes that may need both objects
        ' can finish their work.
        Monitor.Exit(ObjectA)

    End If

    If Not TaskCompleted
        ' The task will attempted in the next loop iteration.
        ' First, the code will pause for 60 seconds.
        Thread.Sleep(TimeSpan.FromSeconds(60))
    End If

Loop
```

Listing 6-20 Avoiding deadlocks

Wait, *Pulse*, and the Provider-Consumer Problem

The *Wait* and *Pulse* methods are designed to solve the classic provider-consumer problem. This occurs when one thread (a consumer) needs to acquire information from another thread (the provider). The consumer can use *Wait.Enter* to gain an exclusive lock on the provider and check for the data it needs. If the provider still hasn't created the data, however, acquiring this lock will freeze it, ensuring that the data is never created. In this case, the consumer calls the *Wait* method to move to the wait queue for the consumer object. This indicates that it wants to eventually obtain an exclusive lock on the provider. The provider then calls the *PulseAll* method to notify all the waiting consumers that the data is ready. The consumer threads then move to the ready queue and take turns acquiring the exclusive locks they need to read information from the provider.

Note that to use *Wait* and *PulseAll*, you must call *Enter* to start a synchronized block. The provider-consumer problem rarely appears in a distributed application because .NET handles low-level infrastructure details such as creating class instances for a client and managing remote object lifetime. (These details are beyond the scope of this book.)

Custom Threaded Objects

Technically, there is no relation between threads and objects. A single method in an object can be executed by several different threads, and a single thread can span multiple methods in different objects. However, it's often useful to create a dedicated class that encapsulates everything a thread needs. This provides an easy way to associate pieces of required information with a thread and overcome the fundamental limitation that a thread can execute only methods that take no parameters.

Consider, for example, the asynchronous calls to an imaginary stock quote XML Web service, which we considered earlier in the chapter. The *GetStockQuote* Web method required a single ticker parameter and returned a decimal with price information. You can easily create a class that encapsulates this information (as shown in Listing 6-21).

```
Public Class StockQuoteInfo

    Public TickerParameter As String
    Public PriceReturnValue As Decimal

    Public Sub New(ticker As String)
        TickerParameter = ticker
    End Sub

    Public Sub New()
        ' This is the default constructor.
    End Sub

End Class
```

Listing 6-21 Encapsulating the details of a method call

Now it's just a small leap to incorporate this into a custom threading class that encapsulates the method parameters and the code required to call the stock lookup methods, as shown in Listing 6-22.

```
Public Class StockQuoteLookup

    Public StockCall As New StockQuoteInfo()
    Private Proxy As New StockQuoteService()

    Public Sub DoLookup()
        StockCall.PriceReturnValue = Proxy.GetStockQuote( _
         StockCall.TickerParameter)
    End Sub

End Class
```

Listing 6-22 Creating a custom class for an asynchronous method call

Note that we use the synchronous *GetStockQuote* method from the proxy class, *not* the asynchronous *BeginGetStockQuote*. That's because the entire *DoLookup* method will execute asynchronously from the rest of the application. Essentially, this moves the responsibility for the asynchronous call from the proxy class to our client code (as shown in Figure 6-6).

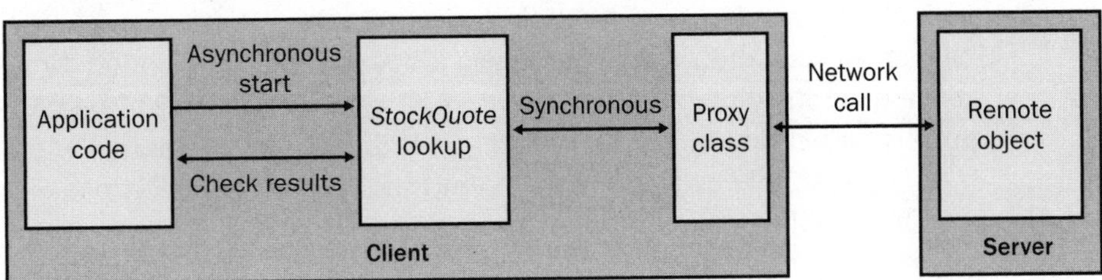

Figure 6-6 Using a custom threaded class

You can easily use the *StockQuoteLookup* class synchronously, as shown in Listing 6-23.

```
Dim Lookup As New StockQuoteLookup()
Lookup.StockCall.Ticker = "MSFT"

Lookup.DoLookup()

MessageBox.Show("MSFT is at: " & _
 Lookup.StockCall.PriceReturnValue.ToString())
```

Listing 6-23 Calling an XML Web service synchronously by using a custom class

You can also use the *StockQuoteLookup* class asynchronously by creating and using a *Thread* object. Listing 6-24 shows an example that uses this technique and then polls the class to determine when processing is complete (at which point it is safe to read the return value).

```
Dim Lookup As New StockQuoteLookup()
Lookup.StockCall.Ticker = "MSFT"

Dim LookupThread As New Thread(AddressOf Lookup.DoLookup)
LookupThread.Start()

Do Until (LookupThread.ThreadState And ThreadState.Stopped)
    ' (Do other tasks if desired)
Loop

MessageBox.Show("MSFT is at: " & _
 Lookup.StockCall.PriceReturnValue.ToString())
```

Listing 6-24 Calling an XML Web service asynchronously by using a custom class

One of the advantages of creating a dedicated object to handle your threaded code is that it allows complete freedom for executing a number of tasks in a set order. With delegates, you're forced to make each method call asynchronous. With a threaded object, you can create a series of method calls that must execute synchronously with respect to each other but can execute asynchronously with respect to the rest of the program. This is particularly useful if you need to call one method with the results of another method.

One simple example is to extend the *StockQuoteLookup* class to support a batch of lookups, as shown in Listing 6-25.

```
Public Class StockQuoteLookup

    Public StockCalls As New ArrayList()
    Private Proxy As New StockQuoteService()

    Public Sub DoLookup()

        Dim StockCall As New StockQuoteInfo()

        ' Iterate through the collection, executing each stock lookup
        ' synchronously.
        For Each StockCall In StockCalls
            StockCall.PriceReturnValue = Proxy.GetStockQuote( _
             StockCall.TickerParameter)
        Next

    End Sub

End Class
```

Listing 6-25 Adding support for multiple method calls

The client code can then create a *StockQuoteLookup* and add a list of the tickers that require quotes, as shown in Listing 6-26.

```
Dim Lookup As New StockQuoteLookup()
Lookup.StockCalls.Add(New StockQuoteInfo("MSFT"))
Lookup.StockCalls.Add(New StockQuoteInfo("AMZN"))
Lookup.StockCalls.Add(New StockQuoteInfo("EGRP"))

Dim LookupThread As New Thread(AddressOf Lookup.DoLookup)
LookupThread.Start()
```

Listing 6-26 Calling a method multiple times asynchronously

In this case, making multiple asynchronous calls would probably still increase performance because the wait time is collapsed. However, this example illustrates how well a threaded object can wrap up all the required information in a single package.

Threading and User Interfaces

A threaded object provides an ideal way to call several required methods, but it doesn't solve one key problem. Namely, how should the thread signal that it's finished its work? In the threading examples used so far, the client has been forced to continuously poll the thread. When the thread has finished, it's safe to access the properties of the *StockQuoteLookup* class. This isn't of much use if you want to return control to the user so that other tasks can be initiated.

One crude solution would be to create a timer that fires in periodic intervals and then polls the in-progress thread. Alternatively, you could let the user dictate when polling should take place, perhaps checking for results whenever the user clicks a Refresh button. Both of these approaches are less than elegant.

A third possibility would be to let the threaded object modify the user interface directly. However, the only safe way that a control can be modified is from code that executes on the thread that owns the user interface. In a Windows application, this is the main thread of your application.

Fortunately, all .NET controls provide a special *Invoke* method (inherited from the base *Control* class) just for this purpose. You call the *Invoke* method and pass it a delegate that points to another method. This method is then executed on the correct user interface thread.

The next example shows a rewritten *StockQuoteLookup* class that implements this pattern to provide safe updating (as shown in Listing 6-27).

```
Public Class StockQuoteLookup

    Public StockCall As New StockQuoteInfo()
    Private Proxy As New StockQuoteService()

    ' By using the base Control class, we have the freedom to use a
    ' variety of controls, including labels, buttons,
    ' and status bar panels.
    Private ControlToUpdate As Control

    Public Sub DoLookup()

        StockCall.PriceReturnValue = Proxy.GetStockQuote( _
         StockCall.TickerParameter)

        ' Marshal the UpdateControl() code to the correct thread.
        ControlToUpdate.Invoke( _
          New MethodInvoker(AddressOf UpdateControl))

    End Sub

    ' This method will execute on the user interface thread.
    Public Sub UpdateControl()

        ControlToUpdate.Text = StockCall.TickerParameter & _
         " = " & StockCall.PriceReturnValue.ToString()

    End Sub

    ' Use a default constructor to force the client to submit
    ' the update control.
    Public Sub New(control As Control)

        ControlToCallback = Control

    End Sub

End Class
```

Listing 6-27 Marshaling calls to the user interface thread

Note that the method you pass to *Invoke* must match the *MethodInvoker* delegate (which means it can't have any parameters or a return value). In Listing 6-27, this method is *UpdateControl*.

> **Note** Interestingly, the *Control* class also provides *BeginInvoke* and *EndInvoke* methods that enable the user interface code to be executed asynchronously, which is rarely required. The *Invoke*, *BeginInvoke*, and *EndInvoke* methods are the only methods that are thread-safe in a Windows control. No other methods should be called from another thread.

You can easily verify that this code is working correctly by naming both threads and calling the *MessageBox.Show* method to display the thread name in the *DoLookup* and *UpdateControl* method. You'll verify that the *DoLookup* executes on the secondary thread, while *UpdateControl* executes on the main thread, which owns the user interface.

To use this code, just supply the control you want updated when you create the *StockQuoteLookup* object:

```
Dim Lookup As New StockQuoteLookup(lblStockResult)
```

Using Callbacks and Locking

One glaring problem in the example we just explored is that the user interface code is tightly coupled with the request processing logic. Ideally, the threading class shouldn't assume the responsibility of updating the client's user interface.

A more traditional approach is for the thread to notify the client that it has finished using an event or a callback. To accommodate this notification technique, you need to add a delegate that represents the callback or a new event to the thread class.

The next example updates the *StockQuoteLookup* class to use a delegate. Note that the delegate variable doesn't use the *AsyncCallback* signature that we used earlier because the threading class doesn't return an *IAsyncResult* object. Instead, it defines a more useful event-type syntax that passes a reference to the *StockQuoteLookup* instance and an empty *EventArgs* object, as shown in Listing 6-28.

```
Public Class StockQuoteLookup

    Public StockCall As New StockQuoteInfo()
    Private Proxy As New StockQuoteService()
```

Listing 6-28 A custom threading class that uses a callback

```
    ' Define callback.
    Public Delegate Sub StockQuoteCallback(_
     sender As StockQuoteLookup, e As EventArgs)

    ' Define callback variable.
    Public StockCallback As StockQuote

    Public Sub DoLookup()

        StockCall.PriceReturnValue = Proxy.GetStockQuote( _
         StockCall.TickerParameter)

        ' Notify the client (and pass instance of this object).
        StockCallback(Me, New EventArgs())

    End Sub

    ' Use a default constructor to force the client to submit
    ' a callback method.
    Public Sub New(callback As StockQuoteCallback)

        StockCallback = callback

    End Sub

End Class
```

The client submits the callback address when creating the custom threaded object:

```
Dim Lookup As New StockQuoteLookup(AddressOf ReceiveResult)
```

Alternatively, you can implement the same sort of logic by using a custom event in the *StockQuoteLookup* instead of storing a delegate. Listing 6-29 demonstrates this approach.

```
Public Class StockQuoteLookup

    Public StockCall As New StockQuoteInfo()
    Private Proxy As New StockQuoteService()

    ' Define the event.
    Public Event Completed(sender As StockQuoteLookup, e As EventArgs)

    Public Sub DoLookup()

        StockCall.PriceReturnValue = Proxy.GetStockQuote( _
```

Listing 6-29 A custom threading class that fires a notification event

```
        StockCall.TickerParameter)

        ' Fire the event.
        RaiseEvent Completed(Me, New EventArgs())

    End Sub

End Class
```

In this case, the client needs to hook up an event handler after creating the object:

```
Dim Lookup As New StockQuoteLookup()
AddHandler Lookup.Completed, AddressOf ReceiveResult
```

Both versions are essentially equivalent. The only difference is that the event-handling version uses a "loosely coupled" design in which multiple clients can handle the same event. However, the *StockQuoteLookup* class won't be aware of which clients are listening.

Both versions also suffer from the same problem. The client callback method will execute on the caller's thread, meaning that you can directly touch any other application variables or modify the user interface. Fortunately, you can still use the *Control.Invoke* method to update the user interface safely. In this case, however, we need to take a further step. You can't directly pass the retrieved information to the method that will update the user interface, so you'll need to store it in a form-level variable first.

Listing 6-30 shows the complete solution.

```
Public Class FormClient
    Inherits System.Windows.Forms.Form

    ' (All other code, including the code to start the threads,
    ' is left out for clarity.)

    Public ResultText As String

    Public Sub ReceiveResult(sender As StockQuoteLookup, _
     e As EventArgs)

        ' Set the update text.
        ResultText = sender.StockCall.TickerParameter & _
         " = $" & sender.StockCall.PriceReturnValue.ToString()

        ' Marshal the UpdateDisplay() code to the correct thread.
        lblResults.Invoke( _
          New MethodInvoker(AddressOf UpdateDisplay))
```

Listing 6-30 A client that uses the custom threading class

```
    End Sub

    Public Sub UpdateDisplay()

        ' Add the recently received text to a label control.
        lblResults.Text &= vbNewLine & ResultText

    End Sub

End Class
```

In the preceding example, we assume that only one thread can contact the application at a time with the result of a stock quote. If, instead, you have multiple requests performing multiple stock lookups and they can all return results at the same time, you need to track information in a collection and add locking. The rewritten example in Listing 6-31 adds this functionality using a *Queue* collection, which retrieves items in the same order they are added.

```
Public Class FormClient
    Inherits System.Windows.Forms.Form

    ' (All other code, including the code to start the threads,
    ' is left out for clarity.)

    Public Results As New System.Collections.Queue()

    Public Sub ReceiveResult(sender As StockQuoteLookup, _
     e As EventArgs)

        ' Set the update text.
        Dim ResultText As String
        ResultText = sender.StockCall.TickerParameter & _
         " = $" & sender.StockCall.PriceReturnValue.ToString()

        ' Add the text to the queue.
        SyncLock Results
            Results.Enqueue(ResultText)
        End SyncLock

        ' Marshal the UpdateDisplay() code to the correct thread.
        lblResults.Invoke( _
          New MethodInvoker(AddressOf UpdateDisplay))

    End Sub

    Public Sub UpdateDisplay()
```

Listing 6-31 A client that uses the custom threading class with multiple simultaneous calls

```
        ' Add the recently received text to a label control.
        Dim ResultText As String

        SyncLock Results
            ResultText = CType(Results.Dequeue(), String)
        End SyncLock

        lblResults.Text &= vbNewLine & ResultText

    End Sub

End Class
```

This might seem slightly excessive for a modest client application, but it does demonstrate how to use locking and marshaling in the same method. This example also provides some more insight into the infamous question "Does locking harm performance?" A healthy dose of common sense can help you determine that in this case locking isn't a problem. The lock on the *Results* object is held for a very brief amount of time. Even if hundreds of stocks are being queried at the same time, the application can easily keep up.

The online samples for this chapter include a simple test program that uses this design and shows how all the pieces work together. It submits a batch of requests simultaneously to a stock quote service, which returns random price information. Figure 6-7 shows this application.

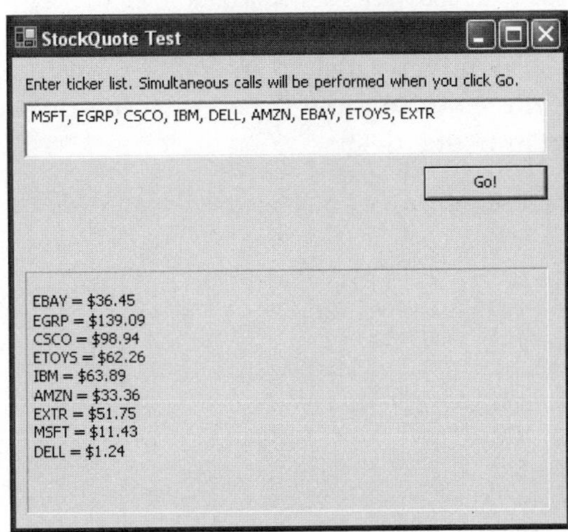

Figure 6-7 The asynchronous Windows client

Sending Instructions to a Thread

The preceding section showed an in-depth example of how a thread can communicate with the rest of your program by raising an event. Sending a message from your application to a worker thread is slightly different. Although a dedicated worker thread could handle an event, this option isn't common and is likely to lead you to tightly bind a thread to a particular user interface model. A better approach is to design the thread with built-in support for certain instructions.

Typically, a client has relatively few instructions to give a thread. The most common type of communication is to order a thread to end gracefully. You can provide this capability by adding a Boolean *Stop* property to the *Thread* class. The thread can then regularly check this value (perhaps after every pass in a loop) and end its processing if it is set to *True*, as shown in Listing 6-32.

```
Public Class ProcessData

    Public Stop As Boolean = False

    Public Sub Process

        Do Until Stop
            ' (Carry out a repetitive processing task).
        Loop

    End Sub

End Class
```

Listing 6-32 A threaded class that recognizes a stop signal

If the thread fails to respond after a short interval of time after the client sets its *Stop* property to *True*, you can take the next, more drastic step, and abort the thread, as shown in Listing 6-33.

```
' Attempt to stop the thread gracefully.
TaskObject.Stop = True

' Wait for the thread for up to 10 seconds.
TaskThread.Join(TimeSpan.FromSeconds(10))

' Check if the thread has ended.
If (TaskThread.ThreadState And ThreadState.Stopped) <> _
 ThreadState.Stopped Then

    ' The thread is still running. Now you must end it forcefully.
    TaskThread.Abort()
    TaskThread.Join()

End If
```

Listing 6-33 Sending a stop signal to a thread

You might want more control over a thread, including the ability to tell a thread to abandon its current work and start processing new data. However, it doesn't make sense to add multiple thread properties to try to accommodate this need. If you do, you will force the application to know far too much about the structure of the *Thread* class. This makes it more difficult to enhance the *Thread* class and might introduce additional vulnerabilities if the *Thread* class properties are not set correctly.

A better approach is to create a dedicated method in the *Thread* class. The client can then call this method when needed. Listing 6-34 presents the outline for one example. In this case, the client can call the *SubmitNewData* method to instruct the thread to abort its current task and start processing different information. The *SubmitNewData* method sets a flag that indicates new data has arrived (the *RestartProcess* variable) and copies the submitted information to a safe place (the *NewData* variable).

```
Public Class ProcessData

    ' The data that is currently being processed.
    ' The integer data type is used as a basic example.
    Private Data As Integer

    ' New data that should be processed as soon as possible.
    Private NewData As Integer

    ' Flags that indicate when processing should stop.
    Private RestartProcess As Boolean
    Private Stop As Boolean = False

    Public Sub Process

        Do Until Stop

            Do Until RestartProcess Or Stop
                ' (Carry out a repetitive processing task).
            Loop

            ' Pick up the new data.
            If RestartProcess And Not Stop Then
                Data = NewData
                RestartProcess = False
            End If

        Loop

    End Sub
```

Listing 6-34 A threaded class that can handle new information

```
    Public Sub SubmitNewData(data As Integer)

        ' Enter the new data.
        NewData = data

        ' Set a flag that will alert the Process method that new
        ' data exists.
        RestartProcess = True

    End Sub

End Class
```

Summary

This chapter dove deep into the intricacies of multithreading with .NET, a technique that's easy to use but difficult to master. Threading works best with an independent task—where the amount of interaction with other threads is minimal and the time required to complete the operation is long enough to warrant the added complexity in design. Judicious, infrequent use of threads can make a client application far more responsive and easier to work with.

In the next chapter, we'll continue our exploration of threading with a look at its role in distributed components.

7

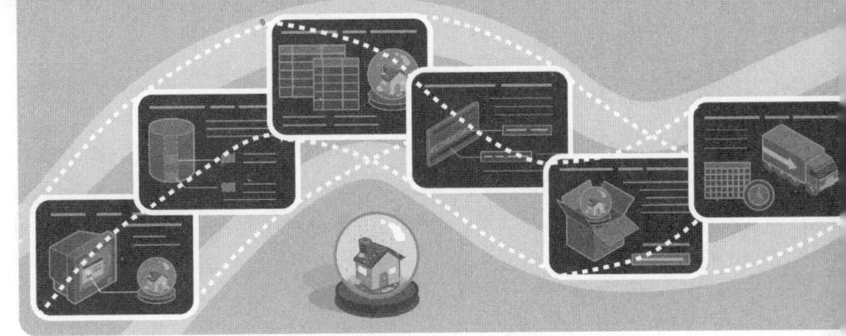

Thread Pools and Services (Scalable Programming)

The preceding chapter showed how you can create multithreaded clients that call XML Web services or remote components asynchronously. Along the way, we sorted through the details of responsible threading, with topics such as synchronization and callbacks. This chapter shifts the focus and asks how threading can be put to use in a remote component.

To answer this question, we need to consider different *singleton* designs. With singleton designs, you are responsible for adding the infrastructure that allows your component to support multiple simultaneous users. You'll need to spawn new threads as needed, track users, and ensure thread safety. Furthermore, if you're expecting a large user load, you must use some type of thread pooling to ensure scalability. This chapter tackles all these considerations. You'll also see how you can create a Microsoft Windows service to act as a .NET Remoting component host.

The Role of Threading in a Distributed System

When designing a component for a distributed application, you have two choices. Your first choice is to use a simple .NET Remoting object (configured as a single-call or client-activated object) or an XML Web service and allow .NET to handle all the details needed to support multiple users. In this case, you don't need to worry about threading at all because .NET automatically creates a separate object instance to serve each client (as shown in Figure 7-1).

Your other choice is to create a custom component designed to handle multiple clients. You can host this component in the ASP.NET application state collection so it's available to all XML Web services and Web pages, or you can host it in a .NET Remoting component host (by configuring it with singleton activation). In these cases, you take on the responsibility for handling multiple clients. This means that you create new state objects and threads to serve client requests as needed (as shown in Figure 7-2). This allows your threads to act in more or less the same way they would in a single-client environment.

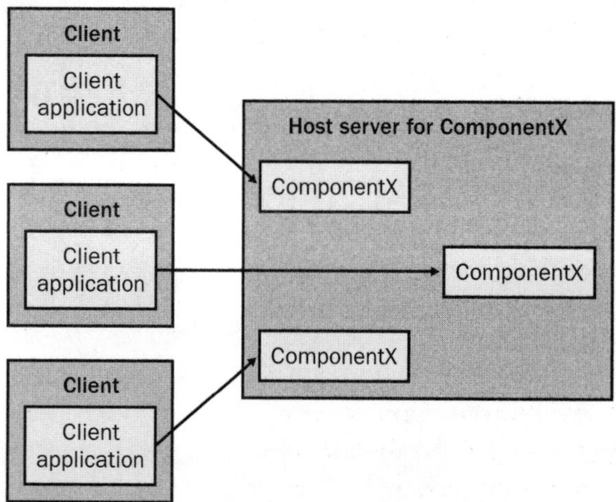

Figure 7-1 Serving multiple clients with a single-call object

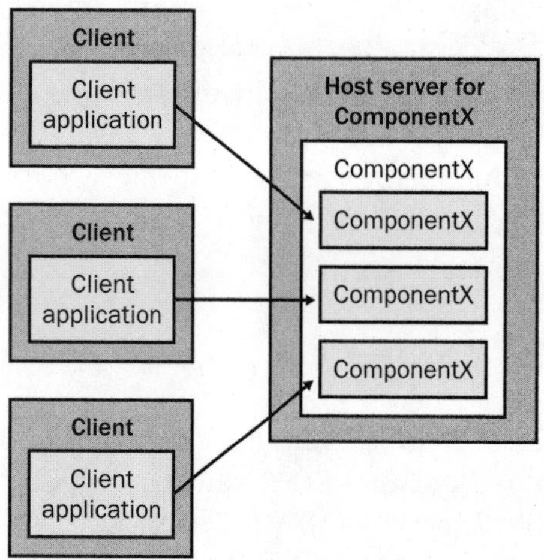

Figure 7-2 Serving multiple clients with a singleton object

Clearly, using singleton designs adds complexity. So why would you want to tackle this approach? Here are some possible reasons:

- You want to create a component where different clients have some measure of interaction or some information is shared. Without using a singleton design, you would need to write this information to an external resource, such as a database, before another client could read it.
- You want to create a component that has unique processing requirements. Using a singleton design gives you complete control over how requests are served. For example, some requests are queued until later, whereas others are processed immediately with high-priority threads. There is no way to use this type of prioritization with an ordinary XML Web service or .NET Remoting.
- You want to create an XML Web service that performs work asynchronously. Ordinarily an XML Web service doesn't hold state and is destroyed after the client call. You can bridge the gap by adding a custom component to an XML Web service. This component can perform a task after the Web method has ended and the XML Web service instance has been destroyed.

Remember that you pay a price for these features. It's fairly easy to create a simple infrastructure for handling multiple clients with a singleton component. However, it's not easy to create an infrastructure that's as robust and efficient as .NET. For example, ASP.NET processes all XML Web service requests using a pool of worker threads and provides a machine.config configuration file that enables you to tailor details such as how often worker processes are recycled. Duplicating these features is a major programming and testing effort, requiring a dedicated software development team doing little else. In general, a singleton server component is easiest to design if you know in advance that it will always be used in a single, specified manner, for a specified task. This chapter doesn't explain everything you need to know (the threading considerations alone could fill an entire book), but it does give you a solid grounding in the core issues you must consider.

Singleton Basics

The lifetime of a typical singleton object is not tied to the client. Consider .NET Remoting, for instance. When a client makes a call, the .NET Remoting service provides a thread from its pool, which then accesses the object. Multiple clients can access the same object on multiple different threads if they make concurrent calls.

If the singleton object is stateless (in other words, it doesn't provide any class properties or member variables), there's really nothing to worry about. Any variables created in a method body are local to the current call. In this case, a singleton object performs like a single-call object. In fact, contrary to what you might expect, a singleton object used in this way might even perform better because it doesn't need to be destroyed and re-created for each call. More likely, however, you'll use a singleton design only if you need to maintain some sort of shared information.

One trivial example is a component that tracks usage information. This logging can be integrated directly into each method or can be applied using a layered interception design. Consider Listing 7-1, in which *ClassA* tracks usage information and *ClassB* performs the actual task.

```
Public Class ClassA
    Inherits MarshalByRefObject

    ' Tracks the number of requests from all clients since the class
    ' was created.
    Private NumberOfCalls As Integer = 0

    Public Function DoSomething() As Integer

        ' Perform usage logging in a thread-safe manner.
        System.Threading.Interlocked.Increment(NumberOfCalls)

        ' Execute the method that does the work.
        Dim TaskB As New ClassB()
        Return TaskB.DoSomething()

    End Function

    Public Function GetUsageInformation() As Integer
        Return NumberOfCalls
    End Function

End Class

Public Class ClassB

    Public Function DoSomething() As Integer
        ' (Code goes here.)
    End Sub

End Class
```

Listing 7-1 Using interception with a singleton

In this case, the client never directly accesses *ClassB*. Instead, it starts a task by calling a method in *ClassA*. This method is really just a front for the functionality in *ClassB*. This layered approach is shown in Figure 7-3.

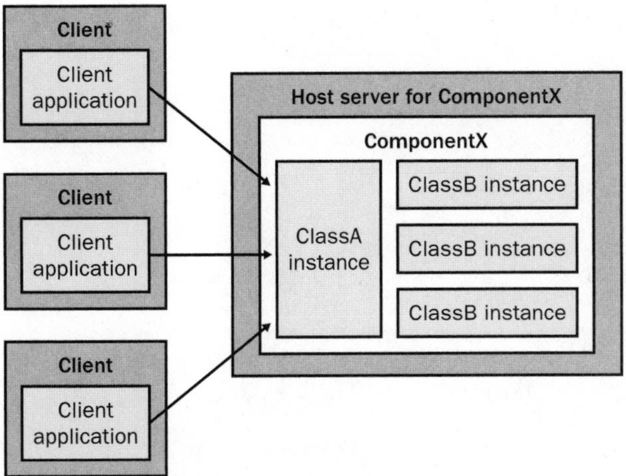

Figure 7-3 Layered singleton design

In a more sophisticated example, the *GetUsageInformation* method might return a collection listing the number of times various methods have been called or might return a custom structure with several pieces of aggregate information. Keep in mind that retaining this information in memory is a good example of how a singleton class works; it isn't a good design choice. In this case, logging information to an external resource (such as a database or event log) is more scalable and durable because the information won't be lost if the component crashes.

Tracking Clients

Another common reason to use the singleton design pattern is to retain client-specific information or even to allow clients to interact. Tracking clients serves two purposes. It enables you to create components that can report on the current user load, or return information about what tasks are currently underway and what clients are connected. To add similar functionality to stateless remote objects, you need to create some sort of shared event log to which each component writes information. The other reason to track clients is to create asynchronous worker services. In this design, clients submit a request for a time-consuming task by calling a method such as *BeginTask* and pick up the results later by calling a method such as *RetrieveTaskResult*. This design can be implemented in an XML Web service or .NET Remoting scenario.

To track clients, *ClassA* needs some sort of collection object. Typically, the *System.Collections.Hashtable* class is the best choice because it can hold any type of object and allows for fast lookup based on a key. This key is some sort of unique value that identifies the client. What you actually store in the *Hashtable* varies, but it might be an instance of the worker *ClassB* that is serving the particular client.

Listing 7-2 shows the bare outline of one possible structure.

```
Imports System.Collections
Imports System.Threading

Public Class ClassA
    Inherits MarshalByRefObject

    ' Tracks clients using this singleton.
    Private ClientTasks As New Hashtable()

    Public Sub StartSomething(clientID As String)

        ' Check if the client already has a task object.
        ' If not, create it.
        Dim Task As ClassB = ClientTasks(clientID)
        If Task Is Nothing Then
            Task = New ClassB()
            ClientTasks(clientID) = Task
        End If

        ' Check if the task is already in progress.
        If Task.InProgress Then
            Throw New InvalidOperationException("Already in progress.")
        Else
            Task.InProgress = True
            Task.Client = clientID

            ' Start the process on another thread.
            Dim TaskThread As New Thread(AddressOf Task.DoSomething)
            Task.ExecutingThread = TaskThread
            TaskThread.Start()
        End If

    End Sub

    Public Function RetrieveResult(clientID As String) As Integer

        ' Check if the task exists and is completed.
        Dim Task As ClassB = ClientTasks(clientID)
        If Task Is Nothing Then
            Throw New InvalidOperationException("No task exists.")
        ElseIf Task.InProgress Then
            Throw New InvalidOperationException("Still in progress.")
        Else
            Return Task.Result
        End If

    End Function
```

Listing 7-2 Client tracking with an asynchronous singleton

```
    Public Sub ReleaseTask(clientID As String)

        Dim Task As ClassB = ClientTasks(clientID)
        If Not (Task Is Nothing) Then

            If (Task.ExecutingThread.ThreadState And _
             ThreadState.Stopped) <> ThreadState.Stopped
                ' We must manually abort the thread.
                Task.ExecutingThread.Abort()
                Task.Join()
            End If

            Task = Nothing
            ClientTasks.Remove(clientID)

        End If

    End Sub

End Class

Public Class ClassB

    Public InProgress As Boolean
    Public Result As Integer

    Public ExecutingThread As Thread
    Public Client As String

    Public Sub DoSomething()
        ' (Code goes here to calculate Result.)

        ' Notify when finished.
        InProgress = False
    End Sub

End Class
```

ClassA acts a dispatcher, creating *ClassB* instances as required and starting them on new threads. If the client calls *RetrieveResult* before the task completes, *ClassB* doesn't wait. Instead, an *InvalidOperationException* is thrown automatically. To get around this limitation, you might want to enhance *ClassB* to include not only a *Result* member variable but also a *Progress* field. The client can then query the progress through a method such as *CheckStatus* in *ClassA*. Alternatively, it might be a more friendly approach to just return *-1* if the result is not yet complete. In either case, you face a common limitation of asynchronous designs: client notification. In an XML Web service, there is no way around this problem because the client cannot accept messages except those returned from a Web method. In a .NET Remoting component, you can use a bidirectional channel and configure the client as a listener, as described in Chapter 4. *ClassB* will then fire an event to *ClassA* to notify that a task had finished, and *ClassA* will notify the client with a callback or another event.

Managing and Cleaning Up Tasks

Our example assumes that the client will release *ClassB* when it completes by calling *ReleaseTask*. If not, the object remains floating in memory endlessly, eventually crippling the server and requiring a server application restart. In our example, the problem is minor because the memory used by *ClassB* is extremely small; this might not always be the case, however, particularly if the component is returning a *DataSet* with a full set of information.

You can improve on this situation by automatically releasing the object when the client retrieves the result, but this still doesn't help if the client disappears and never retrieves the result at all. This is simply not acceptable for a distributed application. To get around it, you need to code your own logic for monitoring in-progress tasks.

A good starting point is to refine the worker class so that it stores the time that the operation began, as shown in Listing 7-3.

```
Public Class ClassB

    Public InProgress As Boolean
    Public Result As Integer

    Public ExecutingThread As Thread
    Public Client As String
    Public StartTime As DateTime

    Public Sub DoSomething()
        StartTime = DateTime.Now
        ' (Code goes here to calculate Result.)

        ' Notify when finished.
        InProgress = False
    End Sub

End Class
```

Listing 7-3 Tracking the task start time

Listing 7-4 shows a sample method that iterates through the *Clients* collection continuously, checking whether any objects are more than 1 hour old.

```
Public Sub CheckClients()

    Dim Limit As TimeSpan = TimeSpan.FromHours(1)

    ' Perform the check.
    Do
        ' Pause briefly.
        Thread.Sleep(TimeSpan.FromMinutes(10))

        Try
            ' Iterate through the collection.
            Dim Task As ClassB
            Dim Item As DictionaryEntry
            For Each Item in ClientTasks
                Task = CType(Item.Value, ClassB)
                If DateTime.Now.Subtract(ClassB.StartTime).TotalMinutes > _
                  Limit.TotalMinutes Then
                    ReleaseTask(ClassB.Client)
                End If
            Next
        Catch
            ' By catching the error, we neutralize it.
            ' The check restarts in ten minutes.
            ' It is a good idea to also log the error, in case
            ' it is a recurring one that is hampering performance.
        End Try
    Loop

End Sub
```

Listing 7-4 Monitoring in-progress tasks

There are two important points about this routine:

- It uses the shared *Thread.Sleep* method to pause execution for 10 minutes after each full check to prevent it from using too many system resources. (Depending on the number of clients, it might make more sense to pause during the iteration, but this is more prone to error if the contents of the collection change while the thread is paused.)
- The entire method is enclosed inside a *Try/Catch* block. This ensures that it can restart the monitoring process even if an error is encountered. Possible errors include checking a *StartTime* value before it is initialized or trying to move to an item in the collection just as it is being removed. Because the *CheckClients* method runs continuously, it is not appropriate to use locking on the *Clients* collection because this would effectively stall other users as they try to register with *ClassA*.

This code should execute on a separate thread, which can be tracked by a member variable:

```
Private MonitorThread As Thread
```

You start this method when *ClassA* is first created:

```
MonitorThread = New Thread(AddressOf Me.CheckClients)
MonitorThread.Priority = ThreadPriority.BelowNormal

' This ensures the thread stops when the main thread terminates.
MonitorThread.IsBackground = True

MonitorThread.Start()
```

Ticket Systems

In the example so far, we've assumed that each client has a unique ID value and that this ID is submitted for every request. This might be the case in a controlled environment in which every user of the component is known. However, this is not likely in a large-scale distributed application. It also exposes obvious potential problems. Clients who submit the wrong ID number might retrieve the results of other users, for example, and there is no way for a single client to start more than one task at a time.

A more common design is to use a ticket system. In this case, a random key is generated for the client when the client first starts the task or logs in to the remote component. You can construct the ticket in a number of ways. One possibility is to use a sequential number. You then keep track of the last issued number in a member variable in *ClassA*. Every time a client makes a request, you increment the number and then use it. To ensure that two clients can't try to increment the number at the same time (and accidentally lead to two clients with the same key), you can use the *System.Threading.Interlocked* class to increment the number, as explained in the preceding chapter. Another approach is to use a random number that has little chance of being duplicated. You can create a number based on the current time (including seconds), for example, and add several random digits to the end.

Both of these ticket-generating systems have a fundamental security flaw, however. With a sequential numbering system, a malicious client can hijack another client's session by guessing the next number. This risk is slightly lessened in the random number situation; because the number is based on the current time, however, a user could guess a valid ticket by issuing several hundred calls. A better approach is to use a statistically unique value such as a globally unique identifier (GUID) for your ticket. GUID values are not related to one another in any kind of sequence and are therefore much more difficult to guess. They correspond to 128-bit integers and are commonly written as a string of lowercase hexadecimal digits in groups of 8, 4, 4, 4, and 12 digits, separated by hyphens. An example is 382C74C3-721D-4F34-80E5-57657B6CBC27. In .NET, you can generate a new GUID by using the *NewGuid* method of the *System.Guid* structure.

Listing 7-5 shows a rewritten *StartSomething* method that uses this technique. Note that it returns the generated key. The client is responsible for holding on to this key and submitting it to the *RetrieveResult* method.

```
Public Function StartSomething() As String

    ' Generate new ticket.
    Dim Ticket As String = Guid.NewGuid().ToString()

    ' Create task and add it to the collection.
    Dim Task As New ClassB()
    ClientTasks(Ticket) = Task

    ' Start the process on another thread.
    Task.InProgress = True
    Task.Client = Ticket
    Dim TaskThread As New Thread(AddressOf Task.DoSomething)
    Task.ExecutingThread = TaskThread
    TaskThread.Start()
    Return Ticket

End Function
```

Listing 7-5 Asynchronous tasks with tickets

> **Note** Ticket-based systems are also used to reduce the cost of authenticating users. This important security technique is covered in depth in Chapter 13. The case study in Chapter 18 also presents ticket-based authentication in a full example and shows how you can create an asynchronous task-based system that doesn't require the complexity of singleton objects.

Locking

The example presented so far is safe only for a single user. To support multiple users, you need to add locking for any shared variables. In this case, the *ClientTasks* collection is the only piece of information shared with all clients.

Before you add locking, it helps to know a little bit about how the *Hashtable* works. The *Hashtable* is designed to support multithreaded access, meaning that an unlimited number of users can read values from the collection at the same time. However, two collection operations aren't considered thread-safe:

- **Writing to the collection** This includes adding a new value or overwriting or removing an existing one.
- **Enumerating through the collection** Because entries can be added or removed while the enumeration is in progress, you might encounter an error (but not data corruption).

To solve the first problem, you just lock the collection before adding the new client task or removing an existing task (as shown in Listing 7-6).

```
Public Function StartSomething() As String

    ' Generate new ticket.
    Dim Ticket As String = Guid.NewGuid().ToString()

    ' Create task and add it to the collection.
    Dim Task As New ClassB()
    SyncLock ClientTasks
        ClientTasks(Ticket) = Task
    End SyncLock

    ' Start the process on another thread.
    Task.InProgress = True
    Task.Client = Ticket
    Dim TaskThread As New Thread(AddressOf Task.DoSomething)
    Task.ExecutingThread = TaskThread
    TaskThread.Start()
    Return Ticket

End Function

Public Sub ReleaseTask(clientID As String)

    Dim Task As ClassB = ClientTasks(clientID)
    If Not (Task Is Nothing) Then

        If Task.ExecutingThread.ThreadState And _
         ThreadState.Stopped <> ThreadState.Stopped
            ' We must manually abort the thread.
            Task.ExecutingThread.Abort()
            Task.ExecutingThread.Join()
        End If

        Task = Nothing
        SyncLock ClientTasks
            ClientTasks.Remove(clientID)
        End SyncLock

    End If

End Sub
```

Listing 7-6 Managing concurrency with locking

Note that this code does not lock the client's *Task* object. It is theoretically possible for more than one client to access the same task (by using the same ticket), but there is no practical reason for this to occur. It's also not necessary to add locking to the *CheckClients* method. Adding this locking can drastically slow down performance because all the new clients would be locked out while the entire collection is scanned. Instead, the *CheckClients* method is prepared to handle an exception resulting from an invalid read.

Instead of using the *SyncLock* statement, you can access a thread-safe wrapper on the collection by using the *Hashtable.Synchronized* method.

```
HashTable.Synchronized(ClientTasks).Remove(clientID)
```

The synchronized version of the collection is just a class that derives from *Hashtable* and that adds the required locking statements. You can easily add this support to your own objects just by creating a derived thread-safe class from an ordinary class.

You might expect that the thread-safe collection would offer the best performance because its locking code has been optimized as required. However, this isn't always the case. For example, if you perform several operations with a synchronized collection, it will acquire and release a lock for each separate operation. If you deal with the basic collection, however, you can acquire a lock and perform a batch of operations all at once, improving overall performance.

Finally, as a matter of good form, it's recommended that when locking a collection that you actually lock the object returned by the *Hashtable.SyncRoot* property. This ensures that even if you are locking on a thread-safe wrapper (such as the one returned through the *Synchronized* property), the underlying collection is still locked, not just the wrapper:

```
SyncLock ClientTasks.SyncRoot
    ' (Do something.)
End SyncLock
```

Advanced Reader-Writer Locking

With collections, you have a better locking choice. You can use the *ReaderWriterLock* from the *System.Threading* namespace, which is optimized to allow a number of readers while locking down write access to a single user. The class provides methods for acquiring and releasing reader and writer locks and for upgrading from a reader lock to a writer lock. The methods for acquiring a lock accept a *TimeSpan* that indicates the maximum wait time.

If you know that your object supports the reader-writer lock semantics, you can dramatically improve concurrency and reduce thread contention by changing from *SyncLock* (and the *Monitor* class) to a *ReaderWriterLock*. First of all, you need to create a member variable in the class that represents the lock:

```
Private ClientTasksLock As New ReaderWriterLock()
```

Listing 7-7 shows the *StartSomething* and *RetrieveResult* methods rewritten in this fashion.

```
Public Function StartSomething() As String

    ' Generate new ticket.
    Dim Ticket As String = Guid.NewGuid().ToString()

    ' Create task and add it to the collection.
    Dim Task As New ClassB()

    ' Specify an infinite wait with the -1 parameter.
    ClientTasksLock.AcquireWriterLock(-1)
    ClientTasks(Ticket) = Task
    ClientTasksLock.ReleaseLock()

    ' Start the process on another thread.
    Task.InProgress = True
    Task.Client = Ticket
    Dim TaskThread As New Thread(AddressOf Task.DoSomething)
    Task.ExecutingThread = TaskThread
    TaskThread.Start()

End Function

Public Function RetrieveResult(clientID As String) As Integer

    ClientTasksLock.AcquireReaderLock(-1)
    Dim Task As ClassB = ClientTasks(clientID)
    ClientTasksLock.ReleaseLock()

    If Task Is Nothing Then
        Throw New InvalidOperationException("No task exists.")
    ElseIf Task.InProgress Then
        Throw New InvalidOperationException("Still in progress.")
    Else
        Return Task.Result
    End If

End Function
```

Listing 7-7 Using reader-writer locking

An XML Web Service Singleton

You can easily adopt the example design pattern in a .NET Remoting scenario by using a component configured as a singleton. In an XML Web service, however, this option doesn't appear. All XML Web services act intrinsically like single-call objects, and separate instances are created for each client. With this hard-wired design, is it possible to create an XML Web service that acts like a singleton?

The short answer is yes. You accomplish this trick by creating the XML Web service as an extra layer. The XML Web service then communicates with a singleton component. There are two possible ways for this communication to take place:

- The XML Web service can communicate with a singleton component over .NET Remoting. This isn't necessarily a bad approach, but it does introduce the overhead of an extra network call, which is not trivial.
- The XML Web service can use a component contained in ASP.NET's application state collection. These objects are global to all Web pages and XML Web services in the Web application.

Using an XML Web service with a singleton enables you to create a task-based service that completes work asynchronously. A full description is outside the scope of this chapter, but you can find an example of this technique at *www.prosetech.com*. In addition, you can refer to Chapter 18 for an example of how to use the asynchronous task-based model *without* a singleton pattern—by storing the task result in a durable data store.

Thread Pools

One problem with the pattern presented so far is that it creates threads indiscriminately. If 10 tasks are underway simultaneously, 10 threads are created. If 100 tasks are requested, the component creates 100 threads, even though this will result in poor performance because the operating system will waste a significant portion of its CPU power just tracking and scheduling all the threads.

Keep in mind that .NET Remoting manages the connection process using its own thread pooling. Therefore, if it receives 100 simultaneous requests, some of these requests will be serialized. In our asynchronous task example, however, even though only a small set of requests might be initiated simultaneously (say, 25 at a time), the tasks continue running after the connection ends. This means that the number of threads can build up without any limit.

You can avoid this problem in several ways. One option is to create your own thread-tracking and thread-processing system. The basic concept is that you don't create a new thread immediately for each client. Instead, you add the information about the client's request to a collection. On a separate thread, another method periodically scans this collection and the current set of tasks, ensuring that new tasks are assigned to existing threads as they become free.

You can even store information about task priority, allowing this monitoring code to make intelligent decisions about which tasks should be processed first. However, this approach requires a major programming project. A better solution is to rely on a special class that .NET provides for this task: the *ThreadPool* class in the *System.Threading* namespace.

The *ThreadPool* class uses a fixed pool of threads to queue tasks. You create work items for the *ThreadPool* class as needed; the number of task items processed simultaneously is automatically limited to 25 per processor, however, because this is the number of threads used. The *ThreadPool* class provides a number of benefits, including a dedicated monitoring thread, reuse of worker threads, and automatic scheduling. However, the *ThreadPool* also introduces a few limitations. First of all, there can only be one *ThreadPool* per application domain. That means that if you use the *ThreadPool* in more than one location in your application to perform more than one type of task, both sets of work items compete for the same limited set of threads. In addition, the *ThreadPool* does not provide any way to prioritize work items or cancel them after they have been submitted.

To find the number of threads allocated to the pool, you can use the shared *ThreadPool.GetMaxThreads* property. To find the number of threads currently free, you can examine the *ThreadPool.GetAvailableThreads* property. To actually queue a work item, you just call the *ThreadPool.QueueUserWorkItem* method with a delegate that points to the method.

Listing 7-8 shows how you would rewrite the *StartSomething* method to use a thread pool.

```
Public Function StartSomething() As String

    ' Generate new ticket.
    Dim Ticket As String = Guid.NewGuid().ToString()

    ' Create task and add it to the collection.
    Dim Task As New ClassB()
    SyncLock ClientTasks
        ClientTasks(Ticket) = Task
    End SyncLock

    ' Queue the task process.
    Task.InProgress = True
    Task.Client = Ticket
    ThreadPool.QueueUserWorkItem( _
      New WaitCallback(AddressOf Task.DoSomething))
    Return Ticket

End Function
```

Listing 7-8 Using a thread pool

> **Note** There's another way to solve this problem. Instead of starting a new thread or queuing a work item when a request is received, you can send a message to a queue. You then have the luxury of retrieving the messages by priority in small batches and deciding how to process them. This approach is described in the next chapter.

Windows Services

Windows services have long been a hot topic in Visual Basic programming circles. The preceding version of the language, Visual Basic 6, included no native support, forcing developers to resort to third-party tools or API wizardry. In the .NET platform, the mystique finally lifts; creating a Windows service is now as easy as creating any other type of application.

Windows services, of course, are long-running applications that have no visual interface and typically work in the background as soon as your computer is started. Services were first introduced with Windows NT and are mediated by the Windows Service Control Manager (SCM). You can start, stop, and configure services through the Computer Management administrative utility.

Services are used to manage everything from core operating system services (such as the distributed transaction coordinator) to long-running engines (such as Microsoft SQL Server and Microsoft Internet Information Services [IIS]). Windows services are ideal for server computers because they enable you to create components that run even while the computer is not logged in. (In fact, it's important to remember that even if a user is logged in, each Windows service runs under a specific fixed account, which is probably not the same as the logged-in user account.) This section shows how you can create a Windows service to use for a long-running task or as a component host.

The .NET support for Windows service applications originates from the *System.ServiceProcess* namespace. The types in this namespace serve three key roles:

- They enable you to create Windows service applications (mainly by deriving a custom class from *ServiceBase*).
- They enable you to install a Windows service (mainly by using *ServiceInstaller* and *ServiceProcessInstaller*).
- They enable you to retrieve information about services installed on the system and programmatically start and stop them (by using *ServiceController*).

Creating a Windows Service

Visual Studio .NET programmers can start by creating a Windows service project. This creates a single class that inherits from *ServiceBase*. This class has the structure shown in Listing 7-9. I've revealed a portion of hidden designer code because it's conceptually important.

```
Imports System.ServiceProcess

Public Class Service1
    Inherits System.ServiceProcess.ServiceBase

    Public Sub New()
        MyBase.New()
        InitializeComponent()
    End Sub

    ' This is the main entry point for the process.
    <MTAThread()> _
    Shared Sub Main()
        ' You could use the method below with an array
        ' of ServiceBase instances to start multiple services in the
        ' same process.
        ServiceBase.Run(New Service1())
    End Sub

    Private Sub InitializeComponent()
        ' (If you have configured Service1 properties at design-time,
        ' the property setting code will be added here.)
        Me.ServiceName = "TestService"
    End Sub

    Protected Overrides Sub OnStart(ByVal args() As String)
        ' Add code here to start your service.
        ' This method might start a timer or a separate thread
        ' before it returns.
    End Sub

    Protected Overrides Sub OnStop()
        ' Add code here to stop your service and release resources.
    End Sub

End Class
```

Listing 7-9 A basic Windows service

When this application is started, the *Main* method runs first. The *Main* method uses the shared *ServiceBase.Run* and passes the new instance of your service. If you want to start multiple services in the same process so they can interact with each other but be stopped and started individually, you can use this method with an array of services, as shown here:

```
Dim ServicesToRun() As ServiceBase
ServicesToRun = New ServiceBase() {New Service1(), New Service2()}
System.ServiceProcess.ServiceBase.Run(ServicesToRun)
```

The *ServiceBase.Run* method doesn't actually start your service—technically, it loads it into memory and provides it to the SCM so that it is *ready* to be executed. What happens next depends on how the service is configured in the SCM. The service itself might be started automatically when the computer boots up, for example, or manually when a user interacts with the Computer Management utility.

When the service is started, the SCM calls the *OnStart* method of your class. However, this method doesn't actually perform the work; instead, it *schedules* the work. If *OnStart* doesn't return after a reasonable amount of time (approximately 30 seconds), the start attempt is abandoned and the service is terminated. Therefore, you shouldn't perform any application-specific processing in the *OnStart* method. Instead, you need to use your *OnStart* method to set up a new thread or timer, which will then perform the real work. Similarly, when the service is stopped, the *OnStop* method is called. This is the point where you will release all in-memory objects and stop the timer or thread processing.

You have two simple tasks to complete to make your Windows service operable. First, you should set all the relevant *ServiceBase* properties. In Visual Studio .NET, you can set these properties using the Properties window in Design view (in which case the property setting code is added to the hidden Windows designer region). Alternatively, you can manually add the property *set* statements to the constructor. Table 7-1 lists the *ServiceBase* properties. Note that properties such as *CanStop* and *CanShutdown* indicate whether a specific feature will be provided to the SCM. If you code the required method but don't set the corresponding property, your code is ignored. Similarly, if you set a property to indicate that your service can perform something it can't, an exception is generated when the command is attempted.

Table 7-1 *ServiceBase* Properties

Property	Description
AutoLog	If this property is *True*, the service uses the Application event log to report command failures and a status message when it is started, stopped, paused, or continued. The name of the service is used as the log's *EventLog.Source*. Alternatively, you can disable this property and use your own custom logging, as discussed in Chapter 14.

Table 7-1 *ServiceBase* Properties

Property	Description
CanHandlePowerEvent	A value of *True* indicates that your service class has overridden the *OnPowerEvent* method to respond to power changes (such as when the computer is suspended).
CanPauseAndContinue	A value of *True* indicates that your service class has overridden the *OnPause* and *OnContinue* methods and therefore supports pausing and continuing.
CanShutdown	A value of *True* indicates that your service class has overridden the *OnShutdown* method to respond when the computer is being powered off.
CanStop	A value of *True* indicates that your service class has overridden the *OnStop* method and therefore supports stopping. As a bare minimum, most services support this feature.
EventLog	Provides a convenient place to store an *EventLog* reference. You can use this log to write additional, custom log messages. Note that this log will not be used by the autologging feature.
ServiceName	The short name used to identify your service.

Next, you need to add the logic to the *OnStart* and *OnStop* methods. In Listing 7-10, this service just starts a thread that writes debug information. Note that you don't need to call the base *OnStart* or *OnStop ServiceBase* methods in your overridden methods because this happens automatically.

```
Imports System.ServiceProcess
Imports System.Threading

Public Class TestService
    Inherits System.ServiceProcess.ServiceBase

    Public Sub New()
        MyBase.New()
        InitializeComponent()
    End Sub

    <MTAThread()> _
    Shared Sub Main()
        ServiceBase.Run(New TestService())
    End Sub

    Private Sub InitializeComponent()
```

Listing 7-10 A test service with threading

```
        Me.ServiceName = "TestService"
    End Sub

    Private ServiceThread As Thread
    Private StopThread As Boolean = False

    Protected Overrides Sub OnStart(ByVal args() As String)
        ServiceThread = New Thread(AddressOf DoWork)
        ServiceThread.Start()
    End Sub

    Protected Overrides Sub OnStop()
        ' We only have 30 seconds to act before the SCM takes matters
        ' into its own hands.

        ' Try to signal the thread to end nicely,
        ' (and wait up to 20 seconds).
        StopThread = True
        ServiceThread.Join(TimeSpan.FromSeconds(20))

        ' If the thread is still running, abort it.
        If ServiceThread.ThreadState And _
          ThreadState.Running = ThreadState.Running Then
            ServiceThread.Abort()
            ServiceThread.Join()
        End If
    End Sub

    Private Sub DoWork()
        Dim Counter As Integer
        Do Until StopThread
            Counter += 1
            Debug.WriteLine("Now Starting Iteration #" & _
              Counter.ToString())
            Thread.Sleep(TimeSpan.FromSeconds(10))
        Loop
    End Sub

End Class
```

Alternatively, you can start a timer (using the *System.Timers.Timer* class), which fires at periodic intervals. A timer is best suited for a short, repeated task, whereas a thread can handle a long-running, continuous task that works through several stages. Listing 7-11 shows an example that uses a custom timer to perform a task.

```
Imports System.ServiceProcess
Imports System.Timers

Public Class TestService
    Inherits System.ServiceProcess.ServiceBase

    Public Sub New()
        MyBase.New()
        InitializeComponent()
    End Sub

    <MTAThread()> _
    Shared Sub Main()
        ServiceBase.Run(New TestService())
    End Sub

    Private Sub InitializeComponent()
        Me.ServiceName = "TestService"
    End Sub

    Private WithEvents ServiceTimer As New Timer(10000)
    Private Counter As Integer

    Protected Overrides Sub OnStart(ByVal args() As String)
        ServiceTimer.Start()
    End Sub

    Protected Overrides Sub OnStop()
        ServiceTimer.Stop()
    End Sub

    Private Sub DoWork(ByVal sender As Object, _
      ByVal e As ElapsedEventArgs) Handles ServiceTimer.Elapsed
        Counter += 1
        Debug.WriteLine("Now Starting Iteration #" & _
          Counter.ToString())
    End Sub

End Class
```

Listing 7-11 A timer-based service

A third option is to not use a timer or thread but use some sort of event handler. For example, you can create a *System.IO.FileSystemWatcher* instance to monitor a directory. The *OnStart* method will connect the handler, and the *OnStop* method will disconnect it. Chapter 16 presents a case study that uses a long-running Windows service to perform directory monitoring.

> **Note** Most services support stopping and starting. When a service stops, any data held in form-level variables should be completely released and the *OnStart* method should perform the required initialization from scratch. If your service retains a significant amount of information, however, you might want to implement *OnPause* and *OnContinue* in addition to *OnStart* and *OnStop*. The pause method will then stop the timer or thread from processing, but it will retain all the state information. The continue method will then resume processing immediately, without requiring any initialization. This pattern isn't used in the example because no significant information is retained while the service is working.

Installing a Windows Service

Unfortunately, Windows service applications cannot be debugged inside Visual Studio .NET because they are controlled by the SCM. To test your service, you first need to create an installer.

The easiest approach is to let Visual Studio .NET perform some of the work for you. Just click your service code file, put it in Design view, and select the Add Installer link that displays in the Properties window (as shown in Figure 7-4).

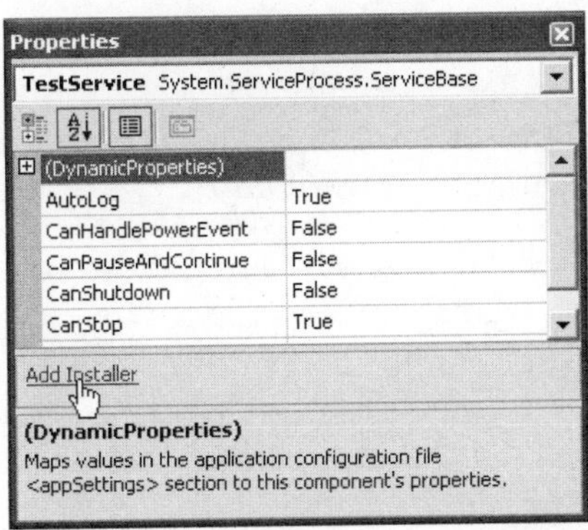

Figure 7-4 Adding an installer in Visual Studio .NET

A new ProjectInstaller.vb file is added to your project. This file contains all the code required to install the service. This installer uses two installer components that are automatically added to the design-time view: *ServiceProcessInstaller1* and *ServiceInstaller1* (as shown in Figure 7-5).

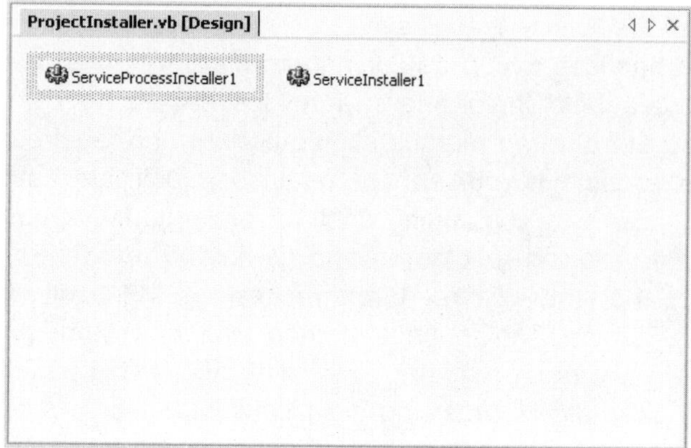

Figure 7-5 The installer components

Taken together, these classes encapsulate the installation process. When included in a setup project, the Windows installer automatically calls the *Install* method of both classes. The classes then write the required Registry information.

Before continuing further, you might want to make two minor modifications:

- The *ServiceProcessInstaller* provides an *Account* property. Set this to *LocalSystem* so that the service runs under a system account rather than the account of the currently logged-in user. (In this case, only an administrator can run the installer.) Alternatively, you can specify the username and password for a specific account.
- The *ServiceInstaller* provides a *StartType* property, which is set to *Manual* by default. If you want to install this service and configure it to start automatically, set this property to *Automatic*.

You can also change these details later by modifying the configuration settings for the service in the Computer Management utility.

The project installer class is very simple and performs most of its work automatically using the functionality it gains from the *Installer* class in the *System.Configuration.Install* namespace (as shown in Listing 7-12).

```
Imports System.Configuration.Install
Imports System.ServiceProcess

<RunInstaller(True)> Public Class ProjectInstaller
    Inherits System.Configuration.Install.Installer

    Public Sub New()
        MyBase.New()
```

Listing 7-12 A sample Windows service installer

```
        InitializeComponent()
    End Sub

    Friend ServiceProcessInstaller1 As ServiceProcessInstaller
    Friend ServiceInstaller1 As ServiceInstaller

    Private Sub InitializeComponent()
        Me.ServiceProcessInstaller1 = New ServiceProcessInstaller()
        Me.ServiceInstaller1 = New ServiceInstaller()

        Me.ServiceProcessInstaller1.Account = _
          ServiceAccount.LocalSystem
        Me.ServiceInstaller1.ServiceName = "TestService"

        ' Add the two installers.
        Me.Installers.AddRange(New Installer() _
         {Me.ServiceProcessInstaller1, Me.ServiceInstaller1})
    End Sub

End Class
```

You can incorporate this installer into a custom setup project, or you can use the InstallUtil.exe utility included with Visual Studio .NET. To do so, build your project, browse to the Bin directory using a command-line window, and type the following instruction (where *WindowsService1* is the name of your application):

```
InstallUtil WindowsService1.exe
```

The output for a successful install operation is shown here:

```
Microsoft (R) .NET Framework Installation utility Version 1.0.3512.0
Copyright (C) Microsoft Corporation 1998-2001. All rights reserved.

Running a transacted installation.

Beginning the Install phase of the installation.
See the contents of the log file for the
 e:\windowsservice1\bin\windowsservice1.exe assembly's progress.
The file is located at e:\windowsservice1\bin\windowsservice1.InstallLog.

Installing assembly 'e:\windowsservice1\bin\windowsservice1.exe'.
Affected parameters are:
   assemblypath = e:\windowsservice1\bin\windowsservice1.exe
   logfile = e:\windowsservice1\bin\windowsservice1.InstallLog

Installing service TestService...
Service TestService has been successfully installed.
```

```
Creating EventLog source TestService in log Application...

The Install phase completed successfully, and the Commit phase is beginning.
See the contents of the log file for the
 e:\windowsservice1\bin\windowsservice1.exe assembly's progress.
The file is located at e:\windowsservice1\bin\windowsservice1.InstallLog.

Committing assembly 'e:\windowsservice1\bin\windowsservice1.exe'.
Affected parameters are:
   assemblypath = e:\windowsservice1\bin\windowsservice1.exe
   logfile = e:\windowsservice1\bin\windowsservice1.InstallLog

The Commit phase completed successfully.

The transacted install has completed.
```

You can now find and start the service using the Computer Management administrative tool (as shown in Figure 7-6).

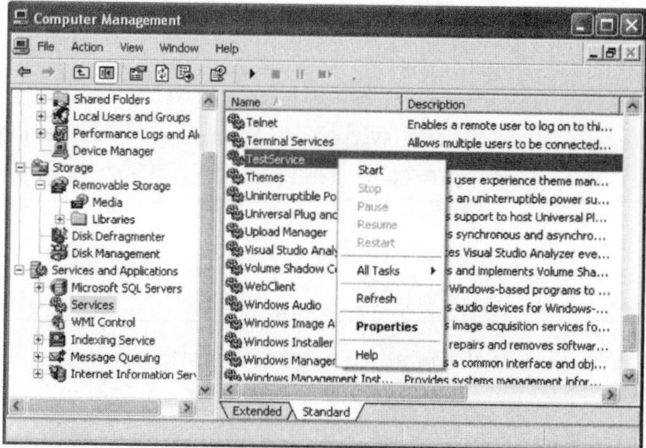

Figure 7-6 The installed service

If you want to update the service, you need to recompile the executable, uninstall the existing service, and then reinstall the new service. To uninstall a service, just use the */u* parameter with *InstallUtil*:

```
InstallUtil WindowsService1.exe /u
```

Debugging a Windows Service

Even though you can't run a Windows service in Visual Studio .NET, it is still possible to debug it with the IDE. You just need to attach to the service after it is already started. Visual Studio .NET then enables you to set breakpoints and single-step through the code.

To attach to a service, begin by loading the appropriate project into Visual Studio .NET. That way, the source code will already be available. Then make sure that the service is installed and currently started by the SCM.

Choose Tools | Debug Processes, and in the Processes window (shown in Figure 7-7) be sure to enable the Show System Processes check box if you are running your service under a system account; otherwise, it won't appear in the list. When you find the matching service, select it by clicking the Attach button.

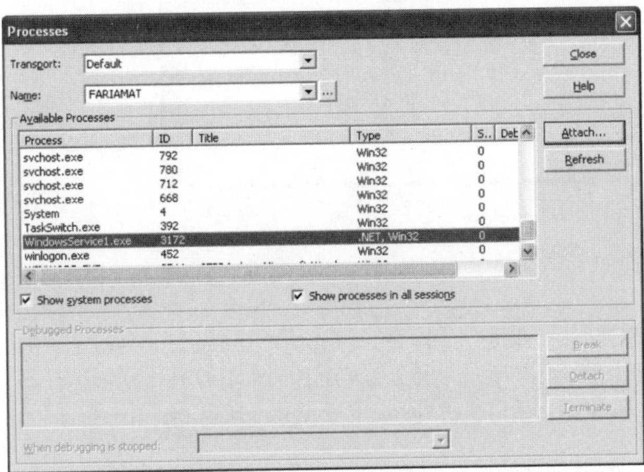

Figure 7-7 Attaching the debugger to a service

In the Attach To Process window, choose to debug the code as a Common Language Runtime application (as shown in Figure 7-8). Then click OK.

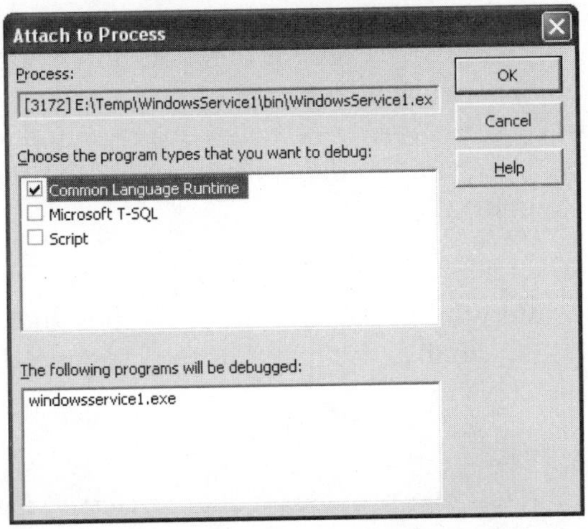

Figure 7-8 Choosing the application type

You are now free to set breakpoints, pause execution, and create variable watches. If you have created the simple debugging service presented previously, some basic information will begin to appear in the Debug window (as shown in Figure 7-9).

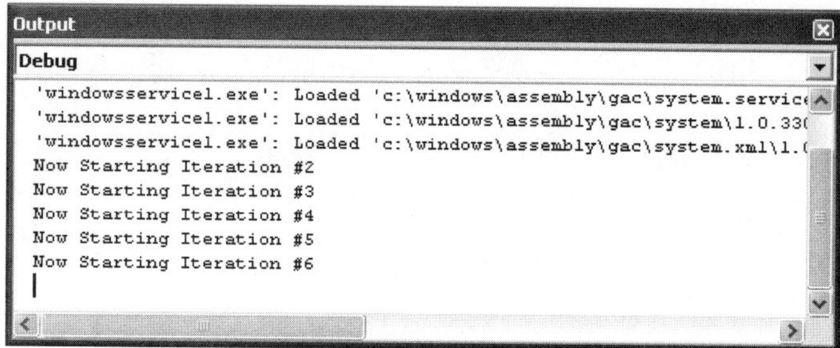

Figure 7-9 Debugging the service

> **Note** The SCM provides only 30 seconds for you to set *OnStart* and *OnStop* breakpoints. If you set a breakpoint and allow the code to be paused for a longer period of time, the service is terminated.

Controlling Windows Services

You don't need to use an administrative tool to start and stop your services. In fact, you can interact directly with services using the *ServiceController* class. This is a useful technique if you want to create your own administrative tool that will monitor your custom services on various computers and that will enable you to manage them from a single location.

For example, you can create a *ServiceController* object bound to a specific service by specifying the service name in the constructor (or the service name and machine name, for a remote service).

```
Dim TestService As New ServiceController("TestService")
```

You are then free to query information from properties such as *Status*, *CanStop*, and *ServiceType*. You can also use methods to programmatically start, stop, pause, or continue the service:

```
TestService.Stop()
```

The *ServiceController* class also provides a shared *GetServices* method, which returns an array of *ServiceController* instances representing all the services on a single computer. You can use this technique to create a simple service manager, as shown in Figure 7-10.

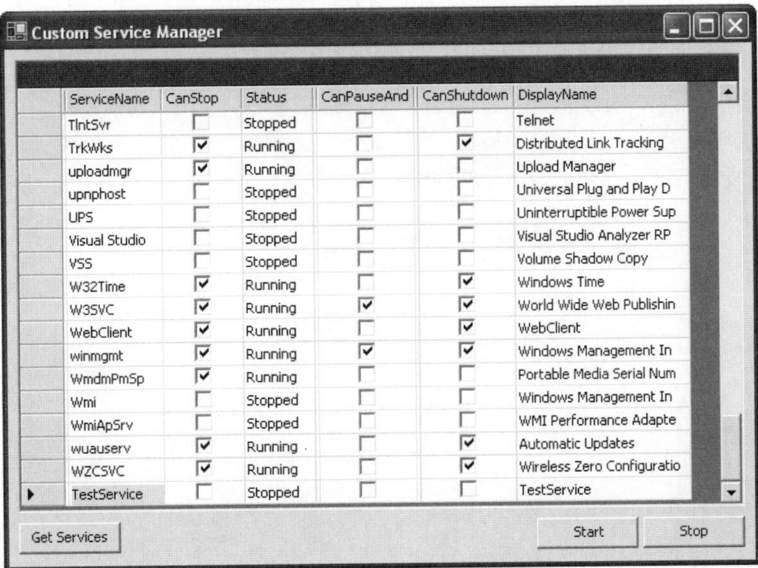

ServiceName	CanStop	Status	CanPauseAnd	CanShutdown	DisplayName
TlntSvr	☐	Stopped	☐	☐	Telnet
TrkWks	☑	Running	☐	☑	Distributed Link Tracking
uploadmgr	☑	Running	☐	☐	Upload Manager
upnphost	☐	Stopped	☐	☐	Universal Plug and Play D
UPS	☐	Stopped	☐	☐	Uninterruptible Power Sup
Visual Studio	☐	Stopped	☐	☐	Visual Studio Analyzer RP
VSS	☐	Stopped	☐	☐	Volume Shadow Copy
W32Time	☑	Running	☐	☑	Windows Time
W3SVC	☑	Running	☑	☑	World Wide Web Publishin
WebClient	☑	Running	☐	☑	WebClient
winmgmt	☑	Running	☑	☑	Windows Management In
WmdmPmSp	☑	Running	☐	☐	Portable Media Serial Num
Wmi	☐	Stopped	☐	☐	Windows Management In
WmiApSrv	☐	Stopped	☐	☐	WMI Performance Adapte
wuauserv	☑	Running	☐	☑	Automatic Updates
WZCSVC	☑	Running	☐	☑	Wireless Zero Configuratio
TestService	☐	Stopped	☐	☐	TestService

Figure 7-10 A custom application for controlling services

This application simply fills a *DataGrid* with a list of services and enables the user to stop or start a selected service. Listing 7-13 shows the form code.

```
Imports System.ServiceProcess

Public Class ServiceManager
    Inherits System.Windows.Forms.Form

    ' (Windows designer code omitted.)

    Friend WithEvents cmdGetServices As System.Windows.Forms.Button
    Friend WithEvents gridServices As System.Windows.Forms.DataGrid
    Friend WithEvents cmdStart As System.Windows.Forms.Button
    Friend WithEvents cmdStop As System.Windows.Forms.Button

    Private Sub cmdGetServices_Click(ByVal sender As System.Object, _
      ByVal e As System.EventArgs) Handles cmdGetServices.Click
        RefreshServices()
    End Sub

    Private Sub cmdStart_Click(ByVal sender As System.Object, _
      ByVal e As System.EventArgs) Handles cmdStart.Click
        If gridServices.CurrentRowIndex > 0 Then
            Dim ServiceName = _
              gridServices.Item(gridServices.CurrentRowIndex, 1)
            Dim Service As New ServiceController(ServiceName)
            Service.Start()
```

Listing 7-13 Managing active services

```
            ' Refresh the display
            RefreshServices()
        End If
    End Sub

    Private Sub cmdStop_Click(ByVal sender As System.Object, _
      ByVal e As System.EventArgs) Handles cmdStop.Click
        If gridServices.CurrentRowIndex > 0 Then
            Dim ServiceName = _
              gridServices.Item(gridServices.CurrentRowIndex, 1)
            Dim Service As New ServiceController(ServiceName)
            Service.Stop()

            ' Refresh the display
            RefreshServices()
        End If
    End Sub

    Private Sub RefreshServices()
        gridServices.DataSource = ServiceController.GetServices()
    End Sub

End Class
```

Note Our example duplicates the basic functionality of the Computer Management utility. To make it truly useful, you can change it to work with a coordinator XML Web service that provides methods such as *RegisterWindowsService* and *GetRegisteredWindowsServices*. Your Windows service can call the *RegisterWindowsService* method when it first starts and then add information about the service and the computer name to a central database. The monitoring utility can call *GetRegisteredWindowsServices* to retrieve the full list of running services. A similar approach is developed in Chapter 11 with remote components.

Using a Windows Service for a Component Host

Now that you have a firm grasp of Windows service programming and how to interact with the SCM, you're ready to adapt the design to a component host.

The code in Listing 7-14 is quite simple: The idea is that you start listening for client connections when *OnStart* is triggered, and you stop listening when *OnStop* is executed.

```
Imports System.ServiceProcess
Imports System.Runtime.Remoting
Imports System.Runtime.Remoting.Channels

Public Class DBComponentHost
    Inherits System.ServiceProcess.ServiceBase

    Public Sub New()
        MyBase.New()
        InitializeComponent()
    End Sub

    <MTAThread()> _
    Shared Sub Main()
        ServiceBase.Run(New TestService())
    End Sub

    Private Sub InitializeComponent()
        Me.ServiceName = "DBComponentHost"
    End Sub

    ' Register the service.
    Protected Overrides Sub OnStart(ByVal args() As String)
        RemotingConfiguration.Configure("SimpleServer.exe.config")
    End Sub

    ' Remove all the listening channels.
    Protected Overrides Sub OnStop()
        Dim Channel As IChannel
        For Each Channel In ChannelServices.RegisteredChannels
            Try
                ChannelServices.UnregisterChannel(Channel)
            Catch
                ' Ignore any channel errors.
            End Try
        Next
    End Sub

End Class
```

Listing 7-14 A Windows service component host

Summary

This chapter covered one of the thornier avenues of custom programming: designing your own singleton components. We looked at the fundamentals, including tracking clients, synchronizing resources, and using custom scheduling and pooling algorithms. However, creating a singleton object that's efficient and robust enough to use in an enterprise system is no small feat. The material covered in this chapter is the essential groundwork, but it doesn't provide the enhancements and experience you'll need to tailor a singleton component to your needs. For some practical examples that bring together threading, multiple clients, and asynchronous task processing, refer to the case studies in the third part of this book.

Finally, we finished up the chapter with a look at creating, installing, and programmatically controlling Windows services.

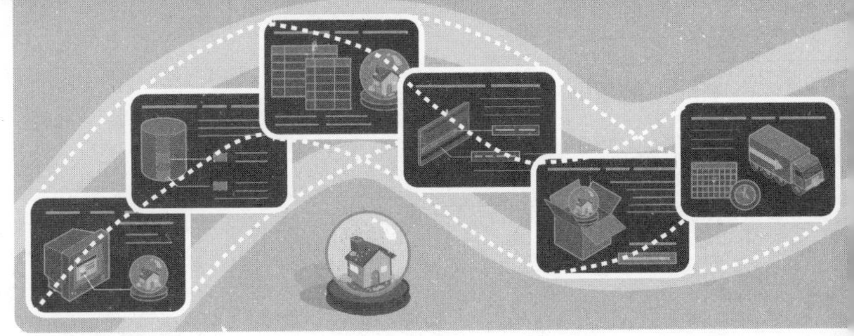

8

Messaging (Lightweight Communication)

In a distributed system, computers are bound together by connections that have widely different characteristics and capabilities. For example, users on an internal network typically have direct, guaranteed access to one or more local servers. They can benefit from proprietary protocols and communicate efficiently over TCP/IP sockets with Microsoft .NET Remoting. Clients that connect over the Internet, however, require different considerations. They are more likely to rely on HTTP and a cross-platform data exchange format such as SOAP. Some users, however, such as those with a dial-up connection or those who use a laptop, can't assume a guaranteed connection of any kind. They might need to perform at least some of their work while disconnected from the rest of the system. In this scenario, the clients can't use XML Web services or .NET Remoting directly. Instead, they need messaging services.

Of course, messaging isn't just a tool to support disconnected clients. It can also ensure scalability and high performance for a large-scale system. Messaging is often described as "lightweight communication" because it allows clients to work asynchronously, sending requests but never waiting for responses. Messaging can also give you the flexibility to even out peak loads and process requests in batches when server hardware is otherwise idle (for example, late at night).

This chapter begins by considering messaging as a natural extension of the asynchronous communication pattern introduced in Chapter 6. We'll look at how you can create true fire-and-forget methods for XML Web services and .NET Remoting components without requiring an asynchronous consumer. Next, and for the majority of the chapter, we'll explore Microsoft Message

Queuing, the messaging service that's built into the Microsoft Windows operating system. We'll also consider when (and where) message queues make most sense in a distributed application.

The Role of Messaging in a Distributed System

Conceptually, Message Queuing is quite simple. Ordinary interaction with an object works like a telephone call: both the client and server participate in a real-time exchange of information. Calling a remote component or XML Web service is conceptually the same.

Technically, an XML Web service call is an exchange of a request and response message. In the .NET way of thinking, these two steps are tightly bound together into a single operation. The proxy class sends a request message and stops to wait for a response message before execution can continue. This guarantees that a certain unit of time is always spent waiting for the server to complete its work.

Messaging is more like sending a fax or an e-mail. A message is sent, and no response is returned (although one might be expected at a later time). The recipient is free to deal with the message immediately or ignore it entirely. The client continues independently, without being notified about the success of the operation or its outcome. However, some messaging services can provide features such as guaranteed delivery or message confirmation for critical tasks.

Clearly, messaging is poorly suited to tasks in which the client needs an immediate answer. However, messaging is ideal in situations where the client just needs to trigger an action or submit a request. When used for this purpose, messaging is fast and efficient because no waiting is required. Messaging is also extremely scalable because an application can receive dozens of messages in an instant and set them all aside for later processing. The message recipient has the luxury of choosing how and when to deal with the received messages. In return, clients don't have to worry about being tied up waiting for a long call to complete if the server is already dealing with several other requests.

Some ideal scenarios for messaging include the following:

- **Submitting an order** Before a typical order can be shipped, a credit check must be made, an inventory check must be made, and a shipping date must be set. These steps can take time. Using messaging ensures that orders aren't lost and client applications aren't delayed in peak times. If the server is in high demand for other tasks, you can even perform all the work during off-hours.

- **Submitting information** For example, a workstation might regularly send data to a remote component, which will be collected and analyzed later. A specialized example of this pattern is with a scientific surveying/monitoring tool that periodically sends a measurement. The method that receives this data is an ideal candidate for a fire-and-forget method.
- **A work-request system** With asynchronous messaging, the server-side component can decide what requests to process first (perhaps depending on the priority) and where to store the information (perhaps in a back-end database). However, there's no way to issue a ticket, so clients will need to supply their own identifiers.

Fire-and-Forget Communication

The first type of messaging we'll consider is fire-and-forget methods, which are supported intrinsically by .NET Remoting and XML Web services. With fire-and-forget methods, the client sends a request message but the server never responds. Therefore, the remote method can't set a *ByRef* parameter or return a value. In addition, if the remote method throws an unhandled exception, it won't be propagated back to the client.

To create a fire-and-forget XML Web service method, you need to apply a *SoapDocumentMethod* attribute to the appropriate Web method and set the *OneWay* property to *True*. Listing 8-1 shows an example.

```
Imports System.Web.Services
Imports System.Web.Services.Protocols

Public Class Stats
    Inherits WebService

    <SoapDocumentMethod(OneWay := True), _
     WebMethod()> _
    Public Sub DoLongTask()
        ' Starts a long database task that doesn't return
        ' information to the client.
    End Sub

End Class
```

Listing 8-1 A one-way Web method

To create a fire-and-forget *Remoting* method, you need to apply the *OneWay* attribute. Listing 8-2 shows an equivalent example for a remote component.

```
Imports System.Runtime.Remoting.Messaging

Public Class Stats
    Inherits MarshalByRefObject

    <OneWay()> _
    Public Sub DoLongTask()
        ' Starts a long database task that doesn't return
        ' information to the client.
    End Sub

End Class
```

Listing 8-2 A one-way method over .NET Remoting

Both of these attributes are often overlooked when developers design distributed systems. If you don't need to return information directly to a client, these methods offer a better option than just calling a normal method asynchronously. Why? Here are the reasons:

- With an asynchronous call, the responsibility falls on the client. If the client neglects to call the method asynchronously, a long wait might be incurred. With one-way methods, client calls are always asynchronous.
- With an asynchronous call, the client waits for a response, but on a separate thread from the rest of the application. With one-way methods, the connection is completely severed after the request and incurs no additional overhead.
- With one-way methods, the client won't receive an unhandled exception. This is generally the desired behavior because the client might not understand the significance of a specific low-level exception and will probably not be able to correct it.

Of course, messaging is not suited for all scenarios. For example, a one-way method has no way to inform the client whether the submitted information is invalid.

You should also remember that one-way methods don't use a dedicated messaging service. They can solve the problem of long method calls that would otherwise tie up clients, but they can't solve the problems of heavy client loads, where requests are received faster than they can be processed. To deal with this reality, you need Message Queuing.

Do One-Way Methods Make Good Event Handlers?

Developers are sometimes advised to use one-way methods with applications that receive events or callbacks over .NET Remoting. The idea is that if you use one-way methods, the server can fire the event without worrying that an unhandled exception on the client end might propagate back to the server. The server also won't be tied up waiting for the client method to finish.

The reality isn't quite as simple. One-way methods are great event handlers if only two parties (one sender and one recipient) are involved. If you're using a singleton component that fires an event to multiple clients, however, they might not be as well suited. This is because the server won't be notified of an error if it attempts to send an event to a one-way method, even if this error occurs because the client has disconnected. If your singleton runs continuously for several days, it might build up a long list of disconnected clients and it will try to send events to all of them, slowing down the overall system performance.

In this case, it is better not to use one-way methods. In fact, it's also better not to use events and to instead communicate with the client through delegates. The server can then store a collection of client delegate references. Every time the singleton component needs to fire an event, it can loop through its collection of delegates and attempt to invoke each one. If an exception is generated, it can just catch the exception and remove the delegate from the collection and thereby clean up disconnected client references.

Introducing Message Queuing

Message Queuing (formerly named MSMQ) is Microsoft's foray into the world of messaging services. Message Queuing first made its appearance as an add-on in an option pack for Windows NT. Message Queuing 2.0, which added support for Active Directory, made its debut with Windows 2000; Windows XP introduced a largely similar Message Queuing 3.0, which includes the added ability to easily send a message to a queue over the Internet in a SOAP package and to forward messages to multiple recipients.

As with all optional Windows components, before you attempt to use Message Queuing, verify that you have it installed by opening the Add/Remove

Windows Components dialog box. As a rule, I try to avoid discussing software setup for Microsoft servers and components in this book because in most large-scale systems, dedicated system administrators will work with developers to create the required environment. However, a brief discussion of Message Queuing installation is important because it is a common source of confusion.

Essentially, you can install Message Queuing in three "modes," as described in the following sections.

> **Note** The MSDN Reference includes information about Message Queuing, but it might not be tailored to the version you're using. For information about setup and configuration, refer to the Message Queuing branch of the Microsoft Management Console (MMC) for help. You can find this information if you press F1 after selecting a queue in Computer Manager.

Message Queuing Server

A Message Queuing server is a dedicated computer that hosts the message queues for your application. A Message Queuing server can be created only on a Windows 2000 Server, Windows 2000 Advanced Server, or Windows .NET Server. Ultimately, you will want to use a Message Queuing server to centralize the queues used in your system so they can be accessed, administered, secured, and protected from a single point.

Ideally, your Message Queuing server will also have Active Directory installed. This provides at least two key benefits:

- **You can use public queues.** That means clients can search for a queue. Otherwise, they must locate the queue using the correct queue and server name—and if you move a queue to another machine, the client application needs to be modified.
- **You can secure your queue with an access control list (ACL).** Queue authentication is quite fine-grained and can prevent users from reading from, sending to, or configuring a specific queue.

Dependent Client

If you have configured a Message Queuing server, you can also create a dependent client. The dependent client can't work in a disconnected environment because it does not have a message store. Instead, it forwards all messages directly to the server (using a special proxy mechanism that's built into Windows). Dependent clients are useful if you want to ensure that messages can't be sent if the server isn't online. Dependent clients are generally less robust and less common than independent clients because they can't weather network problems.

You can configure any Windows 2000 or Windows XP computer to be a dependent client. However, the Message Queuing server and Windows 2000 domain controller must exist before you install the Message Queuing components on the client.

Independent Client

Independent clients can send messages while being connected to a server or without a connection, in which case the message is stored locally until the connection returns. This is a particularly useful trick for laptop users because it enables them to perform work while disconnected and automatically forwards all the appropriate messages when they connect later. This mode of operation is supported by Windows 2000 and Windows XP (but not the server versions) and is also a likely candidate for development testing.

Multiple independent clients can send messages to each other's queues in a workgroup environment, provided they know the computer name and queue name. However, they forgo the ability to look up queues or enforce any type of Windows 2000 queue authentication.

Message Queuing Basics

Database products such as Microsoft SQL Server divide information into multiple databases that contain multiple tables. Message queues separate information into distinct queues that are usually associated with different operations or tasks. For example, an e-commerce program might read order information from a *ProductOrders* queue, and a data-mining component might read from a *RequestedTasks* queue. By default, all queues are stored in the directory C:\[Windows Dir]\System32\Storage of the host computer. Outgoing messages that haven't yet been sent might be stored in memory or they might also be found in the Storage directory on the sending computer, depending on the requested transmission method. Figure 8-1 shows a simplified diagram of Message Queuing.

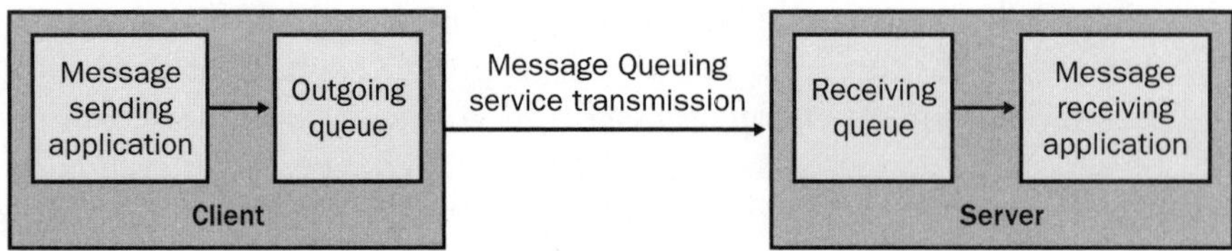

Figure 8-1 Message transmission with Message Queuing

Types of Message Queues

To perform its work, Message Queuing requires several types of message queues. The following sections introduce each one briefly.

Public Queues

Public queues are published in an Active Directory listing and are replicated across a Windows 2000 domain. You can browse or search for a public queue without knowing the name of the computer that hosts it (and therefore you can also move a queue from one computer to another without affecting the client).

Private Queues

Private queues can be used in a workgroup environment without a dedicated Message Queuing server, they don't support authentication, and they can't be located without the computer name. These queues are used most often for development testing before a full deployment or for small-scale use.

Outgoing Queues

Outgoing queues are local internal queues that are used to store messages before they are sent to the destination (remote) queue. Messages can be stored for long periods of time in an outgoing queue if the computer is off line, and they will be automatically sent when connectivity is reestablished. Outgoing queues are generated automatically and can't be created or deleted manually.

Connector Queues

Connector queues reside on Message Queuing servers. They act as a proxy for queues provided by other computers and managed by other messaging systems. For example, you can use Microsoft's MSMQ-MQSeries Bridge (included with the Host Integration Server 2000 product), which allows your .NET applications to interact with IBM MQSeries queues. Similarly, you can use the Microsoft Message Queuing Connector (MQC), which allows connectivity with computers running Message Queuing on non-Windows-based platforms such as UNIX or AS/400. Connector queues handle message transition seamlessly and allow an application to use a foreign queue in the same way it uses an ordinary Message Queuing queue. Without connector queues, there is no interoperability between different Message Queuing products.

Journal Queues

Journal queues contain copies of messages that have been sent or processed, for future reference. There are two types of journaling: source and target.

When sending a message, the sender can elect to use journaling to store a copy of the message on the current computer. Source journaling is therefore controlled on a per-message basis. Target journaling is set on a per-queue basis. If a destination queue has journaling enabled, it stores a copy of every message it receives in a separate journal queue.

Dead-Letter Queues

Dead-letter queues contain messages that expired without being successfully delivered. In some cases, the message might have expired after being forwarded to another computer (or even arriving at the target), in which case it is placed in the dead-letter queue of the computer where it was when it expired. Messages for transactional queues (discussed later in this chapter) are stored in a separate transactional dead-letter queue.

What makes a message undeliverable? A number of factors can intervene, including the following:

- The queue is full, cannot be found, or is not known to the sender.
- A nontransactional message was sent to a transactional queue, or vice-versa.
- The message exceeds its maximum number of allowed hops or its maximum allowed lifetime. For example, it might have exceeded the time-to-reach-queue (TTRQ) limit (which is set by the sender) or its time-to-be-received (TTBR) limit (which the recipient sets).

Administration Queues

Administration queues just store acknowledgement messages (for example, messages that confirm that another message was received). They shouldn't be confused with internal private queues, which Message Queuing uses behind the scenes to manage other queues and record diagnostic information. This chapter does not discuss internal queues.

Report Queues

The report queue is used to track the route a sent message takes if message route tracking is enabled. There can only be one report queue per computer.

The Message Queue Service

If you're new to Message Queuing, you're probably wondering about the underlying technology that drives it. Basically, Message Queuing uses a Windows service to dispatch and receive messages. You can find the service listed, like all others, in the Computer Management utility (as shown in Figure 8-2). This service actually has a fair bit of responsibility, including reading from queues, writing to queues, and working across the network with other Message Queuing services to route messages to their destination.

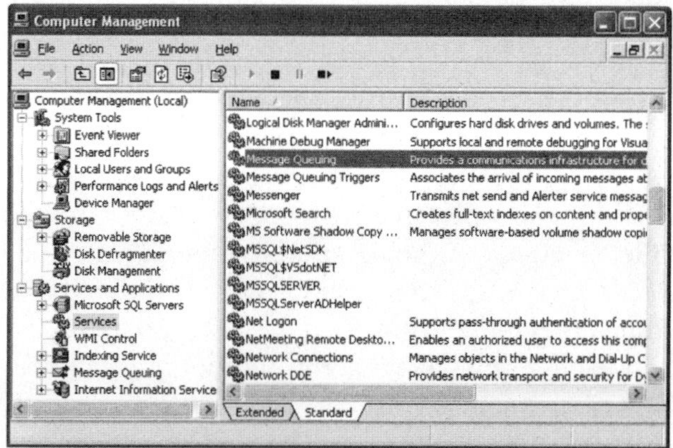

Figure 8-2 The Message Queuing service

Configuring Message Queues

You can perform every Message Queuing task, including creating and removing queues, from a .NET application. In the majority of cases, however, you will create your queues manually with the Computer Management tool and then use .NET code just for sending messages. This is much the same way you would use a server-side database.

You can configure queues by expanding the Message Queuing node under the Services And Application node. You can right-click on a queue category folder to create a new queue for your application. You'll be prompted to enter a queue name and indicate whether the queue is transactional. Transactional queues ensure that messages arrive in the same order they were sent (and hence the message priority is ignored). Transactional queues also guarantee that messages arrive only once. Transactional message queues do *not* enlist the message sending and message receiving into a single atomic operation, as you might assume. Even with transactional queues, Message Queuing uses a disconnected model in which send and receive operations are decoupled from one another.

After creating a queue, you can right-click and modify its properties (as shown in Figure 8-3).

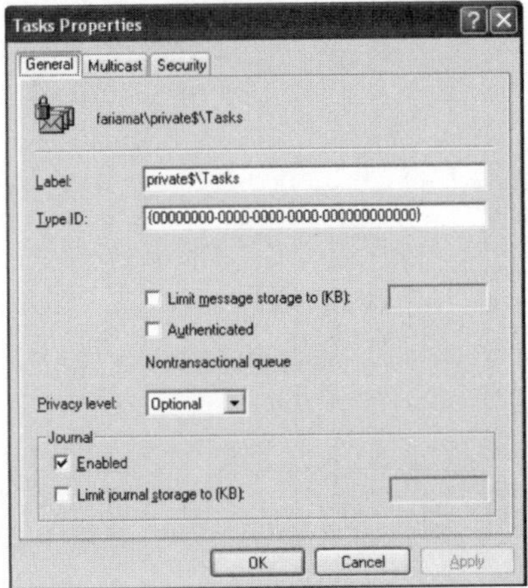

Figure 8-3 Message queue properties

The options you can configure include the following:

- **Label** A string that can identify the queue to allow easy searching.
- **Type ID** Enables you to group multiple queues into a category with a shared GUID. You can generate a GUID using a tool such as guidgen.exe or uuidgen.exe; these are included with the .NET Framework.
- **Maximum Size** Ensures that you won't fill a disk with messages. Otherwise, Windows XP allows unlimited message storing, and Windows 2000 allows up to 2 GB of messages.
- **Privacy Level** Determines whether the message will be encrypted. Optional indicates that the sender can choose, whereas Body indicates that unencrypted messages will be rejected. Note that message queue encryption requires Active Directory.
- **Journal** If this option is enabled, a journal queue is created for this queue with copies of all received messages. This is primarily useful for debugging purposes. You can also limit the size of the journal queue.

Finally, it's worth noting that you can perform all the same tasks for creating and managing queues using the Server Explorer window in Visual Studio .NET (as shown in Figure 8-4).

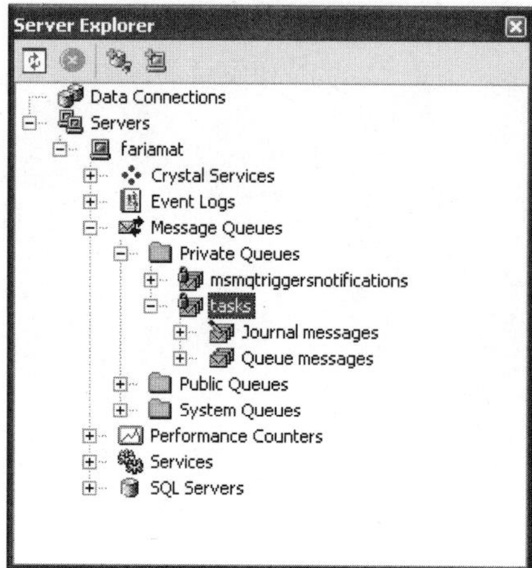

Figure 8-4 Configuring queues in Visual Studio .NET

The Anatomy of a Message

So far we've defined message queues as message lists, but we haven't really considered what a message contains. Every Message Queuing message consists of a few basic properties, such as a label (the title of the message), a priority (which determines the order in which the receiving application reads the messages, assuming they are nontransactional), and the body (which contains the actual message content). The message body is not limited to textual data. Instead, it can include any type of data formatted using binary or XML encoding. However, the recipient application assumes the responsibility of recognizing and reconstructing the appropriate object based on the message data. .NET can't enforce any type of compile-time type safety, which means that invalid messages will lead to runtime errors, which should be caught with exception handlers.

In addition, the message sender sets additional properties that configure the timeout and identify who sent the message. The message sender can also choose the delivery mode. With Express mode, messages are transmitted very quickly and serialized to memory until they can be sent to their network destination. With Recoverable mode, messages are stored in a file first, ensuring that even if the computer crashes no information is lost. When creating a client that might be disconnected from the network, you should use Recoverable mode. Otherwise, unsent messages are lost as soon as the operating system shuts down.

Are Message Queues Suitable for Cross-Platform Programming?

Message Queuing is a Windows operating system service. Non-.NET clients won't be able to make use of it directly. However, that doesn't mean that Message Queuing can't play a large part in a cross-platform application. Remember, part of .NET's strategy is to provide clients on other platforms with a facade through XML Web services (for application programmers) or ASP.NET Web pages (for application users). In a typical cross-platform system, you might use an XML Web service or Web page to receive an order and then send a message through a message queue, which will be read and processed by another .NET component. The message queue, like the database, plays an internal or "back-end" role and is never directly accessed by the client.

Manipulating Queues in .NET

.NET provides a *System.Messaging* namespace that provides types used for formatting, sending, and receiving messages as well as for programmatically discovering, creating, and configuring message queues. Table 8-1 lists the key types in this namespace. The *MessageQueue* class is the heart of this namespace because it provides instance-based members that enable you to interact with a specific queue and shared methods for retrieving information about all the queues on a computer.

Table 8-1 ***System.Messaging*** **Classes**

Class	Description
BinaryMessageFormatter	Serializes or deserializes a .NET object (or an entire graph of connected objects) to or from the body of a Message Queuing message using a binary format.
Message	Encapsulates a Message Queuing message and its properties.
MessageQueue	Provides access to a queue on a Message Queuing server, enabling you to send or retrieve messages.
MessageQueueException	Represents an internal Message Queuing error.

Table 8-1 *System.Messaging* Classes *(continued)*

Class	Description
MessageQueueInstaller	Enables you to install and configure a message queue. This class can be added to a custom setup project or used with the InstallUtil.exe utility.
XmlMessageFormatter	Serializes or deserializes a .NET object (or an entire graph of connected objects) to or from the body of a Message Queuing message using an XML format based on the XSD schema definition.

Before continuing with the following examples, be sure to add a reference to the System.Messaging.dll assembly and import this namespace:

```
Imports System.Messaging
```

Selecting a Queue

You can take two approaches to finding a queue. You can create the message queue by name or you can search through all the message queues available on a computer or in Active Directory.

To create a link to a known message queue, you just create a new *MessageQueue* object and specify the name in the constructor. A good approach is to use the *Exists* method first to verify that the desired queue can be found before you attempt to create it.

Queues are identified using a path-like syntax, which you might have already seen in the MSMQ configuration windows. The first portion of the path indicates a computer or domain name or uses a period (.) to indicate the current computer. The second portion indicates the public queue name. Therefore, Listing 8-3 creates a *MessageQueue* object for the public queue called *MyQueue* and displays its public GUID:

```
If MessageQueue.Exists(".\MyQueue") Then

    Dim Queue As New MessageQueue(".\MyQueue")

    ' Display the unique ID, which is set when the queue is created.
    Console.WriteLine(Queue.Id.ToString())

End If
```

Listing 8-3 Selecting a queue

If you want to connect to a private queue, the second portion of the queue path should always be *Private$* and the third portion should be the queue name.

For example, the following code statement creates a reference to a private queue on the current computer:

```
Dim Queue As New MessageQueue(".\Private$\MyQueue")
```

Occasionally, you might want to open another type of queue. Table 8-2 lists the required queue path formats.

Table 8-2 Queue Path Formats

Queue Type	Path Format
Public	[MachineName]\[QueueName]
Private	[MachineName]\Private$\[QueueName]
Journal	[MachineName]\[QueueName]\Journal$
Machine journal	[MachineName]\Journal$
Machine dead-letter	[MachineName]\DeadLetter$
Machine transactional dead-letter	[MachineName]\XactDeadLetter$

All the rules change when you're working in a disconnected environment. In this case, the queue is not available when the *MessageQueue* object is constructed (and when the message is sent). You need to use the format name rather than the queue name. The format name takes one of several formats, some of which use the GUID that identifies the queue or the machine. Here's an example:

```
' This works even if the queue is not currently available.
Dim Queue As New MessageQueue( _
  "FormatName:PUBLIC=382c74c3-721d-4f34-80e5-57657b6cbc27")
```

Table 8-3 lists the supported format names. Note that to determine a queue's GUID or number, you must either look it up with the Computer Management utility or create a test application. This test application creates a *MessageQueue* object using the name of the queue while connected to the network and then displays the required information.

Table 8-3 Queue Path Formats

Type	Syntax
Public queue	FormatName:PUBLIC=[QueueGUID]
Private queue	FormatName:PRIVATE=[MachineGUID]\[QueueNumber]
Queue by machine	FormatName:DIRECT=OS:[MachineName]\[QueueNumber]
Queue with protocol	FormatName:DIRECT=[Protocol]:MachineName]\[Queue-Number]

Note that you can't use the "queue with protocol" option equivalently on all systems. For example, Message Queuing 3.0 supports the HTTP protocol, whereas Message Queuing 2.0 does not.

After you have a *MessageQueue* object, you can retrieve or set a great deal of information, including all the properties shown in the Computer Management administrative tool. The .NET class library reference describes all the queue properties that you can access.

Searching for a Queue

Another way to find a queue is to use the shared *MessageQueue.GetPublicQueues* method, as shown in Listing 8-4.

```
Dim Queues As MessageQueue() = MessageQueue.GetPublicQueues()
Dim Queue As MessageQueue

' Add the path for every queue to a list control.
For Each Queue In Queues
    lstQueues.Items.Add(Queue.Path)
Next
```

Listing 8-4 Browsing all public queues

You can also use an overloaded version of the *GetPublicQueues* method that accepts a *MessageQueueCriteria* instance. You can use this object to define filter criteria for the queues you want to retrieve, including label, category, and machine information. There are also specialized methods such as *GetPublicQueuesByMachine*, *GetPublicQueuesByCategory*, and *GetPublicQueuesByLabel*.

With private queues, you're constrained to a single *GetPrivateQueuesByMachine* method, which enables you to retrieve the queues for a single machine (as shown in Listing 8-5).

```
Dim Queues As MessageQueue()

' Get the private queues for the current machine.
Queues = MessageQueue.GetPrivateQueuesByMachine(".")
```

Listing 8-5 Browsing all private queues

Creating a Queue

Programmatically creating a queue is just as easy after you understand the queue path syntax. For example, you can create a public queue using the shared *MessageQueue.Create* method, as shown in Listing 8-6.

```
Dim Queue As MessageQueue
Queue = MessageQueue.Create("MyDomain\TestPublicQueue")

Console.Write("Created: " & Queue.Path)
Console.WriteLine("at " & Queue.CreateTime.ToString())
```

Listing 8-6 Creating a public queue

Listing 8-7 generates a new private queue on the current computer.

```
Dim Queue As MessageQueue
Queue = MessageQueue.Create(".\Private$\TestPrivateQueue")
```

Listing 8-7 Creating a private queue

The next code snippet uses the only other version of the *Create* method. This accepts a Boolean parameter that, if *True*, creates a transactional queue:

```
Dim Queue As MessageQueue
Queue = MessageQueue.Create(".\Private$\TestTransactionalQueue", True)
```

The *MessageQueue* class also exposes a shared *Delete* method, which removes the named queue entirely, and an instance *Purge* method, which clears out all the messages from a queue.

Sending a Message

To send a message, you use the *MessageQueue.Send* method. This method accepts the object you want to send and the label (title) of the message. Listing 8-8 shows an example.

```
Dim Queue As MessageQueue

If MessageQueue.Exists(".\Private$\TestQueue") Then
    Queue = New MessageQueue(".\Private$\TestQueue")
Else
    Queue = MessageQueue.Create(".\Private$\TestQueue")
End If

Queue.Send("Inventory Request Order Item #222", "Test Message")
```

Listing 8-8 Sending a simple text message in XML

Figure 8-5 shows the retrieved message.

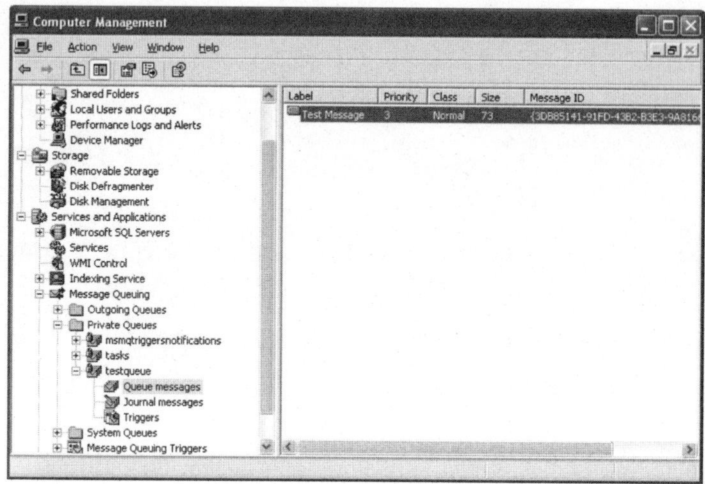

Figure 8-5 Receiving a message

By default, the message is serialized to an XML format. Figure 8-6 shows the message body in the Computer Management tool.

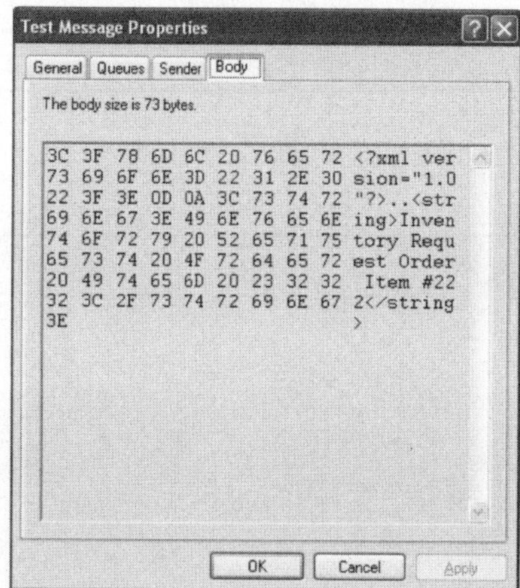

Figure 8-6 The XML-formatted message body

Alternatively, you can set the *MessageQueue.Formatter* property to an instance of the *BinaryMessageFormatter*, which ensures a more compact message (and thereby lessens network traffic). (See Listing 8-9.)

```
Dim Queue As MessageQueue

If MessageQueue.Exists(".\Private$\TestQueue") Then
    Queue = New MessageQueue(".\Private$\TestQueue")
Else
    Queue = MessageQueue.Create(".\Private$\TestQueue")
End If

Queue.Formatter = New BinaryMessageFormatter()
Queue.Send("Inventory Request Order Item #222", "Test Message")
```

Listing 8-9 Sending a simple text message in binary

Figure 8-7 shows the same message in a binary format. The size has dwindled from 73 to 57 bytes.

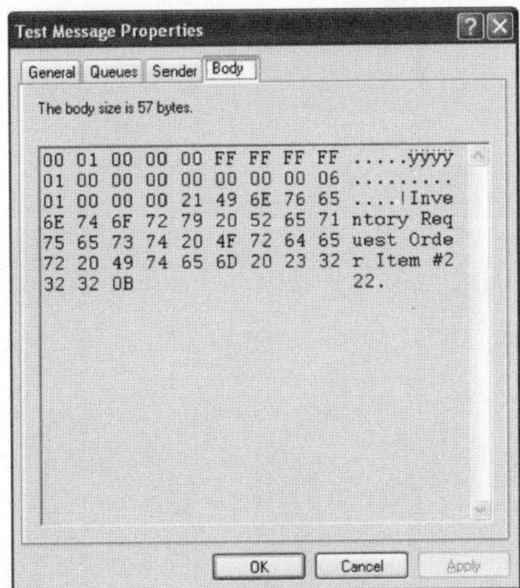

Figure 8-7 The binary-formatted message body

Sending Object Messages

Of course, message queues would be fairly awkward if they accepted only text messages. Instead, you can submit any type of object as long as it satisfies three criteria:

- The class must have a public constructor with no arguments. .NET uses this constructor to re-create the object when the message is received.
- The class must be marked as serializable.
- All class properties must be readable and writable. Read-only properties won't be serialized because .NET won't be able to restore the property values when re-creating the object.

Listing 8-10 shows an ideal *Message* class. It encapsulates information about an order, which the message recipient can then process.

```
<Serializable()> _
Public Class Order

    Public OrderCode As String
    Public ClientName As String
    Public Items As ArrayList

    Public Sub New()
        ' No actions are required in the default constructor.
    End Sub

    Public Sub New(ByVal code As String, ByVal client As String)
        OrderCode = code
        ClientName = client
    End Sub

End Class
```

Listing 8-10 A serializable message class

The code to send this custom object is trivially easy (as shown in Listing 8-11).

```
Dim Ord As New Order("283c74c3-721d-4f34-80e5-57657b6cbc27", _
  "Smith & Smith")
Queue.Send(Ord, "Test Order")
```

Listing 8-11 Sending an object message

> **Note** When you use objects in a message queue, be sure to clearly identify the object type before creating the queue. Trying to determine what type of object has been received can be a nightmare for the server-side application. It's far easier if a queue is restricted to one type of object. However, the server application will always need to check the object type when retrieving a message, or at least use error-handling code for its casting operation. This is because there is no way to enforce queue type safety and restrict clients from submitting incorrect objects in a message. You will also run into problems if clients send the same type of object but encode it with the wrong formatter.

Advanced Message Configuration

None of these examples shows you how to send a message with encryption, a high priority, or a customized timeout. All these options, and more, are available through the *Message* class. To use them, just create a *Message* instance and pass the custom object that you want to send in the *Message* constructor. Then send the message object using the *MessageQueue.Send* method. This two-step process looks like Listing 8-12.

```
Dim Ord As New Order("283c74c3-721d-4f34-80e5-57657b6cbc27", _
  "Smith & Smith")

' Create the message wrapper.
Dim OrderMessage As New Message(Ord)

' Enable encryption (requires access to Active Directory).
OrderMessage.UseEncryption = True
OrderMessage.EncryptionAlgorithm = Messaging.EncryptionAlgorithm.Rc2

' Store the outgoing message in a file before sending it.
OrderMessage.Recoverable = True

' Make it high priority.
OrderMessage.Priority = Messaging.MessagePriority.VeryHigh

' Give it an hour to make it to the destination queue.
OrderMessage.TimeToBeReceived = TimeSpan.FromHours(1)

' Store a copy of the outgoing message on this computer.
OrderMessage.UseJournalQueue = True

Queue.Send(OrderMessage, "Encrypted Order")
```

Listing 8-12 Sending a configured message with the message class

The *Message* class doesn't provide any methods, but it does contain a slew of properties you can set. The reasons why you might create a *Message* wrapper include the following:

- To enable Recoverable mode if you're working in Offline mode. Otherwise, outgoing messages are lost when the computer is rebooted.
- To set a specialized priority. When receiving messages from a nontransactional queue, the application receives the highest (priority level 6) messages first, according to its receipt date, followed by the next highest priority, and so on.

- To specifically use the journal queue to store a copy of the outgoing message.
- To configure a nonstandard timeout value.
- To enable encryption. Encrypted messages use a private/public key system supported by Active Directory. Note, however, that the encryption lasts only while the message is in transit, after which the message is decrypted by the recipient and stored in the destination queue in plain text. This might not be secure enough for some applications, in which case you might want to control the encryption and decryption programmatically, as discussed in Chapter 13.
- To enable the dead-letter queue so you will have a record if the message could not be sent successfully to the target queue within the specified amount of time.
- To enable message acknowledgement. You do this by setting the *AcknowledgeType* and specifying the administration queue that should receive the acknowledgement in the *AdministrationQueue* property.
- To read the *Message.Id* property after sending the message, which will indicate the unique GUID that was generated to identify this message. You can use this ID later to confirm that a message was received.

Table 8-4 lists some key properties and the defaults that are used if you don't modify the *Message* class.

Table 8-4 Message Property Defaults

Property	Default
AcknowledgeType	*AcknowledgeType.None*
AdministrationQueue	A null reference (*Nothing*)
AttachSenderId	*True*
AuthenticationProviderName	Microsoft Base Cryptographic Provider version 1.0
AuthenticationProviderType	*CryptoProviderType.RSA_FULL*
CorrelationId	An empty string ("")
EncryptionAlgorithm	*EncryptionAlgorithm.RC2*
Extension	A zero-length array of bytes
Formatter	*XmlMessageFormatter*
HashAlgorithm	*HashAlgorithm.MD5*

Table 8-4 Message Property Defaults *(continued)*

Property	Default
Label	An empty string ("")
Priority	*MessagePriority.Normal*
Recoverable	*False*
ResponseQueue	A null reference (*Nothing*)
SenderCertificate	A zero-length array of bytes
TimeToBeReceived	*Message.InfiniteTimeout*
TimeToReachQueue	*Message.InfiniteTimeout*
TransactionStatusQueue	A null reference (*Nothing*)
UseAuthentication	*False*
UseDeadLetterQueue	*False*
UseEncryption	*False*
UseJournalQueue	*False*
UseTracing	*False*

Receiving a Message

Typically, a server-side application uses the *Receive* method to read a single message from the queue. For a nontransactional queue, this is the message with the highest priority. If multiple messages exist with the same priority, the oldest one is read first. For a transactional queue, the message received first is simply the message that was sent first.

Before you can receive a message, you need to create a formatter that is configured to recognize specific .NET types. You identify the allowed types using an array of *Type* objects. In the following example, the code is searching for *Order* types in the message body:

```
' Set the allowed types.
Dim AllowedTypes() As Type = {GetType(Order)}
Queue.Formatter = New XmlMessageFormatter(AllowedTypes)
```

Note, however, that this code won't prevent you from attempting to download a message of another type, at which point an exception will be generated.

A server-side application might use this type of logic to receive all the messages in the queue (as shown in Listing 8-13).

```
Dim Queue As New MessageQueue(".\Private$\TestQueue")
Dim ReceivedMessage As Message

' Set the allowed types.
Dim AllowedTypes() As Type = {GetType(Order)}
Queue.Formatter = New XmlMessageFormatter(AllowedTypes)

Do

    ReceivedMessage = Queue.Receive()

    ' Check if it is the expected type.
    If TypeOf ReceivedMessage.Body Is Order Then
        ' Process message here.
        Dim ReceivedOrder As Order = CType(ReceivedMessage.Body, Order)
        Console.WriteLine(ReceivedOrder.OrderCode)
    End If

Loop
```

Listing 8-13 Receiving all messages

If there is no message in the queue when you call *Queue.Receive*, your code just stops, waiting indefinitely for the next message to be received. Alternatively, you can use an overloaded version of the *Receive* method that accepts a *TimeSpan*. If no message is received after the specified amount of time, the code continues. This enables you to create a component that can intelligently check whether it should shut down (perhaps in response to a user interface action or a signal set by another component). Without using a *TimeSpan*, the code could block perpetually and remain unresponsive (as shown in Listing 8-14).

```
Do

    ReceivedMessage = Queue.Receive(TimeSpan.FromSeconds(60))

    ' Check if a message was received.
    If ReceivedMessage = Nothing Then
        ' Yield the processor for some other work, unless
        ' a stop is requested.
        If Not Me.ShouldStop Then
            Thread.Sleep(TimeSpan.FromSeconds(60))
        End If
    Else
        ' (Process message here.)
    End If

    ' Check for a requested shutdown.
    If Me.ShouldStop Then Exit Loop

Loop
```

Listing 8-14 Polling for messages

The *MessageQueue* class also supports asynchronous reads through its *BeginReceive* and *EndReceive* methods. These work the same as the asynchronous methods examined in Chapter 6 and are useful when receiving large data objects.

Sometimes Polling Isn't a Problem

When you create a server-side message processor, you will probably create it as a stand-alone Windows service that periodically checks a queue for messages. For experienced developers, this type of design might set off warning bells because it uses polling, which typically reduces scalability in any system.

The problem with polling is that as more users poll, what begins as minor overhead can become a significant performance hit. If you have hundreds of clients polling a database, for example, connections will become harder to obtain and queries will execute much more slowly. (With thousands of clients, the system will probably stop working altogether.) With Message Queuing, however, polling isn't a problem because with a server-side queue, generally multiple clients send messages but only one application retrieves messages. Therefore, only one application is polling the queue at a time. Similarly, client queues are local to the client computer. Even if every client is polling continuously for a response message, they will all be polling separate queues. Furthermore, each queue is located on a local workstation, which means that polling it has no effect on server resources.

Browsing Messages

When a message is received, it is removed from the queue, even if your application does not use it. To retrieve a copy of the first message but leave the message in the queue, you can use the *MessageQueue.Peek* method. However, this technique is inconvenient because if called multiple times, you will always receive the same message. A better approach is the *For Each* syntax, which enables you to walk through all the messages without removing them.

Listing 8-15 shows an example that iterates through all the messages and displays the title of each one in a list control.

```
Dim Queue As New MessageQueue(".\Private$\TestQueue")
Dim Message As Message

' Configure the list to show the message title.
lstMessages.DisplayMember = "Label"

For Each Message In Queue
    lstMessages.Items.Add(Message)
Next
```

Listing 8-15 Reading messages without receiving them

Note that the whole object is stored in the list control. This enables you to retrieve more message information after the user makes a selection. Or, the user can choose a message, and you can use the *MessageQueue.ReceiveById* method to download and remove the selected message, regardless of where it is positioned in the queue.

Response and Acknowledgement Messages

Conceptually, there are two types of message acknowledgements: automatic and manual. Automatic acknowledgements are sent to a dedicated administration queue. The Message Queuing service sends the acknowledgement message to indicate that a message was received or processed, without requiring the receiving application to take any action (as shown in Listing 8-16).

```
Dim Queue As New MessageQueue(".\Private$\TestQueue")
Dim Ord As New Order("283c74c3-721d-4f34-80e5-57657b6cbc27", _
  "Smith & Smith")
Dim OrderMessage As New Message(Ord)

OrderMessage.AdministrationQueue = New _
  MessageQueue(".\Private$\TestAcknowledgement")
OrderMessage.AcknowledgementType = AcknowledgementTypes.PositiveArrival

Queue.Send(OrderMessage, "Order")

' Hold on to the correlation ID.
' It's required in order to check for an acknowledgement.
Dim CorrelationID As String = OrderMessage.Id
```

Listing 8-16 Requesting an acknowledgement message

Here's how it works: Before you send the message, you set the *Message.AdministrationQueue* property to the administration queue that will receive the message. Then you indicate the desired type of acknowledgement by setting *Message.AcknowledgementType* to one of the values listed in Table 8-5.

Table 8-5 Values from the *AcknowledgementTypes* Enumeration

Value	Description
None	No acknowledgement message is sent. This is the default.
FullReachQueue	The acknowledgement is sent if the message reached the queue successfully, timed out, or was denied access.
PositiveArrival	The acknowledgement is sent if the message reached the queue successfully. However, that doesn't mean the application has processed this message.
NotAcknowledgeReachQueue	This is an "anti-acknowledgment" message. It's sent only if the message can't reach the queue, either because it timed out or access was denied.
FullReceive	The acknowledgement is sent if the message was received by an application or if a timeout occurred.
NegativeReceive	The acknowledgement is sent only if the message could not be read from the queue successfully.
PositiveReceive	The acknowledgement is sent if the message was received (although there is no way to know who has read it from the queue).
NotAcknowledgeReceive	This is an "anti-acknowledgment" message. It's sent only if the message can't be retrieved from the queue, usually because its TTBR timeout has expired.

After sending the message, you should examine and record the *Message.Id* property (perhaps using a local XML file or text file). You can then retrieve the corresponding acknowledgement message from the administration queue, when it arrives, by using the *MessageQueue.ReceiveByCorrelationId* method and specifying the ID of the message you sent (as shown in Listing 8-17). Acknowledgement messages don't have any interesting content. However, you can examine the *Message.Acknowledgement* property of an acknowledgement message to determine whether the message was received, timed out, and so on.

```
Dim AcknowledgementMessage As Message
AcknowledgementMessage = Queue.ReceiveByCorrelationId(CorrelationId)

If AcknowledgementMessage.Acknowledgement = Acknowledgement.ReachQueue
    ' (The order reached the queue. It may or may not have been
    ' processed.)
End If
```

Listing 8-17 Retrieving an acknowledgement message

Response queues operate under a similar principle, but they require the receiving application to take some action. They can also contain additional information. For example, a response message to an order might be a custom structure with information about the order date and shipping charges. To use a response queue, the sending application creates a *MessageQueue* object that identifies the response queue (which is an ordinary queue) and sets it in the *Message.ResponseQueue* property (as shown in Listing 8-18).

```
Dim Queue As New MessageQueue(".\Private$\TestQueue")

Dim Ord As New Order("283c74c3-721d-4f34-80e5-57657b6cbc27", _
  "Smith & Smith")
Dim OrderMessage As New Message(Ord)

' Specify a response queue.
Dim ResponseQueue As New MessageQueue(".\Private$\TestQueueResponse")
OrderMessage.ResponseQueue = ResponseQueue

Queue.Send(OrderMessage, "Order")
```

Listing 8-18 Identifying a response message

The receiving application must then examine this property, create a new message, and set the *Message.CorrelationId* property of the response message to match the *Message.Id* of the received message. This allows the client to determine what the message is responding to. Unlike with acknowledgement messages, it's the recipient's responsibility to perform these tasks. The Message Queuing infrastructure doesn't send a response message automatically.

Message Queues in a Distributed Application

Message Queuing is new to many developers, and we've spent the large part of this chapter examining Message Queuing fundamentals, such as sending and processing messages. The unanswered question that all this raises is where a message queue should enter into your distributed application designs.

Unlike databases, message queues lack almost all error-checking capabilities. That, coupled with the fact that they are tightly bound to the Windows operating system, makes them poorly suited for client use in a distributed application. They also tend to bind a specific user to a fixed machine. In a production-level application, the amount of code you need to write to check for error conditions and respond appropriately might become cumbersome. There is also the fact that dead-letter, confirmation, and journaled outgoing messages might end up scattered on computers throughout the enterprise, making it difficult to track down problems or perform meaningful diagnostics.

However, Message Queuing works much better when it serves as an internal backbone for your components. For example, you might create an XML Web service that uses a message queue to forward work requests to another server-side component. This design neatly sidesteps the problems of other asynchronous approaches and guarantees scalability and high-performance. In Chapter 17, we'll consider a case study that puts Message Queuing to work coordinating an XML Web service and an internal client.

COM+ Queued Components

Experienced COM+ developers might know about queued components, an abstraction that enables you to call a method on a server-side component in an asynchronous, disconnected fashion. Essentially, your call is intercepted by a specialized "recorder" that translates the method call into a message. The message is received on the destination computer, which uses a specialized "player" to invoke the requested method on the component.

The best part about this approach is that it all takes place transparently. When you call the queued component, you don't need to use any special Message Queuing code or classes. It seems that this could be an ideal solution for dealing with heavy user loads in the world of .NET.

Unfortunately, as you'll discover in the next chapter, COM+ components aren't easily remotable unless you either embrace DCOM again (shudder) or create a .NET wrapper component. Because calls to an ordinary .NET component can't be queued, this approach removes most of the benefits that queued components provide. However, all is not lost—several programming gurus have remarked that the pluggable .NET Remoting infrastructure can easily accommodate a Message Queuing channel, which would allow transparent component interaction through a message queue. This functionality hasn't been developed, but it seems like a logical next step for Microsoft as it adds to its infrastructure support in coming upgrades to .NET. In the meantime, you can create one-way, fire-and-forget methods for XML Web services and .NET Remoting components.

Summary

This chapter introduced messaging concepts, including fire-and-forget methods and the Message Queuing service built into the Windows operating system. Message Queuing illustrates an important point. Sometimes creating an efficient, scalable distributed application isn't a matter of adding hardware or optimizing code, but just making compromises. If you have some tasks that can be performed at nonpeak times and you can change synchronous communication into an exchange of one-way messages, you can dramatically lessen the burden on parts of your distributed application.

For an example of the role Message Queuing can play in an application, refer to the case study in Chapter 17.

9

COM+ (Component Services)

A core part of the Microsoft philosophy is that programmers should be able to concentrate on coding the business-specific logic for an application and not have to code the infrastructure for their distributed systems. COM+ extends this philosophy by providing prebuilt services for enterprise applications. It includes solutions such as object pooling, transactions, and role-based security so you don't have to waste valuable time troubleshooting low-level problems and reinventing the wheel.

The name COM+ is a little confusing. Some programmers make the mistake of assuming that COM+ is an enhanced version of COM. Strictly speaking, this assumption isn't correct. Both COM and Microsoft .NET are technologies designed for creating discrete, reusable binary components. COM+ doesn't replace either of these technologies. Instead, it provides services that can be leveraged by a COM or .NET component.

COM+ is a huge subject. Most books about .NET programming list the numerous COM+ options and their .NET equivalents but provide little advice to help a programmer decide where COM+ should fit into an enterprise application. This chapter takes a different approach. It considers some sample cases in which COM+ can be useful in .NET and also identifies COM+ features that are less .NET-friendly. That means the chapter focuses primarily on instance management and transactions. Along the way, it will answer questions such as "Does COM+ belong on the server or client?" and "What's the difference between a database transaction and a COM+ transaction?" and "Is ADO.NET connection pooling better than COM+ object pooling?"

The Role of COM+ in a Distributed System

Here's a surprising claim: COM+ isn't perfect. Here's another: In .NET distributed applications, you don't always need COM+.

COM+ is designed to solve some common problems with large-scale enterprise applications. In the past, it just wasn't possible to design a scalable distributed application without COM+. In .NET, that isn't necessarily the case. Some .NET features compete with or duplicate COM+ functionality. Others complement it. And because COM+ is based on COM and DCOM, a few useful COM+ features are prohibitively difficult to integrate into a .NET application.

It's important to understand that COM+ was initially designed to work with COM components. Many COM+ services can be reused in .NET, but some fit into .NET solutions much more effectively than others. Some of the COM+ services that are ideally suited for .NET include the following:

- **Object pooling** This service enables you to pool objects that are expensive to create and reuse them for different client requests.
- **Just-in-time (JIT) activation** With this service, an object isn't created until the client invokes a method call. JIT activation is also used in conjunction with object pooling, which allows an object to be deactivated when not in use and reused to serve another client, even while the original client maintains its reference to the object.
- **Automatic transactions** Automatic transactions allow components to be used in a transaction without specifically knowing anything about the transaction itself. This service also provides support for distributed transactions.

COM+ also provides some services that are generally less elegant to implement (or less important to use) in a .NET application:

- **Queued components** This service enables you to create components that execute asynchronously by using a transparent Microsoft Message Queuing (MSMQ) interface.
- **Loosely coupled events** This service provides publish and subscribe communication between objects. However, the publisher and the subscriber require no knowledge of each other.
- **Role-based security** This service enables you to group application users into logical roles and assign them different permissions without having to embed security code into the component itself.

Before we consider the individual services COM+ offers and how they fit into the .NET picture, we need to take a closer look at COM interoperability and registration with a serviced component.

MTS, COM+, and COM+ 1.5

COM+ is the successor to Microsoft Transaction Server (MTS). Most developers agree that the MTS moniker is at least as confusing as COM+. Although MTS and COM+ both support distributed transactions, both support several other services as well. In .NET, COM+ services are usually referred to as *enterprise services*, and a .NET component that uses enterprise services is called a *serviced component*.

COM+ 1.5 is yet another version of COM+; it first shipped with Microsoft Windows XP. It adds the ability to expose a COM+ serviced component as a SOAP-based XML Web service, the ability to configure components to be recycled periodically, and configurable transaction levels that can improve performance by reducing the level of failsafe protection.

COM and Interop

We haven't yet examined how a .NET application can use COM components. This level of COM interop is usually seamless and is well documented in almost every book about .NET fundamentals. The basic idea is to create a wrapper between the .NET application and the COM component. The .NET application communicates directly with this wrapper (often called a *runtime callable wrapper* [RCW]), which in turn communicates with the unmanaged COM component. Figure 9-1 depicts this arrangement.

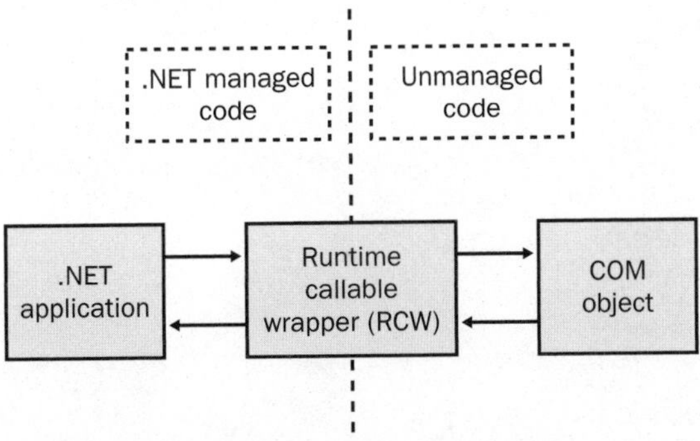

Figure 9-1 The runtime callable wrapper

The RCW is an ordinary .NET assembly that must be deployed with the .NET application. Some vendors provide an RCW assembly with their COM components. If they don't, you can create an RCW for an existing COM component using one of two techniques. The fastest approach is to add a reference to the COM component in Microsoft Visual Studio .NET. Visual Studio .NET will then generate the RCW assembly and place it in the project directory. Your second option is to generate the RCW manually using the tlbimp.exe command-line utility included with the .NET SDK. Chapter 16 presents a case study that uses the COM interop features of .NET.

For most developers, this automatic support provides everything they need. Of course, the actual .NET code in the RCW performs the real heavy lifting and it makes use of a slew of .NET types (mainly from the *System.Runtime.InteropServices* namespace) that allow explicit communication between managed and unmanaged code and mapping between .NET and COM types. It is possible to delve deeper into these details and create your own custom RCW, but this is a task best suited for a seasoned COM expert. If you plan to dive into these lower-level details, I suggest a dedicated book such as *.NET and COM: The Complete Interoperability Guide* by Adam Nathan (Sams, 2002).

COM interoperability isn't just a .NET nicety—it's a core part of the .NET Framework. In fact, Microsoft originally planned to rewrite COM+ entirely in managed .NET code, and future versions of .NET might still pursue this goal. Because of the scope and ambition of the .NET Framework, however, some plans had to be scaled back. COM+ was eventually implemented with heavy use of COM interop.

Of course, creating a .NET serviced component isn't the same as consuming a COM component from a .NET application, so you don't need to use an RCW. Instead, .NET simplifies development of components that use COM+ services (called *serviced components*) through the special *ServicedComponent* class (as discussed in the next section).

COM+ Registration Basics

To create a COM+ component, you must first start a new class library project and add a reference to the System.EnterpriseServices.dll assembly. You can then derive custom classes from the *System.EnterpriseServices.ServicedComponent* class. Listing 9-1 shows a basic example.

```
Imports System.EnterpriseServices

Public Class MyServicedClass
    Inherits ServicedComponent

    Public Function GetHello() As String
        Return "Hello"
    End Function

End Class
```

Listing 9-1 A simple .NET serviced component

Behind the scenes, every serviced component is hosted by a COM+ application, which is really nothing more than a collection of serviced components along with COM+ configuration information. Every COM+ application is registered in the COM+ catalog. Using the administrative tools included with Windows, you can browse the COM+ catalog and modify the settings for various COM+ applications and their components.

With .NET, you have the freedom to place several serviced components into a single COM+ application or separate them into multiple COM+ applications. However, it's recommended that you use a one-to-one mapping between .NET assemblies and COM+ applications, as shown in Figure 9-2. Although it is technically possible to register the serviced components in a single assembly in different COM+ applications, this adds additional versioning and registration headaches.

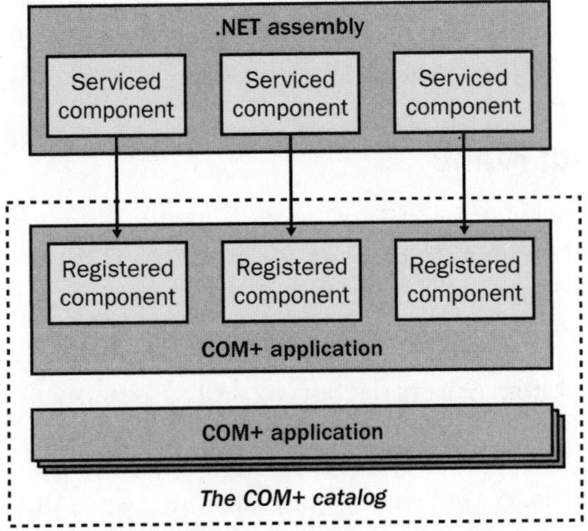

Figure 9-2 Mapping classes to a COM+ application

To browse the COM+ catalog, select Component Services from the Administrative Tools section of Control Panel. Then burrow down to the COM+ Applications node, as shown in Figure 9-3. You'll see a list of all the currently registered COM+ applications and be able to configure them.

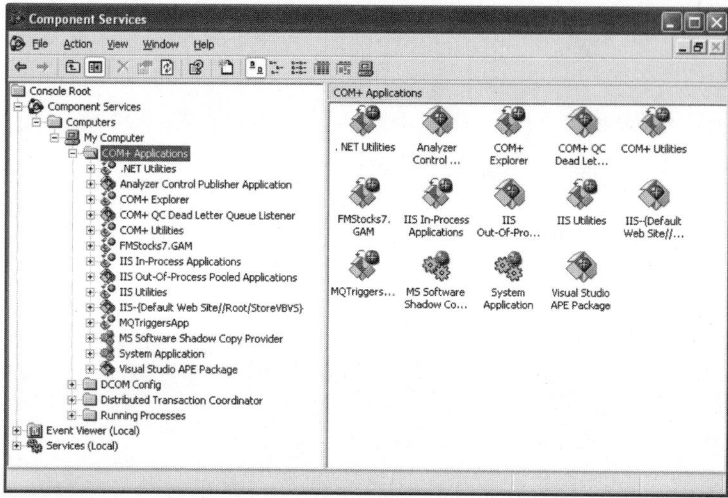

Figure 9-3 The Component Services console

Unfortunately, the serviced component shown earlier in Listing 9-1 isn't ready to use and won't appear in the Component Services utility. Furthermore, if a .NET client attempts to create this class, it will receive an error. Before putting a serviced component to work, you need to go through a few extra registration steps, as discussed in the next few sections.

Giving Your Assembly a Strong Name

Every serviced component needs a strong name that uniquely identifies your class and maps it to a component in a COM+ application. The process for generating a strong-named assembly is covered in detail in Chapter 2. Here's a quick overview of the steps you need to follow:

1. Create a new class library project.
2. Add *MyServicedClass* to the project, as shown earlier in Listing 9-1.
3. If you don't already have a key pair, generate one using the sn.exe command-line utility.
4. Add an *<Assembly:AssemblyKeyFile>* attribute to your class library project, identifying the file with the key pair.
5. Compile the class library into an assembly.

After you've given your assembly a strong name, you're ready to register the component. You have two registration options: dynamic registration and manual registration.

Dynamic Registration

Dynamic registration, also known as "lazy registration," is a COM+ convenience that particularly shines when you test a serviced component. With dynamic registration, a serviced component is registered in the COM+ catalog as soon as it is instantiated by a .NET client.

If you create a simple client and add a reference to the test component shown earlier, for instance, you can instantiate *MyServicedClass* as you would any other .NET object:

```
Dim MyServicedObject As New MyServicedClass()
```

When you instantiate the object, a slight delay will occur. If you refresh the view in the Component Services utility, you'll see a new COM+ application with an application name that matches the assembly name used for your component (in this case, TestComponent). This COM+ application contains one configured class—*MyServicedClass*—as shown in Figure 9-4.

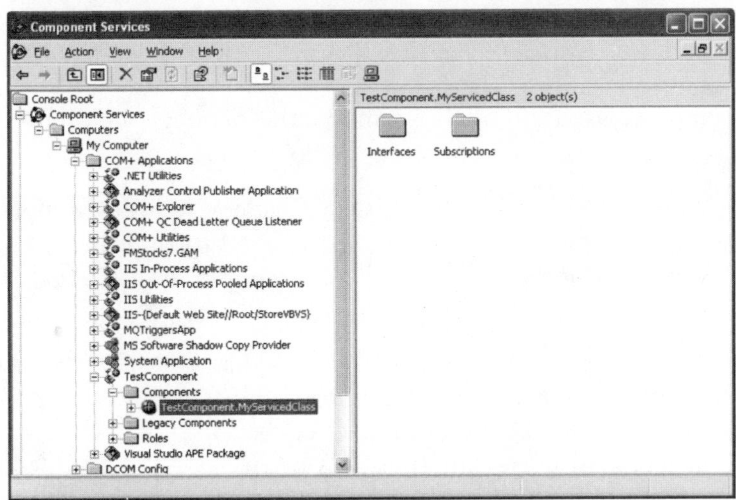

Figure 9-4 The dynamically configured *MyServicedClass*

If you examine the configured component in any detail, you'll notice that the *GetHello* method isn't listed. That's because COM is based on interfaces.

If you rewrite your class as shown in Listing 9-2, the members of *IHello* will appear. This will also get you on the path to exposing your serviced components to legacy COM applications (in other words, unmanaged applications that don't use .NET). This integration task is beyond the scope of this book, however. Creating a compatible .NET interface isn't difficult in principle, but it does require good knowledge of COM and the mapping between COM and .NET types. You are also exposed to the traditional COM versioning nightmares, including the problems that can occur if you create a new, incompatible interface under an existing interface GUID.

```
Public Interface IHello
    Function GetHello() As String
End Interface

Public Class MyServicedClass
    Inherits ServicedComponent
    Implements IHello

    Public Function GetHello() As String Implements IHello.GetHello
        Return "Hello"
    End Function

End Class
```

Listing 9-2 A .NET serviced component with an interface

Dynamic registration might seem like the perfect solution to using COM+ in .NET, but it does suffer from a few quirks:

- Registering a component in the COM+ catalog requires administrator privileges. If the component is instantiated for the first time in an account without these privileges (for example, the ASP.NET worker process that handles XML Web service requests), it will fail.
- The component won't be reregistered unless you increase the version number. When you apply COM+ registration changes in your component code, they won't take effect because the component isn't reregistered. In these situations, it's often easiest just to delete the registration from the catalog manually and restart the application.
- Dynamically registered serviced components can't be installed in the global assembly cache (GAC). This isn't a problem, just a common source of confusion.

For these reasons, it's often recommended that you use manual registration.

Manual Registration

To use manual registration, you use the regsvcs.exe command-line utility included with .NET. You need administrative rights to run this utility. Here's how you register TestComponent from the command line:

```
regsvcs.exe TestComponent.dll
```

The regsvcs.exe utility performs several tasks and informs you of any error it encounters on the way.

1. It generates and registers a COM type library for the component, which might be useful if unmanaged clients need to use this component. In the preceding example, the type library has the name TestComponent.tlb.
2. It searches the COM+ catalog for an application with a matching name (in this case, TestComponent). If it doesn't find one, it creates one. You can override the name choice by adding the */appname* parameter or override it declaratively in the component code itself using *<ApplicationNameAttribute>* (as discussed shortly).
3. It reads the metadata, determines the classes and interfaces to expose, and applies any configured COM+ settings. In the case of *MyServicedClass*, we haven't added any COM+ configuration attributes yet.

Here's the output you're likely to see:

```
Microsoft (R) .NET Framework Services Installation Utility
Copyright (C) Microsoft Corporation 1998-2001.  All rights reserved.

Installed Assembly:
        Assembly: C:\DistributedCode\COM+Component\bin\TestComponent.dll
        Application: TestComponent
        TypeLib: c:\DistributedCode\COM+Component\bin\TestComponent.tlb
```

Alternatively, you can register a component programmatically by using the *System.EnterpriseServices.RegistrationHelper* class in a .NET application. This is a powerful but rarely used feature. In fact, the regsvcs utility uses the *RegistrationHelper* class behind the scenes.

It's also recommended that you install serviced component assemblies into the GAC. This isn't strictly necessary for library activation mode, although it is required for server activation. The key benefit of using the GAC is location transparency—you won't need to worry about which version of an assembly is registered (and which version a given client is using).

COM+ and the Declarative Model

One of the core ideas in COM+ is that a component's behavior can be configured declaratively using attributes. In other words, if you want to create a component that uses transactions or object pooling in COM+, you don't code low-level API calls directly into your component code. Instead, you use attributes to declare to the COM+ runtime that your component needs certain services. The COM+ runtime then supplies these services transparently. These types of attributes (which are conceptually similar to but different from .NET attributes) can apply to an entire component, an individual class, or even a single method and can control everything from security to instance management.

In the past, these details were usually configured using the Component Services utility. You can try this out with the TestComponent application by right-clicking on the component itself or the contained *MyServicedClass* and then choosing Properties. Figure 9-5 shows some of the application-wide settings for TestComponent.

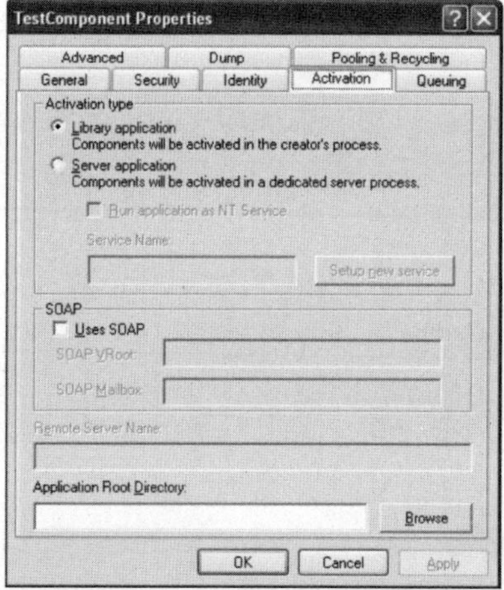

Figure 9-5 COM+ application settings

The COM+ catalog is still a part of the .NET world because it gives developers a flexible way to configure components in a production environment without recompiling. It also allows administrators to fine-tune components to match server hardware and software resources. For example, you might use object pooling to limit an object so it never exceeds the number of available licenses. If you install more licenses, however, you won't want to recompile the component. In this case, you can just tweak the settings by using the Component Services utility.

.NET extends the declarative COM+ model by allowing you to use special .NET attributes to mark up your code. These attributes replicate the settings you can configure using the Component Services utility. To configure the activation type for your COM+ application, for example, you can add an assembly-level attribute (typically to the AssemblyInfo.vb file):

```
<Assembly: ApplicationActivation(ActivationOption.Library)>
```

It's important to understand that this attribute is never directly executed as code. Instead, when your component is registered, all the COM+ attributes are used to configure the COM+ catalog settings. You can then override these settings by modifying them in the Component Services utility. Similarly, if you modify these attributes and recompile the component but you don't change the version number or reregister the application, the COM+ catalog settings won't be changed.

Most COM+ features are exposed through class-level or method-level attributes. However, you can use a few assembly-level attributes. You can specify the COM+ application that will be registered by using the *<Assembly:ApplicationName>* or *<Assembly:ApplicationID>* attribute. The former specifies the name of a COM+ application, and the latter specifies the globally unique identifier (GUID). Without the *<Assembly:ApplicationID>* attribute, .NET will generate a GUID automatically.

```
<Assembly: ApplicationName("TestComponent")>
```

You can also specify the activation type (server or library) using the *<Assembly:ApplicationActivation>* attribute.

```
<Assembly: ApplicationActivation(ActivationOption.Library)>
```

The default activation mode, if not specified, is library. In library activation mode, the components are executed in the client's process. Remember that in this case, the client process is the process that instantiates the serviced component, which will probably be a .NET Remoting component host or an XML Web service on the same machine. Using library activation will ensure the fastest possible communication.

If you use server application, all the components will be executed by dllhost.exe, the COM+ server process. You should be aware that in server activation mode, the component might not terminate when your application does, leading to "permission denied" errors when you attempt to rebuild the component and the .pdb debugging file. To put an end to this frustration, you must either wait until COM+ terminates the process (typically, after three minutes of inactivity) or shut it down manually using the Component Services utility. When using server activation, you also need to ensure that all method parameters and return values use serializable types.

COM+ Versioning

COM is extremely restrictive when it comes to versioning, largely because COM components are usually shared globally on a computer. Even a small change to a component's interface can cause existing applications to break.

When you create a serviced component, you will experience some of the hangover from the legacy of DLL Hell. By default, COM+ serviced components are registered in the Windows Registry using GUIDs to identify applications, components, and interfaces. When you register your serviced component, .NET generates a GUID automatically using a hash of the assembly's strong name and the version number. If you register your component again and the version number has changed, a new entry will be created in the COM+ catalog. Eventually, the clutter will build up and countless unneeded entries that reference old component versions will remain (as shown in Figure 9-6).

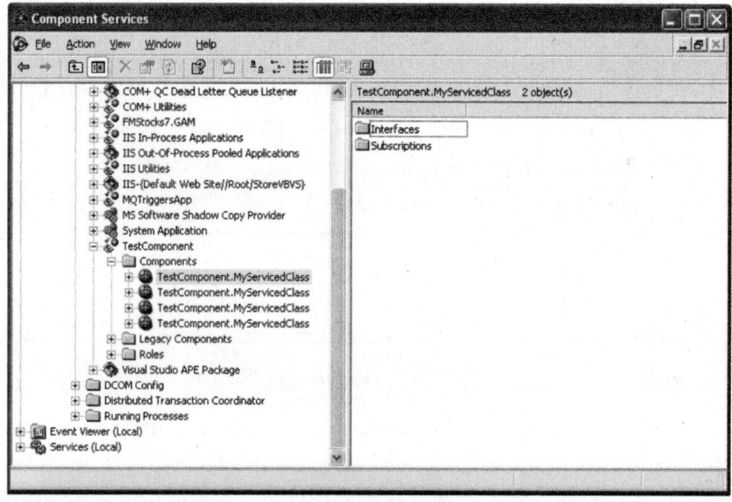

Figure 9-6 A COM+ versioning headache

To tackle this issue, you should lock down your assembly's version number while testing. Then modify the appropriate assembly attribute in the AssemblyInfo.vb file. For example:

```
<Assembly: AssemblyVersion("1.3.0.0")>
```

Of course, after you fix the version number, it's up to you to ensure that you increment the version number and generate a new set of GUIDs when it really is required—namely, when you're ready to distribute a component that has a different interface. Once again, this will primarily be a consideration if you're in the unenviable position of interoperating with unmanaged clients. Another option is to lock down your GUIDs by specifying them in the code using the *<Assembly:Guid>* attribute for the assembly and the *<Guid>* attribute for each class or interface. In a complex component with multiple interfaces and classes, this approach requires significantly more code.

Using a COM+ Component

Now that you have a serviced component, how can you use it? You have three basic options:

- **DCOM** This is the same approach you would use in Visual Basic 6.0. It's heartily discouraged, however, because DCOM is difficult to configure properly and inflexible in the enterprise (especially if your server is behind a firewall).
- **XML Web services** In this case, your XML Web service effectively acts as a layer in between the COM+ component and the client. The XML Web service instantiates the COM+ component directly, just as it would with any other .NET assembly.
- **Remoting** This is often the most flexible approach. Using a component host, you can expose a serviced component exactly as you would expose any other .NET object.

So far, we've explored how you can create and register a serviced component. The next few sections dive into the real details of COM+ programming and consider why you might want to use it.

Object Pooling

A traditional client/server application maps clients directly to server resources in a one-to-one relationship. If there are 10 clients in a system, 10 data objects will be in use. If 1000 clients are attempting to commit data, there will be 1000 data objects and potentially 1000 simultaneous database connections—a much less scalable situation.

To counter this problem, COM+ introduces different types of instance management: object pooling and JIT activation. Object pooling is the most significant of the two. It allows a small set of objects to be reused for a large number of clients. Object pooling is conceptually similar to connection pooling: A "pool" of available, instantiated objects is retained permanently. When a client creates the object, the client actually receives a preinitialized copy of the object from the pool. When the client releases the object, it isn't destroyed. Instead, it's returned to the pool, where it's ready to serve another client. You can configure the minimum and maximum size of the pool, ensuring that the server never attempts to create more objects than it can support.

Object pooling provides the following benefits:

- **Reduced object creation cost** Technically, the cost of creating the object is spread over multiple clients. Although 1000 clients might need to use the object, only 50 objects might need to be created. Even better, these 50 objects will be created only once and then reused.
- **Early object creation** You can specify a minimum pool size, which ensures that the pool will be populated with the first client request. If an object is particularly expensive to create, you can submit the first request yourself, ensuring that the objects are created and ready for subsequent clients.
- **Resource management** You also can specify a pool maximum. This doesn't just determine the maximum number of objects in the pool, but also the maximum number of objects that can be created at any one time, whether they are available in the pool or currently in use. If you specify a maximum of 10 and all 10 instances are in use, for instance, the next client request is put on hold until an instance is free. Therefore, you can use a pooled object to wrap limited resources.

If you understand these three benefits, you understand the motivation behind object pooling. The first advantage, reduced object creation cost, allows distributed applications to support high-client, low-throughput systems in which the cost of creating an object is nontrivial. This problem was introduced in Chapter 1. The third benefit, resource management, is equally important. It enables you to limit the use of objects when they require specialized hardware resources or individual licenses. In this way, large client loads can be served slowly yet effectively. Without this technique, the entire system fails when the load is too great.

The Ideal Pooled Component

Object pooling isn't suited for all situations. An ideal candidate for object pooling has the following characteristics:

- **It performs time-consuming work in the constructor.** By pooling the object, you save time by reducing the number of times the constructor logic must execute.
- **It is stateful.** Presumably, the time-consuming logic in the constructor initializes the object to a certain state. You want to maintain this state so you don't need to perform time-consuming code to re-create it.

- **It doesn't hold client-specific state.** A pooled object typically has a long lifetime, during which it is reused by more than one client. You can't maintain client-specific information when the object is released because the client changes.

One exception applies to this list. If you're creating a pooled object solely to gain the benefit of resource management (in other words, you need to limit access to a scarce resource), your object could theoretically still be stateless. In this case, however, it's still likely (and usually more efficient) that the object holds some information about the limited resource in memory.

Creating any object requires basic overhead. This overhead is quite small with COM, however, and even smaller with .NET. You should *never* use object pooling just to avoid the overhead of creating an ordinary object. As a rule, the types of objects that benefit most from object pooling are those that take a long time to initialize relative to the amount of time required to execute an individual method.

> **Note** This point is worth repeating: the benefits of object pooling are minimal if the object is inexpensive to create. COM+ uses extra memory and processing time to manage an object pool. A good pooled object performs as much work as possible in its constructor (such as connecting to a file or database and retrieving information).

Pooling and State

One confusing point about object pooling is that it's almost always used in conjunction with stateful objects. There's not much benefit to pooling a stateless object—you're better off just re-creating the object for each new client. However, modern programming practices encourage you to use stateless objects. Stateless objects are easier to scale to multiple machines, have minimal overhead, and lend themselves well to .NET Remoting and XML Web services. So why would you ever use a stateful object?

The answer is that pooled objects are never provided directly to clients in a .NET distributed application. Instead, the client contacts a service provider object, which in turn uses the pooled object to perform a specific task. The service provider retrieves the pooled object at the beginning of every method call and releases it at the end, before returning any information to the client. In this way, the client gains all the benefits of stateless objects and your internal system uses its limited resources in the most effective manner possible. Figure 9-7 depicts the arrangement.

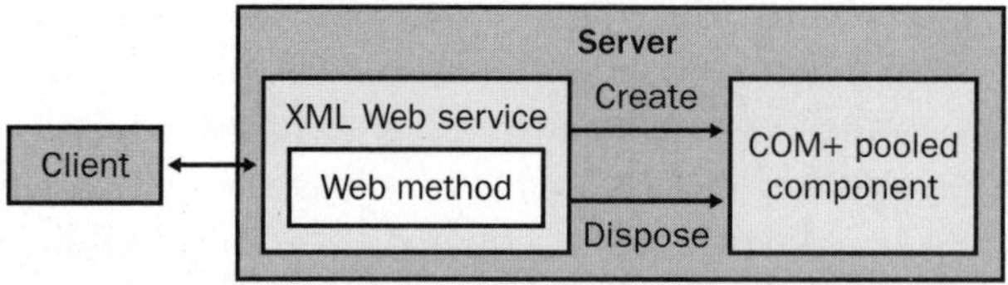

Figure 9-7 A design pattern for pooled object use

One nice aspect of this design is that it prevents so-called *greedy clients*—clients that refuse to release an object so it can be made available for other requests. You can use JIT activation to prevent this behavior, but doing so adds complexity and overhead. With object pooling, the problem disappears because the client never interacts with the pooled object directly. It can retain a reference to the service provider, but the actual pooled object will be held only during the execution of a service provider method.

The approach shown in Figure 9-7 also neatly sidesteps DCOM questions because the service provider and pooled component are hosted on the same computer (the remote server) and can communicate directly. However, the service provider must be an XML Web service or a remote component.

Pooled Behavior in Windows 2000 vs. Windows XP

Pooled behavior is different in Windows 2000 and in Windows XP. This difference largely results from the fact that Windows XP introduces COM+ 1.5 (which is discussed at the end of this chapter). In Windows 2000, a serviced library component is created in a default application domain and can be shared between all clients machine-wide. In Windows XP, pooled applications are limited to the application domain where they were created. This means that to share a pooled object between clients, you should ensure that all requests are served in the same application domain (possibly the application domain of a component host or the application domain used by the ASP.NET worker processes). If you use server activation, this difference does not appear, and pooled objects are always created in their own application domain.

A Pooled Component Example

This chapter has explained how you should use a pooled component, but it hasn't done much to demonstrate what a pooled component really is. The next example examines the difference between ordinary and pooled objects.

Consider the serviced component shown in Listing 9-3. When it's first created, it opens a connection to a database, retrieves some information, and stores it in the *_Data* member variable. This information can be retrieved through the *Data* property.

```
Public Class NonPooledDataReader
    Inherits ServicedComponent

    Private ConnectionString = "Data Source=localhost;" + _
      "Initial Catalog=Store;Integrated Security=SSPI"

    Private _Data As DataSet

    ' The constructor opens a database connection, and retrieves a list
    ' of products.
    Public Sub New()

        Dim con As New SqlConnection(ConnectionString)
        Dim cmd As New SqlCommand("SELECT * FROM Products", con)

        Dim adapter As New SqlDataAdapter(cmd)
        Dim ds As New DataSet()

        con.Open()
        adapter.Fill(ds)
        con.Close()

        _Data = ds

    End Sub

    Public ReadOnly Property Data() As DataSet
        Get
            Return _Data
        End Get
    End Property

End Class
```

Listing 9-3 A nonpooled data class

Let's design a simple client that uses this component. (See Listing 9-4.) It creates an instance of the *NonPooledDataReader* class each time a button is clicked and displays the retrieved data. Figure 9-8 shows the results.

```
Public Class NonPooledClientTest
    Inherits System.Windows.Forms.Form

    Private Sub cmdGetData_Click(ByVal sender As System.Object, _
      ByVal e As System.EventArgs) Handles cmdGetData.Click

        DataGrid1.DataSource = Nothing

        Dim DBReader As New TestComponent.PooledDataReader()
        DataGrid1.DataSource = DBReader.Data

    End Sub

End Class
```

Listing 9-4 A client for the nonpooled class

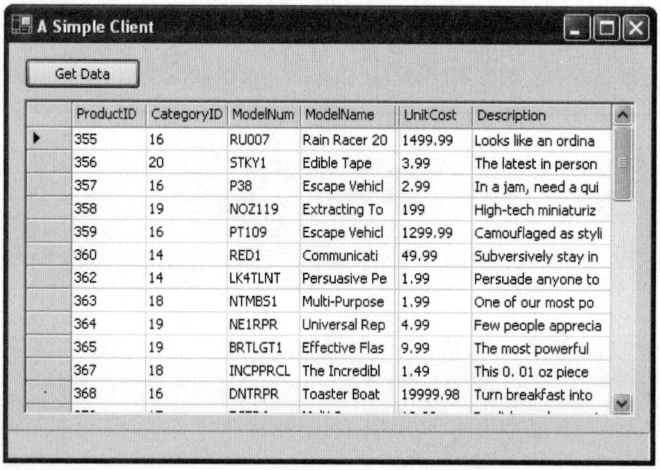

A Simple Client

Get Data

ProductID	CategoryID	ModelNum	ModelName	UnitCost	Description
355	16	RU007	Rain Racer 20	1499.99	Looks like an ordina
356	20	STKY1	Edible Tape	3.99	The latest in person
357	16	P38	Escape Vehicl	2.99	In a jam, need a qui
358	19	NOZ119	Extracting To	199	High-tech miniaturiz
359	16	PT109	Escape Vehicl	1299.99	Camouflaged as styli
360	14	RED1	Communicati	49.99	Subversively stay in
362	14	LK4TLNT	Persuasive Pe	1.99	Persuade anyone to
363	18	NTMBS1	Multi-Purpose	1.99	One of our most po
364	19	NE1RPR	Universal Rep	4.99	Few people apprecia
365	19	BRTLGT1	Effective Flas	9.99	The most powerful
367	18	INCPPRCL	The Incredibl	1.49	This 0.01 oz piece
368	16	DNTRPR	Toaster Boat	19999.98	Turn breakfast into

Figure 9-8 The simple client

So far, this is a fairly predictable segment of code. Every time the button is clicked, the object is reconstructed, the data is requeried, and the *DataGrid* is updated.

Consider what happens when this object is replaced by the pooled equivalent shown in Listing 9-5. You'll see several highlighted changes. The *<ObjectPooling>* attribute is added to indicate that this object should be pooled. The *CanBePooled* method is overridden so it returns *True*, ensuring the object is placed in the pool when it is released. Finally, an additional variable, named *ConstructorFlag*, is set to *True* every time the constructor executes. This *ConstructorFlag* isn't a detail you would implement in your own pooled objects, but it proves useful in this simple test.

```
<ObjectPooling()> _
Public Class PooledDataReader
    Inherits ServicedComponent

    Private ConnectionString = "Data Source=localhost;" + _
      "Initial Catalog=Store;Integrated Security=SSPI"

    Private _Data As DataSet

    Public ConstructorFlag As Boolean

    Public Sub New()

        Dim con As New SqlConnection(ConnectionString)
        Dim cmd As New SqlCommand("SELECT * FROM Products", con)

        Dim adapter As New SqlDataAdapter(cmd)
        Dim ds As New DataSet()

        con.Open()
        adapter.Fill(ds)
        con.Close()

        _Data = ds

        ' Indicate that the constructor has just executed.
        ConstructorFlag = True

    End Sub

    Public ReadOnly Property Data() As DataSet
        Get
            Return _Data
        End Get
    End Property

    Protected Overrides Function CanBePooled() As Boolean
        Return True
    End Function

End Class
```

Listing 9-5 A pooled data class

The client code is also tweaked, which Listing 9-6 shows. Every time it creates the object, it checks the *ConstructorFlag* to determine whether the constructor executed. It then sets the *ConstructorFlag* to *False* and calls *Dispose* on the object to explicitly release it. Note that to call *Dispose*, your client application requires a reference to the System.EnterpriseServices.dll assembly because the implementation for this method is defined in the base *ServicedComponent* class.

> **Note** If *Dispose* isn't called, the object won't be returned to the pool until the .NET garbage collector tracks it down, which will adversely affect other clients, particularly if the pool is small enough that you might quickly run out of instances to satisfy ongoing requests. This is another reason that external clients shouldn't have the ability to directly interact with a pooled object. Instead, your service provider should be the only class that uses a pooled component. It can then ensure that the pooled object is properly released at the end of every method call.

```
Public Class PooledClientTest
    Inherits System.Windows.Forms.Form

    Private Sub cmdGetData_Click(ByVal sender As System.Object, _
      ByVal e As System.EventArgs) Handles cmdGetData.Click

        DataGrid1.DataSource = Nothing

        Dim DBReader As New TestComponent.PooledDataReader()
        DataGrid1.DataSource = DBReader.Data.Tables(0)

        If DBReader.ConstructorFlag Then
            lblInfo.Text = "This data was retrieved from the " + _
                           "database in the constructor."
        Else
            lblInfo.Text = "This data was retrieved from memory."
        End If

        DBReader.ConstructorFlag = False

        ' Return the object to the pool.
        DBReader.Dispose()

    End Sub

End Class
```

Listing 9-6 A client for the pooled class

The pooled object will behave in a very interesting way. The first time you click the Get Data button, the *ConstructorFlag* variable will be *True*, indicating that the information was retrieved from the database. On subsequent clicks, however, the *ConstructorFlag* variable will be *False* because the constructor hasn't executed. Instead, the already instantiated object is provided directly to your client, as indicated by the client form in Figure 9-9. The information is retrieved from memory (the *_Data* property) and the database won't be touched—in fact, you can even take if off line. This behavior is even more powerful when you consider that the pooled object won't just be reused for requests from the same client; it will also be used to serve requests from different clients.

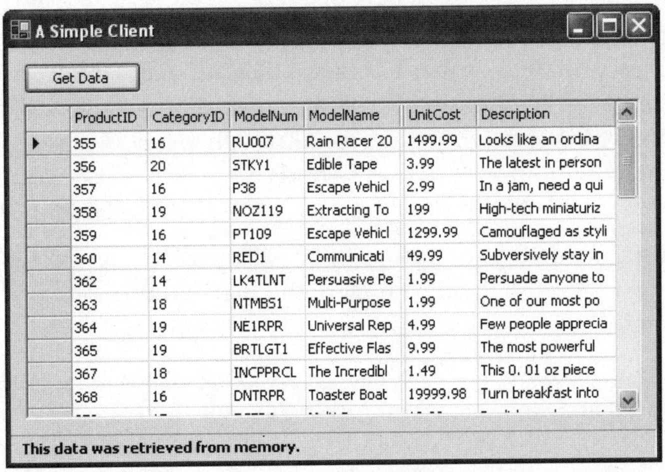

A Simple Client

Get Data

ProductID	CategoryID	ModelNum	ModelName	UnitCost	Description
355	16	RU007	Rain Racer 20	1499.99	Looks like an ordina
356	20	STKY1	Edible Tape	3.99	The latest in person
357	16	P38	Escape Vehicl	2.99	In a jam, need a qui
358	19	NOZ119	Extracting To	199	High-tech miniaturiz
359	16	PT109	Escape Vehicl	1299.99	Camouflaged as styli
360	14	RED1	Communicati	49.99	Subversively stay in
362	14	LK4TLNT	Persuasive Pe	1.99	Persuade anyone to
363	18	NTMBS1	Multi-Purpose	1.99	One of our most po
364	19	NE1RPR	Universal Rep	4.99	Few people apprecia
365	19	BRTLGT1	Effective Flas	9.99	The most powerful
367	18	INCPPRCL	The Incredibl	1.49	This 0. 01 oz piece
368	16	DNTRPR	Toaster Boat	19999.98	Turn breakfast into

This data was retrieved from memory.

Figure 9-9 The simple client with a pooled object

In this case, we're using a Windows Forms client for testing purposes. Remember that when you deploy this solution, you'll want to wrap the calls to the pooled component with a stateless service provider, as shown in Listing 9-7.

```
Public Class ServiceProvider

    <WebMethod()>_
    Public Sub GetData() As DataSet

        Dim DBReader As New TestComponent.PooledDataReader()
        Return DBReader.Data

    End Sub

End Class
```

Listing 9-7 A service provider that uses a pooled object

In this example, the *PooledDataReader* provides a form of caching. The data is retrieved once from the data source and reused for multiple requests. You don't need to use a pooled component to get this ability. XML Web services have built-in caching support, as you'll see in Chapter 12, which allows objects to be retained in memory according to set expiration policies. Components exposed through .NET Remoting have no such capability, however, and might benefit more from pooled component designs.

Establishing a Pool

COM+ gives you the power to fine-tune some aspects of connection pooling, including the following:

- **Minimum pool size** This is the number of objects created with the first request and the number of objects that are maintained and available in the pool at all times. COM+ automatically creates new objects as needed when the pool size dips. Although the pool size can grow above the minimum size, COM+ periodically performs a cleanup and reduces the number of pooled objects to the specified minimum size.
- **Maximum pool size** If a client requests the object and the number of existing objects is already equal to the maximum pool size, the client is forced to wait.
- **Creation timeout** If a client is forced to wait for this amount of time, in milliseconds, an exception is thrown.

> **Note** Remember that the minimum pool size determines the number of *available* objects that are maintained in the pool. In other words, if the minimum size is 10, COM+ reserves 10 free objects above and beyond those that are in use. The maximum pool size specifies the maximum number of objects that can be created at any one time, irrespective of how many objects are actually available.

Here's an example attribute that configures a minimum pool size of 5 and a maximum size of 20:

```
<ObjectPooling(5, 20)> _
```

You can use event logging to verify that the pool you expect is actually being created. For example, you can add the following code to the constructor of the *PooledDataReader*:

```
' Define a log message with the unique hash code for this object.
Dim LogMessage As String = "Pooled " & Me.GetHashCode()

' Write the message.
EventLog.WriteEntry("TestComponent", LogMessage)
```

The first time you run the component, you'll see several entries added to the event log: one entry for each object that was created. The total number of entries should correspond to the minimum pool size plus one. The additional object is used to satisfy the current client.

Consider Figure 9-10, for example, which shows six entries. The extra object was created so COM+ could maintain five available objects. After the client releases the extra object, it will return to the pool. Eventually, COM+ will notice the unneeded extra object and remove it.

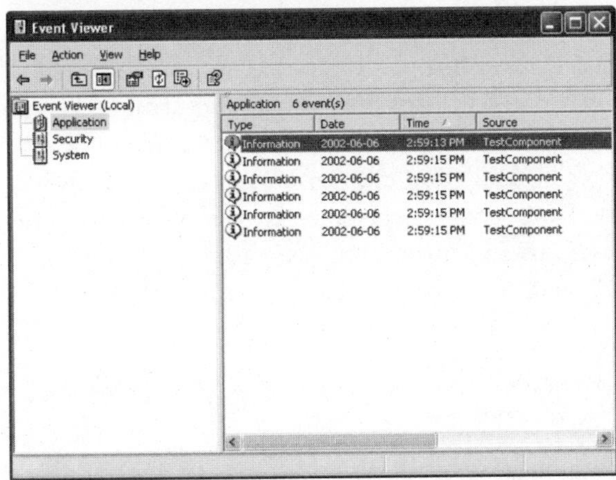

Figure 9-10 Event log entries for a pooled object

Keep in mind that the earlier example in Listing 9-6 might not work as expected if you use a minimum pool size because you might not receive the same object that you release. If you receive another object from the pool, the *ConstructorFlag* won't have been set to *False*.

The maximum pool size always takes precedence over the minimum pool size setting. Consider a case where you have a minimum pool size of 10 and 5 connections are currently in use. In this case, 10 additional connections will be created and added to the pool, provided the maximum pool size allows it. If the maximum pool size is less than 15, the number of new connections is constrained. If the maximum pool size is 10, however, there will be only 5 additional objects in the pool rather than the requested minimum of 10.

There are no definitive rules for optimum pool size settings. These settings depend on your system's processing capabilities and on the nature of the resource. (If you're wrapping a limited resource such as a license, for example, you should make the maximum pool size equal to the number of installed concurrent licenses.) Note that if you specify a large minimum pool size, the first request might take a long time to return.

Activation, Deactivation, and Conditional Pooling

Every pooled component can add additional object pooling logic by overriding three methods from the *ServicedComponent* class: *Activate*, *Deactivate*, and *CanBePooled*.

Deactivate is called by the .NET infrastructure every time a component is released and returned to the pool. It enables you to ensure that the object's in-memory data is in a reasonable state. *Activate* is called when the object is resurrected, just before it is presented to the client.

COM+ also enables you to programmatically determine whether an object should be pooled by using the *CanBePooled* method. If you have determined that the object has expired data or is in an inconsistent state, however, you can return *False* in this method. The object is destroyed when the client calls *Dispose*. Listing 9-8 shows an example that extends the caching approach by returning *False* if the object was created more than one hour ago.

```
<ObjectPooling()> _
Public Class PooledDataReader
    Inherits ServicedComponent

    Private ConnectionString = "Data Source=localhost;" + _
      "Initial Catalog=Store;Integrated Security=SSPI"

    Private _Data As DataSet
    Private CreateTime As DateTime

    Public Sub New()

        Dim con As New SqlConnection(ConnectionString)
        Dim cmd As New SqlCommand("SELECT * FROM Products", con)

        Dim adapter As New SqlDataAdapter(cmd)
        Dim ds As New DataSet()

        con.Open()
        adapter.Fill(ds)
        con.Close()
```

Listing 9-8 Customizing the *CanBePooled* method

```
        _Data = ds

        CreateTime = DateTime.Now

    End Sub

    Public ReadOnly Property Data() As DataSet
        Get
            Return _Data
        End Get
    End Property

    Protected Overrides Function CanBePooled() As Boolean

        If CreateTime.AddHours(1) > DateTime.Now
            Return True
        Else
            Return False
        End If

    End Function

End Class
```

Pooling and Data Providers

Technically, the *PooledDataReader* class that we examined earlier encapsulates a block of data. However, it's more common to create a pooled object that represents a handle to a data source. Consider the somewhat artificial example shown in Listing 9-9, which holds an open handle to a text file. The assumption here is that with multiple clients, the overhead of initializing this connection is significant compared to the actual file reading operation. (This probably isn't the case with a file, but it is likely with a database.)

```
Public Class PooledFileReader
    Inherits ServicedComponent

    Private fs As FileStream
    Private r As StreamReader

    Public Sub New()
        fs = New FileStream("C:\data.txt", FileMode.Open)
        r = New StreamReader(fs)
    End Sub
```

Listing 9-9 Using pooling with a data provider

```
    Public Function GetData() As String
        fs.Position = 0
        Return r.ReadToEnd
    End Function

    Protected Overrides Function CanBePooled() As Boolean
        Return True
    End Function

End Class
```

When implementing a data provider, you commonly need to restrict access. For example, consider the result of using this code in a client:

```
Dim r1 As New PooledTextReader()
Dim r2 As New PooledTextReader()
```

In the Windows operating system, only one process at a time can open a text file. In this case, the second line generates an exception resulting from a file access error. You can defend against this error by implementing a pooling restriction:

```
<ObjectPooling(1, 1)> _
Public Class PooledFileReader
```

Because both the minimum and maximum pool size are set to *1*, there will only ever be one instance of the *PooledTextReader* object. Technically, it's a singleton component (although it's different from a .NET Remoting singleton in that only one client at a time can use it). Now, when another client attempts to create the object, a COM+ timeout error is eventually generated rather than a file access error.

This approach doesn't appear to be much of an improvement—either way, the second line causes an error. However, consider what happens in a more sophisticated case in which the data-provider object corresponds to a licensed resource. If you don't use pooling, when the number of clients rises above the number of licenses, every client starts to experience license violation errors as it attempts to invoke methods. Therefore, the entire system is compromised by the heavy client load. On the other hand, if you use object pooling to restrict the maximum number of objects to the number of available licenses, additional clients are prevented from connecting. Some users (the additional clients) are affected, but those who are currently using the system can carry on, finish their work, and eventually release their objects back to the pool. This scenario also applies when a pooled object is protecting a resource that taxes the server hardware or memory. If too many clients are allowed to connect, the entire system can fail. Resource management entails limiting the maximum client load to guarantee a certain baseline level of connectivity.

Object Pooling vs. Connection Pooling

Most ADO.NET providers include support for connection pooling. Connection pooling is conceptually similar to object pooling. As with object pooling, its goal is to set usage maximums and avoid the overhead of repeatedly creating connections. With connection pooling, the connection is released to the pool when the *Close* method is called and is acquired when the *Open* method is invoked. With object pooling, the process is similar: the object is released using a *Dispose* method and is acquired automatically when it's instantiated.

You can look at connection pooling as a special case of object pooling. In many distributed systems, however, connection pooling provides all the object pooling you need because the key server resource being exposed to remote clients is the database. This is certainly true of the service provider example introduced in Chapter 2.

In the past, connection pooling wasn't sufficient because many forms of connection pooling didn't enforce minimum and maximum pool sizes. They might have reduced the overhead required to acquire a connection, but they failed miserably at restricting the load when too many clients connected at once. OLE DB resource pooling still suffers from this problem. For that reason, developers were sometimes encouraged to disable this OLE DB pooling and use COM+ object pooling in its place. If you're using an OLE DB resource with a large client load, you might still choose to do so (or develop your own custom pooling strategy, as briefly outlined in Chapter 7).

However, both the SQL Server provider and the Oracle .NET provider use their own form of connection pooling that is conceptually similar to COM+ object pooling. That means pool maximums and minimums are strictly enforced. Chapter 12 describes how connection pooling can be configured through connection string settings and develops a sample application to test its success with an XML Web service. With either the SQL Server or the Oracle .NET provider, you have the best that COM+ object pooling can offer, completely for free. The pooling mechanism is also optimized for speed and handily outperforms OLE DB resource pooling.

Just-in-Time Activation

JIT activation is another form of instance management. Whereas object pooling reduces the overhead involved with creating objects, JIT activation can reduce the overhead needed to maintain objects. To understand why JIT activation was developed, you need to consider the types of clients used in common distributed systems with COM.

Object pooling solves the problem that occurs when an object is expensive to create and must be created frequently. This problem typically appears with stateless client models. In the past, these problems were most commonly seen with ASP Web sites. Typically, when a client interacts with a Web page in ASP (or its successor, ASP.NET), a database object is created, used, and then disposed of. If the client performs several tasks (such as adding items to a shopping basket, configuring account information, and placing an order), these database objects might be re-created and disposed several times in a short period of time. This is where object pooling or connection pooling can dramatically reduce the load.

With rich clients, the situation was a little different. Typically, a rich client in a COM-based distributed application would create a reference to a remote database component (using DCOM) and potentially hold this reference for a long period of time. This is known as the "greedy client" problem, and it's a large part of the reason that JIT activation was invented.

With the greedy client problem, an object might be kept alive for a long period of time, wasting server resources. To compensate for this behavior, JIT activation automatically destroys the object at the end of each method call. The next time the client performs a method invocation, a new object is created to serve the request. Therefore, the client can maintain a permanent reference but no object is tied up at the server end.

JIT activation trades performance for scalability—a common pattern in distributed applications. Re-creating an object each time the client needs it requires some work at the server side, and it adds time to the method request. However, the benefit is seen when the number of clients increases. Without JIT activation, greedy clients could starve a server of all its resources (typically memory and database connections), compromising the entire system. With JIT activation, the server footprint is lessened.

To mark a component for JIT activation, you need to add the *<JustInTimeActivation>* attribute to the class definition:

```
<JustInTimeActivation()> _
Public Class JITTest
```

By default, a JIT-activated object isn't automatically destroyed unless you explicitly state at the end of a method that it should be. You can do this in one of two ways. The first way is to add the *<AutoComplete>* attribute to the method, ensuring that the object is always deactivated when the method terminates, as follows:

```
<AutoComplete()> _
Public Sub DoSomething()

    ' Object is destroyed when this method ends.

End Sub
```

Another option is to use the *ContextUtil.SetComplete* method. This enables you to make the deactivation decision programmatically. If you determine that the object has important information in state, for example, you can refrain from calling *SetComplete* and keep it alive:

```
Public Sub DoSomething()

    If Data Is Nothing Then
        ContextUtil.SetComplete()
    End If

End Sub
```

> **Note** JIT activation is one rare case in which deterministic finalization returns to .NET programming. Because the serviced component deactivates itself, you can be sure it will be released after you call *SetComplete* or an *<AutoComplete>* method returns.

JIT-activated objects don't need to be stateless, but they lose all their state every time they are destroyed. Consider the serviced component in Listing 9-10.

```
<JustInTimeActivation()> _
Public Class JITTest
    Inherits ServicedComponent

    Public ConstructorFlag As Boolean
    Public Data As String

    Public Sub New()
        ConstructorFlag = True
    End Sub

    Public Sub DoSomething()
        ' Test method.
        ContextUtil.SetComplete()
    End Sub

End Class
```

Listing 9-10 A simple JIT class

This object stores state in two member variables: *ConstructorFlag* and *Data*. However, this information is abandoned after every method call. Consider the following client code:

```
Dim JIT As New TestComponent.JITTest()

JIT.ConstructorFlag = False
JIT.Data = "My String"

' After this method the object will be deactivated.
JIT.DoSomething()

Dim Status As String

If JIT.ConstructorFlag
    Status = "The constructor executed again. "
    Status &= "The object was reconstructed."
Else
    Status = "The constructor did not execute."
End If

Status &= Environment.NewLine
Status &= "Data is: " & JIT.Data

MessageBox.Show(Status)
```

Figure 9-11 shows the result of this code. Clearly, the JIT object was reconstructed and the data set by the client was lost.

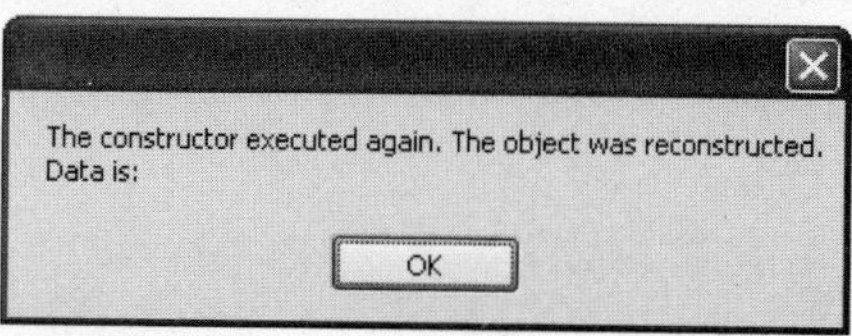

Figure 9-11 Testing a JIT object

JIT-activated objects can override the *Activate* and *Deactivate* methods to serialize state to some sort of durable storage between method calls, but this isn't generally recommended. To tie an object with a specific state record, you need to use some sort of ticket system. For example, the object returns a ticket value to the client, and the client then needs to submit this ticket as an additional parameter for every method call, to allow the object to look up the saved state. The ticket can be a unique number or GUID. Chapter 13 describes ticket systems in detail.

JIT Activation and Object Pooling

JIT activation becomes particularly useful when combined with object pooling. This combination enables you to avoid having to re-create objects. Instead, objects are immediately released and returned to the pool at the end of every method call. In this case, a JIT object can also retain state. It's important to remember, however, that the only valid state you can use is information that is generic to all clients because a single client might receive a different instance of the object with each method call. That means it doesn't make sense for an object that uses JIT activation and object pooling to have a property procedure such as the one shown earlier in Listing 9-10.

Remember that with object pooling you need to override the *CanBePooled* method to specify whether the object should be destroyed or returned to the pool. (See Listing 9-11.) When you combine JIT activation and pooling, .NET first examines the context to determine whether the object should be deactivated. If you have called *SetComplete* or your method uses the *<AutoComplete>* attribute, .NET calls the *CanBePooled* method to determine whether the object should be destroyed or placed in the pool. If you have not called *SetComplete* or used the *<AutoComplete>* attribute, the object remains alive and is not pooled.

```
<JustInTimeActivation (), ObjectPooling()> _
Public Class JITTest
    Inherits ServicedComponent

    Public ConstructorFlag As Boolean

    Public Sub New()
        ConstructorFlag = True
    End Sub

    Public Sub DoSomething()
        ' Test method.
        ContextUtil.SetComplete()
    End Sub

    Protected Overrides Function CanBePooled() As Boolean
        Return True
    End Function

End Class
```

Listing 9-11 A simple pooled JIT class

If you test the class shown in Listing 9-11, you'll discover that the *ConstructorFlag* is not set on subsequent method invocations. That's because the object is served from the pool, not re-created.

JIT Activation and .NET

For the .NET programmer, JIT activation is probably not as useful as object pooling because the greedy client problem is rare in the world of .NET. In fact, .NET tackles this problem by using a stateless model with XML Web services and single-call .NET Remoting objects. These objects follow the same activation pattern as JIT-activated objects in COM+: They are created at the start of a method call and are destroyed at the end, even though the client might maintain a reference over the lifetime of the application. In fact, the only way to hold a direct reference to a remote COM+ object in .NET is through a COM proxy that uses DCOM. This is already unlikely due to the complexity of DCOM!

Conversely, this means that pooling (either COM+ object pooling or ADO.NET connection pooling) is that much more important because objects are typically created and destroyed frequently in a typical .NET distributed system. JIT activation is still useful when you don't have any control over the client that is using the COM+ component—but these situations are far less common in .NET than they were with COM-based applications.

Automatic Transactions

Transactions are one of the best-known features of COM+. In fact, Microsoft Transaction Server (MTS), the predecessor to COM+, was even named after them. That said, a surprising amount of confusion surrounds exactly what a COM+ transaction is and what it is supposed to accomplish. This confusion leads many developers to implement COM+ transactions in places where they only slow performance.

A COM+ transaction isn't a replacement for client-initiated ADO.NET transactions or stored procedure transactions. These types of transactions are handled directly by the data source, which allows them to complete much more quickly. In the case of a transaction encapsulated by a stored procedure, the entire process can take place on the server without requiring any additional network calls. This provides excellent performance.

With a COM+ transaction, the COM+ runtime is in charge, along with the Distributed Transaction Coordinator (DTC) built into Windows. The first consequence of this fact is that if you want to use a COM+ transaction, the data source (or *resource manager*) must be able to work with COM+. Technically, it must support a protocol known as OLE Transactions. Quite a few data sources meet these requirements, including SQL Server (from version 6.5 later), Oracle 8i and 9i, MSMQ, and IBM DB2, just to name a few.

Using the Component Services utility, you can disable the DTC service, monitor a transaction underway, or study transaction statistics (as shown in Figure 9-12).

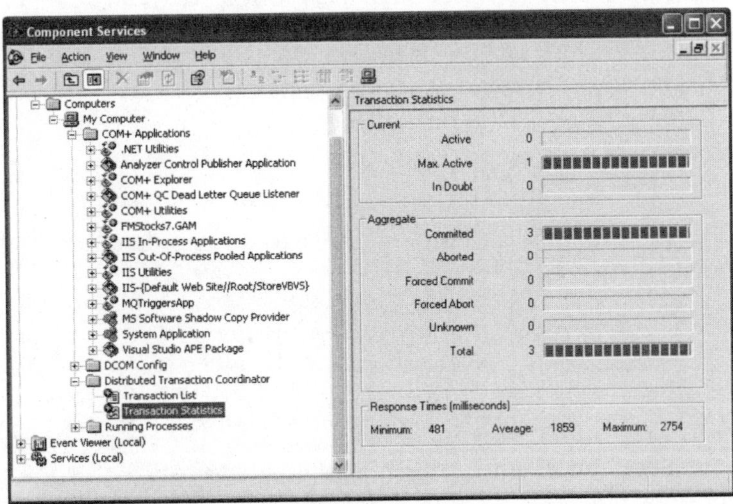

Figure 9-12 The DTC service

Although one DTC coordinates every COM+ transaction, multiple DTCs might be involved in the transaction. If you have data sources on different machines, the DTC service on multiple servers participates in managing the transaction, as shown in Figure 9-13.

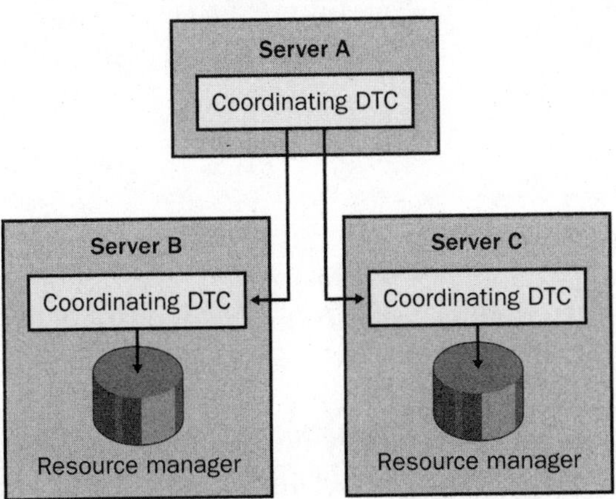

Figure 9-13 Multiple DTCs in a transaction

COM+ uses a two-stage commit process. In the first stage, it asks all the involved resource managers, "If I asked you to commit the changes, could you?" If all the resource managers can apply the change, it uses the second stage to tell all the resource managers to go ahead and commit changes. If any one resource manager responds that it can't commit the changes, COM+ and the DTC instruct all the resource managers to roll back the changes.

Therefore, two of the key characteristics of COM+ transactions are as follows:

- They are slower than database transactions. They also require more network traffic because of the interaction required between COM+ and the data source.
- They require support for resource managers. Most database products will work, but a transaction that involves actions that modify the file system will not be reversible.

Of course, COM+ services provide some advantages:

- They allow transactions to span multiple data sources and multiple servers. These are known as *distributed transactions*.
- They allow transactions to be completed automatically. The component does not need to have any knowledge of the underlying data source and how it manages transactions.
- They give the programmer the freedom to tie together different processes into a single transaction. The components don't require any knowledge of the scope of the transaction.

The first point represents the most common reason that COM+ transactions are used. If you need this ability or you need to tie together a set of processes in a number of varying processes, COM+ transactions just might be the ticket.

Objects and Transactions

Under COM+, transactions are not started and committed explicitly. Instead, you use attributes to identify transactional objects. A transaction is automatically created when a method is executed in a transactional object. If the object encounters an error, the transaction is rolled back and any changes made to a compatible resource manager are canceled.

COM+ transactions can be conceptually divided into two types: those that take place inside a single object (and span a single method call) and those that span multiple objects and multiple method calls. You specify the way that your object can be used in a transaction by adding the <*Transaction*> attribute to the class definition of the serviced component. This attribute generally indicates that your class requires a transaction or will optionally run inside the caller's transaction context, depending on the value you use from the *TransactionOption* enumeration. Table 9-1 lists the *TransactionOption* values.

Table 9-1 Values from the *TransactionOption* Enumeration

Value	Description
Required	This object must run in a transaction. If the caller has already started a transaction, this object participates inside that transaction. Otherwise, a new transaction is created.
RequiresNew	This object must run in a transaction. If the caller has already started a transaction, a new transaction is created for this object. This isn't a nested transaction but a completely independent transaction. Therefore, you must be careful when using this setting to make sure that it can't violate the consistency of the system if it commits but the caller's transaction is rolled back.
Supported	This object can run in a transaction and is enlisted in the caller's transaction if it exists. Otherwise, it does not run in a transaction.
NotSupported	This object does not participate in a transaction. If the caller has a current transaction, this object can't vote on it. However, this object could generate an exception, which, if not handled by the caller, will end up rolling back the transaction.
Disabled	The object doesn't have any transaction requirements or contact a database. This is the default value. It is similar to *NotSupported*, but the object might execute faster because it might be activated in the caller's context, saving the overhead of cross-context calls.

If you're using COM+ to allow one object to perform a distributed transaction that updates multiple data sources, you will probably use *TransactionOption.Required*. Listing 9-12 shows an example.

```
<Transaction(TransactionOption.Required)> _
Public Class TransactionTest
    Inherits ServicedComponent

    Public Sub CommitChanges()

        Try
            ' (Perform changes.)

            ' No errors were encountered.
            ' Vote to commit the transaction.
```

Listing 9-12 A simple transactional class

```
            ContextUtil.MyTransactionVote = TransactionVote.Commit

        Catch Err As Exception
            ' An error was detected. Vote to abort the transaction.
            ContextUtil.MyTransactionVote = TransactionVote.Abort

        Finally
            ' The object must be deactivated before COM+ will perform
            ' the final commit or abort.
            ContextUtil.DeactivateOnReturn = True

        End Try

    End Sub

End Class
```

Consider, for example, what will happen if a client uses the transactional component in Listing 9-12 as follows:

```
Dim DBComponent As New TransactionTest()
DBComponent.CommitChanges()
```

When the *CommitChanges* method is invoked, several steps will happen:

1. COM+ checks whether a transaction is in progress in the caller's context. Because one is not, it starts a new transaction.
2. COM+ intercepts all the database operations and performs them in the scope of the new transaction (provided the data source supports OLE Transactions).
3. If an error isn't encountered, the component votes to commit the transaction.
4. The component sets itself to deactivate.
5. When the component deactivates, COM+ checks to see whether the component voted to commit. If it has, COM+ attempts to apply the transaction using its two-stage commit process.

Listing 9-12 uses an explicit syntax to help make it clear exactly what is taking place. However, you can use the *<AutoComplete>* attribute to save a considerable amount of code. When you apply *<AutoComplete>* to a method, the component deactivates immediately when the method ends. Furthermore, the transaction is automatically committed, assuming no unhandled exceptions are encountered. If an unhandled exception is generated, the transaction is rolled back.

Listing 9-13 shows the equivalent code with *<AutoComplete>*.

```
<Transaction(TransactionOption.Required)> _
Public Class TransactionTest
    Inherits ServicedComponent

    <AutoComplete>
    Public Sub CommitChanges()

        ' (Perform changes.)

        ' If any errors are encountered, the transaction will be
        ' rolled back.
        ' Otherwise, it will be committed when this method ends.

    End Sub

End Class
```

Listing 9-13 A simple transactional class with *AutoComplete*

Even when you use *<AutoComplete>*, you can still vote explicitly. In fact, you might need to. If you call another component that returns an error code instead of throwing an exception, for instance, you need to signal to COM+ that a problem has been encountered and the transaction should not continue.

Remember that the reason the *CommitChanges* method is implemented as a COM+ transaction is because it modifies more than one data source. If it modified only one data source, it could use an ADO.NET client-initiated transaction. If it performed all its work in a single stored procedure, it could use an even more efficient stored procedure transaction.

The next section examines how more than one transactional component can work together.

> **Note** You must be careful when mixing transactional and nontransactional components. If a transactional component calls a method in a nontransactional component and that method commits a change to a data source, that change is applied immediately. That means it won't be undone if the caller's transaction fails and is rolled back.

Rolling a Custom Transaction

If you're using transactions so a client has the option of tying several object methods together in a single atomic unit, you will probably use *TransactionOption.Supported*, which is more flexible than *TransactionOption.Required*. For example, a service provider object might use *TransactionOption.Supported* to mark a method such as *AddCustomer*. This allows the client to call *AddCustomer* on its own, without incurring the overhead of a transaction. However, it also allows the client to bind together several methods in one transaction (such as *AddCustomer* and *AddOrder*), ensuring that they fail or succeed as a unit.

The simplest case occurs when one transactional component calls another *TransactionOption.Supported* or *TransactionOption.Required* component. In either case, the second component is enlisted in the first component's transaction. If either component votes to abort the transaction, COM+ rolls back all the operations made by both components.

Another possibility is that a nontransactional client calls several transactional components. By default, each transactional component is placed in a distinct transaction that is committed or aborted separately. To overcome this problem, you need to make use of an unmanaged DLL called comsvcs.dll. You can add a reference to this COM object easily in a .NET project (as shown in Figure 9-14). No RCW interop class needs to be generated because one is already provided with the .NET Framework. (Look for the file named Interop.ComsvcsLib.dll.)

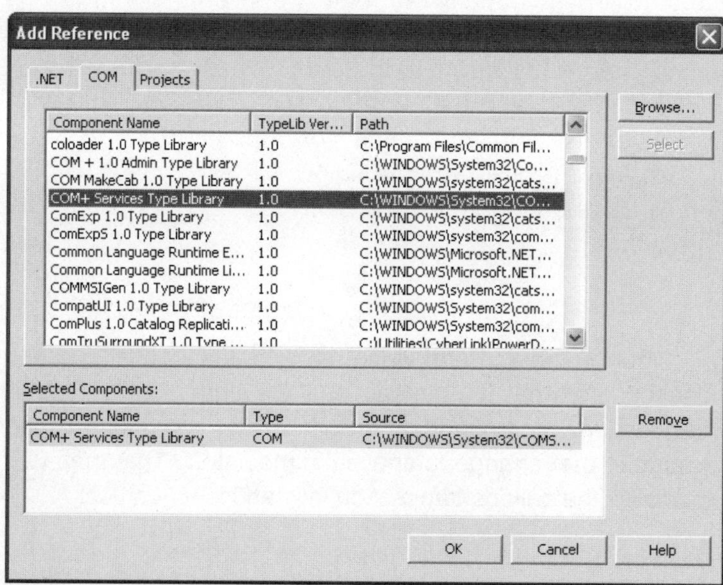

Figure 9-14 Adding a reference to comsvcs.dll

Next, you import the COM+ services namespace:

```
Imports COMSVCSLib
```

Finally, with a little more work and the help of the *TransactionContext* class, you can create a new transaction and place multiple objects inside it, as shown in Listing 9-14.

```
' Create the transaction.
Dim Tran As New TransactionContext()

' Define the objects.
Dim ObjA As TransactionalClassA
Dim ObjB As TransactionalClassB

' Create the objects inside the transaction context.
ObjA = Tran.CreateInstance("TestComponent.TransactionalClassA")
ObjB = Tran.CreateInstance("TestComponent.TransactionalClassB")

Try
    ' Attempt to use the two classes in this transaction
    ObjA.DoSomething()
    ObjB.DoSomething()

    ' No errors were encountered.
    ' Commit the transaction.
    Tran.Commit()

Catch err As Exception
    ' Roll back the transaction.
    Tran.Abort()

End Try
```

Listing 9-14 Hosting a transaction with a nonserviced client

> **Note** Chapter 10 introduces another way to look at combining objects in a transaction: with the facade pattern. This approach is less flexible (it won't support multiple data sources at once), but it performs better and doesn't require COM+ serviced components.

Isolation Levels

By default, COM+ transactions use an isolation level of Serializable. This is the best choice for data integrity, but it can also hamper performance because it requires stricter locks at the data source level. If your component is running under COM+ 1.5, it can take advantage of a configurable transaction isolation level:

```
<Transaction(TransactionOption.Required, _
 Isolation := TransactionIsolationLevel.Serializable> _
Public Class TransactionalClass
```

Note that no constructor for the *<Transaction>* attribute accepts a *TransactionIsolationLevel* value, so you need to specify the property by name. You can set one of five values for the *Isolation* property, as described in Table 9-2. The list is ordered from least to greatest protection.

Table 9-2 Values from the *TransactionIsolationLevel* Enumeration

Value	Description
Any	The calling component's isolation level is used. If this is the root component, the isolation level used is Serializable.
ReadUncommitted	The transaction can read uncommitted updates left by another transaction (even though these changes might be rolled back).
ReadCommitted	The transaction will not read uncommitted data from another transaction, but another user can change the data that this transaction is using. This is the default isolation level that a SQL Server transaction uses.
RepeatableRead	Locks are placed on any data this transaction reads, ensuring that other users can't modify it. However, a row can be inserted that changes the results of your transaction. This is a subtle issue know as *phantom inserts*.
Serialized	Prevents updating or inserting until the transaction is complete. Therefore, no changes can be made that could change the outcome of your transaction while it is in progress.

Be careful when changing the *TransactionIsolationLevel*. The root component of a transaction can't call another component that requires a higher level of protection. (For example, a root *ReadCommitted* object can't enlist a *RepeatableRead* object in the same transaction.)

Also keep in mind that these transaction isolation levels are not absolute because they are not really in the control of COM+. Rather, they must be respected by the resource managers taking part in the transaction.

Web Method Transactions

Web methods have built-in support for COM+ transactions. However, this support comes with a significant limitation. Because of the stateless nature of the

HTTP protocol, an XML Web service method can participate only as the root of a transaction. That means you can't enlist more than one Web method into a single transaction. You can create other transactional components, however, and have them take part in a Web method transaction.

To enable transaction support for a Web method, you use the *TransactionOption* property of the *WebMethod* attribute (as shown in Listing 9-15). Although this property accepts all the standard *TransactionOption* values, they don't have the expected meanings. For example, *Disabled*, *NotSupported*, and *Supported* all have the same effect: They disable transaction support. Similarly, *Required* and *RequiresNew* both enable transaction support *and* start a new transaction. I recommend that you use *RequiresNew* in your Web methods because this most clearly matches the actual behavior.

Inside your transactional Web method, you can perform a variety of tasks, such as updating one or more data sources. You also can create serviced components that will run inside this transaction (provided they are marked with *TransactionOption.Required* or *TransactionOption.Supported*).

```
<WebMethod(TransactionOption := TransactionOption.RequiresNew)> _
Public Sub DoSomething()

    ' (Create other serviced components if desired.)
    ' (Attempt some tasks.)

    ' This transaction will be committed when the method ends,
    ' assuming no unhandled exceptions were encountered.

End Sub
```

Listing 9-15 A transactional Web method

Web methods behave as though you have applied the *<AutoComplete>* attribute. The Web method transaction is committed when the Web method completes, provided no exceptions are encountered. If an unhandled exception is thrown, the transaction is rolled back. The case study in Chapter 18 presents a good example of how a COM+ transaction can be used in a Web service.

Less Useful COM+ Services

Unfortunately, not every COM+ feature is as easy to use as instance management and automatic transactions. Although in principle it is possible to use any COM+ feature with a .NET-serviced component, some place additional restrictions, don't play well with other .NET technologies, or just aren't needed anymore.

The following sections describe several features of COM+ that .NET developers probably won't use, at least in this release of .NET. Keep in mind that these are general recommendations only. You might develop a design that uses one or more of these features effectively. However, most of these features are constrained by .NET interop issues and aren't as important as they are in the COM-based world of programming.

> **Note** Some of these COM+ features will have improved support in future versions of the .NET Framework. Others might be replaced by new features written entirely in managed code.

Currently, COM+ services are used by the CLR but are *provided* by the COM+ runtime, not the CLR. In the future, the managed equivalent of COM+ services will most likely be integrated directly into the CLR, as garbage collection is in the current .NET Framework. In fact, this design was initially planned for the first release of .NET, but it couldn't be accomplished in the set timeframe.

Queued Components

Queued components enable you to use Message Queuing to communicate between components. To your code, a queued call looks like an ordinary method call. But behind the scenes the call is recorded, queued, and then replayed on the real object sometime in the future. Queued components are very scalable, provide automatic message retransmission, and can transmit role-based security information from the caller.

Queued components work best with a dedicated COM proxy. If you don't use COM/DCOM, all calls must flow through a .NET layer, like an XML Web service or a .NET Remoting component host. This .NET layer reduces the value of queued components because it means that the server can't be off line when the call is made. The problem is that even though the component itself is queued, there is no way to create a queued XML Web service or .NET Remoting host.

One alternative is to access Message Queuing directly, as described in Chapter 8. This provides the same functionality as a queued component but forces you to write tightly coupled code that uses specific Message Queue objects. In the future, a .NET Remoting channel may be developed that flows over Message Queuing, allowing developers to communicate transparently with queued components once again.

Role-Based Security

Role-based security allows you to define logical roles for your application such as Administrator, Manager, and so on. After you associate a role with an object, interface, or method, COM+ ensures that only the users in the appropriate roles can access the object. Best of all, the process of creating and associating roles is performed through the Component Services utility so your component doesn't need to contain security code. Unfortunately, role-based security information isn't available to nonserviced components and does not flow over a .NET Remoting channel. This makes it unsuited for any system that isn't entirely built on COM+. .NET provides other role-based security systems, including ones based on Windows accounts or an ASP.NET configuration file. These are generally less powerful but better integrated into the .NET Framework. Chapter 13 discusses the options and shows you how to build your own custom role-based authentication.

Synchronization

Synchronization controls how multiple threads can access your object simultaneously. It isn't required in most .NET scenarios. Instead, you can use .NET threading, which isn't declarative and requires dedicated threading code. .NET includes ample features for handling locks, synchronization, and so forth, as described in Chapter 7 and Chapter 8.

Loosely Coupled Events

A *loosely coupled event* is a publisher-subscriber event model in which COM+ handles the event delivery, and the sender is unaware of whether or not specific clients receive the event. This event handling model is very scalable, but it suffers from some limitations (such as no intrinsic support for firing events across machine boundaries). It's also much more work to implement in .NET.

Instead of using COM+ loosely coupled events, you can use .NET events or callbacks and bidirectional .NET Remoting channels where needed. These communication methods also have limitations, but certain techniques (such as using the <*OneWay*> attribute) can help ensure scalability and optimum performance, without the complexity of COM+ integration.

Object Construction String

An *object construction string* enables you to specify a string of configuration information in Component Services. This string is then provided to the component. This feature is still available in .NET. However, .NET already enables you to set configuration information without recompiling the code through XML configuration files, which is generally a more convenient approach.

SOAP Services (Only in COM+ 1.5)

SOAP services allow you to expose a COM+ application as a .NET XML Web service if you configure it in the Component Services tool. This feature uses the .NET runtime. It's not needed in .NET. You have more flexibility using .NET Remoting or XML Web services directly.

Summary

As one developer put it so well, "The overwhelmingly positive benefits COM+ offered to COM development aren't so overwhelmingly positive in .NET." It's often said that the *EnterpriseServices* namespace gives .NET access to the full set of COM+ features. This is more or less true, but it doesn't tell the whole story. In .NET, you can't apply COM+ services in the same way that you would in a COM-based application. First of all, if you do, you could end up with DCOM nightmares and distribution headaches. Second, some COM+ features bring their own .NET baggage, including limitations that compromise their use with other types of components or managed code (such as role-based security or queued components). Third, you don't have to apply COM+ services in .NET—many features of .NET mirror COM+ services, although they can't replace them in all situations. Using COM+ effectively in .NET means knowing where COM+ can truly provide a benefit that the CLR can't—and how to integrate it into the service provider model with XML Web services and .NET Remoting.

Part II

Developing an Architecture

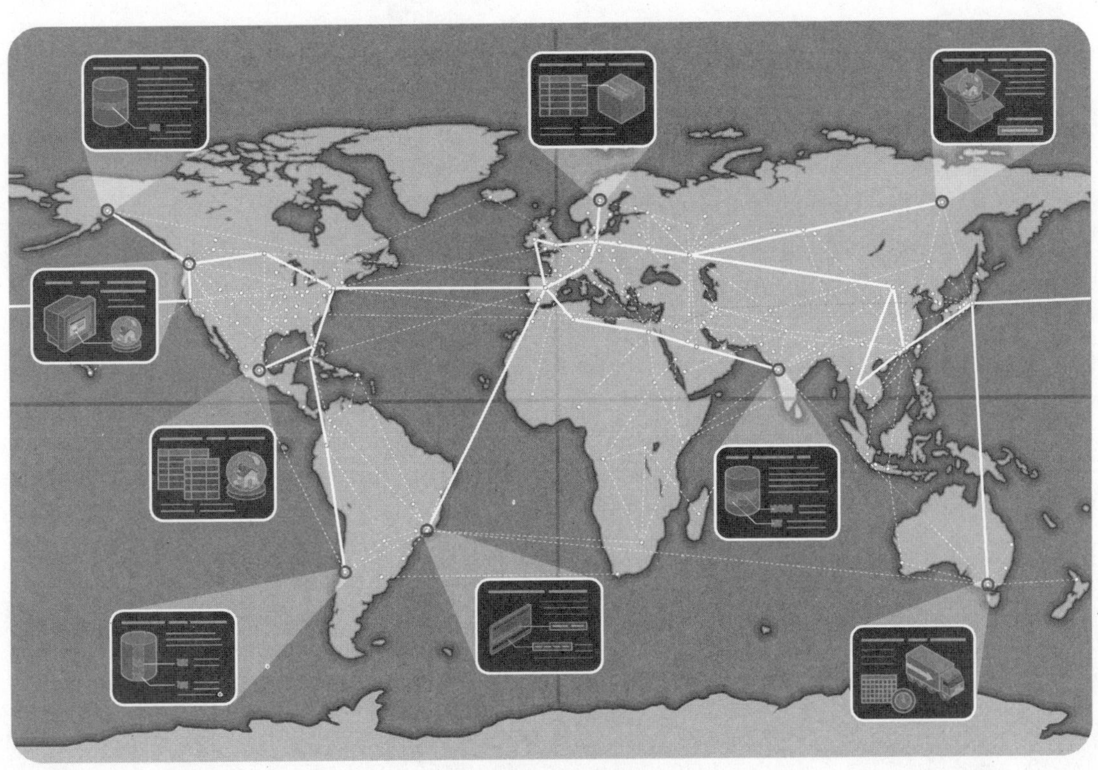

10

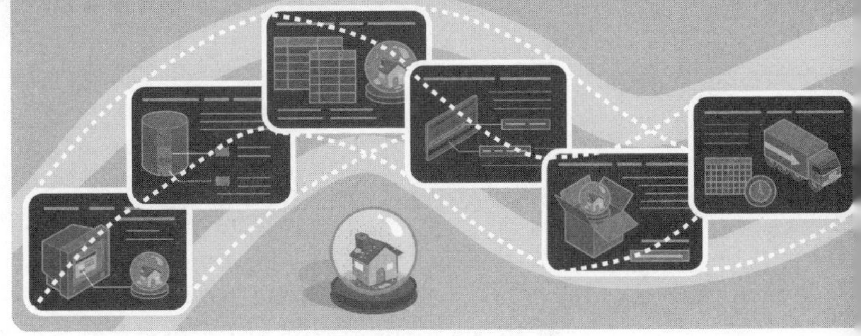

Enterprise Application Modeling

Part I of this book presented the .NET technologies that you need to create distributed applications. Each one of these technologies is a key to solving a particular problem or unlocking a particular feature for a distributed system. However, you can't apply these technologies blindly. If you do, the result will be a disorganized, poorly performing tangle of code. Your use of features such as XML Web services, .NET Remoting, threading, and COM+ services must emerge from a well-planned design.

This chapter considers the fundamental considerations for planning a distributed system. These include the role each component should play, how different parts of the system should communicate, and where business rules should take effect. We'll also tackle the question of state, a few key design patterns (factories, facades, and interfaces), and some guidelines to follow when choosing among different .NET technologies.

Key Considerations for Distributed Components

One of the most harmful myths in software development is that server-side components should act the same way as local objects. Experienced developers realize that a distributed application design must begin and end with practical consideration of the existing technologies. Otherwise, it's all too easy to create an elegant, carefully planned architecture that is fundamentally unworkable. Usually these flawed designs are implemented to some degree before their shortcomings are discovered and quickly reach a bottleneck that can't be overcome.

One common mistake is to look at distributed components as full partners in object-oriented design. Unfortunately, distributed programming represents a compromise between networking technology and object-oriented practices, not a union. Some of these limitations can be overcome with ingenious workarounds (and many articles demonstrate these sorts of coding hacks), but performance almost always suffers.

The next two sections consider two fundamental differences between local code and server code and the design implications of these differences.

Cross-Process and Cross-Computer Communication

One key difference between local and remote code is that remote object communication takes a nontrivial amount of time. This is true whether you are calling a time-consuming method or just setting a simple property. Interacting with an object in another application domain can be hundreds of times slower than interacting with an in-process component. Interacting with a component on another computer or a remote Web server can easily be another order of magnitude slower, even over the fastest possible network connections.

From the developer's point of view, calling a method in a remote object is just as easy as invoking a local method. However, you should always keep in mind that the code you write is just an abstraction over a complex infrastructure that creates a network connection, dispatches a request, and waits for a response. That means if you design your remote object in a traditional style, with numerous properties that need to be set in conjunction, you add extra latency, increase network traffic, and slow down the performance of the entire system.

If the client needs to set four properties before calling a method, for example, that translates into four network calls and four small but measurable delays. The result is a sluggish client application that only grows slower as the load increases. The costs become even higher if you need to create a transaction that spans more than one object interaction because the Microsoft Distributed Transaction Coordinator (DTC) service must be invoked.

The communication problem is one of the reasons that remote objects are always designed as a collection of utility functions (like an old-fashioned DLL) rather than as an abstraction over a real-word entity. Another reason is state.

The Question of State

The other difference between remote objects and local objects is that remote objects rarely retain in-memory information, or state. Some developers have discovered the problems of stateful server components the hard way—by creating components that work perfectly well at first but bring the server to a near standstill as the number of clients grows and the memory load soars. Even a small amount of information can become a heavy burden when multiplied by hundreds or thousands of clients, particularly if they don't signal when they are complete and allow the required cleanup.

Using up server memory isn't the only problem with stateful server-side components. If you store state information in server memory, you effectively tie that instance of the object to a single machine and make it impossible to load-balance the system. If you try to load-balance a stateful system, a client request might be routed to a different computer that doesn't have the correct in-memory information and the state data will be lost.

The two remote object technologies in .NET—XML Web services and .NET Remoting—handle the issues of state very differently. .NET Remoting encourages you to create single-call stateless objects, but it also provides support for stateful client-activated and singleton objects. XML Web services are inherently stateless. Memory can be stored in server memory using the ASP.NET session state service, but there are several limitations:

- The client needs to receive an HTTP cookie and maintain it. If this cookie is lost, the client neglects its duty, or the method of communication is not over HTTP, state management is not possible.
- The state information is tied to a cookie, which contains a randomly generated unique string for the client. Programmatically, state is managed through a key-based dictionary collection. There is no way to associate state with a specific class instance—or even with a specific class.
- The state information is held in perpetuity unless you programmatically remove it or the session times out (typically after 20 minutes without any use).

Interestingly, ASP.NET resolves the load-balancing dilemma by allowing multiple computers to store state information on a single designated server or in a shared database. This solution is far from perfect, however. For one thing, it sacrifices one of the main benefits of in-memory state: performance. By storing state information in another process or on another computer, you ensure that calls to store or retrieve a piece of state data will execute much more slowly. Most of the examples in this book avoid session state and its limitations or use a more flexible alternative such as caching (discussed in Chapter 12).

The Difference Between Stateless Singleton and Single-Call Objects

Here's a question you can use to puzzle a seasoned .NET guru: If you create a stateless object for .NET Remoting, is there any difference between single-call and singleton activation types?

You'll remember that with singleton objects, all clients access the same object. In fact, multiple clients can access the object at the same time because .NET uses a thread pool to handle concurrent requests. As you saw in Chapter 7, if multiple clients try to access a member variable in a singleton object at the same time, you need to add some synchronization code to make sure nothing goes wrong. But here's the twist: In a stateless object, there are no member variables. Therefore, there are no possible threading conflicts!

The answer to this riddle is that a stateless class performs about the same whether it is a singleton object or a single-call object. In fact, the singleton object might even perform a little better because .NET doesn't need to create the object for each new client request. The reason Microsoft recommends that you use single-call objects rather than singleton objects is to ensure that you follow stateless design practices, which will make your life simpler in the long run.

Are Remote Objects Really Objects?

What I've said so far should suggest to you that remote objects aren't exactly objects—at least not in the traditional object-oriented sense of the word. A good example of this difference is an imaginary *Account* class. Listing 10-1 shows how you might implement this class in a traditional object-oriented application.

```
Public Class Account

    ' For simplicity's sake we use public variables instead of
    ' full property procedures.
    Public AccountID As Integer
    Public Balance As Decimal

    Public Sub Update()
        ' (Update this record in the database.)
    End Sub
```

Listing 10-1 A stateful account class

```
Public Sub Insert()
        ' (Insert a new account record using the information in this
        '  class.)
    End Sub

    Public Sub Delete()
        ' (Delete the database record that matches this class.)
    End Sub

    Public Sub Fill()
        ' (Get the database record that matches this class.)
    End Sub

End Class
```

To transfer money between accounts, the client can follow a sequence like the one shown in Listing 10-2.

```
Dim AccA As New Account(), AccB As New Account()

' Retrieve the balance for account 1001.
AccA.AccountID = 1001
AccA.Fill()

' Retrieve the balance for account 1002.
AccB.AccountID = 1002
AccB.Fill()

' Transfer the money.
Dim Transfer As Decimal = 150
AccA.Balance += Transfer
AccB.Balance -= Transfer

' Save both records.
AccA.Update()
AccB.Update()
```

Listing 10-2 Using the stateful account class

This code is clean and straightforward. Unfortunately, it's hopelessly inefficient if the *Account* class is a remote object. The problems are many:

- In total, there are eight remote calls (assuming no action is taken when the objects are first created). Even though the actual message size is small, the basic latency of a cross-process and cross-machine call is not trivial.

- The account objects are stateful. Therefore, they each retain the account number and balance information in server memory. Although this problem is not apparent at design time and under a small load, with thousands of clients performing the same tasks it can become a disaster.
- The account updates are atomic. To ensure that the updates either succeed or fail together, you need to create a client-side transaction. The only way to support a client-side transaction in an object is through COM+, which isn't nearly as efficient as using a database transaction.

The ideal stateless version of this object might be called *AccountUtility*. It would provide straightforward, targeted methods that are centralized around common tasks, such as *UpdateAccount* and *TransferFunds*. Listing 10-3 shows an example.

```
Public Class AccountUtility

    Public Sub UpdateAccount(accountID As Integer, balance As Decimal)
        ' (Update the account record in the database.)
    End Sub

    Public Sub InsertAccount(accountID As Integer, balance As Decimal)
        ' (Insert a new account record.)
    End Sub

    Public Sub Delete(accountID As Integer)
        ' (Delete the corresponding database record.)
    End Sub

    Public Sub TransferFunds(accountIDFrom As Integer, _
      accountIDTo As Integer, transferAmount As Decimal)
        ' (Start a database transaction, and modify the two accounts.)
    End Sub

End Class
```

Listing 10-3 A stateless *AccountUtility* class

It's impossible to claim that the *AccountUtility* represents a real-world entity. You can't even state that *AccountUtility* represents the actions you can take with an account because it includes a method that spans more than one account (*TransferFunds*) and it might well include other methods that perform related updates to several different database records. *AccountUtility* is a group of related functionality, not a true object. In other words, *AccountUtility* is a service provider.

Listing 10-4 shows the same fund-transfer task using the *AccountUtility* class.

```
Dim AccUtility As New AccountUtility()
AccUtility.TransferFunds(1001, 1002, 150)
```

Listing 10-4 Using the stateless *AccountUtility* class

There are a number of benefits in this rewritten version:

- **There is only one remote call.** This can dramatically increase the client's performance and cut down on network traffic.
- **No memory is held in server state.** This ensures scalability but also means that every subsequent method call will need to resubmit the same parameters (such as an account ID), which can become quite tedious and increase the network traffic of the total system.
- **The transfer logic happens on the server, not the client.** This allows the server-side component to use an ordinary database transaction. It also helps separate the business logic from the presentation code (a principle we'll return to later in this chapter).

One of the chief drawbacks to stateless programming is that each method call typically requires a lot of information. In the preceding example, this isn't a problem because only two pieces of information are associated with an account. However, consider the less attractive method that might be required to create a new customer record:

```
Public Sub InsertCustomer(firstName As String, lastName As String, _
  userID As String, password As String, email As String, _
  streetAddress As String, city As String, postalCode As String, _
  country As String)

    ' (Code omitted)

End Sub
```

This is clearly some messy code. Worst of all, because all these parameters are strings, the client program could easily make a mistake by submitting information in the wrong order, which wouldn't generate an exception but would lead to invalid information in the database.

To overcome these issues, we generally deal with structures that encapsulate several related pieces of information. However, these structures differ dramatically from the traditional approach shown with the *Account* class because they include only data, not functionality. Often, these classes have names that end with *Info* or *Details* to highlight this distinction. This convention is used in many of the examples in this book and some Microsoft case studies, but it is by no means universal.

Here's a typical *AccountInfo* structure that a client might use to pass information to an *InsertAccount* method:

```
Public Class AccountDetails

    Public AccountID As Integer
    Public Balance As Integer

End Class
```

Of course, this is the approach you've already seen in the early chapters of this book. It divides a traditional stateful object into a stateless information package and a remote service provider class. The information package is never run out of process; it's just a method of delivering information. The service provider, on the other hand, is entirely stateless and built out of utility functions, ensuring optimum performance.

Performance vs. Scalability

One key theme in distributed application design is the tradeoff between performance and scalability. Performance is a measure of the application's speed, whereas scalability indicates how this speed varies as the client load increases or the server hardware is upgraded.

We've already considered one example of the difference between performance and scalability with session state. In ASP (the previous version of ASP.NET), Web pages that use session state almost always perform faster for small numbers of clients. Somewhere along the way, however, as the number of simultaneous clients increases, they reach a bottleneck and perform terribly. Figure 10-1 diagrams this relationship.

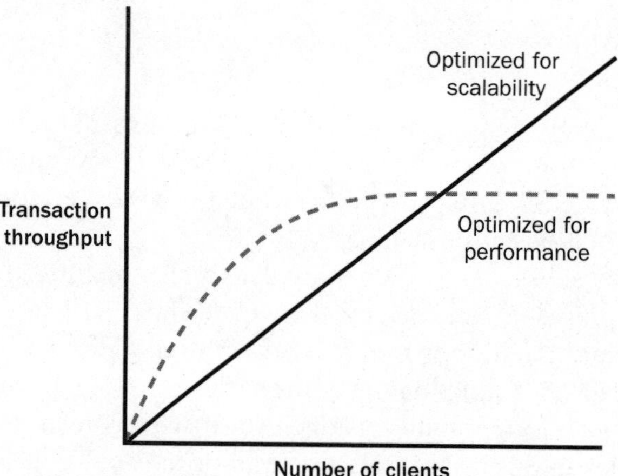

Figure 10-1 Performance vs. scalability

The distinction between performance for small numbers of users and scalability to large numbers is alive and well in the .NET world. One of the best examples occurs with database connection pooling.

Consider, for example, a system with a stateless database component and two Windows clients (on two separate computers). Each method in the database component follows best practices: It creates a connection, performs an operation, and then closes the connection immediately. In configuration A, both clients have local copies of the database component (as shown in Figure 10-2). Therefore, they can use it locally (and speedily) in-process. Connections can't be pooled between the two, however, because the component is always instantiated in the process of the client.

In configuration B, the database component lives on the database server and communicates with out-of-process clients through .NET Remoting (as shown in Figure 10-3). This intrinsically adds overhead because all calls must travel over process boundaries and the network. However, it allows connections to be pooled among all clients.

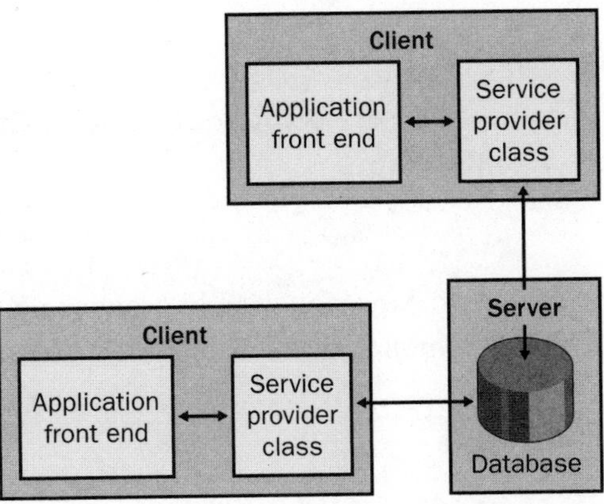

Figure 10-2 Configuration A: best performance for small client numbers

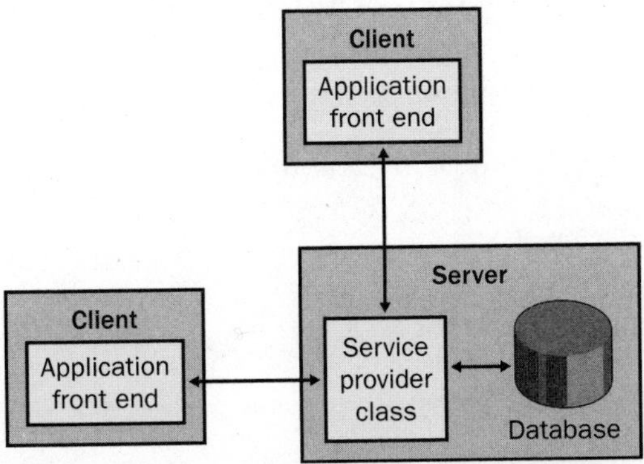

Figure 10-3 Configuration B: best scalability

So which approach is better? Typically, configuration A is best for small client situations. For systems with a large number of clients that perform a relatively small number of database transactions, configuration B is the best choice because it leverages all the advantages of connection pooling.

The conclusion you should draw is that you can't design every type of system in the same way (although you can often use the same technologies and very similar code). Distributing the layers of a small-scale system might only slow it down. On the other hand, a system that supports a heavy client load needs the features; otherwise, it will encounter a bottleneck—essentially becoming a victim of its own success.

There is one piece of good news, however. If you follow good design practices, the amount of work required to transfer design A into design B can be quite small. Ideally, you would design the database component using the service provider model presented in the earlier chapters. This approach works equally well for a local object as for a server-side object. In fact, you can even derive the local service provider from *MarshalByRefObject* and mark the information package with the *Serializable* attribute. These features won't add any extra overhead if you choose not to use them.

When you need to make the transition from design A to design B, you simply modify how the client creates the service provider object. The code used to interact with this object is unchanged.

> **More Info** Chapter 12 takes a closer look at best practices for using connection pooling with .NET Remoting and XML Web services.

The Lessons Learned

The best approach is to design your components with distributed architecture in mind but distribute them to separate computers only when required. So when is distributed architecture required? You might need to shift to a distributed architecture for either of the following reasons:

- You need to support legacy applications that can't be modified or third-party applications that run on different platforms. Server-side components allow business logic to be centralized in one place but used by a wide range of different clients.
- Your system is used heavily enough that scalability issues are overtaking small-scale performance considerations. This is the expected

course for e-commerce shops and companies that expose business-to-business services.

As you've seen, when you design components for a distributed environment, you must keep a number of considerations in mind. Here are some points to remember:

- **Strive to reduce communication frequency.** So-called "chunky" interfaces that exchange large amounts of information perform better than "chatty" interfaces that frequently exchange small bits of information. Chatty interfaces require more overhead. Even worse, they don't just slow down the system on a single-client level—frequent communication also leads to systems that can't scale because they impose too much overall network traffic.
- **Strive to be stateless.** Not only do stateless components make the best use of server resources, they also enable you to implement load balancing later.
- **Keep objects that need to talk close together.** If you need to distribute a data component, for example, create a single remote object that includes all the data classes. If you create multiple data objects and host them on separate servers, performance will suffer when they need to communicate. (For example, if the *OrdersDB* class needs to retrieve the current customer using the *CustomersDB* class and the component is hosted in a different process, the call is subjected to increased overhead.)

Finally, remember that remote objects aren't true players in object-oriented design. If you are in danger of forgetting this principle, remind yourself of some of these limitations:

- **XML Web services can't hold state.** ASP.NET session state is tied to a user cookie, not an object.
- **XML Web services return XML, not objects.** .NET can convert some recognized objects into .NET types, but most of the classes in the common language runtime (CLR) can't make the jump.
- **Remote components can't easily raise events and make use of bidirectional communication.** Bidirectional communication is possible with .NET Remoting—but only if the client has an open channel listening.

Not only is it a mistake to try to create remote components that model ordinary objects, but it's also bad idea to try to create an intermediary layer of objects that masks this reality. The more you distance yourself from the practical reality of your system, the more you risk encouraging a client to ignore this reality and use your component inefficiently. A successful distributed application should guide the client toward proper use and restrict options (such as a *GetAllAccounts* method) that might reduce performance. This approach isn't insulting. In fact, it's the same principle that Microsoft has followed in constraining the ADO.NET *DataSet* to disconnected use and in defaulting XML Web services and remote objects to stateless behavior.

Designing in Tiers

Terms such as *three-tier*, *n-tier*, and *multitier* have been hotly hyped in programming circles. These terms mean widely different things to different people. Some use them to refer to the process of physically partitioning an application, and others use them to talk about logically separating the functionality of an application into layers. This book uses the latter approach.

Three-tier architecture began as an extension of the commonsense idea that different code performs different types of tasks. Three-tier architecture separates an application's functionality into three categories: presentation logic, business logic, and data logic (as shown in Figure 10-4). The presentation logic handles the user interface tasks. The business logic handles the company-specific processes. The data logic just inserts, deletes, modifies, and retrieves records from a back-end data store such as a database. The critical concept in three-tier design is that code in a given layer can communicate only with an adjacent layer. In other words, the presentation logic can't communicate directly with the database. Instead, it has to forward its request through a layer of business objects.

Three-tier design was a fundamental improvement over most client-server designs and was critically important in the world of Visual Basic, where developers were often seduced into placing database logic directly in form event handlers. By adopting a strict three-tier design, it became easier to separate application logic and thereby easier to reuse, replace, and test individual units of functionality.

There's no way to escape three-tier design as a basic organizing principle. A Web page or Windows Forms page should never create an ADO.NET object directly. By creating a separate class to handle this task, you ensure that the code can be easily updated to use a different database structure or data access technology. Your changes are confined to one component instead of being spread haphazardly throughout the user interface logic of a client application.

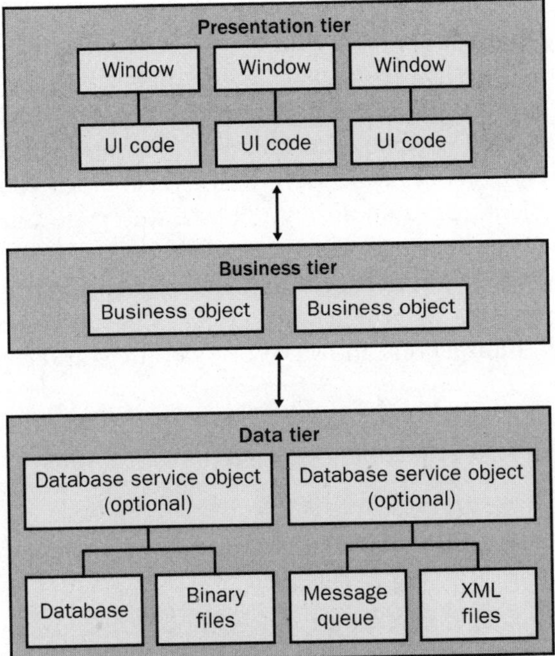

Figure 10-4 Three-tier design

Business Objects

If you're a diehard programming veteran, you've probably noticed that I haven't yet used the term *business objects* in this chapter. There is a definite reason for this omission. Quite simply, many business object designs just don't work.

One of the most common problems in three-tier design is the requirement that business rules be placed exclusively in the middle tier. To achieve this goal, many developers created three-tier designs based on stateful objects (such as the *Account* class used earlier in Listing 10-1) that could validate settings through property procedures. These applications were perfect examples of object-oriented three-tier design—and they performed horribly.

For that reason, I concentrate on a different type of modeling in this book. I call this design *information packages and service providers*, but it's also sometimes known as *entity/service modeling*. Later, when we explore distributed design patterns, you'll discover that the old rules of three-tier design are just as important with service providers and information packages, provided you understand the tradeoffs.

Rules

When designing a new system, the first task you undertake is to determine how you can divide the functionality into components. The second task is to decide where business rules (typically company-specific rules for data validation and data processing) will take place.

In three-tier design, the goal is to place as many rules as possible in the business layer of the application. This has many benefits. It enables you to modify the rules, which tend to change frequently, without disturbing the rest of the application or redeploying new software. It also enables you to support more than one type of client (for example, an ASP.NET Web page and a Windows desktop application) without creating two copies of the same code. And, as you saw earlier with the *AccountUtility.TransferFunds* method in Listing 10-3, moving the business logic away from the client also makes it easier to optimize this code (for example, with transactions and stored procedures) and can even help to keep it secure.

However, the ideal of locating business rules in middle-tier components is not always practical, for both performance and usability reasons.

User Interface Rules

For example, some business rules absolutely belong in the user interface—such as those that restrict invalid options in a window. An application that needs to query a remote object before it can report a user input error just isn't intuitive enough for the average user, who needs to be guided at every step of the way and—more importantly—prevented from entering invalid input in the first place. Leaving these rules out of the presentation tier can also hamper performance.

Consider, for example, the extreme example of what might happen if you create a window that doesn't prevent users from typing letters into an Account ID text box. The user of this application might mistakenly type a name. The application will then contact the remote object, attempt the operation, and generate an error, which it will report back to the client. By the time the information is correctly entered and submitted, the poor design might have already resulted in several additional network calls, reducing the overall performance of the system.

> **Note** One good rule of thumb is that if you have enough information in the client (presentation layer) to do data validation, do it there. Remember that you should try not to hard-code any information. For example, enforcing field-length restrictions in a text box can cause quite a headache if the allowed length of the underlying database field changes. The best approach is to determine the length of the field programmatically, if possible, perhaps by reading the *DataColumn* information in the *DataSet* and then configuring the corresponding user interface controls dynamically. Of course, this requires additional coding.

Data Layer Rules

Other rules are always dealt with in the data layer. These include the rules that verify referential integrity (for example, ensuring that you can't create a child record that refers to a nonexistent parent) and identity integrity (for example, ensuring that you can't create two identical copies of a unique field). In some cases, the business layer might perform a similar check before attempting the operation, which might allow it to save a database trip in the case of an error. However, most of these rules depend on the information that is already in the database, and the business object is in no position to query additional rows just to verify that this restriction is followed.

The Database Can Execute Business Logic

Performance tests indicate that in many cases you can improve application performance by moving business logic to the stored procedure layer. Instead of creating a component that iterates through a collection of order items and inserts each one separately, for example, you can create a more powerful stored procedure that inserts all the orders simultaneously and performs any required validation or preprocessing. Typically, the database can precompile the stored procedure code and thereby execute it more quickly.

Think carefully, however, before you move your logic to the database layer. Advanced stored procedures can be quite difficult to create because you must use script-based languages such as Transact-SQL and deal with custom error codes and database-specific commands. Generally, most systems are better off including the business rules in .NET objects, where they are easier to alter and troubleshoot. In addition, placing time-consuming logic in the database can increase performance at the cost of scalability because the database can't be load-balanced in the same way that a stateless component can. If sheer performance is absolutely critical, however, you might want to try some performance testing to determine whether data layer business logic can save you some time.

Distributed Design Patterns

Over the past few years, the concept of *design patterns*—reusable architecture "recipes" that can be applied to solve similar problems in multiple applications—

has received a good deal of interest. Unfortunately, design patterns are usually demonstrated with toy code that can't be applied directly to most applications.

To truly understand design patterns, you need to realize that different design patterns are designed for different application layers, and many design patterns are already hard-wired into .NET. If you want to create a remote singleton component, for example, you won't add any logic to the class constructor. Instead, you'll use a configuration file to specify the appropriate .NET Remoting activation type.

We'll look at three design patterns that are keenly important for pluggable applications, where components are built separately and snapped together to create a larger system. These design patterns are particularly useful with distributed applications.

Interfaces

Interfaces specify the public properties and methods that a component must provide. More precisely, interfaces define the outward appearance of a class. They don't contain any information about how a property or method actually works.

Conceptually, you can think of an interface as a control panel for a class. Like the buttons on a microwave oven, the interface controls define the range of actions the user can perform. The actual implementation that translates the user's key presses into specific electronic settings is less obvious and is hidden from view.

When you design a distributed system, it helps to create an interface before you actually develop a component. This step forces you to lock down the method that different classes will communicate and the division of functionality between classes before you write any implementation code. Interfaces are also useful because an object can implement more than one interface. The client can choose the appropriate interface and not be distracted by methods that aren't important for the task at hand.

> **Note** Interfaces aren't fully supported in XML Web services, where every method requires a unique URI endpoint. You can use an interface to develop your Web service, but a client can't use it to interact with your service.

Interfaces also have some specialized uses with distributed applications. They allow parts of an application to be developed independently. For example, you can code a client that communicates with a server object using the server object interface. At the same time, you can code a server that communicates with a client using the client's interface. Without interfaces, you would probably need to copy the server and client assembly files back and forth and update project references endlessly (as you might have experienced if you modified some of the examples in Chapter 4).

In this part of the book, Part II, you'll see two critical examples of interfaces at work:

- In Chapter 11, we'll use interfaces to simplify communication with .NET Remoting.
- In Chapter 15, we'll use interfaces to build a modular Windows Forms application that downloads itself piece by piece from a server.

Another reason that you might use interfaces is to tame versioning problems. This technique is a standard part of traditional COM programming, but it's also useful in .NET. Finally, you might need interfaces to expose .NET objects to COM clients. Chapter 9 introduced this topic.

Factories

Factories are classes that create other classes. Factories abstract away the class creation process. This is particularly useful in a system that uses .NET Remoting. Using a factory, the client can create a remote object. The class factory can examine an additional piece of information—perhaps a configuration file setting value—and decide whether to return a local instance of the object or return a proxy that communicates with a remote instance. This location transparency makes it easy to migrate from one architecture to another and hides the .NET Remoting details from the client application. You'll see location transparency in action in the next chapter.

Facades

In all enterprise applications there is a tension between upgradability and performance optimization. The closer the middle-tier components match the database, the easier it is to optimize database queries and indexes but the more difficult it is to modify the structure of the database or introduce an entirely new data source or data access methodology. This tension can never be completely resolved, but facades offer one technique that can help.

A *facade* is a layer between the service provider components and the client. Here's the distinction: A service provider encapsulates a service, such as a database operation. A facade encapsulates a higher-level task, such as committing an order (as shown in Figure 10-5).

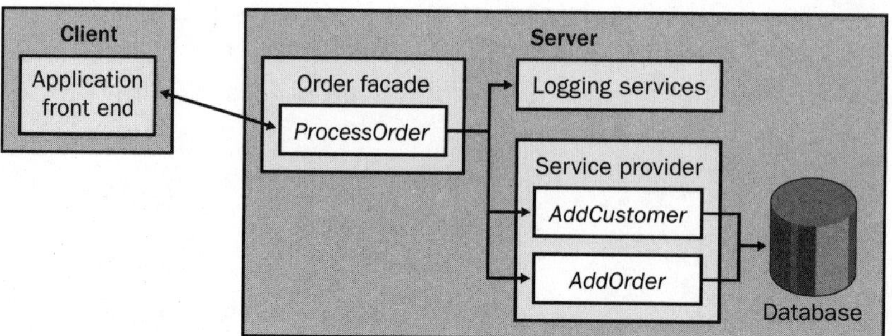

Figure 10-5 Using a facade

However, the facade layer can't ignore database realities. If a given business task corresponds to several database operations, however, it's inefficient to obtain a new connection for each operation. Instead, the facade layer needs to retrieve a connection object from the data source layer.

The next three code listings offer a helpful comparison. Listing 10-5 shows the traditional service provider–based approach to creating a new order.

```
Dim Customer As New CustomerDetails()
Dim Order As New OrderDetails()

' (Code to fill these objects omitted.)

Dim CustDB As New CustomersDB()
Dim OrdDB As New OrdersDB()
If Not CustDB.Exists(Customer) Then
    CustDB.AddCustomer(Customer)
End If

OrdDB.AddOrder(Order)
```

Listing 10-5 Client code using a service provider

Listing 10-6 shows one way to write the equivalent code using a business facade.

```
Dim Customer As New CustomerDetails()
Dim Order As New OrderDetails()

' (Code to fill these objects omitted.)

Dim Bus As New OrderFacade()
Bus.ProcessOrder(Order, Customer)
```

Listing 10-6 Client code using a business facade

Now the business facade (shown in Listing 10-7) takes over the processing, inserting the customer if necessary:

```
Public Class OrderFacade

    Public Sub ProcessOrder(Customer As CustomerDetails, _
      Order As OrderDetails)

        Dim CustDB As New CustomersDB()
        Dim OrdDB As New OrdersDB()

        If Not CustDB.Exists(Customer) Then
            CustDB.AddCustomer(Customer)
        End If

        OrdDB.AddOrder(Order)

    End Sub

End Class
```

Listing 10-7 The business facade

In this case, adding the facade enables you to move some of the business logic away from the client, which is always beneficial. It also increases the overall speed of the operation because fewer network calls are required (only one rather than two or three). Technically, the facade approach is less flexible because it only allows a client to use operations in a set combination. However, if the client needs to be able to call these methods individually, you can add more methods to your facade.

It is possible to introduce one further refinement to the facade. Currently, each individual database operation creates a new connection. Because facades tend to aggregate several database operations, this adds up to additional overhead and inefficiency. You can improve the situation by creating a dedicated helper class that provides and opens a connection object at the beginning of the façade method and closes it at the end. You then pass this connection object to the service provider layer.

Note that the connection object is returned as the base *System.Object* type. This ensures that you don't tightly couple the business facade to a specific data technology. The connection can represent an ADO.NET connection object or a message queue, or it can just be a null reference. Before you implement the approach shown in Listing 10-8, remember to profile its performance. If you keep the connection open while you are performing a time-consuming processing or validation task, performance might suffer.

```
Public Class OrderFacade

    Public Sub ProcessOrder(Customer As CustomerDetails, _
      Order As OrderDetails)

        Dim DB As New DBHelper()
        Dim Conn As Object = DB.GetConnection()

        Dim CustDB As New CustomersDB(Conn)
        Dim OrdDB As New OrdersDB(Conn)

        If Not CustDB.Exists(Customer) Then
            CustDB.AddCustomer(Customer)
        End If

        OrdDB.AddOrder(Order)

        DB.ReleaseConnection(Conn)

    End Sub

End Class
```

Listing 10-8 A facade that aggregates connections

In theory, facades enable you to alter the data layer without changing the client code. In practice, however, this isn't always possible because the client is always tied to a specific representation of the data. In other words, if you modify the database by splitting information into different tables or introducing new stored procedures, the client won't be affected. If you add new information, however, the client will probably need an updated version of the *CustomerDetails* object and might need user interface changes to request or display this information where appropriate. If used properly, however, facades almost always help to standardize an application's design.

> **Note** A good example of how a facade can help is if you need to migrate the design of an e-commerce system from synchronous-based communication through a data access layer to asynchronous connection using message queues. If you've designed your facade carefully, you can implement this change without disturbing the client at all.

Facades and Interception

Another advantage of facades is that they allow you to add interception services. For example, you can use a facade to decouple the error-checking and logging functionality from your data access code, rendering it more reusable and extensible. Listing 10-9 shows an example of this approach, where the facade integrates the logging, validation, and database access tasks using distinct components.

```
Public Class OrderFacade

    Private Validation As New ValidationServices()
    Private Logging As New LoggingServices()

    Public Sub ProcessOrder(Customer As CustomerDetails, _
      Order As OrderDetails)

        Dim CustDB As New CustomersDB()
        Dim OrdDB As New OrdersDB()

        If Not CustDB.Exists(Customer) Then

            ' If the customer is not valid, this method throws an
            ' exception that will be handled by the client.
            Validation.Test(Customer)

            CustDB.AddCustomer(Customer)

        End If

        ' If the customer is not valid, this method throws an
        ' exception that will be handled by the client.
        Validation.Test(Order)

        OrdDB.AddOrder(Order)

        Logging.Log("Order Successful")

    End Sub

End Class
```

Listing 10-9 A facade that incorporates logging and validation

Facades and XML Web Services

The previous examples show the code for various facade classes, but they don't specify whether the facade is an XML Web service or a remote *MarshalByRefObject*. (It can be either.) The important point to remember is that the client will communicate infrequently with the facade, whereas the facade will probably communicate frequently with the service provider classes. For example, one call from the client to a facade might result in several method invocations on various database components. This means that the communication overhead between the facade and the service providers should be as low as possible.

Ideally, the service providers will be ordinary classes that the facade can create in-process. This is the pattern used in all the case studies in the third part of this book. All database access code is encapsulated by a dedicated component that runs on the server. Outside clients never access this component directly. Instead, they use a higher-level XML Web service method.

Facades and Transactions

Yet another reason that you might use facades is to add a transactional capability to higher-level processes that incorporate multiple database operations. Without a facade, a transaction might not be possible. If it is, the client is forced to initiate and control it. This means that a distributed transaction is required to coordinate the communication between the client and server-side database objects. With a facade, transactions are much more efficient because they can be implemented entirely on the server side.

You can add transactional support to a facade in a number of ways. One approach is to create two additional methods in your database class: *StartTransaction* and *CommitTransaction*. The *StartTransaction* method returns a transaction object. All the other methods in the database class accept the transaction object as a parameter. If the transaction object is provided, they use it to enlist any commands. If it isn't (and contains a null reference instead), they just run normally. Listing 10-10 shows sample facade code that uses a transaction. A similar approach is used in the case study in Chapter 17.

```
Public Class OrderFacade

    Public Sub ProcessOrder(Customer As CustomerDetails, _
      Order As OrderDetails)

        Dim CustDB As New CustomersDB()
        Dim OrdDB As New OrdersDB()
        Dim DB As New DBHelper()

        Dim Transaction As Object
        Transaction = DB.StartTransaction()
        If Not CustDB.Exists(Customer) Then
            CustDB.AddCustomer(Customer, Transaction)
        End If

        OrdDB.AddOrder(Order, Transaction)

        DB.CommitTransaction(Transaction)

    End Sub

End Class
```

Listing 10-10 A facade that uses provider-controlled transactions

Note that the transaction object is retained in the *OrderFacade* class as a generic object. This allows the facade to be independent of the database code, which might use a *SqlTransaction* object, an *OleDbTransaction* object, or something entirely different.

Another option is to use a COM+ transaction, which requires slightly more overhead (because it uses a two-stage commit process) but doesn't require a specially designed database component. This technique (shown in Listing 10-11) is particularly easy if your facade is implemented as an XML Web service, in which case you can just use the *TransactionOption* property of the *<WebMethod>* attribute. The transaction is automatically committed unless an exception is thrown. This technique is used in Chapter 18.

```
Public Class OrderFacade

    <WebMethod(TransactionOption := TransactionOption.RequiresNew)> _
    Public Sub ProcessOrder(Customer As CustomerDetails, _
      Order As OrderDetails)

        ' (Code omitted.)

    End Sub

End Class
```

Listing 10-11 A facade that uses a COM+ transaction

Choosing the Right .NET Technology

One principle I've stressed throughout this book is that every .NET technology has an ideal niche. To build a successful distributed application, you need to understand not only how to use these technologies but also when to use them. The next sections consider a few miniature scenarios and the designs they lead to.

Internal and External Systems

The internal system is the proprietary software that manages some part of the day-to-day tasks of running a business. It can include bug tracking or project-management software used by the development department, or a custom sales-tracking and inventory-management application. In either case, you have two choices.

A .NET Remoting–based solution provides the best possible communication speed. Of course, internal systems often don't stay that way. If the system is successful, you'll often require some sort of bridge to expose some functionality to other systems. In this case, an XML Web service–based solution provides an easy migration path if you need to open up parts of the system to a third party. XML Web services also provide ASP.NET services such as caching an integrated authentication that can enhance performance or simplify coding. Either way, the client portion is usually created using Windows Forms. This provides the most flexible user interface and enables you to create different application types, such as long-running system tray applications.

Systems exposed to outside parties (such as e-commerce storefronts) can rely on ASP.NET or an XML Web service backbone. The key consideration is determining whether you should use a disconnected architecture that relies on message queues or a similar technology to distribute client requests. If you are expecting a heavy load concentrated in peak hours and clients do not need an immediate response, this type of disconnected architecture maximizes the processing capabilities of the server.

Hybrid Internal/External Systems

Some systems combine XML Web services and .NET Remoting in parallel. .NET Remoting is used for internal clients, and XML Web services expose a subset of the same features to third parties or other platforms. The success of this approach depends on ensuring that both the XML Web services and the remoted components use the same service provider components to perform the heavy lifting (such as accessing the database). Although the XML Web services and remoted components will execute separately, they will be sharing the same version of the service provider components, as shown in Figure 10-6.

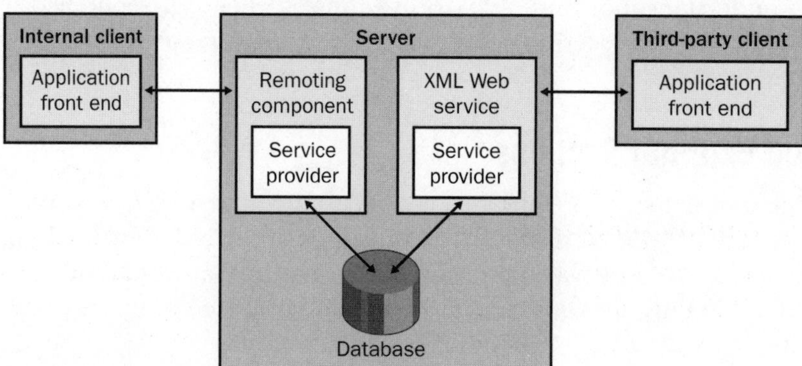

Figure 10-6 A hybrid system

> **Note** Technically, it is possible to create a component that can work as an XML Web service and a remote object. You just need to derive the class from *MarshalByRefObject* to enable .NET Remoting support, and add the <*WebMethod*> attribute and create an .asmx file to expose Web methods. However, this approach is strongly discouraged. You will still have to host the component separately, and the subtle differences in the way XML Web services and .NET Remoting handle issues such as serialization mean that this is a recipe for future headaches. Instead, move shared functionality into a separate component.

The Common Back End

The disadvantage with hybrid systems is that they are inefficient for large client loads. For example, connections can't be pooled between XML Web services and components exposed through .NET Remoting, and load balancing is more complicated because you are dealing with two duplicate implementations.

The solution is to create a common back end of processing components exposed through .NET Remoting (as shown in Figure 10-7). This extra layer results in additional cross-process communication, so it will reduce performance for small numbers. However, it is much more scalable in the long run.

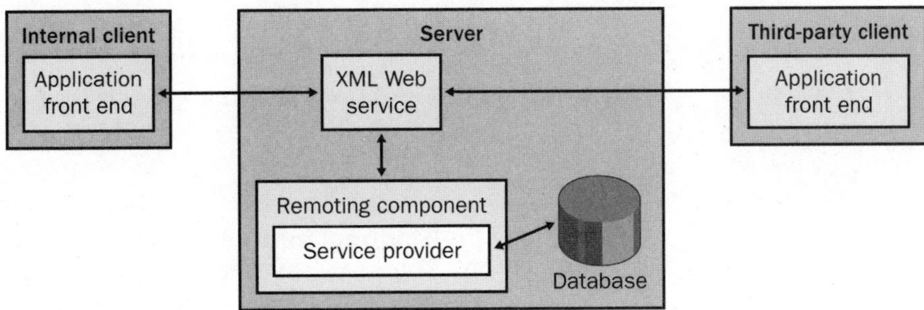

Figure 10-7 A common back end

Partially Disconnected Systems

Partially disconnected systems include clients that aren't always connected and therefore can't always interact with server-side components. For example, you might create a program that logs expenses for traveling employees. When the computer reconnects to the network, these expense reports are inserted into the central database. Another example of a disconnected system is some sort of tool that you distribute to a third party. For example, you might provide authorized dealers with a sales-ordering tool. However, you probably can't assume that these dealers will have a continuous connection to the Internet when they use your application (and you definitely can't assume they will have a connection to your internal network).

There is more than one possible approach to communication in a disconnected system. One option is to use message queues (as shown in Figure 10-8), in which case Windows automatically sends the messages when the connection returns. This approach is helpful because it enables you to use the same application design for connected clients that you use for disconnected clients. Either way, a message is sent when an operation is complete; the only difference is when Windows dispatches the message.

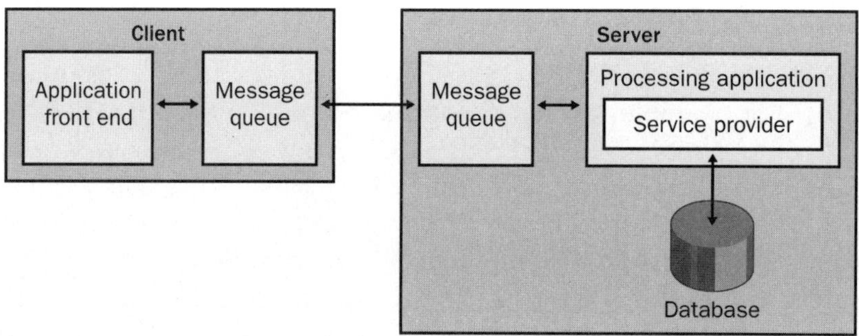

Figure 10-8 A disconnected client with a message queue

In other cases, you might have specific requirements that require the development of a custom solution. You can create an application that polls for a network connection or manually waits for the user to tell it that a connection is available. This is conceptually similar to the way an e-mail program works. If you send an e-mail message while disconnected, exit the program, and then reconnect, the message won't be sent until you reload the program.

A final approach is to create a dedicated Windows service that handles the submission of information to a central service. This service will run perpetually on the computer, checking for a connection. If one exists, it transmits the information stored by the client program. This approach is conceptually similar to a message queue. It's most common if you can't be sure all clients have the Message Queuing software installed or configured correctly.

> **More Info** Chapter 16 presents a case study in which a legacy disconnected system must be migrated into the .NET world.

Upgrading from COM

In today's world, distributed systems commonly need to evolve from existing COM architecture. .NET makes this process relatively easy. Migrating from COM to .NET is a major shift, however, and it's important to follow a disciplined, phased approach to ensure that the system works. For most organizations, this will mean a considerable amount of time spent with a hybrid system that includes both COM and .NET components.

When you upgrade a legacy multitier application, it's best to begin by recoding the client program because it's easier for a .NET client to communicate with a COM component than for a COM-based client to communicate with a .NET component. The first stage of any migration should be to rewrite the presentation layer using ASP.NET or Windows Forms, as shown in Figure 10-9. You can use .NET's built-in COM interop support to access the middle-tier COM objects.

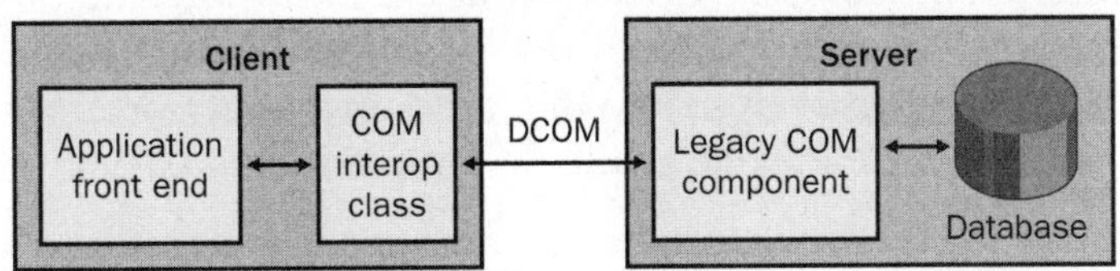

Figure 10-9 Phase-one migration

As long as clients communicate directly with the COM layer, it is difficult to update the business components. In addition, if the components are located on another computer, you must use DCOM for remote communication. The next phase is to correct this problem by moving the COM interop layer to the server, as shown in Figure 10-10. You can do this by creating another .NET layer using XML Web services or components exposed through .NET Remoting. The clients connect directly with this layer of .NET components, which just forwards requests and retrieves the results from the underlying COM components.

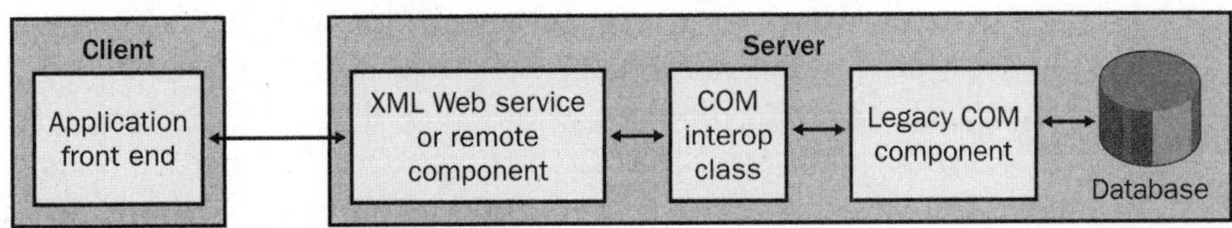

Figure 10-10 Phase-two migration

The final stage is to rebuild the business layer using .NET components, as shown in Figure 10-11. In the best-case scenario, you will be able to deploy these components one by one. The client code won't require any modifications at all—you'll just need to update the layer of .NET XML Web services or remote components.

Figure 10-11 Phase-three migration

Physical Architecture

One topic we haven't examined in much detail is designing the physical infrastructure for a distributed application. The focus of this book is on distributed application programming, not networking, firewalls, or Web servers—although the best programmers will know more than a little about all of these topics. If you are interested in taking a closer look at the hardware side of things, you might want to consider referring to a book such as *Deploying and Managing Microsoft .NET Web Farms* by Barry Bloom (Sams, 2001) or one of the titles from Microsoft Press. Here, we'll just look at the absolute basics.

Scaling

When improving a system's hardware, system architects generally distinguish between the following two types of scaling:

- **Scaling up (vertical scaling)** This is the process of upgrading server hardware—for example, adding new memory or upgrading the CPU.
- **Scaling out (horizontal scaling)** This is the process of adding additional computers to the system, usually as load-balanced servers that share part of the workload.

Scaling up can improve performance and scalability. Scaling out can only improve scalability because each individual client still makes use of only one computer. However, scaling out is generally the best approach and is the Holy Grail of distributed applications because scaling up is expensive and constrained by absolute limits. (For example, you can't yet purchase a 4000 GHz CPU.) Scaling up also encourages a single point of failure. If the server fails, there might be no other server to offer even reduced capacity. Scaling out, on the other hand, is by comparison quite cheap. You just need to add another inexpensive Windows server.

To support horizontal scaling, you need to implement some sort of load-balancing solution. You also need to use .NET Remoting or XML Web services to move the logic of your application out of the client and to the server, where it can be load-balanced.

Load Balancing

Enterprise systems use load balancing to distribute the burden of an application over multiple servers. You can implement load balancing in countless ways, and some are more efficient than others. For instance, you can implement a crude form of load balancing by deploying two versions of a client application that differ only by a single configuration file setting. One group of clients is directed to connect to server A, and the other uses server B. This is a type of static load balancing, and it tends to perform poorly because there is no guarantee that the workload will be evenly shared. It's possible that a large number of clients in the first group will connect at the same time, taxing server A while server B remains underused. Even worse, if one server fails, the other clients won't be redirected to the available computer.

Using a server-side list, you can implement an improved form of load balancing called *round-robin* load balancing. In round-robin load balancing, the client retrieves the name of the server to use when it initializes. It then uses that server for the duration of the current session. The server is chosen randomly from an available list. This approach gives you the freedom to dynamically modify the server configuration, adding or removing computers. It doesn't guarantee that the load will always be evenly distributed, however, because some clients might perform much more intensive tasks or hold a connection for much longer periods of time than others. In addition, as with static load balancing, this system has a single point of failure—the computer that hosts the server lookup service.

Other forms of load balancing require dedicated hardware or software. Hardware load balancing works by analyzing network traffic and is effective but expensive. Software load balancing is most commonly used through Microsoft Application Center 2000. This product provides a robust clustering service that allows a group of computers to be exposed under a single IP address. The Application Center software dynamically routes requests to the server with the lightest load. The only concern you should have when programming a server component for an Application Center environment is ensuring that it is stateless, because subsequent requests from the same client are likely to be routed to different computers. For more information (or to download a trial version), you can visit the Application Center site at *http://www.microsoft.com/applicationcenter*.

Finally, you also can use features in your RDBMS to scale out the database server. The current version of SQL Server (SQL Server 2000) can't be scaled in a manner analogous to Application Center load balancing. Instead, you must use federated database servers to partition the database over multiple servers. After they have been configured, these servers work together to satisfy a query and retrieve information. Ideally, the data will be partitioned in such a way that related information is kept together. You might simply divide tables (for example, putting a product catalog on one server and an employee list on another), or you might partition large database tables according to criteria such as geographic region or date. Microsoft has achieved extremely good performance results using federated database servers (see, for example, *http://www.microsoft.com/sql/evaluation/compare/benchmarks.asp*), but these systems are still exposed to a single point of failure because none of the data is shared. Microsoft also promises that subsequent SQL Server versions will add support for shared clustering as well as partitioning.

Summary

Application architecture is a science of compromises. Developers of distributed applications face countless design issues as they move local components to the server and bring three-tier design into the .NET world. In this chapter, you learned basic concepts about how to balance the reality of network communication and limited server resources with solid, extensible designs. To see these principles in action, you can refer to the case studies that make up Part III of this book.

11

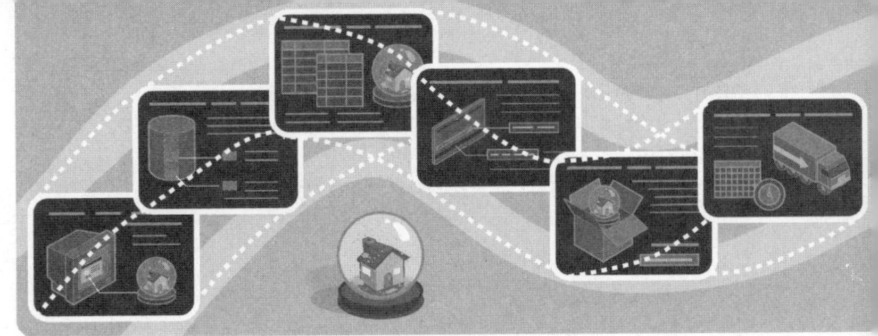

Advanced Remoting Techniques

.NET Remoting is a remarkable topic. Just when you think you've finally mastered every aspect, a new dimension unfolds. At its simplest, .NET Remoting requires little more than a *MarshalByRefObject* and a configuration file. At its most complex, .NET Remoting enables you to build your own custom pieces of its infrastructure, such as sinks that compress data or channels that pass messages over SMTP. This sort of low-level grunt work rarely pays off—quite simply, it's time-consuming, error-prone, and difficult to do correctly. With most enterprise applications, you can't afford to introduce new vulnerabilities and security headaches. Instead, you should let hardened Microsoft programmers create the plumbing for you.

That said, there are still several important topics that we haven't considered yet, which can help you make the jump from creating remote components to designing complete .NET Remoting solutions. These include topics such as remote component versioning and interface-based programming. This chapter examines these issues and identifies some techniques for coordinating remote objects through dynamic registration and publication.

Developing with .NET Remoting in Mind

Using remote components requires some special considerations. These finer points are easily overlooked and can pose quite a bit of trouble for the novice .NET Remoting programmer. The next few sections consider several of them.

ByRef and *ByVal* Arguments

Microsoft Visual Basic .NET defaults to *ByVal* for all its arguments, which is different from the previous version of the language. That means the parameter is passed by value and copied into the new application domain. If it's a custom type and it's not marked *<Serializable>*, or if the remote object doesn't have a reference to the appropriate assembly, a *SerializationException* is thrown.

You also can mark arguments *ByRef*. In this case, you receive an exception unless the type in question is remotable (in other words, derives from *MarshalByRefObject*). If you pass an object that derives from *MarshalByRef* as a parameter, you actually end up passing a proxy to the object across the network. The recipient can then invoke the methods of this object, which will be executed on the computer where the object was created. Of course, for these methods to be executed successfully, the client that called the method and sent the remotable object must have an open channel listening for requests.

Finally, to make matters even more interesting, you can have a class that is both remotable and serializable. In this case, it's important that you choose the appropriate *ByRef* or *ByVal* identifier. Generally, *ByVal* is the behavior you want—but it pays to be vigilant.

Exception Propagation

When you call a method of a remote object, any exceptions in that method are propagated back to your code. Therefore, you must be ready to handle errors such as *SocketException*, *SerializationException*, and *RemotingException*, as well as any other application-specific error condition. Ideally, the remote method will use exception handling to ensure that it catches all errors and throws a higher-level exception, such as *ApplicationException*, to inform the client of a problem.

You also need to think carefully about using custom exception classes. If you define these, both the server and the client need to reference an assembly where they are defined. Otherwise, the client won't recognize the specialized exception class. You must also ensure that all custom exceptions are marked with the *<Serializable>* attribute so they can be sent across the network.

> **Note** One way to avoid some of these exception propagation problems is to add a *<OneWay>* attribute (found in the *System.Runtime.Remoting.Messaging* namespace) to the method of a remotable object. This indicates that the method doesn't provide a return value and does not return any information to *ByRef* parameters. The client's method call will return immediately, and exceptions won't be propagated. This also means that the remote method will probably execute asynchronously to the client and that the client can't assume that the remote method has completed by the time the client call returns. Chapter 8 discusses one-way messages in detail.

Static Members

Static members are never remoted. In other words, if you execute a static member for a remote object, the code is executed locally in the client's application domain.

Another interesting point concerns the virtual methods that every object inherits from the base *System.Object* class. These methods, which include *GetHashCode*, *ToString*, *Equals*, and *MemberwiseClone*, will always execute locally unless they have been overridden with a custom implementation. This behavior is designed to ensure optimal performance—if a remote call were required just to get the string representation of an object, it would result in an unnecessary slowdown in performance.

Private Methods

Private methods are never accessible anywhere outside the class in which they were created and are therefore not available in other application domains. Suppose, for example, that you have two *MarshalByRefObject* instances in two different application domains. Object A passes a delegate to object B, which points to a private method in object A. Even though object A is remotable, and even though object B has a reference to the metadata for object A, it won't be able to invoke the delegate.

Listing 11-1 shows the faulty code. Execution begins with *ObjectA.CallObjectB* and ends when *ObjectB.DoSomething* throws an unhandled exception.

```
Public Class ObjectA
    Inherits MarshalByRefObject

    Private ObjB As ObjectB

    Public Sub CallObjectB()
        ' Create a delegate.
        Dim Ref As New MethodInvoker(AddressOf NonRemoteable)

        ' Pass the delegate to a remote object.
        ObjB.DoSomething(Ref)
    End Sub

    Private Sub NonRemoteable()
        ' This method cannot be invoked remotely.
    End Sub

End Class


Public Class ObjectB
    Inherits MarshalByRefObject

    Public Sub DoSomething(ByVal Ref As MethodInvoker)
        ' The Ref parameter is received successfully.
        ' However it cannot be invoked.
        ' The next statement will fail.
        Ref.Invoke()
    End Sub

End Class
```

Listing 11-1 Invalid delegate use with .NET Remoting

Public Members

If you create a public member variable, .NET automatically creates property *get* and property *set* methods. These methods execute remotely. If .NET didn't take this extra step, public member variables could lead to lost updates or inconsistent data.

A better approach is to use property procedures rather than public member variables with any object that will be exposed to other applications. And the best approach is to make server-side objects entirely stateless.

Versioning

Handling versioning issues in .NET Remoting can be a thorny problem because you need to consider the version of the assembly that exists on more than one computer. You not only have to worry about clients that try to activate older or invalid assemblies, but you might have additional headaches when remote objects attempt to exchange incompatible versions of a serializable object.

Versioning with Server-Activated Objects

To begin with, server-activated objects (singleton and *SingleCall* activation types) have no form of version control. Even if you create these objects using strongly named assemblies and place multiple versions in the global assembly cache (GAC), the component host always activates the most recent version when it receives a request, regardless of the version that the client expects.

The best way to avoid this problem is to never update a remote object after it is in use. Instead, you should place new versions of the server-side object at a new URI endpoint and allow the clients to migrate by updating their configuration files. This technique works well, but it does force you to update the client-side configuration files. You might be able to automate this process using some of the dynamic registration techniques described at the end of this chapter.

So how do you create multiple endpoints for different versions of a single component? You have two choices. First, you can create and host an entirely new assembly. The second (and more common) choice is to use the strong-naming tool (sn.exe) described in Chapter 2 and install your server-side objects into the GAC. You can then modify the component host's configuration file to include version information in the *type* attribute.

Consider Listing 11-2, for example, which registers two versions of *DBComponent* at two different endpoints. Note that you need to include the exact version number and public key token (which is displayed in the Windows Explorer GAC plug-in).

```
<configuration>
   <system.runtime.remoting>
      <application name="SimpleServer">
         <service>
            <wellknown mode="SingleCall"
              type="RemoteObjects.RemoteObject,
              RemoteObjects, Version 1.0.0.1, Culture=neutral,
              PublicKeyToken=8b5ed84fd25209e1"
              objectUri="RemoteObject" />
```

Listing 11-2 Providing multiple versions of a server-side object

```
            <wellknown mode="SingleCall"
              type="RemoteObjects.RemoteObject,
              RemoteObjects, Version 2.0.0.1, Culture=neutral,
              PublicKeyToken=8b5ed84fd25209e1"
              objectUri="RemoteObject_2" />
          </service>
          <channels>
            <channel ref="tcp server" port="8080" />
          </channels>
      </application>
  </system.runtime.remoting>
</configuration>
```

The client configuration file won't change (aside from updating the URI, if required). Keep in mind, however, that you can't specify version information for a server-activated object in the client configuration file. Doing so will have no effect.

Versioning with Client-Activated Objects

With a client-activated object, the rules differ completely. When the client creates the remote object, a message is passed that includes the version assembly information for the remote assembly, provided it has a strong name. The component host then creates the requested version of the assembly. Any version information in the server configuration file is ignored.

Remember that the client automatically uses the version of the assembly that it was compiled with, provided it has a strong name. You don't specify the version information in the configuration file. If you want to alter the binding version, however, the same rules apply as those used for local development. As described in Chapter 2, you can add the *<bindingRedirect>* tag to the client's configuration file to explicitly override the binding behavior and instruct it to use a different version.

Versioning with Serializable Objects

The rules change yet again for serializable objects that can be exchanged between clients. The .NET Remoting framework has two different ways to pass information. It can relax the rules and use a nonversioned system (somewhat like XML Web services), where missing information is ignored if possible. Alternatively, it can tighten the rules, send a strong assembly name with every serialized object, and require an exact version match. Otherwise, a *SerializationException* is thrown.

By default, the SOAP Formatter uses the relaxed rules and the Binary Formatter applies the strict verification. However, you can change these options by modifying the *includeVersions* attribute of the formatter tag. This setting applies to outgoing messages and can be applied to the server or client configuration file. Listing 11-3 shows an example that tightens requirements for the SOAP Formatter.

```
<configuration>
   <system.runtime.remoting>
      <application name="SimpleServer">

         <service>
            <wellknown mode="SingleCall"
              type="RemoteObjects.RemoteObject, RemoteObjects"
              objectUri="RemoteObject" />
         </service>

         <channels>
            <channel ref="http server" port="8080">
               <formatter ref="soap" includeVersions="true" >
            </channel>
         </channels>

      </application>
   </system.runtime.remoting>
</configuration>
```

Listing 11-3 Modifying versioning rules

This is all well and good from a theoretical viewpoint, but you're probably wondering what the practical effects of strict and relaxed versioning are. As you might expect, using relaxed versioning can mean trading short-term convenience for long-term suffering. It works fairly well when you send a serialized object (either as a parameter or as a method return value). However, receiving a serialized object is more error-prone because the expected properties might not exist.

Some coding workarounds can defend against these problems. You can implement custom serialization in your serializable types, for example, and explicitly use error-handling logic when you attempt to retrieve information that might not exist in older versions. However, these workarounds are themselves subject to error and are time-consuming to implement and maintain. I don't recommend this approach. Now that the DLL is finally eradicated from the Windows world, there is no reason to reintroduce it with your own custom logic.

In a real, evolving enterprise application, the only solution is to avoid incremental updates. If you need to update a serializable class, you should create a new version of the serializable class and put a new version of the server-activated object at a different URI. This allows a phased migration approach, which is always more successful than trying to handle multiple-client versions with a single-server version.

Interface-Based Programming

One of the most useful design techniques for .NET Remoting is interface-based programming. With interface-based programming, you define a contract that the client and server must follow. You also specify details for supplementary classes such as custom exceptions, *EventArgs*, and other information packages.

The goal is to concentrate all the shared information about all the remotable and serializable objects in a single assembly. You then distribute this assembly to the client and the server. The client can activate the remote type through the interface, without requiring a direct reference to the remote object's assembly. This simplifies distribution and improves security because there's no longer a need to copy the remote object assembly and distribute it to each client. It also enables you to develop the client application and server components independently after the interface has been defined. Without this technique, it becomes almost impossible to keep track of changing assemblies and update all the references appropriately.

Consider the *CustomerDB* and *CustomerDetails* example demonstrated in Chapter 2. To use interface-based programming, you create four separate projects:

- A class library project that contains the interfaces and serializable classes (in this case, called *CustomerInterfaces*).
- A client project that uses a local copy of the *CustomerInterfaces* assembly.
- A remote object project that uses a local copy of the *CustomerInterfaces* assembly.
- The component host project. This project still requires a local copy of the remote object assembly because it has the responsibility for creating the object. You can add a reference to this project or copy the assembly to the appropriate directory manually.

The complete Visual Studio .NET solution is included online with the code samples for this chapter.

The *CustomerInterfaces* Assembly

The *CustomerInterfaces* assembly includes all the information required by the client and the server-side component. To start with, this information includes the serializable *CustomerDetails* information package (as shown in Listing 11-4). (Alternatively, you can include just the interface for this class if it is subject to change. The remote object assembly will then implement the interface with a specific class.)

```
<Serializable()> _
Public Class CustomerDetails

    Private _ID As Integer
    Private _Name As String
    Private _Email As String
    Private _Password As String

    ' (Constructors and property procedures omitted.)

End Class
```

Listing 11-4 The serializable *CustomerDetails*

Next you need to define an interface for the *CustomerDB* component. This interface lists every public method and property (as shown in Listing 11-5).

```
Public Interface ICustomerDB

    Function GetCustomerDetails(ByVal customerID As Integer) _
     As CustomerDetails

    Function GetCustomerDetails() As ArrayList

    Sub AddCustomer(ByVal customer As CustomerDetails) _

    Sub UpdateCustomer(ByVal customer As CustomerDetails)

    Sub DeleteCustomer(ByVal customerID As Integer)

End Interface
```

Listing 11-5 The interface for *CustomerDB*

In this case, the communication will be one-way (from the client to the *CustomerDB* object), so you don't need to define an interface for the client. If you were using bidirectional communication, you would create an *IClient* interface, which would allow the server to send messages to the client without having a copy of the client's assembly.

The Remote Object

The remote object changes very little. The *CustomerDB* class (shown in Listing 11-6) is identical except that it implements all the members of the interface and adds any private member variables.

```
Public Class CustomerDB
    Inherits System.MarshalByRefObject
    Implements CustomerDBInterfaces.ICustomerDB

    Private Shared ConnectionString As String = _
     "Data Source=MyServer;Initial Catalog=MyDb;" & _
     "Integrated Security=SSPI"

    Public Function GetCustomerDetails(ByVal customerID As Integer) _
      As CustomerDetails Implements ICustomerDB.GetCustomerDetails
        ' (Code omitted.)
    End Function

    Public Sub AddCustomer(ByVal customer As CustomerDetails) _
      Implements ICustomerDB.AddCustomer
        ' (Code omitted.)
    End Sub

    Public Sub UpdateCustomer(ByVal customer As CustomerDetails) _
      Implements ICustomerDB.UpdateCustomer
        ' (Code omitted.)
    End Sub

    Public Sub DeleteCustomer(ByVal customerID As Integer) _
      Implements ICustomerDB.DeleteCustomer
        ' (Code omitted.)
    End Sub

    Public Function GetCustomer(ByVal customerID As Integer) _
      As CustomerDetails Implements ICustomerDB.GetCustomerDetails
        ' (Code omitted.)
    End Function

    Public Function GetCustomers() As ArrayList _
      Implements ICustomerDB.GetCustomerDetails
        ' (Code omitted.)
    End Function

    ' (Private ExecuteNonQuery() method omitted.)

End Class
```

Listing 11-6 The remotable *CustomerDB*

The Component Host

The component host uses exactly the same model as in Chapter 4. The *CustomerDB* object is referenced directly in the configuration file, not the interface because the component host needs to be able to instantiate the object. An interface is enough to communicate with an object once it exists, but not enough to create it.

The *CustomerDB* remote object is entirely stateless, so it is perfectly suited for a server-activated *SingleCall* object. Listing 11-7 shows the appropriate configuration file.

```
<configuration>
   <system.runtime.remoting>
      <application name="SimpleServer">
         <service>
            <wellknown
             mode="SingleCall"
             type="DatabaseComponents.CustomerDB, DatabaseComponents"
             objectUri="CustomerDB" />
         </service>
         <channels>
            <channel ref="tcp server" port="8080" />
         </channels>
      </application>
   </system.runtime.remoting>
</configuration>
```

Listing 11-7 The component host configuration file

Once again, the component host is designed as a Windows application (as shown in Listing 11-8). On startup, it just begins listening for client requests (as shown in Figure 11-1).

```
Imports System.Runtime.Remoting

Public Class HostForm
    Inherits System.Windows.Forms.Form

    ' (Windows designer code omitted.)

    Private Sub HostForm_Load(ByVal sender As System.Object,
      ByVal e As System.EventArgs) Handles MyBase.Load

        ' Configure the server channel.
        RemotingConfiguration.Configure("ComponentHost.exe.config")
        lblStatus.Text = "Listening for client requests ..."

    End Sub

End Class
```

Listing 11-8 The component host form

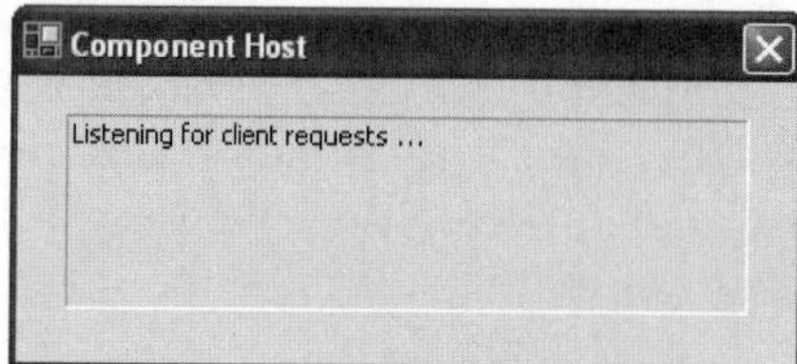

Figure 11-1 The component host

The Client

The client code needs a couple of small changes. Because it is activating the remote object through an interface, it can no longer create it directly by using the *New* keyword. Instead, it needs to use the *System.Activator* class, which provides a shared *GetObject* method.

Listing 11-9 shows the complete code. The remote object reference is created on startup. The *GetCustomers* method is invoked in response to a button click, and a *DataGrid* control is filled with the results (as shown in Figure 11-2).

```
Imports System.Runtime.Remoting
Imports CustomerDBInterfaces

Public Class ClientForm
    Inherits System.Windows.Forms.Form

    ' (Windows designer code omitted.)

    ' Holds the reference to the transparent CustomerDB proxy.
    Private CustomerDB As ICustomerDB

    Private Sub ClientForm_Load(ByVal sender As System.Object, _
      ByVal e As System.EventArgs) Handles MyBase.Load

        ' Configure client channel.
        RemotingConfiguration.Configure("Client.exe.config")

        ' Retrieve a reference to the remote object.
        Dim RemoteObj As Object
        RemoteObj = Activator.GetObject( _
                    GetType(CustomerDBInterfaces.ICustomerDB), _
                    "tcp://localhost:8080/SimpleServer/CustomerDB")

        ' Access the remote object to the interface.
        CustomerDB = CType(RemoteObj, CustomerDBInterfaces.ICustomerDB)

        statusBar.Text = "Configuration successful"
```

Listing 11-9 Activating *CustomerDB* through an interface

```
    End Sub

    Private Sub cmdGetAll_Click(ByVal sender As System.Object, _
      ByVal e As System.EventArgs) Handles cmdGetAll.Click

        ' Access a remote method.
        ' Because CustomerDB is a SingleCall object, this is the point
        ' at which it will be created.
        gridCustomers.DataSource = CustomerDB.GetCustomerDetails()

    End Sub

End Class
```

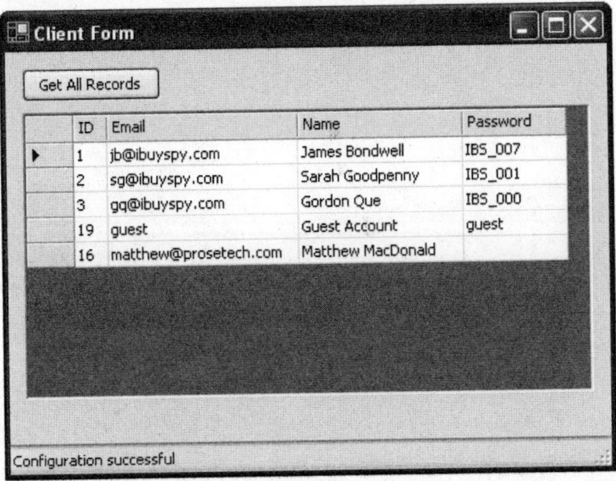

Figure 11-2 The *CustomerDB* client

The configuration file no longer specifies the object URI, just the channel and formatter information (as shown in Listing 11-10).

```
<configuration>
   <system.runtime.remoting>
      <application name="SimpleClient">
         <channels>
            <channel ref="tcp client"/>
         </channels>
      </application>
   </system.runtime.remoting>
</configuration>
```

Listing 11-10 The client configuration file

Figure 11-3 shows the full set of four projects, and the required references, as a single Visual Studio .NET solution.

The solution is configured to start both the component host and the client project simultaneously (as shown in Figure 11-4), allowing easy debugging in the Visual Studio .NET IDE.

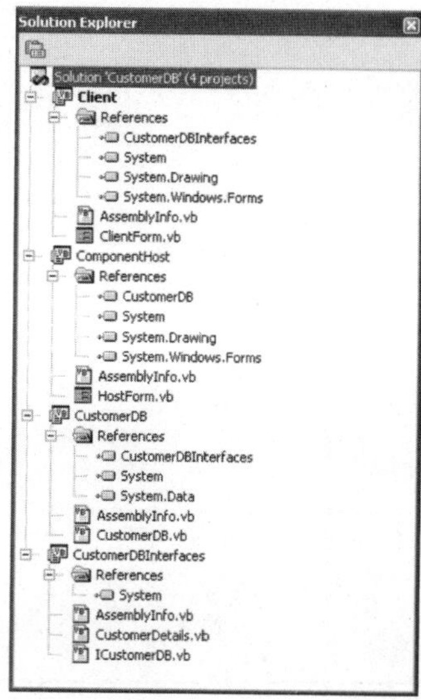

Figure 11-3 An interface-based *CustomerDB* solution

Note Interfaces are particularly useful when you're using bidirectional communication because you can easily define all the interfaces in one assembly (such as *IServer* or *IClient*). This is the only assembly that needs to be distributed. The server references this assembly to gain the ability to talk to the client. The client also references this assembly to gain the ability to talk to the server. We'll use a similar approach to allow different parts of an application to communicate in Chapter 15.

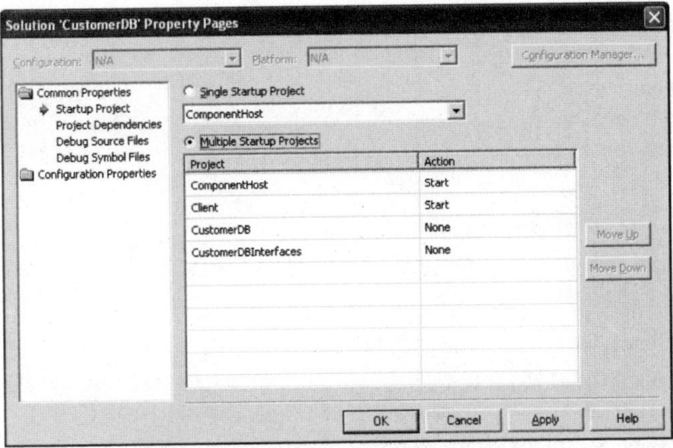

Figure 11-4 *CustomerDB* solution settings

Problems with Interface-Based Remoting

Interface-based programming isn't without a few quirks. The client can no longer use the simple approach of creating a remote object by using the *New* keyword because the client does not have a reference to the full assembly. An interface can't be instantiated directly because it is just an object definition, not an object. The solution—using the *Activator* class—is not ideal because it bypasses the configuration file. You can still use a configuration file and the *RemotingConfiguration.Configure* method to apply channel and formatter settings. However, you have to specify the object URI in your code. This means that if the object is moved to another computer or exposed through another port, you need to recompile the code.

You can solve this problem in several ways. One approach is just to create your own custom configuration setting in the custom *<appSettings>* section of the client configuration file, as shown in Listing 11-11.

```
<configuration>

  <appSettings>
    <add key="CustomerDB"
         value="tcp://localhost:8080/SimpleServer/CustomerDB" />
    </appSettings>

   <system.runtime.remoting>
      <application name="SimpleClient">
```

Listing 11-11 Putting the object URI in the configuration file

```
        <channels>
           <channel ref="tcp client"/>
        </channels>
      </application>
    </system.runtime.remoting>

</configuration>
```

You can then retrieve this setting using the *ConfigurationSettings.AppSettings* collection:

```
Dim RemoteObj As Object
RemoteObj = Activator.GetObject( _
            GetType(CustomerDBInterfaces.ICustomerDB), _
            ConfigurationSettings.AppSettings("CustomerDB"))
```

To simplify life even more, you can create a custom factory class. A *factory* is a dedicated class that abstracts the object-creation process. It allows your client code to remain blissfully unaware of whether the returned object is a remote object created through the *Activator* class or a class that's instantiated locally. In Listing 11-12, the factory uses a shared method so that the client won't need to create an instance of the factory class before using it.

```
Public Class CustomerDBFactory

    Public Shared Function Create() As ICustomerDB
        Dim RemoteObj As Object
        RemoteObj = Activator.GetObject( _
            GetType(CustomerDBInterfaces.ICustomerDB), _
            ConfigurationSettings.AppSettings("CustomerDB"))

        Return CType(RemoteObj, CustomerDBInterfaces.ICustomerDB)

    End Function

End Class
```

Listing 11-12 Using a factory

The client now needs only a single line of code to create the object:

```
CustomerDB = CustomerDBFactory.Create()
```

If you want, you can expand the intelligence of the *CustomerDBFactory*. For example, it might read a configuration file or contact an XML Web service to determine whether it should create a local or remote *ICustomerDB* instance.

Stubs

You can solve the assembly distribution problem in another way. You can create a separate "stub" class that represents the remote object instead of using an interface. A *stub* is a bare skeleton of class. It contains all the public members, but it doesn't define any implementation. Listing 11-13 shows a stub for the *CustomerDB* class.

```
Public Class CustomerDB
    Inherits System.MarshalByRefObject

    Public Function GetCustomerDetails(ByVal customerID As Integer)
      As CustomerDetails
    End Function

    Public Sub AddCustomer(ByVal customer As CustomerDetails)
    End Sub

    Public Sub UpdateCustomer(ByVal customer As CustomerDetails)
    End Sub

    Public Sub DeleteCustomer(ByVal customerID As Integer)
    End Sub

    Public Function GetCustomer(ByVal customerID As Integer) _
      As CustomerDetails
    End Function

    Public Function GetCustomers() As ArrayList
    End Function

End Class
```

Listing 11-13 A *CustomerDB* stub

The client can use this stub to create the remote *CustomerDB* object, as long as the fully qualified class name of the stub matches the fully qualified class name of the remote class. Visual Studio .NET won't raise a compile-time error because it has the metadata it needs to validate your client code:

```
' Configure the client.
RemotingConfiguration.Configure("SimpleClient.exe.config")

' Create the object using the stub.
Dim CustomerDB As New CustomerDB.CustomerDB()
```

The stub approach is really a crude way to simulate an interface. Generally, interfaced-based programming is preferable. One potential problem with the stub approach is that the client might accidentally create a local copy of the stub rather than the remote object. This occurs if the stub namespace differs even slightly from the remote object namespace. To defend against this possibility, you should add code to the constructor that throws an exception, or just make the default constructor private. Listing 11-4 shows the first approach.

```
Public Class CustomerDB
    Inherits System.MarshalByRefObject

    Public Sub New()
        Throw New ApplicationException("Stub cannot be instantiated.")
    End Sub

    ' (Remainder of code omitted.)

End Class
```

Listing 11-14 A stub that cannot be instantiated

.NET Remoting and XML Web Services Revisited

Stubs and interfaces both solve one of the key problems with distributed applications and .NET: deploying the metadata to the client. Without this metadata, the client can't interact with the remote object.

The .NET Remoting solution is quite different from the approach taken with XML Web services. With XML Web Services, the client retrieves the metadata as a human-readable WSDL document. This allows applications on other platforms to interact with XML Web services, and it allows .NET to create a proxy class without requiring the original remote object assembly or even an interface.

Interestingly enough, .NET blurs the distinction between XML Web services and .NET Remoting and enables you to use some XML Web service features with components over .NET Remoting. We'll look at two examples, one that uses WSDL description and one that uses ASP.NET hosting.

Soapsuds and WSDL Description

Here's the first surprise: XML Web services aren't the only server-side technology that uses WSDL. In fact, you can retrieve a WSDL document for a component that's exposed through .NET Remoting, provided the server is using the HTTP channel.

Consider the *CustomerDB* example we looked at in the preceding section. To test this, modify the component host to use the HTTP channel, start the application, and enter the object URL in a browser, with *?WSDL* appended at the end:

```
http://localhost:8080/SimpleServer/CustomerDB?WSDL
```

A complete WSDL document displays in the browser. Interestingly, this WSDL document isn't completely compatible with those generated by an XML Web service. If you try to use this URL to add a Web reference in Visual Studio .NET, the process fails.

However, you can use a dedicated command-line tool to create a proxy class using this document. The tool is called soapsuds.exe, and it plays the same role that wsdl.exe served for XML Web services. To dynamically create a proxy class for the *CustomerDB* object, use the *–url* parameter to specify the URL and the *–gc* parameter to instruct soapsuds to create a code file. It names the file according to the remote object's class name. The client can create the remote object using the generated class, which encapsulates all the .NET Remoting details.

```
soapsuds -url:http://localhost:8080/SimpleServer/CustomerDB?WSDL -gc
```

Soapsuds can create a proxy only in compiled form or C# source code; it does not support Visual Basic. Therefore, before you can use it in a Visual Basic .NET project, you need to compile the proxy class using the csc.exe compiler.

Incidentally, you can retrieve the WSDL documents for all the remote objects in a component host by omitting the object name and specifying *RemoteApplicationMetadata.rem* instead:

```
http://localhost:8080/SimpleServer/RemoteApplicationMetadata.rem?WSDL
```

This always works in Visual Studio .NET 2002. In Visual Studio .NET 2003, however, this option is restricted by default as a security measure. You will need to enable it by modifying the channel information in the configuration file as shown here:

```
<channel ref="tcp client" remoteApplicationMetadataEnabled="true" />
```

Remember that this doesn't mean that .NET Remoting can assume the role played by XML Web services. .NET Remoting still provides fewer options for cross-platform interaction and assumes that both client and server are .NET applications. However, the soapsuds tool provides some interesting insight into how .NET Remoting can work and provides another approach for distributing metadata. Interface-based development is generally preferred, but the soapsuds utility gives the client the ability to create a proxy class independently, as long as the component host is running. The interface-based and stub-based approaches require the server developers to go to the extra work of distributing the interface or stub assembly.

Finally, remember that soapsuds and WSDL description work only if the object is exposed by an HTTP channel. However, you can freely use the Binary Formatter.

ASP.NET Hosting

WSDL isn't the only surprise with .NET Remoting. You also can host a remote component in Microsoft Internet Information Services (IIS) and ASP.NET just as easily as you can with an XML Web service. The only required change is a little bit of configuration file tweaking.

First, consider the long list of prerequisites and limitations:

- As with XML Web services, you must create a virtual directory for your remote component.
- You must use the HTTP channel. However, you're free to use the Binary Formatter for smaller message sizes and more efficient communication (which isn't an option with XML Web services).
- You must use a *SingleCall* object. Client-activated and singleton objects are not supported by the ASP.NET infrastructure because the ASP.NET infrastructure periodically recycles processes.
- You can't specify a specific port number for listening. IIS listens on all the HTTP ports you have configured in the IIS manager. Typically, this will be port 80.
- The object URI must end with *.rem* or *.soap*. This curious requirement isn't found in any other hosting environment.
- You can't directly debug the remote object in the Visual Studio .NET IDE. However, you can manually attach a debugger to the aspnet_wp.exe worker process. You use the same process we followed in Chapter 7 to attach a debugger to a Windows service.

Configuring a remote object to run under ASP.NET is an easy process. All you do is copy your remote object assembly to the \Bin subdirectory of a virtual directory on the server. Alternatively, you can place it in the Web server's GAC. Then you create a configuration file for the Web application. This file must be named web.config, which is the only file ASP.NET recognizes. Listing 11-15 shows an example that uses the Binary Formatter.

```
<configuration>
   <system.runtime.remoting>
      <application>
         <service>
            <wellknown mode="SingleCall"
              type="RemoteObjects.RemoteObject, RemoteObjects"
              objectUri="RemoteObject.rem" />
         </service>

         <channels>
            <channel ref="http">
               <serverProviders>
                  <formatter ref="binary"/>
               </serverProviders>
            </channel>
         </channels>

      </application>
   </system.runtime.remoting>
</configuration>
```

Listing 11-15 Configuring a remote object for ASP.NET

The configuration file is almost identical to the ones we created earlier. The only difference is that you can't specify the application name in the service attribute. Instead, the virtual directory name automatically becomes the application name. If the web.config file shown above is hosted in the virtual directory http://localhost/ASPHost, for example, the full URI is as follows:

```
http://localhost/ASPHost/RemoteObject.rem
```

One advantage to this approach is that the remote object also gains the ability to use IIS authentication features (such as SSL) and the built-in ASP.NET objects. Add these features at your peril—when you add ASP.NET-specific code, you give up the flexibility for other types of component hosts.

Keep in mind that hosting an object in ASP.NET doesn't make it an XML Web service. The same distinction still applies: If you need support for flexible discovery and description or cross-platform use, an XML Web service is best. If you can assume that all clients are written using languages supported by .NET, you can use .NET Remoting.

Programmatic Registration

In Chapter 2, you learned how to register .NET Remoting channels for a component host and a client that uses configuration files. As with most tasks in .NET, anything you can do, you can do in code.

Consider the following configuration file, which you might remember from Chapter 2. It defines a single registered *SingleCall* object type and a TCP/IP listening channel on port 8080.

```
<configuration>
   <system.runtime.remoting>
      <application name="SimpleServer">
         <service>
            <wellknown mode="SingleCall"
                       type="RemoteObjects.RemoteObject, RemoteObjects"
                       objectUri="RemoteObject" />
         </service>
         <channels>
            <channel ref="tcp server" port="8080" />
         </channels>
      </application>
   </system.runtime.remoting>
</configuration>
```

Using types in the *System.Runtime.Remoting* and *System.Runtime.Remoting.Channels* namespaces, you can perform the same work at startup, as shown in Listing 11-16.

```
Imports System.Runtime.Remoting
Imports System.Runtime.Remoting.Channels.
Imports System.Runtime.Remoting.Channels.Tcp

Public Class HostForm
    Inherits System.Windows.Form

    ' (Windows designer code omitted.)

    Private Sub HostForm_Load(ByVal sender As System.Object, _
     ByVal e As System.EventArgs) Handles MyBase.Load

    RemotingConfiguration.ApplicationName = "SimpleServer"

    ' Define the channel.
    Dim Channel As New TcpServerChannel(8080)

    ' Register the channel.
```

Listing 11-16 Server-side dynamic registration

```
        ChannelServices.RegisterChannel(Channel)

        ' Register the remote object type.
        RemotingConfiguration.RegisterWellKnownServiceType( _
          GetType(RemoteObjects.RemoteObject), _
          "RemoteObjects.RemoteObject", _
          WellKnownObjectMode.SingleCall)

    End Sub

End Class
```

This example uses the *TcpServerChannel* class, although you also can use *TcpChannel* for a bidirectional channel or *TcpClient* for a client channel. Similarly, the *System.Runtime.Remoting.Channels.Http* namespace includes an *HttpServerChannel*, an *HttpClientChannel*, and an *HttpChannel.*

The only difference between this code and the Chapter 2 example (other than the fact that you no longer need a configuration file) is that the component host requires a reference to the remote object assembly. Otherwise, the call to the *RemotingConfiguration.RegisterWellKnownServiceType* method generates a compile-time error. Specifically, .NET won't be able to retrieve a *Type* object that represents the class. The offending code is shown here:

```
RemotingConfiguration.RegisterWellKnownServiceType( _
  GetType(RemoteObjects.RemoteObject), _
  "RemoteObjects.RemoteObject", _
  WellKnownObjectMode.SingleCall)
```

The *RegisterWellKnownServiceType* method enables you to register *SingleCall* and singleton object types. You can also use the *RegisterActivatedServiceType* for a client-activated object.

Just as you can register channels, you also can unregister them. This can come in handy because attempting to reregister a channel that's already registered will fail.

Listing 11-17 uses the *ChannelServices.RegisteredChannels* to retrieve all the currently registered channels and systematically unregisters each one.

```
Dim Channel As IChannel

For Each Channel In ChannelServices.RegisteredChannels
    ChannelServices.UnregisterChannel(Channel)
Next
```

Listing 11-17 Unregistering all channels

At this point, you might be wondering why you would want to perform programmatic registration. One of the most obvious problems is that programs that use this technique need to be recompiled if you want to use a different server, port, or communication method. However, programmatic registration also makes possible some new registration techniques.

Consider the case in which you want to register a component host that listens on several different channels. In a configuration-file-based approach, this is awkward because of naming collisions. With programmatic registration, it's easy. All you do is specify a unique name when you create the channel or use an empty string. The empty string tells .NET to ignore names but prevent naming conflicts.

```
' Listen for object requests over TCP/IP on several different ports.
Dim Channel1 As New TcpChannel("", 8000)
Dim Channel2 As New TcpChannel("", 8040)
Dim Channel3 As New TcpChannel("", 8100)
```

Another trick is to create a generic component host that automatically exposes any remotable types in a referenced assembly. Listing 11-18 demonstrates this technique.

```
Dim RemoteObjects As System.Reflection.Assembly

' Find the System.Reflection.Assembly object representing the assembly
' where the RemoteObject type is defined.
RemoteObjects = GetType(RemoteObject).Assembly

' Process all the types in this namespace.
Dim Obj As Type
For Each Obj in RemoteObjects.GetTypes()

    ' Check if the type is remotable.
    If Obj.IsSubclassOf(GetType(MarshalByRefObject)) Then

        ' Register each type using the fully qualified type name
        ' (like RemoteObjects.RemoteObject).
        RemotingConfiguration.RegisterWellKnownServiceType( _
          Obj, Obj.FullName, WellKnownObjectMode.SingleCall)

    End If

Next
```

Listing 11-18 Exposing all the remotable types in an assembly

With this technique, you might still use a configuration file to specify channel information, but you use runtime logic to determine what objects to provide through .NET Remoting.

> **Note** You might want to enhance this example by developing a custom attribute. The component host can then examine the attributes applied to each type in the assembly and instantiate them only if it finds your custom attribute. Alternatively, the attribute might indicate which URI or activation type it should use when registering the type.

Dynamic Publication

Programmatic registration is really just a tool that can enable you to implement your own custom registration schemes. This can prove useful if you have several servers that host different remote components and run different component hosts. Keeping track of the active component hosts, available channels, and usable URL endpoints is no small task.

One interesting approach is to borrow an idea from peer-to-peer programming and create a centralized discovery and lookup server. The idea is that one XML Web service (and one database) can store information that tracks all your active objects. This gives you an easy way to query summary information and troubleshoot connection problems.

Recording Connection Information with an XML Web Service

The next example shows a simple coordination XML Web service designed to help clients find the remote objects they need. A single server is used to run the coordination XML Web service and host the database, which contains a RemoteObjects table listing all the currently available endpoints. This table pairs remote object type names with a URL where they can be found. Figure 11-5 shows that there are two component servers that provide three endpoints, plus two distinct objects (*CustomerDB* and *OrderDB*).

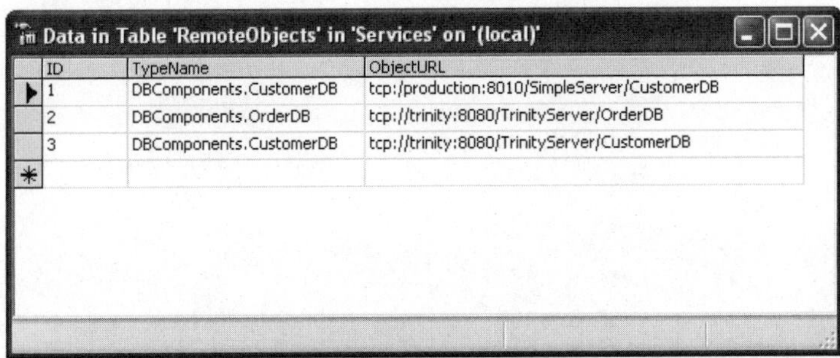
Data in Table 'RemoteObjects' in 'Services' on '(local)'

ID	TypeName	ObjectURL
1	DBComponents.CustomerDB	tcp:/production:8010/SimpleServer/CustomerDB
2	DBComponents.OrderDB	tcp://trinity:8080/TrinityServer/OrderDB
3	DBComponents.CustomerDB	tcp://trinity:8080/TrinityServer/CustomerDB

Figure 11-5 The RemoteObjects table

The coordination XML Web service provides three Web methods: *RegisterUrls*, *UnregisterUrls*, and *GetUrls*. The *RegisterUrls* and *UregisterUrls* methods require an object name and an array of URLs in string format. These allow a component host to submit all the registration information for a remote object in one message rather than suffer the increased latency of multiple messages. However, the component host still needs to send a separate message for every object type. To overcome this limitation and further optimize performance, you can create a custom structure that encapsulates the type name and URL information.

Listing 11-19 shows the Web methods for registering and unregistering objects.

```
Public Class CoordinationService

    Private ConnectionString As String = _
     "Data Source=localhost;Initial Catalog=Services;" & _
     "Integrated Security=SSPI"

    <WebMethod()> _
    Public Sub RegisterUrls(typeName As String, urls As String())

        Dim Sql As String

        Dim con As New SqlConnection(ConnectionString)
        Dim cmd As New SqlCommand(con)

        Try
            con.Open()

            ' Insert a record for each URL.
            Dim Url As String
            For Each Url In urls

                Sql = "INSERT INTO RemoteObjects "
                Sql &= "(TypeName, ObjectURL) VALUES ('"
                Sql &= typeName & "', '"
                Sql &= Url & "')"

                cmd.CommandText = Sql
                cmd.ExecuteNonQuery()

            Next

        Catch Err As Exception
            ' Use "caller inform" exception handling pattern.
            Throw New ApplicationException( _
             "Exception encountered when executing command.", Err)
```

Listing 11-19 The *RegisterUrls* and *UnregisterUrls* Web methods

```
        Finally
            con.Close()

        End Try

    End Sub

    <WebMethod()> _
    Public Sub UnregisterUrls(typeName As String, urls As String())

        Dim Sql As String

        Dim con As New SqlConnection(ConnectionString)
        Dim cmd As New SqlCommand(con)

        Try
            con.Open()

            ' Insert a record for each URL.
            Dim Url As String
            For Each Url In urls

                Sql = "DELETE FROM RemoteObjects "
                Sql &= "WHERE TypeName='"
                Sql &= typeName & "' AND ObjectURL='"
                Sql &= Url & "'"

                cmd.CommandText = Sql
                cmd.ExecuteNonQuery()

            Next

        Catch Err As Exception
            ' Use "caller inform" exception handling pattern.
            Throw New ApplicationException( _
             "Exception encountered when executing command.", Err)

        Finally
            con.Close()

        End Try

    End Sub

    ' (RetrieveUrls method omitted.)

End Class
```

Each component host uses these methods to publish information about its available types. For example, on startup a component host might register its *CustomerDB* URLs by using the code in Listing 11-20. This approach requires the component host to know which types it exposes. Optionally, you can move this information into a custom configuration file or use the *ChannelServices.GetUrlsForObject* method.

```
' Retrieve a reference to the first channel.
Dim Channel As TcpServerChannel = ChannelServices.RegisteredChannels(0)

' This value could be retrieved from a configuration file.
Dim TypeName As String = "CustomerDB.CustomerDB"

' Determine the CustomerDB URLs this channel exposes.
Dim Urls As String() = Channel.GetUrlsForUri(TypeName)

' Register the channels.
Dim Proxy As New localhost.CoordinationService()
Proxy.RegisterUrls(Typename, Urls)
```

Listing 11-20 Registering remote URLs with the coordination service

The component host would have to take similar steps to unregister all channels before it shuts down.

The next ingredient is the *GetUrls* method in the coordination service, which returns a string array with all the current URL endpoints for that object on the system (as shown in Listing 11-21).

```
Public Function GetUrls(typeName As String) As ArrayList

    Dim Sql As String
    Sql = "SELECT * FROM RemoteObjects WHERE TypeName ='"
    Sql &= typeName & "'"

    Dim con As New SqlConnection(ConnectionString)
    Dim cmd As New SqlCommand(Sql, con)
    Dim Reader As SqlDataReader

    Dim Matches As New ArrayList()

    Try
        con.Open()
        Reader = cmd.ExecuteReader()
```

Listing 11-21 The *GetUrls* Web method

```
        ' Add the retrieved URLs to the ArrayList.
        Do While Reader.Read()
            Matches.Add(Reader("ObjectURL"))
        Loop

    Catch Err As Exception
        ' Use caller inform pattern.
        Throw New ApplicationException( _
         "Exception encountered when executing command.", Err)

    Finally
        con.Close()

    End Try

    Return Matches

End Function
```

Now a client can retrieve the URLs for a given object programmatically (as shown in Listing 11-22).

```
' Configure client channel.
RemotingConfiguration.Configure("Client.exe.config")

' This value could be retrieved from a configuration file.
Dim TypeName As String = "CustomerDB.CustomerDB"

' Retrieve the URL.
Dim Proxy As New localhost.CoordinationService()
Dim Urls As ArrayList = Proxy.GetUrls(TypeName)

' Try to connect with the first URL.
Dim RemoteObj As Object
RemoteObj = Activator.GetObject( _
                   GetType(CustomerDBInterfaces.ICustomerDB), _
                   ArrayList(0))

' Access the remote object to the interface.
CustomerDB = CType(RemoteObj, CustomerDBInterfaces.ICustomerDB)
```

Listing 11-22 Finding an URL using the coordination service

This design is more complicated, but it can prove extremely useful in a network where components hosts are not permanently online. The client can wrap its *Activator.GetObject* method calls in exception-handling code and try multiple URLs until one succeeds. This might be necessary in an environment in which the client is separated from some component hosts by a firewall.

You can implement the coordination service design in countless other ways. In this example, the component host still has the power to determine what ports and channels to use based on the configuration file settings. However, you can modify the component host code so that it retrieves the port number or channel it should use (or even the type name of the objects it should register). The component host can then create these endpoints using dynamic registration, which we discussed in the preceding section.

Another option is to store more information about each object. You might store version number information, for example, allowing a client to find the version it requires or choose the closest similar version. You also can include a priority field that indicates the relative network speed or server throughput of a given endpoint. This allows your client to implement a "quality-of-service" approach, in which it attempts the best link first and then moves progressively through the list if the connection can't succeed. All of these ideas represent different ways that you might want to enhance this example to meet your own needs when coordinating a large network of client and distributed Remoting providers.

> **Note** You can implement a basic form of static load balancing (called *round-robin* load balancing) using the coordination service design. Here's how it works. Your coordination XML Web service stores links to remote objects on several servers. Each time a client makes a request, it randomly chooses one. Over time, the client load is distributed over the available servers. This can't replace the sophisticated load balancing of a product such as Microsoft Application Center 2000, but it's useful when you create a coordination service. In the preceding example, there's a good chance that all clients will just try to connect to the first server on the list. If the database doesn't change frequently, this will be the same server, and it will receive a disproportionate amount of the client load.

A Closer Look at *ObjRef*

There is another approach to linking remote components hosted at different places on the network. It involves using the power of object references.

You'll no doubt remember that when a client creates a remote object, the client doesn't really hold a reference to the object. Instead, the client holds the reference to a proxy object. The CLR generates this proxy using the information sent by the server, which includes the following:

- The fully qualified type name of the remote object, including its assembly
- The type names of all the remote object's base classes and all the interfaces implemented by the remote object
- The object URL

All this information is wrapped in a special .NET object: *System.Runtime.Remoting.ObjRef*. This is a serializable class type, which means it can be sent to any .NET client. You can think of the *ObjRef* object as a sort of network pointer. It can be shipped around the network anywhere you want, but it always points to a specific instance on the originating computer.

Now consider this scenario. A client creates a remote object and passes the remote object reference to a different remote object. This second remote object attempts to call a method on the first remote object. What happens?

This scenario is actually no different from the normal one in which a client deals with a remotable object it created directly. The *ObjRef* transmits all the information required. Therefore, the second remote object contacts the first remote object directly (provided no firewall or other network issue intervenes). The client will no longer play any part. It can even shut down.

This gives you an idea of another way that remote objects can be related. For example, you might connect to several different remote applications through one component host. Alternatively, you might create a master remote component that creates other remotable components and returns references to them. Remember, however, that as interesting as these designs are, you should introduce only as many features as you need to simplify your setup. Centralizing remote components to a single server (or a load-balanced set of servers) will always be the easiest approach to manage.

Summary

This chapter took a closer look at .NET Remoting—not the low-level details of the platform but the development techniques you need to master it. We covered a considerable amount of ground, including interface-based development and dynamic registration. The former is the key to locking down distributed designs, and the latter is the key to managing the enterprise-wide configuration of remote objects on multiple servers. In the next chapter, we'll shift our focus to the data tier.

12

Optimizing the Data Tier

Most distributed applications rely on a data tier: a single layer where all information resides. The data tier is one of the most critical areas of a distributed application because a disproportionate amount of the weight tends to fall on it. All too often, the data tier becomes the first bottleneck of a growing system as demand outstrips the system's ability to create connections or retrieve data.

Fortunately, a wealth of tools are available for optimizing the data tier. We'll explore the options in Microsoft .NET, first by developing a connection pooling test and considering the best data-transfer plans, and then by adding dynamic data caching. Finally, this chapter will discuss some of the features available in the data source itself and explain how you can optimize a database, looking specifically at Microsoft SQL Server.

Connection Pooling

Chapter 1 covered some of the issues that face traditional client/server applications. One of the most significant problems for systems with a large number of relatively low-volume clients is the overhead needed to acquire a limited resource. Database connections are an ideal example: They are finite in number and take a measurable amount of time to create. Without some pooling mechanism to reuse and share connections, the time needed to create a connection for each client request will definitely create a bottleneck.

You could try to address this issue by creating a dedicated database component and then using the pooling features available with COM+. Alternatively, you could try to create a server object that manually creates a pool of connections and hands them out to clients. With a fair bit of effort, both of these approaches could work. Fortunately, Microsoft and other database vendors usually provide an alternative: connection pooling built into the data access technology.

In the case of the managed OLE DB or ODBC .NET provider, you rely on the session pooling mechanism of OLE DB or the connection pooling resources of the ODBC driver manager. Both of these tasks are handled transparently and require no additional settings or extra work. In the case of OLE DB drivers, there might be more connection string settings you can use to configure pool sizes and other variables. (Consult the documentation included with the database product.) For ODBC connection pooling, you can configure some options from the Data Sources window in Control Panel. In both cases, a wealth of information is available online in the Microsoft MSDN Library.

The .NET providers for SQL Server and Oracle also provide their own built-in connection pooling, which doesn't rely on any other standard (such as COM+). This connection pooling is automatically enabled by default and, as discussed in Chapter 9, is quite a bit better than the connection pooling available with the OLE DB and ODBC .NET providers because it enables you to enforce connection maximums. Maximums ensure that the system remains reliable even under a heavy client load. To achieve the same benefits with the OLE DB provider, you need to disable connection pooling and implement a custom object pooling system using COM+.

You can customize connection pooling for the SQL Server and Oracle providers using the connection string settings detailed in Table 12-1.

Table 12-1 SQL Server and Oracle Connection Pooling Settings

Setting	Description
Connection Lifetime	Specifies the maximum amount of time that a connection can live in the pool (in seconds). Every time a connection is returned to the pool, its creation time is compared against this value. If it is older than the specified lifetime, it is destroyed. The default is 0, which specifies that all connections are retained for the life of the process. The Connection Lifetime setting proves useful when you need to recycle a large number of connections simultaneously, such as when you want to balance the load with a new server that has just been brought online.
Connection Reset	If *True*, the connection state is reset when a pooled connection is reused. This requires an extra round-trip but makes for easier programming. State includes session-level *SET* statements and the currently selected database. This setting is recommended and is *True* by default.

Table 12-1 SQL Server and Oracle Connection Pooling Settings *(continued)*

Setting	Description
Enlist	When *True* (the default), the connection is enlisted in the current transaction context of the creation thread.
Max Pool Size	The maximum number of connections allowed in the pool (100 by default). If the maximum pool size is reached and no connection is free, the request is queued and performance suffers.
Min Pool Size	The minimum number of connections always retained in the pool (0 by default). This number of connections is created when the first connection is created, leading to a minor delay for the first request.
Pooling	When *True* (the default), connection pooling is used. The *SqlConnection* object is drawn from the appropriate pool when needed or is created and added to the pool.

It's important to remember that most forms of connection pooling, including those used in the managed providers for SQL Server and Oracle, use the connection string to determine whether a connection can be reused. If there is any difference in the connection string used by different clients, the connections are created and maintained in separate pools. This is true whether the connection string specifies a different user for authentication and even if the connection string just has an extra space or changes the order of identical settings because connection pooling algorithms require a full-text match. This is an excellent reason to deny the client the chance to specify the connection string directly. Instead, this variable should be hard-coded in a centrally located configuration file, as demonstrated in Chapter 2, so that the component is guaranteed to use the same string for each client.

As a side effect, this also means that you can't viably enforce security at the database layer because every client would need to use a connection string that specifies a distinct user ID. The option for integrated security (SSPI) might appear to solve this problem; it is just as limited, however, because it always uses the security context of the process on the machine where it is running, not the security context of the requesting client. The only viable way to implement security is at the business level, through your code (typically, by using roles). Chapter 13 returns to this subject.

Connections and Application Domains

Connection pooling won't immediately benefit your client/server applications because it's tied to the application process. This means that if you have multiple independent clients using a local database component, they will each have their own local pool. Connections won't be shared between clients, and scalability will suffer (as shown in Figure 12-1).

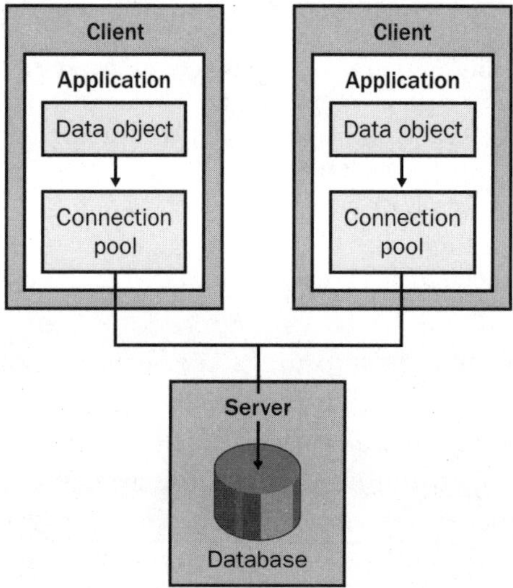

Figure 12-1 Local connection pools

If, on the other hand, all these clients access the same database component through an XML Web service or .NET Remoting, the remote component can use connection pooling and a single pool can serve all clients (as shown in Figure 12-2).

Does this mean all your database components should be remote? Not necessarily—remote components can be much slower because of the network latency and increased overhead in making a cross-process call. This is another example of the key tradeoff between scalability and performance examined in Chapter 10.

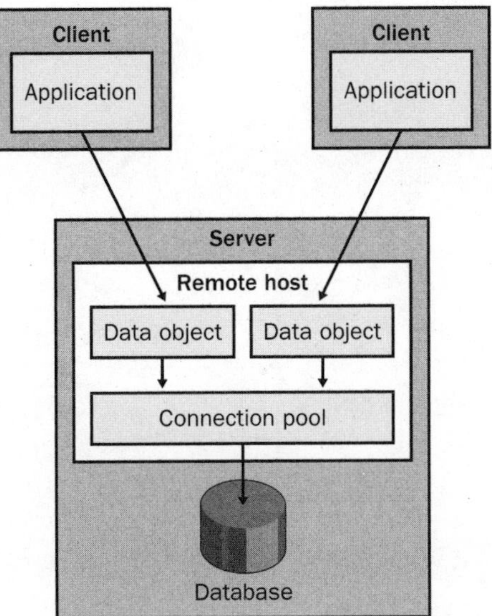

Figure 12-2 A shared connection pool

Testing Connection Pooling

To determine the ideal connection pooling settings, you might need to profile your application with performance counters. .NET includes performance counters specifically designed for the task under the .NET common language runtime (CLR) Data counter group. However, these counters work only with the SQL Server provider. You also might be able to use provider-specific counters. For example, SQL Server includes a counter that shows the current number of open connections.

One way to get a better understanding of how connection pooling works is to create a simple test application that opens and closes a connection to a database. You can use this application in conjunction with performance counters to monitor the effect of different connection string settings. This is the approach we'll take in the following example. It assumes you're using Microsoft Windows 2000 or Windows XP, but the process is similar in most Windows versions.

1. Start Performance Monitor by choosing Programs | Administrative Tools | Performance from the Start menu.
2. In the Performance window, click each existing counter and then click Delete to remove it. Continue this process until all the counter entries (in the lower right of the window) are removed.

3. Right-click on the graph display and choose Add Counters. Select the SQLServer:GeneralStatistics category and the User Connections counter (as shown in Figure 12-3).

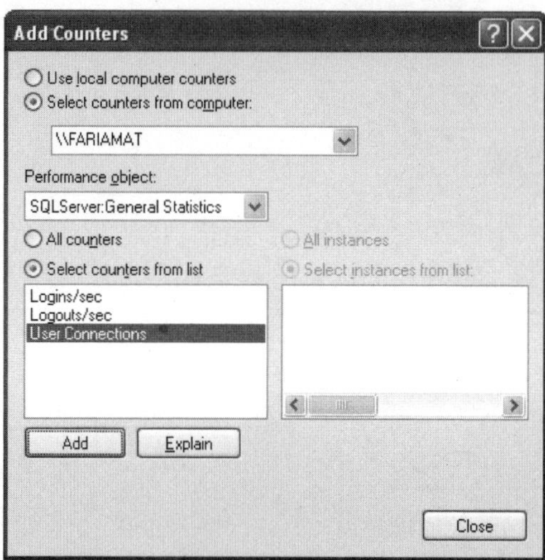

Figure 12-3 The SQL Server connection counter

Now create the simple XML Web service shown in Listing 12-1. Take note of the connection string—it defines several important pooling settings, including the minimum number of pooled connections (5), the maximum simultaneous connections allowed (10), and the timeout before an error is delivered if a client attempts to create an 11th connection (5 seconds).

```
Imports System.Data.SqlClient
Imports System.Web.Services

Public Class ConnectionPoolTest
    Inherits System.Web.Services.WebService

    Private ConnectionString As String = "Data Source=localhost;" & _
     user id=sa;Min Pool Size=5;Max Pool Size=10;Connect Timeout=5"

    <WebMethod()> _
    Public Sub TestConnect()

        Dim con As New SqlConnection(ConnectionString)
        con.Open()
```

Listing 12-1 An XML Web service that tests connection pooling

```
        con.Close()

    End Sub

End Class
```

The *TestConnect* method simply creates a connection and releases it immediately. You can test this method by triggering it with the Microsoft Internet Explorer test page. The result is reflected in the performance counter, as shown in Figure 12-4.

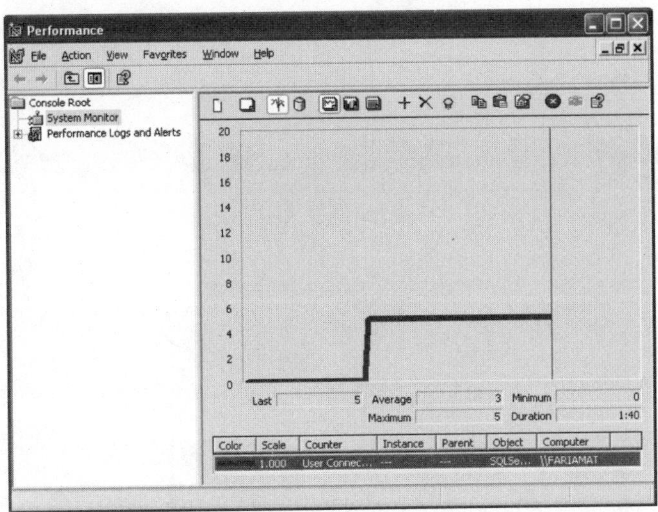

Figure 12-4 Opening a single connection

Because the minimum pool size is set to 5, five connections are created the moment the first connection is requested. Invoking the *TestConnect* method more than once doesn't change the number of connections because the required connection is reused from the pool. All five connections are tied to the lifetime of the ASP.NET application. They live until you manually terminate the ASP.NET worker process (using Task Manager) or until you recompile the application, at which point your XML Web service is automatically migrated to a new application domain, which doesn't yet have a pool of existing connections.

Listing 12-2 shows another interesting test you might want to perform with the ConnectionPoolTest XML Web service. It opens two connections, one that uses a slightly different connection string (it has an extra space character added to the end). This minor difference is enough to trigger the creation of two pools. Therefore, when you invoke this method you'll end up with a total of 10 connections (as shown in Figure 12-5).

```
<WebMethod()> _
Public Sub TestTwoPools()

    Dim conA As New SqlConnection(ConnectionString)
    conA.Open()
    conA.Close()

    ' Modify the second connection string ever-so-slightly.
    Dim conB As New SqlConnection(ConnectionString & " ")
    conB.Open()
    conB.Close()

End Sub
```

Listing 12-2 Creating two pools

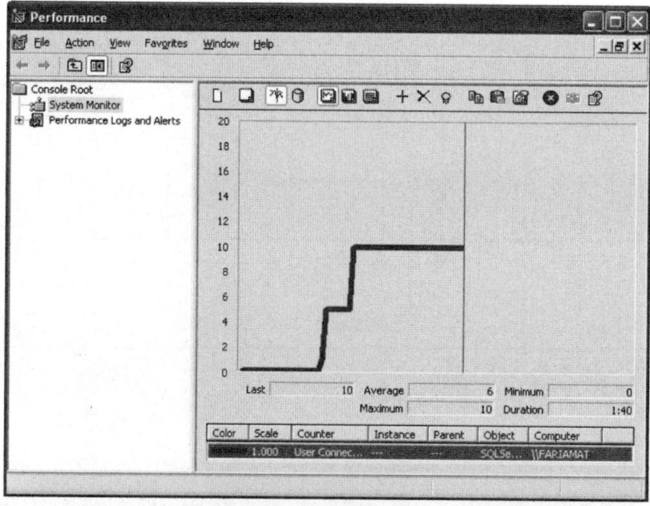

Figure 12-5 Opening two connections in separate pools

Listing 12-3 shows two new Web methods designed to test the effect of opening 10 connections, both consecutively and concurrently. When the connections are opened one after another (using the *TestMultipleConsecutive* method), there is no effect on the total number of connections. The pool of 5 connections remains, as shown in Figure 12-4. Each of the 10 new connections is drawn from this pool and returned in time for subsequent requests.

However, the story changes when the connections are opened at the same time (using the *TestMultipleConcurrent* method). Now 10 connections are required, and the pool is expanded to accommodate this need. This graph matches the display shown in Figure 12-5.

```
<WebMethod()> _
Public Sub TestMultipleConsecutive()

    ' Open 10 connections, one after the other.
    Dim i As Integer
    For i = 1 To 10
        Dim con As New SqlConnection(ConnectionString)
        con.Open()
        con.Close()
    Next

End Sub

<WebMethod()> _
Public Sub TestMultipleConcurrent()

    ' Open 10 connections at the same time.
    Dim Connections As New ArrayList()
    Dim i As Integer
    For i = 1 To 10
        Dim con As New SqlConnection(ConnectionString)
        Connections.Add(con)
        con.Open()
    Next

    ' Close all connections.
    Dim OpenConnection As SqlConnection
    For Each OpenConnection In Connections
        OpenConnection.Close()
    Next

End Sub
```

Listing 12-3 Testing consecutive and concurrent connections

As a final test, consider what happens if you modify the *TestMultipleConcurrent* method so that it attempts to open 11 connections simultaneously. In this case, the 11th connection attempt is stalled (because there are no available connections and no new connections can be created without violating the maximum pool size setting). Now the code generates a timeout error after 5 seconds.

Experiment with these examples until you have a thorough understanding of how connection pooling works. You should understand that even when your code closes a connection, it actually remains open in the pool. However, it's imperative that you call *Close* as soon as possible because this makes the connection available to serve another client request.

> **Note** This example concentrated on an XML Web service application. Connection pooling works identically with .NET Remoting. The only difference is that the lifetime of the pool is tied to the lifetime of the component host, not the ASP.NET application.

Developing a Data Transfer Plan

In Chapter 10, we examined the first stage of planning an application, which involves separating the parts of the system into components and tiers. The next step is to determine exactly how these parts should communicate and how data should be shuttled back and forth over the network. This decision can go a long way toward determining how frequently the client and server need to exchange information and how large each communication is, which ultimately affects the overall scalability of the system.

The first goal is to strive to use "chunky" rather than "chatty" communication. For example, you should provide methods that return an entire structure of related entity information, such as *GetCustomerDetails*, rather than methods that provide individual details, such as *GetCustomerName* and *GetCustomerAddress*. The disadvantage of this approach is that a client might wind up with more information than is needed. Clients that need several pieces of information won't need to call multiple methods, however, which would impose additional network overhead and require additional database trips. As a side benefit, you'll also find it's easier to tune a database for optimum performance if it provides only a few stored procedures rather than every imaginable combination, depending on the required information.

The same reasoning applies when you commit updates to the data source. You should follow the service provider pattern demonstrated in the first part of this book and create a generic *Update* method that accepts a custom structure, instead of implementing multiple separate methods, such as *UpdateCustomerName* and *UpdateCustomerStatus*. In some cases, you can create Web methods that represent higher-level business tasks (such as *CommitOrder*), accept related pieces of information (such as a customer record and an order record), and perform all the work with a single connection.

If the client requires a group of information, a custom collection or array of custom structures is generally ideal. However, you should limit the client's ability to perform wide-open queries without limiting criteria. It might even be a good idea for your remote methods to verify the submitted criteria and reject queries that would return a large number of results (such as date ranges that span 10 years).

Batch Updates

The principles discussed so far are all a matter of common sense. However, one data task can be particularly complicated: batch updates. If your system needs this ability, you might add a method such as *UpdateCustomers* that accepts an array of customer structures. This works well if all you need to do is commit record changes. However, this approach is less ideal if the client needs to perform updates and additions and record deletions simultaneously. You can create separate dedicated methods for each function (*UpdateCustomers*, *DeleteCustomers*, and *AddCustomers* methods), but the client programming will become more cumbersome. You also will be forced to use three connections for a task that would otherwise only take one.

.NET provides the perfect package for this type of problem: the *DataSet*. Chapter 3 showed an example (in Listing 3-18) of a *SubmitBatchChanges* method that accepts a *DataSet* and commits all the contained changes, including additions, deletions, and insertions. Unfortunately, that *SubmitBatchChanges* method is far from ideal for a distributed application. First of all, it requires an entire *DataSet*, which might contain many unchanged rows that will just waste network bandwidth. Even worse, the method returns the *DataSet* to the client after it has been updated, doubling the amount of network traffic required to perform this task.

Here's a better approach:

1. The client uses the *DataSet.GetChanges* or *DataTable.GetChanges* method to create a duplicate *DataSet* or *DataTable* that includes only changed rows.

2. The client submits this smaller *DataSet* to the remote method.

3. The remote method applies the changes in the best possible way using a single connection. If you're using relational data, you might need to separate the *DataSet* into multiple *DataSet* objects that each contain a subset (one with deleted rows, one with updated rows, and so on). This technique is shown in Chapter 3.

4. Assuming the remote method does throw an exception, the client should assume that all the changes are committed and should call the *DataSet.AcceptChanges* method to update the original database so that it reflects the changes. The *AcceptChanges* method updates all the original values to match the current values and sets the state of each row to *DataRowState.Unchanged*.

Listing 12-4 shows the implementation of this changes-only *DataSet* approach.

```
Dim Proxy As New CustomerDBService()
Dim ds As DataSet = Proxy.GetCustomers()

' (Modify the DataSet here.)

' Create the DataSet with the changed rows.
Dim dsChanges As DataSet = ds.GetChanges()

' Submit the DataSet with the changes.
Proxy.SubmitBatchChanges(dsChanges)

' Update the DataSet to reflect the fact that the changes have been
' applied.
ds.AcceptChanges()
```

Listing 12-4 Submitting *DataSet* changes only

One drawback with this approach is that it requires clients to be on their best behavior. If clients submit a large *DataSet* object that includes unchanged rows, it might put an unnecessary strain on the network. One way to discourage this sort of abuse is to examine the *DataSet* in the *SubmitBatchChanges* method and immediately throw an exception if an unchanged row is detected.

The *SubmitBatchChanges* method requires only a minor modification to change it from a function to a subroutine (as shown in Listing 12-5).

```
Public Sub SubmitBatchChanges(ds As DataSet)

    Dim Sql As String = "SELECT * FROM Customers"

    Dim con As New SqlConnection(ConnectionString)
    Dim cmd As New SqlCommand(Sql, con)
    Dim Adapter As New SqlDataAdapter(cmd)

    ' Generate insert, delete, and update commands.
    Dim Builder As New SqlCommandBuilder(adapter)
    Adapter.InsertCommand = Builder.GetInsertCommand()
    Adapter.UpdateCommand = Builder.GetUpdateCommand()
    Adapter.DeleteCommand = Builder.GetDeleteCommand()

    Try
        con.Open()
        Adapter.Update(ds, "Customers")

    Catch Err As Exception
        ' Use caller inform pattern.
```

Listing 12-5 The revised *SubmitBatchChanges*

```
        Throw New ApplicationException( _
         "Exception encountered when executing command.", Err)

    Finally
        con.Close()

    End Try

End Sub
```

Of course, the *DataSet* is notorious for concurrency problems, and it is quite possible that at least one row in the submitted *DataSet* will fail to be properly updated. Ideally, the remote method won't just abandon processing if an error is encountered. Instead, it should report the problem to the client.

Listing 12-6 shows a rewritten *SubmitBatchChanges* method that uses error handling. Note that it no longer returns the updated *DataSet*. Instead, it returns an array of rows that could not be updated.

```
Public Function SubmitBatchChanges(ds As DataSet) As DataRow()

    Dim Sql As String = "SELECT * FROM Customers"

    Dim con As New SqlConnection(ConnectionString)
    Dim cmd As New SqlCommand(Sql, con)
    Dim Adapter As New SqlDataAdapter(cmd)

    ' Generate insert, delete, and update commands.
    Dim Builder As New SqlCommandBuilder(adapter)
    Adapter.InsertCommand = Builder.GetInsertCommand()
    Adapter.UpdateCommand = Builder.GetUpdateCommand()
    Adapter.DeleteCommand = Builder.GetDeleteCommand()

    Adapter.ContinueUpdateOnError = True

    Try
        con.Open()
        Adapter.Update(ds, "Customers")

    Catch Err As Exception
        ' Use caller inform pattern.
        Throw New ApplicationException( _
         "Exception encountered when executing command.", Err)
```

Listing 12-6 *SubmitBatchChanges* with error handling

```
    Finally
        con.Close()

    End Try

    ' Return the rows that were not updated.
    Return ds.Tables("Customers").GetErrors()

End Function
```

The client needs to check these errors to determine whether the *DataSet* was successfully updated (as shown in Listing 12-7). Depending on the type of error, it might need to refresh its *DataSet* by retrieving the original *DataSet* again.

```
Dim Proxy As New CustomerDBService()
Dim ds As DataSet = Proxy.GetCustomers()

' (Modify the DataSet here.)

' Create the DataSet with the changed rows.
Dim dsChanges As DataSet = ds.GetChanges()

' Submit the DataSet with the changes.
Dim RowErrors() As DataRow() = Proxy.SubmitBatchChanges(dsChanges)

' Check for errors, and refresh the DataSet.
If RowErrors.Length = 0 Then
    ds.AcceptChanges()
Else
    ' Re-query the DataSet.
    ds = Proxy.GetCustomers()
End If
```

Listing 12-7 Checking for errors at the client

Caching

Retrieving information from a database takes time. With careful optimization, you can reduce the time and lessen the burden imposed on the server to a certain extent, but you can never eliminate it. Caching is an elegant solution to this problem. With a system that uses caching, some data requests won't require a database connection and a query. Instead, they'll retrieve the information directly from server memory—a much faster proposition.

Of course, storing information in memory isn't always a good idea. Server memory is a limited resource; if you try to store too much, some of that information will be paged to disk, potentially slowing down the entire system. That's why the best caching strategies are self-limiting. When you store information in a cache, you expect to find it there on a future request, most of the time. However, the lifetime of that information is at the discretion of the server. If the cache becomes full or other applications consume a large amount of memory, information will be selectively evicted from the cache, ensuring that performance is maintained. It's this self-sufficiency that makes caching so powerful (and so complicated to implement on your own).

With .NET programming, you can take advantage of a powerful caching system, provided you use XML Web services. That's because caching is built into the ASP.NET platform. It isn't available to components that use .NET Remoting. In fact, caching is so valuable that you might want to implement a data-intensive part of your application using XML Web services rather than .NET Remoting, even though the cost of SOAP communication will be higher.

ASP.NET provides two types of caching. Output caching works declaratively through the *<WebMethod>* attribute and reuses an entire response. Data caching needs to be coded programmatically, but it enables you to implement more flexible caching strategies. Microsoft's case studies generally favor output caching because of its simplicity, but there's no reason that you can't combine both, even in a single XML Web service.

Output (Response) Caching

Output caching stores the result of a Web method invocation and reuses it for other clients for a set amount of time. Output caching is coarser than data caching because it can be used only on a per-method basis. You enable output caching by setting the *CacheDuration* property of the *<WebMethod>* attribute.

Listing 12-8 shows a simple example of output caching. It caches the result of the *GetDate* method for 3 minutes (180 seconds).

```
<WebMethod(CacheDuration := 180)> _
Public Function GetDate() As String

    Return System.DateTime.Now.ToString()

End Function
```

Listing 12-8 Enabling output caching

You can test this Web method using the Internet Explorer test page. The first time you call the method, you'll receive the current time. If you call the method a second time within the allotted 3 minutes, you'll receive the same result. In fact, ASP.NET bypasses the code completely and just returns the result stored inside its cache. (You can test this by setting a breakpoint in the *GetDate* Web method. When ASP.NET reuses a result from the cache, your code won't run and the breakpoint won't be triggered.)

In fact, any client who makes a request in the 3-minute time period receives the exact same result. After the time limit has expired, the result is removed from the cache. On the next request, ASP.NET runs the *GetDate* function, adds the result to the cache, and reuses the new result for another 3 minutes.

Things get a little more interesting if you create a Web method that accepts parameters. In this case, ASP.NET reuses a request only if every parameter matches exactly. Consider, for example, the *GetStockQuote* method shown in Listing 12-9.

```
<WebMethod(CacheDuration := 60)> _
Public Function GetStockQuote(ticker As String) As Decimal

    ' (Lookup code omitted.)

End Function
```

Listing 12-9 Output caching with parameters

In this case, every time ASP.NET receives a request with a new ticker parameter, it caches a separate result. If it receives a request for three different stocks, it caches three different stock quotes and reuses each one for 60 seconds from the time that it was placed in the cache. (To test this, create a modified version of the *GetDate* method that accepts a string parameter. Then try invoking the method with different parameters.)

Considerations for Output Caching

Output caching isn't suitable for every method. In fact, caching is always a compromise. If you cache too little for too short a time, your code will need to query the database frequently. On the other hand, if you cache too much, you'll risk forcing important information out of the cache prematurely. Generally, you should try to apply output caching to methods with the following characteristics:

- **They take time or encapsulate a limited resource.** If a method just wraps some trivial code that never hits a database, you can't realize much savings by adding output caching.
- **They depend only on their parameters.** For example, the *GetDate* method isn't a perfect caching candidate because it depends on the computer clock. When a request is reused, ASP.NET can't take into account that the clock has changed, so the response is inaccurate. Similarly, if you have a Web method that reads user-specific information from a cookie or ASP.NET's session state, it isn't a good caching choice.

- **They have a limited set of possible input parameters.** This is the single most important factor with output caching. It doesn't make sense to cache a method that accepts a wide range of parameters because the cache will fill up with a separate response message for each distinct request. Instead, you should cache methods that take only a few possible values.
- **They don't perform other tasks.** In other words, if you have logging code included in your Web method, this code won't run when the cached response is reused. If you need to get around this limitation, you can use data caching to reuse cached data but still execute the method and some code.

Although these are all solid guidelines, making hard decisions about caching can actually be as much an art as a science. Consider this sample Web method:

```
<WebMethod> _
Public Sub GetProductDetails(ID As Integer) As ProductDetails

    ' (Code omitted.)

End Sub
```

Does it make sense to add output caching to this method? The answer depends on the specific usage patterns of the system. If you have a small number of products in the database and this method is used frequently, this might be an ideal scenario for data caching because you could save numerous trips to the database. On the other hand, if this method is part of the back end of a high-volume e-commerce site, you'll probably have far too many different products to cache them efficiently, and more cached responses will expire without being used.

> **Note** You should use performance counters, as described in Chapter 14, to study the effectiveness of your caching strategies. The ASP.NET Applications Counter category includes performance counters such as Output Cache Hits, Output Cache Misses, and Output Cache Turnover Ratio, which are designed for this purpose. You also can profile data caching with counters such as Cache API Hits, Cache API Misses, Cache API Hit Ratio, and Cache API Turnover Rate.

Data Caching

Data caching enables you to store specific pieces of information in a *Cache* object and reuse them as needed. In many ways, data caching is more powerful than output caching. Unfortunately, it also requires you to intermingle your business code with some ASP.NET-specific caching code. That means that from a design point of view, it's not as elegant as the declarative model used with output caching.

One reason you might use data caching is if you have several methods that need to reuse the same information. Suppose, for example, that you have an XML Web service with two methods: *GetStockQuote* and *GetStockQuoteDetails*. The second method is the same as the first but provides extra information, such as the daily high and low for the stock, in a custom structure. You could apply output caching to both these methods and cache their results separately. On the other hand, you might want to cache a single piece of information in a data cache—the *StockDetails* structure—and use it in both methods. With this approach, you could potentially reduce the number of trips to the database by half.

Data caching works through the *System.Web.Caching.Cache* object. You can access the current instance of this object through the *Context.Cache* property of your XML Web service, assuming your XML Web service class inherits from the base *System.Web.Services.WebService* class. If your class doesn't inherit from *WebService*, you can still access the cache using a slightly longer name: *HttpContext.Current.Cache*. This uses the shared *Current* property of the *System.Web.HttpContext* class, which always returns the current context object. The *Cache* object is not limited to a single service; instead, the information it stores is global to your entire Web application.

To add an item to the cache, you can just assign it using a new key name:

```
Context.Cache("key") = ObjectToCache
```

This technique is rarely used, however, because it doesn't enable you to specify the expiration policy for the cached item. Instead, you'll more commonly use the overloaded *Insert* method. Here's the most commonly used version of the *Insert* method:

```
Context.Cache.Insert(key, value, dependencies, _
                     absoluteExpiration, slidingExpiration)
```

This method takes the string key (which you'll use to index the cached object), the value (the object you want to place in the cache), and an absolute and sliding expiration policy (which enable you to specify how long the object will exist in the cache). Note that even though the *Cache.Insert* method provides parameters for both sliding expiration and absolute expiration, you can't set both of them at once. If you attempt to do so, you'll receive an *Argument-Exception*.

The *Cache* object also provides other methods to clear the cache, retrieve all the cached items, and set file and object dependencies. For more information about these details, refer to the MSDN Reference.

Absolute Expiration

Absolute expiration invalidates cached items after a fixed period of time. It works like output caching, setting a "best before date" on the cached information. Absolute expiration is the best approach if you need to store information that changes frequently and that needs to be periodically refreshed. For example, you could use absolute expiration to keep a stock quote for 10 seconds or a product catalog for 1 hour.

Listing 12-10 shows an example of absolute expiration that stores an object (named *ObjectToCache*) for 10 minutes. The *TimeSpan.Zero* parameter is used simply to disable ASP.NET's other form of caching policy, sliding expiration.

```
Context.Cache.Insert("key", ObjectToCache, Nothing, _
                     DateTime.Now.AddMinutes(10), TimeSpan.Zero)
```

Listing 12-10 Using absolute expiration

Sliding Expiration

Sliding expiration sets an idle timeout on an object. If the cached information is not reused within that amount of time, it's removed from the cache. However, every time it is used, the object's lifetime is reset. Sliding expiration works similarly to the lifetime lease policy with components over .NET Remoting. Sliding expiration works well when you have information that is always valid but is not always being used. One example is historical data. This information doesn't need to be refreshed, but it shouldn't be kept in the cache if it isn't being used.

To use sliding expiration, you need to set the *absoluteExpiration* parameter to *DateTime.Max*. You can then use the *slidingExpiration* parameter to indicate the number of minutes for the object's timeout. The example in Listing 12-11 stores an object until it has been idle for 10 minutes.

```
Context.Cache.Insert("key", ObjectToCache, Nothing, _
                     DateTime.MaxValue, TimeSpan.FromMinutes(10))
```

Listing 12-11 Using sliding expiration

Note that it's impossible to predict how long this object will be in the cache. The item could be invalidated in as few as 10 minutes or kept indefinitely if it is in continuous demand.

Retrieving a Cached Item

To retrieve a cached item, you just look it up using the string key you used to store it. Keep in mind that all objects are stored in the cache as generic *System.Object* types, so you need to cast the object to its real type.

```
Dim MyObject As MyClass
MyObject = CType(Cache("key"), MyClass)
```

Never assume that an object exists in the cache. ASP.NET has complete freedom to remove the object at any time, ensuring optimum performance. If you try to retrieve an object that doesn't exist in the cache, you won't receive an error, just a null reference. Therefore, you must explicitly test the object before you attempt to use it (as shown in Listing 12-12).

```
Dim MyObject As MyClass
MyObject = CType(Cache("key"), MyClass)

If MyObject Is Nothing Then
    ' Object does not exist in the cache.
    ' You must reconstruct it (for example, re-query the database).
End If

' (Process MyObject here.)
```

Listing 12-12 Retrieving a cached item

To consider how you might want to integrate data caching into your XML Web services, let's return to the example of a service that exposes both a *GetStockQuote* and a *GetStockQuoteDetails* method, which return similar information based on the cache. Here's the custom *StockQuoteDetails* structure:

```
Public Class StockQuoteDetails

    Public Name As String
    Public CurrentValue As Decimal
    Public DailyHigh As Decimal
    Public DailyLow As Decimal

End Class
```

Listing 12-13 shows both Web methods. They rely on a private *LookupStockQuote* method, which checks the cache and performs the database lookup only if required.

```
<WebMethod()>
Public Function GetStockQuote(ticker As String) As Decimal

    Dim Quote As StockQuoteDetails = LookupStockQuote(ticker)
    Return Quote.CurrentValue

End Function

<WebMethod()> _
Public Function GetStockQuoteDetails(ticker As String) As StockDetails

    Dim Quote As StockQuoteDetails = LookupStockQuote(ticker)
    Return Quote

End Function

Private Function LookupStockQuote(ticker As String) _
  As StockQuoteDetails

    ' If the quote is in the cache, it will be indexed under
    ' the ticker symbol.
    Dim Quote As StockQuoteDetails
    Quote = CType(Cache(ticker), StockQuoteDetails)

    If Quote Is Nothing Then
        ' Object does not exist in the cache.
        ' It must be retrieved from the database
        ' (using a custom database component).
        Quote = DBComponent.GetStockQuote(ticker)

        ' Once it's retrieved, it should be added to the cache
        ' for future requests.
        Cache.Insert(ticker, Quote, Nothing, _
                     DateTime.Now.AddMinutes(15), TimeSpan.Zero)
    End If

    Return Quote

End Function
```

Listing 12-13 Using data caching in an XML Web service

It's probably not practical to create an XML Web service with two such similar methods, but this is a good example of how you can separate your data caching code from your business logic. Both methods are entirely unaware of how the stock quote was retrieved and whether it required a database lookup.

> **More Info** To see data caching at work, see the case study in Chapter 18, which uses it to store session tickets and save time when authenticating Web method requests. Chapter 17 also puts caching to work to store pricing data.

Determining a Caching Strategy

Caching provides a simple way to achieve some staggering results. In the *GetStockQuote* example, you could save dozens of database calls every minute, vastly reducing the overhead of your application. In fact, caching is unique in the world of distributed programming because it improves both performance and scalability. Cached requests bypass your code and are returned much faster than normal, thereby improving performance. As you add more clients to the system, the number of trips to the database might not change very much, and therefore the overall burden on the system will start to level off (as shown in Figure 12-6), demonstrating admirable scalability.

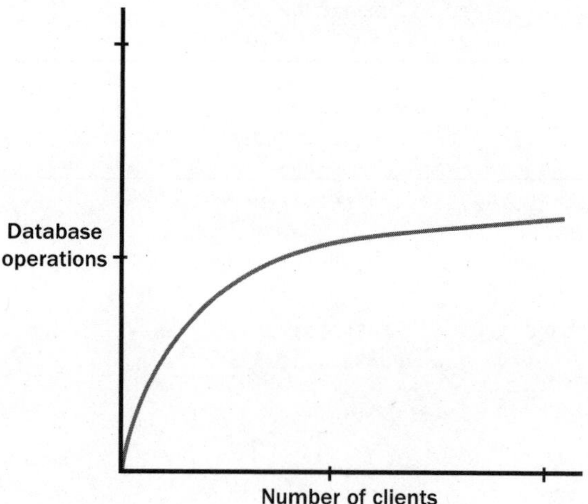

Figure 12-6 The effect of good caching

Caching also represents a compromise that sacrifices complete accuracy and instantaneous updates. There is no easy (or scalable) way to make a cached object dependent on content in a database. This means that cached data is often stale data, which presents a snapshot of how the information looked several minutes in the past. In most applications, this is not a problem—in fact, the need for immediate updates is often overstated. An e-commerce application, for example, can use caching without worrying that new product categories will appear an hour or two after the changes are committed. Of course, a system that provides volatile or time-sensitive data might not have this luxury. For example, many financial applications can't afford to cache a currency exchange rate.

Here are a few more tips for incorporating caching into your applications:

- Microsoft recommends that you design distributed applications with caching in mind. Ideally, you should plan for caching in the design stage and identify its most useful niche.
- Don't be afraid to cache for a long time. Microsoft's IBuySpy case studies, for example, store the output for some pages for 100 minutes. Stale data is generally a minor inconvenience compared to the performance improvements you'll see.
- Don't worry about testing XML Web services that use output caching. ASP.NET automatically creates a dependency on the XML Web service assembly file for all items in the output caching. Every time you recompile the XML Web service, the cache is emptied, enabling you to execute your new code.
- You can manually empty out the cache in a hurry in several ways. The easiest way is just to open the web.config file for the application and save it. When ASP.NET detects the file change, it automatically migrates the application to a new application domain, which won't contain the cached items.

> **Note** You can implement a crude form of caching by creating a singleton .NET Remoting component that stores some data and uses a sliding lifetime policy that keeps it alive only while it is being used. You could create a more sophisticated form of homegrown caching using a COM+ pooled component, as demonstrated in Chapter 9. However, neither of these approaches is as efficient or reliable as the built-in ASP.NET caching service. This is one of the main reasons you might favor using an XML Web service over a .NET Remoting component for high-volume use.

Optimizing the Database

The data tier is the part of a distributed application where information is centralized. That means it's one of the most difficult parts of a distributed application to scale out because it maintains state. It's worth squeezing out every extra ounce of performance you can.

Modern database products have come a long way. Microsoft architects confess that, only a few years ago, almost all the leading PC-based relational database management system (RDBMS) products had major limitations with reliability and data integrity. Today these problems have been fixed across the board, and all enterprise-level databases provide a sophisticated set of features for optimizing the speed that queries and updates execute.

Unfortunately, these considerations require an entirely separate book and are to some degree vendor-specific. I heartily encourage you to read a book that's targeted to your RDBMS. If you're using SQL Server, you might want to look at *SQL Server 2000 Performance Tuning Technical Reference* (Microsoft Press, 2001), which considers every aspect from capacity planning to index tuning. You also can find white papers on MSDN at *http://msdn.microsoft.com/library/en-us/optimsql/odp_tunovw_9mxz.asp.*

With that in mind, the next sections consider some more general guidelines.

Stored Procedures

You should use stored procedures whenever possible. Not only can stored procedures be precompiled with an optimized execution plan, but they also tend to limit the different types of queries that will be performed on a data source. If you shift from a system that uses 40 possible dynamic queries to one that uses a set of 20 stored procedures, for example, it becomes much easier to optimize the database.

Indexes

Use indexes. Quite simply, indexes are the only way that a database server can retrieve a specific row without performing a time-consuming full scan through every record. However, modern databases are brilliant at combining existing indexes in various ways to perform complex queries. This process is fairly involved, so you should not decide yourself which indexes to create. Instead, use the tools included with the RDBMS. In SQL Server, the Index Tuning Wizard can recommend new indexes based on a "snapshot" of the system workload or by analyzing a set of problematic (slow) queries. Keep in mind that having too many indexes can also slow down performance because it requires that more data be stored (and that the average query traverse more space on the hard drive). This is another reason you need a utility such as the Index Tuning Wizard to recommend an optimum set of indexes.

It's also worth considering a clustered index. A typical, nonclustered index is just a long list of row pointers sorted according to the values in one or more data columns. For example, the index for an ID column is just a long list sorted by ID number. Using the list, SQL Server can quickly locate a specific ID, read the pointer that indicates where to find the full record, and jump to that position. A clustered index, however, determines the physical order of the data on the disk. If you create a clustered index for an ID column, records with lower ID values will actually be stored before records with higher ID values. Because you can physically arrange data only in one way, there can be only a single clustered index on a table. With SQL Server, the primary key index is by default clustered, which is a decidedly mixed blessing.

Clustered data is a great help with range queries. If your data is clustered by date, for example, a query that selects a range of dates from a single month will find all its data close together on the disk, decreasing transfer times. Of course, in an elaborate system with multiple RAID drives, this is not always an advantage. Clustering too much related data close together can lead to disk contention as multiple queries fight to access the same area on the disk. This is known as a *hot spot*. There is no easy answer to this tradeoff. It's best to work closely with your database administrator and weigh the options.

Of course, life isn't always this painful. Consider a table that consists of Invoice Number, Invoice Date, Invoice Amount, and Sales Office columns. Now suppose that 10,000 records are inserted into this table every day and users most often query data based on Sales Office. This makes Sales Office an ideal column for a clustered index. However, because the new rows will likely originate from a range of different sales offices, inserts will still be spread evenly across the table, reducing the hot spot danger.

Profiling

Most modern RDBMS products include profiling tools. With SQL Server, you can use the included Profiler, which provides a slew of useful features:

- You can monitor the performance of SQL Server and keep track of issues such as failed connections or denied logins.
- You can identify slow-executing queries, which pose a potential problem for your system.

- You can debug Transact-SQL statements and stored procedures.
- You can capture a log of events and replay them later on another system. You can even use this snapshot to determine the optimal set of indexes for your data.

In short, tools such as Profiler provide you with some very useful tools for gauging performance and the effect of database optimizations. Use them.

Partition Large Data Tables

You can use horizontal or vertical partitioning of large data tables to increase processing speed. Horizontal partitioning segments a large table into multiple tables, each containing a subset of the total rows. One table might contain records for the current year, for instance, whereas another table might contain records with an Older Date column. Alternatively, you might divide a customer table based on the customer's last name.

Vertical partitioning segments a table with a large number of columns into multiple tables that contain the same number of rows but only some of the columns. These rows are linked by matching a unique row identifier contained in both tables. This approach is most successful if the separate tables are used independently in queries. If one table contains all the information normally required by a query, for example, the query will execute much faster. The other table can store data that is used only occasionally.

In a large environment, partitioning can extend across several database servers. This presents the application programmer with new challenges. Ideally, you should strive to meet two goals:

- Distribute the workload evenly.
- Ensure that every server contains enough information to satisfy an average query.

If you divide order records over two tables, for example, your first goal is to split the traffic between these two servers so that they both serve approximately the same number of requests. If you divide a Customers table by last name, you'll accomplish this goal. If you divide an Orders table by date, you probably won't because there will be much more interest in recent orders than in extremely old orders. If you perform a query that retrieves a single customer or order record, the request will be satisfied by a single database server. If you perform a query that retrieves a group of orders by date, you'll also likely need only one server. If you try to retrieve all the orders submitted by a given individual, however, you might need to read order information from more than one server, which will increase overhead and slow down the query.

Once again, these considerations are not trivial and require careful consideration when you're creating the physical infrastructure of a system. When creating a system that spans multiple servers, you need to work closely with an experienced database administrator. Large databases are possible, however. Microsoft touts its live example of a 1.5-terabyte database of satellite imagery, which is available at its TerraServer Web site (*http://terraserver.homeadvisor.msn.com*).

Placing Code in the Data Tier

Most distributed applications use stored procedures to wrap simple SQL statements that correspond to queries, or to record updates, inserts, or deletions. However, it's possible to create a much more intelligent stored procedure that can perform several related tasks (and even enforce business rules).

If the time taken to perform this logic is short (and it usually is), you can achieve a substantial performance improvement by reducing the number of required round-trips. For example, most applications use separate stored procedures to add order records (which link an order to a customer) and individual order item records (which detail each purchased product). That means it takes 10 round-trips to commit an order with nine order items. If you create an intelligent stored procedure, it can perform the work required to insert all these records simultaneously, dramatically reducing overhead.

However, stored procedure programming isn't without a healthy share of headaches. Almost every RDBMS uses a vendor-specific form of SQL that forces you to use primitive script commands to complete your work. Some of the problems you'll encounter include the following:

- The lack of robust error handling. You must rely on cryptic error codes instead.
- The need to get work at a lower level by manually creating and managing cursors.
- No direct support for arrays, making it difficult to accept a variable list of items. One common workaround is to encode this information in some sort of XML document.
- Primitive support for debugging, code reuse, and other object-oriented niceties.

In a future version of SQL Server, Microsoft aims to enable developers to code stored procedures using object-oriented .NET code. This has the potential to dramatically change the development model of distributed applications. Until then, you're probably better off placing your data logic in a dedicated .NET data component (if your system is not extremely performance-sensitive).

Normalizing

Normalization is the process by which you break data down into multiple tables. For example, it's customary to split the table of order information from the table that contains the customers who place the orders. This normalized form has several advantages:

- It reduces duplicate data (which indirectly improves performance).
- It eliminates the possibility for conflicting data.
- It greatly simplifies some queries and data analysis tasks. If you were to place customer information in the order table, you would require some extremely awkward SQL code to coax out a distinct list of customers. It would be even harder (and extremely inefficient) to modify customer information because it would exist in multiple order records.
- It speeds up index creation and modification because normalized tables generally have fewer columns. This can also improve the performance of Update commands.
- It allows better locking because locking works on a row basis. With normalization, the data is factored into more than one table, and a typical transaction has to lock only some of the rows in one of the tables.

That said, deviating from good normalization practices is sometimes a worthwhile and practical tradeoff. Normalized databases generally require more complex queries. Before retrieving data, an application often needs to perform intricate subqueries or multiple joins. In addition, these steps can actually reduce performance—both because the required data is fragmented into several different places on the hard drive and because the table joining adds extra time.

Selective denormalization can improve performance. However, the associated cost (generally a loss of flexibility, future scalability, data integrity, or even performance for other tasks) is often too high. For these reasons, I rarely recommend denormalization—in fact, I mention it here only because it is a recurrent issue of interest to developers and a valid performance-optimizing tactic. For more information about the risks involved and how you might code around them, I encourage you to read the article "Responsible Denormalization" by Michelle Poolet in *SQL Server* magazine, which is provided online by Microsoft at *http://msdn.microsoft.com/library/en-us/dnsqlmag2k/html/ResponsibleDenormalization.asp*.

Summary

The data tier will make or break most distributed applications. This chapter considered some principles that no distributed programmer can afford to ignore, including connection pooling, caching, and optimization. All of these techniques are useful ingredients in the programmer's toolbox, but it's not always obvious when you should use them. As with any performance-optimization strategy, the only way to gauge the value of a change is to perform stress testing and profiling. Without this step, you might spend a great deal of time perfecting code that will achieve only a minor improvement in performance or scalability, at the expense of more effective changes. Chapter 14 introduces the art and science of profiling.

Finally, every programmer would do well to consider three basic tips for ensuring good database performance:

- Optimize the SQL in your stored procedures. Writing SQL might not be as exciting as writing .NET code, but you ignore doing so at your own risk. Excessive joins or misuse of data types can exert a performance toll.
- Although hardware can't solve poor design or coding, the database server is generally one of the best places to spend your hardware budget. A database should have the fastest possible hard drive and enough cache memory to optimize reads. SQL Server optimizes its cache automatically, but other RDBMS products might benefit from fine-tuning and manual enlargement of in-memory cache sizes.

Learn the enhancement techniques for your RDBMS. Database products almost always support standardized SQL syntax and similar features, but they differ widely in performance optimization techniques. You need to understand these to coax the best possible performance from them.

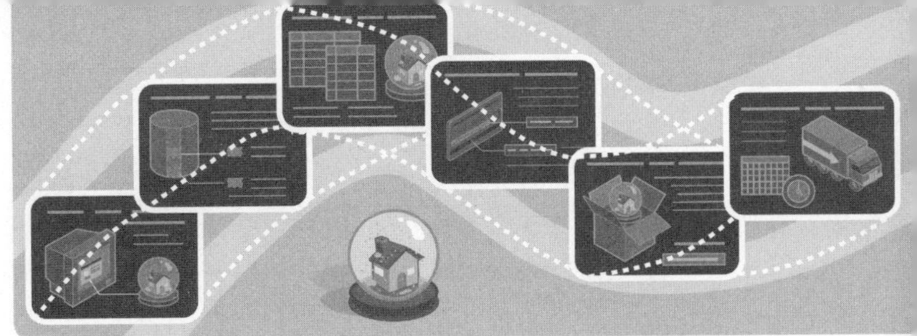

13

Implementing Security

Security is one of the subtlest aspects of distributed application design because it must be implemented at many different levels. When programmers talk about securing an application, they might be referring to any of the following:

- Using authorization and authentication to ensure that users can perform only specific, allowed tasks
- Filling coding holes that could enable a crafty attacker to read files or execute SQL statements beyond the intended permissions
- Using encryption to encode information sent between application components
- Using code access security to prevent malicious code from executing
- Implementing some sort of licensing or copy protection to prevent users from redistributing the application without permission

In fact, these topics only scratch the surface of security, which includes everything from locking the server-room door to auditing program actions with a log (so suspicious behavior can be discovered and investigated). The real challenge with security is determining where the most significant vulnerabilities in an application are. No company has unlimited resources to tackle every possible security problem. For that reason, an experienced developer doesn't aim to make a perfectly invulnerable application—just one that's secure for all practical purposes. This means that the encryption used to protect information might not be unbreakable—it might just be strong enough that by the time the code is cracked, the information is no longer useful. Similarly, a distributed system might use ticket-based authentication with expiration dates, limiting the effect of a security breach to a single session. Therefore, when implementing security you have to start by deciding what level of security you need and what risks you're prepared to accept. A system that uses security to provide subscription access to news articles probably requires a lower level of security than one that handles information about financial transactions. Similarly, a system is only as strong as its weakest point. That means there's little point in perfecting an advanced encryption system if you're also in the habit of e-mailing user passwords to individuals in clear text.

This chapter explores some of the techniques you can use to secure remote components and XML Web services. We'll consider Microsoft Windows authentication and custom role-based authentication as well as the advantages and limitations of both approaches. We'll also delve into encryption with the Microsoft .NET Framework and explore how you can implement encryption on your own or acquire it for free with the Secure Sockets Layer (SSL) protocol. Finally, this chapter introduces the code access security model that's hard-wired into the common language runtime (CLR).

Authentication and Authorization

Authentication is the process of determining a user's identity. Often, authentication is described as forcing users to prove that they are who they claim to be. *Authorization* is the process of assigning permissions and restrictions to a given user after the user has been authenticated. If authentication fails, the user probably won't be able to use the application at all. If authorization fails, the requested action is aborted. In the Windows operating system, for example, users are authenticated at startup when they supply a username and password combination. Authorization is performed for operations such as deleting a file or attempting to launch Control Panel.

Authentication and authorization are what most programmers think of first when they tackle security. Using authentication and authorization, you can create an application that provides different features to different user classes. The distributed application programmer has two options when incorporating authentication into an application:

- Use Windows authentication, which enables you to leverage existing account information and use the automatic directory-based security provided by IIS

- Develop a custom authentication system, which will typically use a relational database (although other data stores are possible)

Windows authentication enables you to use built-in operating system services to manage and verify users. Some of the reasons you might use Windows authentication include the following:

- To provide automatic authentication with IIS. This enables you to use challenge/response user verification, which is more secure than just sending username and password information over the Internet.
- To use existing login accounts. If you're allowing remote access to an internal application, for example, users will already have an account on your domain server. No additional setup or configuration is required.
- To use existing per-user permissions (such as access control lists). If you use Windows authentication with impersonation, the remote object executes under the identity of the client, ensuring that the client's permissions are evaluated for tasks such as reading a file.

A custom authentication system is generally the most flexible, scalable, and portable choice (meaning it can easily be migrated to a new system), but it also requires the most work. Custom authentication almost always works in tandem with a database. The reasons developers use custom authentication include the following:

- To include additional user-specific information. This information can be added in a Users table or another linked table in a database. It can include everything from address or credit card information to application preferences.
- To use a custom permissions system. You can associate users with groups that have application-specific permissions you define, without having to create numerous Windows groups.
- To store user information independent of the Windows operating system, making it easier to move to another platform.
- To give the application the complete capability to add, remove, or otherwise manipulate user records.
- To optimize performance. Windows authentication can become a bottleneck. Database operations, on the other hand, can be optimized using connection pooling, query optimization, and caching.

- To store other tables in a database that directly link to user records. Although you can simulate this with Windows authentication by using the user login name, it becomes more difficult to design queries for aggregate reports (such as a list of products ordered by a specific user).

In the enterprise world, Windows authentication is most often used when you're Web-enabling an internal application. In this situation, most users will already have login accounts. Custom authentication is the system of choice when your application is serving a third-party audience (such as eager e-shoppers) rather than a known audience of employees or associates.

That said, it is possible to use custom authentication with an internal audience. This approach (which you'll see again in the Chapter 18 case study) is particularly common when you need to store additional information about a user in a database or audit a user's actions. It's also possible, but impractical, to use Windows authentication with a large audience. One key stumbling block is that you have no easy way to provide self-registration (for example, a sign-up page on a Web site that enables customers to create their own accounts).

Windows Authentication

The first thing you need to know about Windows authentication is that it's practical only if you're using IIS to host your remote components. If you're adding authentication to an XML Web service, this level of support is automatic. If you're using .NET Remoting, you must use IIS as the component host (as described in Chapter 11). If you need the freedom to switch your remote component technology in the future, to use a custom component host, or to use a binary-encoded channel, you need the flexibility of custom authentication instead of Windows authentication.

You should also realize that even when you use Windows authentication, your code won't run under the identity of the authenticated user. Instead, your code runs under a local ASP.NET account that has carefully restricted privileges. It is possible to change this behavior using impersonation (discussed later in this chapter), but it's generally not recommended. A better approach is to use the *HttpContext.User* property to retrieve information about the authenticated user, such as the username and the groups to which the user belongs.

To illustrate how Windows authentication works, it helps to create a simple XML Web service, as shown in Listing 13-1.

```
Imports System.Web.Services
Imports System.Security.Principal

Public Class AuthenticationTest
    Inherits System.Web.Services.WebService

    ' Retrieves the identity used to execute this code.
    <WebMethod()> _
    Public Function GetCurrentUser() As String

        Return WindowsIdentity.GetCurrent.Name

    End Function

    ' Retrieves the authenticated IIS user.
    <WebMethod()> _
    Public Function GetIISUser() As String

        ' You could also retrieve the same information from
        ' System.Threading.Thread.CurrentPrincipal.Identity.Name
        Return User.Identity.Name

    End Function

End Class
```

Listing 13-1 A simple XML Web service that tests authentication

> **Note** Listing 13-1 uses the *User* property that is inherited from the base *WebService* class. *User* is an instance of an identity object that implements *System.Security.Principal.Identity*. You can access the same object through the *Thread.CurrentPrincipal.Identity* property. You use this technique with a component exposed through .NET Remoting because it doesn't derive from *WebService*.

You can test both of these Web methods using the Internet Explorer test page. If you don't enable IIS directory security, no user will be authenticated. The *GetIISUser* method returns an empty string. The *GetCurrentUser* method, however, returns the account used for the ASP.NET worker process. This account is defined in the <processModel> section of the machine.config file on the Web server. The name takes the form [MachineName]\[UserName] or [DomainName]\[UserName]. Typically, *GetCurrentUser* returns a string such as *WEBSERVER\ASPNET*. This test demonstrates the default case, in which no client authentication is performed.

IIS Authentication Settings

To enable directory-based authentication, run IIS Manager. (Choose Settings | Control Panel | Administrative Tools | Internet Services Manager from the Start menu.) Find the appropriate virtual directory, right-click on it, and choose Properties. Click on the Directory Security tab (shown in Figure 13-1).

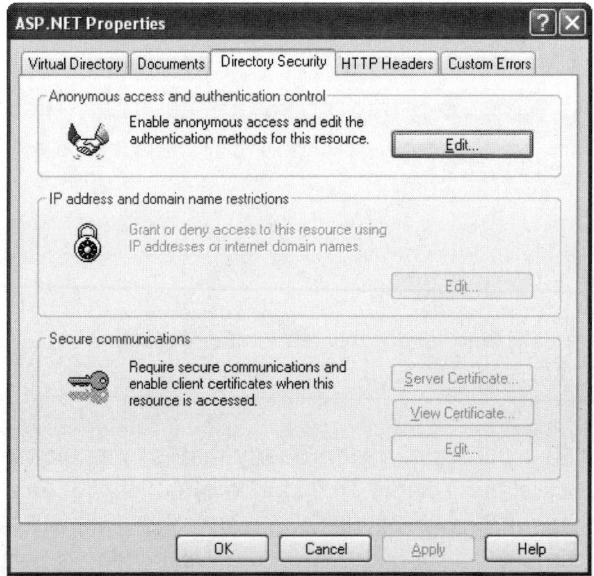

Figure 13-1 Directory security settings

You can secure a directory using IIS authentication, IP address restrictions (to restrict or allow clients based on the IP address of their computer), or certificates (which are extremely secure but must be created and distributed to every client). Click the Edit button in the Anonymous Access And Authentication Control section to display options for IIS authentication (as shown in Figure 13-2).

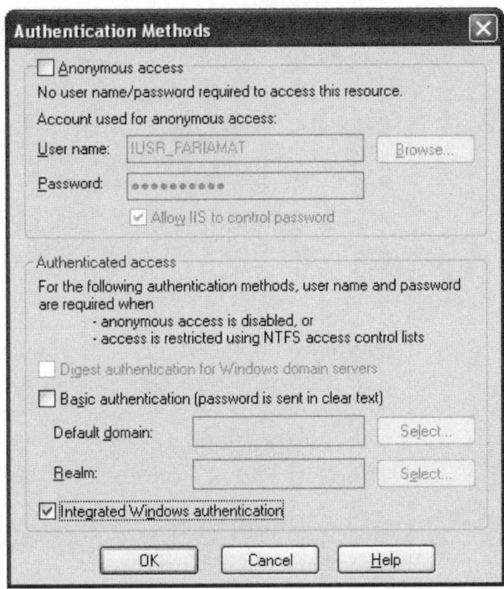

Figure 13-2 IIS directory authentication options

By default, anonymous access is enabled. When anonymous access is enabled, IIS never authenticates a client, regardless of what other authentication settings you specify. To change this behavior, deselect Anonymous Access and select one or more of the other authentication methods (listed in Table 13-1). Note that although these methods differ in strength, they all have the same goal: to match a username and password supplied by the user (or client application) with a user account in a valid Windows user account on a domain controller, in Active Directory, or on the local machine. If you enable multiple authentication methods, IIS automatically attempts to use the strongest method first.

Table 13-1 IIS Authentication Options

Authentication Method	Description
Basic authentication	The username and password information are passed to the server, encoded using Base64 encoding. Basic authentication is generally used only for personalization services or in conjunction with SSL encryption because its password encoding is essentially equivalent to clear text and can be "sniffed" from the network by an attacker.

Table 13-1 IIS Authentication Options

Authentication Method	Description
Digest authentication	Similar to basic authentication, but it encrypts the user's password information using a hashing algorithm called Message Digest 5 (MD5) before it sends it over the network. Digest authentication requires a user account to be stored in Active Directory.
Integrated Windows authentication	Uses a challenge/response mechanism (with Kerberos, if Active Directory Services is installed on the server). Unlike basic or digest authentication, password credentials are never sent across the network, making this the most secure option. However, this standard won't work across a proxy computer and requires the opening of additional ports before it will work with a firewall. Therefore, it is best suited to internal clients.
Certificate authentication	Uses signed client-side certificates that map each client to a specific user account. This method is extremely secure but difficult to implement. You must purchase certificates from a third party, such as VeriSign, and deploy them to each client computer. For this reason, certificate authentication is rarely used outside of specialized setups.

Note that these authentication standards have different levels of support in various Internet browsers. However, Table 13-1 doesn't note these differences because they won't apply to XML Web services or remote components. In these scenarios, the client is always a dedicated .NET Web or Windows application, not an Internet browser. .NET clients support all of these authentication methods.

To test IIS authentication, modify the directory settings for the test XML Web service by disabling anonymous access and enabling integrated authentication (as shown in Figure 13-2). Then run the XML Web service with the Internet Explorer test page. You'll discover that *GetCurrentUser* still returns the ASP.NET account, whereas *GetIISUser* returns the name of the user account you're currently logged on to (as in MYLOCALCOMPUTER\MATTHEW). Internet Explorer automatically submits the required credentials to validate the user with IIS.

Setting Authentication Information with an XML Web Service Client

The preceding example relies on Internet Explorer to submit the required information to the XML Web service. In a distributed application, however, clients don't interact with a remote XML Web service through a browser—instead, they use a dedicated client application.

To pass a user's credentials from a client application to an XML Web service, you have to tell the XML Web service proxy which user information it should transfer. If you're using Windows integrated authentication, you can configure your proxy class to use the security credentials of the current user's account, using the *System.Net.CredentialCache* class, as shown in Listing 13-2.

```
' Create the XML Web service proxy.
Dim Proxy As New localhost.AuthenticationTest()

' Assign the current user's credentials to the proxy class.
Proxy.Credentials = System.Net.CredentialCache.DefaultCredentials

' Perform an authenticated call to a Web method.
MessageBox.Show(Proxy.GetIISUser())
```

Listing 13-2 Transparent authentication using the current user

This is a simple, elegant approach in which authentication is performed transparently, without the user being aware of any part of the process. If you try to make the same call to *GetIISUser* without assigning any credential information, the call will fail and an exception will be thrown.

If you aren't using Windows integrated authentication or you want the ability to use a different user account for making remote class, you need to create a *NetworkCredential* object manually (as shown in Listing 13-3).

```
' Create the XML Web service proxy.
Dim Proxy As New localhost.AuthenticationTest()

' Create the credential objects.
Dim Credentials As New System.Net.NetworkCredential("name", "password")

' Assign the credentials to the proxy class.
Proxy.Credentials = Credentials

' Perform an authenticated call to a Web method.
MessageBox.Show(Proxy.GetIISUser())
```

Listing 13-3 Manual authentication with a *NetworkCredential*

This technique is useful if the computer always runs under a fixed account, but different users use the application to perform Web method calls. In this case, your client application will probably retrieve the user information from a custom login dialog box. Alternatively, you can retrieve the information from the registry or configuration file if you intend to use a fixed account, no matter which user is currently using the application. In this case, remember to encrypt or hash passwords before you store them anywhere, using the cryptography classes discussed later in this chapter.

Setting Authentication Information with a .NET Remoting Client

You have the same two options with a .NET Remoting client, each with slightly different syntax. Because you don't directly interact with the proxy for the remote object, you must use the *ChannelServices* class (from the *System.Runtime.Remoting.Channels* namespace) to add the credential information to the channel.

Listing 13-4 shows an example that uses the credentials of the current user. It assumes that you've imported two .NET Remoting namespaces: *System.Runtime.Remoting* and *System.Runtime.Remoting.Channels*.

```
' Configure the client using a configuration file.
RemotingConfiguration.Configure("Client.exe.config");

' Create the remote object.
Dim RemoteObject As New RemoteClass()

' Find the properties for the channel used to communicate with
' the remote object.
Dim Properties As IDictionary
Properties = ChannelServices.GetChannelSinkProperties(RemoteObject)

' Assign the current user's credentials to the channel.
Properties("credentials") = CredentialCache.DefaultCredentials

' Perform an authenticated call to the remote object.
MessageBox.Show(RemoteObject.GetIISUser())
```

Listing 13-4 Transparent authentication in .NET Remoting

Listing 13-5 shows similar code that assigns the security information using a new *NetworkCredential* class.

```
' Configure the client using a configuration file.
RemotingConfiguration.Configure("Client.exe.config");

' Create the remote object.
Dim RemoteObject As New RemoteClass()

' Find the properties for the channel used to communicate with
' the remote object.
Dim Properties As IDictionary
Properties = ChannelServices.GetChannelSinkProperties(RemoteObject)

' Assign the credentials to the proxy class.
Properties("username") = "name"
Properties("password") = "password"

' Perform an authenticated call to a Web method.
MessageBox.Show(RemoteObject.GetIISUser())
```

Listing 13-5 Manual authentication in .NET Remoting

Available User Information

With the approach shown so far, access is allowed for any user who can be authenticated on your server. This is a starting point, but it probably doesn't satisfy your security needs. To provide fine-grained authentication, your server-side object needs to investigate the caller's identity and determine whether the user has sufficient permissions to perform the requested task. This is generally described as *role-based security*. With Windows authentication, each role corresponds to a Windows group, as shown in Figure 13-3.

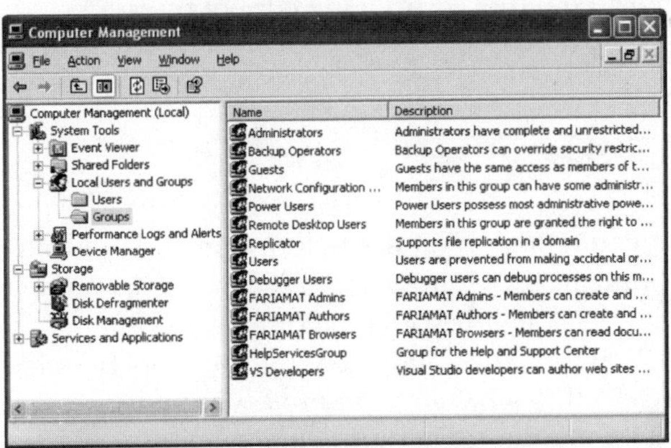

Figure 13-3 Sample Windows groups

To create new groups or to add or remove users to and from a group, choose Settings, Control Panel, Administrative Tools, Computer Management from the Start menu. The process is quite straightforward: Any Windows user can belong to as many groups as required. Some built-in groups are always available and don't need to be created, including Guests, Administrators, and Power Users.

In your application, groups identify access levels. For example, you might create a group called Project Managers and give it a different level of permissions than the Programmers group in an incident-tracking application. However, using Windows, you can only add the groups and configure group membership, not define the permissions assigned to a group. It's up to your application to assign application-specific privileges to the appropriate group.

To test whether an authenticated user is in a given role, you use the *IsInRole* method of the current security principal. This method accepts a single string parameter, which represents the group name, and returns *True* if the user is a member of the requested group. Here's the code you would use in an XML Web service:

```
If User.IsInRole("Manager") Then
    ' (Perform requested task here.)
Else
    Throw New SecurityException("Invalid role.")
End If
```

If you're accessing another server or domain controller, you need to use the path notation introduced earlier, which uses the syntax *[MachineName]\[GroupName]* or *[DomainName]\[GroupName]*.

The logic is similar in a component over .NET Remoting, although the security principal must be retrieved from the current thread:

```
If Thread.CurrentPrincipal.IsInRole("Manager") Then
    ' (Perform requested task here.)
Else
    Throw New SecurityException("Invalid role ")
End If
```

In both cases, you're accessing the security principal through the *IPrincipal* interface (found in the *System.Security.Principal* namespace). The *IPrincipal* interface provides only a single method (*IsInRole*) and a single property (*Identity*). You can gain some more functionality by casting the security principal object to the *WindowsPrincipal* type, which represents Windows-authenticated information. The *WindowsPrincipal* object provides three overloaded versions of the *IsInRole* method: one that takes a string name, one that takes an enumerated value representing one of the built-in Windows groups, and one that takes an integer that represents the unique role ID (RID) assigned to the group.

Listing 13-6 shows a test method you can add to an XML Web service to determine whether a user is an administrator.

```
<WebMethod()> _
Public Function IsAdministrator() As Boolean

    Dim Principal As WindowsPrincipal
    Principal = CType(User, WindowsPrincipal)

    Return Principal.IsInRole(WindowsBuiltInRole.Administrator)

End Function
```

Listing 13-6 Manual authentication in .NET Remoting

What's lacking from all this is a way to separate the security code from the business logic (as you can with COM+ role-based security). Unfortunately, .NET does not provide any equivalent for declarative security. Although the .NET Framework does include a *PrincipalPermission* attribute that allows only a specific user or role to access a method, it works on the account of the current user (which will be the ASP.NET worker process or the account used to run the component host), not the IIS-authenticated user. This makes it relatively useless unless you're using impersonation.

Impersonation

Impersonation is the process by which certain actions are performed under a different identity. You can use impersonation with a remote component to execute code under the caller's identity rather than the identity of the ASP.NET worker process or the account running the component host.

Impersonation is generally discouraged because it complicates and often weakens security. If you use impersonation with an XML Web service, for example, you also need to grant the user (or the user's group) permissions to server-side resources such as files and databases. This is a slightly uncomfortable situation because it could potentially allow the client to access the server and perform other operations that should be disallowed (such as deleting files). Usually, it's more secure to grant access only to the account used by the server-side object, which can then use these permissions to access server resources on behalf of the client.

In some cases, however, impersonation might be useful. If you have a file-lookup service, for example, you might want to use Windows ACLs to determine whether a given user can retrieve a specific file. Without impersonation, you have to write all the security code yourself, and your service could be "tricked" into accessing a file it shouldn't if the code contains an error. If you use impersonation, however, you don't have to write any security code. If the code attempts to access a disallowed file, an exception will be thrown.

With an XML Web service, you can enable impersonation using the web.config file:

```
<configuration>

    <system.web>
        <!-- Other settings omitted. -->
        <identity impersonate="true" />
    </system.web>

</configuration>
```

In this case, the entire Web method executes under the caller's security context. However, it's more common to use programmatic impersonation. This gives you the freedom to use impersonation for some methods and not for others. It also enables you to use impersonation just for certain segments of code.

> **Note** If you must use impersonation, programmatic impersonation is generally much more practical and flexible. Otherwise, you might need to grant additional unrelated permissions to the users who need to access your XML Web service. For example, XML Web service users will require read/write access to the Temporary ASP.NET Files directory where the compiled ASP.NET files are stored. This directory is located under the following path: C:\WINNT\Microsoft.NET\Framework\[version]\Temporary ASP.NET Files.

To use programmatic impersonation, you use the *WindowsIdentity.Impersonate* method. This enables you to execute some code in the identity of a specific user (such as your file access routine) but run the rest of your code under the local ASP.NET account, which ensures that it won't encounter any problems.

Listing 13-7 presents an example of programmatic impersonation. It retrieves the identity object, performs some actions under its context, and then reverts to the original ASP.NET account. You can use the same process with

.NET Remoting; just remember to retrieve the identity from the *Thread.CurrentPrincipal* property.

```
If Not User.GetType() Is WindowsPrincipal

    ' User was not authenticated with Windows authentication.
    Throw New SecurityException( _
      "Windows authentication was not performed.")

Else

    ' Retrieve the identity object.
    Dim Identity As WindowsIdentity
    Identity = CType(User.Identity, WindowsIdentity)

    ' Impersonate the identity.
    Dim ImpersonateContext As WindowsImpersonationContext
    ImpersonateContext = ID.Impersonate()

    ' (Perform tasks under the impersonated account.)

    ' Revert to the original ID.
    ImpersonateContext.Undo()

End If
```

Listing 13-7 Using programmatic impersonation

> **Note** Other forms of ASP.NET authentication, such as Forms-based authentication and Passport authentication, aren't supported in XML Web services (or .NET Remoting). This limitation results from the fact that there is no way to submit the user credentials with each request.

Custom Role-Based Authentication

With custom authentication, your code performs the work that IIS accomplishes automatically: investigating the supplied account information and verifying it with a database lookup. As with IIS, you need to perform this authentication at the beginning of every request or develop a ticket-issuing system, as described in the next section.

Most developers have used some form of custom authentication in their applications. Often, custom authentication just verifies that a user exists in the database and then allows access to the rest of the application. Chapter 18 presents one such example of a security system that can easily be integrated into any distributed application.

A more sophisticated system will use multiple tables, as shown in Figure 13-4. Here, tables track users, roles, and the permissions granted to each role. Two other tables are used to create many-to-many relationships between these three entities.

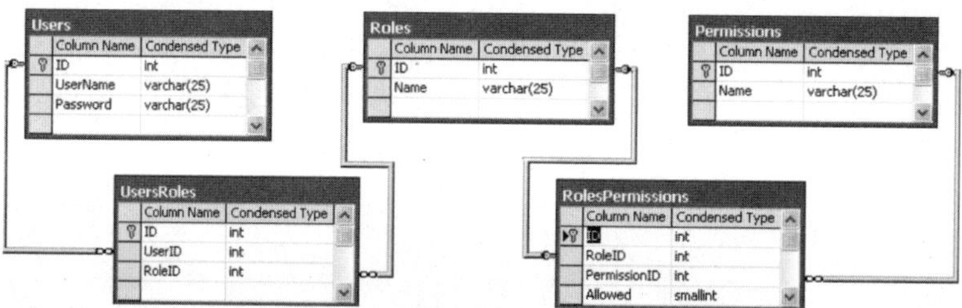

Figure 13-4 Database tables for custom authentication

It helps to consider a simple example. Figure 13-5 shows sample information: a single user, a role, and a permission record. Figure 13-6 shows the data used to link these records together, effectively giving the administrator the ability to delete records and assigning the testuser account to the Administrator role. If the Allowed column of the Permissions table has a value of 1, the permission is granted. If the Allowed column contains a 0, the permission is denied.

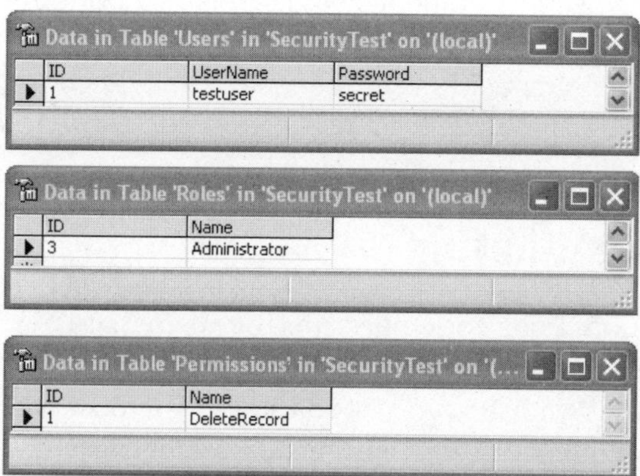

Data in Table 'Users' in 'SecurityTest' on '(local)'

ID	UserName	Password
1	testuser	secret

Data in Table 'Roles' in 'SecurityTest' on '(local)'

ID	Name
3	Administrator

Data in Table 'Permissions' in 'SecurityTest' on '(...

ID	Name
1	DeleteRecord

Figure 13-5 Creating a user, a role, and a permission

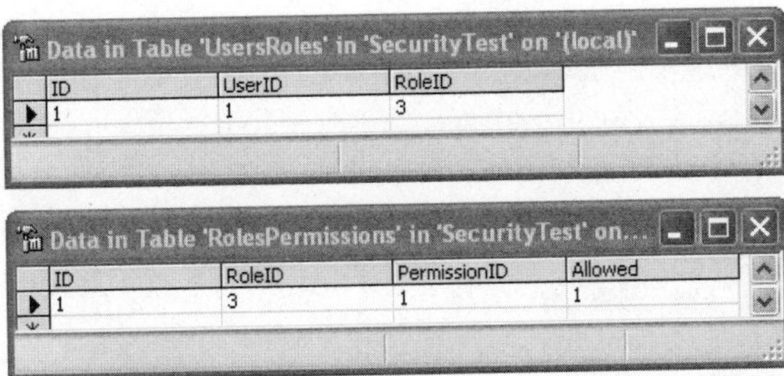

Figure 13-6 Linking users, roles, and permissions

> **Note** For tighter security, you should encrypt the password in the database. When the user accesses your XML Web service, you encrypt the supplied password and then see whether it matches the value in the database. Encryption is discussed later in this chapter.

To bring this all together in a simple, maintainable way, you can include in your remote components a private method that checks for a requested permission. To support this method, you need to add a dedicated stored procedure, as shown in Listing 13-8.

```
CREATE Procedure CheckPermission
 (
   @UserName    varchar(25),
   @Permission    varchar(25)
 )
 AS

SELECT MIN(Allowed) FROM RolesPermissions
    INNER JOIN Permissions ON Permissions.ID = PermissionID
    INNER JOIN Roles ON Roles.ID = RoleID
    INNER JOIN UsersRoles ON Roles.ID = Roles.ID
    INNER JOIN Users ON Users.ID = UsersRoles.UserID
WHERE Users.UserName=@UserName AND
    Permissions.Name=@Permission
```

Listing 13-8 A stored procedure for verifying a permission

The *CheckPermission* stored procedure joins together all the tables to find out whether a given permission is provided to a given user. The *MIN* function returns the lowest value from the Allowed column of all matching records. This handy trick allows permissions to be both granted and denied. This logic springs into action when a user matches more than one group. Consider, for instance, the case in which testuser is a member of both a Programmers and a Contractors group. Table 13-2 summarizes the possible outcomes.

Table 13-2 Authorization with Multiple Group Membership

Permission in Programmers Group	Permission in Contractors Group	Authorization Outcome
Granted (Allowed = 1)	Granted (Allowed = 1)	Granted (Returns 1)
Granted (Allowed = 1)	Denied (Allowed = 0)	Denied (Returns 0)
Granted (Allowed = 1)	Not specified (no record for this permission)	Granted (Returns 1)

Listing 13-9 shows the private .NET function you can use to test a permission. Note that this method assumes that the user's password information has already been verified. Alternatively, you can alter the stored procedure to also accept and use password information.

```
Private Function PermissionDemand(user As String, _
  permission As String) As Boolean

    Dim con As New SqlConnection(ConnectionString)
    Dim cmd As New SqlCommand("CheckPermission", con)
    Dim r As SqlDataReader

    cmd.CommandType = CommandType.StoredProcedure
    Dim Param As SqlParameter

    Param = cmd.Parameters.Add( _
     "@UserName", SqlDbType.NVarChar, 25)
    Param.Value = user

    Param = cmd.Parameters.Add( _
     "@Permission", SqlDbType.NVarChar, 25)
    Param.Value = permission

    Dim Allowed As Integer = 0

    Try
        con.Open()
        r = cmd.ExecuteReader()

        If r.Read() Then
            Allowed = r(0)
        Else
```

Listing 13-9 Authorizing a permission

```
            ' No matching permission record.
            Allowed = 0
        End If

        r.Close()

    Finally
        con.Close()

    End Try

    If Allowed = 1 Then
        Return True
    Else
        Return False
    End If

End Function
```

The client uses the following pattern:

```
If PermissionDemand(userName, "DeleteRecord")
    ' (Allow record deletion.)
Else
    Throw New SecurityException("Insufficient permissions.")
End If
```

Optionally, you can change the *PermissionDemand* function into a subroutine and give it the responsibility of throwing an exception if the permission is denied. The client would then use this pattern:

```
' Attempt to validate the user.
PermissionDemand(userName, "DeleteRecord")

' If the code reaches this point, no exception was thrown.
' (Allow record deletion.)
```

Ticket Systems

This custom authorization system suffers from one flaw. The user's authentication information (username and password) must be submitted with each method call. This leads to the cumbersome coding style shown here, in which two unrelated parameters are tacked onto every method:

```
Public Function GetProductInfo(productID As Integer, _
  username As String, password As String) As ProductDetails

    ' (Authenticate user.)
```

```
    ' (Perform task.)

End Function
```

Worse yet, the XML Web service has to validate this information every time. This can lead to a significant scalability bottleneck, especially if you store user information using the same data source as the rest of the application data (which is more than likely).

To counter these problems, you need to implement some sort of ticket system. With a ticket system, the client begins a session by calling a remote *Login* method with user account information. The *Login* method authenticates the user and issues a new ticket. Typically, this ticket is a globally unique identifier (GUID). You can use random numbers or some other ticket scheme, but this raises the possibility that a hacker might guess a ticket value based on previous values.

The client then submits this ticket on subsequent method calls. Every other server-side method performs its authentication by validating the ticket.

If properly implemented, a ticket system provides a number of benefits:

- **It can drastically improve performance when combined with caching.** If you store tickets in an in-memory cache, ticket validation is almost instantaneous and doesn't require a trip to the database.
- **It limits the effects of a security breach.** If hackers intercept a Web method request, they can (at worst) steal the session ticket and hijack a user session. However, they won't have the account information to log in to the system on their own.
- **It enables you to use SSL effectively.** SSL encrypts communication between a client and an XML Web service. However, it imposes additional overhead. With a ticket system, you can use SSL to encrypt requests to the *Login* method and protect user account information, but you won't need to use it for other methods.

The remainder of this section focuses on the essentials of a ticket system that uses ASP.NET application state. This removes some of the need for database access but can hamper performance for large systems because of the amount of information that needs to be stored in memory. Chapter 18 shows a case study with a complete example of a ticket system that incorporates caching rather than application state.

The first step is to create a class that represents the ticket information you need to retain, as shown in Listing 13-10. In this example, the ticket class stores a UserID, which would allow you to look up application-specific permission information from the database. Alternatively, you might want to store this type of information in the ticket class itself so that you could fill it once and then access it easily in any method.

```
Public Class TicketIdentity

    ' The unique value (e.g. 382c74c3-721d-4f34-80e5-57657b6cbc27).
    Public Ticket As Guid

    ' The IP address of the client.
    Public HostAddress As String

    ' The user identity information.
    Public UserID As Integer

    Public Sub New()
        ' Create a new GUID when the class is created.
        Me.Ticket = Guid.NewGuid()
    End Sub

End Class
```

Listing 13-10 A ticket class

Then you create the remote *Login* Web method (as shown in Listing 13-11). This method issues a new ticket, stores the ticket information in server memory, and returns the ticket to the user.

```
Public Function Login(userName As String, password As String) _
  As Guid

    ' Verify that the user name and password are in the database.
    ' (Database code omitted.)

    ' If they are, create a new ticket.
    Dim Ticket As New TicketIdentity()

    ' Store the user address information.
    Ticket.HostAddress = Context.Request.UserHostAddress

    ' Add this ticket to Application state.
    Application(TicketIdentity.Ticket.ToString()) = TicketIdentity

    ' Return the ticket GUID.
    Return TicketIdentity.Ticket

End If
```

Listing 13-11 The *Login* Web method

The third ingredient is the private server-side method that performs the authentication (as shown in Listing 13-12). It accepts the ticket, looks up the full ticket information, and then performs any additional authorization steps that are necessary.

```
Private Sub AuthenticateSession(ByVal ticket As Guid)

    Dim Ticket As TicketIdentity
    Ticket = Application(ticket.ToString())

    Dim Success As Boolean = False

    If Not Ticket Is Nothing

        ' Matching ticket was found.
        Success = True

        ' You could also verify that the IP address is unchanged by
        ' uncommenting the following code.
        ' If Ticket.HostAddress <> Context.Request.UserHostAddress
        '     Success = False
        ' End If

    End If

    If Not Success Then
        Throw New Security.SecurityException("Session not valid.")
    End If

End Sub
```

Listing 13-12 The authentication logic

Note that the *Login* method stores the user's IP address to prevent hijacked sessions. When the ticket is authenticated, the XML Web service can verify that the IP address hasn't changed (in other words, that the request is being made from the same computer). However, this system won't always work, particularly if the user is behind a proxy server that uses a dynamic IP address that changes unpredictably. Therefore, you should uncomment the preceding code only if you're working with a known (probably internal) environment in which this technique is practical.

Now that these ingredients are in place, every method can make use of the *AuthenticateSession* method. Listing 13-13 presents an example.

```
<WebMethod()> _
Private Function GetProductName(ID As Integer, ticket As Guid) _
  As String

    ' Attempt to validate the ticket.
    AuthenticateSession(ticket)

    ' Now perform the task.
    ' (Method-specific code omitted.)

End Function
```

Listing 13-13 Authenticating a ticket

The client follows the pattern shown in Listing 13-14.

```
Dim Proxy As New localhost.TicketServiceTest()

' Get the ticket.
Dim Ticket As Guid = Proxy.Login("testuser", "secret")

' Perform some work using the ticket.
Dim Product As String
Product = Proxy.GetProductName(234, Ticket)
```

Listing 13-14 Using a ticket on the client side

Passing Tickets Automatically

The ticket-based system we've considered so far doesn't solve the problem of additional method parameters. The client still needs to hold onto the ticket and submit it with every request. An easier approach is possible—one that automatically tracks and submits the ticket transparently.

With an XML Web service, the secret is to develop a custom SOAP header. The SOAP header (which contains the ticket GUID) is transmitted automatically with every Web method request. The client doesn't need to perform any additional actions. Listing 13-15 shows a sample SOAP header class.

```
Public Class TicketHeader
    Inherits SoapHeader

    Public Ticket As Guid

End Class
```

Listing 13-15 A SOAP ticket header

This technique is demonstrated in detail with the case study in Chapter 18, and so we won't delve into it in any more detail here.

With .NET Remoting, a similar technique is available with the *CallContext* class. The first step is to create a custom object that encapsulates the information you need to transmit automatically. (This plays the same role as a SOAP header in ASP.NET.) This object must be serializable and must implement the *ILogicalThreadAffinative* interface (in the *System.Runtime.Remoting.Messaging* namespace) for it to make the jump to other application domains. Note that both the client and the server need a copy of this class definition, so it should be placed in a separate assembly. If you're using interface-based programming (always a good idea), you can place this class in the same assembly that's used to define the required interfaces. Listing 13-16 uses this technique.

```
<Serializable()> _
Public Class TicketData
   Implements ILogicalThreadAffinative

    Public Ticket As Guid

End Sub
```

Listing 13-16 An *ILogicalThreadAffinative* object

Your client can create this object and use the *CallContext.SetData* method to attach it to the current context, as shown in Listing 13-17. It is automatically transmitted to the remote component with every request.

```
Dim RemoteObject As New RemoteClass()

' Get the ticket.
Dim Ticket As Guid = RemoteObject.Login("testuser", "secret")

' Set the ticket.
Dim TicketObj As New TicketData()
TicketObj.Ticket = Ticket
CallContext.SetData("ticket", TicketObj)

' Perform some work.
' The ticket is transmitted automatically (and seamlessly)
' with each call.
Dim Product As String
Product = Proxy.GetProductName(234)
```

Listing 13-17 Using an automatic ticket on the client side

The remote component can use *CallContext.GetData* to retrieve this information and validate it, as shown in Listing 13-18.

```
Dim TicketObj As TicketData
TicketObj = CType(CallContext.GetData("ticket"), TicketData)
```

Listing 13-18 Retrieving an automatic ticket on the server side

Encryption

So far, we've discussed only one aspect of security: authenticating users and authorizing tasks. Authentication is the heart of security design, but it's not the only consideration. With a network sniffer, a malicious user could extract ticket GUIDs, usernames, and passwords as they flow between client and server, not to mention sensitive data such as credit card information. If you use integrated Windows authentication, malicious users won't be able to retrieve passwords and account information, but they will still have easy access to any other sensitive data transmitted between the client and the server-side object. In fact, if you're using the SOAP format, this information is sent in clear-text messages.

The only way to protect communication in a distributed system is to use encryption. There are two basic approaches:

- Use SSL to enable automatic encryption. This is supported only by components hosted in IIS.
- Use the cryptography classes in the .NET Framework to selectively encrypt sensitive data.

The first approach is far easier to implement, provided you're using an XML Web service or a remote component hosted in IIS. It also ensures industrial-strength protection. The second option is significantly more work, but it allows you to protect sensitive data in specialized scenarios (for example, where you want to encrypt only a portion of the data exchanged between client and server) or when the environment doesn't support IIS and SSL.

> **Note** Even if you use SSL encryption to secure distributed communication, it's still worthwhile to explore the custom cryptography classes provided with the .NET Framework. You can use these classes in a variety of scenarios. For example, the same code you use to encrypt messages can be applied to secure persisted data, such as files on the hard drive or binary fields in a database.

SSL

SSL technology is used to encrypt communication between a client and a Web site. SSL is well known for its use in commercial Web sites, but it is equally valuable in almost any type of distributed application.

For a server to support SSL connections, it must have an X.509 digital certificate. This certificate indicates that the server identity is registered with a valid Certificate Authority (CA). We'll consider how to obtain a certificate in the next section.

A secure SSL session unfolds over several steps. The process is outlined here:

1. The client requests an SSL connection.
2. The server signs its certificate and sends it to the client.
3. The client verifies that the certificate was issued by a CA it trusts, matches the expected server, and has not expired or been revoked. The client continues to the next step only if all this information is validated.
4. The client tells the server what encryption key lengths it supports.
5. The server chooses the strongest key length that is supported by both the client and server, and informs the client what it is.
6. The client randomly generates a session key, encrypts it using the server's public key, and sends it to the server.
7. The server decrypts the session key using its private key. Both the client and server now have a session key they can use to encrypt communication for the duration of the session.

SSL and Certificates

To use SSL, you first need to install a server-side certificate using IIS. You can generate your own certificate for testing (using Certificate Server from Windows 2000 Server or Windows .NET Server, which requires Active Directory). When deploying a public application, however, you will probably want to use a genuine certificate authority such as VeriSign (*http://www.verisign.com*).

One of the easiest ways to purchase a certificate is to create and e-mail a *certificate request* to the appropriate Certificate Authority. IIS Manager allows you to create a certificate request automatically by following these steps:

1. Expand the Web Sites group, right-click on your Web site (often called Default Web Site), and choose Properties.
2. In the Directory Security tab, click the Server Certificate button. This starts the IIS Certificate Wizard that requests some basic organization information and generates a request file.
3. Complete all steps of the wizard. Figure 13-7 shows one step, where you must choose the Web site name and key length. The larger the bit length, the stronger the key.

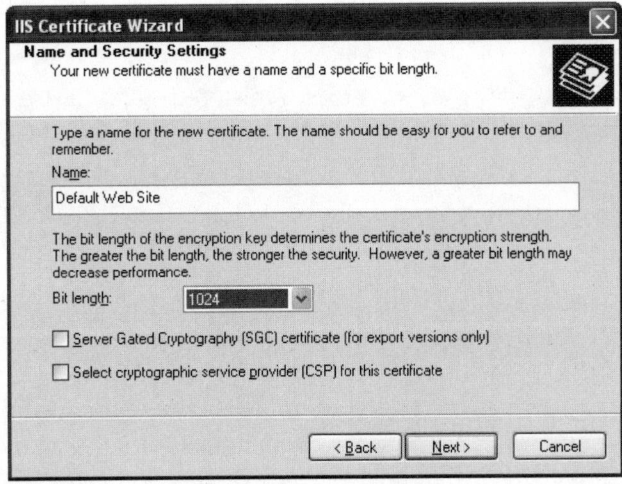

Figure 13-7 The IIS Certificate Wizard

4. E-mail the generated request file (which is automatically encrypted using the public key of the Certificate Authority) to the CA.
5. You will receive a certificate that you can install in IIS to complete the request, along with additional step-by-step instructions from the CA.

You can read much more information about certificate requests and how to use certificates with IIS in detail in the online IIS help, at *http://localhost/iisHelp*.

Certificates Establish Trust

In a distributed application, identity verification is a thorny problem. Just how can a client be sure that the server is who it claims to be? A clever attacker could use IP spoofing or some other advanced technique to masquerade as the server, create a secure SSL session with an unsuspecting client, and then seamlessly decrypt all the sensitive information the client sends.

SSL solves this problem using digital certificates. Certificates have two purposes:

- They show that the server is registered with a Certificate Authority (CA). In other words, the CA vouches for the server's identity.
- The server is not known to be malicious. If it is, its certificate will be revoked.

Clients use certificates to partially validate the server's identity. In other words, clients make the decision "I will trust this server because the CA vouches that it is Amazon.com," not "I trust this server because it claims to be Amazon.com." Every computer is preconfigured with a list of trusted CAs. This list can be modified using a tool such as makecert.exe (which is installed with the .NET Framework). Certificates also contain a small set of identifying information, including the holder's name, organization, and address; the holder's public key; validation dates; and a unique serial number.

Certificates are fundamentally limited in scope. They don't indicate that the server application is free from error, trustworthy, secure against outside attackers, or provided by a reliable business. They simply allow you to validate its identity through a third party.

Communicating with SSL

After you've installed your certificate, you just need to ensure that client requests use a URL that starts with *https:* rather than *http:* to use SSL encryption. If you're using an XML Web service, you can modify the base *Url* property of the generated proxy class (inherited from the *WebClientProtocol* class in the *System.Web.Services.Protocols* namespace), as shown in Listing 13-19.

```
Dim Proxy As New localhost.SSLServiceTest()
Proxy.Url = "https://localhost/DistributedCode/SSLServiceTest.asmx"

' (You can now send an SSL-encrypted message).

Proxy.Url = "http://localhost/DistributedCode/SSLServiceTest.asmx"

' (You can now send normal unencrypted requests).
```

Listing 13-19 Enabling SSL on the client side

This technique is particularly useful when you work with a service that uses ticket-based authentication. In this case, you might want to use SSL only when calling the *Login* method. To perform the required URL manipulations without hard-coding the URL, you can use the *System.Uri* class:

```
Dim Proxy As New localhost.SSLServiceTest()
Dim WSUri As New Uri(Proxy.Url)

' Use SSL.
' WSUri.Host = "localhost" and
' WSUri.Path = "/DistributedCode/SSLServiceTest.asmx"
Proxy.Url = "https://" & WSUri.Host & WSUri.AbsolutePath

' Use ordinary HTTP.
Proxy.Url = "http://" & WSUri.Host & WSUri.AbsoultePath
```

In your XML Web service code, you can check whether a user is connecting over a secure connection using the *HttpRequest.IsSecureConnection* property, as shown in Listing 13-20.

```
If Not Context.Request.IsSecureConnection Then

    Throw New SecurityException( _
      "This page must be requested through SSL.")

Else

    ' (Perform action.)

End If
```

Listing 13-20 Verifying SSL on the server side

In a .NET Remoting scenario, you just modify the URL in the client's configuration file so that it starts with *https:* rather than the *http:* prefix.

Keep in mind that when you use SSL, all traffic is encrypted, not just the data you're exchanging. For example, the text in an XML Web service request message that identifies the method to execute is encrypted, along with the body of the message, the envelope, and all SOAP headers. This is one reason why SSL has a reputation for being slow.

The .NET Encryption Classes

SSL is an ideal solution for protecting mission-critical applications. But there are situations in which you might want the flexibility to encrypt only small details in large data messages or use encryption outside of IIS. The .NET Framework includes a full complement of cryptography classes that can help you with this task in the *System.Security.Cryptography* namespace.

Before you can harness encryption for use in a distributed system, you need to know a little about cryptography and the two forms of encryption in common use today. These standards form the basis of SSL and the .NET Framework cryptography classes.

Cryptographic algorithms use keys to scramble information. The two kinds of encryption are secret key (symmetric) encryption and public key (asymmetric) encryption. Both schemes rely on the strength of the keys, not on the secrecy of the algorithms used to perform the encryption. The algorithms aren't secret. In fact, they've been subject to public scrutiny by the cryptographic community, and their strengths and limitations are well known.

Symmetric encryption is the form of encryption that most individuals are familiar with. It uses the same key to both encrypt and decrypt information. Symmetric encryption is extremely fast, but it's easily compromised if another user knows the secret key value. Unfortunately, because this key has to be known by both the server and the client, it usually has to be transmitted in some way, making it very vulnerable.

The .NET Framework provides the following classes that implement private-key encryption algorithms:

- *DESCryptoServiceProvider*
- *RC2CryptoServiceProvider*
- *RijndaelManaged*
- *TripleDESCryptoServiceProvider*

Asymmetric encryption uses a key pair that consists of a public key and a corresponding private key. This is the type of encryption used natively by .NET to create strong-named assemblies, and we considered it in Chapter 2. With asymmetric encryption, information encrypted using the public key can be decrypted only using the matching private key. The reverse also applies: The public key is the only key that can decrypt data encrypted with the private key. Asymmetric encryption is mathematically complex. (For example, some algorithms depend on the fact that although multiplying two prime numbers to generate a new number is computationally easy, factoring the result to rediscover the original pair of prime numbers is quite difficult, especially for large numbers.) With asymmetric encryption, the private key is guarded carefully, whereas the public key value is published. If client A wants to send information to client B, it uses client B's public key to encrypt the data. This information can then be decrypted only using client B's private key, meaning that even the client that creates the message can't read it.

Asymmetric encryption is an elegant solution to the problems faced by symmetric encryption, but its added complexity comes with a significant cost: Using it is hundreds of times slower. Often, symmetric and asymmetric encryption are combined, such that asymmetric encryption is used to distribute a random key. This random key is then used to encrypt subsequent messages using symmetric encryption. This technique is used natively in SSL. If you attempt to encode all communication using asymmetric encryption, your application will probably perform terribly.

The .NET Framework provides the following classes that implement public-key encryption algorithms:

- *DSACryptoServiceProvider*
- *RSACryptoServiceProvider*

.NET also provides additional classes in the *System.Security.Cryptography* namespace that generate random numbers and create hash values and digital signatures, which can be used to verify data and ensure that it hasn't been altered in transmission. Some of these classes actually perform the appropriate cryptographic tasks in managed .NET code, while others are just thin .NET wrappers over the unmanaged CryptoAPI library.

Selective Asymmetric Encryption

Selective encryption is an attractive option if you need to create a remote component that isn't hosted in IIS, doesn't use SOAP, or just needs improved performance over SSL. The key disadvantage with selective encryption is that both the client and server need to participate actively. If the client accidentally submits unencrypted information, for example, an error might occur—or at worst, invalid data could be committed to the database. For that reason, selective encryption is best when you have complete control over the client code, and it is less attractive for cross-platform or third-party integration projects. This section considers how you can add selective encryption to an XML Web service.

In most cases, a secure interaction begins when a client sends a request attempting to log in. Typically, this request contains two pieces of information: a username and a password. The password must be kept secret; otherwise the security of the entire application is compromised. Therefore, in a secure system, the client must begin by encrypting the password before sending the request. In this case, asymmetric encryption is the only option unless you have already distributed some sort of secure password to each and every client.

Fortunately, asymmetric encryption is quite easy to use, provided that the XML Web service exposes a public key. The client can encode its password using the XML Web service's public key, ensuring that only the XML Web service can decode this information. Figure 13-8 diagrams the process.

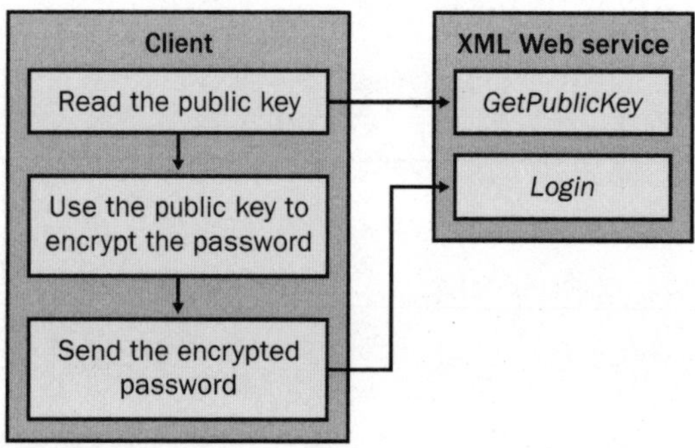

Figure 13-8 Encrypting information at the client

Listing 13-21 shows an XML Web service that creates a key and stores it in application state so that it can be reused for all requests. In this case, the key is used for RSA encryption (a standard developed by Ronald L. Rivest, Adi Shamir, and Leonard M. Adleman in 1977), and the default key size is used. Note that to use 128-bit encryption with Windows 2000, both the client and server require the Windows 2000 high-encryption pack (downloadable from Microsoft at *http://www.microsoft.com/windows2000/downloads/recommended/encryption*) or the Windows 2000 Service Pack 2.

```
Imports System.Web.Services
Imports System.Security.Cryptography
Imports System.Text

Public Class CryptographyTest
    Inherits System.Web.Services.WebService

    <WebMethod()> _
    Public Function GetPublicKey() As String

        ' Retrieve the key object.
        Dim Key As RSACryptoServiceProvider = GetKeyFromState()

        ' Return the private portion of the key only.
        Return Key.ToXmlString(False)

    End Function

    Private Function GetKeyFromState() As RSACryptoServiceProvider

        Dim Key As RSACryptoServiceProvider

        ' Check if the key has been created yet.
        ' This ensures that the key is only created once.
        If Application("Key") Is Nothing Then

            ' Create a key for RSA encryption.
            Dim Parameters As New CspParameters()
            Parameters.Flags = CspProviderFlags.UseMachineKeyStore
            Key = New RSACryptoServiceProvider(Parameters)

            ' Store the key in the server memory.
            Application("Key") = Key

        Else
            Key = CType(Application("Key"), RSACryptoServiceProvider)

        End If

        Return Key

    End Function

End Class
```

Listing 13-21 An XML Web service that exposes a public key

The XML Web service client can retrieve the key and use it to encrypt data. Keep in mind that encrypted data is always translated into a byte array. You could attempt to convert it back to a string using an *Encoding* object, but the resulting special characters might interfere with the XML serialization process required to send a SOAP message. Therefore, this approach is not recommended.

Incidentally, the XML version of the key looks something like this:

```
<RSAKeyValue>
<Modulus>xMOD47YH9sadjqccA3mZZAuvFcUqfQ4pc9KzU6A6/BPTEKtrK3GY3jRkamwZ21JCht7/
12AQqatfSfmIav8Lqi3Jb8RwsG471XdHJBG80Aa717q3Mc8/QNiESNo7cWC/5scCa/
38r+57fqVtH4zChXxmxFL2fwm+dLS0dTyiMmE=</Modulus>
<Exponent>AQAB</Exponent>
</RSAKeyValue>
```

To test the encryption, you need to add a Web method that actually requires encrypted information. In this case, we'll use the *Login* method shown in Listing 13-22.

```
<WebMethod()> _
Public Function Login(ByVal userName As String, _
  ByVal password As Byte()) As Boolean

    ' Retrieve the key object.
    Dim Key As RSACryptoServiceProvider = GetKeyFromState()

    ' Decrypt the password.
    Dim DecryptedPassword As String
    Dim Enc As New UnicodeEncoding()
    DecryptedPassword = Enc.GetString(Key.Decrypt(password, False))

    ' This code simply uses a hard-coded password.
    ' Typically, you would look this value up in a database.
    ' You would then create and return a ticket to indicate the
    ' user is allowed, as demonstrated earlier.
    If DecryptedPassword = "secret" Then
        Return True
    Else
        Return False
    End If

End Function
```

Listing 13-22 A *Login* method that requires an encrypted password

Note that the password parameter is a byte array, not a string. This hints at one unpleasant consequence of using manual encryption: You need to change the interface of the remote class to accommodate it. Of course, this change has at least one benefit. Namely, the client is unlikely to accidentally submit a clear-text password because the proxy class will throw an error if it doesn't receive the expected byte array data type.

To test this implementation, you can create a client-side method that reads the Web server's key, encrypts a password, and verifies that authentication succeeds (as shown in Listing 13-23).

```
Dim Proxy As New localhost.CryptographyTest()

Dim Password As String = "secret"

' Construct a key object using the public portion of the key.
' The client will be able to encode, but not decode information.
Dim Key As New RSACryptoServiceProvider()
Key.FromXmlString(Proxy.GetPublicKey())

' Encrypt the password.
Dim Enc As New UnicodeEncoding()
Dim EncryptedPassword As Byte()
EncryptedPassword = Key.Encrypt(Enc.GetBytes(Password), False)

' Attempt to call Login() with the encrypted password.
If Proxy.Login("test", EncryptedPassword) Then
    MessageBox.Show("Authentication succeeded.")
End If
```

Listing 13-23 Encrypting information at the client end

> **Note** For this encryption scheme to work properly, both the XML Web service and the client must use the same encoder (in this case, the *System.Text.UnicodeEncoding* class). If the client encodes information using the *ASCIIEncoding* class while the server uses *UnicodeEncoding*, the correct value won't be retrieved.

If you use a SOAP tracing tool (such as the one included with the Microsoft SOAP Toolkit), you can examine the request message as it is sent over the network. In an unencrypted XML Web service, the message appears as shown in Listing 13-24. With encryption, the message is more like that shown in Listing 13-25. (In this case, each number represents a byte value that can't be representable as text.)

```
<?xml version="1.0" encoding="utf-8"?>
<soap:Envelope xmlns:xsi="http://www.w3.org/2001/XMLSchema-instance"
      xmlns:xsd="http://www.w3.org/2001/XMLSchema"
      xmlns:soap="http://schemas.xmlsoap.org/soap/envelope/">

  <soap:Body>
    <Login xmlns="http://tempuri.org/">
      <userName>testuser</userName>
      <password>secret</password>
    </Login>
  </soap:Body>

</soap:Envelope>
```

Listing 13-24 An unencrypted SOAP message

```
<?xml version="1.0" encoding="utf-8"?>
<soap:Envelope xmlns:xsi="http://www.w3.org/2001/XMLSchema-instance"
      xmlns:xsd="http://www.w3.org/2001/XMLSchema"
      xmlns:soap="http://schemas.xmlsoap.org/soap/envelope/">

  <soap:Body>
    <Login xmlns="http://tempuri.org/">
      <userName>testuser</userName>
      <password>56 67 16 180 176 188 160 39 187 29 85 204 163 243 149
       16 222 138 75 56 117 61 128 87 218 83 223 121 22 206 129 33 117
       7 197 181 89 230 216 17 174 0 34 96 111 177 60 163 107 99 6 12
       223 176 143 251 85 76 50 143 19 202 50 20 14 153 59 158 116 156
       187 28 183 194 0 198 61 115 10 214 211 146 240 80 130 55 199 84
       50 37 33 172 136 111 11 62 117 106 13 178 96 214 31 157 19 235
       170 240 222 44 51 253 176 44 116 241 15 245 218 129 34 182 213
       32 149 86 54 67</password>
    </Login>
  </soap:Body>

</soap:Envelope>
```

Listing 13-25 An encrypted SOAP message

Note that it's still possible to retrieve information such as which method the user is calling. If this information must also be protected, you're better off encrypting the entire message with SSL.

> **Note** You also can implement encryption by creating a custom SOAP extension for an XML Web service or a custom channel sink for .NET Remoting. Both of these approaches require more work and tightly couple your solution to a specific technology. They also encrypt the entire message, which means they perform more slowly than the selective encryption techniques shown in this example. However, these specialized solutions might be appealing if you need to reuse a specific encryption scheme that's independent of the actual business code and the type of data. You can find more information about both of these approaches in the MSDN reference.

Selective Symmetric Encryption

After a session has been started, it's imperative to switch to secret key encryption as soon as possible. Asymmetric encryption and decryption are computationally expensive, and encoded messages are significantly larger than they would be with symmetric encryption. To make the switch, the client and the XML Web service need to agree on a common secret key. You can use the user's existing password for this purpose, if it is sufficiently long, or the server can randomly generate a new key, in which case it needs to use asymmetric encryption to pass the key to the client. In both cases, the remote object will probably need to store the client's key in some type of state.

Whereas asymmetric encryption uses a public and a private key, symmetric encryption uses both a secret key and an *initialization vector*, which is a sequence of random bytes added to the message. Typically, a client will always use the same secret key (perhaps one derived from the user password) while selecting a different initialization vector for each session. However, this book doesn't consider these details at length. If you want to implement industrial-strength encryption, you might want to refer to a dedicated book about encryption theory. (In fact, entire technical works are devoted to explaining single-encryption algorithms, including Rijndael, the symmetric algorithm used in the next example.)

The first task is to define a structure in the XML Web service that represents the client key information:

```
Public Class ClientKey

    Public Key As Byte()
```

```
    Public IV As Byte()

End Class
```

Next, you modify the *Login* Web method to accept client key information and store it in the *Application* collection, indexed by the client's username (as shown in Listing 13-26). As you might expect, the *Key* and *IV* values are actually encrypted before transmission using the XML Web service's public key. To ensure optimal performance, the *Login* method decrypts these values before storing the key. Otherwise, they would need to be decrypted each time the *ClientKey* object is used, which would impose a noticeable performance burden.

```
<WebMethod()> _
Public Function Login(ByVal userName As String, _
  ByVal password As Byte(), ByVal clientKey As ClientKey) As Boolean

    ' Retrieve the key object.
    Dim Key As RSACryptoServiceProvider = GetKeyFromState()

    ' Decrypt the password.
    Dim DecryptedPassword As String
    Dim Enc As New UnicodeEncoding()
    DecryptedPassword = Enc.GetString(Key.Decrypt(password, False))

    If DecryptedPassword = "secret" Then
        ' Store the client's key in Application state.
        ' To optimize performance, it must be decrypted first.
        clientKey.IV = Key.Decrypt(clientKey.IV, False)
        clientKey.Key = Key.Decrypt(clientKey.Key, False)
        Application(userName) = clientKey

        Return True

    Else
        Return False

    End If

End Function
```

Listing 13-26 A *Login* method that stores client key information

A new method is added, which returns a string of secret data, encrypted using the client's key (as shown in Listing 13-27). Note that once again both the client and server must agree on the same encryption and encoding standard; otherwise, this system will break down.

```
<WebMethod()> _
Public Function GetSecretData(ByVal userName As String) As Byte()

    ' Create a key object that is identical to the client's key.
    Dim Key As ClientKey = CType(Application(userName), ClientKey)
    Dim RM As New RijndaelManaged()

    ' Create a memory stream.
    Dim s As New MemoryStream()

    ' Encrypt information into the memory stream.
    Dim CryptStream As New CryptoStream(s, _
      RM.CreateEncryptor(Key.Key, Key.IV), CryptoStreamMode.Write)
    Dim w As New StreamWriter(s)
    w.WriteLine("Secret data!")
    w.Flush()

    ' Now move the information out of the stream,
    ' and into an array of bytes.
    Dim r As StreamReader
    Dim Bytes As Byte()
    ReDim Bytes(s.Length)
    s.Position = 0
    s.Read(Bytes, 0, s.Length)

    ' Clean up.
    s.Close()

    ' Return the final byte array of encrypted data.
    Return Bytes

End Function
```

Listing 13-27 Encrypting data at the server

The code required for this task is somewhat complicated by the fact that symmetric encryption is stream-based. The string of information must be written to an in-memory cryptographic stream, which is automatically scrambled. Then the information must be read from the stream and converted to an array of bytes so that it can be safely returned from the Web method. (The *Stream* object is not natively supported as an XML Web service data type.)

The client code to retrieve the encrypted information is shown in Listing 13-28.

```
Dim Proxy As New localhost.CryptographyTest()

Dim Password As String = "secret"

' Construct a key object using the public portion of the key.
Dim Key As New RSACryptoServiceProvider()
Key.FromXmlString(Proxy.GetPublicKey())

' Encrypt the password.
Dim Enc As New UnicodeEncoding()
Dim EncryptedPassword As Byte()
EncryptedPassword = Key.Encrypt(Enc.GetBytes(Password), False)

' Create a secret key for the server to send back data.
' This will be a symmetric key to ensure optimum performance.
Dim RM As New RijndaelManaged()
Dim ClientKey As New localhost.ClientKey()

' The values for this key are encrypted with the XML Web service's
' public key.
ClientKey.Key = Key.Encrypt(RM.Key, False)
ClientKey.IV = Key.Encrypt(RM.IV, False)

If Proxy.Login("test", EncryptedPassword, ClientKey) Then

   MessageBox.Show("Authentication succeeded.")

   ' Try to retrieve some information.
   Dim Data As Byte() = Proxy.GetSecretData("test")

   ' Place the array of bytes into a memory stream.
   Dim s As New MemoryStream()
   s.Write(Data, 0, Data.Length)

   ' Decrypt and display the data.
   Dim cs As New CryptoStream(s, RM.CreateDecryptor(RM.Key, RM.IV), _
     CryptoStreamMode.Read)
   Dim r As New StreamReader(s)
   s.Position = 0
   MessageBox.Show("Retrieved: " & r.ReadToEnd())

   s.Close()

End If
```

Listing 13-28 Decrypting data at the client end

Now the encrypted string "*Secret data!*" will be successfully retrieved, decrypted, and displayed.

> **Note** Future versions of the .NET Framework will likely abstract away parts of this process with a declarative model. For example, you might be able to add a specific attribute to a class member or parameter to specify that it must be encrypted automatically by the runtime before transmission. Microsoft recently released the Web Services Enhancements kit (WSE) as a separate add-on, which can be downloaded from *http://msdn.microsoft.com/webservices/building/wse*. It includes support for using the emerging SOAP security standard WS-Security in an XML Web service. These extensions will likely be integrated into the core .NET Framework in future releases.

Why Custom Encryption is Not SSL

It's easy to be lured into the belief that this custom encryption scheme provides the equivalent of an SSL-encrypted session. This "do-it-yourself" frame of mind is often encouraged in programming books, although it's quite dangerous.

SSL is a mature, sophisticated protocol. As such, it provides some features that are not implemented in the above example. The problems in the custom implementation include the following:

- **No message authentication codes** In other words, even though a malicious user can't read an encrypted message, the attacker could alter it, without the client or server realizing what had happened. This would probably lead to an application error, but it could be used as part of a more sophisticated exploit. To overcome this problem, you need to add keyed hash codes to every encrypted message. This is possible with the .NET cryptography classes, but it's more work.
- **No identity verification** Because the custom authentication approach doesn't use certificates, there's no way for a client to be sure that the server it is communicating with isn't really a crafty hacker. Currently, the .NET Framework doesn't include any classes for validating certificates.

The lack of these features might be only a minor drawback if you're designing an internal application and the threat risk is small. However, if

> your application is dealing with highly sensitive information, these limitations might be unacceptable. The best approach is to carefully model the security risks and the types and motivations of potential attackers. If you could be subject to a man-in-the-middle attack (where an attacker uses privileged network access to intercept communication or even steal another computer's IP address), SSL might be the only viable choice. If you do decide to use the .NET cryptography classes, write as little code as possible, and always have it reviewed by a security expert.

Selective Encryption with .NET Remoting

You can use selective encryption in a .NET Remoting scenario in much the same way that you use it with a Web service, and with the same classes from the *System.Security.Cryptography* namespace. The process becomes quite a bit more complicated if you use *SingleCall* objects, however, because *SingleCall* objects are destroyed at the end of each method invocation. Unlike an XML Web service, .NET Remoting doesn't provide a global state store (such as the *Application* collection) to store keys, so a *SingleCall* .NET Remoting object would need to manually serialize its information to some data source. This process would not only be difficult to code, but it would also be subject to other security breaches (for example, if a malicious user accesses the database and reads the remote object's private key).

A much better approach is to use client-activated objects. Using encryption with a client-activated object is actually quite a bit easier than using it with an XML Web service because the remote object will need to serve only a single user—the user who created the object. The remote object will also remain running so that all the required information can be retained in memory. This means you don't need to worry about using the *Application* collection or a database. Instead, the remote object uses a private member variable to store the automatically generated asymmetric server key and the client-submitted symmetric key. You can allow the client to retrieve the former and submit the latter using property procedures or methods.

Using Custom Classes to Wrap Encryption

If you're designing a secure service with .NET Remoting, you might be able to abstract away some of the encryption details by using custom objects. The basic strategy is to wrap the information that needs to be transmitted between the client and server in a custom object. This object can use property procedure logic to perform the encryption automatically. (This solution isn't possible with XML Web services because the property procedure logic for custom classes won't appear in the automatically generated proxy file.)

For example, you can use a *UserInfo* class to wrap the account information that must be submitted to the *Login* method, as shown in Listing 13-29. The constructor requires that you provide an *RSACryptoServiceProvider* instance when you create the object.

```
<Serializable()> _
Public Class UserInfo

    <NonSerialized()> Private _RSA As RSACryptoServiceProvider
    Private Encoding As New UnicodeEncoding()

    Private _UserName As String
    Private _Password As Byte()

    Public Property RSA() As RSACryptoServiceProvider
        Get
            Return _RSA
        End Get
        Set(ByVal Value As RSACryptoServiceProvider)
            _RSA = Value
        End Set
    End Property

    Public Property UserName() As String
        Get
            Return _UserName
        End Get
        Set(ByVal Value As String)
            _UserName = Value
        End Set
    End Property

    Public Property Password() As String
        Get
            Return Encoding.GetString(_RSA.Decrypt(_Password, False))
        End Get
        Set(ByVal Value As String)
            _Password = _RSA.Encrypt(Encoding.GetBytes(Value), False)
        End Set
    End Property

    Public Sub New(ByVal encryptor As RSACryptoServiceProvider)
        RSA = encryptor
    End Sub

End Class
```

Listing 13-29 Automatic encryption with a custom class

The *Login* method will then be slightly modified:

```
Public Sub Login(userInfo As UserInfo)
    ' (Code omitted.)
End Sub
```

The *RSACryptoServiceProvider* used for the encryption and decryption is specifically marked with a *<NonSerialized>* attribute. This ensures that the sensitive key information can't be sent over the wire. However, when receiving the *UserInfo* object, you'll need to set the *RSA* property before you can access any properties. If your *RSACryptoServiceProvider* encapsulates the full key pair, you'll be able to set and retrieve the password information. If the *RSACryptoServiceProvider* includes only the public key information, you'll be able to set the password information (encrypt) but not read it (decrypt).

Be warned, however, that although this approach simplifies the client code, it can make it difficult for you to extend the system or modify the encryption techniques. You might also end up with an unmanageable number of new classes. To counteract this tendency, you can create a generic encryption package that will work with any string, as shown in Listing 13-30.

```
<Serializable()> _
Public Class EncryptionPackage

    <NonSerialized()> Private _RSA As RSACryptoServiceProvider
    Private Encoding As New UnicodeEncoding()

    Private _Encoded As Byte()

    Public Property RSA() As RSACryptoServiceProvider
        Get
            Return _RSA
        End Get
        Set(ByVal Value As RSACryptoServiceProvider)
            _RSA = Value
        End Set
    End Property

    Public Property Text() As String
        Get
            Return Encoding.GetString(_RSA.Decrypt(_Text, False))
        End Get
        Set(ByVal Value As String)
            __Encoded = _RSA.Encrypt(Encoding.GetBytes(Value), False)
        End Set
    End Property

    Public Sub New(ByVal encryptor As RSACryptoServiceProvider)
        RSA = encryptor
    End Sub

End Class
```

Listing 13-30 A generic encrypted information package

The client will then immediately recognize a method that requires encrypted information because it will use the *EncryptionPackage* data type. As written, this approach has two minor drawbacks. First, it supports only asymmetric encryption, which is slower and produces a larger encrypted message than symmetric encryption. Second, it doesn't support extremely large strings. The *Encrypt* method can work only with data up to one block size large. If the data is larger than one block, you must break it down into separate blocks, encrypt them separately, and then reassemble the encrypted blocks. Because it is stream based, symmetric encryption doesn't have this limitation. The example in the next section takes this limitation into account with a lengthier example.

Using .NET Serialization to Encrypt Classes

Another interesting approach is to serialize objects to byte arrays using .NET object serialization. This is particularly useful when you want to encrypt a group of related information. The basic approach is as follows:

- Create a class that contains the information you want to encrypt. Make sure that it is serializable (as explained in Chapter 4).
- Create an *EncryptionPackage* class that wraps this class. The *EncryptionPackage* class should provide methods that allow you to encrypt and decrypt the contained object.
- Make the *EncryptionPackage* class serializable so that it can be sent to a remote component using .NET Remoting.

Listing 13-31 shows a class that follows this design and can be used to encrypt the contents of any serializable object. A full discussion of this code is beyond the scope of this chapter. However, the basics are easy to understand. The object is first converted to a stream of bytes using binary serialization. It is then asymmetrically encrypted and stored in a private memory stream named *SerializedObject*. The *Deserialize* method decrypts this data to a second memory stream and then deserializes and returns the original object.

The code is much longer than the previous example because it breaks down the data into the appropriate block size before it is encrypted, allowing you to asymmetrically encrypt data no matter what its size. You could develop a simpler class using symmetric encryption.

```
<Serializable()> _
Public Class EncryptionPackage

    Private SerializedObject As New MemoryStream()

    ' Encrypt the object and store it internally.
    Public Sub New(ByVal objectToEncrypt As Object, _
      ByVal rsa As RSACryptoServiceProvider)

        ' Serialize a copy of objectToEncrypt in memory.
        Dim f As New BinaryFormatter()
        Dim ObjectStream As New MemoryStream()
        f.Serialize(ObjectStream, objectToEncrypt)
        ObjectStream.Position = 0

        ' The block size depends on the key size.
        Dim BlockSize As Integer
        If rsa.KeySize = 1024 Then
            BlockSize = 16
        Else
            BlockSize = 5
        End If

        ' Move through the data one block at a time.
        Dim RawBlock(), EncryptedBlock() As Byte
        Dim i As Integer
        Dim Bytes As Integer = ObjectStream.Length
        For i = 0 To Bytes Step BlockSize

            If Bytes - i > BlockSize Then
                ReDim RawBlock(BlockSize - 1)
            Else
                ReDim RawBlock(Bytes - i - 1)
            End If

            ' Copy a block of data.
            ObjectStream.Read(RawBlock, 0, RawBlock.Length)

            ' Encrypt the block of data.
            EncryptedBlock = rsa.Encrypt(RawBlock, False)

            ' Write the block of data.
            Me.SerializedObject.Write(EncryptedBlock, _
              0, EncryptedBlock.Length)
        Next
```

Listing 13-31 Encrypting a serializable object with a wrapper

```
    End Sub

    ' Decrypt the stored data, deserialize it, and return it as
    ' a generic Object (because the code does not know the original type).
    Public Function Decrypt(rsa As RsaCryptoServiceProvider) As Object

        ' Create the memory stream where the decrypted data
        ' will be stored.
        Dim ObjectStream As New MemoryStream()

        ' Determine the block size for decrypting.
        Dim keySize As Integer = Rsa.KeySize / 8

        ' Move through the data one block at a time.
        Me.SerializedObject.Position = 0
        Dim DecryptedBlock(), RawBlock() As Byte
        Dim i As Integer
        Dim Bytes As Integer = Me.SerializedObject.Length
        For i = 0 To bytes - 1 Step keySize

            If ((Bytes - i) > keySize) Then
                ReDim RawBlock(keySize - 1)
            Else
                ReDim RawBlock(Bytes - i - 1)
            End If

            ' Copy a block of data.
            Me.SerializedObject.Read(RawBlock, 0, RawBlock.Length)

            ' Decrypt a block of data.
            DecryptedBlock = rsa.Decrypt(RawBlock, False)

            ' Write the decrypted data to the in-memory stream.
            ObjectStream.Write(DecryptedBlock, 0, DecryptedBlock.Length)
        Next

        ObjectStream.Position = 0
        Dim f As New BinaryFormatter()
        Return f.Deserialize(ObjectStream)

    End Function

End Class
```

To encrypt an object, you supply it in the *EncryptionPackage* constructor:

```
' MyObject is the object you want to encrypt.
Dim MyObject As New MyClass()

Dim Package As New EncryptionPackage(MyObject, publicRsa)
' Package now contains an encrypted copy of the object data.
```

To decrypt the object, you use the *Decrypt()* method, and cast the returned object to the expected type:

```
MyObject = CType(Package.Decrypt(privateRsa), MyClass)
' MyObject now contains the decrypted, deserialized object.
```

Note that both of these steps force you to submit the appropriate *RSACryptoServiceProvider* object representing the public key or the full key pair. To ensure optimum security, this information is never stored in the class.

It's difficult to say categorically whether custom wrappers are a good approach for distributed applications that require a significant amount of encryption. As a general rule, the more custom encryption you add, the more you need to modify the interface of your server-side methods. Over time, this might make the system less manageable.

Authentication and encryption are widely identified as key areas where XML Web services and remote object technologies such as .NET Remoting must be improved—in fact, Microsoft is probably considering these limitations even as you read this chapter. In a future version of the .NET Framework, you can expect more consistent, automated security functions that can be integrated into your code in a declarative fashion (probably with the use of attributes). Until then, you need to make the difficult decision between SSL and custom encryption.

Code Access Security

The final topic in this chapter is code access security, which is a new addition to .NET designed to restrict unknown or suspicious code. You might be aware that Java programs on the Windows platform run inside a protected "sandbox" that restricts the code from directly performing certain low-level operations. .NET extends this concept with code access security. Conceptually, code access security is a dynamic sandbox that gives some assemblies more permissions than others.

When the CLR first loads an assembly, it considers several details to determine the security level that should be allowed. These details, called *evidence*, include the following:

- **Zone** The security level, which is based on whether the code is executed locally or accessed from a remote site. Zones in .NET are the same zones configured in Internet Explorer and include Internet, Local Intranet, Trusted Sites, Restricted Sites, and Local Machine.
- **URL** A specific URL or file location for a specific resource, such as *http://localhost/MyFiles/Assembly.dll* or *file:///c:\temp\Assembly.dll.*
- **Application directory** The directory from which the code is loaded.
- **Site** Similar to the URL but less specific. For example, *www.microsoft.com* is a site.
- **Strong name** The strong-name signature that identifies the assembly.
- **Publisher certificate** The Authenticode digital signature of the assembly.

The CLR evaluates all of this information and then considers the security policy on the current computer. The security policy sets the allowed permissions based on the evidence. The security policy isn't defined anywhere in .NET code. Instead, it's stored in each computer's machine.config configuration file. You can edit this file manually or (more easily) use the .NET Framework Configuration tool to edit it. Just choose Settings | Control Panel | Administrative Tools | Microsoft .NET Framework Configuration. Ideally, you won't need to change security policy at all, particularly on the client side. Applying security policy changes to multiple client computers can be quite a challenge.

By default, code that a user executes directly from a local hard drive has unlimited permissions. Code access security becomes more important when one or more parts of the application are downloaded dynamically from a less-trusted source, such as the Internet. Chapter 15 tackles this issue in detail and shows how you can display the evidence for an assembly and customize security policy when needed.

Security and the Stack Walk

Security policy isn't worth much if there isn't an infrastructure that can enforce it. In .NET, code access security is enforced by the CLR, which uses a *stack walk* technique. The concept is quite simple. In a .NET application, certain actions trigger security checks. These security checks might occur when the program attempts to access a file or display a dialog box using the .NET Framework classes. However, these security checks pertain only to managed code—in unmanaged code, all bets are off. Therefore, to execute any unmanaged code, an assembly needs full permissions.

When a security check is made, the CLR walks the stack to discover all the assemblies involved in the current request. Therefore, if a Windows application (assembly A) calls another component (assembly B), which in turn calls a third component (assembly C), which triggers a security check, the CLR examines the permissions of all three assemblies (as shown in Figure 13-9). If each assembly on the stack has been granted the permission demanded by the security check, the call succeeds. If any assembly has not been granted the demanded permission, the stack walk fails and a security exception is thrown.

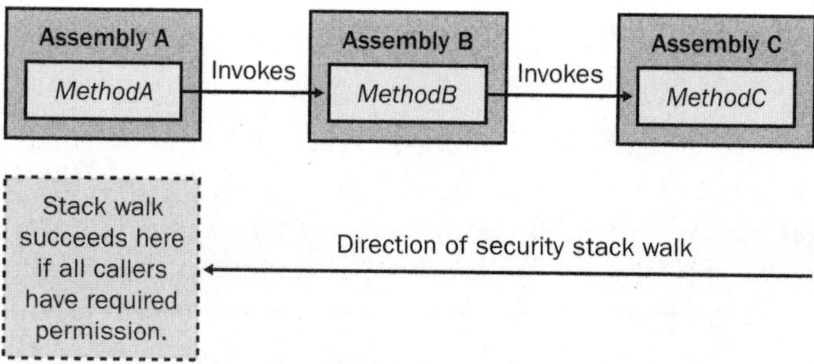

Figure 13-9 A security stack walk

This stack walk process prevents the infamous *luring attack*, in which malicious code tricks more trusted code into doing something it can't do on its own. In other words, an assembly that has limited trust uses an assembly with full trust to perform a nefarious deed. This kind of attack is extremely difficult for developers to guard against without the help of .NET's stack-walking mechanism.

Remember that if you download code and then run it from the local hard drive, it automatically acquires full permissions (unless another rule, such as one that acts based on assembly signature, prevents it). The CLR has no way to know how the code was installed. On the other hand, if you launch the same code from the remote site, increased restrictions come into play. Chapter 15 explores this topic in more detail.

> **Note** Remember that code access security acts in addition to other levels of security. If a user attempts to access a file that is restricted based on the user account, for example, the program won't be able to read the file, regardless of the code access security level. If code access security restricts a given application from accessing the file system, however, the user won't be able to read any file, even one that could be accessed directly using Windows Explorer or another program.

Security Demands

You can trigger a stack walk manually using a security demand. This doesn't necessarily tighten the security for your application or component, but it can save time and simplify error handling. Suppose, for example, that you have a component that requires file access, which is used by another application that doesn't have this permission. If you don't use a security demand, a *SecurityException* will occur when your component attempts to access the file system. You need to specifically catch this exception to distinguish it from other possible problems. Depending on the design of your component, you might need to add this exception-handling code to several methods.

If, on the other hand, you *demand* file access permission in the constructor for your class, a *SecurityException* will be thrown immediately when the client attempts to create the class. This prevents the class from being created and subsequently placed in an invalid state after an operation fails. It also simplifies your exception-handling code and identifies the problem immediately.

You can use security demands in two ways. You can add an imperative security demand at any point in your code by using the appropriate permission class (which always derives from *System.Security.CodeAccessPermission*). Here's a list of permission objects that are a part of the .NET class library:

```
System.Data.Common.DBDataPermission
System.Drawing.Printing.PrintingPermission
System.Messaging.MessageQueuePermission
System.Net.DnsPermission
System.Net.SocketPermission
System.Net.WebPermission
System.Security.Permissions.EnvironmentPermission
```

```
System.Security.Permissions.FileDialogPermission
System.Security.Permissions.FileIOPermission
System.Security.Permissions.IsolatedStoragePermission
System.Security.Permissions.PublisherIdentityPermission
System.Security.Permissions.ReflectionPermission
System.Security.Permissions.RegistryPermission
System.Security.Permissions.ResourcePermissionBase
System.Security.Permissions.SecurityPermission
System.Security.Permissions.SiteIdentityPermission
System.Security.Permissions.StrongNameIdentityPermission
System.Security.Permissions.UIPermission
System.Security.Permissions.UrlIdentityPermission
System.Security.Permissions.ZoneIdentityPermission
```

Listing 13-32 shows how you use an imperative security check to demand a file access permission in a class constructor.

```
Public Sub New(ByVal path as string)

    ' Check for permissions on the specified file.
    Dim Permission As New FileIOPermission( _
      FileIOPermissionAccess.Read, path)

    ' Force a stack walk.
    Permission.Demand()

    ' (Other code omitted.)

End Sub
```

Listing 13-32 An imperative security demand

Declarative demands work similarly but allow neater coding. For every permission class, a corresponding attribute class derives from *System.Security.Permissions.SecurityAttribute*. You use the attribute to mark a method. When the method is invoked (but before any code is executed), the security walk is performed. Listing 13-33 shows an example.

```
<FileIOPermissionAttribute(SecurityAction.RequestMinimum, _
 All := "C:\ ")> _
Public Sub New(ByVal path as string)

    ' (Other code omitted.)

End Sub
```

Listing 13-33 A declarative security demand

Security attributes enable you to separate a code access security demand from the business logic in your code. However, you can't use this technique if you need to evaluate certain conditions and then decide whether to perform a demand or if you want to perform a demand with variable information.

You also can apply a declarative security demand to a class or an assembly, in which case it executes when the class is created or the assembly is accessed.

Security *Assert*, *Deny*, and *PermitOnly*

Code access security also enables you to *assert* permissions to stop a stack walk. By default, a stack walk continues until all assemblies on the stack have been verified. If the stack walk discovers a method that explicitly asserts the permission, however, the CLR stops checking and decides that the security requirement has been met. Therefore, an assertion could allow a less-trusted piece of code to use a more fully trusted assembly to perform an action such as writing to a file. It's the responsibility of the asserting component to ensure that this capability can't be exploited for the wrong purposes.

For example, you might create a component that writes a small amount of information to a predetermined file. To use your class, an assembly will need full file I/O permissions. By using a security assertion, however, you can allow your code to perform its work, regardless of the caller. Of course, there's a darker side to security assertions as well. They make it easy to create code that's susceptible to a luring attack. Quite simply, it is hard to anticipate the ways that a permission could be used maliciously. For example, code might write a large amount of data using your component and fill up the hard drive. Alternatively, if you allow the calling code to specify the filename, the component could be tricked into overwriting a valuable system file.

You can assert permissions imperatively by creating a permission object and using the *Assert* method, or you can assert them declaratively, as shown in Listing 13-34.

```
<FileIOPermission(SecurityAction.Assert, All := "C:\")> _
Public Sub LogData()

    ' If this assembly is permitted to access C:\, this method
    ' will always succeed, even if the caller has insufficient
    ' privileges.

    ' (Code omitted.)

End Sub
```

Listing 13-34 A declarative security assertion

Finally, .NET provides support for revoking permissions. An assembly can use this capability to prevent the other methods it calls from performing certain operations. Listing 13-35 presents an example.

```
' Create a permission set that represents read access to the TEMP
' environment variable and write access to files in C:\

Dim Permissions As New PermissionSet(PermissionState.None)
Permissions.AddPermission( _
  New EnvironmentPermission(EnvironmentPermissionAccess.Read, "TEMP"))

Permissions.AddPermission( _
  New FileIOPermission(FileIOPermissionAccess.Write, "C:\"))

' Deny this permissions from the current stack frame.
Permissions.Deny()

' If the MyComponent.DoSomething() attempts to read a file or
' environment variables that we have denied, a SecurityException will
' occur.
MyComponent.DoSomething()
```

Listing 13-35 Denying access to multiple permissions through a *PermissionSet*

One exception applies to the preceding rule. If you call a method that asserts a required security permission, the action will succeed even if the caller has been denied the permission. This is because the stack walk will never make it to the caller's method, and therefore the denial will never come into effect (as shown in Figure 13-10). Thus, security denials are, on their own, an insufficient way of restricting the permissions of a trusted assembly.

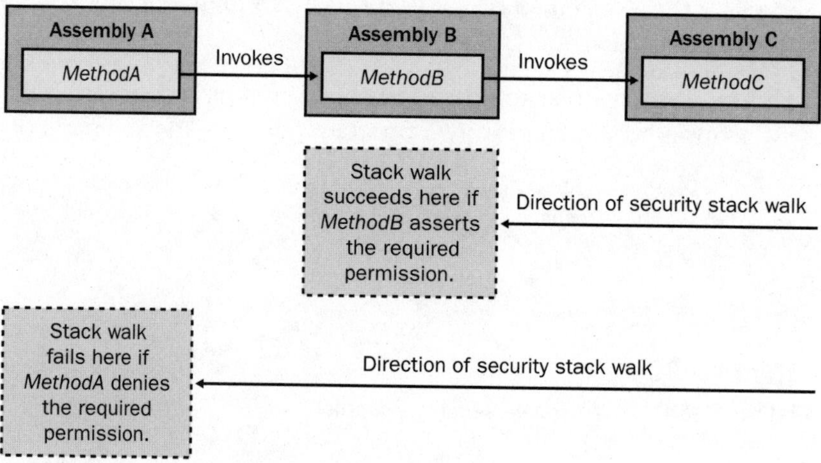

Figure 13-10 Security assertions and denials

Finally, you can use the *PermitOnly* method to revoke all privileges except those you identify specifically. Keep in mind that these permissions are revoked only for the current call. When the stack is cleared and a new method is executed, the permissions will be present and active. If you want to deny a permission for all methods in a class, you can apply a permission attribute to the class declaration.

> **Note** The .NET code access security framework is a rich and extensible model. For more information about how it works and the advanced techniques you can use with it, you can refer to the excellent book *Visual Basic .NET Code Access Security Handbook* (Lippert) from Wrox.

Summary

Security is an enormous topic, and many books are devoted exclusively to explaining cryptography standards and concepts. This chapter considered the fundamentals of integrating security into your distributed applications. It began with an overview of custom and Windows-based authentication and considered the common ticket system design pattern. For an example of custom authentication in action, you can refer to the case study in Chapter 18.

This chapter also explored encryption and how you can protect sensitive data over the wire with SSL or the .NET cryptography classes. Clearly, the heavy lifting required with custom encryption code means it isn't for everyone. In fact, it's dangerously close to so-called infrastructure programming, which can detract from the design of more important business-specific parts of your application. You can rest assured that the security tasks you've learned about in this chapter will become more automated as XML Web services evolve and Microsoft builds new features into future .NET releases.

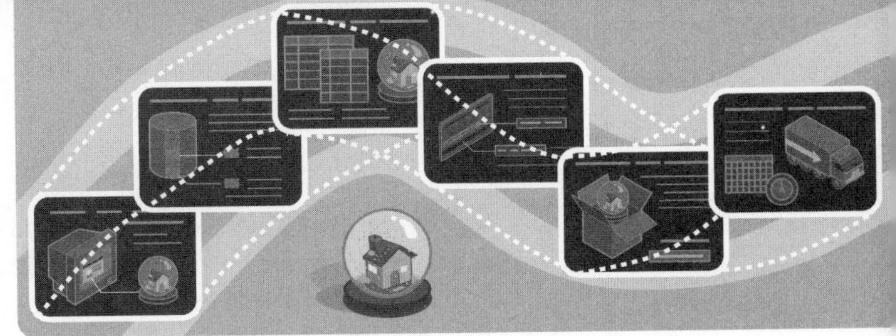

14

Monitoring, Logging, and Profiling

No matter how well you design your system, separate its components, and simplify your architecture, a distributed application is always complicated. As a consequence, when a distributed application fails, it can be difficult to track down not only the cause of the problem but also the component where the error occurred. This is a problem for any large system, but it is particularly painful with distributed systems, where components can be spread across multiple machines, sites, and geographic locations. To manage this difficulty, you need to create a reliable logging infrastructure. Fortunately, the rich class library of the Microsoft .NET Framework makes it easy. This is the topic we'll consider in the first part of this chapter, with both server-side and client-side logging.

Of course, logging isn't just a way to identify errors and their possible causes—it's also a way to record diagnostic information about an application, its usage patterns, and its performance. In this sense, logging is just one way to instrument, or profile, an application. This is the other focus of this chapter: applying the delicate science of profiling. In most cases, this means using and understanding Windows performance counters to help you gauge the performance (and changes in performance) of an application. We'll tackle that topic at the end of this chapter.

Server-Side Logging

The most important place for logging in your application is on the server side, where your remote components execute. The reasons for this include the following:

- The server-side objects perform the majority of the work, including manipulating data and accessing the database. By the time a database error is propagated to the client, it has probably been rethrown as a more generic exception, which hides sensitive details about the internal system of your application. Logging this generic information might not be enough to enable you to diagnose the original problem.
- The server-side objects can track the actions of all clients, which is useful when you are auditing the overall use of a system or searching for suspicious behavior.
- Client-side logs are difficult to retrieve. A client can use a central log through some type of central component (like an XML Web service), but this adds complexity and further possibilities for error.

> **Note** Generally, client-side logging is the best way to identify problems in the client software or connection difficulties. It's a valuable feature but not a replacement for server-side logging. Client-side logging is discussed later in this chapter.

You need to make two decisions when implementing server-side logging: where to log the information and where to add the logging code. .NET provides numerous possibilities, each with its own benefits and drawbacks. Table 14-1 outlines some of your choices.

Table 14-1 Server-Side Logging Approaches in .NET

Logging Approach	Description
Windows event log	A simple, low-overhead way to store error-related information that might be reviewed by an administrator at a later date. The chief drawback is that information is tied to a specific computer and is short-term. You can't assume that it will be reviewed before it expires.
Direct database	Best when the information being collected is more historical than error-related and demands later analysis rather than immediate action. For example, you can store security audit information. The chief drawback is that it requires more resources than some other event logging approaches.

Table 14-1 Server-Side Logging Approaches in .NET *(continued)*

Logging Approach	Description
Message Queuing	Sends error information to a message queue so that it can be retrieved and processed by another component. This approach enables you to use custom classes with logging information. However, it is suitable only if you design an automated utility to read the queue and designate how to further handle the error (for instance, send it to a database or trigger an administrator alert).
Direct mail	Sends an e-mail message with error information to an administrator. Useful for immediate alerts but tends to couple the error logging code with a specific error response strategy. Should be reserved for serious errors because it can easily lead to e-mail clutter (and disregarded messages).

Windows event logging and direct mailing haven't yet been addressed in this book; they are discussed a little later in this chapter.

ADO.NET database interaction and Message Queuing are easy to implement using the information covered in the first part of the book. The Message Queuing approach is particularly interesting and extremely flexible. Although it adds complexity, it enables you to completely separate your error logging code from your error response strategy. The remainder of this section outlines a sample approach you can use with Message Queuing.

First, you define a custom error object that contains information about problems. Listing 14-1 shows an example.

```
' This enumeration represents how a component chooses to react
' to an error.
<Serializable()>_
Public Enum ErrorAction
    Unknown
    RecoveredFull
    RecoveredPartial
    Ignored
    RaisedToClient
End Enum

' This is the class that will be send to the message queue.
<Serializable()> _
Public Class LoggedError

    ' This contains the original (caught) exception.
    Public OriginalException As Exception
```

Listing 14-1 A serializable *LoggedError* class

```
    ' This indicates the name of the component and procedure
    ' where the error occurred.
    Public FailedComponent As String
    Public FailedProcedure As String
    Public FailedComponentVersion As String

    ' A severity level is assigned as an integer from 0 to 10.
    Public SeverityLevel As Integer

    Public ActionTaken As ErrorAction

End Class
```

An exception handler in your component catches an error. It then creates an instance of the error object and calls a helper method to deal with it (as shown in Listing 14-2).

```
Try
    ' (Attempt action here.)

Catch Err As Exception

    Dim LogItem As New LoggedError()
    LogItem.OriginalException = Err

    ' (Other property set statements omitted.)

    ' Log the error. In this case, LogComponent is a member variable
    ' that references an instance of the EventLogger class shown in the
    ' next code listing.
    LogComponent.LogError(LogItem)

    ' (Handle the error accordingly.)

End Try
```

Listing 14-2 Logging the error through a facade

The *LogComponent* object is an instance of the *EventLogger* class shown in Listing 14-3, which sends the error information to a message queue.

```
Public Class EventLogger

    Private Queue As New MessageQueue("MyDomain/MyLogQueue")

    Public Sub LogError(ByVal logItem As LoggedError)
        Dim ErrMessage As New Message(LogItem)
```

Listing 14-3 Sending the error information to a message queue

```
        Queue.Send(LogItem, "Error")
    End Sub

    ' (Other methods could be added to log informational messages
    ' differently from errors or warning, or to change the current
    ' queue.)

End Class
```

Finally, a dedicated listener application receives the error message, examines it, and then decides how to act on it. Figure 14-1 shows the full approach.

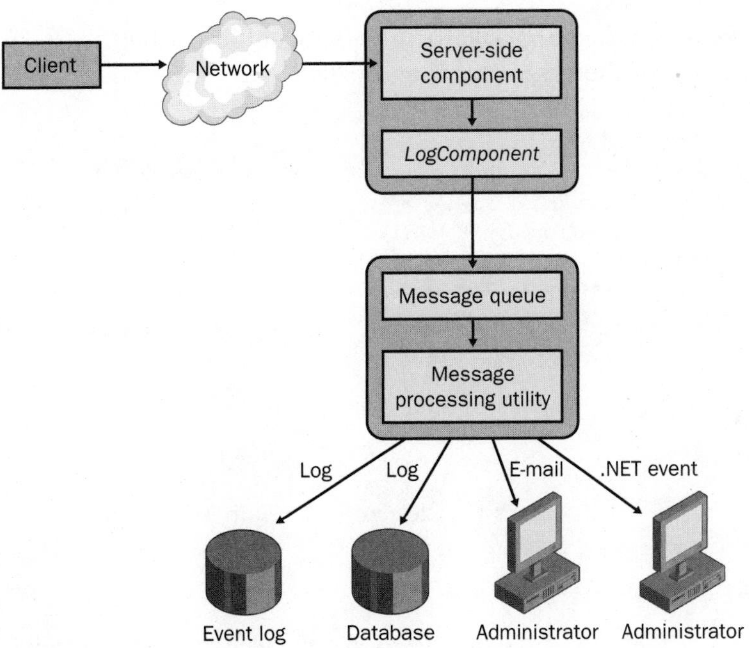

Figure 14-1 Using message queuing to handle error logging

Logging with Facades and Reflection

The Message Queuing example is shows the basic pattern you should follow when adding logging. As much as possible, the code that performs the logging should be isolated from the code that handles the exception. This basic pattern enables you to quickly replace your logging strategies without touching the business code. For example, Listing 14-2 works with any class that exposes a *LogError* method. If you modify the *LogComponent* variable so that it contains an instance of a *DatabaseLogger* class, the application can continue to function seamlessly. This is nothing new—in fact, it's a straightforward implementation of the facade pattern introduced in Chapter 10.

To improve on this approach, you can formalize the arrangement by defining an *ILogger* interface, which might look something like this:

```
Public Interface ILogger

    Sub LogError(logItem As LoggedError)
    Sub LogWarning(logItem As LoggedWarning)
    Sub LogInformation(logItem As LoggedInfo)

End Interface
```

Every logging class will then implement this interface:

```
Public Class EventLogger
    Implements ILogger

    Private Queue As New MessageQueue("MyDomain/MyLogQueue")

    Public Sub LogError(ByVal logItem As LoggedError) _
      Implements ILogger.LogError
        Dim ErrMessage As New Message(LogItem)
        Queue.Send(LogItem, "Error")
    End Sub

    ' (Remainder of implementation code omitted.)

End Class
```

Finally, the business facade can just retain *LogComponent* as an *ILogger* variable:

```
Private LogComponent As ILogger
```

It can then use some initialization code at startup to determine which type of logging to implement. To implement this code, you might use a value in a database or you might use a setting in an application configuration file.

Listing 14-4 shows a constructor for the business facade that retrieves the name of the logging component class and the assembly it is contained in using the application configuration file. Keep in mind that the assembly of the logger component is probably not the same assembly as the one that contains the facade. You can deal with this reality using .NET reflection, which enables you to programmatically load a class from an external assembly using only the filename and class name.

```
Public Sub New()

    ' Retrieve the name of the logger assembly.
    ' This is a full path like "s:\MyAssemblies\Loggers\EventLog.dll"
    Dim File As String
    File = ConfigurationSettings.AppSettings("AssemblyFile")

    ' Retrieve the name of the logger class.
    ' This is a fully qualified name like "Loggers.EventLogger"
    Dim Class As String
    Class = ConfigurationSettings.AppSettings("LogClass")

    ' Load the assembly.
    Dim LoggerAssembly As Sytem.Reflection.Assembly
    LoggerAssembly = System.Reflection.Assembly.LoadFrom(File)

    ' Create an instance of the logger.
    LogComponent = CType(LoggerAssembly.CreateInstance(Class), ILogger)

End Sub
```

Listing 14-4 Instantiating a logger dynamically

For a much closer look at reflection, refer to Chapter 15, where it's used as the basis for a self-updating application and dynamic application browser. For now, note that reflection can come in handy in your exception handling code to determine information about the executing assembly (as shown in Listing 14-5). This way, when you review the logged message later, you'll know exactly which version of the application failed.

```
Try
    ' (Attempt action here.)

Catch Err As Exception

    Dim LogItem As New LoggedError()
    LogItem.OriginalException = Err

    ' Set some properties obtained through reflection.
    Dim CurrentAssembly As Sytem.Reflection.Assembly
    CurrentAssembly = Sytem.Reflection.Assembly.GetExecutingAssembly()
    LogItem.FailedComponentVersion = CurrentAssembly.GetName().Version
    LogItem.FailedComponent = CurrentAssembly.GetName().Name

    ' (Other property set statements omitted.)
```

Listing 14-5 Using reflection to retrieve version information

```
    ' Log the error.
    LogComponent.LogError(LogItem)

    ' (Handle the error accordingly.)

End Try
```

You now know the types of details you need to consider—details that have less to do with .NET technology than they do with the overall design of your logging framework. The next few sections consider how to actually implement the code that goes into an *ILogger* class such as *EventLogger*.

The Windows Event Log

The Windows event log is a repository for information and error-related system and application messages. It provides its own basic management features (for example, a size limit that ensures it won't grow too large) and can be easily examined using the graphical Event Viewer utility included with Windows. The Windows event log offers a number of advantages:

- **Simplicity** Even in the case of a database or system error, attempts to write log messages will probably still succeed. Unlike with simple file logging, concurrency problems won't occur. And because event logs are wrapped with easy-to-use .NET classes, there's little chance that a syntax error in your code will derail an important log message.
- **Standardization** The event log is a basic part of the Windows operating system. You don't need to specifically configure a computer if you relocate your remote components; you can always assume that the event log will work.
- **Remote use** The Windows event log is often criticized because it is machine-specific. Although this is true, you can programmatically log messages to another computer (or retrieve them in the same way)—a requirement in any distributed system.

The Windows event log often has some nontrivial limitations as well, including these:

- **No object support** Log messages are little more than simple strings. You can append binary data, but you need to manipulate it manually. This differs sharply from Message Queuing, which enables you to send custom objects. The lack of object support might not be a disadvantage if an administrator is reviewing the log, but it prevents you from creating an automated utility that scans and interprets log messages.

- **Size restrictions** By default, log entries are automatically overwritten when the maximum log size is reached (typically half a megabyte), as long as these entries are of at least a certain age (typically seven days). This means that application logs can't be easily used to log critical information that you need to retain for a long period of time.
- **Little customizability** You can create a custom log to store your messages. You also can assign an application-defined category number to your messages. However, that is the extent of the event log's customizability. There are no other ways to group or distinguish messages.
- **Location dependency** Log messages are tightly bound to a specific computer. If you have several servers in a Web farm or if you migrate your remote components from one computer to another, you might end up with messages scattered everywhere.

In short, the event log is an ideal place to log short-term information with a minimum of fuss. It's not a suitable location for the long-term storage of auditing or profiling information.

To view the event log on the current computer, select Event Viewer from the Administrative Tools section of Control Panel. By default, you'll see the three standard event logs on the current computer, as described in Table 14-2.

Table 14-2 Standard Event Logs

Log	Description
Application	Used to track errors or warnings from any application. Generally, you will use this log or create your own custom log.
Security	Used to track security-related problems. For the most part, this log is used exclusively by the operating system.
System	Used to track operating system events.

To connect to the event logs on a different computer, right-click on the Event Viewer item at the top of the tree and choose Connect To Another Computer (as shown in Figure 14-2).

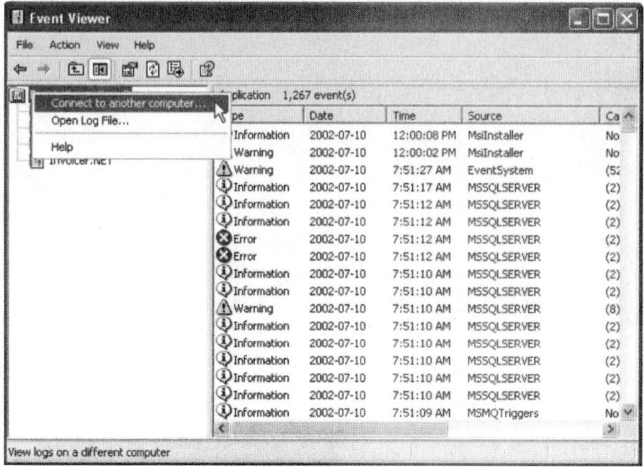

Figure 14-2 The Event Viewer

You also can right-click on one of the logs in the Event Viewer and choose Properties to modify its maximum size and overwrite settings, or you can create a new custom log. Figure 14-3 shows the properties of the Application event log.

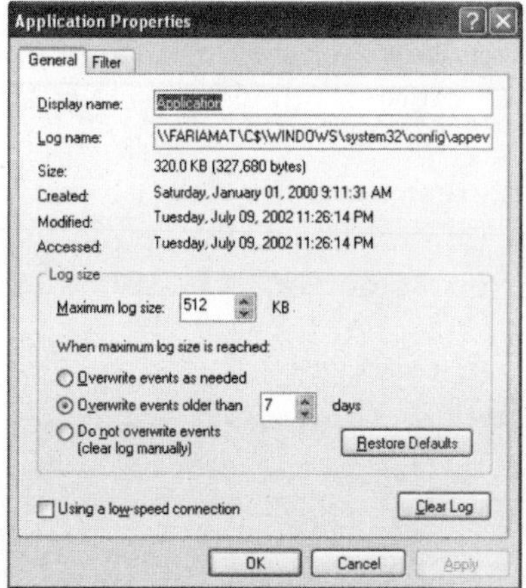

Figure 14-3 Event log properties

To get an idea about what type of information is stored in the log, you might want to look at an average log entry that's been left by another application. You'll find that messages are generally classified as warnings, errors, or notifications. They include time and date information, along with the name of the application or component that entered the event and a full message.

Writing Log Entries

You can interact with event logs using the classes in the *System.Diagnostics* namespace. The *EventLog* class represents an individual log, and it's this class that you need to work with to retrieve and write log entries.

The event log doesn't permit indiscriminate writing. Before you can add a message to a log, you need to register your application as an event-writing source for that log. (Technically, you don't register your application—just a string that identifies it.) You can perform this task manually using the *EventLog.CreateEventSource* method, or you can coax .NET into doing the work for you by setting the *EventLog.Source* property before you attempt to write a message. If you neglect to perform one of these steps, an error will occur.

Listing 14-6 shows the .NET code required to write an error message to the Application log.

```
' Create a reference to the application log.
Dim Log As New EventLog()

' Define an event source. If it is not registered, .NET will register
' it automatically when you write the log entry.
Log.Source = "MyComponent"

' Write the entry.
Log.WriteEntry("This is an error message", EventLogEntryType.Error)
```

Listing 14-6 Windows event logging

Figure 14-4 shows the corresponding item as viewed in the Event Viewer, and Figure 14-5 shows the actual error message content.

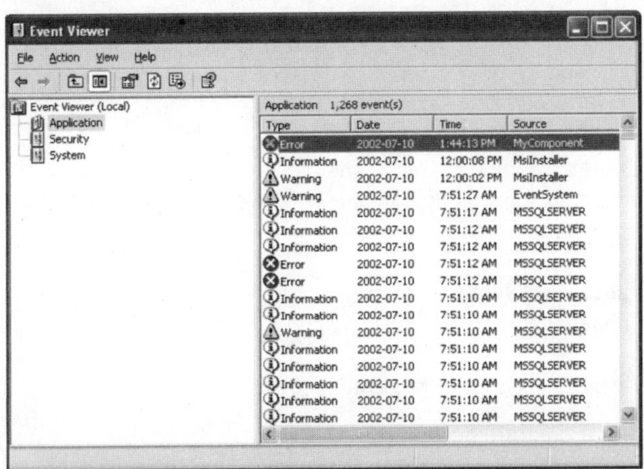

Figure 14-4 The updated error listing

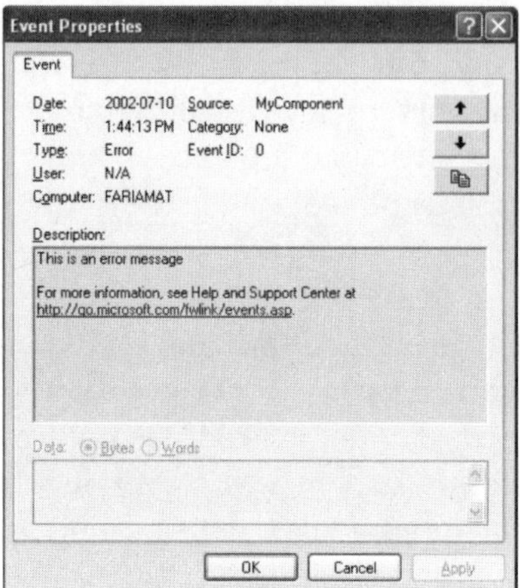

Figure 14-5 The error message

Note that when you create an *EventLog* object without specifying the log you want to use, the Application log on the current computer is used by default. You can change this logic by using a different *EventLog* constructor, as shown here:

```
' Create a reference to the Security log.
Dim SecurityLog As New EventLog("SecurityLog")

' Create a reference to the Application log on a computer
' named MyServer.
Dim RemoteLog As New EventLog("Application", "MyServer")
```

You can even create your own log using the shared *EventLog.CreateEventSource* method. This is a useful way to separate your messages from the clutter of entries added by other applications (as shown in Listing 14-7).

```
' Create the log (and register the event source) if the log does not
' already exist.
If Not EventLog.Exists("MyCustomLog") Then
    EventLog.CreateEventSource("MyComponent", "MyCustomLog")
End If

Dim Log As New EventLog("MyCustomLog")
Log.Source = "MyComponent"

Log.WriteEntry("This is an error message", EventLogEntryType.Error)
```

Listing 14-7 Creating a custom log

When writing a log entry, you have the choice of 10 overloaded versions of the *WriteEntry* method. You can choose to supply an event ID (a number you use to identify the event), a category number (a number you use to group messages), and an array of bytes. The *EventLogEntryType* enables you to indicate how the Event Viewer should classify the entry, according to the values shown in Table 14-3.

Table 14-3 *EventLogEntryType* Values

Value	Description
Information	Logs a non-error condition. The Microsoft recommendation is to use this for "an infrequent but significant successful operation." For example, you might use it to demarcate when a long-running system service starts. However, don't use this for a common occurrence; otherwise, you will quickly exhaust the available space in the event log.
Warning	Indicates a problem that isn't immediately significant (and doesn't result in an exception) but that might cause future complications. Many warning messages deal with resource consumption (for example, when disk space is low). If the application can't recover from the event without loss of functionality or data, it should use an *Error* event instead.
Error	Indicates a significant problem that results in the loss of functionality or data (for example, if a service can't be loaded or can't access a database).
SuccessAudit	A security event that occurs when some sort of security check succeeds (for example, a successful user login).
FailureAudit	A security event that occurs when a security check fails (for example, when a user login attempt fails). Failure audits are important because they can show suspicious patterns that indicate when the system's security has been compromised or when an intrusion has been attempted.

Note Unless you want the responsibility of creating a byte array (and, if needed later, translating it back to its original form), the event log limits you to an ordinary string of human-readable information. If you're logging an error, you can use the *Exception.ToString* method. The *ToString* method returns a string with the name of the class that threw the exception, the exception message, and the stack trace. The return string also includes the result of calling *ToString* on the inner exception.

Retrieving Log Entries

When you create an application that uses a Windows event log, you also create a requirement for someone (generally a system administrator) to review that information. That person can perform this task using the Event Viewer, but the task can be complicated if the log is on another computer that doesn't allow remote access. In this case, you might need to create a remote component or XML Web service that exposes methods that allow authenticated users to retrieve log information. This service can retrieve the log information using the classes in the *System.Diagnostics* namespace.

Consider the Web method shown in Listing 14-8, which uses the *EventLog.Entries* property. This collection represents all the entries added to an event log. The Web method converts this information into a *DataTable*, which can easily be sent to the client and displayed using data binding.

```
<WebMethod()> _
Public Function RetrieveLog(ByVal logName As String) As DataSet

    Dim Log As New EventLog(logName)

    ' Create a table to store the event information.
    Dim dt As New DataTable()
    dt.Columns.Add("EntryType", GetType(System.String))
    dt.Columns.Add("Message", GetType(System.String))
    dt.Columns.Add("Time", GetType(System.DateTime))

    Dim Entry As EventLogEntry
    For Each Entry In Log.Entries

        ' Add this entry to the table.
        Dim dr As DataRow = dt.NewRow()
        dr("EntryType") = Entry.EntryType.ToString()
        dr("Message") = Entry.Message
        dr("Time") = Entry.TimeGenerated
        dt.Rows.Add(dr)

    Next

    ' The DataTable is not a valid XML Web service return type.
    ' Thus, you must add it to a DataSet before returning it.
    Dim ds As New DataSet()
    ds.Tables.Add(dt)

    Return ds

End Function
```

Listing 14-8 Returning log information

The client requires a mere two lines to display this information using a *DataGrid* control:

```
Dim Proxy As New localhost.MyService()
DataGrid1.DataSource = Proxy.RetrieveLog("Application").Tables(0)
```

Figure 14-6 shows the retrieved data.

Log Entries

EntryType	Message	Time
Error	The message '-1073724769' for application 'MSSQLSERVER' could n	2002-07-29
Error	The message '-1073724769' for application 'MSSQLSERVER' could n	2002-07-29
Information	The message '-1073724769' for application 'MSSQLSERVER' could n	2002-07-29
Information	The message '-1073724769' for application 'MSSQLSERVER' could n	2002-07-29
Information	The message '-1073724769' for application 'MSSQLSERVER' could n	2002-07-29
Information	The Search service has started.	2002-07-29
Information	The Message Queuing service started.	2002-07-29
Warning	The COM+ Event System failed to fire the ConnectionMade method	2002-07-29
Information	Message Queuing Triggers started successfully.	2002-07-29
Warning	The COM+ Event System failed to fire the StartShell method on subs	2002-07-29
Warning	Windows saved user FARIAMAT\Faria registry while an application o	2002-07-29
Information	Windows unloaded user FARIAMAT\Faria registry when it received a	2002-07-29
Error	Faulting application wmplayer.exe, version 8.0.0.4477, faulting mod	2002-07-30
Error	Faulting application explorer.exe, version 6.0.2600.0, faulting modul	2002-07-30
Information	The shell stopped unexpectedly and Explorer.exe was restarted.	2002-07-30
Error	Faulting application explorer.exe, version 6.0.2600.0, faulting modul	2002-07-30
Error	Faulting application wmplayer.exe, version 8.0.0.4477, faulting mod	2002-07-30
Information	The shell stopped unexpectedly and Explorer.exe was restarted.	2002-07-30
Error	Faulting application explorer.exe, version 6.0.2600.0, faulting modul	2002-07-30

Figure 14-6 The retrieved log information

Handling Log Events

The *EventLog* class also provides an *EntryWritten* event that enables you to respond when a new entry is added to a log. Using this technique, you can design a utility that waits for events and then attracts the administrator's attention by displaying a message box or playing a sound.

Before using the *EntryWritten* event, familiarize yourself with a few details:

- To receive an event notification, you must set the *EventLog.EnableRaisingEvents* property to *True*.
- Sadly, you can receive event notifications only when entries are written on the local computer. You can't receive notifications for entries written on remote computers, even if you create an *EventLog* object to represent such a log.

- The *EntryWritten* event fires only a maximum of once every 5 seconds, even if log messages are written more frequently.
- If you want to handle the *EntryWritten* event, make sure that you're using a custom log. Otherwise, the event is triggered when other applications add unrelated messages to the same log.

Handling the *EntryWritten* event is as straightforward as any other .NET event. You just connect the event handler (after creating a valid *EventLog* object):

```
Dim Log As New EventLog("MyCustomLog")
Log.Source = "MyComponent"

AddHandler Log.EntryWritten, AddressOf OnEntryWritten
Log.EnableRaisingEvents = True
```

Then you handle the event:

```
Private Sub OnEntryWritten(ByVal sender as System.Object, _
  ByVal e as System.Diagnostics.EventLogEvent)

    ' You can check what source sent the message, if desired.
    If e.Entry.Source = "MyComponent" Then

        MessageBox.Show("Entry written with message: " & _
                        e.Entry.Message)

    End If

End Sub
```

Direct Mail Notification

You can also send e-mail from a .NET application without needing to do much more than create a single object. The only catch is that to use this e-mail capability, you must have a properly configured SMTP server to send the message. (You can configure settings for the SMTP server using IIS manager.) If you don't, you won't be informed of an error and the message will never be received. For more information, refer to Microsoft's excellent introduction to Internet e-mail and mail servers at *http://www.microsoft.com/TechNet/prodtechnol/iis/deploy/config/mail.asp*.

The .NET e-mail features are found in the *System.Web.Mail* namespace. The key classes include *MailMessage* (which represents a single e-mail message), *SmtpMail* (which exposes shared methods you can use to send a message), and *MailAttachment* (which represents a file attachment that you can link to a message).

Sending a message is as simple as creating a new *MailMessage* object; setting some properties to identify the recipient, the priority, the subject, and the message itself; and using the *SmtpMail.Send* method to send it on its way (as shown in Listing 14-9).

```
Dim MyMessage As New MailMessage()
MyMessage.To = "someone@somewhere.com"
MyMessage.From = "Automatic Logger"
MyMessage.Subject = "Error"
MyMessage.Priority = MailPriority.High
MyMessage.Body = "Critical error: " & _
                 LoggedError.OriginalException.ToString()

SmtpMail.SmtpServer = "localhost"
SmtpMail.Send(MyMessage)
```

Listing 14-9 Sending an error e-mail

Client-Side Logging

Client-side logging rarely uses techniques such as Windows event logging, e-mailing, or Message Queuing. The reasons are simple: the client, after it has been deployed, is difficult to update or reconfigure. And furthermore, the client machine isn't guaranteed to provide the necessary ingredients (such as a properly configured Message Queuing service or an SMTP server for mail delivery). Even if it did, there would be no way report network or connection problems if they interfere with these services.

Another, more fundamental, distinction between client and server errors is the fact that server errors represent shortcomings in your code. Client-side errors can also fall prey to coding errors, but they are more likely to result from misconfiguration or connectivity problems. The last thing you want is to clutter your log with hundreds of trivial client events that might be successfully resolved without your intervention.

Generally, client logging takes one of two forms (as described in Table 14-4). If you want to be informed of a particularly significant error that doesn't relate to connectivity issues, you might add an XML Web service that the client can call when the error occurs. The Web method can then log the information, send an e-mail message, or perform whatever additional processing is needed. Of course, this raises the possibility that a user might discover this method and call it for malicious reasons (if it isn't safeguarded with the appropriate authentication code).

Table 14-4 Client-Side Logging Approaches in .NET

Logging Approach	Description
Remote object	Allows clients to report a serious error to the server. The remote component can then decide how to further deal with this information (for example, place it in durable storage such as a database or notify an administrator). This approach isn't commonly used for server-side logging due to the increased overhead and sensitivity to error.
File	Best used to log client-side information (problems with the client-side software or with a connection). Can't be effectively used on the server side due to concurrency/locking problems.

A more common approach is to use the logging features built into .NET. These logging features can be easily enabled, disabled, and further configured through switches. Therefore, in its standard configuration, .NET might ignore the logging code. If a mysterious error develops at the client site, however, the client can instruct the program to log all its actions by changing a simple configuration file setting and e-mail the resulting file to the technical support department. To implement this approach, you must understand .NET tracing and trace switches.

Using Tracing

.NET provides a *Trace* class in the *System.Diagnostics* namespace. The *Trace* class is quite similar to the *Debug* class, which you might have used to write messages to the Output window in Visual Studio .NET while testing an application. The key difference is that the *Debug* class is intended for writing messages that are useful purely in a testing environment. These messages are therefore disabled in the release version of an assembly. Tracing, however, is used to record information that might be useful in the field for instrumentation or diagnostic purposes. For that reason, tracing is enabled by default in the release version of an assembly.

> **Note** Technically, tracing is enabled in the release version when you compile with Visual Studio .NET. This is because Visual Studio .NET automatically adds the */d:Trace=True* switch to the compiler command line. If you're compiling the code manually, you need to add this switch. (Similarly, you can disable it in a Visual Studio .NET project by finding the appropriate section in the project's Properties window and removing the trace switch.)

The *Trace* class provides two important shared methods: *Write* and *WriteLine*. (*WriteLine* is the same as *Write*, but it adds a trailing line break.) The first parameter to the *Write* or *WriteLine* method can be a string containing a message or it can be an object. If it is an object, .NET just calls the object's *ToString* method to arrive at the appropriate trace message. Optionally, you can add a second parameter, which is a category name. The category name is just added to the beginning of the message, followed by a colon (:). It isn't used to determine sorting.

Consider the following code statement:

```
Trace.WriteLine("This is my message", "Category")
```

It produces this output with the default trace listener:

```
Category: This is my message
```

If you add this code to a new .NET application, the message appears in the Debug view of the Output window (as shown in Figure 14-7).

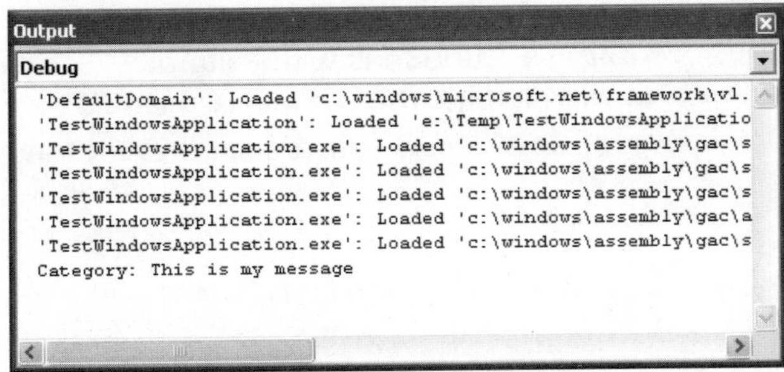

Figure 14-7 Viewing trace information in the Output window

At run time, you won't see anything. However, tracing is still enabled. If you attach the Visual Studio .NET debugger to your application, any subsequent messages appear in the Output window. This technique was demonstrated in Chapter 7 with Windows service debugging.

You also can use trace assertions, which check a condition and only display a message if the result is *False*. Essentially, with a trace assertion you're claiming that a given condition should always hold true. If it doesn't, you want to log this failure.

```
Trace.Assert(Balance >= 0, "Somehow the balance became negative.")
```

Trace assertions don't take the place of the validation code you need to verify user input. Instead, trace assertions are meant to test assumptions in your code that will always hold true unless there is a coding error.

Trace Listeners

Most clients won't be able to attach a debugger just to view a trace message. Fortunately, the *Trace* class can send output to any valid class derived from *System.Diagnostics.TraceListener*. In .NET, there are only three such classes (although it's trivially easy to develop your own): *DefaultTraceListener*, *TextWriterTraceListener*, and *EventLogTraceListener*. The *Trace* class provides a collection of registered listeners through the *Trace.Listeners* property. An instance of the *DefaultTraceListener* class is added automatically, which is why you can see the trace messages appear in the Output window at design time.

If you add an instance of the *EventLogTraceListener*, the trace messages are automatically echoed to an event log, where they are stored permanently:

```
' Define a listener that represents a custom Windows event log.
Dim Listener As New EventLogTraceListener("CustomLog")

' Register the listener so it will receive trace messages.
Trace.Listeners.Add(Listener)
```

Alternatively, you can use the *TextWriterTraceListener* to send trace output to a *TextWriter* or *Stream*. .NET abounds with examples of *Stream*-derived classes, but one of the most relevant for tracing is the *FileStream*. With a *FileStream* and a *TextWriterTraceListener*, you can capture messages in a local file:

```
' Create the log file.
Dim LogFile As FileStream = File.Create("c:\mylogfile.txt")

' Create a new text writer using the output stream,
' and add it to the trace listeners.
Dim FileListener As New TextWriterTraceListener(LogFile)
Trace.Listeners.Add(FileListener)

' Ensure that messages are written to the file immediately.
Trace.AutoFlush = True
```

The last line ensures that messages are written to the file immediately. Otherwise, if you exit the application without calling *Trace.Flush*, *TextWriterTraceListener.Flush*, or *TextWriterTraceListener.Close*, some entries will probably not be written to the file.

When you use a *TextWriterTraceListener*, it's always a good idea to explicitly close the file before the application exits. In a Windows application, you can accomplish this by handling an event such as *Application.ApplicationExit*. In a Windows service, you can respond to the *OnShutdown* or *OnStop* method. Otherwise, the file remains locked open and you can't delete or replace it.

> **Note** By default, both the *Trace* class and the *Debug* class share the same collection of listeners. In other words, the *Trace.Listeners* and *Debug.Listeners* properties both reference the same *TraceListenerCollection*. This means that any messages you write with *Trace.Write* are received by all trace listeners and any messages you write with *Debug.Write* are received by all trace listeners. If this isn't the behavior you want, you must manually create a new *TraceListenerCollection* at startup, assign it to the *Trace.Listeners* property, and then add the appropriate listener objects. Make sure you include an instance of the *DefaultTraceListener* class if you want messages to appear in the Debug window in Visual Studio .NET.

You also can add trace listeners declaratively in the client application's .config file. This gives the user an easy way to specify the filename and enable logging by modifying a simple configuration file setting (as shown in Listing 14-10).

```
<configuration>
<system.diagnostics>

  <trace autoflush="true">
    <listeners>
      <add name="FileListener"
           type="System.Diagnostics.TextWriterTraceListener,System"
           initializeData="c:\mylogfile.txt" />
    </listeners>
  </trace>

</system.diagnostics>
</configuration>
```

Listing 14-10 Adding a listener with the configuration file

Trace Switches

.NET tracing really shines with trace switches. So far, you've learned how to enable and disable tracing en masse. With trace switches, you can separate your trace messages into different categories and allow trace messages for a single category to be enabled or disabled. For example, you might group trace messages for business logic with one switch and group trace messages that indicate remote object invocations with another. The user can then log whichever set of trace messages is relevant to the current problem. You can also use trace switches to configure a variable level of detail for trace messages.

There are two types of tracing switches:

- The *BooleanSwitch*, which represents a group of tracing messages that can be enabled or disabled
- The *TraceSwitch*, which represents a group of tracing messages that display differently depending on the *TraceLevel* (as described in Table 14-5)

Table 14-5 *TraceLevel* Values

Value	Description
Off (0)	Trace messages in this category are disabled.
Error (1)	Only error messages are shown.
Warning (2)	Error messages and warnings are shown.
Info (3)	Error messages and warnings are shown, with additional information.
Verbose (4)	All trace messages are shown, in their most detailed form.

Of course, none of this happens automatically. You need to inspect the properties of the *BooleanSwitch* or *TraceSwitch* class programmatically and then output the appropriate trace messages.

To create a switch, you must first define it in the configuration file. The configuration file names the trace switch and sets its state. The user can therefore modify the configuration file to enable or disable logging or to change its detail level.

In Listing 14-11, two trace switches are defined. One is a *BooleanSwitch*, which is used to enable or disable trace messages related to user interface, and the other is a *TraceSwitch*, which is used to configure the level of standard application-level trace messages.

```
<configuration>
<system.diagnostics>

  <switches>

    <!-- In order to receive user interface related messages, change
         value="0" to value="1" -->
    <add name="UISwitch" value="0" />

    <!-- In order to receive general trace messages, set value to
         something other than 0 (depending on the desired detail
         level) -->
```

Listing 14-11 Defining trace switches

```
    <add name="GeneralSwitch" value="0" />

  </switches>

</system.diagnostics>
</configuration>
```

Now, in your application code you must create an instance of the *BooleanSwitch* class and the *TraceSwitch* class, using the name defined in the configuration file:

```
Private UISwitch As New BooleanSwitch("UISwitch", "User Interface")
Private GeneralSwitch As New TraceSwitch("GeneralSwitch", "General")
```

The only remaining detail is to inspect the *UISwitch* and *GeneralSwitch* and use that information to configure the tracing messages that the application outputs (as shown in Listing 14-12).

```
If UISwitch.Enabled Then
    Trace.WriteLine("User interface loaded", "UI")
End If

' You could also use the equivalent syntax:
' Trace.WriteLineIf(UISwitch.Enabled, "User interface loaded", "UI")


If GeneralSwitch.Level = TraceLevel.Verbose
    Trace.WriteLine("Application started at " & _
      DateTime.Now.ToString(), "General")
End If
' You could also use the equivalent syntax:
' If GeneralSwitch.TraceVerbose
'     ' (Write message here.)
' End If
```

Listing 14-12 Examining trace switches

> **Note** Tracing is not limited to the client side. If you use the *TextWriterTraceListener* with server components, however, you need to take additional steps to ensure that every component writes to a unique file (to prevent locking and concurrency issues). You also need to track all these individual files. Because of the complexity of server-side logging, it's often more useful to design your own generic logger facade, interface (for example, the *ILogger* interface shown earlier), and logging components (for example, *EventLogger*).

Catching Unhandled Errors

.NET provides one interesting feature that's useful in reporting errors that aren't properly handled. A special event, *AppDomain.UnhandledException*, fires if an unhandled exception has occurred, just before the application is terminated. You can handle this event and use it as a last-ditch attempt to log an error.

Here's how you attach an event handler:

```
Dim CurrentDomain As AppDomain = AppDomain.CurrentDomain
AddHandler CurrentDomain.UnhandledException, AddressOf UnhandledError
```

The event handler receives the exception information from the *UnhandledExceptionEventArgs*.

```
Public Sub UnhandledError(sender As Object, _
  e As UnhandledExceptionEventArgs)

    Trace.Write(e.ExceptionObject.ToString(), "Unhandled Error")

End Sub
```

Profiling with Performance Counters

Performance counters—the basic unit of measurement for gauging the performance of your application—were introduced in Chapter 12, when we considered connection pooling. However, a lot more information is available from the performance monitor than the number of open connections, and this information can prove tremendously useful when you're trying to improve an application's performance. Performance counters are particularly useful when you're attempting to identify a bottleneck that's hampering application performance.

To open the Performance window, choose Performance from the Administrative Tools section in Control Panel. By default, you'll see only performance counters for measuring basic information such as the computer's CPU and disk drive use. However, .NET installs much more useful counters for tracking application performance. To add a new counter, right-click on the Counter list, choose Properties, and click on the Data tab. Before continuing, remove all the default counters. You can then click Add to insert some more useful ones (as shown in Figure 14-8).

Note that you can specify a computer name in the Add Counters window. This enables you to monitor the performance of a remote computer without incurring additional overhead that could skew the results.

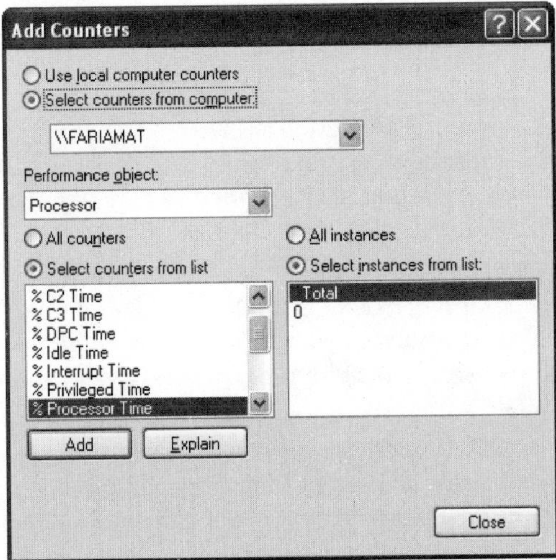

Figure 14-8 Adding performance counters

Essential Performance Counters

On an average computer, dozens of performance counters are available. Examples include data source–specific counters (such as those included with SQL Server), the ten basic .NET performance categories, two ASP.NET categories, and hardware-specific categories that profile memory or CPU usage and disk activity. Clearly, it's not easy to sort out which counters are best for profiling system activity. It can help to refer to the descriptions of some of the most important categories and counters in Table 14-6. You also can refer to the MSDN Help for a full description of every .NET counter.

Table 14-6 Some Valuable Performance Counter Categories

Category	Description
Processor	Studying the % CPU Utilization counter can give you a basic idea of where a bottleneck lies. If your application throughput (requests to server per second) levels off while the CPU utilization is still small (less than 70 percent), a bottleneck exists that isn't related to CPU speed.
.NET CLR Data	Tracks open and pooled connections with the SQL Server data provider. Useful for determining pool usage, in conjunction with any available data source provider counters.
.NET CLR Exceptions	The # of Exceps Thrown counter is a basic measure of health. If it rises unexpectedly, it might indicate that error conditions are being met, although it might also indicate the activation of normal exception handlers in response to a common problem or an invalid user action.

Table 14-6 Some Valuable Performance Counter Categories *(continued)*

Category	Description
.NET CLR Locks and Threads	Tracks thread contention (more than one thread competing for a locked resource, forcing at least one thread to wait). If you're implementing your own threading, as described in Chapter 7, you need to become familiar with these counters.
.NET CLR Memory	Provides information related to .NET garbage collection. This might indicate a problem if large objects are being created and released frequently and are wasting memory before they are garbage collected. Unfortunately, this sort of problem usually can't (and should not) be dealt with manually.
.NET CLR Remoting	Provides useful .NET Remoting counters, such as Remote Calls/sec and Total Remote Calls. These counters can be global or relative to a single component host application (which you must indicate).
.NET CLR Security	Provides information about code access security checks and enables you to determine the performance penalty associated with a check. These counters aren't often used for improving performance, but they can help you understand code access security.
ASP.NET	Useful with XML Web service applications. The Requests Queued counter indicates the number of requests waiting to be processed by an XML Web service. You can study this counter, while changing the workload, to determine the maximum throughput your XML Web service can support. Application Restarts and Worker Process Restarts can indicate whether general health is poor. Remember, however, that the application will be restarted if configuration settings change, and the worker process will be recycled periodically according to the options set in the *<processModel>* section of the machine.config file.
ASP.NET Applications	Similar to the ASP.NET category, but you can choose a single XML Web service application to profile. Requests/sec indicates the application throughput, and Pipeline Instance Count indicates the maximum number of concurrent requests being served. Several counters also enable you to test data caching (including Cache API Hits, Cache API Hit Ratio, and Cache API Turnover Rate) and output caching (Output Cache Hits and Output Cache Turnover Ratio).

You might have noticed one puzzling fact: There are four ASP.NET categories, and some of them seem similar. You'll find an ASP.NET category, which provides information about the overall performance of ASP.NET, and an ASP.NET Applications category, which provides information about a single specified Web application. You'll also find two extremely similar categories with version information (ASP.NET [version] and ASP.NET Apps [version]). These categories are actually the same as the versionless categories.

Technically, the versionless categories map to the latest version of the .NET Framework. If you install multiple versions of the .NET Framework, you will find one ASP.NET [version] category and one ASP.NET Apps [version] category for each version of the framework. However, the ASP.NET and ASP.NET Application categories automatically represent the latest installed version.

Now That I'm Monitoring, What Does It Mean?

As Microsoft tactfully states, "Deciding whether or not performance values are acceptable is a subjective judgment that varies significantly with variations in user environments. The values you establish as the baseline for your organization are the best basis for comparison."

In other words, many numbers don't mean anything, at least not without context. A 90 percent CPU level means your CPU is being used heavily. However, the significance of this fact depends on the test conditions, including the hardware and the current user load. In fact, many of these numbers are most important when they deviate from the expected values. Before evaluating them, you must drive your system through numerous test scenarios and develop a sense of the normal operating ranges for your equipment. You should carefully record these typical values. When you make changes to the system or hardware in the future, you can use these values as a baseline.

Custom Performance Counters

.NET provides classes in the *System.Diagnostics* method that enable you to interact programmatically with Windows performance counters, retrieving the current set of counters, retrieving the current value for a specific counter, or creating and incrementing your own counters. This section examines these tasks.

The first step when you use custom counters is to create the counters and counter category. You can do this manually in Visual Studio .NET using Server Explorer or programmatically using the classes in the *System.Diagnostics* namespace. You can even create a custom installer as part of a Visual Studio .NET setup project, which adds the counters when the application is installed on a computer.

Listing 14-13 shows the code needed to create a custom counter category (provided it doesn't already exist) and add two counters.

```
If Not (PerformanceCounterCategory.Exists("Shopping Counters")) Then

    Dim Counters As New CounterCreationDataCollection()

    ' Create a simple counter that records a total value.
    Dim CountCounter As New CounterCreationData()
    CountCounter.CounterName = "Total Purchases"
    CountCounter.CounterHelp = "Total number of purchases " & _
                               "submitted by this component"
    CountCounter.CounterType = PerformanceCounterType.NumberOfItems32
    ' Create a rate counter that records a per second value.
    Dim RateCounter As New CounterCreationData()
    RateCounter.CounterName = "Purchases/Second"
    RateCounter.CounterHelp = "Current number of purchases per " & _
                              "second submitted by this component"
    RateCounter.CounterType = RateOfCountsPerSecond32

    ' Add both counters to the collection.
    Counters.Add(CountCounter)
    Counters.Add(RateCounter)

    ' Create the custom category.
    PerformanceCounterCategory.Create("Shopping Counters", _
      "Counters for the Shopping.dll component", Counters)

End If
```

Listing 14-13 Creating custom counters

The *CounterType* property identifies the type of counter that you're creating. Although .NET provides several options, most choices are concurrency counters and rate counters. Concurrency counters reflect a simple value. When your program increments a concurrency counter, the new value appears identically in the performance monitor. Rate counters involve an extra calculation. You set rate counters in the same way that you set concurrency counters. Behind the scenes, however, these values are cached for a second. The current value of the counter is always equal to the total count received in the last second.

The *32* at the end of the counter type indicates the size allocated to store the counter data. If you expect to require values larger than a 32-bit integer, you can use the corresponding type that ends with *64*. You also can use more advanced counters such as *AverageCount64* or *CounterDelta32*, which calculate values by comparing the number of counts in a given interval with the number of counts in a previous interval. The formulas used for these calculations are outlined in the MSDN Reference.

When you create counters, it's also a good idea to include some descriptive information. In Listing 14-13, this includes the *CounterHelp* string assigned to each counter and a similar category description. The user can view this information when adding a counter in the Performance window (as shown in Figure 14-9).

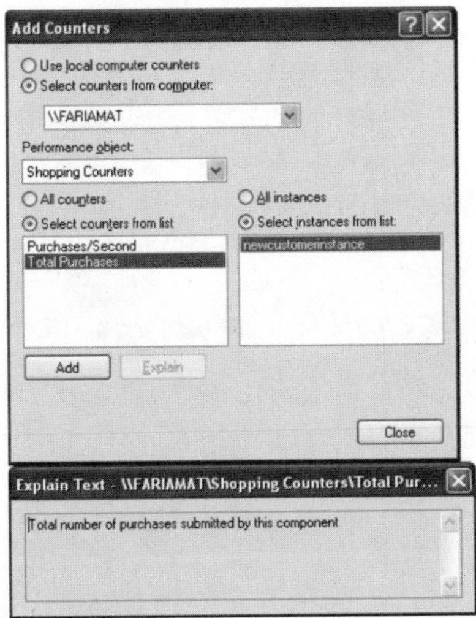

Figure 14-9 Adding custom performance counters

As you might imagine, .NET makes it similarly easy to remove a counter category:

```
PerformanceCounterCategory.Delete("Shopping Counters")
```

If you prefer to create counters at design time with Visual Studio .NET, you can just follow these steps:

1. Open Server Explorer, and expand the node for the server you want to view. Right-click on the Performance Counters node and choose Create New Category.
2. Enter a name and description for the category you want to create in the Performance Counter Builder dialog box.
3. In the New Counter frame, specify the counter name, type, and description. Click Add To List.
4. Repeat step 3 for each new counter you want to create in this category.

To use a counter, you need to create a counter instance. Counter instances relate to performance counters in the same way that objects relate to classes. Although there is only one Purchases/Second counter defined, a server component can create multiple instances. Depending on your needs, a counter might be created for every instance of a server-side component, or a single server-side component might create multiple instances to represent work it is doing for different clients.

Creating a performance counter is easy. You just create an instance of the *PerformanceCounter* class and specify the counter category, counter name, and the instance name. You must also add the optional *False* parameter; otherwise, the counter will be created in read-only mode. (You also can access a counter on another computer by specifying a machine name parameter, but only in read-only mode.)

For example, here's the code that creates an instance of the total counter and increments it by one:

```
Dim TotalCounter As New PerformanceCounter("Shopping Counters", _
  "Total Purchases", "NewCustomerInstance", False)

' Increment the counter by 1.
TotalCounter.Increment()
```

You also can set the *PerformanceCounter.RawValue* property directly, but the *Increment* method ensures that the operation is atomic. This way, multiple threads or components can increment the same counter at once without losing data. Figure 14-10 shows the result in the Performance window after the total counter has been incremented several times.

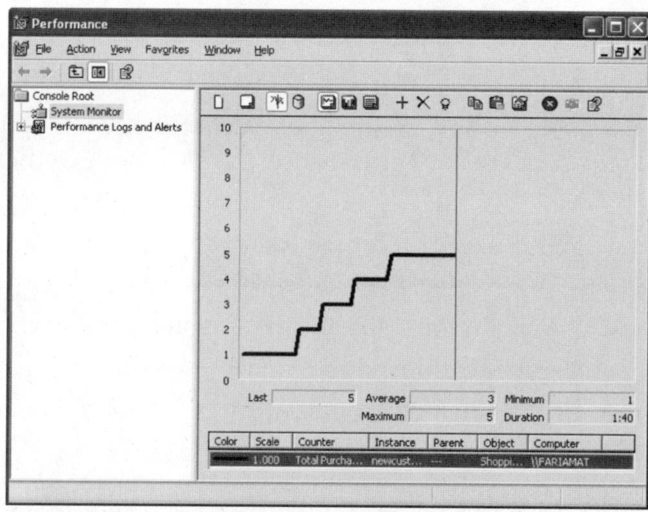

Figure 14-10 Incrementing a custom concurrency counter

You can adjust the rate counter just as easily. If you monitor the performance counter while executing the following code, however, a very different behavior results: The counter spikes to 100 once the code is executed, but falls back rapidly, reaching 0 one second later, as the rate of counts/second dwindles.

```
Dim RateCounter As New PerformanceCounter("Shopping Counters", _
  "Purchases/Second", "NewCustomerInstance", False)

' Increment the counter by 100.
RateCounter.IncrementBy(100)
```

Figure 14-11 shows the results of executing this code multiple times.

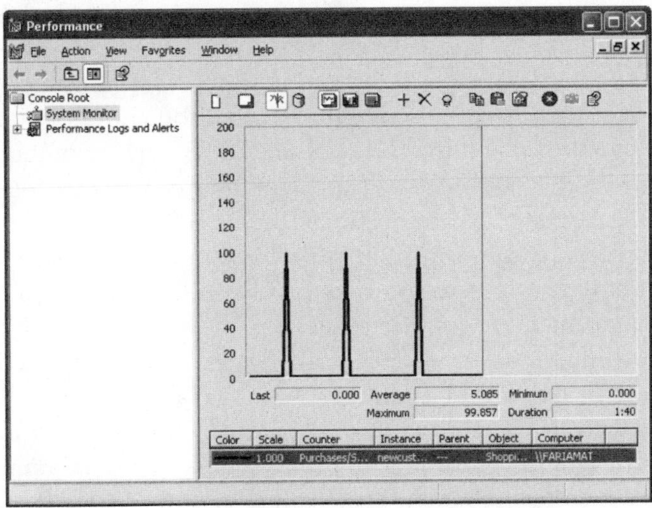

Figure 14-11 Incrementing a custom rate counter

When the application ends or when the counters are no longer needed, be sure to release them. Otherwise, the counters remain until the Performance window is closed.

```
RateCounter.RemoveInstance()
TotalCounter.RemoveInstance()
```

Stress Testing

Performance counters help you gauge how your applications perform; to draw meaningful conclusions, however, you need to study how these counters respond under different loads. Unfortunately, .NET doesn't provide any easy tool to automate this task for you. Although stress-testing tools are available (such as Application Center Test, which is included with some versions of Visual Studio .NET, and its predecessor, Web Application Stress Tool (WAST), which is available for a free download from *http://webtool.rte.microsoft.com*), few tools support .NET Remoting or XML Web services directly. To simulate a realistic load, you will probably need to create your own testing application.

The basic strategy is to design a multithreaded application that makes continuous requests on multiple different threads. You should start with a modest load and gradually increase the number of threads until the application begins to generate timeout errors or manifest other problems. Then step back and use the highest load that doesn't cause any problems.

After you've found the highest load your application can support, the next (and more difficult) step is to determine what the current bottleneck is. One rule of thumb is that if the CPU usage is at 85 percent or more, the CPU is likely to be the bottleneck. If the maximum number of simultaneous requests is reached before this point, the bottleneck lies elsewhere, such as with memory, configuration, thread contention, hard drive speed, or database locking. Discovering this bottleneck requires practice, patience, and performance counter monitoring.

When performing stress testing, you should use a dedicated Web server and a set of dedicated client machines. These client machines should interact with the server over a fast isolated network. If you try to test the server using a load-testing tool running from the same computer, you will retrieve data that is much less accurate and much less useful.

Summary

This chapter considered the technologies to use and best practices to follow when you add logging features to your distributed system. In the real world, these designs are neglected far too often, leading to countless headaches when problems occur in an application that lacks a sufficient way to record them.

You should always consider these three final guidelines:

- **Test your exception handling and logging code.** Some reports suggest that logging code typically contains the highest concentration of errors relative to any other part of an application because it is seldom properly tested.
- **Quantify your theory with stress testing.** Unless you put your system under a heavy load and watch the performance counters, you won't know what unique bottlenecks are holding it back. Without proper profiling, all other considerations are just theory. Well-documented accounts show applications that have increased their performance by several orders of magnitude just by addressing a single bottleneck.
- **Remember the difference between scalability and performance.** When a bottleneck presents itself, ask yourself whether it is a scalability problem that appears only under heavy client loads or whether it is a performance problem that slows down every user. Answering this question will help you determine the most likely course of improvement and prevent you from wasting time with optimizations that won't solve the problem at hand.

15

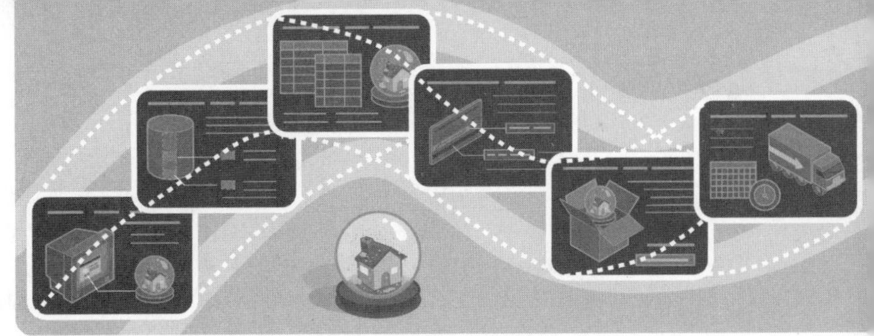

Deployment Strategies

Chapter 2 covered the basics every programmer should know about deploying assemblies in the Microsoft .NET world. First we examined how the common language runtime (CLR) resolves assembly references without needing any additional information from the registry. Next we considered how you can implement your own versioning and binding policies using a few simple configuration file settings. These two features represent a dramatic shift from traditional Microsoft Windows programming, and they distinguish .NET assemblies from traditional COM components.

The easy deployment features in .NET are a great improvement for developers who are trying to keep all the parts of a large distributed application up-to-date. However, they only scratch the surface of what's really possible with .NET. This chapter considers some advanced techniques that enable you to create an automatically updating application—or one that's built dynamically using assemblies from a remote server. These approaches represent a conceptual leap, but not a technological one. In fact, the examples presented in this chapter are still built on the assembly deployment model considered in Chapter 2—they just extend it to entirely new territory by integrating .NET XML Web services.

Traditional Deployment Problems and .NET Solutions

In Chapter 2, you learned how .NET solves the infamous component registration problem, allowing DLL files to be freely copied and used without requiring a separate registration tool (such as regsvr32) or a dedicated setup program. Even better, .NET DLLs can be used from local application directories. A central component repository is available—the global assembly cache (GAC)—but you'll rarely need to use it.

This shift returns programmers to a deployment model similar to the early Windows world. It also gives developers fine-grained control over all the components (and component versions) an application uses. Taken together, these innovations erase the worst nightmares of DLL Hell. They make application updates effortless—almost.

The only remaining problem is that someone still needs to perform the actual file copying. If you're deploying a component to a directory on a server, this step might require only a single step; if you need to distribute an application update to remote clients, however, life isn't as easy.

A good example is a "partly disconnected" system. This is the type of system in which some clients need to be disconnected for some of the time, often because they are using a notebook computer and a network/Internet connection is either not available or not of sufficiently high bandwidth. These clients need to work with a dedicated client application that records information locally and then submits it to the central system when the client reconnects. (We examined this model, and the role disconnected clients play in a distributed system, in Chapter 10.)

In a disconnected system, managing updates can be an extremely tedious, time-consuming, and expensive process. Possible approaches include distributing setup CDs, providing downloadable patches, and e-mailing update notifications. And it's even harder to ensure that clients with the wrong versions can't connect to your XML Web services or interact with your remote components. This version mismatch (for example, old-version clients accessing updated server-side components) can introduce all kinds of compatibility problems unless your system design is carefully controlled.

This chapter considers two basic designs for automated deployment:

- An application launcher that examines the current version of an application and can update it (or recommend an update) automatically. This approach completely removes distribution headaches.
- A modular application that downloads just the required portions of an application. This approach won't work for disconnected clients, but it guarantees that remote clients use the most up-to-date version without ever needing to run an installation. It also allows you to tailor the client application to suit different types of users.

We'll also consider how to make these approaches work in a practical setting and avoid the problems that can occur with code access security.

The Application Launcher

The application launcher developed in this chapter allows an application to update itself with automatic file downloads. This model is used, in a slightly different fashion, in the popular .NET Terrarium learning game developed by

Microsoft architects to demonstrate .NET. (You can download the Terrarium application, but not the source code, from *http://www.gotdotnet.com/terrarium.*)

The key principle in this model is that the user never loads the application directly. Instead, the user launches a stub program called the application launcher. This program queries an XML Web service to determine whether a new version of the target program is available. If it is, the launcher notifies the user or installs it automatically. When this process is complete, the most recent version of the application is started.

The example presented in this chapter uses a polite application launcher that interacts with the user before taking any action. It provides a single window with a display that indicates the current local and server version of the requested application and a brief message indicating whether an upgrade is recommended. The application launcher then enables the user to decide whether the upgrade will be made before continuing. There's no reason to adopt this behavior, however. You can use the same technique to automatically install a critical update—you just omit the steps that asks the user for confirmation. Figure 15-1 diagrams the end-to-end process.

It's up to you to determine how you want to keep track of different versions of the upgradeable application. In the example considered here, a separate directory is created for every new version under the application directory. (For example, MyApp\1.00.22 would hold version 1.00.22 of the application MyApp.) This approach makes it easy to distinguish between different versions and keep a backup in the case an update fails. Optionally, you can configure the application launcher to automatically remove old versions to conserve disk space.

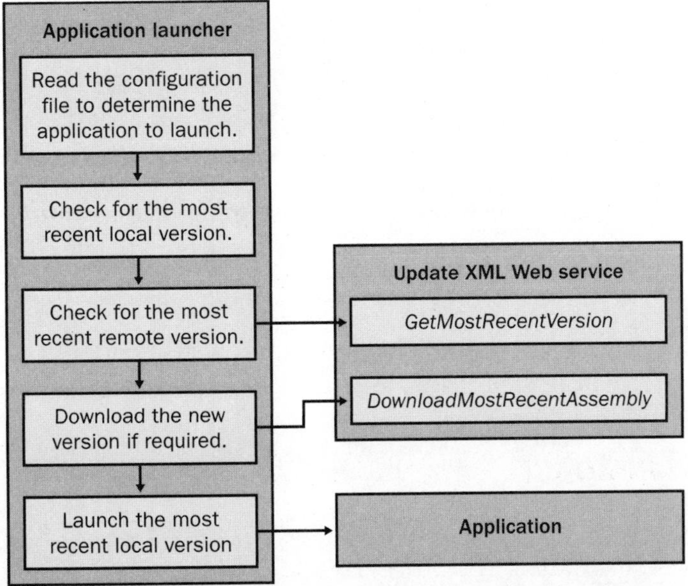

Figure 15-1 The update process with an application launcher

Before embarking on the application launcher project, you need to import several namespaces. The application launcher uses the typical namespaces (such as *System.Windows.Forms*) that are imported at a project-level for every Windows application project in Microsoft Visual Studio .NET, along with the following:

```
Imports System.Configuration
Imports System.IO
Imports System.Environment
Imports System.Reflection
```

The application launcher also defines several form-level variables, as shown in Listing 15-1. These variables track values used in more than one event handler in the application launcher.

```
Public Class LaunchForm
    Inherits System.Windows.Forms.Form

    ' The name of the file to launch (for example, "MyApp.exe").
    Private LocalAppFile As String

    ' The local directory for the most recent version.
    Private CurrentDir As String

    ' The version provided on the server (for example "1.1.0.0").
    Private ServerVersion As String

    ' The proxy object needed for communication with the XML Web service.
    Private UpgradeProxy As New localhost.UpgradeService()

    ' (Other code omitted.)

End Class
```

Listing 15-1 The application launcher startup form

Note that the application launcher holds a reference to an *UpgradeService* XML Web service. We'll show this XML Web service code later, but here's the basic structure:

```
Public Class UpgradeService
    Inherits System.Web.Services.WebService

    <WebMethod()> _
    Public Function GetMostRecentVersion(ByVal appName As String) _
      As String
        ' (Code omitted.)
    End Function
```

```
    <WebMethod()> _
    Public Function DownloadMostRecentAssembly( _
      ByVal appName As String) As Byte()
        ' (Code omitted.)
    End Function

End Class
```

When the application launcher first loads, it checks the most recent local version and the available server version. The call to the XML Web service is executed in a *Try/Catch* block, ensuring that it can recover and continue if the client is currently disconnected from the Internet (or the Web server is offline). If a more recent version of the application is discovered on the server, the Upgrade button is enabled. Listing 15-2 compares the local and server versions on startup.

```
Private Sub Launcher_Load(ByVal sender As System.Object, _
  ByVal e As System.EventArgs) Handles MyBase.Load

    Dim LocalApp As [Assembly]

    ' Retrieve configured file using .config file.
    LocalAppFile = ConfigurationSettings.AppSettings("FileToLaunch")
    lblDisplay.Text = "About to launch: " & LocalAppFile
    lblDisplay.Text &= NewLine

    ' Retrieve a list of all the directories in the current path.
    Dim SourceDir As New DirectoryInfo(Application.StartupPath)

    ' Find highest version by sorting the directories alphabetically.
    ' and taking the first item in the list.
    Dim ContainedDirectories() As DirectoryInfo
    ContainedDirectories = SourceDir.GetDirectories()
    Array.Sort(ContainedDirectories, New DirectoryInfoComparer())

    CurrentDir = ContainedDirectories(0).Name
    lblDisplay.Text &= "About to use version in directory: " & _
                       CurrentDir
    lblDisplay.Text &= NewLine & NewLine

    ' Check what version the XML Web service is providing.
    Try
```

Listing 15-2 Comparing the local and server version on startup

```
        ServerVersion = UpgradeProxy.GetMostRecentVersion(LocalAppFile)
        lblDisplay.Text &= "Server hosts version: " & ServerVersion
        lblDisplay.Text &= NewLine

        ' Determine if the upgrade option should be provided.
        If ServerVersion > CurrentDir Then
            cmdUpgrade.Enabled = True
            lblDisplay.Text &= "An upgrade is recommended."
            lblDisplay.Text &= NewLine & NewLine
        End If

    Catch
        lblDisplay.Text &= "Could not determine server version."
        lblDisplay.Text &= NewLine
        lblDisplay.Text &= "You may not be connected to the Internet."
        lblDisplay.Text &= NewLine & NewLine

    End Try

End Sub
```

This functionality could be incorporated into the updateable application itself, but using a separate application launcher makes life easier and enables you to reuse this design with other upgradeable programs. In fact, because the application launcher uses a configuration file to determine the application to launch, you can use it to launch any .NET application recognized by the remote XML Web service, without changing a single line of code! All you need to do is modify the configuration file.

Figure 15-2 shows the application launcher display when it first loads up.

Figure 15-2 A new file detected by the application launcher

Sorting *DirectoryInfo* Objects

To determine which directory contains the most recent version of the application, the launcher sorts the array of *DirectoryInfo* objects, which represent all the contained directories. The directory with the highest version number will then be placed first in the list.

Unfortunately, *DirectoryInfo* objects have no intrinsic ability to sort themselves. The problem is that there are far too many possible criteria for a sort operation. In the launcher application, it's clear that we need to sort based on the directory name. To actually implement this logic, however, we need to add one additional class: a custom *DirectoryInfo* comparer, as shown here:

```
Public Class DirectoryInfoComparer
    Implements IComparer

    Public Function Compare(ByVal x As Object, ByVal y As Object) _
      As Integer Implements System.Collections.IComparer.Compare

        Dim DirX, DirY As DirectoryInfo
        DirX = CType(x, DirectoryInfo)
        DirY = CType(y, DirectoryInfo)

        ' Compare the DirectoryInfo objects alphabetically
        ' using the name of the directory.
        Return DirX.Name > DirY.Name

    End Function

End Class
```

On the server side, the code needed for the *GetMostRecentVersion* Web method is fairly straightforward (as shown in Listing 15-3). Using an *Assembly* object, the XML Web service loads the requested assembly and returns its version number as a string. Optionally, you can enhance this application so that instead of returning a single string it returns an entire structure that might include additional information (such as a Boolean flag indicating whether the upgrade is recommended or required, or a file size that can be used to estimate the required download time).

```
<WebMethod()> _
Public Function GetMostRecentVersion(ByVal appName As String) As String

    ' Check the version of this executable.
    Dim App As [Assembly]
    App = [Assembly].LoadFrom(Server.MapPath("CodeBase\" & appName))
    Return App.GetName().Version.ToString()

End Function
```

Listing 15-3 Returning the server-hosted file version

Currently, the XML Web service is hard-coded to inspect a directory named CodeBase for the latest assembly versions. You can make this setting dependent on a configuration file, or you can move the assembly information to a database. You can even insert the assembly itself into a database record as a block of binary data.

> **Note** The *Assembly* type (from the *System.Reflection* namespace) must be referenced with a fully qualified name or using square brackets because *Assembly* is a reserved keyword in the Visual Basic language. By default, the Visual Basic compiler assumes you're trying to use the keyword, not the class name.

The next step is the programmatic upgrade of the application. If the user clicks the Upgrade button, the application launcher creates a new directory with the new version number and copies the new version of the assembly into this directory. Listing 15-4 shows the code needed for this process.

```
Private Sub cmdUpgrade_Click(ByVal sender As System.Object, _
  ByVal e As System.EventArgs) Handles cmdUpgrade.Click

    ' Show the hourglass while the download is in progress.
    Me.Cursor = Cursors.WaitCursor

    ' Create a directory for the new version.
    CurrentDir = Application.StartupPath & "\" & ServerVersion
    Directory.CreateDirectory(CurrentDir)

    ' Download the new version.
    Dim Download() As Byte
```

Listing 15-4 Upgrading the application

```
    Download = UpgradeProxy.DownloadMostRecentAssembly(LocalAppFile)
    Dim fs As New FileStream(CurrentDir & "\" & LocalAppFile, _
                             FileMode.CreateNew)
    fs.Write(Download, 0, Download.Length)
    fs.Close()

    lblDisplay.Text &= "New version downloaded to " & CurrentDir

    ' (You could add optional code here to delete directories
    ' that correspond to old versions.)

    cmdUpgrade.Enabled = False
    Me.Cursor = Cursors.Default

End Sub
```

This code uses the *DownloadMostRecentAssembly* XML Web service method shown in Listing 15-5. Once again, this method works with any assembly, provided it's in the correct directory. The server-side code just opens a read-only file stream and returns the assembly as an array of bytes.

```
<WebMethod()>
Public Function DownloadMostRecentAssembly(ByVal appName As String) _
  As Byte()

    ' The best approach is to create a FileInfo object, then a
    ' FileStream. This way you can specify a read-only stream.
    ' Otherwise, the code may fail because the GetMostRecentVersion()
    ' method creates an assembly reference to the file, preventing it
    ' from being modified or opened in a writeable mode.
    Dim f As New FileInfo(Server.MapPath("CodeBase\" & appName))
    Dim fs As FileStream = f.OpenRead()

    ' Create the byte array.
    Dim Bytes As Byte()
    ReDim Bytes(fs.Length)

    ' Read the file into the byte array.
    fs.Read(Bytes, 0, fs.Length)
    fs.Close()

    Return Bytes

End Function
```

Listing 15-5 Returning the latest file as a byte array

Note that you can't create the *FileStream* directly by using its constructor and passing in the file path. If you do so, .NET attempts to create a writable stream. The problem is that the *GetMostRecentVersion* method has already created a reference to the assembly file in order to retrieve its version information. This means that the assembly is currently loaded in the XML Web service application domain. If you attempt to open a writable stream to a file that is in use, a runtime exception will occur (even if you don't write any data to the stream). In .NET, there is no way to unload an assembly reference without unloading the entire *AppDomain*. The solution is to explicitly open a read-only stream. (If you're feeling particularly sharp as you read this, an alternative solution might have already occurred to you. You can modify the *GetMostRecentVersion* method so that it creates a new *AppDomain* and loads the requested assembly into the new *AppDomain*. Then, the method can unload the entire domain by using the *AppDomain.Unload* method. This is an equivalent solution, although it requires a little more code.)

Finally, the application launcher starts the most recent version of the application when the Continue button is clicked, as shown in Listing 15-6.

```
Private Sub cmdContinue_Click(ByVal sender As System.Object, _
  ByVal e As System.EventArgs) Handles cmdContinue.Click

    ' Load the assembly for the most recent application version.
    Dim LocalApp As [Assembly]
    LocalApp = [Assembly].LoadFrom(CurrentDir & "\" & LocalAppFile)

    ' Retrieve the name of the startup class for the application.
    Dim ClassName As String
    ClassName = ConfigurationSettings.AppSettings("StartupClass")

    ' Create an instance of the startup form.
    Dim AppForm As Form
    AppForm = LocalApp.CreateInstance("UpgradeableApp.StartupForm")

    ' Show the form.
    Me.Hide()
    AppForm.ShowDialog()
    Me.Close()

End Sub
```

Listing 15-6 Launching the application startup form

In this case, the code turns to the configuration file again to determine which class it should use to start the application. This setting must be a fully qualified class name (in this case, *UpgradeableApp.StartupForm*, the name of a Windows Form in the assembly). The full configuration file is shown here:

```
<?xml version="1.0" encoding="utf-8" ?>
<configuration>

  <appSettings>
    <add key="FileToLaunch"
         value="UpgradeableApp.exe" />
    <add key="StartupClass"
         value="UpgradeableApp.StartupForm" />
  </appSettings>

</configuration>
```

After the first window has been created for the form, the user can seamlessly branch out to any other part of the application. For example, if the *UpgradeableApp.StartupForm* attempts to launch another form from the assembly (such as *Form2*), the CLR automatically searches for the requested type in the same assembly. There is only one potential stumbling block. When an application is launched in this way, you can't use the *Application* class (in the *System.Windows.Forms* namespace) to correctly retrieve information such as the application's version number. If you do, this information will correspond to the hosting assembly, which in this case is the application launcher. If you want to retrieve version information dynamically, you must use the reflection types instead to retrieve a reference to the application assembly. (You can use a method such as *Assembly.GetExecutingAssembly*.)

The application launcher is a simple, reusable utility for automating deployment. You can use similar techniques to create a transparent application launcher that performs required upgrades in the background, without requiring any user interaction. You can even dedicate a separate thread to the process. This way, the version will be downloaded while the user works. The next time the user exits and restarts the application, the application launcher will start the newly downloaded version. Alternatively, you can make the process entirely optional. You might want to advertise on the application status bar when a new version is available and enable the user to ignore the message, for example, or initiate a download by choosing an Upgrade Now menu option.

Security Holes in the Upgrade XML Web Service

As it stands, the code has a significant but subtle security vulnerability. In fact, it's a good example of what can go wrong with an XML Web service. Clearly, the *DownloadMostRecentAssembly* Web method enables any user to retrieve a file from the CodeBase directory. If you needed to protect these files, you could create some sort of authentication system, as discussed in Chapter 13. The user would have to call a Web method to become authenticated before calling the

XML Web service and then present some sort of user credential (such as a ticket) to the other XML Web service methods to be allowed to download a file.

This is straightforward enough, but it doesn't plug the real security hole. The problem is that the *DownloadMostRecentAssembly* XML Web service method provides an unchecked window onto the server's file system. Instead of submitting a valid filename, a client could submit a qualified path name such as "*..\myfile*". If this sequence were inserted into the path name, the Web method would actually download the file named myfile from the parent of the CodeBase directory. ("..\" means to move one directory up the tree.) Because the XML Web service is limited only by the restrictions of the ASP.NET worker process, this could enable a user to download a sensitive server-side file. This type of problem, which depends on being able to specify a path outside of the intended bounds, is called a *canonicalization error*. It's one of the most common but least high-tech security errors that an application can suffer from.

It's easy enough to create a more resilient Web method. One technique is to ensure that you strip out only the filename from the user's submitted string before processing it. For example, the following line of code uses the *Path* class (from the *System.IO* namespace) to remove only the final filename portion of the string. By inserting this line at the beginning of the *DownloadMostRecentAssembly* Web method, you ensure that the user is constrained to the correct directory.

```
appName = Path.GetFileName(appName)
```

If the user has behaved responsibly and submitted only a filename with no path characters, the *appName* string will be unchanged. Otherwise, the returned *appName* will include only the final filename portion.

Other Enhancements to the Application Launcher

The application launcher is a simple utility that works admirably well. If you want to incorporate this design into your own projects, you might consider a few enhancements:

- Instead of returning just the version of server-side assemblies, you can return other information in a custom class. This might allow a client to choose whether a download is necessary, select among multiple versions (perhaps depending on regional settings), or even download optional features.
- The upgrade XML Web service should log every download and use the properties of the *Context.Request* object to store additional information about the user. This helps both to identify suspicious

behavior that might indicate downloads by the wrong users and, more commonly, errors in the application launcher or upgrade XML Web service that result in unnecessary downloads. If the Web server becomes a file server dedicated to constantly transmitting large binary files, performance will suffer.

- To force the user to use the application launcher, you should modify the target application so that it can't be started independently. There are several possible ways to do this, but the easiest is just to compile the application as a DLL assembly. In Visual Studio .NET, this just involves tweaking the project properties. The next example uses this approach.

The Application Browser

The application browser presents a somewhat different solution to the same problem. With an application browser, the entire application is dynamic, and it usually cannot operate in disconnected mode (although you can add code to ensure that it does). The basic principle behind an application browser is that the functionality of the target application is partitioned into distinct modules. When a given user logs in, the application browser queries an XML Web service to determine which modules are allowed for this user. It uses this information to configure the interface (perhaps adding a list of options to a menu or creating a group of buttons). When the user attempts to use one of the modules, the application browser downloads it from the server.

Several key differences exist between application launchers and application browsers:

- With an application browser, the target application is designed in several distinct pieces. This gives you the freedom to download only the required components. On the other hand, a self-updating application might restrict some users from using some features, but it is always a single file and therefore a single download.
- Because of the additional complexity with application browsers, the download process is rarely managed manually by your code (although there is no reason it can't be). Instead, assemblies are usually loaded directly from the server using the *Assembly.LoadFrom* method. The CLR then shadow-copies a local version if it doesn't already exist. The process is completely transparent.

- Application browsers dictate the user interface to some degree. In our example, the application browser is implemented as a multiple document interface (MDI) window, inside of which MDI child windows can be created. Application launchers play a lesser role, generally disappearing quietly after the program is started.

You can think of an application browser as a Windows Forms equivalent of an Internet browser. Like an Internet browser, it retrieves its content from the Internet. As soon as you change the contents of the Web server, all users of the application are affected—there is no manual download process. However, the application browser has greater processing power than what is available in traditional client-side scripting languages. It can handle a rich graphical user interface with all the customary GUI frills and windowing. Figure 15-3 diagrams how an application browser works. As with all XML Web services, this technique can be used over the Internet with a remote server or locally over an intranet.

Note that the assemblies must be hosted in a public directory on the server because the XML Web service no longer shoulders the burden of transmitting the files. You should protect this directory with Microsoft Internet Information Services (IIS) authentication settings (or network security settings with a network share in an intranet scenario). If Windows authentication won't work for your environment, you might want to steer away from the application browser approach and the possible security risks.

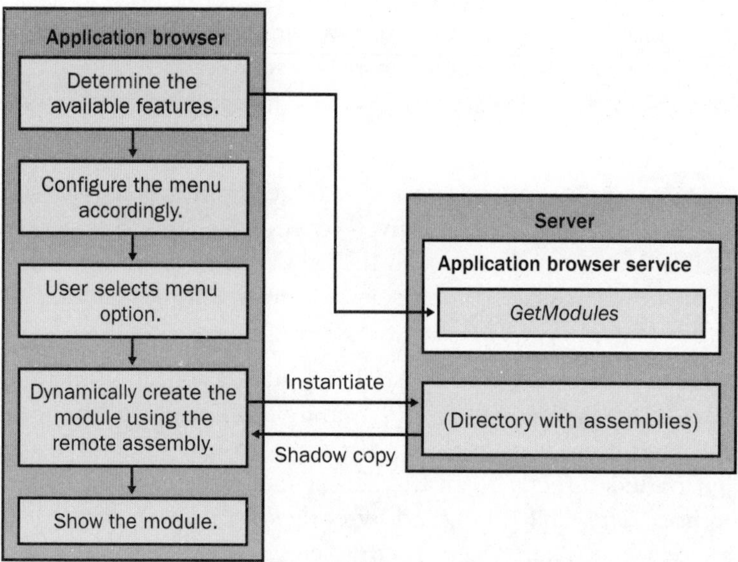

Figure 15-3 Using an application browser

The Application Browser XML Web Service

The first step in creating the application browser XML Web service is to define a custom structure or class that encapsulates the information about an application module. In our simple example (the *BrowserModule* class shown in Listing 15-7), this information includes the friendly (display) name and the URL for the corresponding assembly. If you want, you can add additional information such as the application browser menu under which a given module should appear.

```
Public Class BrowserModule
    Public MenuName As String
    Public AssemblyUrl As String

    ' Could add addition properties to configure
    ' order, menu shortcuts, and so on.

    Public Sub New()
        ' A default public constructor is required for XML Web service
        ' serializable types.
    End Sub

    Public Sub New(ByVal menuName As String, _
     ByVal assemblyUrl As String)
        Me.MenuName = menuName
        Me.AssemblyUrl = assemblyUrl
    End Sub

End Class
```

Listing 15-7 The module information

Note that you need to include a default constructor. This is because the version of this class that the client will use will contain only the public members. It won't contain any constructor logic.

Next you must create the single required Web method, which returns an array of *BrowserModule* objects, as shown in Listing 15-8. Note that the array is strongly typed. If you use a generic collection of objects (such as an *ArrayList* or a *Hashtable*), .NET wouldn't create a copy of the *BrowserModule* class in the client's proxy file and the client wouldn't be able to retrieve *BrowserModule* properties.

```
Public Class AppBrowser
    Inherits System.Web.Services.WebService

    <WebMethod()> _
    Public Function GetModules() As BrowserModule()

        Dim Modules As New ArrayList()

        ' In this service, every custom setting corresponds to a
        ' module. A more powerful approach would be to create a custom
        ' configuration file section just for modules,
        ' and use a custom configuration file reader class to get the
        ' settings.
        Dim Keys() As String
        Keys = ConfigurationSettings.AppSettings.AllKeys
        Dim Key As String
        For Each Key In Keys
            Dim Item As New BrowserModule(Key, _
              ConfigurationSettings.AppSettings(Key))
            Modules.Add(Item)
        Next

        ' It's important for this method to return a strongly-typed
        ' BrowserModule array, not an ArrayList. Otherwise, the
        ' BrowserModule class will not be included in the automatically
        ' generated proxy, because .NET will not be able to tell that
        ' it's required.
        Return Modules.ToArray(GetType(BrowserModule))

    End Function

End Class
```

Listing 15-8 The application browser XML Web service

The information about available browser modules is stored in a configuration file that looks like this:

```
<?xml version="1.0" encoding="utf-8" ?>
<configuration>

 <appSettings>
   <add key="Product Catalog"
     value="http://localhost/AppBrowser/CodeBase/ProductCatalog.dll" />
   <add key="Invoice Module"
     value="http://localhost/AppBrowser/CodeBase/InvoiceModule.dll" />
  </appSettings>
```

```
  <!-- System.web settings omitted -->

</configuration>
```

This is the only code that's required on the server side. However, you must create the modules before continuing. We'll tackle this task next.

The Application Browser Modules

Each application browser module should be created in a separate project, compiled as a DLL assembly, and deployed to the CodeBase virtual directory on the server. In Visual Studio .NET, you can just create a new Windows Forms project and change the output type to Class Library, as shown in Figure 15-4. Note that the namespace has also been modified to *ApplicationBrowser*.

The form itself is nothing remarkable. It's just given a text caption "Product Catalog" so you can quickly determine whether the application browser test is successful.

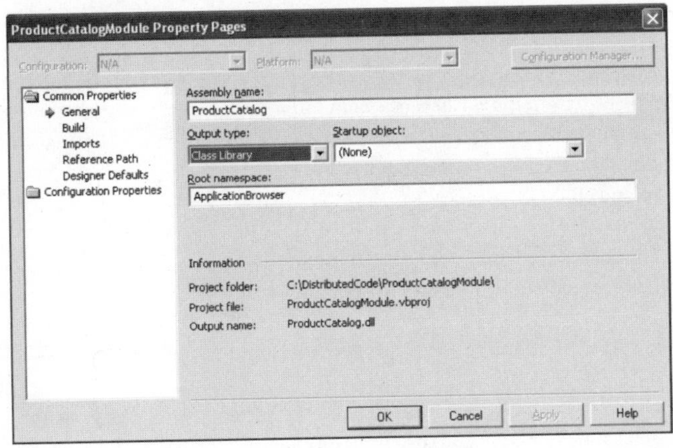

Figure 15-4 Configuring project properties for a browser module

The Application Browser

The application browser is created as another Windows Forms project. On startup, it loads an MDI parent window and configures its menu with a list of supported modules. You need only three steps to implement this design:

1. Set the *Form.IsMdiContainer* property to *True* for the startup form.

2. Create a menu with two main headings: an Action heading (which will display the supported modules) and a Windows heading (which will list the currently displayed modules).

3. Set the *MenuItem.MdiList* property for the Window item to *True*. That way, .NET will automatically create and manage the list of MDI children without requiring any code.

The form stores a form-level variable for a *Hashtable* that tracks all the supported modules:

```
' Stores a collection of BrowserModule objects.
' Each object is indexed using the menu item that displays the
' corresponding module.
Public AvailableModules As New Hashtable()
```

On startup, the program contacts the XML Web service and retrieves the array of *BrowserModule* objects (as shown in Listing 15-9. Each *BrowserModule* object is added to the menu using its friendly name. The complete object is added to the *AvailableModules* collection so that it can be retrieved later.

```
Private Sub ApplicationBrowser_Load(ByVal sender As System.Object, _
  ByVal e As System.EventArgs) Handles MyBase.Load

    Dim Proxy As New localhost.AppBrowser()
    Dim mnu As MenuItem

    Dim BrowserModule As localhost.BrowserModule
    For Each BrowserModule In Proxy.GetModules()

        mnu = mnuAction.MenuItems.Add(BrowserModule.MenuName)

        ' Add the item so we can retrieve it later (when the menu
        ' option is clicked) and determine the necessary DLL.
        AvailableModules.Add(mnu, BrowserModule)

        ' Connect the event handler for the menu option click.
        AddHandler mnu.Click, AddressOf mnu_Click

    Next

End Sub
```

Listing 15-9 Initializing the application browser

Figure 15-5 shows the lists of retrieved modules on the application browser menu.

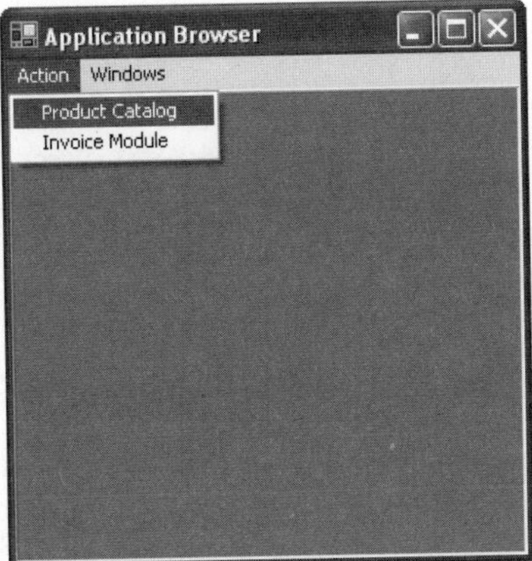

Figure 15-5 The list of dynamic modules

The event handler for the corresponding menu item is also hooked up dynamically using the *AddHandler* statement. When the menu item is clicked, the event handler in Listing 15-10 looks up the corresponding *BrowserModule* item and loads the appropriate assembly using the *Assembly.LoadFrom* method with the full URL. The startup form is then instantiated as an MDI child.

```
Private Sub mnu_Click(ByVal sender As System.Object, _
  ByVal e As System.EventArgs)

    ' Get the related BrowserModule object.
    Dim BrowserModule As localhost.BrowserModule
    BrowserModule = AvailableModules(sender)

    ' Load the corresponding assembly.
    Dim ModuleAssembly As [Assembly]
    ModuleAssembly = [Assembly].LoadFrom(BrowserModule.AssemblyUrl)

    Dim ModuleForm As Form
    ModuleForm = _
      ModuleAssembly.CreateInstance("ApplicationBrowser.ModuleForm")

    ' Show the module as an MDI child.
    ModuleForm.MdiParent = Me
    ModuleForm.Show()

End Sub
```

Listing 15-10 Dynamically loading a module

Note that the fully qualified name for the startup class is hard-coded. A better approach is for this piece of information to be a public property of the *BrowserModule* class. The current design for the application browser uses custom configuration settings, however, which means it can store only two pieces of information about each module. To allow for more information, you need to create a custom configuration section or just read the information out of a database.

The process that takes place behind the scenes is quite interesting. Every time this method runs, it instructs .NET to use an assembly from the remote computer. However, .NET does not treat the remote assembly like a local component—if it did, the application could slow down dramatically for low-bandwidth clients. Instead, .NET checks the version of the remote file and downloads a cached copy, if required. If it already has the most recent version cached locally, it won't take any additional action. This is similar to the logic we coded manually in the application launcher. The most significant difference is that the cached file is not stored in the local application directory. Instead, it's placed in the GAC so that it can be used by multiple applications if required.

You can verify this by browsing the GAC on your computer. Just navigate to C:\[WindowsDir]\Assembly\Download using Windows Explorer. (Download is the special subdirectory used for cached assemblies.) Figure 15-6 shows the automatically downloaded assembly.

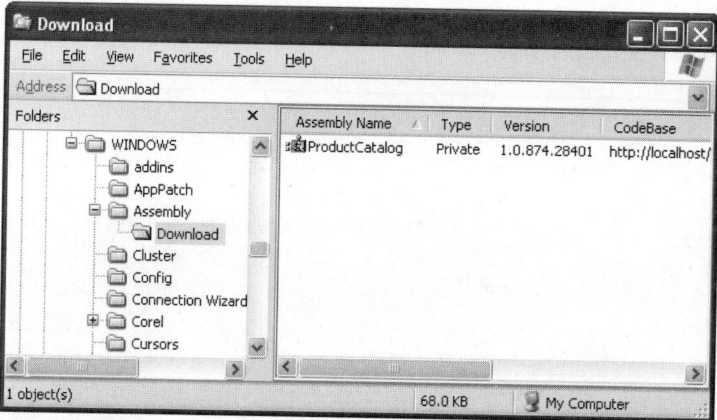

Figure 15-6 The dynamically downloaded assembly

There's only one problem with the application so far: as written, it won't work. As soon as you attempt to launch an application module, you'll receive a security exception because .NET knows that the assembly originated from a remote location. The default code access security policy doesn't give remote code the execute permission. As you'll see, you can fine-tune these settings by adding a known trusted source.

> **Note** Based on the analysis in Chapter 13, you might believe that you can solve this problem by using a security assertion. However, this won't work because .NET always walks *up* the stack. That means it checks the downloaded assembly for permission and then it checks the application browser code. You can't assert the permission in your application browser code because a security exception will have already been thrown.

Code Access Security

Code access security can be a confounding issue for new .NET developers because it springs into action at the most unexpected times. Consider, for example, our application launcher. Because it manually downloads the assembly as a stream of bytes and then re-creates the file on the local computer, .NET has no way to know it originally came from the Internet. When we run the application, it's identified as a component from the local computer zone and given full trust. With the application browser, on the other hand, the assembly is executed directly from the Internet using the *LoadFrom* method. In this case, the assembly will have markedly different evidence and be granted a much lower level of trust.

> **Note** The same considerations that apply to code access security with the *LoadFrom* method also apply if you're using a configuration file with the *<codeBases>* setting (as demonstrated in Chapter 2). If you specify a URI, .NET will use the same process to download the assembly into the GAC and will apply the same security restrictions.

To test this principle, you can add a little code to the application browser and application launcher to display the evidence for the assembly you want to use. In this case, we want to examine the host evidence (which includes information such as the origin of the code). Assembly evidence is not important because we haven't digitally signed the assembly.

Listing 15-11 shows a rewritten version of the menu event handler, which just displays the evidence piece by piece in separate message boxes.

```
Private Sub mnu_Click(ByVal sender As System.Object, _
  ByVal e As System.EventArgs)

    ' Get the related BrowserModule object.
    Dim BrowserModule As localhost.BrowserModule
    BrowserModule = AvailableModules(sender)

    ' Load the corresponding assembly.
    Dim ModuleAssembly As [Assembly]
    ModuleAssembly = [Assembly].LoadFrom(BrowserModule.AssemblyUrl)

    ' Get an enumerator that allows us to walk through the
    ' host evidence.
    Dim Enumerator As IEnumerator
    Enumerator = ModuleAssembly.Evidence.GetHostEnumerator()

    Do While Enumerator.MoveNext()
        ' Show the current piece of evidence.
        MessageBox.Show(Enumerator.Current.ToString())
    Loop

End Sub
```

Listing 15-11 Displaying assembly evidence

Notice two significant items. First of all, the security zone is recognized as the intranet:

```
<System.Security.Policy.Zone version="1">
   <Zone>Intranet</Zone>
</System.Security.Policy.Zone>
```

This is the piece of evidence that ultimately causes the code to be denied permission to execute.

The URL identifies the location more specifically:

```
<System.Security.Policy.Url version="1">
   <Url>http://localhost/AppBrowser/CodeBase/ProductCatalog.dll</Url>
</System.Security.Policy.Url>
```

And the site pinpoints the server:

```
<System.Security.Policy.Site version="1">
   <Name>localhost</Name>
</System.Security.Policy.Site>
```

So how has .NET made these decisions? Clearly, the URL is drawn directly from the parameter used in the *LoadFrom* method. What might not be immediately clear, however, is how .NET analyzes this parameter. If it is a path name (or a URL that begins with *file:///*), the CLR identifies that the request is attempting to access the local computer. If the URL begins with *http://*, the CLR performs a little more sleuthing. In this case, because the first 3 bytes of the IP address match, .NET determines that the computer is on the same network. (The first 3 bytes of the IP address are the first three numbers separated by periods. In other words, the address 127.2.44.11 is on the same intranet as 127.2.44.300 but not the same intranet as 127.2.46.300, provided you use a subnet mask of 255.255.255.0. For more information, you might want to consult a detailed book about networking.)

Incidentally, in this case the URL is using the localhost loopback alias, which points to the current computer. However, .NET cannot identify this fact and therefore still denies the request.

You can solve this problem in more than one way. You can disable the security policy altogether for the client computer, using the caspol.exe command-line utility included with .NET. This is the most radical approach. Alternatively, you can create a new security rule that will recognize your strongly signed assemblies. The easiest approach, however, is to configure a new security group for the remote server. This is the approach we'll take in the next section.

To change the security policy, you can manually edit the machine.config file or you can use the .NET Framework Configuration tool, which is by far the easiest option. Just choose Settings, Control Panel, Administrative Tools, Microsoft .NET Framework Configuration.

The basic approach we'll take is to create a code group that includes any assembly downloaded from the localhost computer. You need to create this code group as a subset of the *LocalIntranet_Zone* code group. Conceptually, you're adding a special case that modifies how .NET processes an assembly from the local intranet. If you try to create your custom code group as a subset of *My_Computer_Zone*, it won't work because the ProductCatalog.dll assembly is not being executed from the local computer.

Adding the code group is easy. First of all, find the Runtime Security Policy, Machine, Code Groups, LocalIntranet_Zone node (as shown in Figure 15-7).

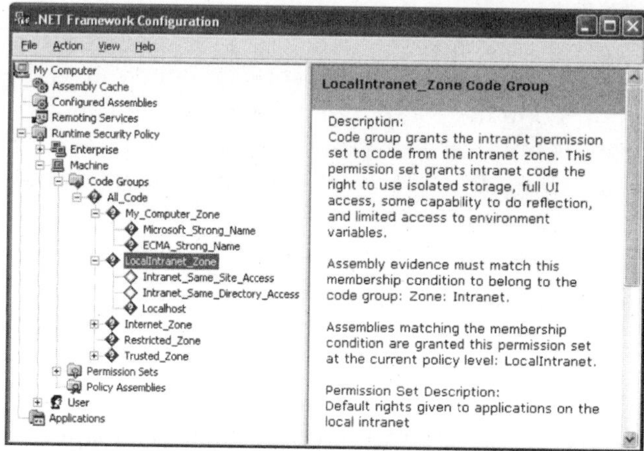

Figure 15-7 Adding a custom group for localhost

Right-click on this node and choose New. You'll travel through a three-step wizard that prompts you to first create a descriptive name and then select the type of code group. In this case, you can create a site-specific or URL-specific code group. The site-specific code group includes all the assemblies downloaded from a specific server. The URL-specific code group is similar but more granular. It enables you to specify a specific directory on a server. Figure 15-8 shows the URL-specific condition that will allow any assembly downloaded from a URL that begins with *localhost*.

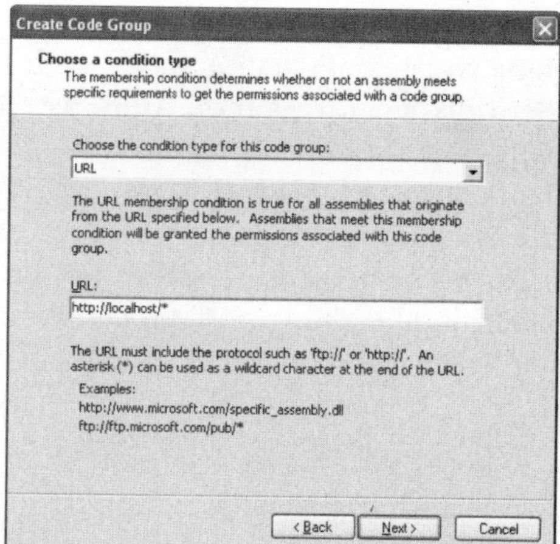

Figure 15-8 The code group URL

The final step is to select the permissions for this code group. In this case, the full trust permission set is recommended.

> **Note** Keep in mind that this condition applies only to URLs that match exactly. If the client tries to download a file from the same server computer using its IP address, the security *LocalIntranet_Zone* security restrictions apply because .NET won't match the code group. You can alter this behavior by adding multiple URL rules.

If you run the simple evidence tester shown in Listing 15-11 again, you'll find that the same evidence still appears. However, the matched code group now has increased permissions. With this change, the application browser runs smoothly and loads the remote form seamlessly, albeit with an unremarkable user interface (as shown in Figure 15-9). The MDI list even tracks the currently displayed modules.

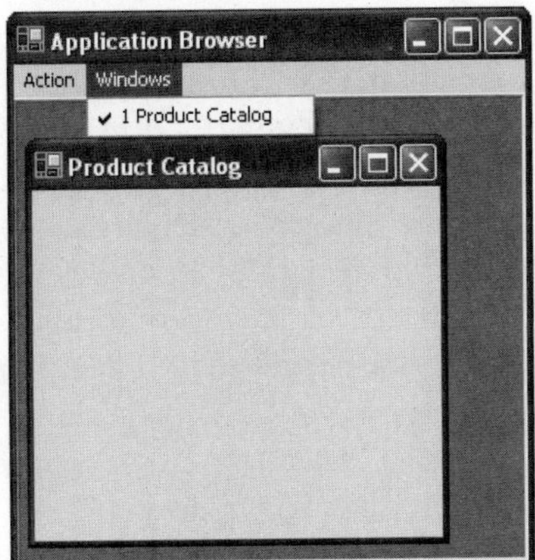

Figure 15-9 The application browser at work

However, life isn't perfect for the administrator of a large distributed system, who must coordinate the security policy updates to hundreds or thousands of client computers! The easiest way to manage this feat is to export a separate XML file that contains the new security settings and run the caspol.exe command-line utility on each client computer to apply the settings. The following caspol.exe command applies the custom security settings from the CustomPermissions.xml file. Keep in mind that the user running this utility needs administrator privileges.

```
caspol-machine -addpset CustomPermissions.xml
```

The MSDN reference has much more information about the caspol.exe utility and the steps required to administer code access security. Be warned, however—making and deploying code access security changes will complicate your system.

Improving Communication in the Application Browser

One of the challenges with creating an application browser is striking the right balance when you divide functionality between modules. Ideally, the modules will perform completely independent tasks and require no interaction. In some cases, however, a little bit more cooperation is required.

For example, the application module might need to tailor the application browser interface, perhaps modifying the window caption and adding a new set of menu items when it gains the focus. You can implement these features by using the *Form.MdiParent* property of the child window. Using this property, you can give the application module direct access to the parent and allow it to perform any basic modification supported by the *Form* class (such as modifying the window text or obtaining reference to the overhead menu). However, this direct approach can run into a good deal of trouble.

As most .NET developers realize, it's rarely a good idea for one form to tinker directly with the controls and properties of another form. Instead, the child form should call a custom method that you've added to the parent form. The custom parent method can then perform the required modifications. This extra layer of indirection improves encapsulation and ensures that you can modify the application browser (for example, renaming control variables) without causing mysterious errors to appear in the application modules.

All this is well and good, but it's not necessarily easy to implement. What happens, for instance, if you develop the application browser and application modules separately? To call a custom method in a *Form* class, you need to have a reference to the assembly that contains the form. Or do you?

As with .NET Remoting, the solution to this problem is to program using interfaces. The basic technique is to define a contract that the application browser must respect and a separate contract that all application modules must respect. The application browser can rely on the application module interface to interact with the application module, and the application module can rely on the browser interface to interact with the application browser.

Consider the application module interface shown in Listing 15-12. It defines a *ModuleClosed* event and a dedicated *Start* method. Neither of these details is required, but they enable you to write cleaner code in the application browser. They also make the overall logic clearer. Looking at this interface, it's immediately apparent that the application browser needs to know when the module closes and relies on this notification to perform some task.

```
Public Interface IApplicationModule

    Sub Start(ByVal parent As Form)
    Event ModuleClosed(ByVal sender As Object, ByVal e As EventArgs)

End Interface
```

Listing 15-12 The application module interface

Listing 15-13 shows the revised application module code required to implement the *IApplicationModule* interface.

```
Public Class ModuleForm
    Inherits System.Windows.Forms.Form
    Implements AppBrowserInterfaces.IApplicationModule

    ' Implement the required event.
    Public Event ModuleClosed(ByVal sender As Object, _
      ByVal e As System.EventArgs) _
      Implements AppBrowserInterfaces.IApplicationModule.ModuleClosed

    ' Use the Start() method to show the window.
    ' By putting this logic in the application module, you
    ' gain the ability to configure the window display, choosing
    ' a default size or even showing it as a non-MDI modal window.
    Public Sub Start(ByVal parent As System.Windows.Forms.Form) _
      Implements AppBrowserInterfaces.IApplicationModule.Start

        Me.MdiParent = parent
        Me.Show()

    End Sub

    ' Raise the appropriate event when the form closes.
    Private Sub ModuleForm_Closed(ByVal sender As Object, _
      ByVal e As System.EventArgs) Handles MyBase.Closed

        RaiseEvent ModuleClosed(Me, New EventArgs())

    End Sub

End Class
```

Listing 15-13 Implementing *IApplicationModule*

This interface-based approach proves useful if you need to limit the user to a single instance of an application module. Currently, the application browser enables the user to start any number of instances of the same module. Using interfaces, you can easily modify this logic. There are several possible solutions, but one is to just disable a menu item when it is clicked and re-enable it when the module form closes. The next example demonstrates this technique.

Listing 15-14 shows the revised code that the application browser uses to create the module and to subscribe to the *ModuleClosed* event. Note that the menu item that triggered the action is disabled after the method has completed successfully. The changed lines are highlighted in bold.

```
Private Sub mnu_Click(ByVal sender As System.Object, _
  ByVal e As System.EventArgs)

    ' Get the related BrowserModule object.
    Dim BrowserModule As localhost.BrowserModule
    BrowserModule = AvailableModules(sender)

    ' Load the corresponding assembly.
    Dim ModuleAssembly As [Assembly]
    ModuleAssembly = [Assembly].LoadFrom(BrowserModule.AssemblyUrl)

    ' Create the module through the interface.
    Dim ModuleForm As AppBrowserInterfaces.IApplicationModule
    ModuleForm = _
      ModuleAssembly.CreateInstance("ApplicationBrowser.ModuleForm")

    ' Disable the menu item so the module can't be loaded twice.
    CType(sender, MenuItem).Enabled = False

    ' Keep track of the disabled menu item.
    DisabledMenuItems(ModuleForm) = sender

    ' Subscribe to the close event.
    AddHandler ModuleForm.ModuleClosed, AddressOf ModuleClosed

    ' Display the module.
    ModuleForm.Start(Me)

End Sub
```

Listing 15-14 Creating the module through its interface

When the module is closed, the application browser responds to the *ModuleClosed* event, checks which module has been deactivated, and then reenables the corresponding menu item, as shown in Listing 15-15.

```
Private Sub ModuleClosed(ByVal sender As Object, _
  ByVal e As System.EventArgs)

    Dim mnu As MenuItem = CType(DisabledMenuItems(sender), MenuItem)

    ' Re-enable the menu.
    mnu.Enabled = True

    ' Remove the menu from the collection.
    DisabledMenuItems.Remove(sender)

End Sub
```

Listing 15-15 Handling the *ModuleClosed* event

Communication from the module to the browser can be just as important. Consider the application browser interface shown in Listing 15-16. It defines a method that allows application modules to add and remove a linked menu of options.

```
Public Interface IApplicationBrowser

    Sub AddMenu(ByVal menu As MenuItem)
    Sub RemoveMenu(ByVal menu As MenuItem)

End Interface
```

Listing 15-16 The application browser interface

In this case, the *MenuItem* corresponds to a top-level menu with a collection of contained menu options. The application browser attaches this top-level menu to the main MDI menu. Whenever an option is selected, however, the event is handled by the appropriate module (as shown in Figure 15-10).

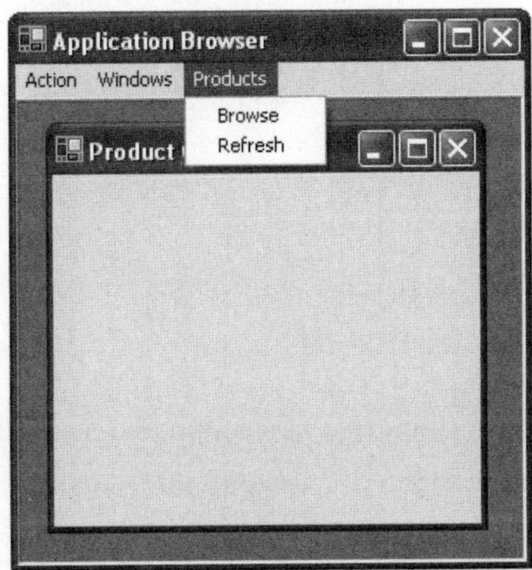

Figure 15-10 Attaching dynamic menus

Listing 15-17 shows the implemented code in the application browser.

```
Public Class ApplicationBrowser
    Inherits System.Windows.Forms.Form
    Implements AppBrowserInterfaces.IApplicationBrowser

    Public Sub AddMenu(ByVal menu As System.Windows.Forms.MenuItem) _
      Implements AppBrowserInterfaces.IApplicationBrowser.AddMenu

        mnuMain.MenuItems.Add(menu)

    End Sub

    Public Sub RemoveMenu(ByVal menu As _
      System.Windows.Forms.MenuItem) _
      Implements AppBrowserInterfaces.IApplicationBrowser.RemoveMenu

        mnuMain.MenuItems.Remove(menu)

    End Sub

    ' (Other code omitted.)

End Class
```

Listing 15-17 Implementing *IApplicationBrowser*

Finally, Listing 15-18 shows how the application module can use the *IApplicationBrowser* interface to communicate with the parent, adding a menu at startup and removing it when the module closes.

```
Public Class ModuleForm
    Inherits System.Windows.Forms.Form
    Implements AppBrowserInterfaces.IApplicationModule

    ' Add the menu.
    Private Sub ModuleForm_Load(ByVal sender As System.Object, _
      ByVal e As System.EventArgs) Handles MyBase.Load

        Dim Parent As AppBrowserInterfaces.IApplicationBrowser
        Parent = CType(Me.MdiParent, _
                 AppBrowserInterfaces.IApplicationBrowser)
        Parent.AddMenu(mnuProducts)

    End Sub
```

Listing 15-18 Using *IApplicationBrowser* to add a dynamic menu

```
    ' Remove the menu.
    Private Sub ModuleForm_Closed(ByVal sender As Object, _
      ByVal e As System.EventArgs) Handles MyBase.Closed

        Dim Parent As AppBrowserInterfaces.IApplicationBrowser
        Parent = CType(Me.MdiParent, _
          AppBrowserInterfaces.IApplicationBrowser)
        Parent.RemoveMenu(mnuProducts)

        RaiseEvent ModuleClosed(Me, New EventArgs())

    End Sub

    ' (Other code omitted.)

End Class
```

In short, interface-based programming is a key technique for programming application browsers. When in doubt, however, strive for the least amount of interaction possible. The more your forms interact, the greater the chance that an unusual combination of different modules will lead to an unexpected error.

A More Dynamic Application Browser

The application browser developed in this chapter uses a static set of available modules. In this case, the list of available modules will change only when you modify the application. Alternatively, you could create an XML Web service in which the user needs to log in before calling the *GetModules* method. In this case, the list of module names might correspond to the allowed user functions.

In a bug-tracking (incident-reporting) application, for example, some users will be allowed to report bugs, whereas others might have access to task-assignment or user-configuration modules. This approach of partitioning an application into dynamic modules is extremely useful for low-bandwidth clients because users won't need to wait while the assemblies are downloaded for features they will never use. It also tightens security one more notch, ensuring that users won't ever see the code that contains the restricted functionality (unless more than one individual uses the same workstation). However, there are some drawbacks. The dynamic interface can lead to unnecessary support headaches because different users will end up using subtly different hybrid versions of the application. You might need to test the application under these different scenarios. It also becomes impossible for different modules to communicate with one another unless the application browser takes on the responsibility of facilitating this communication.

Summary

This chapter presented two approaches to automated deployment. The application launcher design is a "common-sense" solution: It doesn't involve a new .NET redesign, and it works well with disconnected clients that require only periodic updates. For most distributed systems, the application launcher is the best solution.

The application browser is a more ambitious approach that breaks down an entire application into distinct components. It takes more time to develop and test and introduces new issues such as code access security. If you need to create an extremely configurable and automatically updatable application, however, it might be exactly what you need.

Keep in mind that you don't necessarily need these approaches if you just want to create a fixed client application that downloads dynamic (and frequently changing) data from a Web server. The case study in Chapter 17 presents an example with a dynamic client that periodically retrieves a product catalog, stores it locally in XML, and uses the information to tailor its interface accordingly.

Part III

Case Studies

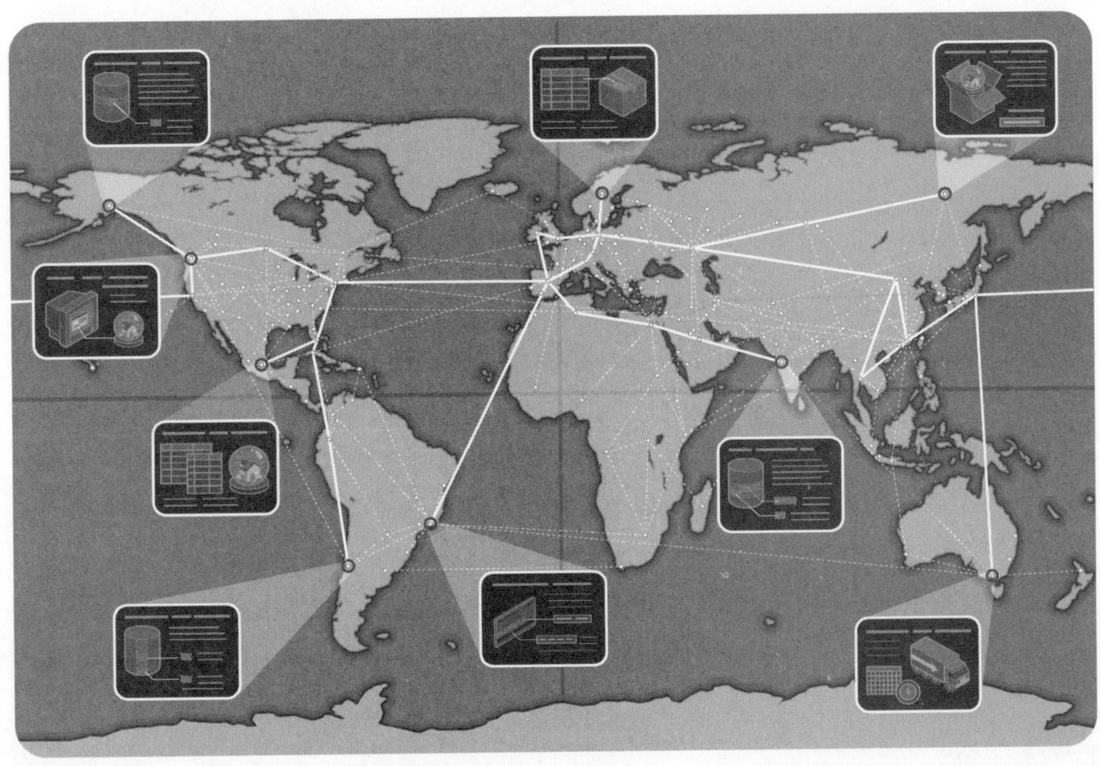

16

Invoicer.NET Traveling Sales

This chapter explores the solution to a common problem: coordinating the work of employees in the field. To make this example more relevant, we won't build the solution from scratch. Instead, we'll consider a scenario in which the new system must be based on an existing ad-hoc solution that uses Microsoft Access and Microsoft Excel. Many companies begin with these simple tools to save small amounts of repetitive work and then encounter painful stumbling blocks as they try to apply this technology to serve a much larger audience. In this chapter, we'll look at a migration path you can take to ease this setup into the Microsoft .NET world, beginning with a few server-side components to coordinate the data and gradually moving to a dedicated end-to-end solution.

The solution presented in this chapter includes a server-side Windows service that uses file system events, a simple XML Web service, a SQL Server database, and two client front ends (Windows Forms and ASP.NET). We'll also dig through some optimized ADO.NET code. In this case, we won't use .NET distributed technology to solve a performance bottleneck but to address a significant data integrity problem—quite simply, how to consolidate the information of hundreds of users who work independently and are disconnected from the system for long periods of time.

Defining the Problem

The Graphic Design Institute, a fictional company, sells trade show materials, including graphics and hardware that can be used to construct booths and displays. As the company grew from a small startup with a dozen full-time employees to a larger player, the regular paperwork involved in tracking sales and inventory purchases became impossible to manage. Eventually, the sales team standardized on using an Excel template (which was distributed around the office) to record new sales. These sales records were typically filled out in the field on a notebook computer by traveling sales staff. When a new sales order was completed, the sales associate would e-mail the spreadsheet to a sales manager at the Graphic Design Institute, who would add the information to an Access database using a Visual Basic macro program developed in-house. Then problems began to appear.

Here are some of the problems the Graphic Design Institute found with their ad hoc system:

- More than one employee needs to use the data in the Access database file. For example, different individuals use it to create sales projections, determine the inventory requirements for next quarter, and draw up monthly performance bulletins. Unfortunately, even though the database is hosted on an internal network, it cannot reliably support concurrent users. As a result, the company periodically distributes separate copies to individuals who need the data, resulting in additional coordination and distribution headaches.
- The sales template fluctuates regularly. Each version has a separate Access module coded using Visual Basic for Applications (VBA). Determining which version to use—and validating the entries—is a difficult and error-prone task.
- As the sales force expands, the regular work of inspecting the sales e-mail messages, saving the attachments, and running the Access module has become very time-consuming, and as a result the inventory supply isn't keeping up with demand. The sales force is currently up to about 100 individuals.
- The sales database is growing extremely large and is performing poorly for the aggregate queries needed to generate historical reports.
- The sales employees are demanding a way to retrieve information about the sales they submit. Unfortunately, they currently have no choice but to query the sales manager directly.

These growing pains are typical of an expanding company that's trying to evolve from a patchwork of simple stopgap solutions to an integrated system. Management has decided that the current year's budget doesn't allow for the development of a traditional end-to-end proprietary solution for data management. However, management is interested in a solution that might naturally evolve into a more customized system in the future.

Key Analysis

Some of the problems facing the Graphic Design Institute are the result of the company outgrowing its current system. At this point, it's clear to all involved that Access can't scale to store the large amount of data required or serve the multiple users who need to access the data. The Graphic Design Institute needs to start by installing an enterprise database engine (in this example, Microsoft SQL Server) and building a new table structure. This is the most time-consuming step, but it won't necessarily involve a large expense because the sales employees won't need to access the server directly. Instead, the Graphic Design Institute only needs to add licenses for the server-side components, which will connect directly to the database as needed.

Beyond the upgrade to SQL Server, the problems—and the possible solutions—become a little more complicated. There are two important points about the way this system is used:

- The sales employees perform their work in a disconnected state, without necessarily having a network or Internet connection. Therefore, the solution must allow the completed invoice to be submitted after it is created.
- The sales employees don't receive any immediate result or response when they submit their orders. This means the server doesn't need to process client requests synchronously. Instead, it can take full advantage of asynchronous processing and handle the work when convenient.

Finally, the upgradeability of any solution is a key concern. Many of the problems that the Graphic Design Institute is experiencing are a direct result of not having planned for the future. In crafting a new solution, it's all too easy to meet the current needs by creating a system that will be just as difficult to enhance as their current one.

Although Excel will remain the sales reporting tool for the near future, it would be a dangerous mistake to assume that it will always be the best approach for the Graphic Design Institute. In the future, the problems inherent in using Excel to create orders (such as the lack of strict validation at the time of entry and the difficulty in managing new versions of the custom spreadsheet) might require the development of a proprietary order-entering client. If the new system is designed using server code that is tightly coupled to Excel, this enhancement won't be easy. In our solution, we'll consider carefully how the various parts of the system can be separated and what future improvements can be made without requiring a full rewrite.

Evaluating Different Paths

The disconnected nature of this system is the most significant factor in determining how to architect the solution. In Chapter 8, we considered using message queues for this task. In this case, message queues aren't a viable option because they require a dedicated client program, which the Graphic Design Institute isn't ready to develop or support. In addition, message queues aren't included with older Windows operating systems, and the Graphic Design Institute isn't prepared to tackle the effort required to upgrade or reconfigure sales notebooks. Only one assumption can be made about the notebooks used by the sales staff: They support e-mail and basic Internet access. Therefore, an ASP.NET front end is an ideal choice. However, ASP.NET would require the sales staff to be connected to the Internet at the time of order entry, which might not be practical. To overcome this limitation, we can use an ASP.NET page just to upload the completed orders, not to enter and process them. This fits with the Graphic Design Institute's plans to stay with the Excel format for the present.

Of course, the ultimate solution needs to be implemented in separate stages—development, deployment, and testing. Here's a recommended migration strategy:

1. Replace the manual steps that the sales manager currently takes to add the information into the Access database. The new process should also be implemented generically enough that new spreadsheet versions can be created without causing confusion or requiring a recompile.

2. Provide a consistent way for order files to be transferred from the sales notebooks to the central system. Ideally, this transfer method will bypass the sales manager completely unless a problem occurs.

3. Consider some future enhancements, such as creating a dedicated Windows Forms front end and moving validation to the client.

Defining the Solution

The new system will be named Invoicer.NET, and will consist of several parts. The core of the new system will be an *OrderProcessor* component that will run on the server, reading information from the Excel file and committing it to a record in the SQL Server database. This component will run continuously on a server computer and will be implemented as a Windows service. This component is used in both the first and second stage of the design.

Of course, the client won't interact directly with the *OrderProcessor* component. Instead, the sales manager will receive the e-mail and forward the spreadsheet to the *OrderProcessor*. Figure 16-1 diagrams the first iteration of the system. Notice that the sales manager just copies the e-mail file to the appropriate directory. The *OrderProcessor* component uses Windows file system events to ensure that it is notified whenever a file arrives. This is a simple, robust approach to implementing a queue-like behavior. Polling a database or manually scanning a directory would incur more system overhead. Another benefit to this approach is that it is quite effective for a smaller organization that might not have a Web server where it can host an ASP.NET Web site or an XML Web service. However, the sales manager is still a bottleneck and a possible single point of failure for this system because all traffic must be routed through that e-mail.

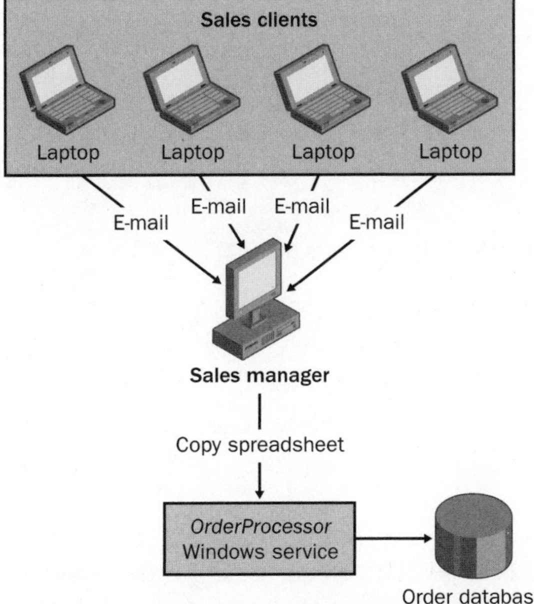

Figure 16-1 Architecture of the system: stage 1

As the system enters its second stage, a dedicated ASP.NET client will perform the task that the sales manager performs manually—transferring the files. On the back end, the *OrderProcessor* will still perform the raw data crunching, but the ASP.NET Web page will enable sales staff to upload their spreadsheets directly. Optionally, a Windows client can be added to perform a similar task through an XML Web service. Figure 16-2 shows both of these approaches.

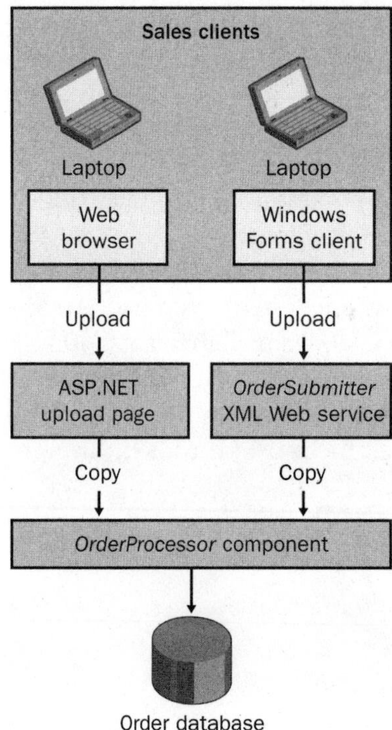

Figure 16-2 Architecture of the system: stages 2 and 3

Finally, a more advanced Windows client can be developed that works natively with an XML Web service and bypasses the Excel layer. We'll explore how you can prepare for this design at the end of this chapter.

The Data Layer

The first step in creating this system is to build the database. In our case, we'll use a fairly simple set of tables so we can focus on the overall architecture rather than mundane details such as setting multiple fields and adding stored procedure parameters. In a typical business system, the logic would closely match our example, but the database tables would be expanded. For example, the Products table would probably require additional fields to track detailed product information. The database might also include additional tables such as ProductCategories.

Figure 16-3 shows the business-specific tables for our stripped-down data layer. Essentially, there are two order-specific tables: Orders, which includes a record for each Excel file that is processed, and the child table OrderItems, which contains the list of ordered items for every order. There are also a Products table, which lists the services and items the Graphic Design Institute sells; a SalesAgent table, which includes a record for every sales associate; and a Customers table, which tracks the companies that buy from the Graphic Design Institute.

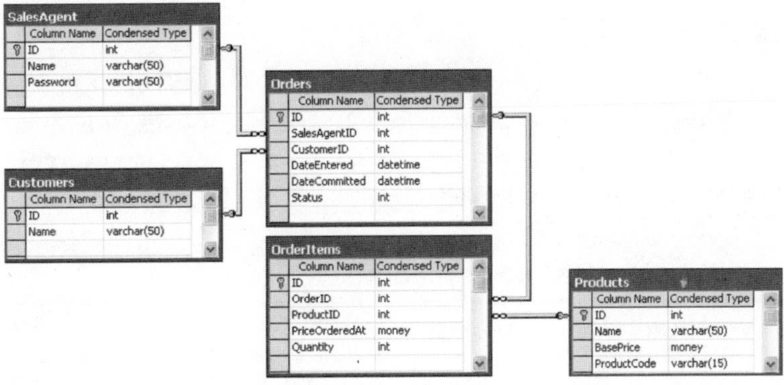

Figure 16-3 The business tables

> **Note** As with just about any financial or commerce-based database, the price of a product has to be recorded in the actual order record. This is common sense because the price might fluctuate after the order is committed and the sale price is important for billing and historical data.

The database includes an additional table that's intended for internal use by the *OrderProcessor* component. This table, called ExcelMappings, is a critical part of the puzzle because it allows the program code to be abstracted away from the structure of the Excel spreadsheet (as shown in Figure 16-4). This enables the Graphic Design Institute to create new spreadsheets without needing to create new versions of the server-side code for order processing. The details behind this approach are explained a little later.

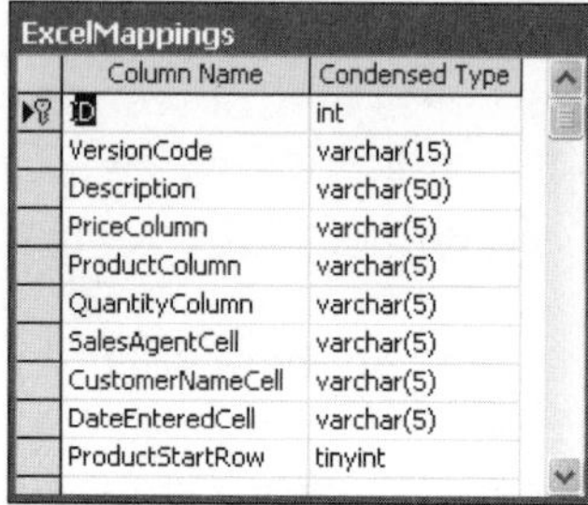

Figure 16-4 The internal ExcelMappings table

Stored Procedures

To perfect this database, you would probably want to add a full complement of views, indexes, and stored procedures. For our purposes, however, we'll focus on adding the functionality required by the order-processing server component. There are six stored procedures (described in Table 16-1).

Table 16-1 Invoicer Stored Procedures

Stored Procedure	Description
CustomerAdd	Inserts a new record into the Customers table.
OrderAdd	Inserts a new record into the Orders table.
OrderItemAdd	Inserts a new record into the OrderItems table. There is one record for every product purchased as part of an order.
GetCustomerIDByName	Retrieves the ID column for the customer record that matches the supplied name. This allows the code to determine whether a customer exists in the database or whether one must be added.
GetProductIDByCode	Retrieves the ID column for the product record that matches the supplied product code. This is important because products are linked to orders by their unique ID numbers but the Excel spreadsheet lists only the product code.
GetExcelMappings	Retrieves a row from the ExcelMappings table with the specified version code. This row describes all the information the code needs to find values on the spreadsheet.

Listing 16-1 presents the combined code for the first three stored procedures (*CustomerAdd*, *OrderAdd*, and *OrderItemAdd*), which are dedicated to adding database records.

```
CREATE Procedure CustomerAdd
 (
    @Name   nvarchar(50),
    @ID     int OUTPUT
 )
 AS
 INSERT INTO Customers
 (
    Name
 )
 VALUES
 (
    @Name
 )
 SELECT
    @ID = @@Identity


CREATE Procedure OrderAdd
 (
    @SalesAgentID int,
    @CustomerID   int,
    @DateEntered  datetime,
    @Status       int,
    @ID           int OUTPUT
 )
 AS
 INSERT INTO Orders
 (
    SalesAgentID,
    CustomerID,
    DateEntered,
    Status,
    DateCommitted
 )
 VALUES
 (
    @SalesAgentID,
    @CustomerID,
    @DateEntered,
    @Status,
```

Listing 16-1 Stored procedures for inserting data

```
    GETDATE()
  )
  SELECT
    @ID = @@Identity


CREATE Procedure OrderItemAdd
  (
    @OrderID        int,
    @ProductID      int,
    @PriceOrderedAt money,
    @Quantity       int,
    @ID             int OUTPUT
  )
  AS
  INSERT INTO OrderItems
  (
    OrderID,
    ProductID,
    PriceOrderedAt,
    Quantity
  )
  VALUES
  (
    @OrderID,
    @ProductID,
    @PriceOrderedAt,
    @Quantity
  )
  SELECT
    @ID = @@Identity
```

Optionally, you could create a more complex stored procedure that adds an order record and all subitems in one step. This would reduce the number of round-trips and would improve performance, but it would require some more intricate SQL, it would be more difficult to maintain, and it would offer reduced opportunity for code reuse.

Listing 16-2 shows the stored procedure code used for the *GetCustomerIDByName* and *GetProductIDByCode* stored procedures, which accept a unique value and return the corresponding identifier.

```
CREATE PROCEDURE GetCustomerIDByName
 (
    @Name varchar(50)
 )
 AS
    SELECT [ID] FROM Customers
    WHERE [Name] = @Name

CREATE PROCEDURE GetProductIDByCode
 (
    @Code varchar(15)
 )
 AS
    SELECT [ID] FROM Products
    WHERE ProductCode = @Code
```

Listing 16-2 Stored procedures for retrieving data

Finally, another stored procedure is required to return the list of Excel mappings for a specific version code. This stored procedure is quite simple:

```
CREATE PROCEDURE GetExcelMappings
 (
    @VersionCode varchar(15)
 )
 AS
    SELECT * FROM ExcelMappings
    WHERE VersionCode = @VersionCode
```

The Excel Spreadsheet

The Excel file is the least flexible part of the system. Because it is already in widespread use and is distributed to dozens of sales associates, it cannot be easily changed. However, one change is required: the addition of a dedicated version code field that distinguishes the different spreadsheet versions. This version code is set in cell F2, which is the only hard-coded cell value. This cell was chosen based on the current Graphic Design Institute spreadsheet; all future spreadsheets must adhere to this convention. Most of the other details will be customizable.

Fortunately, the Graphic Design Institute already uses a system in which orders are given unique filenames that combine the date, customer, and sales agent code (for instance, 2003-03-03_FRX_JM.xls). This ensures that all filenames are unique. At the end of this chapter, we'll consider some techniques you could use if unique filenames weren't guaranteed.

Figure 16-5 shows a sample Excel spreadsheet. For the sake of simplicity, we are assuming that only a single workbook sheet is used in the file. In most scenarios, the Excel file will be far more complicated and might include a significant amount of information that isn't relevant to the order (such as a recent price list). In fact, many companies develop multipage spreadsheets that compute the final order values to read-only fields on a separate sheet using Excel macros. These details don't change the validity of our approach, however, which is to abstract the structure of the Excel file as much as possible.

Microsoft Excel - test.xls

	A	B	C	D	E
1					
2	Customer:	Northwind Traders			Version Code: 2003-001
3					
4	Product Code	Price	Quantity	Total	
5	133AE	$14.99	10	$149.90	
6	422-XG	$1,012.01	1	$1,012.01	
7	3A22	$49.75	2	$99.50	
8	149AE	$2,000.00	1	$2,000.00	
9					
10					
11			Grand Total:	$3,261.41	
12			Date:	2003-05-05	
13					
14					
15					
16	Sales Agent:	Eli Bowen	221		
17					

Figure 16-5 The order spreadsheet

To create the mapping record for this version (2003-001), you need to specify the row where order items start (5); the columns for price (B), product (A), and quantity (C) information; and the cell where the sales associate (C16) and customer (B2) are recorded. Figure 16-6 shows the complete ExcelMappings row.

Data in Table 'ExcelMappings' in 'Invoicer' on '(local)'

ID	VersionCode	PriceColumn	ProductColumn	QuantityColumn	SalesAgentCell	CustomerNameCell	DateEnteredCell	ProductStartRow
1	2003-001	B	A	C	C16	B2	D12	5

Figure 16-6 The Excel mapping

The Data Component

The first step in creating the data component is to define the record structures, as shown in Listing 16-3. Note that the code doesn't currently include definitions for all the tables, just those that the application will manipulate.

```
Public Class Customer
    Public ID As Integer
    Public Name As String
End Class

' This enumeration contains custom status codes that are used to
' fill the Status field of the Order table.
Public Enum StatusCode
    Open = 501
    Waiting = 502
    Fulfilled = 503
    Problem = 504
End Enum

' CustomerName is included as a member of this structure, even though
' it is technically part of the linked customer record. The reason is
' that the Excel file only specifies customer names, not the unique ID
' numbers.
Public Class Order
    Public ID As Integer
    Public OrderItems As New ArrayList()
    Public SalesAgentID As Integer
    Public CustomerID As Integer
    Public CustomerName As String
    Public DateEntered As Date
    Public Status As StatusCode
End Class

' OrderItem instances can be added to the OrderItems property of the
' Order class. A more defensive approach would be to use a custom class
' to restrict invalid objects from being assigned to the OrderItems
' property, as demonstrated in Chapter 3.
Public Class OrderItem
    Public ID As Integer
    Public OrderID As Integer
    Public ProductID As Integer
    Public ProductCode As String
    Public PriceOrderedAt As Decimal
    Public Quantity As Integer
End Class
```

Listing 16-3 Data entities

Public member variables are used rather than full property procedures because these structures will be used only in the server-side code, and there aren't any rules that you need to enforce there. By the time the data is transferred to the server, it's too late to identify input problems and correct them. Instead, the client needs to assume this responsibility. In addition, any server methods that receive data from the client need to be equipped with the appropriate validation logic.

> **Note** As always, it is valid for an information package to exist even if not all the fields are set to valid values. For example, you might receive an *OrderItem* instance from a method that sets only some of the properties, or you might have an *Order* class that doesn't provide its linked *OrderItem* instances. Similarly, a newly created *Order*, *OrderItem*, or *Customer* object won't yet have its unique ID property set.

As with all well-designed data components, functionality is restricted to using stored procedures that exist in the database. This makes it easier to introduce changes and optimizations later on. Dynamic SQL statements, which are every developer's favorite trick, are notoriously difficult to optimize and more fragile because the database administrator will have no way of knowing the dependencies of your code.

> **Note** To really round out this solution, you would probably want to create dedicated administrative tools to automate every database interaction. With our implementation, a SQL Server–savvy user would be required to commit the details for new Excel sheet versions and new products into the database using a tool such as SQL Server Enterprise Manager.

The *CustomersDB* Class

Listing 16-4 shows the service provider code for the Customers table. Note that even though each table provides only one or two functions, the code has been organized into two table-specific classes. This isn't necessary, but it provides a solid framework for adding database functionality in the future.

```
Public Class CustomersDB

    Private ConnectionString As String

    Friend Sub New(Connection As String)
        Me.ConnectionString = Connection
    End Sub

    ' AddCustomer uses the CustomerAdd stored procedure.
    Public Function AddCustomer(customer As Customer) As Integer

        Dim con As New SqlConnection(ConnectionString)
        Dim cmd As New SqlCommand("CustomerAdd", con)

        cmd.CommandType = CommandType.StoredProcedure
        Dim Param As SqlParameter

        Param = cmd.Parameters.Add( _
         "@Name", SqlDbType.NVarChar, 50)
        Param.Value = customer.Name

        ' Add the output parameter.
        Param = cmd.Parameters.Add("@ID", SqlDbType.Int)
        Param.Direction = ParameterDirection.Output

        Try
            con.Open()
            cmd.ExecuteNonQuery()

        Catch Err As Exception
            ' Use "caller inform" exception handling pattern.
            Throw New ApplicationException( _
             "Exception encountered when executing command.", Err)

        Finally
            con.Close()

        End Try

        ' Return the unique ID output parameter.
        Return Param.Value

    End Function

    ' CheckIfCustomerExists uses the GetCustomerIDByName stored
    ' procedure.
```

Listing 16-4 The *CustomersDB* service provider

```
    Public Function CheckIfCustomerExists(Name As String) As Integer

        Dim con As New SqlConnection(ConnectionString)
        Dim cmd As New SqlCommand("GetCustomerIDByName", con)
        Dim r As SqlDataReader

        cmd.CommandType = CommandType.StoredProcedure
        Dim Param As SqlParameter

        Param = cmd.Parameters.Add( _
         "@Name", SqlDbType.NVarChar, 50)
        Param.Value = Name

        Dim ID As Integer = 0

        Try
            con.Open()
            r  = cmd.ExecuteReader(CommandBehavior.SingleRow)
            If r.Read() = True
                ' A customer exists with this name.
                ID = r("ID")
            End If

        Catch Err As Exception
            ' Use "caller inform" exception handling pattern.
            Throw New ApplicationException( _
             "Exception encountered when executing command.", Err)

        Finally
            If Not (r Is Nothing) Then r.Close()
            con.Close()
        End Try

        Return ID

    End Function

End Class
```

The *OrdersDB* Class

The *OrdersDB* class is a little more complex. It provides a public *AddOrder* function and a private *AddItem* function. Here's the basic structure:

```
Public Class OrdersDB
    Private ConnectionString As String

    Friend Sub New(Connection As String)
        Me.ConnectionString = Connection
    End Sub

    ' Encapsulates the logic needed to add an order and its sub-items.
    Public Function AddOrder(ByVal order As Order) As Integer
        ' (Code omitted.)
    End Function

    Private Function AddItem(ByVal item As OrderItem, _
     ByVal con As SqlConnection)
        ' (Code omitted.)
    End Function

End Class
```

AddItem is private so that it can be called only as part of an *AddOrder* operation. This allows the *OrdersDB* class to implement a more optimized design. Essentially, it works like this: the *AddOrder* method opens the connection to the database, calls *AddItem* as required, and then closes the connection. *AddItem* receives a reference to the database connection, and assumes that it is open. It uses this connection to execute its commands directly. This way, you can add an order that includes multiple products without incurring the additional overhead of repeatedly opening and closing new connections.

Listing 16-5 shows the logic for the *AddOrder* method:

```
Public Function AddOrder(ByVal order As Order) As Integer

    Dim con As New SqlConnection(ConnectionString)
    Dim cmd As New SqlCommand("OrderAdd", con)

    cmd.CommandType = CommandType.StoredProcedure
    Dim Param As SqlParameter

    Param = cmd.Parameters.Add("@SalesAgentID", SqlDbType.Int)
    Param.Value = order.SalesAgentID
```

Listing 16-5 The *OrdersDB.AddOrder* method

```
        Param = cmd.Parameters.Add("@CustomerID", SqlDbType.Int)
        Param.Value = order.CustomerID
        Param = cmd.Parameters.Add("@DateEntered", SqlDbType.DateTime)
        Param.Value = order.DateEntered

        Param = cmd.Parameters.Add("@Status", SqlDbType.Int)
        Param.Value = order.Status

        ' Add the output parameter.
        Param = cmd.Parameters.Add("@ID", SqlDbType.Int)
        Param.Direction = ParameterDirection.Output

        Try
            con.Open()
            cmd.ExecuteNonQuery()

            ' Now add the order items.
            Dim Item As OrderItem
            For Each Item In order.OrderItems
                ' Set the ID of the parent order record
                ' that was just inserted.
                Item.OrderID = Param.Value
                AddItem(Item, con)
            Next

        Catch Err As Exception
            ' Use "caller inform" exception handling pattern.
            Throw New ApplicationException( _
             "Exception encountered when executing command.", Err)

        Finally
            con.Close()

        End Try

        ' Return the unique ID output parameter.
        Return Param.Value

    End Function
```

The *AddItem* method has an additional responsibility. Because the spreadsheet lists only product codes, not product IDs, the *AddItem* method must look up the corresponding ID for each item before it can insert the order item record, as shown in Listing 16-6.

```
Private Function AddItem(ByVal item As OrderItem, _
 ByVal con As SqlConnection)

    Dim Param As SqlParameter
    Dim cmd As SqlCommand

    ' Check if the ProductID is 0. If so, the number must be looked
    ' up using the ProductCode property.
    ' This could be implemented as a separate public method in a
    ' ProductsDB class, but the overhead of continuously opening and
    ' closing the connection to check each product would slow down
    ' the application.
    If item.ProductID = 0 Then
        cmd = New SqlCommand("GetProductIDByCode", con)
        cmd.CommandType = CommandType.StoredProcedure
        Param = cmd.Parameters.Add("@Code", SqlDbType.VarChar, 15)
        Param.Value = item.ProductCode

        Dim r As SqlDataReader
        r = cmd.ExecuteReader(CommandBehavior.SingleRow)
        r.Read()
        item.ProductID = r("ID")
        r.Close()
    End If

    cmd = New SqlCommand("OrderItemAdd", con)
    cmd.CommandType = CommandType.StoredProcedure

    Param = cmd.Parameters.Add("@ProductID", SqlDbType.Int)
    Param.Value = item.ProductID

    Param = cmd.Parameters.Add("@OrderID", SqlDbType.Int)
    Param.Value = item.OrderID

    Param = cmd.Parameters.Add("@PriceOrderedAt", SqlDbType.Money)
    Param.Value = item.PriceOrderedAt

    Param = cmd.Parameters.Add("@Quantity", SqlDbType.Int)
    Param.Value = item.Quantity

    ' Add the output parameter.
    Param = cmd.Parameters.Add("@ID", SqlDbType.Int)
    Param.Direction = ParameterDirection.Output

    cmd.ExecuteNonQuery()

End Function
```

Listing 16-6 The private *OrdersDB.AddItem* function

The *InvoicerTables* Class

With this factored design, the client needs to use two classes: *OrdersDB* and *CustomersDB*. The *InvoicerTables* class (shown in Listing 16-7) wraps these two classes, so that they client does not need to create them separately. It also includes the code that retrieves and applies the connection string information from a configuration file.

```
Public Class InvoicerTables
    Public Customers As CustomerDB
    Public Orders As OrderDB

    Public Sub New()
        ' Retrieve the connection string.
        Dim Connection As String = ConfigurationSettings.AppSettings( _
          "InvoicerConnection")
        Customers = New CustomerDB(Connection)
        Orders = New OrderDB(Connection)
    End Sub

End Class
```

To accommodate this design, you should mark the constructors for *CustomersDB* and *OrdersDB* with the accessibility keyword *Friend*. This means that only code in the same assembly (for example, code in the *InvoicerTables* class) can create a *CustomersDB* or *OrdersDB* instance.

The configuration file that *InvoicerTables* uses is shown in Listing 16-7.

```
<?xml version="1.0"?>
<configuration>

  <appSettings>
    <add key="InvoicerConnection"
         value="Data Source=localhost;Initial Catalog=Invoicer;
                Integrated Security=SSPI" />
  </appSettings>

</configuration>
```

Listing 16-7 Composition with *InvoicerTables*

There's one other part of the database—the class that will allow access to the Excel mapping information. To ensure that the Excel processing code isn't tied too closely to the business logic, you implement it in a separate class (as discussed in the next section).

The *ExcelTranslator* Class

The next step is to prepare the server-side code that scans the submitted Excel files and inserts the required database records. This task conceals another key design decision.

A programmer who attacks this problem directly might be tempted to perform all the work in a single method call. The original Access program uses this approach and steps through the Excel file, generating and executing a new database command for each line item. This approach will work, but it is extremely inflexible. If you decide later to upgrade the application by adding a dedicated Windows client that submits order requests directly, you need to rewrite the database code completely. As mentioned at the beginning of this case study, one of the key requirements for this system is the ability to migrate to a more sophisticated design in the future.

To ensure that your solution isn't tightly coupled to the Excel format, you must separate the logic that scans the Excel spreadsheet from the logic that inserts the order and order item records. Thanks to the careful design of the database component, this task is easy—all you need to do is rely on the *Order* information package class to transfer the retrieved data.

The *ExcelTranslator* encapsulates all the logic needed to scan through the Excel spreadsheet and convert its information in an *Order* object. The two methods of the *ExcelTranslator* class are implemented as shared helpers, which means the client won't need to create a class instance in order to use them.

The private *GetMappings* function retrieves the required mapping information from the database and returns it using a custom *ExcelMapping* class:

```
Public Class ExcelMapping
    Public ID As Integer
    Public VersionCode As String
    Public Description As String
    Public PriceColumn As String
    Public ProductColumn As String
    Public QuantityColumn As String
    Public SalesAgentCell As String
    Public CustomerNameCell As String
    Public DateEnteredCell As String
    Public ProductStartRow As Integer
End Class
```

Listing 16-8 shows the *ExcelTranslator.GetMappings* function. The same configuration file is used to retrieve the database connection string.

```
Private Shared Function GetMappings(ByVal version As String) _
 As ExcelMapping

    Dim Mapping As New ExcelMapping()

    ' Retrieve the connection string.
    Dim ConnectionString As String
    ConnectionString = ConfigurationSettings.AppSettings( _
      "InvoicerConnection")

    ' Define and execute the GetExcelMappings stored procedure.
    Dim con As New SqlConnection(ConnectionString)
    Dim cmd As New SqlCommand("GetExcelMappings", con)
    Dim r As SqlDataReader

    cmd.CommandType = CommandType.StoredProcedure
    Dim Param As SqlParameter

    Param = cmd.Parameters.Add( _
     "@VersionCode", SqlDbType.NVarChar, 15)
    Param.Value = version

    Try
        con.Open()
        r = cmd.ExecuteReader(CommandBehavior.SingleRow)

        r.Read()
        Mapping.ID = r("ID")
        Mapping.Description = r("Description")
        Mapping.VersionCode = r("VersionCode")
        Mapping.PriceColumn = r("PriceColumn")
        Mapping.ProductColumn = r("ProductColumn")
        Mapping.QuantityColumn = r("QuantityColumn")
        Mapping.SalesAgentCell = r("SalesAgentCell")
        Mapping.CustomerNameCell = r("CustomerNameCell")
        Mapping.DateEnteredCell = r("DateEnteredCell")
        Mapping.ProductStartRow = r("ProductStartRow")

    Catch Err As Exception
        ' This error is not packaged inside a custom application
        ' exception because this is a private function.
        ' The public function that calls this method can rethrow
        ' this exception to the client with a more suitable wrapper.
        Throw Err

    Finally
        If Not (r Is Nothing) Then r.Close()
```

Listing 16-8 The private *ExcelTranslator.GetMappings* function

```
            con.Close()

        End Try

        Return Mapping

    End Function
```

The *ConvertExcelFileToOrder* method is the most interesting part of the *ExcelTranslator* class. It accepts a file path to an Excel file and uses the Excel Automation objects to process the file. The Excel Automation objects are a COM-based library of controls that enable you to control (or "drive") Excel, provided Excel is installed on the current computer. You can use the Automation objects to open files, read values, or do anything else you can do manually through the Excel GUI.

To use the Excel Automation objects in .NET, you need to create a *runtime callable wrapper* (RCW), which is essentially a proxy through which your .NET code can interact with a COM object. You can create this wrapper by using the tlbimp.exe command-line utility or by adding a Visual Studio .NET project reference (as shown in Figure 16-7). Just choose Add Reference from the Project menu, and then click on the COM tab of the Add Reference window. The actual name of the Automation objects depends on the version of Excel you have installed. With Excel 2000, the library is version 9.0, whereas Excel 2002 (included with Microsoft Office XP) uses version 10.

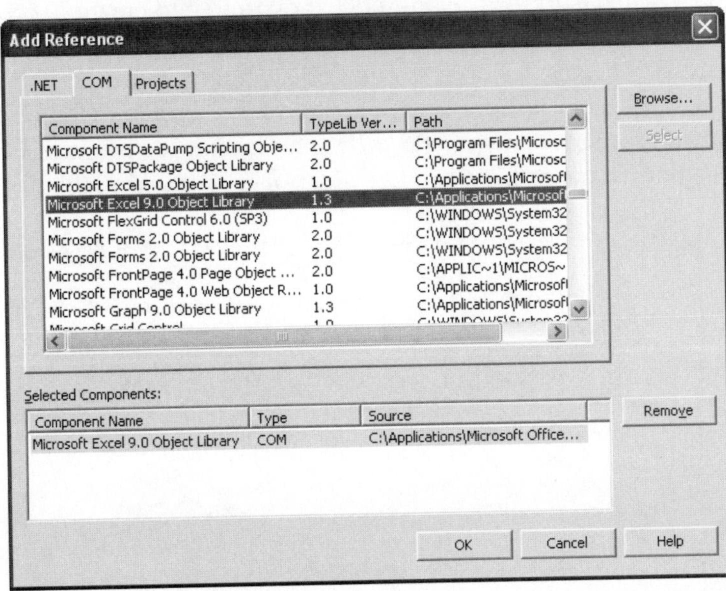

Figure 16-7 The Excel Automation object

The newly added RCW objects use the same name as the COM library. The assemblies are generated in the project output directory and are visible in Solution Explorer (as shown in Figure 16-8).

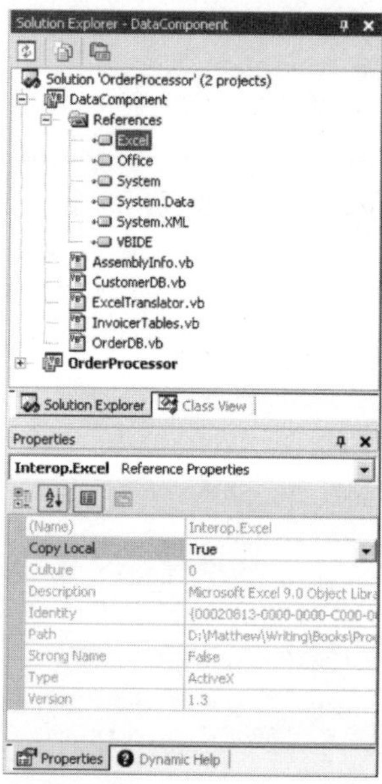

Figure 16-8 The RCW for the Excel Automation object

After you have added the reference, you're free to create *Excel.Application* and *Excel.Worksheet* objects. Listing 16-9 shows the code that parses the Excel file and creates the *Order* object. The code interacts with the Excel document through a worksheet wrapper, which provides a *Range* method that enables you to retrieve a value in specific cells. The lookup cells are not hard-coded, however; they're drawn from the ExcelMappings database table.

```
Public Shared Function ConvertExcelFileToOrder(ByVal path As String) _
 As Order

    Dim Order As New Order()

    ' This is the programmatic equivalent of starting the
    ' Excel application.
    Dim ExcelApp As New Excel.Application()

    Try
        ExcelApp.Workbooks.Open(path)

        ' Select the first sheet (note that this object uses
        ' 1-based, not zero-based counting, unlike .NET.
```

Listing 16-9 The *ExcelTranslator.ConvertExcelFileToOrder* method

```
        Dim Sheet As Excel.Worksheet = ExcelApp.Workbooks(1).Sheets(1)

        ' Determine the version code.
        Dim Version As String = Sheet.Range("F2").Value

        ' Get mappings for this version.
        Dim Mappings As ExcelMapping = GetMappings(Version)

        ' Convert the sheet into an order.
        Order.SalesAgentID = Sheet.Range(Mappings.SalesAgentCell).Value

        Order.DateEntered = Sheet.Range(Mappings.DateEnteredCell).Value
        Order.CustomerName = _
         Sheet.Range(Mappings.CustomerNameCell).Value
        Order.Status = StatusCode.Open

        ' Store the cell column for each piece of information that must
        ' be retrieved.
        Dim Counter As Integer = Mappings.ProductStartRow
        Dim Prod As String = Mappings.ProductColumn
        Dim Price As String = Mappings.PriceColumn
        Dim Q As String = Mappings.QuantityColumn

        Do Until Sheet.Range(Prod & Counter.ToString()).Value = ""
            ' Add item at current row.
            Dim Item As New OrderItem()
            Item.ProductCode = Sheet.Range(Prod & _
                                 Counter.ToString()).Value
            Item.PriceOrderedAt = Sheet.Range(Price & _
                                 Counter.ToString()).Value
            Item.Quantity = Sheet.Range(Q & Counter.ToString()).Value

            Order.OrderItems.Add(Item)

            Counter += 1
        Loop

    Catch Err As Exception
        ' Use "caller inform" exception handling pattern.
        Throw New ApplicationException( _
         "Exception encountered when executing command.", Err)

    Finally
        Excel.Workbooks.Close()
        Excel.Quit()

    End Try

    Return Order

End Function
```

The Back-End *OrderProcessor* Service

Now that the data classes have abstracted away the heavy lifting, the *OrderProcessor* has only one task remaining: to scan the Excel file and invoke the methods needed to add the order and order item records.

The *OrderProcessor* is created as a Windows service that runs uninterrupted on any computer (including a server or the sales manager's workstation). For most of its life, it remains quietly idle. When a new Excel file appears in the designated directory, however, it springs into action, transferring the information into the database and moving the file to a new directory. To automate this task, the *OrderProcessor* uses the *FileSystemWatcher* class from the *System.IO* namespace. This class has a single purpose in life: to forward notification from the operating system to your program when certain changes occur to the file system. This enables you to respond to actions such as the creation, deletion, or modification of a file without resorting to resource-intensive polling. Your code is automatically notified when a change occurs through a standard .NET event.

To use the *FileSystemWatcher* class, you need to take three simple steps:

1. Set the *Path* property to indicate the directory you want to monitor (for instance, E:\ExcelFiles).
2. Set the *Filter* property to indicate the types of files you are monitoring for (for instance, *.xls).
3. If you're monitoring changes, set the *NotifyFilter* to indicate the type of changes you want to monitor for. In our case, we're monitoring file creation, so we don't need to use the *NotifyFilter*.

The *FileSystemWatcher* class raises four events: *Changed*, *Created*, *Deleted*, and *Renamed*. If you need to, you can disable these events by setting the *EnableRaisingEvents* property to *False*.

The *Created*, *Deleted*, and *Renamed* events are easy to handle. If you want to use the *Changed* event, however, you need to use the *NotifyFilter* property to indicate the types of changes you're looking for (for example, a file size change or filename change). Otherwise, your program might be swamped by an unceasing series of events as files are modified. If you're monitoring changes, you might also need to tweak the *InternalBufferSize* property to make sure that changes aren't lost if they occur in quick succession. The *InternalBufferSize* property should be left alone if possible, however, because it uses nonpaged memory that cannot be swapped to disk. The default buffer is 8192 bytes (8 KB).

Listing 16-10 shows the basic structure for the *OrderProcessor* service.

```
Public Class OrderProcessor
    Inherits System.ServiceProcess.ServiceBase

    ' This class will notify the code when a new Excel appears.
    Private Watcher As New FileSystemWatcher()

    ' This provides the link to the database tables.
    Private Tables As InvoicerTables

    ' This stores the directory where files should be placed after they
    ' are processed.
    Private CompleteDirectory As String

    ' Fires when the service is started.
    Protected Overrides Sub OnStart(ByVal args() As String)
        ' (Code omitted.)
    End Sub

    ' Fires when the service is stopped.
    Protected Overrides Sub OnStop()
        ' (Code omitted.)
    End Sub

    ' Handles the FileSystemWatcher.Created event and processes
    ' the new file.
    Private Sub Watcher_Created(ByVal sender As Object, _
     ByVal e As System.IO.FileSystemEventArgs)
        ' (Code omitted.)
    End Sub

    ' Used to log diagnostic messages.
    Private Sub Log(ByVal message As String)
        ' (Code omitted.)
    End Sub

    ' Creates the service instance when it is first loaded.
    Public Shared Sub Main()
        Dim Process As New OrderProcessor()
        ServiceBase.Run(Process)
    End Sub

End Class
```

Listing 16-10 The *OrderProcessor* service

You'll notice that a private *Log* function handles any diagnostic messages the code needs to output. This is an important step because Windows services are notoriously difficult to debug. The *OnStart* code, for example, will complete before you have the chance to attach a debugger. If an unhandled exception is thrown, you won't receive an informative message; instead, the Service Control Manager will just inform you that the service has started and stopped.

To help track problems, the *Log* function adds messages to the Application event log, as shown in Listing 16-11.

```
Private Sub Log(ByVal message As String)

    ' Place the message in the event log.
    Dim Log As New EventLog("Application")
    Log.Source = "OrderProcessor"
    Log.WriteEntry(message)

    ' Echo the message to any debug listeners.
    Debug.WriteLine(DateTime.Now.ToLongTimeString() & " ------------")
    Debug.WriteLine(message)

End Sub
```

Listing 16-11 Logging messages

The *OnStart* method for the service performs several tasks (as shown in Listing 16-12). First of all, it reads the required information from the application configuration file. This step could be performed in the *Main* method or the constructor, but placing it in the *OnStart* method ensures that any changes to the configuration file are picked up when the service is stopped and restarted. The *OnStart* method also creates a new instance of the *InvoicerTables* class, allowing it to read the same configuration file to determine the database connection string. Finally, the *FileSystemWatcher* class is configured and the event handler is attached.

```
Protected Overrides Sub OnStart(ByVal args() As String)

    ' Determine the path to monitor.
    Watcher.Path = ConfigurationSettings.AppSettings("MonitorPath")
    CompleteDirectory = _
     ConfigurationSettings.AppSettings("CompletePath")

    Tables = New InvoicerTables()

    ' Configure the FileSystemWatcher for Excel files.
    Watcher.Filter = "*.xls"

    ' Enable events.
    Watcher.EnableRaisingEvents = True
    AddHandler Watcher.Created, AddressOf Watcher_Created

    Log("Started watching " & Watcher.Path)

End Sub
```

Listing 16-12 Starting the service

The configuration file is shown here in its entirety:

```
<?xml version="1.0"?>
<configuration>

  <appSettings>
    <add key="InvoicerConnection"
         value="Data Source=localhost;Initial Catalog=Invoicer;
                Integrated Security=SSPI" />
    <add key="MonitorPath"
         value="E:\ExcelFiles" />
    <add key="CompletePath"
         value="E:\ExcelFiles\Complete" />
  </appSettings>

</configuration>
```

The *OnStop* method detaches the event handler and releases the *InvoicerTables* instance (as shown in Listing 16-13).

```
Protected Overrides Sub OnStop()

    Watcher.EnableRaisingEvents = False
    RemoveHandler Watcher.Created, AddressOf Watcher_Created

    Tables = Nothing

    Log("Stopped")

End Sub
```

Listing 16-13 Stopping the service

Finally, the most important work is performed in response to the *FileSystemWatcher.Created* event (as shown in Listing 16-14). The file is processed in four stages:

1. The file is submitted to the *ExcelTranslator.ConvertExcelFileToOrder* method, which returns the corresponding *Order* object.
2. The *Order.CustomerName* property is checked against the database using the *CheckIfCustomerExists* method of the *CustomersDB* class. If a record exists for this customer, the appropriate ID is added to the order. Otherwise, the customer record is inserted.
3. The *Order* object is submitted to the *AddOrder* method of the *OrdersDB* class.
4. The Excel file is copied to the directory for completed files. This step isn't necessary, but it enables you to see at a glance (using Windows Explorer) which files have been processed. This last step

is performed only if the file is successfully imported, so it also enables you to see which files haven't been imported (perhaps due to an unrecoverable error).

```
Private Sub Watcher_Created(ByVal sender As Object, _
 ByVal e As System.IO.FileSystemEventArgs)

    Log(e.FullPath)

    Try
        ' A new Excel file has appeared. Process it.
        Dim NewOrder As Order
        NewOrder = ExcelTranslator.ConvertExcelFileToOrder(e.FullPath)

        ' If the order is from a new customer, insert the customer
        ' record.
        NewOrder.CustomerID = _
          Tables.Customers.CheckIfCustomerExists(NewOrder.CustomerName)

        If NewOrder.CustomerID = 0 Then
            Dim NewCustomer As New Customer()
            NewCustomer.Name = NewOrder.CustomerName
            NewOrder.CustomerID = _
              Tables.Customers.AddCustomer(NewCustomer)
        End If

        ' Commit the order to the database.
        NewOrder.ID = Tables.Orders.AddOrder(NewOrder)

        ' Move the file to a new directory.
        File.Move(e.FullPath, CompleteDirectory & "\" & e.Name)

        Log("Order " & NewOrder.ID.ToString() & " added")

    Catch Err As Exception

        ' Additional logging code can be added here.
        ' For example, you might want to send an email to the sales
        ' manager.
        Log("Failure " & Err.ToString())

    End Try

End Sub
```

Listing 16-14 Importing a new file

With this code, the solution is complete in its first stage. You can run the *OrderProcessor* component and manually copy Excel file attachments to the appropriate directory for automatic processing.

The Web Front End

The next step is to remove the requirement for the sales manager to download and copy the Excel files. The easiest approach that is guaranteed to be supported for all sales notebooks is to create a basic ASP.NET upload page.

ASP.NET allows uploads through the HtmlInputFile control. To allow a user-initiated upload, you need to take three steps:

1. Set the encoding type of the form to *"multipart/form-data"*. You can do this by setting a property of the *HtmlForm* control class, or you can just find the tag in your ASPX file and modify as shown here. If you don't make this change, your uploading code won't work.

   ```
   <form id="Form1" enctype="multipart/form-data" runat="server">
     <!--
    Server controls go here, including the HtmlInputFile control. -->
   </form>
   ```

2. Add the HtmlInputFile control, either by hand as an *<input type="file" runat="server">* tag or by using Visual Studio .NET, in which case you must right-click on the HTML control and choose Run As Server Control.
3. Add a button that triggers the upload and saves the file to the server's hard drive. (The Browse button functionality is hard-wired into the browser.) You can use the *HtmlInputFile.PostedFile.SaveAs* method.

Figure 16-9 shows the simple ASP.NET page used by the Graphic Design Institute.

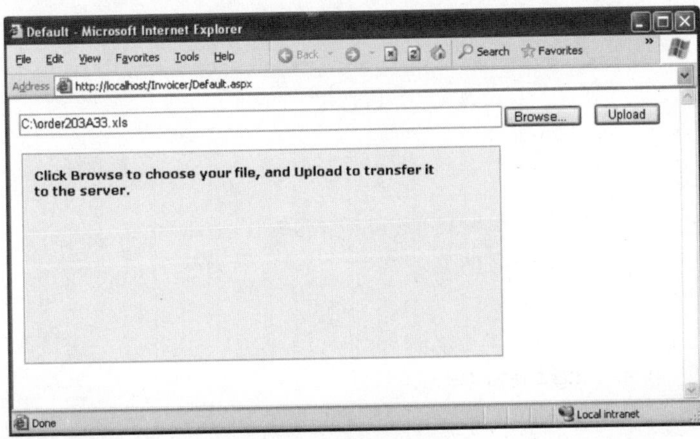

Figure 16-9 The ASP.NET upload page

The class code for the page is shown in Listing 16-15. The code reacts when the Upload button is clicked. It checks whether the file is valid (and not suspiciously large) and then transfers it to the location specified in the *MonitorPath* setting in the web.config file. The *OrderProcessor* then takes over the rest of the work.

```
Public Class Upload Page
    Inherits System.Web.UI.Page

    Protected WithEvents FileUpload As HtmlInputFile
    Protected WithEvents FileInput As HtmlInputFile
    Protected WithEvents lblInfo As Label
    Protected WithEvents cmdUpload As Button

    Private Sub cmdUpload_Click(ByVal sender As System.Object, _
     ByVal e As System.EventArgs) Handles cmdUpload.Click

        ' Check that a file is actually being submitted.
        If FileInput.PostedFile Is Nothing Then

            lblInfo.Text = "No file specified."

        Else

            If Not FileInput.PostedFile.FileName.EndsWith(".xls") Then
                lblInfo.Text = "You can only upload Excel files."

            ElseIf FileInput.PostedFile.ContentLength > 20000 Then
                lblInfo.Text = "The file is too large to be permitted."

            Else

                Try
                    ' The saved file will retain its original file
                    ' name, but be stored in the ExcelFiles directory.

                    Dim SavePath As String
                    SavePath = _
                      ConfigurationSettings.AppSettings("MonitorPath")

                    SavePath &= "\" & Path.GetFileName( _
                      FileInput.PostedFile.FileName)

                    ' Save the file.
                    FileInput.PostedFile.SaveAs("E:\ExcelFiles\" & _
                                                ServerFileName)
```

Listing 16-15 The ASP.NET upload page code

```
                lblInfo.Text = "File " & SavePath
                lblInfo.Text &= " uploaded successfully."

            Catch Err As Exception
                lblInfo.Text = Err.Message

            End Try

        End If
    End If

End Sub

End Class
```

Alternatively, the ASP.NET page could perform the processing of the order file itself, by interacting directly with the component. However, we didn't choose this approach for a few reasons:

- While transitioning to this new solution, it's logical to expect that some users will continue to e-mail the orders instead of uploading them. Using the *OrderProcessor* component simplifies life by ensuring that all files are processed in exactly the same manner.
- By using the *OrderProcessor* component, you gain the flexibility to process files in batches or when a computer is available. If the ASP.NET page were to take over this responsibility, the user would need to wait while the file was being processed before receiving a response. This could also lead to problems if the user assumed there was a problem and refreshed the page, which would send the same file multiple times.

The XML Web Service Layer

You can introduce a similar upload strategy through a dedicated XML Web service and Windows client. The XML Web service plays the same role as the ASP.NET Web page: It accepts a buffer of bytes and writes them to the *OrderProcessor* directory. At this point, the *OrderProcessor* takes over. Listing 16-16 shows the XML Web service.

```
Public Class OrderService
    Inherits System.Web.Services.WebService

    <WebMethod()> _
    Public Sub UploadExcelFile(ByVal filename As String, _
     ByVal bytes As Byte())

        ' Determine the location and name for the new file.
        Dim SavePath As String
        SavePath = ConfigurationSettings.AppSettings("MonitorPath")
        SavePath &= "\" & filename

        ' Create a FileStream.
        Dim fs As New FileStream(SavePath, FileMode.CreateNew)

        ' Write the received bytes to the file.
        fs.Write(bytes, 0, bytes.Length)
        fs.Close()

    End Sub

End Class
```

Listing 16-16 The Excel upload XML Web service

The Windows client provides the functionality for selecting a file and transmitting it to the XML Web service (as shown in Figure 16-10).

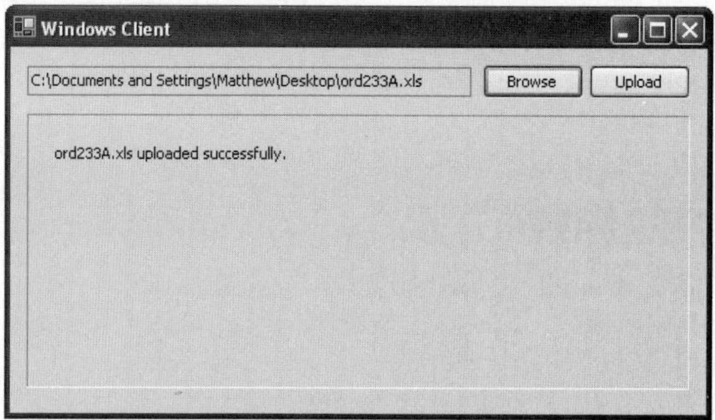

Figure 16-10 The Windows upload client

The code shown in Listing 16-17 is similar to the ASP.NET upload page, although the file selection is provided through the *OpenFileDialog* class.

```
Public Class WindowsClient
    Inherits System.Windows.Forms.Form

    Friend WithEvents cmdBrowse As Button
    Friend WithEvents cmdUpload As Button
    Friend WithEvents Label1 As Label
    Friend WithEvents lblInfo As Label
    Friend WithEvents dlgOpenFile As OpenFileDialog
    Friend WithEvents txtFile As TextBox

    Private Sub cmdBrowse_Click(ByVal sender As System.Object, _
     ByVal e As System.EventArgs) Handles cmdBrowse.Click

        dlgOpenFile.ShowDialog()
        txtFile.Text = dlgOpenFile.FileName

    End Sub

    Private Sub cmdUpload_Click(ByVal sender As System.Object, _
     ByVal e As System.EventArgs) Handles cmdUpload.Click

        ' Check that a file is actually being submitted.
        If txtFile.Text = "" Then
            lblInfo.Text = "No file specified."

        ElseIf Not txtFile.Text.EndsWith(".xls") Then
            lblInfo.Text = "You can only upload Excel files."

        Else
            Dim fs As FileStream

            Try
                ' Create the byte array.
                fs = New FileStream(txtFile.Text, FileMode.Open)
                Dim Bytes As Byte()
                ReDim Bytes(fs.Length)
                fs.Read(Bytes, 0, fs.Length)

                ' Submit the byte array to the XML Web service.
                Dim Proxy As New localhost.OrderService()
                Dim FileName As String = Path.GetFileName(txtFile.Text)
                Proxy.UploadExcelFile(FileName, Bytes)

                ' Display the confirmation message.
                lblInfo.Text = FileName & " uploaded successfully."
                txtFile.Text = ""
```

Listing 16-17 The Windows client form code

```
            Catch Err As System.Web.Services.Protocols.SoapException
                lblInfo.Text = "Server error: " & Err.Message

            Catch Err As Exception
                lblInfo.Text = Err.Message

            Finally
                If Not (fs Is Nothing) Then
                    fs.Close()
                End If

            End Try

        End If

    End Sub

End Class
```

Migration Strategies

As it stands, our solution addresses all the requirements identified in the problem analysis. It also provides a SQL Server database as a scalable backbone to build further enhancements, such as client programs that can query real-time sales data. However, the system also has a few potential headaches as a result of its evolution from Excel and Access. This final section addresses some of these problems and considers how the application might be enhanced in the future.

Adding Security

Currently, the ASP.NET page allows fairly open access to the database. Any individual who submits an Excel file that matches the prescribed format can commit order information. A better approach is to implement some sort of authorization that restricts uploads to valid clients. If nothing else, this can prevent the server hard drive from becoming clogged with invalid Excel files submitted by anyone else.

Adding this logic is quite easy. The SalesAgent table stores an optional password for every sales employee. To support authorization, you add a password text box to the ASP.NET page. When an upload is initiated, it compares the supplied password against the sales agent ID in the Excel file and stops the upload if the two don't match. This technique is best designed by adding a new *ValidateAgent* stored procedure along with additional methods.

Adding Early Validation

To further limit invalid data, the ASP.NET can perform the processing synchronously by communicating directly with the component and by assuming the responsibility currently assigned to the *OrderProcessor* component. This way, errors in the Excel file can be reported automatically. Currently, the sales administrator must check the *OrderProcessor* directory periodically for files that couldn't be successfully processed.

Using Unique Filenames

The current system assumes that the submitted files contain unique names. Otherwise, the attempt to move the Excel file to the completed directory or the attempt to save it to the processing directory might fail. This approach matches the organization of the Graphic Design Institute, in which orders are given unique filenames that combine the date, customer, and sales agent code. It also ensures that the same order file can't be inadvertently submitted twice.

If duplicate filenames are possible, it's easy to implement a more robust approach using the XML Web service and ASP.NET page. (No alternative is available for the first stage, direct e-mailing, although the sales manager can manually rename the file.) Before saving the file, the XML Web service and ASP.NET page can generate a unique identifier using the current date and time (along with a random number) or by creating a new GUID through the *System.Guid* class. This string can then be incorporated in the filename. The problem with this approach is that the same order can be submitted twice and added separately to the database. Unfortunately, as long as Excel is used to create orders, there is no easy way to prevent this possibility.

Excel Headaches and a Dedicated Windows Client

Even with these enhancements, a few stumbling blocks are inherent in using Excel to track orders. For example, using the Excel Automation objects imposes a basic overhead that might seriously degrade performance if hundreds of orders need to be processed simultaneously. On some computers, the Excel Automation objects don't release properly from memory and can quickly use up valuable server resources (because each Excel instance will use several megabytes of RAM). When using the *OrderProcessor* component, you might also run into difficulty because the component runs under a different account from the one Excel has been configured under. To solve this problem, you might need to log in and run Excel under the *OrderProcessor* account at least once, so all the required initial settings are configured properly. Alternatively, you could configure the *OrderProcessor* service to use a specific user account.

No obvious alternatives to the Excel Automation objects are available in this scenario. There are open-source projects on the Internet dedicated to reading the Excel file format, but because the format is extremely complex, this code requires a considerable investment of time, and there is no guarantee that the format will remain fixed in future versions of Microsoft Office. Excel files can be read through ADO.NET using an OLE DB provider, but the query-like syntax required to select cell values is awkward at best. And no matter how you retrieve the information from the Excel file, you will always be left with at least two inherent problems:

- There is no easy way to track whether the same Excel file is submitted twice. This can lead to duplicate order records in the database.
- There is no sure-fire way to enforce validation in an Excel spreadsheet. You can use read-only password-protected fields and a proprietary format, but adding these VBScript macros (and maintaining them with the correct business logic) is a time-consuming and error-prone task.

Eventually, if the Graphic Design Institute continues to prosper, these problems will become too significant. For this reason, we've designed our solution using a carefully standardized database and an intermediary layer of entity objects such as the *Order* class and the *Customer* class. The best migration plan is to encourage sales associates to use the dedicated Windows upload client. You can then take one of two approaches:

- Add the ability for the Windows client to process the order and submit the *Order* object through an XML Web service. This approach requires some form of automated deployment (as discussed in Chapter 15) because the business-processing logic changes frequently. But it removes the burden from the server and makes it easier to alert the client if the Excel file is invalid and prevent duplicate submissions.

- Enable sales associates to enter orders directly using the Windows client interface and save these files using a proprietary format. The development of this solution requires considerable extra work, but it solves all validation problems.

Best of all, with either of these approaches you can continue to use the same database and database components. You just need to add new methods to the *OrderService* XML Web service, as shown in Listing 16-18. Notice that this code is quite similar to the code used in the *OrderProcessor* service, but it's simplified because it doesn't have to deal with the Excel file.

```
Public Class OrderService
    Inherits System.Web.Services.WebService

    Private Tables As New InvoicerTables()

    <WebMethod()> _
    Public Function InsertOrder(ByVal order As Order) As Integer

        ' If the order is from a new customer, insert the customer
        ' record.
        Order.CustomerID = _
          Tables.Customers.CheckIfCustomerExists(Order.CustomerName)

        If Order.CustomerID = 0 Then
            Dim NewCustomer As New Customer()
            NewCustomer.Name = Order.CustomerName
            Order.CustomerID = _
              Tables.Customers.AddCustomer(NewCustomer)
        End If

        ' Commit the order to the database.
        Return Tables.Orders.AddOrder(Order)

    End Function

End Class
```

Listing 16-18 The *InsertOrder* XML Web service method

Summary

This chapter walked through a common nightmare in a growing company and showed how .NET can complement a legacy application rather than replace it. The Graphic Design Institute doesn't need the highest possible degree of sheer processing power because its sales force is relatively small. However, it can still benefit from .NET's capability to help centralize information.

The next chapter shifts to a different type of distributed application—one that places a premium on efficiency and is designed in .NET from the ground up.

17

Transact.NET Order Fulfillment

Distributed application programming is, at least partly, a science of compromises. When building a distributed application, you need to decide which parts of the system will bear the greatest burdens. If you choose carefully and balance the workload between client and server according to the available resources, you can create the foundation for a scalable application. If you rely on a shortcut, however, you might create a bottleneck that won't appear until later, when the load increases and your system becomes a victim of its own success.

This chapter's case study considers a company that wants immediate order notification and processing and is willing to go to a little more trouble to make it possible—and scalable. The solution is end-to-end Microsoft .NET, with a smart Microsoft Windows client, an order-processing XML Web service, and an internal Windows application used to fulfill orders. One interesting aspect of this system is that Microsoft Message Queuing is used to send notification messages when orders arrive. Another interesting factor is the Windows client, which sports a data-driven interface. It provides an excellent example of how you can make a dynamically updatable Windows application without relying on automatic downloads.

Defining the Problem

A. Datum Corporation is a computer vendor with a difference. It specializes in complex setups for server-based computers. A. Datum deals primarily with orders from local software companies in the area. (A. Datum's office is located in the heart of Silicon Valley.)

A. Datum has been using an informal model in which orders are placed by phone. Upon receiving an order, the sales staff informs the production staff immediately by phone and sends an internal e-mail with full details. Wherever possible, orders are processed in a matter of hours and sent by courier the very same day. The sales staff also logs order records to an internal database hosted by Microsoft SQL Server, but there is no process in place to ensure that this step is taken. The production staff doesn't interact with the SQL Server database at all; instead, they receive the order information through internal e-mail.

Now A. Datum is growing, primarily because it has a reputation for meeting orders with record speed. Management is well aware that the current infrastructure can't handle their growing needs. They don't have enough employees to create a dedicated call center to handle incoming orders, and they need to enforce a more consistent, standardized approach. However, A. Datum is unwilling to surrender its reputation for the fastest possible response times. Their challenge is to implement a system that enables them to have this instantaneous notification without sacrificing scalability and to have the ability to grow the organization if it meets with continued success.

Fortunately, A. Datum also has a considerable amount of in-house development expertise. Therefore, it can handle a more complex system than a less tech-savvy company might. In fact, A. Datum developers have already begun to develop a test version of a Windows ordering client to distribute to interested parties. A. Datum hopes that this application will become the standard order-submission tool used by its clients. The company could use ASP.NET to allow clients to submit orders, but it has avoided this option because it limits the functionality the application can provide. In the future, A. Datum would like to add tools such as wizards and network diagramming to help clients specify the configuration for the extremely technical systems they order. A. Datum also wants to enable clients to draw up orders without an Internet connection. Both of these considerations have steered the company toward Windows Forms.

Key Analysis

A. Datum isn't seeking a traditional solution. It has specific needs and wants to gain a competitive edge with a slightly unusual approach.

The traditional approach to this type of application would be to create a simple ASP.NET Web site for order submission and an internal Windows client for order fulfillment. The Windows client would probably not receive individual order notification. Instead, it would query the database for outstanding orders at the user's request. Figure 17-1 shows this model.

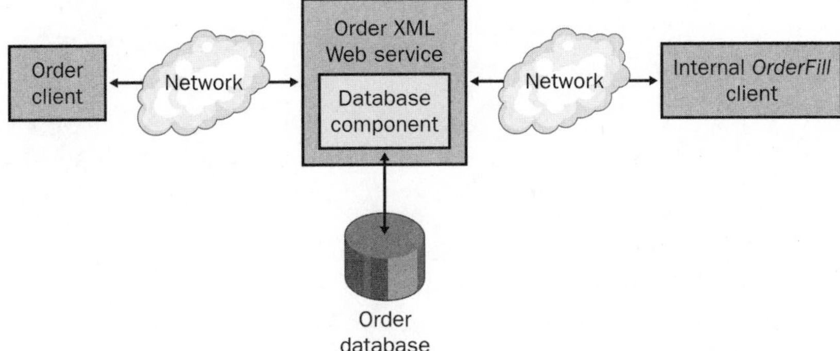

Figure 17-1 A centralized system with an XML Web service

However, A. Datum isn't interested in this approach. It wants the internal client to be alerted immediately if an order exists. This alert will enable the production staff to begin working immediately. Currently, this notification is performed by a phone call, which raises numerous potential problems, including the possibility that the order the company fulfills won't exactly match the order entered in the database, which can lead to future inventory, invoicing, and accounting headaches. To avoid these problems, A. Datum needs to centralize their workflow around the database.

The easiest part of the design to implement is the client application for submitting orders. A. Datum already has a clear idea about how it wants this application to function. The client application will periodically download a price-information file and then use this information file to tailor its user interface. The client configures an order using the downloaded price information, and then submits the order through an XML Web service hosted by A. Datum.

The key question is determining the ideal method for notifying the internal client about new orders. Some possibilities include:

- Poll the database at a regular interval. This is one of the least scalable approaches. It can impose a significant burden on the database if the polling is performed frequently and by several clients. (In this case, the database usage is analogous to a denial-of-service attack.)
- Add a database trigger that creates a file when a record is inserted. This is really a "code-around" tactic rather than a real solution. It can't distinguish between records added for different reasons (for example, order records that have already been fulfilled), and it requires the client to poll a directory on the server.

- Use an order XML Web service that sends a message via Message Queuing. This approach has a low overhead and doesn't require excessive coding.
- Use an order XML Web service that sends a message via .NET Remoting. This approach is fairly easy to implement, but it requires more code to deal with potential connection and serialization errors.

The last two options represent the most reasonable choices for A. Datum. They offer similar performance, but the Message Queuing option is the least complicated to implement and therefore has the least possibility for error. Message Queuing is also supported by their internal network environment, and will work over a company firewall that could thwart a TCP Remoting channel.

Defining the Solution

A. Datum is a growing company, and it understands the importance of avoiding poor design practices that can hamper growth. Database polling is a particularly good example of what not to do because it imposes a serious burden and prevents scalability beyond a small set of users.

With earlier programming technologies, instant notification would be unrealistic or prohibitively difficult and time-consuming to code. However, with .NET you can create a robust, high-performance solution with only a few ingredients: a central database, a client-servicing XML Web service, two independent Windows Forms applications, and a simple Message Queuing notification system. Figure 17-2 diagrams the proposed system, which is named Transact.NET.

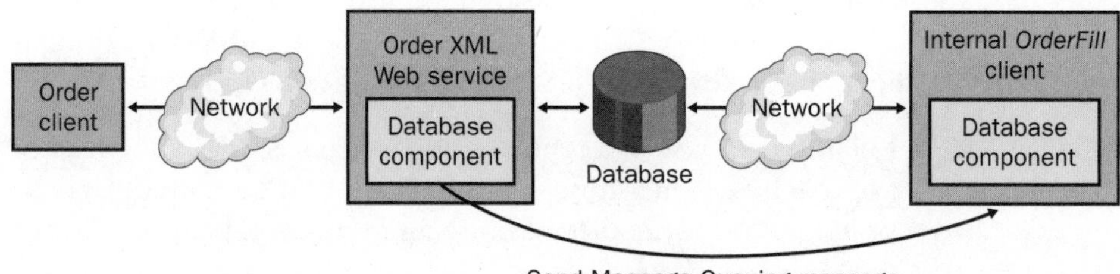

Figure 17-2 The Transact.NET system with notification

Note that Message Queuing acts *in addition* to the basic infrastructure and isn't a key part of it. It notifies the client that a new order is available and indicates the order number. However, it doesn't try to send the full package of order information. This has several important consequences:

- If the Message Queuing service fails, the application still works as designed. The only missing functionality is the instant notification.
- Message Queuing is optional. If the order-filling client doesn't have an available message queue, it doesn't need to use this service.
- Programming is vastly simplified, and scalability is ensured. If you try to use Message Queuing exclusively to route order information to the order-filling client, you face a number of dangers, including losing the order on the wrong computer, difficulty tracking in-progress orders, and the inability to move the order-filling client to another computer while it has outstanding orders.
- The Message Queuing service can be easily replaced with a different notification method (such as events over .NET Remoting) without redesigning the entire solution.

On startup, the order-filling client registers its notification queue with the XML Web service. The XML Web service automatically sends a notification message when it receives an order, provided there is a registered queue. This loosely coupled design is conceptually similar to a callback, but as you've learned in this book, a callback isn't as easy or reliable when it needs to cross machine boundaries. Messaging, however, is a lightweight form of communication that quickly frees the ASP.NET worker thread so that it can handle new requests.

The order-filling client uses a background thread to monitor for new messages and maintains a list of available orders. The client can "check out" any orders that it intends to fill and then either return them to the pool or complete them and create a shipment record.

The external client doesn't require the same threading or messaging capabilities, but it does present an interesting way to use the *DataSet*. Pricing and product information is stored locally in an XML file that contains the serialized content of a *DataSet*. When the application starts, it checks this XML file (which has a server-assigned expiry date) and decides whether to download a new version from the XML Web service. The application then dynamically creates and fills Windows controls to represent the product options in the pricing file. This case study uses a simple version of the client that lacks basic capabilities such as saving and loading order files. However, it provides a good example of how you can distribute dynamically updated product and pricing information.

The Data Layer

The Transact database has two types of tables: those that store product and pricing information (as shown in Figure 17-3) and those that store order and shipment information (as shown in Figure 17-4).

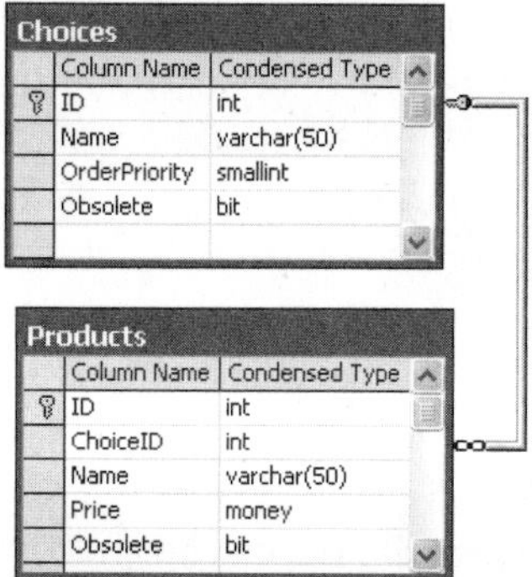

Figure 17-3 Product tables

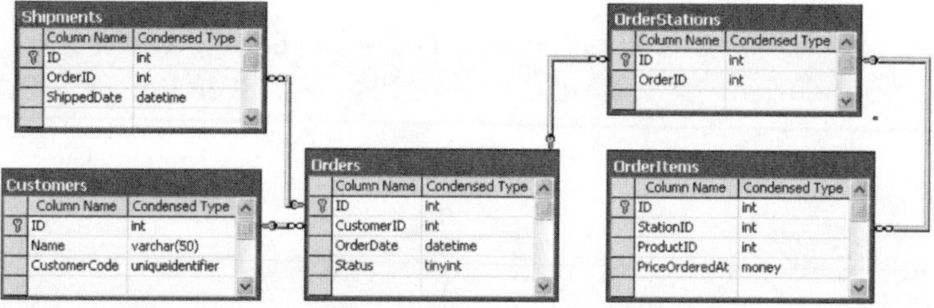

Figure 17-4 Order tables

A standard order consists of one or more computers, each of which is entered separately in the OrderStations table. Each computer is composed of several parts (a CPU, a hard drive, a motherboard, and so on), each of which is represented by a separate record in the OrderItems table. A record is added to the Shipments table after the internal order-filling client has processed an order.

The Products table lists all the available products and their prices. (Other information, such as a description, isn't included but can easily be added.) The Choices table determines how the products are grouped. Essentially, products that reference the same choice record are grouped as mutually exclusive options. When choosing the parts for a computer, the client selects exactly one item out of each choice grouping.

Figure 17-5 shows the sample data preloaded into the Products and Choices tables. There are 4 choice groups defined, and a total of 12 products.

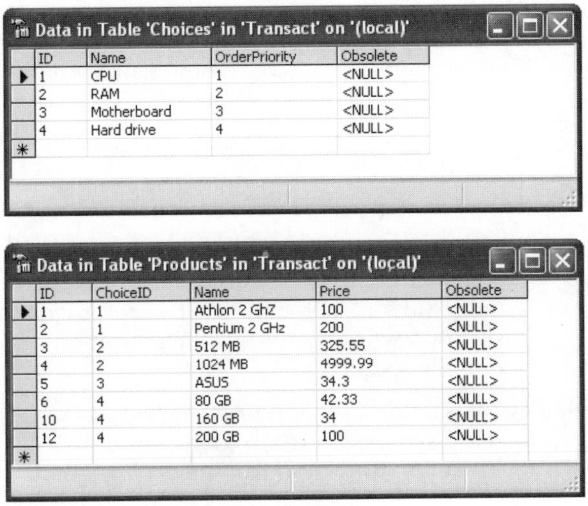

Data in Table 'Choices' in 'Transact' on '(local)'

ID	Name	OrderPriority	Obsolete
1	CPU	1	<NULL>
2	RAM	2	<NULL>
3	Motherboard	3	<NULL>
4	Hard drive	4	<NULL>

Data in Table 'Products' in 'Transact' on '(local)'

ID	ChoiceID	Name	Price	Obsolete
1	1	Athlon 2 GhZ	100	<NULL>
2	1	Pentium 2 GHz	200	<NULL>
3	2	512 MB	325.55	<NULL>
4	2	1024 MB	4999.99	<NULL>
5	3	ASUS	34.3	<NULL>
6	4	80 GB	42.33	<NULL>
10	4	160 GB	34	<NULL>
12	4	200 GB	100	<NULL>

Figure 17-5 Sample product data

Both the Products and Choices tables contain a true/false Obsolete column. When this value is set to *True (1)*, the stored procedure code automatically ignores these rows when returning pricing information. This allows products to be removed from the catalog without deleting the records, ensuring that old order records are still interpretable. More complex logic that links choices to previous selections (for example, logic that allows SCSI hard drives only if the order includes a compatible motherboard or SCSI controller) is typically implemented in the client application because it is extremely difficult to model in the database.

Stored Procedures

The Transact database uses eight stored procedures, as described in Table 17-1. The first three are used to commit a new order (*AddOrder*, *AddOrderItem*, and *AddStation*). Four more (*SetOrderInProgress*, *SetOrderAvailable*, *CompleteOrder*, and *GetAvailableOrders*) are used by the internal order-filling client when processing orders. The final stored procedure, *GetPriceInfo*, is used to retrieve the current product catalog.

Table 17-1 Transact Stored Procedures

Stored Procedure	Description
AddOrder	Adds a new order record and returns the unique ID.
AddOrderItem	Adds a new order item for a new station and returns the unique ID.
AddStation	Adds a new computer as part of a new order and returns the unique ID.
SetOrderInProgress	Changes the status of an order from available (*Status 0*) to in-progress (*Status 1*) and returns all the associated information (the order, station, and order item records).
SetOrderAvailable	Changes the status of an order from in progress to available. This is used when the order-filling client returns an unfilled order to the pool.
CompleteOrder	Changes the status of an order to shipped (*Status 2*), generates a new shipment record, and returns the shipment ID for confirmation purposes.
GetAvailableOrders	Returns all the orders that are available (*Status 0*). However, this stored procedure returns only the ID column. This is because there could be hundreds of orders but the order-filling client only needs the information for orders that are being filled.
GetPriceInfo	Returns all the information (except obsolete records) from the Choices and Products tables. This then becomes the product catalog that the remote client downloads from the XML Web service.

Listing 17-1 shows the stored procedure code used for *GetPriceInfo*. Note that this stored procedure returns two separate result sets. This information could be combined into a single table using a join query, but it's easier to manipulate if it's kept as separate tables.

```
CREATE PROCEDURE GetPriceInfo
 AS
    SELECT * FROM Choices
    WHERE NOT (ISNULL(Obsolete,0)=1) ORDER BY OrderPriority

    SELECT * FROM Products
    WHERE NOT (ISNULL(Obsolete,0)=1)
```

Listing 17-1 Returning the product catalog

Listing 17-2 shows the stored procedures used to commit a new order to the database. They all use fairly straightforward insert commands and return the unique identity value. The date for a new order is inserted automatically using SQL Server's *GetDate* function.

```
CREATE Procedure AddOrder
(
    @CustomerID int,
    @ID         int OUTPUT
)
AS

INSERT INTO Orders
(
    CustomerID,
    OrderDate,
    Status
)

VALUES
(
    @CustomerID,
    GETDATE(),
    0
)

SELECT
    @ID = @@Identity


CREATE Procedure AddStation
(
    @OrderID int,
    @ID      int OUTPUT
)
AS

INSERT INTO OrderStations
(
    OrderID
)

VALUES
(
    @OrderID
)
```

Listing 17-2 Stored procedures for adding a new order

```
SELECT
    @ID = @@Identity


CREATE Procedure AddOrderItem
(
    @StationID      int,
    @ProductID      int,
    @PriceOrderedAt money,
    @ID             int OUTPUT
)
AS

INSERT INTO OrderItems
(
    StationID,
    ProductID,
    PriceOrderedAt
)

VALUES
(
    @StationID,
    @ProductID,
    @PriceOrderedAt
)

SELECT
    @ID = @@Identity
```

The order-filling client uses all the other stored procedures. First of all, the client needs a way to determine what orders are in the queue to be shipped (as shown in Listing 17-3). Orders are automatically sorted by date, ensuring a first-in-first-out (FIFO) process.

```
CREATE PROCEDURE GetAvailableOrders
 AS
    SELECT ID FROM Orders
    WHERE Status = 0
    ORDER BY OrderDate
```

Listing 17-3 Finding available orders

Listing 17-4 shows the stored procedures used for setting the status of an order to in-progress or available. Conceptually, the *SetOrderInProgress* stored procedure retrieves an order from the pool of available orders so that another order-filling client won't try to ship it at the same time. The *SetOrderAvailable* stored procedure is used only if a previously selected order can't be completed and needs to be returned to the pool.

```
CREATE Procedure SetOrderInProgress
 (
    @ID int
 )
 AS

UPDATE Orders
    SET Status = 1
    WHERE ID = @ID

SELECT * FROM Orders WHERE ID = @ID
SELECT * FROM OrderStations WHERE OrderID = @ID
SELECT * FROM OrderItems
    INNER JOIN Products ON Products.ID = OrderItems.ProductID
    INNER JOIN OrderStations ON OrderStations.ID = OrderItems.StationID
    WHERE OrderID = @ID


CREATE Procedure SetOrderAvailable
 (
    @ID int
 )
 AS

UPDATE Orders
    SET Status = 0
    WHERE ID = @ID
```

Listing 17-4 Changing the order status

One interesting fact about the *SetOrderInProgress* stored procedure is that it ends by returning three result sets: the order record, the related stations, and the order items for all the stations. Therefore, when the order-filling client selects an order, it automatically receives the required information.

Finally, after an order has been filled, the order-filling client needs to update the database accordingly. The *CompleteOrder* stored procedure updates the order status and inserts a new shipment record with the current date (as shown in Listing 17-5).

```
CREATE Procedure CompleteOrder
 (
    @OrderID int,
    @ShipID  int OUTPUT
 )
 AS

UPDATE Orders
    SET Status = 2
    WHERE ID = @OrderID

INSERT INTO Shipments
(
    OrderID,
    ShippedDate
)

VALUES
(
    @OrderID,
    GETDATE()
)

SELECT
    @ShipID = @@Identity
```

Listing 17-5 Completing the order

The Data Component

The database component wraps all these stored procedures using two classes, *ProductDB* and *OrderDB*. There are also three entity classes used to model the parts of an order (as shown in Listing 17-6). We won't create entire classes for the other tables because the application doesn't need to work with this information directly.

```
' Note that these structures do not define the full records,
' only the pieces that are relevant in this solution.
Public Class Order

    Public OrderID As Integer
    Public CustomerID As Integer
    Public Stations As Station()
    Public OrderDate As Date

    ' This sets the automatic list box display for the
    ' OrderFillClient.
    Public Overrides Function ToString() As String
        Return OrderID & ": " & Stations.GetLength(0).ToString() & _
               " station(s)"
    End Function

End Class

Public Class Station

    Public OrderItems As OrderItem()
    Public OrderID As Integer

End Class

Public Class OrderItem

    Public StationID As Integer
    Public PriceOrderAt As Decimal
    Public ProductID As Integer

    ' This is not truly a part of the OrderItems table,
    ' but is included here for convenience when retrieving
    ' order information. It displays the product name that
    ' corresponds to the order's ProductID.
    Public ProductName As String

End Class
```

Listing 17-6 Data entities

The *ProductDB* Class

The *ProductDB* class provides a single method, *GetPricingDataSet*, that retrieves the Choices and Products information and returns this information in a *DataSet*. When the *SqlDataAdapter.Fill* method is executed, two tables are created in the *DataSet*, with the default names Table and Table1. The code in Listing 17-7 uses table mapping to rename these tables to the more descriptive Choices and Products.

```
Public Class ProductDB

    Private ConnectionString As String

    Friend Sub New(ByVal connectionString As String)
        Me.ConnectionString = connectionString
    End Sub

    Public Function GetPricingDataSet() As DataSet

        Dim con As New SqlConnection(ConnectionString)
        Dim cmd As New SqlCommand("GetPriceInfo", con)
        cmd.CommandType = CommandType.StoredProcedure

        Dim Adapter As New SqlDataAdapter(cmd)

        ' Apply table mappings.
        ' This ensures that the tables are renamed with
        ' more descriptive titles.
        Adapter.TableMappings.Add("Table", "Choices")
        Adapter.TableMappings.Add("Table1", "Products")

        Dim ds As New DataSet("Pricing")

        Try
            con.Open()

            ' Because this stored procedure returns two result sets,
            ' two tables will be inserted in the DataSet.
            Adapter.Fill(ds)

        Finally
            con.Close()

        End Try

        ' Add a data relation to link the two tables.
```

Listing 17-7 The *ProductDB* service provider

```
        ' This allows the client to use an easier navigation model.
        Dim parent As DataColumn = ds.Tables(0).Columns("ID")
        Dim child As DataColumn = ds.Tables(1).Columns("ChoiceID")
        Dim relation As New DataRelation("Choices_Products", _
                                         parent, child)
        ds.Relations.Add(relation)

        Return ds

    End Function

End Class
```

For convenience, the *GetPricingDataSet* method adds a *DataRelation* to link the two tables before it returns them.

The *OrderDB* Class

The *OrderDB* class is by far the most detailed part of the data component. Its basic structure and public methods are shown here:

```
Public Class OrderDB

    Private ConnectionString As String

    Friend Sub New(ByVal connectionString As String)
        Me.ConnectionString = connectionString
    End Sub

    Public Function CommitNewOrder(ByVal order As Order) As Integer
        ' (Code omitted.)
    End Function

    Public Function GetAvailableOrderIDs() As Integer()
        ' (Code omitted.)
    End Function

    ' Returns the structure that represents the full order,
    ' with all contained items.
    Public Function SetOrderInProgress(ByVal ID As Integer) As Order
        ' (Code omitted.)
    End Function

    Public Sub SetOrderAvailable(ByVal ID As Integer)
        ' (Code omitted.)
```

```
    End Sub

    ' Returns the unique ID of the shipment record for confirmation.
    Public Function CompleteOrder(ByVal ID As Integer) As Integer
        ' (Code omitted.)
    End Function

End Class
```

The *CommitNewOrder* method is particularly interesting; it makes use of three private methods to insert the separate order, station, and order items records (as shown in Listing 17-8). This logic is divided so that it is more maintainable. It also gives you the option to add other methods to the component that insert records in only one of the three tables.

It's important to note that these three methods (*InsertOrder*, *InsertStation*, and *InsertOrderItem*) are all private. They can't be made public because they all require an open connection. The public *CommitNewOrder* method opens this connection, performs all the database work by calling these methods multiple times, and then closes the connection. The only other option—opening and closing the connection with each database operation—would suffer much worse performance.

```
Public Function CommitNewOrder(ByVal order As Order) As Integer

    Dim Item As OrderItem
    Dim Station As Station

    ' Execute all steps in a single ADO.NET transaction.
    Dim tran As SqlTransaction
    Dim con As New SqlConnection(ConnectionString)

    Dim OrderID As Integer

    Try
        con.Open()
        tran = con.BeginTransaction

        OrderID = InsertOrder(order, con, tran)

        For Each Station In order.Stations
            Station.OrderID = OrderID
            Dim StationID As Integer
            StationID = InsertStation(Station, con, tran)
            For Each Item In Station.OrderItems
                Item.StationID = StationID
                InsertOrderItem(Item, con, tran)
```

Listing 17-8 Inserting a new order

```
            Next
        Next

        tran.Commit()

    Catch Err As Exception
        tran.Rollback()

        ' Rethrow the exception.
        Throw Err

    Finally
        con.Close()

    End Try

    Return OrderID

End Function

Private Function InsertOrder(ByVal order As Order, _
  ByVal con As SqlConnection, ByVal tran As SqlTransaction) As Integer

    Dim cmd As New SqlCommand("AddOrder", con)

    ' If this parameter is a null reference (Nothing)
    ' no transaction will be used.
    cmd.Transaction = tran

    cmd.CommandType = CommandType.StoredProcedure
    Dim Param As SqlParameter

    Param = cmd.Parameters.Add("@CustomerID", SqlDbType.Int)
    Param.Value = order.CustomerID

    ' Add the output parameter.
    Param = cmd.Parameters.Add("@ID", SqlDbType.Int)
    Param.Direction = ParameterDirection.Output

    cmd.ExecuteNonQuery()

    Return Param.Value

End Function

Private Function InsertStation(ByVal station As Station, _
  ByVal con As SqlConnection, ByVal tran As SqlTransaction) As Integer
```

```
    Dim cmd As New SqlCommand("AddStation", con)
    cmd.Transaction = tran

    cmd.CommandType = CommandType.StoredProcedure
    Dim Param As SqlParameter

    Param = cmd.Parameters.Add("@OrderID", SqlDbType.Int)
    Param.Value = station.OrderID

    ' Add the output parameter.
    Param = cmd.Parameters.Add("@ID", SqlDbType.Int)
    Param.Direction = ParameterDirection.Output

    cmd.ExecuteNonQuery()

    Return Param.Value

End Function

Private Function InsertOrderItem(ByVal orderItem As OrderItem, _
  ByVal con As SqlConnection, ByVal tran As SqlTransaction) As Integer

    Dim cmd As New SqlCommand("AddOrderItem", con)
    cmd.Transaction = tran

    cmd.CommandType = CommandType.StoredProcedure
    Dim Param As SqlParameter

    Param = cmd.Parameters.Add("@StationID", SqlDbType.Int)
    Param.Value = orderItem.StationID

    Param = cmd.Parameters.Add("@ProductID", SqlDbType.Int)
    Param.Value = orderItem.ProductID

    Param = cmd.Parameters.Add("@PriceOrderedAt", SqlDbType.Money)
    Param.Value = orderItem.PriceOrderAt

    ' Add the output parameter.
    Param = cmd.Parameters.Add("@ID", SqlDbType.Int)
    Param.Direction = ParameterDirection.Output

    cmd.ExecuteNonQuery()

    Return Param.Value

End Function
```

Notice also that all these database operations run under a single ADO.NET transaction. This ensures that an order can't be partially committed—if it contains invalid items, no part of the order is added to the database.

> **Note** The private methods can be run in the context of an ADO.NET transaction or independent of one. If the caller passes in a null reference (*Nothing*) for the transaction object, the command executes normally.

Listing 17-9 shows the *GetAvailableOrderIDs* method, which just wraps the *GetAvailableOrder* stored procedure and returns an array of integers. For the sake of easier coding, the method iterates through the retrieved results, adds them to an *ArrayList*, and then converts them to a strongly typed integer array on the last line. (Another approach is to use an ordinary array and to use the *ReDim* command to expand it with each pass while reading the results.)

```
Public Function GetAvailableOrderIDs() As Integer()

    Dim con As New SqlConnection(ConnectionString)
    Dim cmd As New SqlCommand("GetAvailableOrders", con)
    Dim r As SqlDataReader
    Dim IDs As New ArrayList()

    cmd.CommandType = CommandType.StoredProcedure

    Try
        con.Open()
        r = cmd.ExecuteReader()
        Do While r.Read
            IDs.Add(CType(r("ID"), Integer))
        Loop

    Finally
        con.Close()

    End Try

    Return IDs.ToArray(GetType(Integer))

End Function
```

Listing 17-9 Retrieving available orders

Listing 17-10 shows the methods used to mark an order in-progress (*SetOrderInProgress*) and return it back to the pool (*SetOrderAvailable*). The *SetOrderInProgress* method is more complicated because it needs to step through the retrieved results (three tables in total) and build up the corresponding *Order*, *Station*, and *OrderItem* objects.

```
Public Function SetOrderInProgress(ByVal ID As Integer) As Order

    Dim con As New SqlConnection(ConnectionString)
    Dim cmd As New SqlCommand("SetOrderInProgress", con)
    cmd.CommandType = CommandType.StoredProcedure
    Dim Param As SqlParameter

    Param = cmd.Parameters.Add("@ID", SqlDbType.Int)
    Param.Value = ID

    Dim Adapter As New SqlDataAdapter(cmd)
    Dim ds As New DataSet()

    Try
        con.Open()
        Adapter.Fill(ds)

    Finally
        con.Close()

    End Try

    ' Add order information from first table.
    Dim row As DataRow = ds.Tables(0).Rows(0)

    Dim Order As New Order()
    Order.OrderID = row("ID")
    Order.CustomerID = row("CustomerID")
    Order.OrderDate = row("OrderDate")

    Dim OrderStations, OrderItems As New ArrayList()

    ' Add station information from second table.
    For Each row In ds.Tables(1).Rows
        Dim Station As New Station()
        OrderStations.Add(Station)
```

Listing 17-10 Retrieving and releasing an order

```
        ' Add order item information from third table.
        Dim rowChild As DataRow
        For Each rowChild In ds.Tables(2).Select("StationID='" & _
          row("ID") & "'")
            Dim Item As New OrderItem()
            Item.ProductName = rowChild("Name")
            Item.PriceOrderAt = rowChild("PriceOrderedAt")

            OrderItems.Add(Item)
        Next

        Station.OrderItems = OrderItems.ToArray(GetType(OrderItem))
    Next

    Order.Stations = OrderStations.ToArray(GetType(Station))
    Return Order

End Function

Public Sub SetOrderAvailable(ByVal ID As Integer)

    Dim con As New SqlConnection(ConnectionString)
    Dim cmd As New SqlCommand("SetOrderAvailable", con)
    cmd.CommandType = CommandType.StoredProcedure

    Dim Param As SqlParameter
    Param = cmd.Parameters.Add("@ID", SqlDbType.Int)
    Param.Value = ID

    Try
        con.Open()
        cmd.ExecuteNonQuery()

    Finally
        con.Close()

    End Try

End Sub
```

Finally, the *CompleteOrder* method wraps the *CompleteOrder* stored procedure and returns the shipping confirmation number (as shown in Listing 17-11).

```
Public Function CompleteOrder(ByVal ID As Integer) As Integer

    Dim con As New SqlConnection(ConnectionString)
    Dim cmd As New SqlCommand("CompleteOrder", con)
    cmd.CommandType = CommandType.StoredProcedure

    Dim Param As SqlParameter
    Param = cmd.Parameters.Add("@OrderID", SqlDbType.Int)
    Param.Value = ID

    ' Add the output parameter.
    Param = cmd.Parameters.Add("@ShipID", SqlDbType.Int)
    Param.Direction = ParameterDirection.Output

    Try
        con.Open()
        cmd.ExecuteNonQuery()

    Finally
        con.Close()

    End Try

    Return Param.Value

End Function
```

Listing 17-11 Completing an order

The *TransactTables* Class

The *TransactTables* class provides a gateway to the other database classes (as shown in Listing 17-12), just as in the preceding case study. It accepts a connection string argument and passes it to a new instance of the *ProductDB* and *OrderDB* classes.

```
Public Class TransactTables

    Public Product As ProductDB
    Public Order As OrderDB

    Public Sub New()

        ' Retrieve the connection string.
        Dim Connection As String = ConfigurationSettings.AppSettings( _
          "TransactConnection")
```

Listing 17-12 Composition with *TransactTables*

```
        ' Create the table classes.
        Product = New ProductDB(Connection)
        Order = New OrderDB(Connection)

    End Sub

End Class
```

The Order Submission XML Web Service

The *OrderService* provides the functionality for three tasks:

- It allows the client to download product information through its *GetPricingDataSet* method.
- It allows the client to submit a new order through the *SubmitOrder* method.
- It allows the internal client to register for notification through the *RegisterNotifyQueue* method.

The structure of the *OrderService* is shown here:

```
Public Class OrderService
    Inherits System.Web.Services.WebService

    Private DB As New DBComponent.TransactTables()

    <WebMethod()> _
    Public Function GetPricingDataSet() As DataSet
        ' (Code omitted.)
    End Function

    <WebMethod()> _
    Public Function SubmitOrder(ByVal order As Order, _
      ByVal customerCode As Guid) As OrderState
        ' (Code omitted.)
    End Function

    <WebMethod()> _
    Public Function RegisterNotifyQueue(ByVal queuePath As String)
        ' (Code omitted.)
    End Function

End Class
```

In a more elaborate setup, the *RegisterNotifyQueue* method would be part of a separate XML Web service and would use some sort of authentication to ensure that it is accessible only to the internal client. Alternatively, the queue information could be stored in another location (such as an XML file or a separate table in the database).

The basic code for the *RegisterNotifyQueue* method is shown in Listing 17-13.

```
<WebMethod()> _
Public Function RegisterNotifyQueue(ByVal queuePath As String)

    ' Store the queue path in application state.
    Application("NotifyQueue") = queuePath

End Function
```

Listing 17-13 Registering a notification queue

A. Datum's product catalog changes infrequently, but remote clients might request it often. To ensure optimum performance, the *OrderService* uses ASP.NET's caching capabilities to store the product information for 30 minutes. In this case, data caching is used rather than output caching. This allows the same product data to be retrieved from the cache in other Web methods. For example, the *SubmitOrder* Web method makes use of the cached product catalog to verify pricing information.

To provide data caching, the *OrderService* includes a private *LookupPricing* method. This method checks the cache and, if it can't find the *DataSet*, uses the database component to retrieve the information (as shown in Listing 17-14).

```
<WebMethod()> _
Public Function GetPricingDataSet() As DataSet

    Return LookupPricing()

End Function

Private Function LookupPricing() As DataSet

    Dim ds As DataSet = Context.Cache("Pricing")

    If ds Is Nothing Then

        ds = DB.Product.GetPricingDataSet()
```

Listing 17-14 Retrieving the product catalog

```
            ' Add an expiration date of 30 days to the DataSet.
            ds.ExtendedProperties.Add("ExpiryDate", _
              DateTime.Now.AddDays(30))

            ' Insert the DataSet into the cache, and keep it there
            ' for 30 minutes.
            Context.Cache.Insert("Pricing", ds, Nothing, _
              DateTime.Now.AddMinutes(30), TimeSpan.Zero)

        End If

        Return ds

    End Function
```

The *LookupPricing* method also inserts an additional piece of information into the *DataSet*: an extended property that stores the suggested expiry date. The client uses this information to determine when to query the service again for new product information. Currently, the *DataSet* is set to expire 30 days into the future, but you could also implement a fixed date that depends on the start of a business quarter, the first day of the month, or any other criteria.

The final part of the XML Web service is the *SubmitOrder* method, which adds the order information to the database. This method is the most complex part of the XML Web service, and we'll examine it piece by piece.

First of all, the XML Web service defines an enumeration that represents possible order outcomes. (There is no value for a failed order insertion because this generates an unhandled exception that propagates back to the client. The client should use error-handling code to catch this exception and inform the user.)

```
Public Enum OrderState

    SentToCoordinator
    LoggedInDatabaseOnly

End Enum
```

The *SentToCoordinator* value indicates that the order was added and that a notification message was sent. The *LoggedInDatabaseOnly* value indicates that the order was added but the notification message was not sent. Possible reasons include a missing notification queue (which is possible if no order-filling client is currently running) or an error that occurred while the service was attempting to send the message.

The first task the *SubmitOrder* method performs is to set the price for each item in the order. The XML Web service doesn't use the pricing data set by the client. That would constitute a serious security hole, allowing the client to manually edit the client-side *DataSet* and insert impossibly low prices. Instead, the current pricing information is retrieved and applied to each item. This process completes quite quickly because it uses the cached pricing information from the *LookupPricing* function (as shown in Listing 17-15).

```
Dim ds As DataSet = LookupPricing()

Dim Ord As OrderItem
Dim Station As Station

For Each Station In order.Stations

    For Each Ord In Station.OrderItems

       ' Retrieve the corresponding price.
       Dim Product As DataRow
       Product = ds.Tables(1).Select( _
                 "ID=" & Ord.ProductID.ToString())(0)

       Ord.PriceOrderAt = Product("Price")

    Next
Next
```

Listing 17-15 Updating order prices

The XML Web service just applies the correct prices without examining the prices that were set by the client. This is the least disruptive approach, but there are other possibilities. For example, you can modify the code so that the XML Web service looks at the client prices and throws an exception if it finds an invalid price. This prevents the problem where a client orders a product at a different price than expected, but it can also lead to annoying errors if the client-side pricing is slightly out-of-date. A third approach is to return the final adjusted order from the Web method so that the client application can display the *PriceOrderedAt* values that were committed to the database.

Next, the XML Web service inserts the order into the database (by using the *CommitNewOrder* method from the database component) and sends the notification message, provided a notification queue is registered. The message simply consists of the newly added order ID. Alternatively, you could use a custom object for the message, but in this case only one piece of information is required. Using a simple message format ensures that you do not need to distribute an assembly to the order-filling client.

The code for committing the order and sending the notification message is shown in Listing 17-16.

```
' Add the order to the database.
Dim ID As Integer = DB.Order.CommitNewOrder(order)

' Notify queue.
Dim QueuePath = Application("NotifyQueue")
If QueuePath <> "" Then

    ' User error handling here.
    ' An error should be harmless, and not propagate back to the
    ' caller.
    Try
        Dim NotifyQueue As New MessageQueue(QueuePath)

        NotifyQueue.Send(ID)
        Return OrderState.SentToCoordinator

    Catch
        Return OrderState.LoggedInDatabaseOnly

    End Try

Else
    Return OrderState.LoggedInDatabaseOnly

End If
```

Listing 17-16 Committing the order and sending the notification

The Order Client

This case study includes a stripped-down order client that includes the ability to send orders, download the product catalog, and create orders based on the current products and choice groupings. However, it lacks many features that would be part of a complete application, including the ability to save a local copy of an order file and print order information. Figure 17-6 shows the main window for the order client.

When the application first launches, it attempts to load the *DataSet* XML file. If it can't locate or read the file, it warns the user and attempts to download the product catalog. If it finds the *DataSet* XML but the *DataSet* object's expiration date has passed, it recommends an update, but gives the user a choice. This enables the user to continue working with a slightly outdated pricing file if the client computer doesn't currently have an Internet connection.

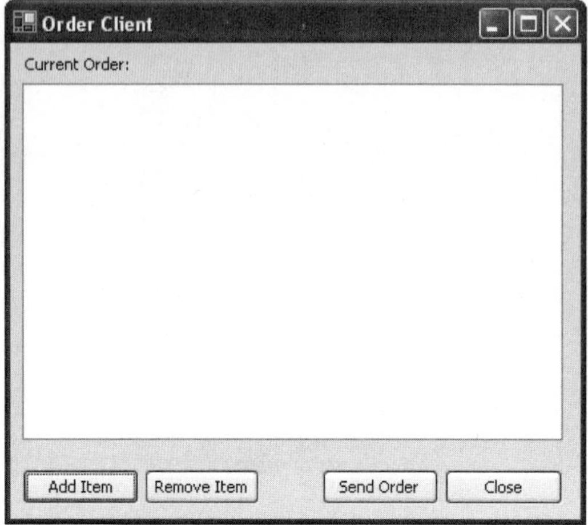

Figure 17-6 The order client

> **Note** Technically, the *DataSet* serialization is a form of client-side caching. It ensures that the client won't need to download huge amounts of data each time the application is started.

All the download logic is wrapped into a special startup module shown in Listing 17-17. (Remember that a module is just a class in which all the members are shared.) Other parts of the program can retrieve the pricing information from the public *Startup.Pricing* member variable.

```
Public Module Startup

    Public Pricing As New DataSet()

    Public Sub Main()
        ' Check if it's time to download the pricing file.
        CheckExpiration()

        Application.Run(New Main())
    End Sub

    Private Sub CheckExpiration()

        Dim ExpiryDate As DateTime
```

Listing 17-17 The startup module

```
        Try
            ' Attempt to open the DataSet and read the expiry date.
            Pricing.ReadXmlSchema(Application.StartupPath & _
              "\pricing.xsd")
            Pricing.ReadXml(Application.StartupPath & "\pricing.xml")

            ExpiryDate = CType( _
              Pricing.ExtendedProperties("ExpiryDate"), DateTime)

            ' Determine if an upload is required.
            If ExpiryDate < DateTime.Now Then
                ' Recommend a download.
                Dim Result As DialogResult
                Result = MessageBox.Show("Your current pricing " & _
                  "data is out-of-date. It is recommended that " & _
                  "you click OK to perform an automatic pricing " & _
                  "download. This requires an Internet connection.", _
                  "Confirm Download", MessageBoxButtons.OKCancel, _
                  MessageBoxIcon.Question)

                If Result = DialogResult.OK Then
                    DownloadData()
                End If
            End If

        Catch
            MessageBox.Show("Error reading file. Click OK to " & _
              "attempt to download the price data.", "Error", _
               MessageBoxButtons.OK)
            DownloadData()

        End Try

    End Sub

    Private Sub DownloadData()

        ' Download the DataSet.
        Dim Proxy As New localhost.OrderService()
        Pricing = Proxy.GetPricingDataSet()

        ' Save the DataSet file.
        Pricing.WriteXmlSchema(Application.StartupPath & _
          "\pricing.xsd")
        Pricing.WriteXml(Application.StartupPath & "\pricing.xml")

    End Sub

End Module
```

When the user chooses to add an item, a second window appears (as shown in Figure 17-7). This window dynamically creates and fills the required drop-down list controls by inspecting the choice groupings (as shown in Listing 17-18). For each row in the Choices table it creates a new label and combo box control. It then fills the combo box with all the rows from the Products table that match the corresponding choice.

```
Private Sub Choices_Load(ByVal sender As System.Object, _
  ByVal e As System.EventArgs) Handles MyBase.Load

    Dim y As Integer = 20

    Dim rowChoice, rowProduct As DataRow
    For Each rowChoice In Startup.Pricing.Tables(0).Rows

        ' Create the text label.
        Dim lbl As New Label()
        lbl.Text = rowChoice("Name") & ":"
        lbl.Left = 10
        lbl.Top = y + 5

        ' Create the listbox.
        Dim lst As New ComboBox()
        lst.DropDownStyle = ComboBoxStyle.DropDownList
        lst.Width = 200
        lst.Left = 90
        lst.Top = y
        y += 40

        For Each rowProduct In rowChoice.GetChildRows( _
          Startup.Pricing.Relations(0))
            lst.Items.Add(New OrderItem(rowProduct("ID"), _
              rowProduct("Name"), rowProduct("Price")))
        Next

        lst.SelectedIndex = 0
        pnl.Controls.Add(lst)
        pnl.Controls.Add(lbl)

        Choices.Add(lst)
    Next

End Sub
```

Listing 17-18 Dynamically creating the order interface

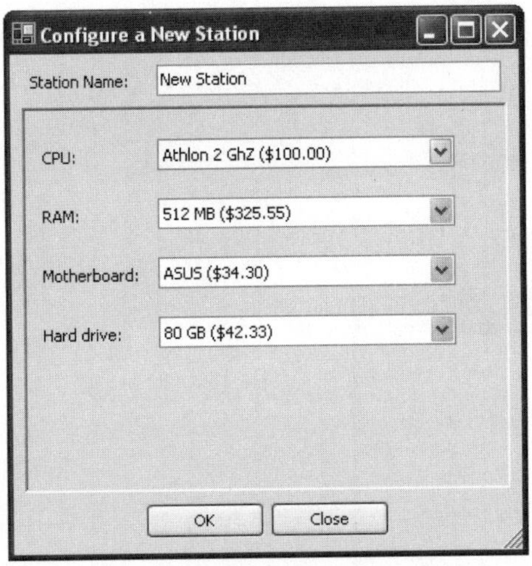

Figure 17-7 Adding an order station

When the window closes, the current selections are provided in the *Choice* property of the form (as shown in Listing 17-19).

```
Public Choice As Station

Private Sub cmdOK_Click(ByVal sender As System.Object, _
  ByVal e As System.EventArgs) Handles cmdOK.Click

    Choice = New Station()
    Choice.Name = txtStation.Text

    Dim lst As ComboBox
    For Each lst In Choices
        Choice.OrderItems.Add(lst.SelectedItem)
    Next

    Me.DialogResult = DialogResult.OK
    Me.Close()

End Sub
```

Listing 17-19 Returning a new station

The main form then adds the completed station to the list of computers that represents the current order:

```
Dim frm As New Choices()
If frm.ShowDialog() = DialogResult.OK Then
```

```
    ' Add station.
    lstStations.Items.Add(frm.Choice)

    frm.Dispose()

End If
```

Figure 17-8 shows an order with several stations.

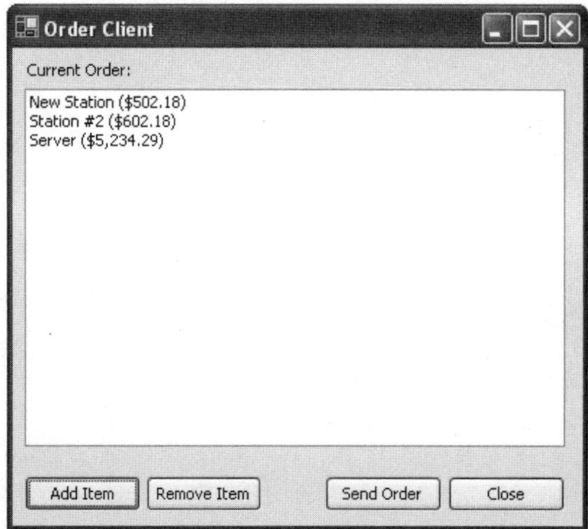

Figure 17-8 A sample order

The order can then be sent using the *OrderService*. The code in Listing 17-20 reacts when the client clicks the Send Order button.

```
Private Sub cmdSend_Click(ByVal sender As System.Object, _
  ByVal e As System.EventArgs) Handles cmdSend.Click

    ' Change the cursor to indicate that the operation is in progress.
    Me.Cursor = Cursors.WaitCursor

    Dim Ord As New Order()

    Dim OrdStation As Station
    Dim Stations As New ArrayList()

    For Each OrdStation In lstStations.Items
        Stations.Add(OrdStation)
    Next

    Ord.Stations = Stations.ToArray(GetType(localhost.Station))
    Dim Proxy As New localhost.OrderService()
```

Listing 17-20 Submitting an order

```
    If Proxy.SubmitOrder(Ord, CustomerGuid()) = _
      OrderState.LoggedInDatabaseOnly Then
        MessageBox.Show("Order sent successfully.", _
          "Order Registered")
    Else
        MessageBox.Show("Order sent successfully and is currently " & _
          "in progress.", "Order Registered")
    End If

    lstStations.Items.Clear()
    Me.Cursor = Cursors.Default

End Sub
```

The client displays a confirmation message that varies based on the return value of the service. If the *OrderService* was able to send a notification message, the client indicates to the user that the order is currently being processed.

The Internal *OrderFill* Client

The internal client provides the features needed to process orders after they've been submitted. It also has the ability to dynamically receive a message and update the interface accordingly, thanks to some careful threading code. Figure 17-9 shows the interface that appears when the internal client is started.

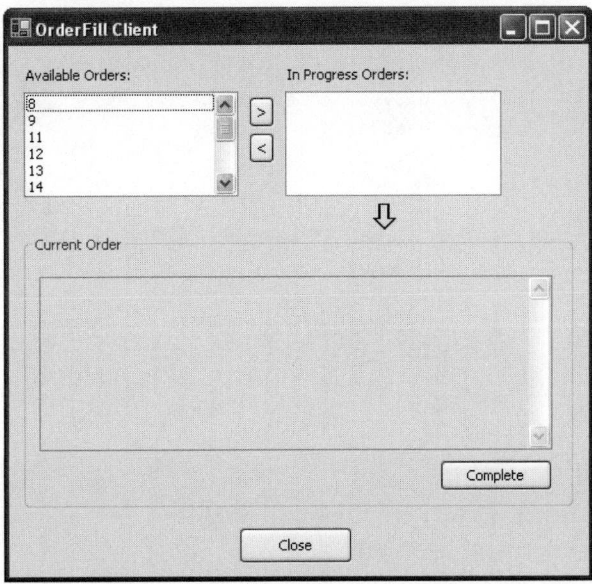

Figure 17-9 The *OrderFill* client at startup

The first step is to register the current queue and retrieve the IDs for all the available orders. The database connection and queue path are drawn from the configuration file shown here:

```
<?xml version="1.0" encoding="utf-8" ?>
<configuration>

  <appSettings>
    <add key="TransactConnection"
         value="Data Source=localhost;Initial
                Catalog=Transact;Integrated Security=SSPI" />
    <add key="MessageQueue"
         value="FARIAMAT\private$\TransactNotify" />
  </appSettings>

</configuration>
```

Listing 17-21 shows the code that runs when the internal client starts. It registers the queue, retrieves the order IDs, and starts a separate thread that monitors the queue for new messages. (We'll deal with the threading code that's involved a little later.)

```
' The remote OrderService.
Private Proxy As New localhost.OrderService()
' The local database component.
Private DB As New DBComponent.TransactTables()

' The custom threaded object that monitors the queue.
Private WithEvents Monitor As New QueueMonitor()
' The thread where the QueueMonitor performs its work.
Private MonitorThread As New Thread(AddressOf Monitor.DoWatch)

Private Sub OrderFillClient_Load(ByVal sender As System.Object, _
  ByVal e As System.EventArgs) Handles MyBase.Load

    ' Register queue.
    Proxy.RegisterNotifyQueue( _
      ConfigurationSettings.AppSettings("MessageQueue"))

    Dim ID As Integer
    For Each ID In DB.Order.GetAvailableOrderIDs()
        lstAvailable.Items.Add(ID)
    Next

    ' Start the queue monitor.
    MonitorThread.Priority = ThreadPriority.BelowNormal
    MonitorThread.Start()

End Sub
```

Listing 17-21 Configuring the internal client on startup

The two arrow buttons enable users to place orders in progress or return them to the available pool. The client can place multiple orders in progress at the same time, which can be useful as different teams in the production center work to assemble the parts for different orders. Often, while one order is underway but waiting (for example, while special software is being installed), another order is filled.

When an order is checked out, a full structure is returned with all the order information. This object is placed directly in the in-progress list control (as shown in Listing 17-22). The list control calls the object's *ToString* method to determine what text it should display. In the case of the *Order* object, this method is overridden to return some useful information, including the order ID and the total number of stations.

```
Private Sub cmdCheckOut_Click(ByVal sender As System.Object, _
  ByVal e As System.EventArgs) Handles cmdCheckOut.Click

    ' Ensure an item is currently selected.
    If lstAvailable.SelectedIndex <> -1 Then
        Dim Ord As Order

        Try
            ' Put the record in progress.
            ' This step allows you to run multiple OrderFillClient
            ' instances at the same time without conflict.
            Ord = DB.Order.SetOrderInProgress(Val(lstAvailable.Text))

            ' Move the item from one listbox to the next.
            ' Note that the item in lstInProgress is a full-fledged
            ' Order object, with all the order information.
            lstInProgress.Items.Add(Ord)
            lstAvailable.Items.Remove(lstAvailable.SelectedItem)

        Catch Err As Exception
            MessageBox.Show(Err.ToString, "Error")

        End Try

    End If

End Sub
```

Listing 17-22 Putting an order in progress

Whenever an item is selected from the in-progress list control, the corresponding order information is displayed (as shown in Figure 17-10). Listing 17-23 shows the event-handling code that displays the information.

```
Private Sub lstInProgress_SelectedIndexChanged( _
  ByVal sender As System.Object, ByVal e As System.EventArgs) _
  Handles lstInProgress.SelectedIndexChanged

    If lstInProgress.SelectedIndex <> -1 Then
        Dim Ord As Order = CType(lstInProgress.SelectedItem, Order)
        Dim Display As String
        Display = "Order ID: " & Ord.OrderID.ToString()
        Display &= Environment.NewLine
        Display &= "Customer ID: " & Ord.CustomerID & _
        Display &= Environment.NewLine

        Dim Station As Station, Item As OrderItem
        For Each Station In Ord.Stations
            Display &= Environment.NewLine
            Display &= " **** STATION ****" & Environment.NewLine
            For Each Item In Station.OrderItems
                Display &= "     * ITEM *       "
                Display &= Item.ProductName & ": "
                Display &= Item.PriceOrderAt.ToString("C")
                Display &= Environment.NewLine
            Next

        Next
        txtOrderInfo.Text = Display

    Else
        ' This automatically clears the order display when the list
        ' is emptied.
        txtOrderInfo.Text = ""

    End If

End Sub
```

Listing 17-23 Displaying order information

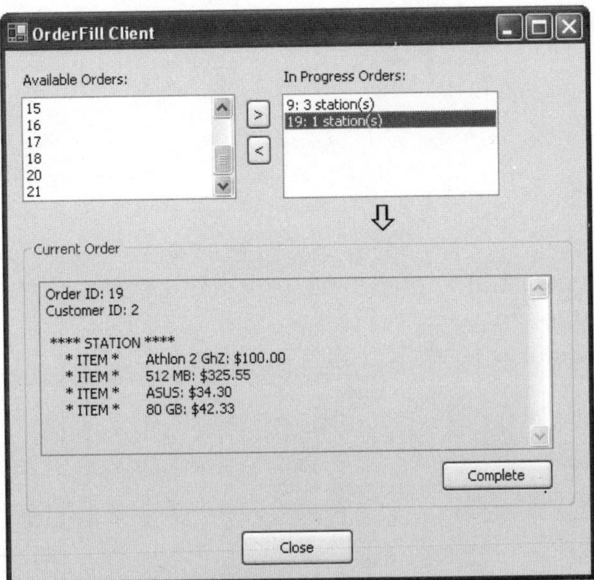

Figure 17-10 Displaying information for an in-progress order

Orders can be returned to the pool just as easily as they are retrieved, as shown in Listing 17-24.

```
Private Sub cmdReject_Click(ByVal sender As System.Object, _
  ByVal e As System.EventArgs) Handles cmdReject.Click

    If lstInProgress.SelectedIndex <> -1 Then

        Try
            Dim ID As Integer
            ID = CType(lstInProgress.SelectedItem, Order).OrderID
            DB.Order.SetOrderAvailable(ID)

            ' Move the item from one listbox to the next.
            lstAvailable.Items.Add(ID)
            lstInProgress.Items.Remove(lstInProgress.SelectedItem)

        Catch Err As Exception
```

Listing 17-24 Returning an in-progress order

```
            MessageBox.Show(Err.ToString, "Error")

        End Try

    End If

End Sub
```

To complete an order, the ID is retrieved from the currently selected item and submitted to the database component (as shown in Listing 17-25). The unique ID for the shipping record is displayed in a message box so it can be noted in the production paperwork.

```
Private Sub cmdComplete_Click(ByVal sender As System.Object, _
  ByVal e As System.EventArgs) Handles cmdComplete.Click

    Try
        ' Complete the order.
        Dim OrderID, ShipID As Integer
        OrderID = CType(lstInProgress.SelectedItem, Order).OrderID
        ShipID = DB.Order.CompleteOrder(OrderID)

        ' Update the list.
        lstInProgress.Items.Remove(lstInProgress.SelectedItem)

        ' Notify the user.
        MessageBox.Show("Confirmation for this shipment is: " & _
          ShipID.ToString, "Shipment Recorded")

    Catch
        MessageBox.Show(Err.ToString, "Error")

    End Try

End Sub
```

Listing 17-25 Completing an order

Note that error-handling code is always used when the application performs a database operation. Otherwise, an unhandled error could cause the application to end and jeopardize any other orders that are currently in progress.

When the application closes, it automatically returns all in-progress orders and terminates the queue-monitoring thread (as shown in Listing 17-26). It also unregisters the queue to inform the XML Web service that notification messages are no longer required.

```
Private Sub OrderFillClient_Closing(ByVal sender As Object, _
  ByVal e As System.ComponentModel.CancelEventArgs) _
  Handles MyBase.Closing

    ' Unregister the queue.
    Proxy.RegisterNotifyQueue("")

    ' You must use this method to reject all the currently in-progress
    ' orders. Otherwise, they will not be available in the future.
    Dim Ord As Order
    For Each Ord In lstInProgress.Items
        DB.Order.SetOrderAvailable(Ord.OrderID)
    Next

    ' It is safe to abort this thread while it is sleeping
    ' or waiting for messages.
    MonitorThread.Abort()
    MonitorThread.Join()

End Sub
```

Listing 17-26 Returning orders on shutdown

The Queue Monitor

The final ingredient in the order-filling client is the custom queue-monitoring class. It follows the threading guidelines set out in Chapter 6. The process can be divided into five steps:

1. Check the queue for messages. If messages aren't found, pause the thread for a few seconds.
2. If a message is found, fire an event to the client. The custom *EventArgs* object for transmitting the message is shown here:

```
Public Class MessageEventArgs
    Inherits EventArgs

    Public Message As Integer

    Public Sub New(ByVal message As Integer)
        Me.Message = message
```

```
    End Sub

End Class
```

3. Handle the event and add the message information to an *ArrayList* member variable. (A collection is used in case several messages are received in quick succession, before the interface can be updated. This approach allows the client to use locking to protect against concurrency errors.)
4. Invoke a method to refresh the user interface display.
5. Read the message information from the *ArrayList*. For each new order ID found, add an entry to the available list.

Listing 17-27 shows the custom object for monitoring the queue. The actual monitoring is performed in the *DoWatch* method. It loops continuously (so long as the *RequestStop* flag is not set). Each time it attempts to retrieve a message for 30 seconds. If no message is found, an exception is thrown and the thread is temporarily suspended.

```
Public Class QueueMonitor

    Public Event MessageReceived(ByVal sender As Object, _
      ByVal e As MessageEventArgs)

    Public RequestStop As Boolean = False

    Public Sub DoWatch()

        Dim Queue As New MessageQueue( _
          ConfigurationSettings.AppSettings("MessageQueue"))
        Dim Message As System.Messaging.Message

        Do Until RequestStop

            Dim AllowedTypes() As Type = {GetType(Integer)}
            Queue.Formatter = New XmlMessageFormatter(AllowedTypes)

            Try
                Message = Queue.Receive(TimeSpan.FromSeconds(30))

                If Not Message Is Nothing Then
                    RaiseEvent MessageReceived(Me, _
                      New MessageEventArgs(Message.Body))
                End If
```

Listing 17-27 Monitoring the queue

```
            Catch e As MessageQueueException
                ' No message was received after 30 seconds.
                If Not RequestStop Then
                    Thread.Sleep(TimeSpan.FromSeconds(30))
                End If

            End Try

        Loop

    End Sub

End Class
```

You could use the *MessageQueue.Receive* method without specifying a timeout, but this would tie up the thread indefinitely. By using the looping approach, the thread can still respond (within no more than 30 seconds) if the *RequestStop* variable is set to *True*. Incidentally, the code performs equally well if you loop more aggressively, reducing the timeout and thread sleep to 5 or fewer seconds. However, A. Datum considers a notification time of 30 seconds to be satisfactory. Optionally, you can retrieve the wait time from a configuration file and set it programmatically.

When the event is fired, the update takes two steps. First, the event is handled and the message information is recorded. Second, the *AddNewFromQueue* method is invoked to update the user interface (as shown in Listing 17-28).

```
Private Messages As New ArrayList()

Private Sub Monitor_MessageReceived(ByVal sender As Object, _
  ByVal e As MessageEventArgs) Handles Monitor.MessageReceived

    SyncLock Messages
        Messages.Add(e.Message)
    End SyncLock
    Me.Invoke(New MethodInvoker(AddressOf AddNewFromQueue))

End Sub
```

Listing 17-28 Handling the *MessageReceived* event

Remember that the *MessageReceived* event takes places on the *QueueMonitor* thread, so it can't update the user interface directly. Instead, the *Control.Invoke* method marshals this code to the user interface thread, where it can perform its work safely. The private *AddNewFromQueue* function then updates the interface (as shown in Listing 17-29).

```
Private Sub AddNewFromQueue()

    SyncLock Messages
        Dim Message As String
        For Each Message In Messages
            lstAvailable.Items.Add(Message)
        Next
        Messages.Clear()
    End SyncLock

End Sub
```

Listing 17-29 Updating the interface

No additional order information is required. The full order is retrieved if the order is selected and placed in progress.

Future Directions

The current solution meets all the requirements of the problem analysis. It allows disconnected clients to create orders and coordinates the workflow so that orders can be filled mere moments after they've been received. However, a number of additional features can be added to this basic infrastructure.

Adding Security

You might want to add increased security or a ticket-based authentication system, such as the one presented in the next chapter. This authentication code might make use of the customer GUID, which is present in the Customers database but isn't used.

Currently, the XML Web service takes one important precaution: it applies the current pricing to all submitted orders to prevent malicious clients from purchasing items at incorrect prices. However, there is no way to prevent nonregistered users from using the service and submitting invalid orders or just wasting server resources.

Adding Confirmation GUIDs

Another useful change would be to create a unique GUID value to identify orders. This GUID could be inserted into the order record and returned to the client as a confirmation value.

If you choose to implement this approach, make sure you identify orders with GUIDs, not just sequential numbers. You should never use the unique identity field as a confirmation number because it allows clients to make false order claims easily. For example, a client that receives confirmation number 200 might claim to have submitted order 201. However, a client that receives a GUID confirmation code such as 382c74c3-721d-4f34-80e5-57657b6cbc27 will have no idea what other confirmation codes are used by the system and won't be able to guess another valid value.

Supporting Multiple Order-Filling Clients

One of the most obvious changes you might make is to modify the *OrderService* so that it can support multiple order-filling clients. This change is quite easy; you just have to replace the notify queue string with a collection that contains multiple queue paths. The *RegisterNotifyQueue* method then adds or removes entries from this collection, using a *SyncLock* statement to prevent errors.

```
<WebMethod()> _
Public Function RegisterNotifyQueue(ByVal queuePath As String, _
  ByVal remove As Boolean)

    Dim NotifyList As ArrayList = Application("NotifyQueueCollection")

    SyncLock NotifyList

        If Not remove Then
            NotifyList.Add(queuePath)
        Else
            NotifyList.Remove(queuePath)
        End If

    End SyncLock

End Function
```

When an order is submitted, the *OrderService* would then step through the full list and attempt to send a message to each queue:

```
Dim NotifyList As ArrayList = Application("NotifyQueueCollection")
Dim QueuePath As String

SyncLock NotifyList

    For Each QueuePath in NotifyList
        Try
            Dim NotifyQueue As New MessageQueue(QueuePath)
            NotifyQueue.Send(ID)

        Catch Err As Exception
```

```
            ' (Depending on the error, you might want to remove the
            ' queue from the list here.)

        End Try
    Next

End SyncLock
```

You'll also need to make some minor modifications to the order-filling clients. For example, they need to prevent users from processing an order that is already being filled by another client. To support this feature, the logic in the *SetOrderInProgress* stored procedure needs to be tightened so that in-progress orders can't be requested, as shown here:

```
CREATE Procedure SetOrderInProgress
 (
    @ID int
 )
 AS

UPDATE Orders
    SET Status = 1
    WHERE ID = @ID AND Status = 0
```

If no matching record is found, the stored procedure should refrain from returning any rows to the client. You can accomplish this by checking that the global SQL Server variable *@@ROWCOUNT* is 0. This variable always returns the number of rows affected by the most recent operation.

```
IF @@ROWCOUNT = 1
  BEGIN
    SELECT * FROM Orders WHERE ID = @ID
    SELECT * FROM OrderStations WHERE OrderID = @ID
    SELECT * FROM OrderItems
      INNER JOIN Products ON Products.ID = OrderItems.ProductID
      INNER JOIN OrderStations
        ON OrderStations.ID = OrderItems.StationID
      WHERE OrderID = @ID
  END
```

The *OrderDB.SetOrderInProgress* method must then check how many records were updated by the command. If the command succeeds, it will return one affected row. If it returns zero affected rows, the database component should throw an error to notify the client. The client can interpret this error as indicating that the row is currently in progress, notify the user accordingly, and remove the item from the list.

Summary

This case study presents a solution that uses .NET technologies to accomplish automatic notification. The most important design decision in this example is separating the Message Queuing logic from the rest of the application. This allows the instant notification to act as an enhancement to the core service and dodges several problems that would otherwise harm the overall maintainability and reliability of the system.

The next chapter considers another case study, one that shows how .NET distributed technology can allow clients to tap into the server's processing power.

18

SuperCompute.NET Work Requests

Client/server programming is notoriously inflexible. In a typical setup, the weakest part of the system—the client—is forced to perform almost all the processing work. Too often, the server acts as a glorified data store and file server.

However, distributed application architecture gives you the flexibility to distribute the workload among the different parts of the system as you see fit. In many cases, this means centralizing logic in a middle tier, where you can pool objects, reuse connections, and cache data. In other cases, this might mean taking some of the work away from the server and splitting it among multiple idle workstations.

In the case study presented in this chapter, we examine a company that's migrating from a simple client/server based application to a full distributed system. This company, Trey Research, has a simple need: to move the functionality of its server-side application to the client while still retaining the processing power of the server. Our solution is simple, logical, and far easier to maintain than a comparable client/server approach would be. It also demonstrates best practices for a ticket-based security system, a COM+ transaction, and a dash of asynchronous programming.

Defining the Problem

Trey Research is a graphic design company that does print media and video work. As part of a typical project, Trey Research generates dozens of samples from which the client can choose. This process involves rendering source files into photorealistic three-dimensional images and animated sequences. This rendering process is computationally expensive and can't be performed on the ordinary client workstations used to design the source files. Up to now, a single individual has managed this process: the graphic coordinator.

When a sample is completed, the source files are passed along to the graphic coordinator. Usually, an individual places the source files on the internal network and notifies the coordinator by e-mail. The graphic coordinator then runs a custom batch program on a special server computer. This server computer runs the Microsoft Windows operating system and has an impressive complement of hardware, including a RAID array of SCSI drives and eight high-performance CPUs.

The Trey Research solution suffers from several problems, however, including the following:

- The graphic coordinator is often so busy managing the transfer of files for various projects that little time is left for other work.
- The rendering process is long, and the projects are time-sensitive. Unfortunately, there is no way to start the rendering process unless the graphic coordinator is available, which leads to some last minute, late-night work binges.
- There's no automated way to track projects as they are submitted and completed. The graphic coordinator is completely responsible for fielding questions about in-progress rendering operations, completed tasks, and unrecoverable errors. Sometimes projects are submitted more than once, leading to an increased burden on the server.
- There's no way to attribute projects to their owners. The graphic coordinator is forced to spend extra time tracking down the appropriate individual when a rendering operation is complete, and sometimes the results are delivered to the wrong people.
- The graphic coordinator retains critical pieces of information about the system and current workflow. If the graphic coordinator is ill (or worse yet, leaves the company), work is interrupted.

Trey Research is planning to solve these problems on an internal level and is willing to distribute a client program internally. It would like the option, however, of adding remote use (over the Internet) in the future if it moves its Web site to an in-house server.

Key Analysis

Trey Research has the hardware it needs. What's lacking is the process. The company needs a convenient, efficient, automated workflow that can route tasks directly to the custom processing application, without requiring any human intervention. This system also needs to send a notification back to the original client when the task is completed.

This situation is quite a bit different from the Transact.NET case study in Chapter 17. First of all, the task typically takes much longer (several hours) to complete, and the client isn't necessarily available when it's finished. Similarly, the client and server don't require instantaneous notification. They are best served by a straightforward, reliable infrastructure. For that reason, the ideal solution is unlikely to use events with .NET Remoting. A disconnected message-based approach is more reliable and scalable. Microsoft Message Queuing is a possibility, but it might not be needed if we can develop a centralized interface that allows all clients to submit tasks and get information about outstanding work requests.

As with the previous case studies, it is keenly important to separate the various parts of the solution. For example, the code that triggers the batch-rendering process should not be directly embedded in the XML Web service, and all database access should be encapsulated by a dedicated component. In addition, it's important to realize that the rendering process isn't like the typical server-side functionality we've looked at in the two preceding case studies, which focus primarily on adding or retrieving information from a database. Unlike these tasks, the rendering process has several unique characteristics:

- **It takes a significant amount of time.** There's no good reason to tie up an XML Web service or a remote component for this amount of time because it can quickly use up the available thread pool and be unable to handle incoming requests.
- **It is computationally expensive.** Because this process has specific needs and imposes an increased demand on the server, it should be isolated from other parts of the system. This prevents service disruption if a software error occurs.
- **It is not always available.** Trey Research can shut down the rendering program when it needs the server for another task. This shouldn't stop other users from submitting requests, checking the progress of existing requests, and downloading rendered files.

Finally, you must consider the security needs of the new system. Initially, it will run on an internal network, which means you can devote less energy to defending against spurious requests and denial-of-service attacks. A practical system is still needed to tie users to specific requests, however, both to prevent confusion and to protect any sensitive content.

Defining the Solution

The new system will use a centralized server that hosts a database of shared information. Clients will retrieve information from the database using a set of dedicated XML Web service methods that wrap all the required functionality.

To ensure optimum performance, the XML Web service should be devoted solely to performing database operations and returning information. A separate server-side component can run continuously (unless stopped by an administrator), performing the actual rendering operation. Figure 18-1 shows a high-level diagram of the system.

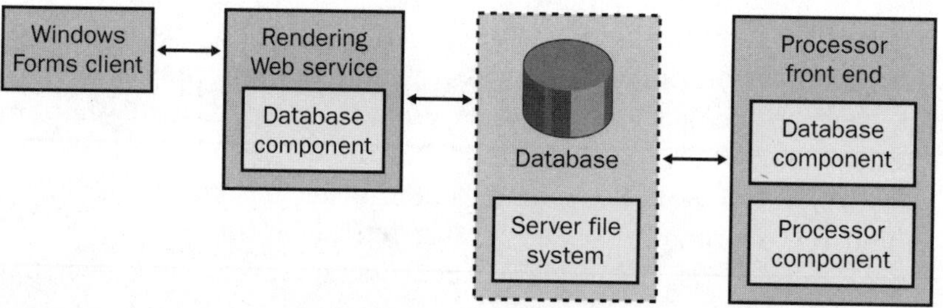

Figure 18-1 The SuperCompute system architecture

One detail Figure 18-1 doesn't show is that the client retrieves the rendered file directly from the server (using a UNC file path stored in the database). It is possible to force the client to work through the XML Web service and to use the "downloading" technique shown in Chapter 15. This approach isn't practical, however, because of the sheer size of the rendered files (potentially hundreds of megabytes). Even though the ASP.NET worker process can easily handle the task, multiple downloads would tie up all the available worker threads, rendering the server unable to handle other requests. This would seriously affect scalability and reduce the overall reliability and availability of the XML Web service.

The final part of the SuperCompute architecture is the authentication model. Even though Trey Research has modest security needs, you need a disciplined system in place that ensures that tasks are linked to users. This not only makes it easier for clients to retrieve information about the tasks they have submitted, but it also enables the system administrator to track usage information and determine which users and projects have the highest processing requirements.

Trey Research has the choice of either using Windows authentication and leveraging the current set of user logins on the network server or developing a custom authentication system that retrieves user account information from the network server. Trey Research favors the latter because it allows task records to be easily linked to the corresponding user record in the database. It also separates the information, allowing the network and rendering-service users to be managed separately (one group by the network administrator and the other group by the graphic coordinator). In the future, this system could be the foundation for a more elaborate permission-based system that imposes strict limits on the types of projects that can be submitted and how the processor prioritizes them.

Figure 18-2 shows the current system, which uses the ticket approach described in Chapter 13. When a ticket is generated (by the *Login* method), a record is written to the database with a GUID, identifying the client. On subsequent requests, the ticket is used to validate the session. Finally, the ticket is removed using a dedicated *Logout* method, custom expiration logic in the XML Web service, or a stored procedure that performs batch cleanup.

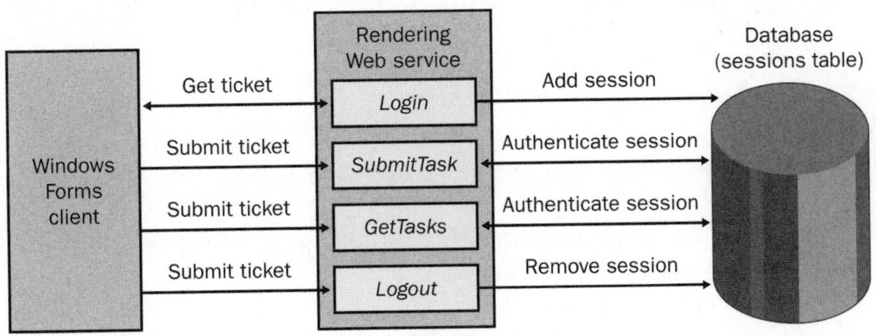

Figure 18-2 Authentication with a custom ticket system

By default, this custom authentication system is less secure at the transport level than Windows authentication is. This means that it is technically possible for network traffic between the client and XML Web service to be intercepted and passwords to be "sniffed" out. To defend against this possibility, Trey Research plans to install a server certificate and enable SSL security before rolling out the new application.

The security model has one limitation as it stands. Because users download their rendered files manually, without connecting through the XML Web service, it is possible for users to download rendered files that they did not create. The network administrator can apply directory restrictions that limit which groups of users can access rendered files, but there is no automatic way to set up a finer-grained system that sets individual permissions on each file. In the internal network used by Trey Research, this isn't considered a problem. However, the company might want to improve on it in a number of ways in the future. One approach would be to store files in a virtual directory and expose them over HTTP. This directory would not allow file browsing, so users would be restricted to making requests for specific files. Because the filename uses a GUID, it is unique enough to ensure that no user could ever guess another user's filename (and hence download it).

> **Note** Security-free downloading is desirable under certain circumstances because it allows easier team use. (One user can upload the file, for example, and another can download it.) If security is added at a later date, this requirement should still be considered. GUID filenames represent a good compromise because all members of a team can be informed about a given project file, and passwords need never be shared.

The Data Layer

This solution requires three tables: Users, Sessions, and Tasks. Figure 18-3 shows the table relationships.

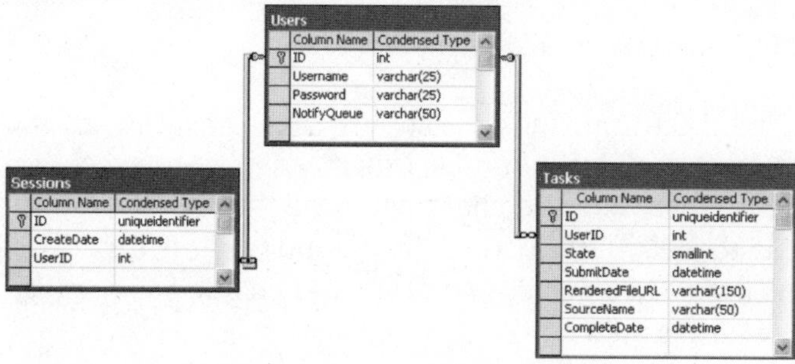

Figure 18-3 The SuperCompute tables

The Users table contains the logic information for all the users who will access the rendering service. The password is stored in plain text, and all password comparisons default to SQL's standard non-case-sensitive behavior. For increased security, this field could hold encrypted binary information. In addition, the Users table includes an optional NotifyQueue column, which is designed to hold the path to a Message Queuing private queue on the user's computer, which can be used for notification. This feature isn't currently implemented, but is designed for possible future enhancements. If you are installing this case study from the code download, you will find only a single defined user, with the user name *testuser* and the password *secret*.

The Sessions table is used for the ticket-based authentication. It stores a record for each session currently in progress. Sessions are identified by their unique GUID column, which is passed back to the client. The Sessions table also indicates the date the session was started, which is useful if you need to implement an expiration policy, and the client who is authorized to perform actions with this session ticket.

Finally, the Tasks table lists the jobs that have been submitted for rendering. The Tasks table includes file information, a numeric status that indicates whether the task is new (0), in progress (1), completed (3), or halted with an error (2), and the date the task was submitted and completed. The *SourceFile* corresponds to the original name of the source file, which is retained to help the client identify the task later. The *RenderedFileURL* provides a UNC or URL path to the rendered file after the rendering has been completed.

Stored Procedures

The basic implementation of the SuperCompute system requires 11 stored procedures, as described in Table 18-1. These stored procedures represent the tasks required by the rendering service and task processor. They don't include any additional functionality to add new user records or profile the system's overall performance.

Table 18-1 SuperCompute Stored Procedures

Stored Procedure	Description
GetUser	Retrieves a user ID that matches the supplied login information. Used to authenticate a user.
AddSession	Creates a new session record for a logged-in user and returns the generated GUID session ticket.

Table 18-1 SuperCompute Stored Procedures *(continued)*

Stored Procedure	Description
GetSession	Retrieves the session for the specified user.
DeleteSession	Removes the session for the specified user. Used when the user logs out.
GetTasksByUser	Retrieves all the task records for a specified user.
GetCompletedTasksByUser	Retrieves all the completed task records for a specified user.
AddTask	Adds a new task record.
GetAvailableTasks	Retrieves the task records that are not in progress, completed, or halted with an error. The task processor will then begin to process these records.
UpdateTaskStatus	Modifies the status of a task.
CompleteTask	Modifies the status of a task, sets the complete date, and adds the UNC file path for the rendered file.
DeleteOldSessions	Enables the administrator to remove old session records that are no longer in use.

Listing 18-1 shows the stored procedure code required to validate a user. If a match is found, the unique numeric ID is returned.

```
CREATE PROCEDURE GetUser
 (
    @UserName   varchar(25),
    @Password   varchar(25)
 )
 AS
    SELECT [ID] FROM Users
    WHERE UserName = @UserName AND [Password]=@Password
```

Listing 18-1 Stored procedures for validating a user

Listing 18-2 presents the four stored procedures used to manage session records. The GUID is generated using the *NEWID* function built into SQL Server.

```
CREATE Procedure AddSession
 (
    @UserID     int,
    @GUID       uniqueidentifier OUTPUT
 )
 AS

   SELECT
       @GUID = NEWID()

 INSERT INTO Sessions
 (
    [ID],
    UserID,
    CreateDate
 )
 VALUES
 (
    @Guid,
    @UserID,
    GETDATE()
 )


CREATE PROCEDURE GetSession
 (
    @GUID    uniqueidentifier,
    @UserID  int
 )
 AS
    SELECT CreateDate FROM Sessions
    WHERE [ID] = @GUID AND UserID=@UserID
    ORDER BY CreateDate DESC


CREATE PROCEDURE DeleteSession
 (
    @GUID    uniqueidentifier
 )
 AS
    DELETE FROM Sessions
    WHERE [ID] = @GUID


CREATE PROCEDURE DeleteOldSessions
 AS
    DELETE FROM Sessions
    WHERE DATEDIFF(day, CreateDate, GETDATE()) > 5
```

Listing 18-2 Stored procedures for managing sessions

The *GetSession* stored procedure sorts the retrieved rows so that the largest creation date (representing the most recent session) is at the top of the list. It does this because the XML Web service assumes that there is only a single session per user and reads the first record from the list.

Typically, there should be only one session record for a given user at a time, but it is possible for an orphaned session record to exist if a user disconnects without calling the *Logout* XML Web service method. In this case, the session remains until the database administrator executes the *DeleteOldSessions* stored procedure, which removes any session record created more than five days earlier.

The remainder of the stored procedures deal with tasks. The *GetTasksByUser* and *AddTask* stored procedures shown in Listing 18-3 are the two stored procedures indirectly available to the user through the render XML Web service.

```
CREATE PROCEDURE GetTasksByUser
 (
    @UserID int
 )
 AS
    SELECT * FROM Tasks
    WHERE UserID = @UserID


CREATE Procedure AddTask
 (
    @UserID     int,
    @Status     int,
    @SourceName varchar(50),
    @GUID       uniqueidentifier OUTPUT
 )
 AS

SELECT
   @GUID = NEWID()

 INSERT INTO Tasks
 (
    [ID],
    UserID,
    State,
    SourceName,
    SubmitDate
 )
```

Listing 18-3 User-specific stored procedures for tasks

```
VALUES
(
   @Guid,
   @UserID,
   @Status,
   @SourceName,
   GETDATE()
)
```

The task processor uses the *GetAvailableTasks*, *UpdateTaskStatus*, and *CompleteTask* stored procedures to retrieve the tasks that should be processed, to manage the status for each task, and to update the record when the rendering process completes, as shown in Listing 18-4.

```
CREATE PROCEDURE GetAvailableTasks
 AS
    SELECT * FROM Tasks
    WHERE State = 0
    ORDER BY SubmitDate


CREATE Procedure UpdateTaskStatus
 (
    @GUID uniqueidentifier,
    @Status int
 )
 AS
     UPDATE Tasks
     SET State = @Status
     WHERE [ID] = @GUID


CREATE Procedure CompleteTask
 (
    @GUID             uniqueidentifier,
    @RenderedFileURL nvarchar(100),
    @Status           int
 )
 AS
    UPDATE Tasks
    SET State = @Status,
    RenderedFileURL = @RenderedFileURL,
    CompleteDate = GETDATE()
    WHERE [ID] = @GUID
```

Listing 18-4 Processor-specific stored procedures for tasks

Note that the *GetAvailableTasks* stored procedure sorts the results so that the earliest dates are first. This ensures that tasks are processed in first-in-first-out (FIFO) order.

The Data Component

As with the previous case studies (and every well-designed enterprise application), database access takes place solely through a dedicated database component. Both the rendering XML Web service and the server-side task processor use this database component. Listing 18-5 shows the entity portion of the database component, which defines classes to represent the rows in each table.

```
Public Class UserDetails

    Public UserID As Integer
    Public UserName As String
    Public Password As String
    Public Queue As String

End Class

Public Class SessionDetails

    Public CreateDate As DateTime
    Public UserID As Integer
    Public Ticket As Guid

End Class

Public Enum TaskStatus
    NewAdded = 0
    InProgress = 1
    HaltedWithError = 2
    Complete = 3
End Enum

Public Class TaskDetails

    Public SourceName As String
    Public TaskGUID As Guid
    Public Status As TaskStatus
    Public SubmitDate As DateTime
    Public RenderedFileUrl As String
    Public UserID As Integer
    Public CompleteDate As Date

End Class
```

Listing 18-5 Data entities

Note You can add property procedures to the entity classes, but they will not be usable in an XML Web service client. When an XML Web service client creates a proxy class, the generated code includes all the required entity classes but the property procedures are converted to public member variables. However, property procedures can still prove useful when you're executing server-side code.

The *UserDB* Class

The *UserDB* class, shown in Listing 18-6, is the simplest part of the database component. It exposes a single *AuthenticateUser* method, which accepts login information and returns the corresponding numeric user ID if a matching record can be found.

```
Public Class UserDB

    Private ConnectionString As String

    Friend Sub New(ByVal connectionString As String)
        Me.ConnectionString = connectionString
    End Sub

    ' Verify that the specified information is correct.
    ' If it is, return the unique UserID.
    ' Otherwise, return 0.
    Public Function AuthenticateUser(ByVal userName As String, _
      ByVal password As String) As Integer

        Dim con As New SqlConnection(ConnectionString)
        Dim cmd As New SqlCommand("GetUser", con)
        Dim r As SqlDataReader

        cmd.CommandType = CommandType.StoredProcedure
        Dim Param As SqlParameter

        Param = cmd.Parameters.Add( _
         "@UserName", SqlDbType.NVarChar, 25)
        Param.Value = userName

        Param = cmd.Parameters.Add( _
         "@Password", SqlDbType.NVarChar, 25)
```

Listing 18-6 The *UserDB* class

```
Param.Value = password

        Dim UserID As Integer = 0

        Try
            con.Open()
            r = cmd.ExecuteReader()

            If r.Read() Then
                UserID = r("ID")
            Else
                ' No matching user.
                UserID = 0
            End If

            r.Close()

        Finally
            con.Close()

        End Try

        Return UserID

    End Function

End Class
```

Notice that the database classes use exception handling to ensure that the database connection is always closed, even if an error occurs. However, they do not catch the exception or rethrow a higher-level exception (such as an *ApplicationException*). This is because this component is consumed by server-side code (such as the XML Web service) that might need to be informed of lower-level errors. However, this also means that the XML Web service should handle these exceptions. Otherwise, they will be propagated back to the client.

The *SessionDB* Class

The *SessionDB* class wraps the logic for creating, verifying, and removing sessions, in the structure shown here:

```
Public Class SessionDB

    Private ConnectionString As String

    Friend Sub New(ByVal connectionString As String)
        Me.ConnectionString = connectionString
```

```
    End Sub

    Public Function CreateSession(ByVal userID As Integer) As Guid
        ' (Code omitted)
    End Function

    ' Removes the indicated session.
    Public Sub RemoveSession(ByVal ticket As Guid)
        ' (Code omitted)
    End Sub

    ' Returns a null reference if no matching session is found.
    Public Function GetSession(ByVal ticket As Guid, _
      ByVal userID As Integer) As SessionDetails

        ' (Code omitted)

    End Function

End Class
```

The *CreateSession* generates a session record for the specified user and returns the GUID ticket. The *RemoveSession* method deletes a session record. Listings 18-7 and 18-8 show these methods.

```
Public Function CreateSession(ByVal userID As Integer) As Guid

    Dim con As New SqlConnection(ConnectionString)
    Dim cmd As New SqlCommand("AddSession", con)

    cmd.CommandType = CommandType.StoredProcedure
    Dim Param As SqlParameter

    Param = cmd.Parameters.Add("@UserID", SqlDbType.Int)
    Param.Value = userID

    ' Add the output parameter.
    Param = cmd.Parameters.Add("@GUID", SqlDbType.UniqueIdentifier)
    Param.Direction = ParameterDirection.Output

    Try
        con.Open()
        cmd.ExecuteNonQuery()
```

Listing 18-7 The *CreateSession* method

```
    Finally
        con.Close()

    End Try

    ' Return the unique identifier.
    Return Param.Value

End Function
```

```
Public Sub RemoveSession(ByVal ticket As Guid)

    Dim con As New SqlConnection(ConnectionString)
    Dim cmd As New SqlCommand("DeleteSession", con)

    cmd.CommandType = CommandType.StoredProcedure
    Dim Param As SqlParameter

    Param = cmd.Parameters.Add("@GUID", SqlDbType.UniqueIdentifier)
    Param.Value = ticket

    Try
        con.Open()
        cmd.ExecuteNonQuery()

    Finally
        con.Close()

    End Try

End Sub
```

Listing 18-8 The *RemoveSession* method

Finally, the *GetSession* method, shown in Listing 18-9, retrieves the session that matches the specified GUID and user ID. By requiring these two criteria, the code ensures that a ticket can't be used for an ID other than the one that was used to log in.

```
' Returns a null reference if no matching session is found.
Public Function GetSession(ByVal ticket As Guid, _
  ByVal userID As Integer) As SessionDetails
```

Listing 18-9 The *GetSession* method

```
    Dim con As New SqlConnection(ConnectionString)
    Dim cmd As New SqlCommand("GetSession", con)
    Dim r As SqlDataReader

    cmd.CommandType = CommandType.StoredProcedure
    Dim Param As SqlParameter

    Param = cmd.Parameters.Add("@GUID", SqlDbType.UniqueIdentifier)
    Param.Value = ticket

    Param = cmd.Parameters.Add("@UserID", SqlDbType.Int)
    Param.Value = userID

    Dim Session As SessionDetails = Nothing

    Try
        con.Open()
        r = cmd.ExecuteReader
        If r.Read() Then
            Session = New SessionDetails()
            Session.CreateDate = r("CreateDate")
            Session.UserID = userID
            Session.Ticket = ticket
        End If

    Finally
        con.Close()

    End Try

    Return Session

End Function
```

The *TaskDB* Class

The *TaskDB* class contains five methods, which allow tasks to be retrieved and updated in different ways. It is possible to shorten the *TaskDB* class by consolidating some methods—for example, by replacing *UpdateTaskStatus* and *CompleteTask* with a more generic *UpdateTask* method. However, more specific, limited stored procedures can generally be optimized more efficiently by the SQL Server engine. In addition, using carefully targeted methods helps focus the application code, preventing it from being used for tasks that haven't been anticipated beforehand (and therefore not optimized or tested for security).

The structure for the *TaskDB* class is shown here:

```
Public Class TaskDB

    Private ConnectionString As String

    Friend Sub New(ByVal connectionString As String)
        Me.ConnectionString = connectionString
    End Sub

    Public Function GetTasks(ByVal userID As Integer, _
      ByVal completedOnly As Boolean) As DataSet
        ' (Code omitted.)
    End Function

    Public Function GetAvailableTasks() As TaskDetails()
        ' (Code omitted.)
    End Function

    Public Function AddTask(ByVal task As TaskDetails) As Guid
        ' (Code omitted.)
    End Function

    Public Sub UpdateTaskStatus(ByVal taskGuid As Guid, _
      ByVal status As TaskStatus)
        ' (Code omitted.)
    End Sub

    Public Sub CompleteTask(ByVal taskGuid As Guid, _
      ByVal renderedFileUrl As String)
        ' (Code omitted.)
    End Sub

End Class
```

Note Tasks are identified using a statistically unique GUID. Alternatively, you can use an autoincrementing identity column for the same purpose. However, autoincrementing numbers are "guessable"; for example, if you submit a task that is assigned the number 402, it's quite likely that you might find another user's task with an ID such as 400 or 401. A GUID solves this problem because each value is generated independently. Knowing one task GUID can't help a user guess another task's GUID.

Listings 18-10 and 18-11 show the *GetTasks* method and the *GetAvailable-Tasks* method, respectively.

```
Public Function GetTasks(ByVal userID As Integer, _
  ByVal completedOnly As Boolean) As DataSet

    Dim con As New SqlConnection(ConnectionString)
    Dim cmd As New SqlCommand("", con)
    Dim Adapter As New SqlDataAdapter(cmd)
    Dim ds As New DataSet()

    If completedOnly Then
        cmd.CommandText = "GetCompletedTasksByUser"
    Else
        cmd.CommandText = "GetTasksByUser"
    End If
    cmd.CommandType = CommandType.StoredProcedure

    Dim Param As SqlParameter
    Param = cmd.Parameters.Add("@UserID", SqlDbType.Int)
    Param.Value = userID

    Dim Tasks As New ArrayList()

    Try
        con.Open()
        Adapter.Fill(ds, "Tasks")

    Finally
        con.Close()

    End Try

    Return ds

End Function
```

Listing 18-10 The *GetTasks* method

```
Public Function GetAvailableTasks() As TaskDetails()

    Dim con As New SqlConnection(ConnectionString)
    Dim cmd As New SqlCommand("GetAvailableTasks", con)
    Dim r As SqlDataReader

    Dim Tasks As New ArrayList()

    Try
        con.Open()
        r = cmd.ExecuteReader()

        Do While r.Read()
            Dim Task As New TaskDetails()

            Task.TaskGUID = r("ID")
            Task.SourceName = r("SourceName")
            Task.Status = r("State")
            Task.SubmitDate = r("SubmitDate")

            ' Here we use ToString() to defend against a null value,
            ' which would otherwise cause an exception.
            Task.RenderedFileUrl = r("RenderedFileURL").ToString()

            Tasks.Add(Task)
        Loop

    Finally
        con.Close()

    End Try

    Return Tasks.ToArray(GetType(TaskDetails))

End Function
```

Listing 18-11 The *GetAvailableTasks* method

One interesting fact about the *TaskDB* class is that the *GetTasks* method returns a *DataSet*, whereas the *GetAvailableTasks* method returns an array of *TaskDetails* objects. Generally, the second option is better for encapsulation because it hides the database details from the client. However, the second option can't be used in conjunction with client-side data binding because the *TaskDetails* class doesn't provide property procedures. In fact, even if you add property procedures to the *TaskDetails* class, this information will not be added to the automatically generated proxy class that the client uses, and data binding still won't be allowed. The only workaround is to either create a client that doesn't use data binding or return a *DataSet* rather than an array of custom objects. In the interest of simplifying development, the *TaskDB* class adopts the second approach.

The *AddTask* method (shown in Listing 18-12) is quite straightforward. It just calls the *AddTask* stored procedure and returns the generated GUID. This code is typical of a multitier distributed application; if all the components of your system are properly isolated, you'll find that their code is straightforward, logical, and unsurprising.

```
Public Function AddTask(ByVal task As TaskDetails) As Guid

    Dim con As New SqlConnection(ConnectionString)
    Dim cmd As New SqlCommand("AddTask", con)

    cmd.CommandType = CommandType.StoredProcedure
    Dim Param As SqlParameter

    Param = cmd.Parameters.Add("@UserID", SqlDbType.Int)
    Param.Value = task.UserID

    Param = cmd.Parameters.Add("@Status", SqlDbType.SmallInt)
    Param.Value = task.Status

    Param = cmd.Parameters.Add("@SourceName", _
      SqlDbType.NVarChar, 50)
    Param.Value = task.SourceName

    ' Add the output parameter.
    Param = cmd.Parameters.Add("@GUID", SqlDbType.UniqueIdentifier)
    Param.Direction = ParameterDirection.Output

    Try
        con.Open()
        cmd.ExecuteNonQuery()

    Finally
        con.Close()

    End Try

    ' Return the unique identifier.
    Return Param.Value

End Function
```

Listing 18-12 The *AddTask* method

Finally, the *TaskDB* class provides two methods for updating database information. The *UpdateTaskStatus* method (shown in Listing 18-13) allows the internal processor to modify the task status when it is placed in progress or when an error occurs. When the task completes, the *CompleteTask* method (shown in Listing 18-14) modifies the status accordingly and sets the corresponding file path for the *RenderedFileUrl*.

```
Public Sub UpdateTaskStatus(ByVal taskGuid As Guid, _
  ByVal status As TaskStatus)

    Dim con As New SqlConnection(ConnectionString)
    Dim cmd As New SqlCommand("UpdateTaskStatus", con)

    cmd.CommandType = CommandType.StoredProcedure
    Dim Param As SqlParameter

    Param = cmd.Parameters.Add("@GUID", SqlDbType.UniqueIdentifier)
    Param.Value = taskGuid

    Param = cmd.Parameters.Add("@Status", SqlDbType.SmallInt)
    Param.Value = status

    Try
        con.Open()
        cmd.ExecuteNonQuery()

    Finally
        con.Close()

    End Try

End Sub
```

Listing 18-13 The *UpdateTaskStatus* method

```
Public Sub CompleteTask(ByVal taskGuid As Guid, _
  ByVal renderedFileUrl As String)

    Dim con As New SqlConnection(ConnectionString)
    Dim cmd As New SqlCommand("CompleteTask", con)

    cmd.CommandType = CommandType.StoredProcedure
    Dim Param As SqlParameter
```

Listing 18-14 The *CompleteTask* method

```
    Param = cmd.Parameters.Add("@GUID", SqlDbType.UniqueIdentifier)
    Param.Value = taskGuid

    Param = cmd.Parameters.Add("@Status", SqlDbType.SmallInt)
    Param.Value = TaskStatus.Complete

    Param = cmd.Parameters.Add("@RenderedFileURL", _
                               SqlDbType.NVarChar, 150)
    Param.Value = renderedFileUrl

    Try
        con.Open()
        cmd.ExecuteNonQuery()

    Finally
        con.Close()

    End Try

End Sub
```

The *SuperComputeTables* Class

The *SuperComputeTables* class provides a gateway to the other database classes. It accepts a connection string argument and passes it to a new instance of the *UserDB*, *SessionDB*, and *TaskDB* classes. It also retrieves the connection string information. This approach (shown in Listing 18-15) is the same pattern used in the Chapter 16 and Chapter 17 case studies.

```
Public Class SuperComputeTables

    Public Users As UserDB
    Public Sessions As SessionDB
    Public Tasks As TaskDB

    Public Sub New()
        ' Retrieve the connection string.
        Dim Connection As String = ConfigurationSettings.AppSettings( _
          "SuperComputeConnection")

        ' Create the table classes.
        Users = New UserDB(Connection)
        Sessions = New SessionDB(Connection)
        Tasks = New TaskDB(Connection)
    End Sub

End Class
```

Listing 18-15 Composition with *SuperComputeTables*

The Render Web Service

The *RenderService* class provides the functionality that allows the client application to query task information and submit new tasks. To call any *RenderService* Web method, the client must first log on and receive a valid ticket.

RenderService Authentication

The ticket information is encapsulated in a custom *SoapHeader* class called *TicketHeader*. Although this class defines four pieces of information, not all of this information will be present at the same time. That's because username and password information is erased immediately after login, and at the same time the corresponding user ID and ticket GUID are inserted. (See Listing 18-16.)

```
Public Class TicketHeader
    Inherits SoapHeader

    Public UserName As String
    Public Password As String
    Public UserID As Integer
    Public SessionGUID As Guid

End Class
```

Listing 18-16 The SOAP authentication header

The *TicketHeader* class is defined in the XML Web service .asmx file, but it is also added to the proxy file. The first task the client needs to accomplish is to create a *TicketHeader* object, set the username and password information, and apply the header to the proxy class. Then the client can call the *Login* Web method, which examines and modifies the header as required.

Here's an example of the client code, which retrieves the user login information from a login window:

```
Dim Proxy As New localhost.RenderService()

' Create the SOAP header with the user name and password.
Dim Ticket As New localhost.TicketHeader()
Ticket.UserName = frmLogin.UserName
Ticket.Password = frmLogin.Password

' Assign the header to the proxy instance.
Proxy.TicketHeaderValue = Ticket

' Try to log in.
If Proxy.Login() Then
    ' The login attempt was successful.
```

```
Else
    ' The login attempt failed.
End If
```

Listing 18-17 shows the *Login* Web method, which verifies the account information and assigns the ticket. Note that the *Login* method includes a *SoapHeader* attribute. This attribute serves three purposes. First, it indicates that this method requires the authentication header. Without this piece of information, the header will not be sent with the client's request message. Second, it indicates which member variable will be used to receive the header. In this case, the variable is named *Ticket*. Third, the *SoapHeader* attribute adds the optional *Direction* parameter and specifies that the SOAP header should be sent back to the client at the end of the method. Otherwise, the changes to the two ticket values (*Ticket.SessionGUID* and *Ticket.UserID*) wouldn't take effect.

```
' Check user name and password from SOAP header.
' If they can be authenticated, add a session record,
' remove the user password from the header (for security),
' and add the ticket GUID.
' Returns False if the client could not be successfully logged in.
<WebMethod(), _
 SoapHeader("Ticket", Direction:=SoapHeaderDirection.InOut)> _
Public Function Login() As Boolean

    Dim UserID As Integer
    UserID = Tables.Users.AuthenticateUser(Ticket.UserName, _
                                           Ticket.Password)

    If UserID <> 0 Then
        ' Clear the password for enhanced security.
        Ticket.Password = ""
        Ticket.UserName = ""
        Ticket.UserID = UserID

        ' Create the session and assign the GUID to the SOAP header.
        Dim GUID As Guid = Tables.Sessions.CreateSession(UserID)
        Ticket.SessionGUID = GUID

        Return True

    Else
        Return False

    End If

End Function
```

Listing 18-17 The *RenderService.Login* method

After the login has been completed successfully, the client does not need to take any further action. The ticket remains "attached" to the current proxy class instance and is automatically sent with each Web method request that requires the header. Figure 18-4 shows how a typical session record appears in the database.

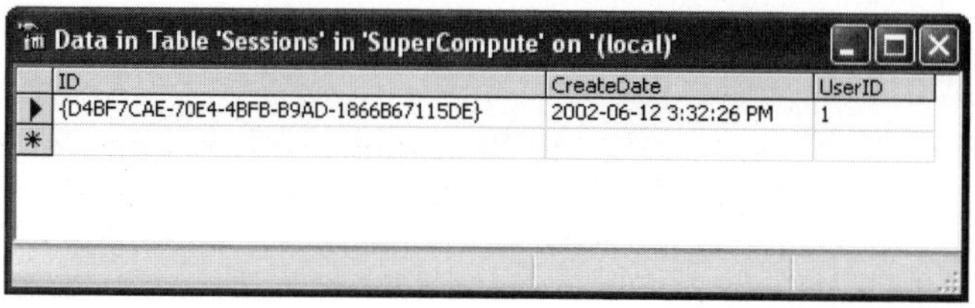

Data in Table 'Sessions' in 'SuperCompute' on '(local)'

ID	CreateDate	UserID
{D4BF7CAE-70E4-4BFB-B9AD-1866B67115DE}	2002-06-12 3:32:26 PM	1

Figure 18-4 A session record

Every other Web method in the *RenderService* class also includes an attribute indicating that it requires the *TicketHeader*. The first line in the method then calls a private *AuthenticateSession* function, which examines the supplied session GUID and user ID information. This pattern is shown in Listing 18-18.

```
<WebMethod(), SoapHeader("Ticket")> _
Public Sub DoSomething()

    AuthenticateSession(Ticket)

    ' (Actual method code goes here.)

End Function

' Throws an exception if the session is not valid.
' Currently, sessions are allowed to exist indefinitely, but you
' could use this method to examine the CreateDate value and impose
' an expiration date.
Private Sub AuthenticateSession(ByVal ticket As TicketHeader)

    If Tables.Sessions.GetSession(ticket.SessionGUID, ticket.UserID) _
      Is Nothing Then
        ' No record was returned. Raise an exception.
        Throw New Security.SecurityException("Session not valid.")

    Else
        ' The session exists. Allow the code to continue.
        ' (This is where you could add an expiration policy.)

    End If

End Sub
```

Listing 18-18 Authenticating a ticket

Optionally, you can use the *AuthenticateSession* function to check the creation date and remove an expired ticket. Because this expiration policy is implemented in code, you have the freedom to tailor it to your needs, possibly creating expiration rules that are user-specific or that depend on the time of day.

> **Note** One reason a session ticket is used is that it can protect user account information. Typically, a system uses an SSL connection to ensure that requests to the *Login* method are encrypted. After that point, requests can use fast, clear-text transmission because the login information is no longer used. At worst, a session GUID could be intercepted and a session could be hijacked until it expires. For more information, refer to the ticket-based security discussion in Chapter 13.

It is possible to use a simpler login approach that doesn't require the client to create a *TicketHeader* object. To do this, you create a *Login* method that accepts username and password information through two parameters:

```
<WebMethod(), _
 SoapHeader("Ticket", Direction:=SoapHeaderDirection.Out)> _
Public Function Login(userName As String, password As String) _
  As Boolean

    ' (Authentication code omitted.)

End Function
```

This approach is sometimes preferred because it is more transparent for the client. However, hiding more details can also confuse the client programmer, who might not be aware of the behind-the-scenes process and what causes a session to time out.

Finally, when the client is finished, it's good practice to call the *Logout* method shown in Listing 18-19 to ensure proper cleanup of the session record.

```
<WebMethod(), SoapHeader("Ticket")> _
Public Sub Logout()

    Tables.Sessions.RemoveSession(Ticket.SessionGUID)

End Sub
```

Listing 18-19 The *RenderService.Logout* method

RenderService Functionality

The *RenderService* class provides two more Web methods: *GetTasks* and *SubmitTask*. The *GetTasks* method (shown in Listing 18-20) is the simplest—it just examines the user ID information in the SOAP authentication header, invokes the database component, and returns a *DataSet* with the corresponding information. The client doesn't need to submit any information in method parameters.

```
' Returns all the tasks for the currently logged in user.
<WebMethod(), SoapHeader("Ticket")> _
Public Function GetTasks(ByVal completedOnly As Boolean) As DataSet '

    AuthenticateSession(Ticket)
    Return Tables.Tasks.GetTasks(Ticket.UserID, completedOnly)

End Function
```

Listing 18-20 The *RenderService.GetTasks* method

The *SubmitTask* method (shown in Listing 18-21) performs a little more work. It adds a record to the database for the new task and copies the file onto the server. The unique-task GUID is used for the filename, ensuring that there can't be a naming conflict (and that malicious users can't guess which project a rendered file corresponds to).

However, there is one wrinkle with this approach: To use the GUID as the filename, the task record must be added *before* the file is transferred. Usually, these two tasks are performed in the opposite order, ensuring that if there is a file-transfer error (which could be caused by network problems), the record isn't added. To overcome this problem, the entire Web method executes inside a COM+ transaction. This means that if an exception is generated while the file is being written, the database insert operation is rolled back.

```
' Transfers the source file as byte array. Returns the GUID
' that identifies the task.
' This method adds a task record, and
' saves a file with the date and GUID as a filename.
<WebMethod(TransactionOption:=TransactionOption.RequiresNew), _
 SoapHeader("Ticket")> _
Public Function SubmitTask(ByVal buffer As Byte(), _
  ByVal fileName As String) As Guid

    AuthenticateSession(Ticket)
```

Listing 18-21 The *RenderService.SubmitTask* method

```
    ' Create a corresponding task record for the transferred file.
    Dim Task As New DBComponent.TaskDetails()
    Task.SourceName = fileName
    Task.Status = DBComponent.TaskStatus.NewAdded
    Task.UserID = Ticket.UserID

    ' You must add the record before the file is transferred,
    ' in order to get the GUID, which is used for the file name.
    ' To ensure that the record is not committed in the case of an
    ' error, this Web method executes inside a COM+ transaction.
    Dim TaskGuid As Guid = Tables.Tasks.AddTask(Task)
    ' Prepare to save the file.
    Dim SavePath As String
    SavePath = ConfigurationSettings.AppSettings("SourceDirectory")

    ' Make sure the directory does not end with a backslash.
    SavePath.Trim("\")

    SavePath &= "\" & TaskGuid.ToString()
    Dim fs As New FileStream(SavePath, FileMode.CreateNew)
    fs.Write(buffer, 0, buffer.Length)
    fs.Close()

    Return TaskGuid

End Function
```

Note The code in Listing 18-21 contains one quirk. The transaction is started in the XML Web service, but the database component also participates. If the transaction fails, the database operations are rolled back. This is exactly what you want, but it might strike you as a little odd because the database component does not use COM+. So how can it participate in a COM+ transaction?

The answer is as follows: when the XML Web service transaction is created, a new unmanaged context is created and associated with the current thread. The database component is not associated with any specific unmanaged context, so the common language runtime (CLR) automatically provides the database component with the current transactional context. In other words, .NET automatically enlists the database object in the transaction.

> This approach is extremely convenient but subject to one caveat: It's not guaranteed to work in future versions of the .NET Framework. If .NET is rewritten entirely in managed .NET code at some point, this behavior will most likely change and you will have to specifically configure transactional components with attributes.

The Client

The client code is a straightforward Windows Forms application that enables the user to upload new tasks and view the progress of current tasks. When the application first starts, the user is prompted to log in (as shown in Figure 18-5).

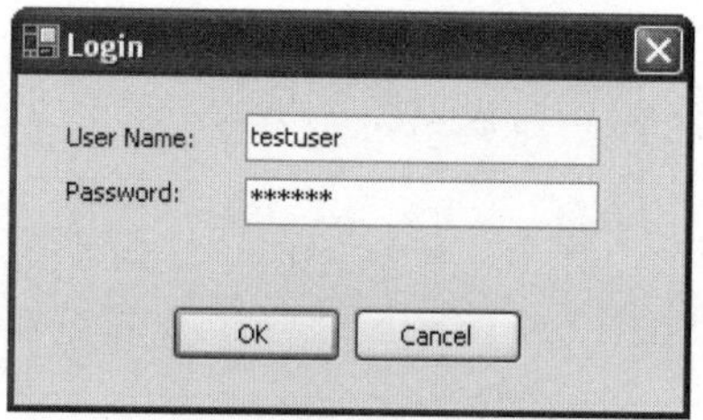

Figure 18-5 The Login window

The client code includes a private *Login* function that shows the login form until the client cancels the attempt or the login succeeds, as shown in Listing 18-22.

```
Private Proxy As New localhost.RenderService()

Private Function Login()

    Dim frmLogin As New Login()

    Do While frmLogin.ShowDialog() = DialogResult.OK

        ' Create the SOAP header with the user name and password.
        Dim Ticket As New localhost.TicketHeader()
        Ticket.UserName = frmLogin.UserName
        Ticket.Password = frmLogin.Password
```

Listing 18-22 The client *Login* method

```
        ' Assign the header to the proxy instance.
        Proxy.TicketHeaderValue = Ticket

        ' Try to log in.
        If Proxy.Login() Then Return True

    Loop

    ' Login was cancelled.
    Return False

End Function
```

If the user can be successfully authenticated by the XML Web service, the application continues by retrieving and displaying the user's list of tasks (as shown in Listing 18-23). Figure 18-6 shows the client form in action.

```
Private Sub Client_Load(ByVal sender As Object, _
  ByVal e As System.EventArgs) Handles MyBase.Load

    ' Try to authenticate the user.
    If Login() Then
        Display("Successfully logged in.")
        SetUpForm()
    Else
        Application.Exit()
    End If

End Sub

Private Sub SetUpForm()

    Dim Tasks As DataSet
    Tasks = Proxy.GetTasks(False)

    Display("List of " & Tasks.Tables(0).Rows.Count.ToString() & _
            " current task(s) retrieved.")

    gridTasks.DataSource = Tasks.Tables(0)

End Sub
```

Listing 18-23 Logging in and retrieving tasks at startup

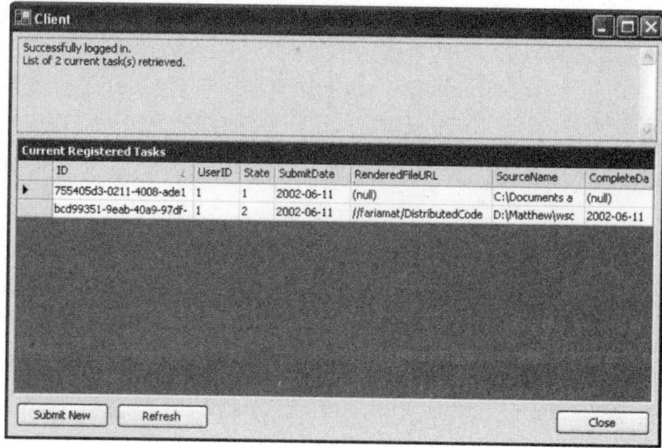

Figure 18-6 The client interface

A custom *Display* method is used to quickly add text to a read-only text box display:

```
Private Sub Display(ByVal message As String)

    txtStatus.Text &= message
    txtStatus.Text &= System.Environment.NewLine

End Sub
```

The remainder of the interface is quite predictable. When the form closes, the *Logout* Web method is called automatically. When the Submit New button is clicked, a common Open dialog box is used to select the file. When the user selects a file, it's transferred to the server using the *SubmitTask* Web method (see Listing 18-24).

Figure 18-7 shows the results.

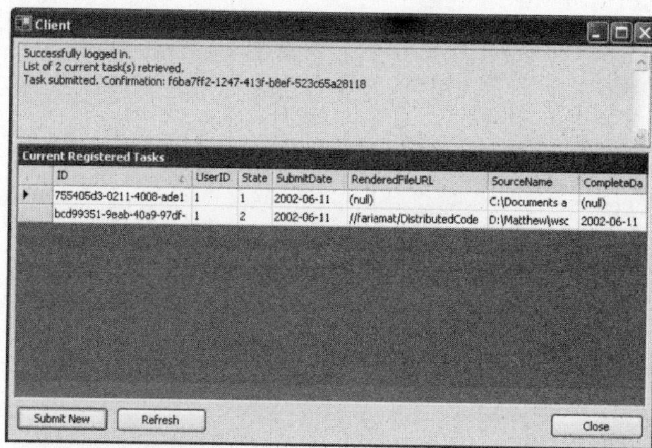

Figure 18-7 Submitting a task

```
Private Sub cmdSubmit_Click(ByVal sender As System.Object, _
  ByVal e As System.EventArgs) Handles cmdSubmit.Click

    If dlgOpen.ShowDialog() = DialogResult.OK Then

        Dim fs As New FileStream(dlgOpen.FileName, FileMode.Open)
        Dim Buffer As Byte()
        ReDim Buffer(fs.Length)
        fs.Read(Buffer, 0, fs.Length)
        fs.Close()

        Dim Guid As Guid = Proxy.SubmitTask(Buffer, dlgOpen.FileName)
        Display("Task submitted. Confirmation: " & Guid.ToString())

    End If

End Sub
```

Listing 18-24 Submitting a new task

> **Note** One interesting technique used in the client interface is a horizontal splitter bar, which enables the user to decide how much of the window is used for the text information display and how much for the list of current tasks. The split display is implemented using separate docked panels. To examine it in detail, download the SuperCompute case study.

The Task Processor

On the server side, a separate application processes tasks one at a time. This application could be modeled as a Windows service (as a similar application was in Chapter 16); but in this case, a Windows Forms application is used, both to allow for a rich user interface complete with a displayed log of information and to demonstrate a few important threading techniques.

The task processor is actually split into two assemblies: a *TaskProcessor* library component that encapsulates the custom rendering code, and a TaskProcessorUI executable application. The TaskProcessorUI application scans through the list of available tasks using the database component and processes each one using the *TaskProcessor* component.

The *TaskProcessor* Component

Listing 18-25 shows the complete *TaskProcessor* component. In this case, a *WasteTime* method is used to stall processing for three minutes, loosely simulating the rendering process.

```
Public Class TaskProcessor

    Public Sub RenderFile(ByVal sourceFile As String, _
      ByVal targetFile As String)

        ' This is where the business-specific code for rendering the
        ' files would go. In this example, the code simply stalls for
        ' three minutes while "processing" the file.
        WasteTime(180)

        ' Create the rendered (in this case, empty) file.
        Dim fs As New FileStream(targetFile, FileMode.CreateNew)
        fs.Close()

    End Sub

    Private Sub WasteTime(ByVal seconds As Integer)

        Dim StartTime As DateTime = DateTime.Now
        Do
        Loop Until DateTime.Now > (StartTime.AddSeconds(seconds))

    End Sub

End Class
```

Listing 18-25 The *TaskProcessor* component

The Task Processor Front End

The task processor application provides a simple user interface that enables the user to quickly suspend and resume processing (as shown in Figure 18-8). This allows the server to be freed up for more time-sensitive tasks as required.

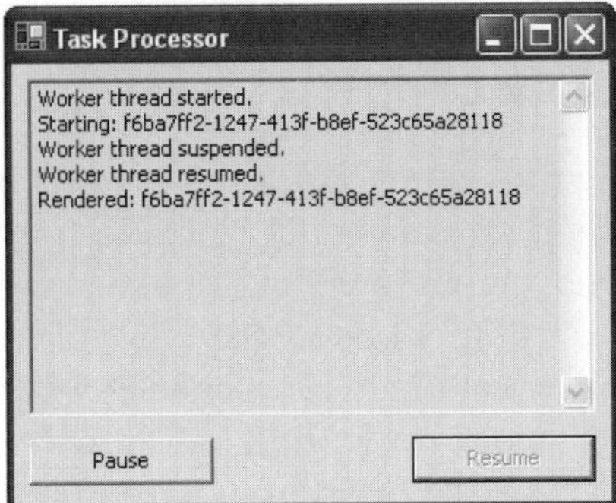

Figure 18-8 The task processor interface

A dedicated object on a separate thread performs all the processing work. This allows the front end to remain responsive, even while the rendering operation is underway. Listing 18-26 shows the code used to set up these objects when the program starts.

```
Private WorkerObject As ProcessThread
Private WorkerThread As Thread

Private Sub Main_Load(ByVal sender As System.Object, _
  ByVal e As System.EventArgs) Handles MyBase.Load

    ' Set up the worker object that will perform the work.
    WorkerObject = New ProcessThread(Me)

    ' Set up the thread where the work will be performed.
    WorkerThread = New Thread(AddressOf WorkerObject.DoWork)

    ' Start the worker process.
    WorkerThread.Start()
    Display("Worker thread started.")

End Sub

Public Sub Display(ByVal message As String)

    txtStatus.Text &= message
    txtStatus.Text &= System.Environment.NewLine

End Sub
```

Listing 18-26 The task processor initialization code

Is This the Best Use of Multiple CPUs?

As described previously, the TaskProcessorUI application renders only one file at a time. However, the server on which this application runs has multiple CPUs available. In this case, we assume that the actual task-processing code has been optimized to use multiple CPUs. This ensures that each individual task will complete several times faster than it would otherwise. If the task-processing code were not optimized, however, you could obtain better performance by creating a more complicated multithreaded front-end application that creates several worker threads that run at the same time.

To make this transition easier, we've designed the front-end application to perform all its work using a custom threaded object. If you decide to implement multiple worker threads in your front-end application, refer to the singleton design shown in Chapter 7. You can control the number of active threads using a preset maximum, or you can make use of the .NET *ThreadPool* object for automatic thread pooling.

Remember that creating a multithreaded front end can increase the overall throughput of the application (because it allows several tasks to be processed at the same time), but it won't reduce the time taken to process an individual task. On the other hand, a multithreaded task processor can both increase the overall system throughput *and* reduce the time taken for a single task, which often makes it a better choice.

Listing 18-27 shows the threaded worker object without the actual processing logic (which is contained in the *DoWork* method).

```
Public Class ProcessThread

    Private SourcePath As String
    Private TargetPath As String
    Private ServerPrefix As String
    Private HostForm As Main

    Private Tables As New DBComponent.SuperComputeTables()
    Private Processor As New TaskProcessor()
```

Listing 18-27 The threaded worker object

```
    Public RequestStop As Boolean = False

    Public Sub New(ByVal form As Main)
        SourcePath = ConfigurationSettings.AppSettings( _
                      "SourceDirectory")
        TargetPath = ConfigurationSettings.AppSettings( _
                      "CompleteDirectory")
        ServerPrefix = ConfigurationSettings.AppSettings( _
                      "ServerPrefix")
        HostForm = form
    End Sub

    Public Sub DoWork()
        ' (Code omitted)
    End Sub

End Class
```

The worker object reads the directories it should process from the configuration file shown in Listing 18-28. In addition, it stores a *Server* prefix that is used to create the UNC path for the rendered filename, which will be stored in the database and used by the client to retrieve the final file.

```
<?xml version="1.0" encoding="utf-8" ?>
<configuration>

  <appSettings>
    <add key="SuperComputeConnection"
         value="Data Source=localhost;Initial
                Catalog=SuperCompute;Integrated Security=SSPI" />
    <add key="SourceDirectory"
         value="c:\SuperCompute\Source" />
    <add key="CompleteDirectory"
         value="c:\SuperCompute\Complete" />
    <add key="ServerPrefix"
         value="\\localhost\CaseStudies\SuperCompute\Complete" />
  </appSettings>

</configuration>
```

Listing 18-28 The task processor configuration file

The *DoWork* subroutine shown in Listing 18-29 retrieves all the available tasks from the database, determines the appropriate source and target filenames, and then submits a request to the *TaskProcessor* component. If there are no waiting requests, the thread is put to sleep for 5 minutes before it requeries the database.

```
Public Sub DoWork()

    Dim Task As DBComponent.TaskDetails
    Dim Tasks As DBComponent.TaskDetails()

    Do
        ' Retrieve all tasks that need to be processed.
        Tasks = Tables.Tasks.GetAvailableTasks()

        For Each Task In Tasks

            ' Mark the record in progress.
            Tables.Tasks.UpdateTaskStatus(Task.TaskGUID, _
              DBComponent.TaskStatus.InProgress)

            Dim Source, Target As String
            FileToRender = SourcePath & "\" & Task.TaskGUID.ToString()
            Target = TargetPath & "\" & Task.TaskGUID.ToString()

            ' Perform the rendering.
            Processor.RenderFile(Source, Target)

            Task.RenderedFileUrl = ServerPrefix & "/" & _
                                   Task.TaskGUID.ToString()
            Task.Status = DBComponent.TaskStatus.Complete

            ' Update the task record.
            Tables.Tasks.CompleteTask(Task.TaskGUID, _
              Task.RenderedFileUrl)

            ' Check if the user is trying to close the application.
            If RequestStop Then Return

        Next

        ' There are no more files.
        ' Pause for five minutes before the next check.
        Thread.Sleep(TimeSpan.FromMinutes(5))
    Loop

End Sub
```

Listing 18-29 Processing tasks

Listing 18-29 leaves out two details. First, the *DoWork* method actually performs the rendering in an exception handler. If an exception occurs, it then updates the task status to indicate that an error occurred and to ensure that it does not attempt to render the file again (which could be a considerable waste of time if a source file error causes a recurring error).

One type of exception gets special treatment, however: the *ThreadAbortException*. The *ThreadAbortException* only occurs if a user attempts to shut down the application while it is in the middle of an operation and the thread can't complete the current operation and end gracefully in the allowed time. A *ThreadAbortException* does not indicate a problem in the file being rendered. Listing 18-30 shows the error-handling code used to deal with this occurrence.

```
Public Sub DoWork()

    Dim Task As DBComponent.TaskDetails
    Dim Tasks As DBComponent.TaskDetails()

    Do
        Tasks = Tables.Tasks.GetAvailableTasks()

        For Each Task In Tasks

            Try

                ' (Processing code omitted.)

            Catch Err As ThreadAbortException
                ' This error only occurs if the thread cannot
                ' end fast enough when a stop is requested. There
                ' is no database problem, so no action is performed.

            Catch
                ' This is a miscellaneous update error.
                ' When an error is encountered, the status of the file
                ' is updated.
                ' This is also a good place to add custom logging code,
                ' or even write a more descriptive error code to the
                ' task record in the database.
                Tables.Tasks.UpdateTaskStatus(Task.TaskGUID, _
                  DBComponent.TaskStatus.HaltedWithError)

            End Try

            If RequestStop Then Return
        Next

        Thread.Sleep(TimeSpan.FromMinutes(5))
    Loop

End Sub
```

Listing 18-30 Exception handling in *DoWork*

The worker thread also provides messages that need to appear directly in the user interface. You can accommodate this design in a number of ways, but the most direct way is just to marshal code to the user-interface thread. The *ProcessThread* class provides a *HostForm* property just for this purpose; it stores a reference to the user-interface form.

Listing 18-31 shows the logging code for the *DoWork* method and the helper methods that allow the call to be marshaled to the user-interface thread.

```
Public Sub DoWork()

    Dim Task As DBComponent.TaskDetails
    Dim Tasks As DBComponent.TaskDetails()

    Do
        Tasks = Tables.Tasks.GetAvailableTasks()

        For Each Task In Tasks

            Try
                Display("Starting: " + Task.TaskGUID.ToString())

                ' (Processing code omitted.)

                Display("Rendered: " + Task.TaskGUID.ToString())
            Catch Err As ThreadAbortException

            Catch
                Tables.Tasks.UpdateTaskStatus(Task.TaskGUID, _
                DBComponent.TaskStatus.HaltedWithError)

                Display("Error with: " + Task.TaskGUID.ToString())

            End Try

            If RequestStop Then Return
        Next

        Thread.Sleep(TimeSpan.FromMinutes(5))
    Loop

End Sub
```

Listing 18-31 User interface messages in *DoWork*

```
' This method allows a method call to be marshaled to
' the user interface thread, allowing a label control update.
Private Sub Display(ByVal message As String)
    NewText = message
    HostForm.Invoke(New MethodInvoker(AddressOf Me.AddText))
End Sub

Private NewText As String

' This method executes on the form thread.
Private Sub AddText()
    HostForm.Display(NewText)
  End Sub
```

Finally, the application needs to take extra care when shutting down. It attempts to terminate the thread gracefully by raising a flag, as shown in Listing 18-32. Note that if the thread is currently suspended, it must be resumed before it can be aborted. If the code fails to end the thread after 3 minutes, the thread is aborted manually. Alternatively, you can set the timeout limit based on a configuration file setting.

```
Private Sub Main_Closing(ByVal sender As Object, _
  ByVal e As System.ComponentModel.CancelEventArgs) _
  Handles MyBase.Closing

     ' Set the stop flag so the thread can finish the current task.
     WorkerObject.RequestStop = True

    If (WorkerThread.ThreadState And ThreadState.WaitSleepJoin) = _
      ThreadState.WaitSleepJoin Then
        ' Thread has put itself to sleep.
        ' It is safe to end the thread.
        WorkerThread.Interrupt()
        WorkerThread.Abort()

    Else
        If (WorkerThread.ThreadState And ThreadState.Suspended) = _
          ThreadState.Suspended Then
            WorkerThread.Resume()
        End If

        ' Attempt to let the worker thread end gracefully.
        WorkerThread.Join(TimeSpan.FromMinutes(3))
```

Listing 18-32 Closing the task processor

```
        If (WorkerThread.ThreadState And ThreadState.Running) = _
          ThreadState.Running Then
            ' Thread is still running.
            ' Time to end it the hard way.
            WorkerThread.Abort()
        End If

    End If

End Sub
```

> **Note** When you test more than one component of this project at the same time, you should use separate instances of Visual Studio .NET or run some of the applications outside the development environment. If you configure your project to start multiple applications for debugging, you might experience a significant slowdown when you attempt to use the client application while a task is being processed. Instead, you should run these applications outside the IDE when you want to test the full solution at once.

Downloading a Rendered File

The final ingredient is allowing the client to download the rendered file. A *MouseDown* event handler is added to the *DataGrid* for this purpose. (See Listing 18-33.) When a right-click is detected on a row that corresponds to a completed item, a special shortcut menu is displayed (as shown in Figure 18-9).

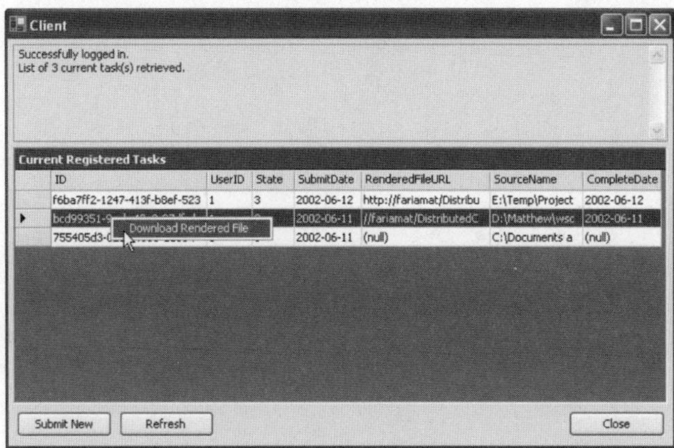

Figure 18-9 Retrieving the rendered file in the client

```
Private Sub gridTasks_MouseDown(ByVal sender As Object, _
  ByVal e As System.Windows.Forms.MouseEventArgs) _
  Handles gridTasks.MouseDown

    If e.Button = MouseButtons.Right Then

        Dim HitInfo As DataGrid.HitTestInfo
        HitInfo = gridTasks.HitTest(e.X, e.Y)

        If HitInfo.Type = DataGrid.HitTestType.Cell Then
            If gridTasks.Item(HitInfo.Row, colRendered).ToString() _
             <> "" Then
                ' This file can be downloaded. Select the row and
                ' show menu.
                gridTasks.CurrentRowIndex = HitInfo.Row
                mnuGrid.Show(gridTasks, New Point(e.X, e.Y))
            End If
        End If

    End If

End Sub
```

Listing 18-33 Showing the right-click download option

If the user chooses the download menu item, a common Save dialog box appears that enables the user to specify where the file should be placed. (See Listing 18-34.) As a nicety, the filename defaults to the original client source name plus the extension rendered.

```
Private Sub mnuDownload_Click(ByVal sender As System.Object, _
  ByVal e As System.EventArgs) Handles mnuDownload.Click

    ' Determine the UNC path to the rendered file.
    Dim FileToDownload As String
    FileToDownload = gridTasks.Item( _
                 gridTasks.CurrentRowIndex, colRendered).ToString()

    ' Default the target filename based on the source filename.
    dlgSave.FileName = gridTasks.Item(gridTasks.CurrentRowIndex, _
                   colSource).ToString() & ".rendered"

    If dlgSave.ShowDialog() = DialogResult.OK Then
        ' Copy the file.
        File.Copy(FileToDownload, dlgSave.FileName)
    End If

End Sub
```

Listing 18-34 Transferring the rendered file

Note that there is currently no way to remove task records from the database. These records should not be deleted automatically when a file is downloaded because they might be useful in the future for tracking old files or reviewing usage information. The best approach is probably to add a new status code that indicates a task that has completed and has been downloaded. The *GetTasksByUser* stored procedure can then be modified to ignore records that have been downloaded.

Future Directions

The current solution addresses all the requirements identified in the problem analysis. It also provides the opportunity for future enhancements, such as a more detailed security model and a reporting tool that can profile rendering usage. As always, however, there is still room for improvement.

Adding Ticket Caching

One of the reasons for using a ticket-based security system is to replace the costly user ID and password lookup with a faster ticket verification. In the example so far, the ticket verification also entails a database trip and still results in unnecessary overhead on every method call.

A better approach is possible by adding caching. With a caching strategy, a ticket object is added to the cache for every ticket, indexed by GUID. Listing 18-35 shows the rewritten *Login* method. A sliding expiration policy is used, ensuring that the ticket is retained for up to three hours after the last request.

```
<WebMethod(), SoapHeader("Ticket", _
 Direction:=SoapHeaderDirection.InOut)> _
Public Function Login() As Boolean

    Dim UserID As Integer
    UserID = Tables.Users.AuthenticateUser(Ticket.UserName, _
                                           Ticket.Password)

    If UserID <> 0 Then
        ' Clear the password for enhanced security.
        Ticket.Password = ""
        Ticket.UserName = ""
        Ticket.UserID = UserID

        ' Create the session and assign the GUID to the SOAP header.
        Dim GUID As Guid = Tables.Sessions.CreateSession(UserID)
        Ticket.SessionGUID = GUID
```

Listing 18-35 Adding a ticket to the cache

```
            ' Store the ticket in the cache.
            Context.Cache.Insert(GUID, Ticket, null, DateTime.MaxValue, 
                     TimeSpan.FromHours(3))

            Return True

        Else
            Return False

        End If

    End Function
```

When authenticating a session, the service first checks the cache and then turns to the database as a last resort, as shown in Listing 18-36.

```
Private Sub AuthenticateSession(ByVal ticket As TicketHeader)

    Dim Success As Boolean = True

    Dim CachedTicket As TicketHeader
    CachedTicket = Context.Cache(ticket.SessionGUID)

    If CachedTicket Is Nothing
        ' Attempt database validation.

        If Tables.Sessions.GetSession(ticket.SessionGUID, _
          ticket.UserID) Is Nothing Then
            ' No record was returned.
            Success = False
        End If

    Else
        ' Ticket was found in the cache. Validate it.
        If CachedTicket.UserID <> ticket.UserID Then
            Success = False
        End If

    End If

    If Not Success Then
        Throw New Security.SecurityException("Session not valid.")
    End If

End Sub
```

Listing 18-36 Checking the cache for the ticket

> **Note** Even with caching, it's still strongly recommended that you store information in a backend database. Otherwise, the session ticket might be removed by ASP.NET if server resources become scarce or the amount of information in the cache increases.

Enhanced Client Cleanup

Currently the client contains a minimum of error-handling code. The problem with this approach is that an unhandled exception could cause the application to terminate without properly logging out. To solve this problem, you can add exception-handling code to the Web method calls and log out if an error occurs. Although this problem is minor (and is addressed by the *DeleteOldSessions* stored procedure), our approach can be improved. One possibility is to use the *AppDomain.UnhandledException* event, which fires whenever an exception occurs that your code doesn't catch. You can then use your event handler to log out. This technique is described in detail in Chapter 14.

Another problem is that the client doesn't consider the possibility that a session could time out. Ideally, the server would create a special *SoapException* class, with some XML information added to the *Detail* property that indicates a security exception. Upon receiving this exception, the client could then attempt to log in again.

Adding Message Queuing

Another nice addition to this application would be the use of Message Queuing. As explained at the beginning of this chapter, a *NotifyQueue* field allows the database to record a client-specific queue path. The task processor front end can retrieve this information after a rendering operation completes and mail a message to the client. The client application can be upgraded to include a worker thread that continuously scans the message queue and reports immediately when rendered files are ready. This is similar to the approach developed in the preceding chapter, and it saves the client from needing to requery the XML Web service.

Adding Load Balancing

The current solution assumes that only one server will be rendering tasks. However, what happens if Trey Research is remarkably successful and wants to add another server to the mix to maximize the throughput of the system?

In fact, only a few simple changes are required to enable the application to support multiple instances of the task processor. The most significant change is that the rendering application can no longer retrieve a list of tasks to process. Instead, it must retrieve the information for a single task.

Here's the current code for retrieving available tasks:

```
Tasks = Tables.Tasks.GetAvailableTasks()

For Each Task In Tasks

    ' Mark the record in progress.
    Tables.Tasks.UpdateTaskStatus(Task.TaskGUID, _
      DBComponent.TaskStatus.InProgress)

    ' (Processing code omitted.)

Next
```

The problem here is that multiple task processors will contain duplicate lists and will probably attempt to process the same task at the same time. Instead, you should replace the *GetAvailableTasks* method (and stored procedure) with a *RequestNextTask* method that returns a single available task.

The task-processing code will now look like this:

```
Tasks = Tables.Tasks.RequestNextTask()

' (Processing code omitted.)
```

Note that the code no longer needs to explicitly set the task record in progress by calling the *UpdateTaskStatus* method because the *RequestNextTask* stored procedure performs this step automatically. If you don't use this approach, you might run into a significant concurrency problem when the actions of more than one processor overlap as follows:

1. The first task processor queries an available task and receives task A.
2. The second task processor queries an available task. Because task A is not yet in progress, it receives the same task.
3. The first task processor marks task A in progress.
4. The second task processor also marks task A in progress.
5. Both servers are performing the same work.

To avoid this problem, steps 1 and 3 must be collapsed into a single *RequestNextTask* stored procedure that uses an embedded SQL transaction. Listing 18-37 shows one example that works by holding a lock on the task record.

```
CREATE Procedure RequestNextTask
 AS

SET TRANSACTION ISOLATION LEVEL REPEATABLE READ
BEGIN TRANSACTION

    -- Find the GUID for the next record.
    DECLARE @GUID uniqueidentifier
    SELECT TOP 1 @GUID = ID FROM Tasks
      WHERE State=0 ORDER BY SubmitDate

    -- Update the status to place it in progress.
    UPDATE Tasks SET State = 1 WHERE ID = @GUID

    -- Return the record.
    SELECT * FROM Tasks WHERE ID = @GUID

COMMIT TRANSACTION
```

Listing 18-37 The new *RequestNextTask* stored procedure

In addition, you might want to expand the *RequestNextTask* stored procedure and the Tasks table so that they record information about which server is processing a given task.

Finally, you might need to tighten the rules of some of the other stored procedures. For example, you might want to add a *Where* clause that makes sure a record status can't be updated to complete unless it is currently marked in progress. Listing 18-38 shows such a change for the CompleteTask stored procedure.

```
CREATE Procedure CompleteTask
 (
    @GUID            uniqueidentifier,
    @RenderedFileURL nvarchar(100),
    @Status          int
 )
 AS
    UPDATE Tasks
    SET State = @Status,
    RenderedFileURL = @RenderedFileURL,
    CompleteDate = GETDATE()
    WHERE [ID] = @GUID
    AND State = 1
```

Listing 18-38 The refined *CompleteTask* stored procedure

Summary

This chapter presented the last of our three case studies. It showed how to implement a scalable and efficient workflow built on .NET technologies. We returned to some common themes:

- Centralize data among all parts of a system by using a database.
- Wrap the client functionality behind an XML Web service facade instead of directly exposing the database component.
- Defend against the security risks that are likely in your scenario, including user error.
- Consider the compromises needed to ensure scalability and performance. In our example, this meant bypassing the XML Web service for a single task (downloading the rendered file).

The next chapter takes a quick look at a few of the case studies provided by Microsoft.

19

Microsoft Case Studies

A daunting gap exists between understanding the technologies that support distributed applications and being able to implement an end-to-end solution. The average distributed application comprises hundreds or thousands of lines of code, split into distinct layers and partitioned over multiple computers. Decisions that affect deployment, security, and scalability are made at every level of distributed application programming, and it's difficult to choose correctly until you've lived through the full design-to-deployment process at least once.

There is one way to pare down the learning curve, however, and that's by poring through the gold standard of distributed application code. I encourage you to examine some of the excellent platform samples available from Microsoft after you've finished reading the case studies in this book. You'll find that many of these samples are long and even tedious—but they are invaluable examples of how to ruthlessly apply the best practices I've explained throughout the previous 18 chapters. In this chapter, I summarize several of these samples, discuss what technologies they demonstrate, and identify where you can find them. Enjoy!

> **Note** This chapter focuses on full-scale case studies. However, the Internet is also home to many other types of resources, including sites that provide code snippets that can help you learn individual topics. Some of the best are at *http://www.gotdotnet.com/quickstart/howto* and *http://www.gotdotnet.com/quickstart*. Although the examples you'll find there are basic, they provide a useful starting point for learning new material.

The IBuySpy Storefront

The IBuySpy case studies represent one of the best ways to learn ASP.NET programming. However, they aren't just for Web developers—their careful use of tiers, database components, and stored procedure code reinforces many of the points I've stressed in this book.

IBuySpy is a fictitious e-commerce company complete with a product catalog, shopping basket, user-comment service, and account information. The IBuySpy site uses output caching to reduce the load on the database by storing rendered HTML for instantaneous reuse, it uses data binding to reduce coding, and it uses ASP.NET user controls to ensure that the site's user interface is modular and reusable. For the distributed application programmer, the most interesting aspect of the IBuySpy store is its use of database classes, which closely follows the service provider model introduced at the beginning of this book. Every database interaction passes through a dedicated table class, which then executes a corresponding stored procedure. The ASP.NET page code contains no dynamic SQL statements or direct database connections. The IBuySpy store also provides XML Web services that allow access to the IBuySpy catalog, but there is no corresponding client application. You can develop your own or test these XML Web services using the Microsoft Internet Explorer test page functionality.

You can download the IBuySpy store code in Visual Basic .NET or C# versions from *http://www.ibuyspy.com*. A setup program creates the required database (provided you have access to Microsoft SQL Server) and virtual directory. You also can run the IBuySpy store online at *http://www.ibuyspystore.com*, as shown in Figure 19-1. In addition, you can browse the well-commented code online at *http://www.ibuyspystore.com/vbdocs/docs/docs.htm*.

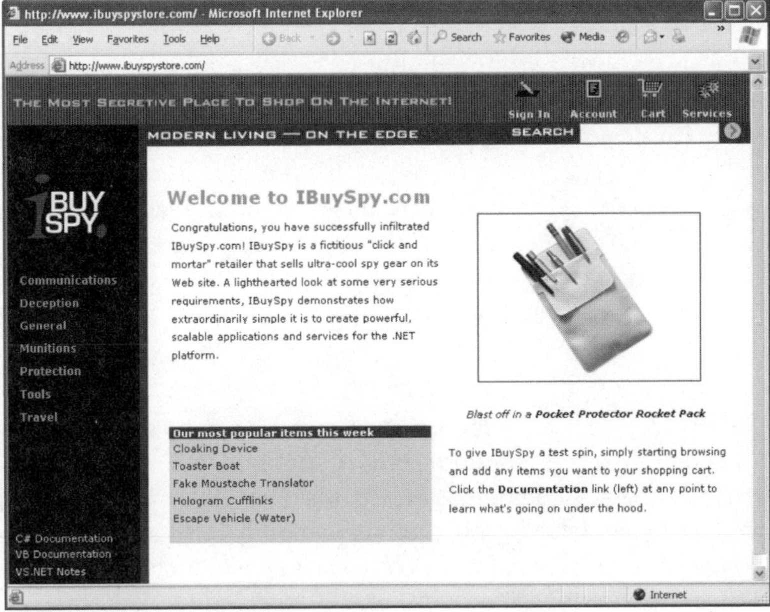

Figure 19-1 The IBuySpy storefront

Does Microsoft Favor ASP.NET?

All Microsoft distributed case studies use ASP.NET because ASP.NET offers the easiest way to implement a distributed application and the shortest path to optimum performance thanks to features such as output caching. ASP.NET also guarantees cross-platform support. Microsoft is facing stiff competition from other server-side technologies such as J2EE, and this ability to support any client with an Internet browser is a key marketing priority.

However, Microsoft has also repeatedly declared that smart Windows Forms are a core part of its strategy and that the company expects to see ongoing development for distributed applications based in the Windows world. In fact, part of the goal of Windows services is to bring Internet functionality into a desktop world. However, Microsoft doesn't provide any complete case studies that use Windows Forms.

The IBuySpy Portal

The IBuySpy portal is a configurable Web portal for an intranet or the Internet that's built out of custom user controls. By default, it's designed as an employee portal for the fictitious IBuySpy company, but you can easily replace the content to create your own custom portal. It even includes ASP.NET administration pages that enable you to customize the content and layout for the portal without altering a line of code. As with all Microsoft case studies, you are free to take as much or as little code as you would like to reuse in your own applications; nothing is restricted or licensed.

> **Note** A portal is a Web site that acts as a hub for a cluster of information organized around some central theme. For example, you might create a company-specific site used by a programming team that contains information such as company bulletins, software development notes, downloadable utilities, contact information, and project deadlines. The portal would combine this information into a small set of pages, allowing a user easy access to a wealth of related information.

In many respects, the IBuySpy portal is more complex than the IBuySpy store. This results from the extreme configurability of the portal. Essentially, the IBuySpy portal site consists of user controls that are loaded dynamically into configurable "slots" on the page. A database determines every aspect of the interface, including the back-end user controls that should be loaded, their positions, and the back-end content. You can easily add your own user control to the page just by adding a record to the database.

As with the IBuySpy store, the IBuySpy portal (shown in Figure 19-2) is primarily of interest to distributed programmers who want a solid example of layered data access and ADO.NET programming. The IBuySpy portal uses output caching, like the IBuySpy store does, but it doesn't include any XML Web services.

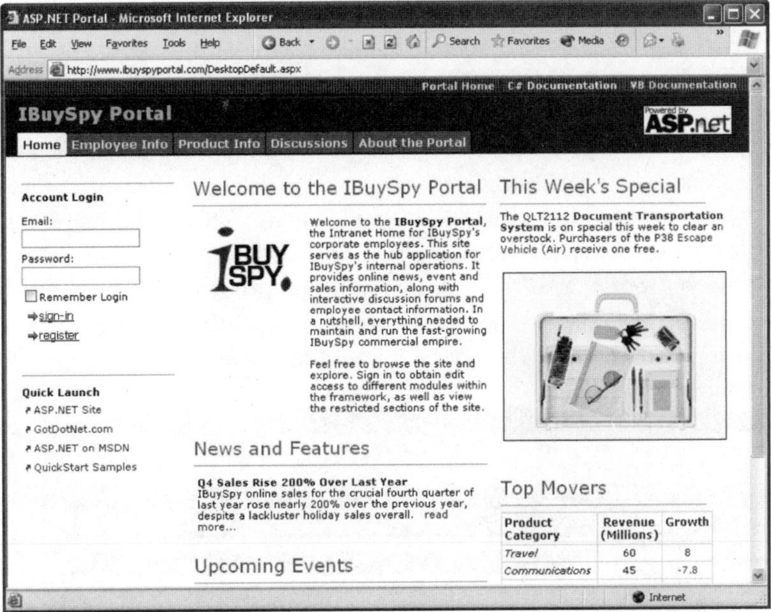

Figure 19-2 The IBuySpy portal

Duwamish 7

Duwamish is an e-commerce site fronted by ASP.NET. Like the IBuySpy store, it is implemented in C# and Visual Basic .NET, uses output caching, accesses the database exclusively through stored procedure code, and provides an optional (but unused) XML Web service. Unlike the IBuySpy case studies, however, Duwamish is an update of a well-known Microsoft platform sample that was previously used to demonstrate the best of Windows DNA coding. As a result, Duwamish follows a more traditional multilayered design, which has both benefits and disadvantages.

In Duwamish, the Web page communicates with a business layer facade, which then interacts with a business rules layer, which ultimately uses the data access layer to send information to and from the database. This design complicates the structure of the applications, but it also allows for some intriguing possibilities. For example, the classes in the business facade layer are all remotable *MarshalByRefObject* types, which means they can be easily hosted on another computer if required. Duwamish also uses a "system framework" component, through which the various parts of the application access configuration information, log messages, and raise exceptions. This is similar to the facade-based designs discussed in Chapter 10.

You can download the Visual Basic version of Duwamish 7 through MSDN at *http://msdn.microsoft.com/code/sample.asp?url=/MSDN-FILES/026/002/073/msdncompositedoc.xml*. It includes a setup program that installs the required information in the database and configures a virtual directory for the ASP.NET front end. The Duwamish Books home page is shown in Figure 19-3.

Figure 19-3 Duwamish Books

> **Note** As with all MSDN pages, the URL for downloading Duwamish 7 is subject to change. If you don't find it in service or if you don't want to type in the full string, you can go to the MSDN Code Center at *http://msdn.microsoft.com/code*. You should be able to browse or search for the required download from there.

.NET Pet Shop

The .NET Pet Shop is another e-commerce and ASP.NET-fronted application from Microsoft that uses more or less the same practices found in the IBuySpy storefront. What makes the .NET Pet Shop notable is that it's a .NET Framework implementation of the Sun J2EE blueprint application (which demonstrates Java best practices). The .NET version requires only one-fourth the number of lines of code and is reputed to be much faster, largely due to ASP.NET's built-in output caching features. (Java has no prebuilt equivalent.) Like the code for the IBuySpy store, the code for the .NET Pet Shop is mostly concentrated in two layers: a user interface and a set of stateless back-end components that access a database. The only difference is that these back-end components make use of the functions in a custom database class to achieve more economical code.

You can download the .NET Pet Shop from *http://www.gotdotnet.com/team/compare/petshop.aspx*, which also provides a performance comparison of the .NET and Java versions and links to documentation and frequently asked questions. It installs the required database and virtual directory automatically. The .NET Pet Shop is provided in C# code only. The home page for the .NET Pet Shop is shown in Figure 19-4.

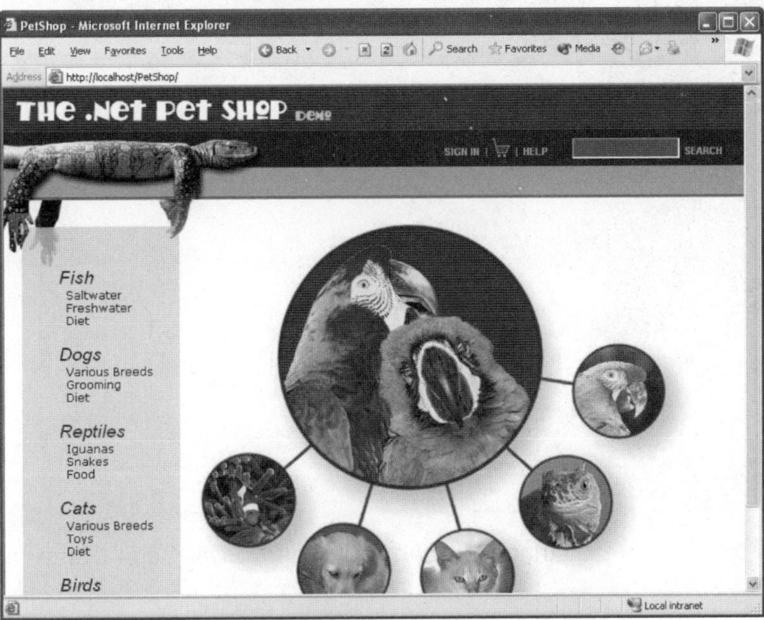

Figure 19-4 The .NET Pet Shop

Fitch & Mather Stocks 7

The Fitch & Mather Stocks 7 application is a rewrite of the Fitch & Mather financial services application. It has a multilayered architecture similar to that of Duwamish, which includes facade layers and business rules that can be remoted on separate computers. The front end consists of ASP.NET Web pages. It includes two advanced features: optional support for an Oracle database and use of a COM+ service component (called a "general accounting module"). This component is developed using Visual C++, not C#, which means that Fitch & Mather cannot be considered a true end-to-end .NET solution. The rest of the project is coded in C#.

You can download the Fitch & Mather project from *http://msdn.microsoft.com/code/sample.asp?url=/msdn-files/026/002/074/msdncompositedoc.xml.* The dedicated setup program installs the database code and configures the database and virtual directory. The Fitch & Mather login screen is shown in Figure 19-5.

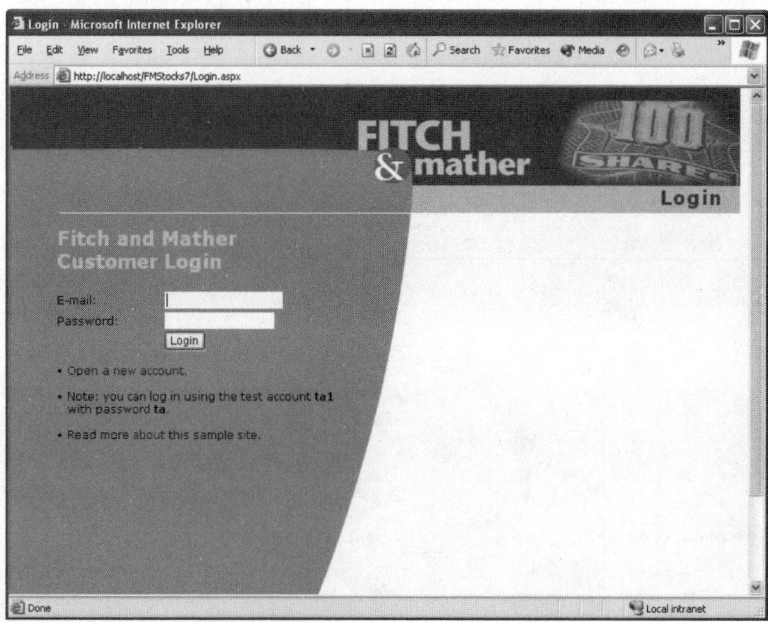

Figure 19-5 Fitch & Mather Stocks

Nile Books

Nile Books is another rewrite of a traditional platform sample—in this case, the Nile Books Doculabs benchmark application. It uses performance-enhancing techniques that are similar to those demonstrated in the other Microsoft case studies, including caching output, stored procedures, and component service providers. Unfortunately, the sample is less useful for learning than it is for benchmarking. There is no Visual Studio .NET project support, the ASP.NET is written inline along with the user interface markup in .aspx files, and there is no setup program to automate the creation of a virtual directory and insertion of database information. The other case studies are generally more useful. You can download Nile Books (in C# code only) from *http://msdn.microsoft.com/library/en-us/dnbda/html/bdasampnilecs.asp*.

ColdStorage

ColdStorage is a set of XML Web services that enable users to upload and download information from a "virtual hard drive" on the server. As with the Favorites Service (described at the end of this chapter), Microsoft's MSDN Web site includes a series of design-to-deployment white papers that cover every aspect of development from envisioning the system to profiling it. These white papers are a treasure trove of minor insights and are generally more interesting than the actual solution. You can download the code (in C# only) from *http://msdn.microsoft.com/code/sample.asp?url=/msdn-files/026/002/529/msdncompositedoc.xml*, or you can browse the white papers at *http://msdn.microsoft.com/library/en-us/dncold/html/storageadsvc.asp*. The setup program for ColdStorage configures the required XML Web service virtual directory and creates the SQL Server database.

Jaggle

Jaggle is a set of XML Web services designed for a real estate application. Jaggle uses a strict separation of layers, so the XML Web service layer is designed as a business facade over a data access layer. You can download Jaggle from *http://msdn.microsoft.com/code/sample.asp?url=/msdn-files/026/002/716/msdncompositedoc.xml*. After you install the setup file, you still need to run the SQL script to install the database and manually create several virtual directories. This process is described in a ReadMe file. Parts of Jaggle are in Visual Basic .NET code, but the majority is C#.

Favorites Service

The Favorites Service is an XML Web service created by the MSDN architecture team. It enables users to save a server-side list of Web links (or favorites) that can be accessed from any computer. The Favorites Service was first built using the previous generation of Microsoft technologies—Visual Studio 6—and you can download the original Favorites Service code from *http://msdn.microsoft.com/code/sample.asp?url=/msdn-files/026/002/332/MsdnCompositeDoc.xml*. Far more useful is the series of architectural white papers about the process of designing the Favorites Service. These papers discuss key basics for caching and implementing security with XML Web services; you can read them online on MSDN at *http://msdn.microsoft.com/library/en-us/dncold/html/ssf1over.asp*. Finally, the .NET incarnation of the Favorites service can be found at *http://msdn.microsoft.com/code/sample.asp?url=/msdn-files/026/002/332/msdncompositedoc.xml*, although you won't find the same useful white papers there.

Index

B

D

E

J

K

L

M

P

Q

R

S

T

W

X

Matthew MacDonald

Matthew MacDonald is an author, educator, and MCSD developer who has a passion for emerging technologies. He is a regular writer for developer journals such as *Inside Visual Basic*, *ASPToday,* and *Hardcore Visual Studio .NET*, a contributor to O'Reilly's series of .NET *Nutshell* titles, and the author of several books about programming with .NET, including *The Book of VB .NET* (No Starch), *ASP.NET: The Complete Reference* (Osborne McGraw-Hill), and *User Interfaces in VB.NET* (Apress). In a dimly remembered past life, Matthew studied English literature and theoretical physics.

Send e-mail to him with praise, condemnation, and everything in between at *distribapps@prosetech.com*.

Chain Hoist Load Hook

Need to lift and move a heavy object? Using a *chain hoist*, you can move automobile and truck engines, transmissions, outboard motors, sound equipment, or anything else that's too heavy for your back and hands to carry. Most chain hoists are motorized. A *load hook* on the end of a pulley in the chain hoist is attached to the object to be lifted, while, as the name implies, a chain passes through the pulley to hoist the load. Just like COM or the Microsoft .NET Framework, a chain hoist makes your work easier by doing the heavy lifting with objects.

At Microsoft Press, we use tools to illustrate our books for software developers and IT professionals. Tools very simply and powerfully symbolize human inventiveness. They're a metaphor for people extending their capabilities, precision, and reach. From simple calipers and pliers to digital micrometers and lasers, these stylized illustrations give each book a visual identity, and a personality to the series. With tools and knowledge, there's no limit to creativity and innovation. Our tag line says it all: the tools you need to put technology to work.

The manuscript for this book was prepared and galleyed using Microsoft Word. Pages were composed by Microsoft Press using Adobe FrameMaker+SGML for Windows, with text in Garamond and display type in Helvetica Condensed. Composed pages were delivered to the printer as electronic prepress files.

Cover Designer:	Methodologie, Inc.
Interior Graphic Designer:	James D. Kramer
Principal Compositor:	Gina Cassill
Interior Artist:	Rob Nance
Copy Editor:	Ina Chang
Proofreader:	nSight, Inc.

Get a **Free**

e-mail newsletter, updates, special offers, links to related books, and more when you

register on line!

Register your Microsoft Press® title on our Web site and you'll get a FREE subscription to our e-mail newsletter, *Microsoft Press Book Connections.* You'll find out about newly released and upcoming books and learning tools, online events, software downloads, special offers and coupons for Microsoft Press customers, and information about major Microsoft® product releases. You can also read useful additional information about all the titles we publish, such as detailed book descriptions, tables of contents and indexes, sample chapters, links to related books and book series, author biographies, and reviews by other customers.

Registration is easy. Just visit this Web page and fill in your information:

http://www.microsoft.com/mspress/register

Microsoft

Proof of Purchase

Use this page as proof of purchase if participating in a promotion or rebate offer on this title. Proof of purchase must be used in conjunction with other proof(s) of payment such as your dated sales receipt—see offer details.

Microsoft® .NET Distributed Applications: Integrating Web Services and Remoting

0-7356-1933-6

____

CUSTOMER NAME

Microsoft Press, PO Box 97017, Redmond, WA 98073-9830